834

THE WORKS OF JONATHAN EDWARDS

VOLUME 5

John E. Smith, General Editor

PREVIOUSLY PUBLISHED

PAUL RAMSEY, ed., *Freedom of the Will*
JOHN E. SMITH, ed., *Religious Affections*
CLYDE A. HOLBROOK, ed., *Original Sin*
C. C. GOEN, ed., *The Great Awakening*

JONATHAN EDWARDS

Apocalyptic Writings

"NOTES ON THE APOCALYPSE"

AN HUMBLE ATTEMPT

EDITED BY STEPHEN J. STEIN

ASSOCIATE PROFESSOR OF RELIGIOUS STUDIES

INDIANA UNIVERSITY

New Haven and London

YALE UNIVERSITY PRESS, 1977

Copyright © 1977 by Yale University.
All rights reserved. This book may not be
reproduced, in whole or in part, in any form
(except by reviewers for the public press),
without written permission from the publishers.

Designed by John O. C. McCrillis
and set in Baskerville type.
Printed in the United States of America by
The Vail-Ballou Press, Inc., Binghamton, New York.

Published in Great Britain, Europe, Africa, and Asia
(except Japan) by Yale University Press, Ltd.,
London. Distributed in Latin America by Kaiman
& Polon, Inc., New York City; in Australia and
New Zealand by Book & Film Services, Artarmon, N.S.W.,
Australia; and in Japan by Harper & Row, Publishers, Tokyo Office.

Library of Congress Cataloging in Publication Data

Edwards, Jonathan, 1703–1758.
    Apocalyptic writings.
    (The works of Jonathan Edwards; v. 5)
    Includes bibliographical references and indexes.
    CONTENTS: Notes on the apocalypse.—An humble attempt.
    1. Bible. N. T. Revelation—Commentaries.
I. Edwards, Jonathan, 1703–1758. An humble attempt to promote
explicit agreement and visible union of God's people ... 1977. II.
Title.
BX7117.E3 1957   vol. 5   [BS2825.A2]   285'.8s   [228'.06]
ISBN 0–300–01945–9   76–30845

CONTENTS

LIST OF ILLUSTRATIONS

FOREWORD

WITH this volume the Editorial Committee for the Works of Jonathan Edwards inaugurates the publication of the major manuscripts of Edwards in the Yale University Press edition. Here and in subsequent volumes of the edition the massive body of Edwards' manuscripts, including notebooks, letters, and sermons, will be made available to the public. These materials promise a full and complete exposure of his ideas in a manner never before possible.

In this volume Edwards' private commentary on the book of Revelation appears for the first time in print. "Notes on the Apocalypse" is a virtually unknown manuscript concealed for more than two centuries by the fortunes of time and the changing winds of cultural favor. The manuscript highlights Edwards' lifelong commitment to apocalyptic speculation—a hitherto inadequately explored facet of his thought— and at the same time reveals the significance of the apocalyptic factor in his pastoral and theological activities. The other materials in this volume show the way in which his private reflections came to public attention in his own day.

The generous support of the Bollingen Foundation for this editorial project again deserves prominent mention.

T HE book of Revelation fascinated Jonathan Edwards, America's premier philosopher-theologian, a fact that has been a source of bewilderment and embarrassment to some students of American thought. For him the Apocalypse came alive with each new reading. Like others in the eighteenth century, Edwards believed that the biblical visions with the mysterious figures and cryptic references could be very useful to the Christian church. He drew heavily in his sermons and treatises upon the Revelation's bizarre and sometimes baffling symbolism, finding it a source of comfort and encouragement for the people of New England. Edwards spent long hours studying the Revelation, the only book of the Bible he favored with a separate commentary; that preoccupation began in early manhood as he searched for the best interpretation of the Apocalypse, and it spanned the full range of his years. Not content with mere curiosities or speculations, he probed for the pastoral and theological implications of the prophecies.

Few people in the twentieth century share his enthusiasm for the Apocalypse; even fewer will find Edwards' interpretation persuasive or intellectually respectable. Many of us today have little patience with such pursuits. Those committed to contemporary apocalypticism will probably judge his reflections inappropriate for devotional literature. This volume does not promise to raise Edwards' intellectual or religious stock, but it will allow a fuller assessment of the apocalyptic factor in his life and thought by publishing for the first time his private "Notes on the Apocalypse," together with his treatise published in 1748, *An Humble Attempt to Promote Explicit Agreement and Visible Union of God's People in Extraordinary Prayer.*[1]

1. *The Apocalyptic Tradition*

Edwards joined a long and curious tradition when he began his notebook on the Apocalypse, a tradition stretching back to early

---

1. "Apocalypse" will be used as a short title for JE's notebook and *Humble Attempt* for the treatise. The abbreviations AP and HA will appear in the notes. The "Apocalypse" must be distinguished carefully from the Apocalypse, or book of Revelation, in the New Testament.

Christianity and embracing a diversity of issues and ideas. Some church fathers, such as Irenaeus (c. 130–c. 200), espoused the hope of an earthly millennium based on selected Old Testament prophecies and the book of Revelation. They expected the whole creation to be restored to its pristine condition upon Christ's return and with redeemed humanity be brought to its intended perfection. Others in the early church, most notably Origen (c. 185–c. 254), denounced such chiliasm as a carnal Jewish dream and would have denied canonical status to the Revelation. With the Constantinian settlement in the fourth century, persecution became nearly a thing of the past, and the original context of Christian apocalyptic literature ceased to exist. Problems of theological adjustment and institutional construction now faced the emerging church. Augustine of Hippo (354–430), the primary architect of the orthodox theological consensus in the West, adopted a new approach to the Apocalypse by translating the eschatological hope from the future to the present and thoroughly spiritualizing it. For him the millennium of Revelation 20 symbolized the present militant age of the church on earth. The first resurrection was a spiritual experience of individuals, and the second was to come at the end of time.[2] Augustine's reinterpretation accentuated the consolatory nature of the Revelation, which he viewed as an account of the victorious struggle of the city of God against the forces of Satan. The western church followed the lead of Augustine; from the fifth through the fifteenth centuries his interpretation prevailed almost unchallenged, with a few notable exceptions.[3]

In the twelfth century Joachim of Flora (c. 1132–1202), a Cistercian monk, devised a different exposition of the Apocalypse as part of a vigorous movement for monastic reform. He explained the course of world history by three successive ages, one for each member of the Trinity. The third age, that of the Spirit, was to be a time of liberty and new spirituality. Joachim's scheme shifted the focus of the Revelation to the future and raised the hopes of his followers. The Spiritual Franciscans declared themselves men of the new era and used the Apocalypse to denounce their adversaries—both the empire and the papacy—as

2. See Appendix A, below, p. 439, for the major divisions of the book of Revelation as seen by JE. *The Interpreter's Dictionary of the Bible* (4 vols., New York, 1962), *4*, 58–71, provides a succinct and intelligible critical analysis of the structure and content of the book.

3. Ernest Lee Tuveson, *Millennium and Utopia: A Study in the Background of the Idea of Progress* (Berkeley, 1949), and Le Roy Edwin Froom, *The Prophetic Faith of Our Fathers: The Historical Development of Prophetic Interpretation* (4 vols., Washington, D. C., 1946–54), offer contrasting perspectives on the tradition.

antichristian. This future-oriented, polemical interpretation was not lost upon other dissident groups. In England the disciples of John Wycliffe (c. 1329–84) sanctioned their cause with the seal of prophecy. John Purvey (c. 1353–1428), a close friend of Wycliffe, wrote a commentary predicting the progressive decline of the papal Antichrist. On the Continent the Taborites, the radical followers of John Huss (c. 1369–1415), preached a chiliastic doctrine, attacking the royalist party in Prague as antichristian and proclaiming their own cities to be centers of the coming kingdom. They took up the sword of revenge to enforce their apocalyptic logic. At the time of the Reformation, Thomas Muentzer (c. 1490–1525), Melchior Hoffmann (c. 1500–43), John of Leyden (1510–36), and other radical Protestants availed themselves of the book of Revelation as a reinforcement for their own programs of reform and revolution, often with devastating results for themselves and their followers.[4] During this period, fervor and fanaticism became synonymous with radical apocalypticism in the minds of many.

It was primarily that association which drove Martin Luther (1483–1546) and John Calvin (1509–64) away from millenarianism.[5] In his early years as a reformer, Luther voiced uncertainty about the Revelation, declaring it neither apostolic nor prophetic. Later he moderated his judgment and argued from the book that the Pope was the Antichrist and the Protestant cause righteous. He searched for historical equivalents—past, present, and future—to fit the details of the visions, though he continued to fear the excesses accompanying extreme apocalypticism. Calvin was the most guarded of all the reformers in his attitude toward the Apocalypse. He stood firmly in the Augustinian line, rejecting chiliasm, eschatological calculations, and millenarian fanaticism. The Revelation was the only book of the Bible on which he did not write a commentary.

The polemical bent of Protestant exegetes produced an inevitable response from the Roman Catholic community. Near the turn of the seventeenth century two prominent Jesuits wrote commentaries offering different interpretations of the Revelation. Francisco Ribera (1537–91) contended that the prophecies of the Antichrist were still unfulfilled.

4. Standard literature includes Marjorie Reeves, *The Influence of Prophecy in the Later Middle Ages: A Study of Joachimism* (Oxford, 1969); Norman Cohn, *The Pursuit of the Millennium* (New York, 1957); and George H. Williams, *The Radical Reformation* (Philadelphia, 1962).

5. T. F. Torrance, *Kingdom and Church: A Study in the Theology of the Reformation* (Fairlawn, N.J., 1956); Paul Althaus, *The Theology of Martin Luther*, trans. Robert C. Shultz (Philadelphia, 1966); and Heinrich Quistorp, *Calvin's Doctrine of the Last Things*, trans. Harold Knight (London, 1955).

The Antichrist was to be a Jewish deceiver of the world who would reign for three and a half years. By contrast, Luis de Alcasar (1554–1613) thought that the prophecies of the Apocalypse had already been fulfilled in the struggles of the early church with Judaism and paganism. The last two chapters of the Revelation, he said, tell of the triumph of the Roman Catholic Church.[6]

The portion of the apocalyptic tradition that developed in post-Reformation England formed the immediate background of Edwards' "Notes on the Apocalypse." In the sixteenth and seventeenth centuries England spawned a host of Protestant commentators who planted a love of the Apocalypse deep in the soul of English Protestantism. John Bale (1495–1563) was one such exegete, a Carmelite monk turned defender of Reformed doctrine. He explained the conflict between Protestant and Catholic powers in terms of a struggle between the church of Christ and the forces of Antichrist, the latter in his eyes the Roman papacy. He in turn influenced another convert to the Reformation, perhaps the most prominent of all English commentators on the Apocalypse, John Foxe (1516–87), whom he met on the Continent during the Marian exile. Foxe's "Book of Martyrs," a chronicle of Protestant suffering in England, combined apocalyptic lore with ecclesiastical history, fervent nationalism, and unbounded hatred of Roman Catholicism. The result was a volume of epic significance for England and a place in the national pantheon for Foxe.[7] Edwards cited the *Acts and Monuments* early in his notebook.

Foxe and Bale retained the Augustinian mode of interpretation, but later generations of English exegetes began to move away from that cautious view of the Revelation. For example, Thomas Brightman (1562–1607), a clergyman with Puritan leanings, spoke of two millenniums instead of one: the first, ending in 1300, was Augustinian in conception; the second, extending for the next thousand years, was inaugurated by the use of the means of grace and promised a future glorious time for the church on earth. Brightman attacked Ribera's idea that the prophecies remained unfulfilled by arguing that three vials already had been poured, beginning with Elizabeth's strictures against the

6. Ribera, *In sacram Beati Ioannis Apostoli & Evangelistae Apocalypsin Commentari* (Lugduni, 1593); and Alcasar, *Vestigatio Arcani Sensus in Apocalypsi* (Antwerp, 1614).

7. Bale, *The Image of Both Churches* (London, 1550); and Foxe, *Acts and Monuments of these Latter and Perilous Days* (London, 1563). See William Haller, *The Elect Nation: The Meaning and Relevance of Foxe's Book of Martyrs* (New York, 1963); and Katharine Robbins Firth, "The Apocalyptic Tradition in Early Protestant Historiography in England and Scotland, 1530 to 1655," Diss. Univ. of Oxford, 1971.

Roman Catholics, and that the remaining four were impending. He was optimistic about the future despite present hardships.[8] John Cotton (1584–1652), a Puritan revered on both sides of the Atlantic, also formulated new ideas about the Revelation. In his sermon-commentaries he affirmed that Rome, the subject of the visions, had passed through three distinct phases: pagan, before Christ; Christian, during the time of the emperors; and anti-Christian, under the popes. The seven trumpets of the Apocalypse were directed against Christian Rome and the seven vials against anti-Christian Rome. Five of the latter had been poured, Cotton maintained, and the beginning of the millennium was imminent—in 1655, to be exact. History was moving rapidly toward a climax in his view.[9]

Seventeenth-century England was ripe for such talk and for even more radical speculation. Unlike the situation on the Continent, there existed no confessional deterrents to chiliasm in England. In this context Joseph Mede (1586–1638), a Cambridge don and biblical scholar, took a new look at millennialism. His *Clavis Apocalyptica*[1] offered a different interpretation of the book of Revelation grounded upon its linguistic structure. He believed that a proper understanding of the text would result from a correct ordering of the visions because the prophecies were not written in the order of their fulfillment. Discovering the synchronisms—that is, the sections agreeing in time and period— unlocks the secrets of the book. The seventh seal, according to Mede, contains the events of the seven trumpets, most of which have been fulfilled in the distant past. When the sixth trumpet sounds, the six vials are poured on the antichristian forces. Four vials, he contended, remain to be emptied on Rome, *the* enemy of the church. The battle of Armageddon under the seventh vial will usher in the reign of the saints on earth for a thousand years. The first resurrection is a bodily resurrection of the martyrs, who will rule with the saints during the millennium.

8. Brightman's *Apocalypsis apocalypseos* (Frankfort, 1609), first translated into English in 1611.

9. Cotton, *The Churches Resurrection, or the Opening of the Fift and sixt verses of the 20th Chap. of the Revelation* (London, 1642); *The Powring out of the Seven Vials: or an Exposition, with Application of the 16 Chapter of the Revelation* (London, 1642); and *An Exposition upon the Thirteenth Chapter of the Revelation* (London, 1655). See the collection of essays edited by Peter Toon, *Puritans, the Millennium and the Future of Israel: Puritan Eschatology 1600 to 1660* (Cambridge, Eng., 1970).

1. Cambridge, 1627, reprinted frequently, translated and published under the auspices of the Westminster Assembly as *The Key of the Revelation* (London, 1643). Mede's collected works were first published in 1648.

Mede's millennialism had an impact upon an important community of English scholars, trained in biblical learning and the new sciences, who had become fascinated with the prospect of coordinating scriptural prophecy with the new theories about the universe. Henry More (1614–87), a student of Mede's, developed the optimism implicit in Mede's ideas in a commentary of his own. Sir Isaac Newton (1642–1727) became the epitome of the old and the new learning in tandem by his attempts to decipher the apocalyptic discourses of the Bible and to fix the chronology of the apocalyptic kingdoms with the aid of the developing sciences. His successor at Cambridge, William Whiston (1667–1752), a mathematician and theologian, devoted himself equally to scriptural chronology and scientific investigation. Edwards knew firsthand the works of all three men.[2]

During the decade of the Civil War in England, a time of heightened interest in the Apocalypse, Mede's writings influenced another group, the social and political activists of all persuasions. Some like William Twisse (1578–1646) and Thomas Goodwin (1600–80), members of the Westminster Assembly, adopted Mede's millennialism and stressed the theological implications of the idea. Others, such as John Archer, a lecturer at All Hallows church in London, carried the millennial speculation further by distinguishing three states of Christ's kingdom: the providential, the spiritual, and the monarchical. The millennium, he concluded, will be a monarchical kingdom inaugurated by the physical return of Christ, shortly after which he will leave the earth and return again at the end of the thousand years. Archer stressed the necessity of divine initiative in the coming of the kingdom.[3] The Fifth Monarchists, by contrast, planned to set up Christ's kingdom by force, a kingdom associated with the mythical society of Daniel 2:44. Therefore they revolted against Charles I and eventually opposed Oliver Cromwell as well, regarding themselves as chosen by God to rule over their oppressors and to restructure society in accord with his will. The movement failed to institutionalize itself, and after 1660 the Fifth Monarchists faded into the ranks of Nonconformity or were suppressed by the authorities.[4]

2. More, *Apocalypsis Apocalypseos; or the Revelation of St John the Divine unveiled* (London, 1680); Newton, *Observations Upon the Prophecies of Daniel, and the Apocalypse of St. John* (London, 1733); and Whiston, *An Essay on the Revelation of St. John, So far as Concerns the Past and Present Times* (Cambridge, 1706).

3. See Twisse's preface to Mede's *Key*; *The Works of Thomas Goodwin* (4 vols., London, 1681–97); and Archer, *The Personall Reigne of Christ Upon Earth* (London, 1642).

4. See the following studies: William Haller, *The Rise of Puritanism* (New York, 1938);

The tumult of the Civil War era discredited the most radical interpretations of the Apocalypse in England and opened the way for other methods of explaining the visions. Hugo Grotius (1583–1645), the Dutch jurist and theologian, introduced one new approach. Irenic in nature and Arminian in theology, Grotius ignored the antipapal, the polemical, and the revolutionary interpretations of the Apocalypse and turned his attention to philological investigation of the text, thereby raising a whole range of new questions. The works of Henry Hammond (1605–60), a biblical annotator of Arminian persuasion, were the chief vehicle for his ideas in England.[5] At the beginning of the eighteenth century the liberal theologian Daniel Whitby (1638–1726) proposed another perspective upon the millennium, arguing that it was not an actual reign of the resurrected saints, but a figurative thousand years when the church will prosper in advance of Christ's return to the earth. Whitby's postmillennialism, so named because the second coming of Christ is positioned after the millennium, was implicit in the work of commentators during the preceding century, and his formulation of the idea won some adherents.[6] Among his disciples on the English scene were Charles Daubuz (1673–1717), a Huguenot exile, and Moses Lowman (1680–1752), a dissenting scholar-divine.[7] Edwards struggled mightily in his notebook with the interpretation of Lowman.

The Christian apocalyptic tradition from Irenaeus to Moses Lowman was rich and varied, but also strange and sometimes perverse. Edwards was acquainted with this heritage of Christian thought; through the years he shaped parts of it into a unique theological con-

John F. Wilson, *Pulpit in Parliament: Puritanism during the English Civil Wars 1640–1648* (Princeton, 1969); William M. Lamont, *Godly Rule: Politics and Religion, 1603–60* (London, 1969); Bernard S. Capp, *The Fifth Monarchy Men: A Study in Seventeenth-Century English Millenarianism* (Totowa, N. J., 1972); Christopher Hill, *The World Turned Upside Down: Radical Ideas during the English Revolution* (New York, 1972); and Tai Liu, *Discord in Zion: The Puritan Divines and the Puritan Revolution 1640–1660* (The Hague, 1973).

5. Grotius, *Explicatio trium utilissimorum locorum Novi Testamenti* (Amsterdam, 1640); and *Commentatio ad loca Novi Testamenti quae de Antichristi agunt* (Amsterdam, 1640). Hammond, *A Paraphrase, and Annotations upon All the Books of the New Testament* (London, 1653).

6. *A Discourse on the Millennium*, in *A Paraphrase and Commentary on the New Testament* (2 vols., London, 1703), 2. Postmillennialism and premillennialism, contrasting categories of theological analysis, are largely inappropriate for seventeenth- and eighteenth-century apocalyptic thought because they imply too rigid a set of opposing assumptions. The terms will be avoided in this volume. For different viewpoints on their usefulness in the period, see C. C. Goen, "Jonathan Edwards: A New Departure in Eschatology," *Church History, 28* (1959), 25–40; and James W. Davidson, "Searching for the Millennium: Problems for the 1790's and the 1970's," *New England Quarterly, 45* (1972), 241–61.

7. Daubuz, *A Perpetual Commentary on the Revelation of St. John* (London, 1720); and Lowman, *A Paraphrase and Notes on the Revelation of St. John* (London, 1737).

figuration consistent with his other ideas and his time and place in the eighteenth century.

2. *The Beginning of the Notebook*

"In America," wrote Perry Miller, "the greatest artist of the apocalypse was, of course, Jonathan Edwards";[8] but he was hardly the only American to form such biblical components into functional designs. Edwards came to his craft naturally, for in New England a long line of colonial spokesmen—most prominently, John Cotton and Roger Williams in the first generation, the historian Edward Johnson, the poet Michael Wigglesworth, Samuel Sewall the commentator, and father and son Increase and Cotton Mather—had made the visions of the Revelation a formative influence upon the consciousness of the people. The Puritans filled their diaries, sermons, and public papers with apocalyptic discourse. After leaving their homes in the old world under duress, they identified their cause in the wilderness with the plight of the persecuted saints in the Revelation and transferred to their commonwealths a sense of divine mission and a spirit of apocalyptic fervor. Later when that sense of election eroded and new waves of settlers buried the religious commitment under a host of competing claims, the clergy rose to castigate the people for their sins and to warn them of impending punishment, drawing upon the imagery and ideas of the Apocalypse. Then the Puritans wrote the history of their experiences as though they were the subjects of the Revelation. In effect, they translated the apocalyptic tradition into a meaningful literature of their own.[9]

The eighteenth century did little to undermine the place of apocalyptic among the people of New England. The children of the Puritans viewed the imperial conflicts of the new century, a dominant social and political reality, as part of the ongoing struggle of the church against the forces of the Antichrist. Edwards was certainly weaned on such anti-Catholicism.[1] During his childhood in Windsor, Queen Anne's War

8. "The End of the World," in *Errand into the Wilderness* (Cambridge, Mass., 1956), p. 233.

9. See Aletha Joy Bourne Gilsdorf, "The Puritan Apocalypse: New England Eschatology in the Seventeenth Century," Diss. Yale Univ., 1965; Sacvan Bercovitch, "Horologicals to Chronometricals: The Rhetoric of the Jeremiad," *Literary Monographs*, ed. Eric Rothstein (Madison, Wis., 1970), *3*, 1–124; Robert Middlekauff, *The Mathers: Three Generations of Puritan Intellectuals, 1596–1728* (New York, 1971); and J. F. Maclear, "New England and the Fifth Monarchy: The Quest for the Millennium in Early American Puritanism," *William and Mary Quarterly*, 3rd ser., *32* (1975), 223–60.

1. See Mary Augustina Ray, *American Opinion of Roman Catholicism in the Eighteenth Century* (New York, 1936). On the English background, see Christopher Hill, *Antichrist in Seventeenth-Century England* (London, 1971); and John Miller, *Popery and Politics in England 1660–1688*

(1702–13) reached into his home when the Connecticut assembly appointed his father Timothy as a chaplain on the expedition against Canada.[2] The colonists imagined antichristian forces conspiring against them at a distance and in the neighboring forests. Captives returning from Canada extolled providence for their release and in the same breath warned their fellow settlers of the dangers from the unholy alliance between the French Jesuits and their Indian subordinates.[3] In 1723 Solomon Stoddard, Edwards' grandfather, called for more active Indian missions in the hope that the natives would not "fall in with the *Papists*," thereby prolonging bloodshed.[4] For New England the struggle with Rome had not ended in 1649 with the execution of Charles I, nor in 1689 with the accession of William and Mary to the throne; it was continuing as the enemy employed new and more dangerous weapons against the Puritans. As a result in 1723 the young Edwards wrote, "The saints shall revenge themselves, no otherwise than by doing their utmost for the destruction of popery" (AP; below, p. 120)—a sentiment favored by the majority of the citizenry.

When Edwards penned that line in his notebook, the furor over events in New Haven during the preceding fall had not yet subsided. Yale College in New Haven had been founded to preserve the Reformed Protestant faith inviolate from new theologies. During his undergraduate days—times of turmoil for the young institution—and during two subsequent years of theological training, Edwards had been exposed to a thoroughly Protestant curriculum.[5] Therefore the "apostasy" of the rector Timothy Cutler, two of his associates, and some of the neighboring ministers to the Anglican Church shocked the religious establishment, which was prepared to defend itself against assaults of Rome from without but not against subversion from within. The pulpits and newspapers of New England screamed alarm and poured forth exhortations.[6] The apostasy provided new incentive to examine the pro-

(Cambridge, Eng., 1973). Also James W. Davidson, "Eschatology in New England: 1700–1763," Diss. Yale Univ., 1973.

2. Timothy Edwards, letter to Mrs. Esther Edwards, Sept. 10, 1711; in Sereno E. Dwight, ed., *The Works of President Edwards with a Memoir of His Life* (10 vols., New York, 1829–30), *1*, 15. Hereafter cited as Dwight ed.

3. E.g., John Williams, *The Redeemed Captive, Returning to Zion* (Boston, 1707).

4. *Whether God is not Angry with the Country for doing So little towards the Conversion of the Indians?* (Boston, 1723), p. 11.

5. Richard Warch, *School of the Prophets: Yale College, 1701–1740* (New Haven, 1973), chs. 8–9.

6. See Carl Bridenbaugh, *Mitre and Sceptre: Transatlantic Faiths, Ideas, Personalities, and Politics 1689–1775* (New York, 1962), ch. 3.

phecies concerning the antichristian conspiracy, which in the Puritans'
eyes included the Church of England. As the reverberations still
sounded among the public, Edwards was writing in his private notebook: "What is said to Pergamos seems very well to suit the case of the
Church of England; 'and where thou dwellest, even where Satan's seat
is' [Rev. 2:13]" (AP; below, p. 99).

Turning to the book of Revelation was natural for Edwards because
by the end of 1722 he had developed a disciplined program of private
study, including the regular investigation of the Bible. As a young man
he resolved "To study the Scriptures so steadily, constantly and frequently, as that I may find, and plainly perceive myself to grow in the
knowledge of the same."[7] There is no evidence that he ever gave up that
resolution, although he frequently chided himself for neglecting study
and losing "that relish of the Scriptures" necessary for faith and
scholarship.[8] Edwards cultivated the habit of biblical study, especially
during the year he served in New York as a supply minister. "I had
then," he later recollected, "and at other times, the greatest delight in
the holy Scriptures, of any book whatsoever."[9] At the same time he became preoccupied with observing the progress of God's kingdom and
praying for its advancement; he watched contemporary events for
signs of divine activity:

> If I heard the least hint of any thing that happened in any part of
> the world, that appear'd to me, in some respect or other, to have a
> favorable aspect on the interest of Christ's kingdom, my soul eagerly
> catch'd at it; and it would much animate and refresh me. I used to
> be earnest to read public news-letters, mainly for that end; to see if
> I could not find some news favorable to the interest of religion in the
> world.[1]

It will become evident that Edwards retained that habit in later years.

In New York Edwards wrote his earliest comments on the Revelation, a group of miscellaneous reflections loosely tied together by the
theme of conflict.[2] According to him, the greatest barrier to the ad-

7. Dwight ed., *1*, 70.
8. "Diary," in Dwight ed., *1*, 85.
9. "Personal Narrative," in David Levin, ed., *Jonathan Edwards: A Profile* (New York, 1969),
p. 32. The narrative was first printed in Samuel Hopkins, *The Life and Character of the Late
Reverend Mr. Jonathan Edwards* (Boston, 1765). See Daniel B. Shea, Jr., *Spiritual Autobiography
in Early America* (Princeton, 1968), pp. 187–208, for a suggestive analysis.
1. Levin, ed., *Jonathan Edwards*, p. 31.
2. "Theological Miscellanies" (MSS, Yale coll.), no. k, EXPOSITION; no. hh, ANTI-
CHRIST; no. uu, APOCALYPSE; no. ww, FOUR BEASTS; no. xx, VIALS; no. yy,

vancement of God's kingdom was the Church of Rome, which he assailed as the most dangerous foe of Christ, worse than the Jews or the Mahometans, an unscrupulous enemy of the church comparable to "a viper or some loathsome, poisonous, crawling monster."[3] Despite this opposition, God will accomplish his purpose in the world because the operation of providence cannot be thwarted. Even at the moment of greatest antichristian oppression, God was not without witnesses; he has always maintained a remnant of an evangelical church. Since the Reformation, God has reversed the fortunes of the church by pouring out the vials of wrath upon his enemies. The memory of persecution and martyrdom will fade in the future as the knowledge of divinity spreads, injustices are rectified, the saints and martyrs vindicated, and men stimulated to greater holiness during the millennium. The promised triumph of the saints is the hope and encouragement of the church on earth.

In the spring of 1723 Edwards increased his commitment to the study of the Apocalypse. After an apparent evaluation of his entire study program, he began a separate notebook for comments on the book of Revelation, the "Notes on the Apocalypse." Earlier he had noted an "Apocalypse" among his contemplated projects and had drawn up a list of "Books to be Inquired for," a partial forecast of the range of interests to be explored in the new notebook:

The best geography.
The best history of the world.
The best exposition of the Apocalypse.
The best general ecclesiastical history from Christ to the present time.
The best upon the types of the Scripture.
Which are the most useful and necessary of the Fathers.
The best chronology.
The best historical dictionary of the nature of Boyle's dictionary.
The best that treats of the cabalistical learning of the Jews.[4]

His fascination with apocalyptic carried Edwards from geography to cabalism before the completion of his quest for the best available

WOMAN IN THE WILDERNESS; and no. 26, MILLENNIUM. Hereafter the series is cited as "Miscellanies" and individual entries as Miscell. no.

3. Miscell. no. hh.

4. "Catalogue" (MS, Yale coll.), letter sheet and p. 1. See Thomas H. Johnson, "Jonathan Edwards' Background of Reading," *Publications of the Colonial Society of Massachusetts, Transactions, 28* (1930–33), 193–222.

volumes. The opening portion of the "Apocalypse" was one product of this flurry of enthusiasm and activity.[5]

The first pages of the notebook provide the most comprehensive analysis of the book of Revelation ever offered by Edwards, a synoptic account in which he commented chapter by chapter upon a range of textual and substantive issues. The usefulness of the visions, he conceded, depends upon their clarity; therefore he probed the complexities of the book in order to untangle its structure and themes. He established to his own satisfaction that "the method of these visions is first, to give a more general representation of things, and then afterwards, a more distinct description of the particular changes and revolutions that are the subjects of them" (AP; below, p. 106), a view reminiscent of Joseph Mede's contention that the book does not proceed in uninterrupted chronological fashion. But other uncertainties nagged Edwards as he searched for a satisfactory interpretation of the figures inhabiting the pages of the Revelation. It did not require special insight to discover that the church will be troubled during much of her earthly sojourn, according to the visions. On that interpreters in every age agreed. However, the nature and duration of the suffering of the faithful, the identity of the persecutors, the time of the end of the persecution, and the prospects for the future—these issues left commentators divided.

Early in the "Apocalypse" Edwards took one unequivocal position from which he never deviated, namely, that the key to the entire book of Revelation, the single issue "it is impossible to be mistaken in the general meaning of," was the description and identity of the Antichrist. Revelation 17:18 "is spoken the plainest of any one passage in the whole book. . . . 'Tis the only part of this prophecy that is spoken without allegory" (AP; below, pp. 107, 120). Edwards was convinced that the Roman papacy was the Antichrist and that the Revelation describes the rise, reign, and fall of the antichristian forces together with the interrelated fortunes of the church. The identification of the Antichrist was not incidental to the central design of the Bible, for as Christ was "the chief subject of the prophecies of the Old Testament," so the Antichrist is of the New. The activities of the Antichrist were purposely shrouded in secrecy until the time of his appearance; this explanation accounts for the obscurity and mystery of the Revelation, according to Edwards. Edwards defined "mystery" as what is concealed or not yet known (AP; below, pp. 118–19); plenty of mystery remained for him in the Revelation.

5. See below, pp. 77 ff., for the dating of the AP.

It was no mystery that the Antichrist and his minions were powerful. The persecutions suffered by the faithful throughout the centuries of church history, in Edwards' mind, established the strength of the coalition. The leaders of the antichristian forces manifest their might through trickery and deception; the clergy dupe their followers by pretended miracles and pretentious displays of pomp. Such deceits as the doctrine of transubstantiation, the claim to infallibility, and dispensations are miracles, Edwards exclaimed, "that God himself cannot do!" Ceremonies, "priest's shews," and similar exhibitions amaze the "gazing multitude" and make them credulous and submissive. Most offensive of all is the attempt of the Antichrist to exalt "himself above all that is called God, or that is worshiped, so that he as God sitteth in the temple of God, shewing himself that he is God" (AP; below, pp. 112, 125). This is the supreme blasphemy.

The antidote to such chicanery and imposture, Edwards insisted, is the manifestation of truth that will dash to pieces the false doctrines and practices of the antichristian kingdom. The light of the gospel will destroy the darkness and deceit. The Word of God cuts through the cloud surrounding the Antichrist, and he stands revealed before his followers, who then desert him. The downfall of the beast signals the beginning of more glorious times for the church on earth. No longer will the faithful be the subjects of persecution and hardship; those who oppressed the church will themselves feel the sting of God's wrath. According to Edwards, when the Antichrist is overthrown, the final joys of the church will be foreshadowed during the reign of the saints on the earth. Ultimately the church militant becomes the church triumphant in the "new heaven and new earth." The "event of things" will show this to be the will of God for his people (AP; below, p. 120).

The visions of the Seer were for Edwards an apocalyptic timetable for the future. Like others in the tradition, he tried his hand at correlating the prophecies with the progression of historical events.[6] He equated the opening of the seals with the then future persecutions of the early church by the heathen Roman Empire, the sounding of the trumpets with the disasters befalling the Christian empire at the hands of the barbarian and Islamic forces, and the pouring of the vials with the assaults upon the antichristian kingdom by her opponents beginning in the days before the Reformation. Edwards calculated that the papacy would fall by 1866 at the end of the traditional forty-two months of the

6. See the diagram of JE's early view of the Apocalypse on p. 14.

EDWARDS' EARLY VIEW OF THE APOCALYPSE

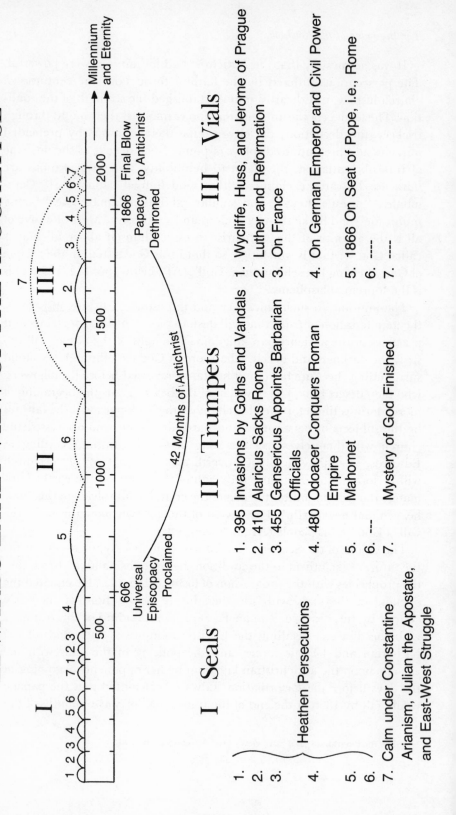

I Seals

1.
2.
3. } Heathen Persecutions
4.
5.
6.
7. Calm under Constantine
     Arianism, Julian the Apostate, and East-West Struggle

II Trumpets

1. 395 Invasions by Goths and Vandals
2. 410 Alaricus Sacks Rome
3. 455 Gensericus Appoints Barbarian
         Officials
4. 480 Odoacer Conquers Roman
         Empire
5. Mahomet
6. ---
7. Mystery of God Finished

III Vials

1. Wycliffe, Huss, and Jerome of Prague
2. Luther and Reformation
3. On France
4. On German Emperor and Civil Power
5. 1866 On Seat of Pope, i.e., Rome
6. ---
7. ---

reign of Antichrist. His interpretation was based on the belief that God works through the historical process to achieve his will, not in spite of or apart from that process.

Edwards' earliest reflections on the Revelation were a natural product of his situation. He soon began to use his new notebook to forge theological concepts from the exegetical materials on the visions.

3. *The "Apocalypse," the Ministry, and the Millennium*

In the years after 1723 it became necessary for Edwards to adapt his study habits to a broadening set of responsibilities. Nonetheless, he persisted with his interest in the Apocalypse and never set aside his notebook for more than limited periods of time. "My heart," he wrote looking back in 1739, "has been much on the advancement of Christ's kingdom in the world. . . . And my mind has been much entertained and delighted, with the Scripture promises and prophecies, of the future glorious advancement of Christ's kingdom on earth."[7] The "Apocalypse" was the private record of his entertainment and delight; his sermons and published writings documented his increasing public involvement in the fortunes of the church and a disposition to apply eschatological notions to contemporary situations. Together private reflections and public representations formed an intriguing and complex, but sometimes contradictory, network of theological ideas.

In the public sphere the most pressing new demand made upon Edwards was as a preacher; as a result he frequently turned to his private notebooks for ideas and themes in his sermons. In 1729 when the mantle of Solomon Stoddard fell squarely upon his shoulders, the young minister faced the task of preaching two or more times each week. He found that the book of Revelation, as well as other parts of the Bible, could be accommodated to virtually any pastoral need by the deft art of sermonizing. Today sixty-six sermons on the Revelation remain among his papers, evidence of a strong homiletical interest in that part of the Bible.[8]

His earliest extant sermon on the Apocalypse shows the youthful preacher weaving his private reflections into a discourse designed to motivate his congregation to greater concern for the things of religion. Edwards explained the text, "And the city was pure gold, like unto

7. "Personal Narrative," in Levin, ed., *Jonathan Edwards*, p. 35.

8. See Appendix B, below, pp. 440–43, for a list of the extant sermons on the Revelation with their stated doctrines or themes. On JE as a preacher, see Wilson H. Kimnach, "The Literary Techniques of Jonathan Edwards," Diss. Univ. of Pennsylvania, 1971.

clear glass" (Rev. 21:18), as a "metaphorical description" of the city of God, the biblical Zion or New Jerusalem.[9] This "new heaven and new earth," the culmination of God's redemptive work, is the reward of the saints. It is fitting, Edwards observed, that a description of the city of God be placed at the conclusion of "the most comprehensive and most particular prophecy of all the changes that should happen to the Christian church that we have in the whole Bible," for it specifies what is the "ultimate end and drift of all these things" (Bk. I, p. 2). But the text is a visionary representation, not a literal description: "there is nothing upon earth that will suffice to represent to us the glories of heaven" (Bk. I, p. 4). All similitudes that shadow forth the heavenly state are inadequate, at best providing only a glimpse of the excellence of that state.

Reason tells man that God's motive for the creation was the communication of his own happiness to "something else." In the "Apocalypse" Edwards found the vision of the four beasts (Rev. 4:6–9) confirmatory; the second beast resembling a calf symbolizes the goodness of God. "Goodness," he wrote, "is the only end why he has created the world, and the ultimate end of every dispensation of whatever nature" (below, p. 137). There will come a time when "God will fully manifest his love to good men, to those that answer the end of their creation," in a manner that Christians have not yet enjoyed here on earth (Bk. I, p. 20). This, he concluded, is evidence of a future state of happiness after death.

If there be such a glorious future, Edwards asked in the sermon, why is the world so dull and neglectful of such things? It is foolish and shameful that Christians think so little about the New Jerusalem, that they fix their hearts on things in the world that are mere "loss and dung" compared to the rewards received with the crown of glory (Bk. II, p. 20). "How unreasonable are they who grudge to deny themselves for the sake of heaven. Truly no rhetoric can represent their folly" (Bk. II, p. 21). By linking the vision of the heavenly Jerusalem with the happiness of all who heard him, Edwards prepared the logical ground for urging his congregation to strive for consistency between their daily activities and the larger purpose of God in the world.

Edwards used the book of Revelation for other homiletical purposes: consolation, imprecation, and preparation for battle as well as for the sacrament. He found it thoroughly suitable to the application of legal terrors. For example, in 1731 or 1732 he preached a sermon with the

9. Sermon on Rev. 21:18, in 2 booklets (MSS, Yale coll.), Bk. I, p. 1.

following stated doctrine: " 'Tis not inconsistent with the attributes of God to punish ungodly men with a misery that is eternal."[1] According to Edwards, the text in Revelation 19:2–3 is a visionary account of the songs of praise upon the occasion of God's "executing vengeance on Antichrist" at the fall of Babylon when the "great whore" is paid in kind for shedding the blood of the saints. The saints sing with delight as they watch the smoke ascend from Babylon after the overthrow of the antichristian church and the punishment of its members. That smoke rises forever.

In this sermon Edwards went from the images of the Apocalypse into the imagination of his congregation. The smoke rising forever is a representation of the eternal torment and misery of those being punished for their sins. Eternal chastisement, he warned, is not inconsistent with the mercy of God, for the nature of the crime dictates the severity of the punishment. Since God is "a Being whose loveliness, honorableness and authority are infinite" (p. 12), the violation of obligations to him demands a commensurate punishment. There will be no respite in hell. The vindication of divine majesty requires that ungodly men be so treated. "When the sun is grown so old that he grows pale and has lost his light, their torments will be as extreme as ever" (p. 5). Eternal punishment will be "always but beginning." Those who think this too cruel a conception of God, Edwards said, have not looked closely at the horrid nature of sin. All agree that the unending punishment meted out to papal persecutors does not seem too harsh or extreme, he reminded his Protestant hearers, because of the terribleness of their manifest crime. So it will appear with the eternal torments for other sins when the saints have an adequate sense of the excellence of God and of the dreadfulness of transgressions against him. Edwards pressed into service a Protestant reading of the Revelation in order to instruct his congregation about the nature and potential consequences of sin.

The Apocalypse proved a rich storehouse of diverse sermonic materials suitable to the range of practical situations confronting Edwards, but pastoral obligations did not dull his fascination with the more speculative apocalyptic issues. During the same years he continued to fill the pages of the notebook with a variety of reflections, including additional conjectures about the meaning of the four beasts of Revelation 4, which he regarded as symbols of God's providential care, and further accounts of the devices of the Antichrist, especially as portrayed in the tale of the two beasts in chapter 13. In this period the millennium

1. Sermon on Rev. 19:2–3 (MS, Yale coll.), p. 4.

remained a matter of consuming private interest for him. In the note-book he compiled more examples of the biblical use of the number "seven" as evidence that the glorious time of the church's prosperity would begin in the "seventh thousand year" of the world, or about 2000 in the present era, a calculation consistent in his judgment with the pattern of sabbaths established by God during the week of creation.[2]

Edwards toyed with the political implications of the "theocracy" that will be established in the millennium, when both civil and ec-clesiastical governments will be overthrown: then "the absolute and despotic power of the kings of the earth shall be taken away, and liberty shall reign throughout the earth." That liberty will not result in anarchy, but neither will it be limited to spiritual freedom, for it includes release "from the tyrannical and absolute power of men." During the millennium kings will be like the judges who ruled ancient Israel before the monarchy was established—a form of government that pleased God greatly, according to Edwards' understanding of the Bible. They will be "as the kings of England now are in civil matters" —a compliment the heirs of Edwards would later revoke in a long list of grievances against George III.[3] In that glorious day, Edwards con-jectured, a variety of forms of government may prevail, but none shall be contrary to "true liberty" (AP; below, p. 137).

The geography of the millennium, another issue that divided com-mentators, attracted his exegetical attention. Edwards found scriptural warrant for placing the land of Canaan at the center of the coming kingdom of Christ. In the "Apocalypse" he noted the geographical advantages of Canaan, located literally at the center of the old world in the midst of three continents and so positioned with respect to waterways that all of the remaining parts of the globe could be reached easily. Canaan, wrote Edwards, was "to be the place from whence the truth should shine forth, and true religion spread around into all parts of the world." Although Israel's strategic location had not been fully exploited, he was confident "that the most glorious part of the church will hereafter be there, at the center of the kingdom of Christ, com-municating influences to all other parts" (below, p. 134).

2. See the continuity in JE's numerical reflections in the AP, nos. 16, 21, 25, 27, 29, 35b, 50, 53, 55, 60, and 69.

3. See Alan Heimert, *Religion and the American Mind from the Great Awakening to the Revolution* (Cambridge, Mass., 1966), pp. 408–12; J. F. Maclear, "The Republic and the Millennium," in *The Religion of the Republic*, ed. Elwyn A. Smith (Philadelphia, 1971), pp. 183–216; and Stephen J. Stein, "An Apocalyptic Rationale for the American Revolution," *Early American Literature*, 9 (1975), 211–25.

In like manner, he speculated that the return of the Jews to their homeland is inevitable because the promises of land made to them have been only partially fulfilled. God intends the Jews to be "a visible monument" of his grace and power. The return to their traditional homeland, however, was premised by Edwards upon a conversion of the Jews to Christianity. Then "religion and learning will be there at the highest; more excellent books will be there written, etc." Canaan will be the spiritual center of the coming kingdom, and Israel will again be a truly distinct nation. Yet other Christians will have access to Jerusalem because the Jews will "look upon all the world to be their brethren, as much as the Christians in Boston and the Christians in other parts of New England look on each other as brethren." The millennium, Edwards reasoned, will be a time of such fraternity and unity (AP; below, p. 135).

In the years after the beginning of the notebook, a pattern emerged in Edwards' treatment of the Apocalypse. Speculation in private but discretion in public came to be characteristic of him. He kept conjectures to himself in the notebook and in his sermons utilized more conventional and less controversial eschatological ideas—heaven, hell, the blessedness of one and the terror of the other. The millennium, a major subject of Edwards' private reflections, was noticeably absent as a leading topic in his early sermons, even on occasions when it would have served his announced ends. Sometimes he avoided explicit reference to it, preferring indirect expressions subject to more than one interpretation, perhaps in order to escape the taint of fanaticism and radicalism associated with the idea.

In no period was Edwards' public discretion on apocalyptic issues more evident than at the time of the surprising conversions in Northampton during the winter of 1734–35. The revival demanded public interpretation by the young preacher. "Pressing into the Kingdom of God," a sermon he preached in February 1735 during the stirring, displayed his characteristic way of dealing with eschatological topics. In the discourse he underscored the "extreme necessity" of his congregation and urged them to get on with the business of heaven because it was the proper objective of the Christian life. There is no safety or refuge outside heaven; men will cry in vain to God as they are swallowed by a "fiery deluge of wrath." "Sacrifice *every thing*," he exhorted his hearers, for the eternal interest of your souls. "You that have a mind to obtain converting grace and to go to heaven when you die, now is your season! Now, if you have any sort of prudence for your own

salvation, and have not a mind to go to hell, improve this season!"
Edwards argued passionately because he was convinced that God might
be gathering his elect a last time "before some great and sore judgment," an argument he based on an interpretation of Revelation 7–8.
In the past, he noted, God has frequently brought "great and destroying
judgments" after a special effusion of his Spirit. "And this may be the
case now," he added, "that God is about, in a great measure, to forsake
this land, and give up this people, and to bring most awful and overwhelming judgments upon it, and that he is now gathering in his elect,
to secure them from the calamity. The state of the nation, and of this
land, never looked so threatening of such a thing as at this day."[4]
Edwards tried to promote a concern for the business of religion by
raising the specter of impending judgment and woe. He did not use a
millennial hypothesis to interpret the affairs of 1734–35 in Northampton.

Edwards displayed the same reluctance in his later accounts of the
revival. Despite the fact that the religious awakening in the community
paralleled his private anticipations of the preparatory period leading to
the future glorious state of the church on earth, he avoided the suggestion that the revival was a beginning or even a type of the millennium.
His earliest description of the affair in a letter to Benjamin Colman
(1673–1747) on May 30, 1735, spoke of the work as "an extraordinary
dispensation of providence" on account of its "universality" among the
people, its "extent" throughout many towns, and its "swift progress
from place to place." But Edwards added, "I forbear to make reflections, or to guess what God is about to do; I leave this to you, and shall
only say, as I desire always to say from my heart, 'To God be all the
glory, whose work alone it is.' "[5] In a longer account written for publication in 1736 when the religious fervor had passed, he placed the
events in an eschatological framework, noting that as religion became
universal, "noise among the dry bones waxed louder and louder. All
other talk but about spiritual and eternal things was thrown by. . . .
The only thing was to get the kingdom of heaven, and everyone appeared pressing into it."[6] Edwards ascribed no millennial significance
or preparatory role to this awakening. Two years later when the full

4. *The Works of President Edwards* (4 vols., New York, 1843), *4*, 385, 389, 392, 396–97.
Hereafter cited as Worcester rev. ed.

5. C. C. Goen, ed., *The Great Awakening*, Vol. 4 of *The Works of Jonathan Edwards* (New
Haven, 1972), pp. 107, 109. Hereafter cited as *Works, 4*.

6. Letter to Benjamin Colman, Nov. 6, 1736, abridged by Colman; in *Works, 4*, 117.

text of the narrative was published in America, it contained more detailed descriptions of the "abiding change" worked on many persons in Northampton: they have "a new sense of things, new apprehensions and views of God, of the divine attributes, and Jesus Christ, and the great things of the Gospel" as well as "new sweetnesses and delights." It is evident, Edwards wrote, that God was manifesting his glory "in this corner of the world."[7] The signs were similar to his expectations for the times preceding the millennial reign, but he did not state that association. When he spoke of the restraints upon Satan during the revival of 1734–35, he did not link them with the traditional binding of Satan (Rev. 20:1–3) during the millennium. He passed by these and other opportunities to make public his private thoughts.

The ministers who wrote the prefaces to the various accounts were less restrained in their judgments. In a letter dated October 12, 1737, the Englishmen Isaac Watts (1674–1748) and John Guyse (1680–1761) were quick to associate the "astonishing exercises" of God's power with "his promises concerning the latter days"—an association, they wrote, that "gives us further encouragement to pray, and wait, and hope for the like display of his power in the midst of us." They regarded the events in America as indicative of "how easy it will be for our blessed Lord to make a full accomplishment of all his predictions concerning his kingdom." They closed their preface with a request that all readers pray for the full accomplishment of God's promises "concerning the large extent of this salvation in the latter days of the world."[8] The four ministers who introduced the American edition of the narrative sounded the same theme, linking the "wonders" of the events in Northampton with the apocalyptic predictions of Scripture. "And as this wonderful work may be considered as an earnest of what God will do towards the close of the Gospel day," they wrote, "it affords great encouragement to our faith and prayer in pleading those promises which relate to the glorious extent and flourishing of the kingdom of Christ upon earth, and have not yet had their full and final accomplishment."[9] Compared to these, Edwards' judgments about the revival of 1734–35 were indeed restrained.

Edwards' restraint did not imply the absence of hope on his part. On

7. *A Faithful Narrative of the Surprising Work of God in the Conversion of Many Hundred Souls*; in *Works, 4*, 208, 210.

8. *Works, 4*, 131–32, 137.

9. Ibid., p. 141. Three of the four signatories—Joseph Sewall, Thomas Prince, and John Webb—later signed the preface of the HA; the fourth minister, William Cooper, died in the intervening years. Cf. HA; below, p. 311.

the contrary, his expectations had been buoyed by the outpouring of the Spirit in Northampton; he eagerly awaited times of greater success for the church.[1] Therefore no one was more disappointed when religious depression set in again and dullness reigned in the hearts of his congregation. The return to a period of spiritual torpor, however, did not end his life of study; in fact, in the years after 1738 his reading raised his sights anew and led him to hope with greater intensity that God might do something special among the people of New England, an expectation he came to partly as a result of studying the commentary on the Revelation by Moses Lowman.[2] With Lowman's *Paraphrase and Notes* in hand, Edwards reevaluated his earlier views of the Apocalypse and began a period of concentrated activity in the notebook.

One public measure of the impact of Lowman upon Edwards was the series of sermons he preached between March and August of 1739, published posthumously as *A History of the Work of Redemption* (1774). Edwards hoped to spark another revival in his congregation with the sermons. As he addressed those who were "neglecting the business of religion and their own souls," he had little good to say about the present very dark times.[3] He prayed for another awakening because he believed that God advances his work of redemption through successive effusions of his Spirit. From the fall of man to the birth of Christ, from the incarnation to the resurrection, and from Christ's resurrection until the end of the world, "it has been God's manner in every remarkable new establishment of the state of his visible church, to give a remarkable outpouring of his Spirit."[4] Therefore, wrote Edwards, "it would be ungrateful in us not to take notice of . . . that remarkable pouring out of the Spirit of God which has been of late in this part of New England, of which we, in this town, have had such a share."[5] God has worked in Northampton and other remote parts of the world—as remote as Muscovy, Malabar, and Saxony—promoting the work of redemption. The kingdom of heaven, a synonym for the evangelical state of things in the church and world, is always advancing toward fullness through successive dispensations of providence, each of which may be described

1. In a letter to Benjamin Colman, May 2, 1738 (MS, Massachusetts Historical Society), JE wrote, "Religion remains much in the same state amongst us that it has lately been; it is not as it was with us three years ago, nor yet is it as it was before that time of great blessing, and I hope never will be."

2. See below, pp. 55–59, for a discussion of Lowman.

3. Worcester rev. ed., *1*, 420.

4. Ibid., p. 380.

5. Ibid., p. 470.

as Christ's coming. Christ came in his kingdom at the time of the apostles and in the fourth century when Christianity gained imperial recognition; he will come again when the Antichrist falls and finally when he himself returns to judge the world and take the saints to eternal glory.

At the present the church is in the third period, the "latter days of the world," according to Edwards, a term he used for all Christian experience after the resurrection. It is a time of trial for the church with only short intermissions or respites. God has always chosen to have "the darkest time with the Christian church just before the break of day"; deliverance follows the dark night of affliction, the time of "greatest extremity."[6] The fortunes of the church during this period of tribulation comprise the subject matter of the major part of the book of Revelation, the one prophetic book in the New Testament. The church now has only the guidance of prophecy: "Where Scripture history fails, there prophecy takes place; so that the account is still carried on, and the chain is not broken till we come to the very last link of it in the consummation of all things."[7]

From the book of Revelation, according to Edwards, the church learns that the Roman papacy fulfills the prophecies of the Antichrist, and that the fall of Antichrist will be a moment of signal importance in history. Earlier he had calculated to his own satisfaction the time of that fall (AP; below, p. 129), but in 1739 he was reluctant to go on record with a public prediction. "I am far," he said in the sermons, "from pretending to determine the time when the reign of Antichrist began, which is a point that has been so much controverted among divines and expositors."[8] Edwards' reluctance to offer specific dates in public was probably reinforced by his reading of Lowman, who had explained the meaning of the first five vials, he thought, "with greater probability perhaps than any who went before him."[9] On the basis of Lowman, he changed his mind and pushed forward his own private apocalyptic timetable. The present age was not under the third vial but the sixth, according to the new interpretation, and fewer events remained to be fulfilled before the inauguration of the millennium than under Edwards' old scheme. Pastorally the change gave Edwards greater cause to direct an urgent summons to his congregation, who seemed to him very far from the state described in the Scriptures. Nevertheless, the recogni-

6. Ibid., p. 449.
7. Ibid., p. 368.
8. Ibid., p. 457.
9. Ibid., p. 462.

tion of God's customary way of accomplishing his salvation "should strengthen our faith in those promises," he wrote, "and encourage us, and stir us up to earnest prayer to God for the accomplishment of the great and glorious things which yet remain to be fulfilled."[1] There was some reason for cautious optimism in the midst of religious stagnation. God works gradually in his kingdom through the means of grace, including preaching, prayer, and the other ordinances. When the kingdom of Antichrist is overthrown, the reign of Christ will follow, and the church will enjoy a state of peace and prosperity.

For Edwards the millennium was not the ultimate goal of the entire work of redemption, but only an earnest of the heavenly state which is the fullness of the kingdom. Accordingly, in the sermons on Isaiah 51:8 the millennium took second place to heaven, the objective of all God's dealings with the church. Following the years of prosperity on earth, a new rebellion will shake the kingdom of Christ, subjecting Christians again to hardship and suffering at the hands of the forces of Satan. Final deliverance comes at a moment of desperation when "the world shall be filled with the most aggravated wickedness that ever it was."[2] Then Christ will appear with his hosts to gather the elect to their reward, but his enemies will stand "before his judgment seat with inconceivable horror and amazement, with ghastly countenances, and quaking limbs, and chattering teeth, and knees smiting one against another" as they prepare to receive their sentence.[3] At that moment begins the "new heaven and new earth."[4]

The sermons on the work of redemption are an important index of Edwards' public views in 1739, prima facie evidence of the role of the "Apocalypse" in his ministry, and further confirmation of the general restraint he showed in statements about controversial issues in the apocalyptic tradition. In addition, they establish indisputably the significance of time and history in his theological reflections.[5] By the end of the 1730s Edwards possessed a new apocalyptic timetable, a considerable body of evidence that God was inclined to pour out his

1. Ibid., p. 480.
2. Ibid., p. 495.
3. Ibid., p. 502.
4. See JE's reflections on the "new heaven and new earth" in the AP, including nos. 41, 59, 62, 64, 65, 73a, 84, and 85.
5. Two thoughtful and provocative interpretations of JE's sermons on the work of redemption are Heimert, *Religion and the American Mind*, esp. pp. 60–61, 98–100; and Peter Gay, *A Loss of Mastery: Puritan Historians in Colonial America* (Berkeley, 1966), pp. 88–117. See also William J. Scheick, "The Grand Design: Jonathan Edwards' *History of the Work of Redemption*," *Eighteenth-Century Studies, 8* (1975), 300–14.

Spirit both locally and universally, and a continuing hope that through his ministrations the church in Northampton would blossom with a new awakening. Edwards and his congregation were primed for the return of the revivals.

The congregation in Northampton did not have long to wait. News of the evangelical successes of the Anglican itinerant George Whitefield (1714–70) began arriving in the colonies, and America prepared to receive the successful young preacher.[6] Whitefield's tour of the colonies began near the end of October, only a few months after Edwards had completed his series of sermons on Isaiah 51. As reports of Whitefield's activities circulated, hopes soared. The contagion spread to Northampton, where Edwards was following closely the news from afar. When he heard that Whitefield planned a journey to New England, he wrote to invite the revivalist to make Northampton a stop on his itinerary, but he also warned that the region might prove unresponsive to his preaching because it was "more hardend" than other places. Nevertheless, he expressed the desire "to see something of that Salvation of God in New-England which he has now begun, in a benighted, wicked and miserable world and age and in the most guilty of all nations." The promises of God and the reports of success led Edwards to share with Whitefield his private hope that the present moment may be "the dawning of a day of Gods mighty Power and glorious grace to the world of mankind." To that end he encouraged the itinerant to continue preaching, "that the work of God may be carried on by a Blessing on your Labours . . . until the Kingdom of Satan shall shake, and his proud Empire fall throughout the Earth and the Kingdom of Christ, that glorious Kingdom of Light, holiness, Peace and Love, shall be Established from one end of the Earth unto the other!" In particular, Edwards wanted his own congregation to take part in the new awakening, and he himself longed to be an "instrument" of God's glory.[7] The prospect of a visit from Whitefield raised his apocalyptic fever to a new high.

The events of the following months, including Whitefield's visit to

6. See Luke Tyerman, *The Life of the Rev. George Whitefield* (2 vols., London, 1876–77); and Stuart C. Henry, *George Whitefield: Wayfaring Witness* (New York, 1957). Although Whitefield was a member of the Church of England, he managed to exploit anti-Anglican sentiments in the colonies. See William Howland Kenney, III, "George Whitefield, Dissenter Priest of the Great Awakening, 1739–1741," *William and Mary Quarterly*, 3rd ser., *26* (1969), 75–93.

7. Letter to Whitefield, Feb. 12, 1740; in Henry Abelove, "Jonathan Edwards's Letter of Invitation to George Whitefield," *William and Mary Quarterly*, 3rd ser., *29* (1972), 488–89. JE expressed the same hopes about Whitefield's visit in a letter to Eleazar Wheelock (1711–79), Oct. 9, 1740 (MS, Forbes Library).

Northampton in October of 1740, did not disappoint him. The town was again filled with the quickening in a measure surpassing the experiences of 1734–35. Edwards became a successful revivalist and eventually the most prominent American spokesman for the new evangelicalism. The months of August and September in 1741 were the "most remarkable" of the revival, according to his report, filled with "great revivings, quickenings, and comforts"; but even in February and March of the following year there was "continual commotion, day and night."[8] During the busiest months he had little time for the "Apocalypse." By the end of 1742 the whole land had experienced the excitement of the Great Awakening.[9]

In that moment of evangelical success and high spirits, Edwards wrote the following conjecture:

> 'Tis not unlikely that this work of God's Spirit, that is so extraordinary and wonderful, is the dawning, or at least a prelude, of that glorious work of God, so often foretold in Scripture, which in the progress and issue of it, shall renew the world of mankind. If we consider how long since the things foretold, as what should precede this great event, have been accomplished; and how long this event has been expected by the church of God, and thought to be nigh by the most eminent men of God in the church; and withal consider what the state of things now is, and has for a considerable time been, in the church of God and world of mankind, we can't reasonably think otherwise, than that the beginning of this great work of God must be near. And there are many things that make it probable that this work will begin in America.[1]

This heady proclamation published in 1743 was neither in character with Edwards' earlier pronouncements on the revivals nor totally consistent with his own private reflections. Within a short time after it was printed, he became defensive about his remarks on the millennium, insisting that they had been misunderstood—a claim that must be

8. Letter to Thomas Prince, Dec. 12, 1743; in *Works, 4,* 547, 550.

9. See Edwin S. Gaustad, *The Great Awakening in New England* (New York, 1957), ch. 4; and Joseph Tracy, *The Great Awakening: A History of the Revival of Religion in the Time of Edwards and Whitefield* (Boston, 1841).

1. *Some Thoughts Concerning the Present Revival of Religion in New England;* in *Works, 4,* 353. JE was not alone in his excitement and optimism. A minister in Boston near the same time wrote, "Let the Guardian Angels carry the News to Heaven of the numerous Converts; the *Millennium* is begun, Christ dwells with Men on Earth." See a letter of John Moorhead to John Willison, July 30, 1742; in Jules H. Tuttle, "The Glasgow-Weekly-History, 1743," *Proceedings of the Massachusetts Historical Society, 53* (1919–20), 213. Hereafter cited as *PMHS.*

checked against the full range of his comments.

In 1743 more than one motive was at work in Edwards' treatise on the revivals. On the one hand, he wanted to celebrate publicly the outpouring upon New England and affirm the religious results of the awakening. He had prayed and worked for precisely such a manifestation of God's presence among his people. Edwards would not and could not turn his back on the revival. On the other hand, the voices of the critics were growing louder as they challenged the divinity and validity of the awakening. The excesses of some with an "enthusiastical spirit" played into the hands of the opponents of the revivals. Indiscretions abounded among the itinerants and lay exhorters. Censoriousness rather than fraternity, division rather than unity, were becoming the prevailing marks of the revival.[2] In this situation someone had to defend the awakening by affirming what was genuine in it and by restraining the radical elements that were discrediting the movement. Edwards elected to take on these tasks in his treatise on the revivals.

From C. C. Goen's analysis of *Some Thoughts*, it is clear that Edwards established to his own satisfaction that the revival was a glorious work of God deserving the support of all parties interested in true religion.[3] He tried to meet the charges of the critics by suggesting that the excesses were insufficient grounds to reject the genuine manifestations of God in the awakening, but he did not deny the reality of the problem. Tactically this argument had the advantage of disarming the critics by removing the onus of extremism from the majority of those favoring the revivals. Edwards' defense was of little pastoral assistance, however, for it left the individual with the difficult task of determining what was true religion and what was not, a dilemma Edwards recognized and tried to solve in his later discourse on the religious affections.[4] The millennial speculations in 1743 were atypical of Edwards' earlier public statements and formed only a small part of the argument of the treatise.[5] Rather than setting to rest the charges of extremism, *Some Thoughts* gave a new target to the opponents of the revivals by adding the issue of the millennium.

2. AP; below, p. 218. See Gaustad, *Great Awakening*, ch. 5.

3. *Works, 4*, 65–78.

4. See John E. Smith's introduction to the *Religious Affections*, Vol. 2 of *The Works of Jonathan Edwards* (New Haven, 1959). Hereafter cited as *Works, 2*.

5. Goen's interpretation follows his own earlier essay, "Jonathan Edwards: A New Departure." The essay has influenced several studies, including Ernest Lee Tuveson, *Redeemer Nation: The Idea of America's Millennial Role* (Chicago, 1968); and Heimert, *Religion and the American Mind*.

In the treatise of 1743 Edwards expressed in public his private commitment to millennialism, although he still chose to avoid use of the term itself. He did not present a very effective case for his ideas. Most of the references to the approaching glorious times of the church are explicitly conjectural or hypothetical, even prefaced by the particle *if*. The concluding paragraphs in his discussion are introduced in the same conditional manner.[6] Edwards spent much of his time belaboring the fact that it was "probable" the millennial age might begin in America, arguing the point with a strange set of reasons.[7] For example, he explained the distant "isles" of Isaiah 60:9, which some interpreters thought a prophecy of the first fruits of the church's glorious age, as a reference to the colonies. "I can't think that anything else can be here intended but America," he wrote, although earlier in his private reflections he had explained the conversion of the isles as pointing to Europe.[8] He argued that the division between the old world and the new, as well as the principle of fairness or equality "in the dispensations of providence," nearly compelled God to give "the honor of communicating religion in its most glorious state" to America as a representative of the new world—after all, the old world had killed Christ, too. He offered this argument in spite of the fact that he had privately reasoned that God had not finished fulfilling his promises to the Jews, and that Canaan was to be the center of the glorious kingdom of God (AP; below, p. 134). He also proposed that America would be the center of the coming kingdom because when God does something great for the church, he commonly begins with the weakest part in order that the last may be first—an evaluation of America in tension with his earlier praise for the first generation of settlers in New England.[9]

These arguments, among the most tortured in his essays, hardly represent the range of Edwards' thinking about the millennium. He seems to have been searching desperately for evidence to support his claims for the millennial role of New England's revivals. It is hard to ignore the charge of Charles Chauncy (1705–87) that Edwards' reasoning was "absolutely precarious."[1] In preceding years Edwards had not

6. Cf. *Works, 4,* 466 and 498.

7. See ibid., 353–58.

8. Compare ibid., 353, with Miscell. no. g. JE had also described a threefold interpretation of the "isles" in the AP; below, p. 142.

9. For example, see Worcester rev. ed., *1,* 468.

1. *Seasonable Thoughts on the State of Religion in New-England* (Boston, 1743), p. 372. Chauncy did not deny the value or importance of the prophecies of the "last days": he denounced those who pretended to calculate the moment of fulfillment. "But it can answer no good End

allowed himself such unguarded statements about the expectations of the church. Nevertheless, at this moment pastoral concerns still motivated him: "I have thus long insisted on this point, because if these things are so, it greatly manifests how much it behooves us to encourage and promote this work, and how dangerous it will be to forbear so to do."[2]

A revealing footnote to his remarks on the millennium is found in Edwards' private correspondence. In a letter to William McCulloch (1691–1771) on March 5, 1744, he complained about a "slanderously reported and printed" account "that I have often said that the millennium was already begun, and that it began in Northampton." He found it especially objectionable that Chauncy had not divulged the source of the report. All of this, Edwards grumbled, "is very diverse from what I have ever said." He acknowledged that he had spoken of the revivals as "forerunners of those glorious times so often prophesied of in the Scripture, and that this was the first dawning of that light, and beginning of that work which, in the progress and issue of it, would at last bring on the church's latter-day glory." But the critics had ignored, he maintained, that he had also pointed to "many sore conflicts and terrible convulsions" and the "returns of dark clouds" before the days of prosperity for the church.[3] By 1744 Edwards was smarting from the criticism directed against his published millennial speculations.

The publication of *Some Thoughts* brought to a close the second period of the "Apocalypse," the period in which the revivals had become the central concern of Edwards' ministry. Throughout the years from 1723 to 1743 he had continued to develop his interpretation of the Revelation in the notebook. By the end of those twenty years, his apocalyptic interest was no longer a private matter because of his leadership in the revivals and his now public commitment to millennialism.

4. *The Aftermath of the Awakening: The* Humble Attempt

After 1743 there were few reasons to be sanguine about the state of religion in New England. In that deteriorating situation Edwards

---

to lead People into the Belief of any *particular* Time, as the Time *appointed* of GOD for the Accomplishment of these Purposes in his mercy; because this is one of those Matters, his Wisdom has thought fit to keep conceal'd from the Knowledge of Man" (pp. 374–75).

2. *Works, 4,* 358.

3. Ibid., 560. The letter is printed in full in Dwight ed., *1,* 211–19. The MSS for this and the other letters exchanged between JE and the ministers in Scotland, except where otherwise indicated, are in the Andover collection of Edwards Papers in the Hills Library, Andover Newton Theological School.

revealed more of his private reflections on the book of Revelation when he published the *Humble Attempt* in 1748. His treatise, highly occasional in nature, was the culmination of many years of study, but also the direct product of his response to the changing circumstances of the decade. In it Edwards called for united prayer, which he defended on a variety of grounds, as a remedy for the problems confronting the evangelical world. The *Humble Attempt* underscored his conception of the significance of prophecy in the life of the church and in turn provided the rationale for his principal use of the "Apocalypse" during the last ten years of his life.

Confusion presided over the religious scene in New England in the mid-1740s. The increasing decay and deadness made Edwards "very melancholy," his high hopes giving way to keen disappointment.[4] The "glorious Things promis'd to the Church in the latter Days" had not materialized despite the prayers of the faithful and the signatures of one hundred and eleven ministers who, like Edwards, were waiting for "the Glory of the latter Days."[5] The ecclesiastical chaos that followed in the wake of the itinerants discredited the awakening and created a centrifugal force in the churches of the land. "In many places where God of late wonderfully appeared," wrote Edwards to a friend, "he has now in a great measure withdrawn; and the consequence is, that Zion and the interest of religion are involved in innumerable and inextricable difficulties."[6] The situation changed little during the next fifteen years; never again during his lifetime did a general awakening return to the colonies. But Edwards was not given to despair; in spite of disappointment he refused to surrender the evangelical cause and held to the hope "that God will revive his work, and that what has been so great and very extraordinary, is a forerunner of a yet more glorious and extensive work."[7]

4. Letter to William McCulloch, Mar. 5, 1744; in Dwight ed., *1*, 212.

5. *The Testimony and Advice of an Assembly of Pastors of Churches in New-England, At a Meeting in Boston July 7, 1743. Occasion'd by the late happy Revival of Religion in many Parts of the Land. To which are added, Attestations contain'd in Letters from a Number of their Brethren who were providentially hinder'd from giving their Presence* (Boston, 1743); excerpted in Richard L. Bushman, ed., *The Great Awakening: Documents on the Revival of Religion, 1740–1745* (New York, 1970), pp. 129–32.

6. Letter to an unnamed correspondent, Nov. 20, 1745; in James Robe, ed., *The Christian Monthly History: or, An Account of the Revival and Progress of Religion, Abroad, and at Home* (2 vols., Edinburgh, 1743–46), No. 8 (Nov. 1745), p. 235. The letter is reprinted in Appendix C, below, pp. 444–60. Concerning the disintegration of the religious community in New England, see C. C. Goen, *Revivalism and Separatism in New England, 1740–1800: Strict Congregationalists and Separate Baptists in the Great Awakening* (New Haven, 1962); and Richard L. Bushman, *From Puritan to Yankee: Character and the Social Order in Connecticut, 1690–1765* (Cambridge, Mass., 1967), esp. pp. 145–232.

7. Letter to McCulloch, Mar. 5, 1744; in Dwight ed., *1*, 213.

Edwards found a bit of comfort in reports of continuing success drifting in from widely scattered places. Some information came through the newly founded evangelical magazines operating on both sides of the Atlantic, clearinghouses for tidings about the revivals.[8] He read carefully the pages of those public prints. Other news filtered through the network of his own correspondents, with whom he shared the watchful and hopeful posture. For example, decline appeared widespread in New England, but reports from Virginia and Maryland told of harvests by the revivalists William Robinson (d. 1746) and Samuel Buell (1716–98), to name but two. The missionary work of David Brainerd (1718–47) among the Indians of the middle colonies was noted with "those things that have a favorable aspect on the interest of religion."[9] Edwards also derived encouragement from the letters sent by the ministers in Scotland with whom he corresponded regularly beginning in the 1740s. A community of interests existed among evangelicals on both sides of the Atlantic.[1] Through the years Edwards and the other clergymen exchanged news of revivals, discussed theological issues, including matters that impinged directly upon the interpretation of the Apocalypse, and traded books of potential interest. Intelligence of the revivals in Scotland and elsewhere lifted his sagging spirits and softened the blow dealt by the decline of the revivals in New England.

The unstable international situation of the 1740s added to the uncertain outlook for evangelicalism in America. The decade witnessed renewed hostilities among the powers of Europe in the War of the Austrian Succession (1740–48), which spilled over into America as King George's War (1744–48), an imperial clash between England and

8. See Thomas Prince, Jr., ed., *The Christian History, Containing Accounts of the Revival and Propagation of Religion in Great Britain and America* (2 vols., Boston, 1744–45), which appeared as a periodical between March 1743 and Feb. 1745; and Robe, ed., *The Christian Monthly History*, which appeared between Nov. 1743 and Jan. 1746. The power behind the Boston publication was Thomas Prince, Sr., a strong supporter of revivalism, later one of the signers of the preface of the HA. See John E. Van de Wetering, "The *Christian History* of the Great Awakening," *Journal of Presbyterian History*, 44 (1966), 122–29. Robe's publication succeeded an earlier periodical edited by William McCulloch, *The Glasgow Weekly History Relating to the Late Progress of the Gospel At Home and Abroad* (Glasgow, 1741–42). See Tuttle, "Glasgow-Weekly-History." The first evangelical magazine began with the encouragement of George Whitefield, *The Weekly History: or, An Account of the most Remarkable Particulars relating to the present Progress of the Gospel* (London, 1741–42). See Roland Austin, "The Weekly History," *Proceedings of The Wesley Historical Society, 11*, Pt. 2 (1917), 39–43.

9. Appendix C, below, p. 449.

1. There is no adequate study of the evangelical community which spanned the Atlantic during the mid-eighteenth century. See Dwight ed., *1*, esp. chs. 15–18, for some of the letters exchanged during this period by JE and his Scottish friends; and Arthur Fawcett, *The Cambuslang Revival: The Scottish Evangelical Revival of the Eighteenth Century* (London, 1971).

the colonial powers of Spain and France.[2] One area of conflict in North America was the southeastern coastal region where the Spanish and English conducted intermittent and indecisive raids upon each other. More persistent struggles took place in another theater, the region of Canada and the adjacent English colonies. There open warfare broke out after March 1744 when France declared war on Britain. At stake in America were territorial claims, trading rights, natural resources, and military advantages—none of these inconsequential. Edwards followed developments closely because the outcome had implications for the view of history he had shaped in his reflections on the Revelation.

For New England the most celebrated campaign of the 1740s was the effort to secure control of Cape Breton, an island in the Gulf of St. Lawrence ceded to France by the Peace of Utrecht in 1713. The French had secured their possession with a strong fort and garrison at Louisburg. Privateers from Cape Breton and from the nearby English territory of Nova Scotia freely sailed the neighboring seas, preying upon vessels of their respective enemies. New Englanders had experienced that annoyance in their trade and in their competition with the French for fisheries. When news of the declaration of war reached Cape Breton, the French commander attacked Canso, a fishing outpost on Nova Scotia. Word of the attack sent shudders through New England and served notice of an impending conflict.

Opinions were divided in New England regarding the best course of action. Robert Auchmuty (d. 1750), an agent of the Massachusetts colony in London, urged immediate attack upon Cape Breton, arguing that the benefits of control of the island would be considerable. Auchmuty's views circulated widely in the press and won support from those inclined to take the offensive.[3] Others favored the more cautious tactic of delaying military action until the official position of the government in England was clear and its assistance assured. In January 1745 Governor William Shirley of Massachusetts proposed an attack, but the General Court refused to go along with his plan. Later the assembly

2. Howard H. Peckham, *The Colonial Wars 1689–1762* (Chicago, 1964), ch. 5; and Douglas Edward Leach, *Arms for Empire: A Military History of the British Colonies in North America, 1607–1763* (New York, 1973), ch. 6.

3. See Auchmuty's letter of Apr. 9, 1744; in *Collections of the Massachusetts Historical Society,* 1st ser., *5* (1798), 202–05. Among other reasons, he argued that England would obtain vast revenues from the fisheries of Cape Breton and correspondingly France would suffer a severe blow from the loss of the island because of the religious dependence of the French Roman Catholics upon fish. JE was familiar with this argument, which he may have read in its newspaper versions (*The Boston Weekly News-Letter,* Nov. 20, 1746, p. 1, and Sept. 3, 1747, p. 1. Hereafter cited as BNL) or in the later publication, *Importance of the Island of Cape Breton considered* (London, 1746). See HA; below, p. 423.

reversed itself and agreed to undertake an expedition against Cape Breton as part of a wider campaign. Edwards obviously favored the decision, as his report of the affair attests. Some twenty members of the congregation in Northampton were part of the expeditionary force. Before departure, he noted, there had been "an extraordinary spirit of prayer given the people of God in New England, with respect to this undertaking, more than in any public affair within my remembrance" (below, p. 449).

From the beginning, according to Edwards, things went well for the English. The harvest of the preceding summer had been plentiful, intelligence about the defenses at Louisburg was seemingly adequate thanks to the timely return of some repatriated prisoners, and there was growing popular support for the campaign.[4] Within two months after the decision had been made, the expedition sailed for Canada, good fortune aiding at every turn. In Edwards' view providence was smiling upon New England. On June 17, 1745, the beleaguered defenders of Louisburg surrendered to the combined forces of the colonial militia under William Pepperell and the English naval squadron commanded by Commodore Peter Warren.[5] News of the victory brought rejoicing to New England and caused Edwards later to declare the siege and surrender of Cape Breton "a dispensation of providence, the most remarkable in its kind, that has been in many ages."[6]

4. Many of the clergy of New England quickly rallied to the cause. For example, Abiel Walley described one response in a letter to an unnamed correspondent, Oct. 15, 1747 (MS, Boston Public Library). "A very remarkable Minister, one Mr. Moody of near four Score years old as Soon as ye Generale was appointed for ye Expedition to Cape Breton, went to him and offer'd to go as a Chaplain, Saying He had been at ye pulling down one Limb of Antichrist in ye Year 1711. a place Called Port Royal in Nova Scotia. (Now Annapolis) and he would go and help pull downe this by his Prayers. it was thought in his advanced age of ye fatigue would be too much for him, thinking a Field Campaign he could not Survive He said He would go for he Should be as willing to go to Heaven (if the time of his Death came) from Cape Britton as any where—when he was there went round ye Camp every Day encouraging the Soldiers not to let their Courage fail they were fighting for God who would give them ye victory, and when ye place was taken and they entred ye City He took an ax went into one of their Churches Cutt downe of their Images or Cross, then preached a Thanksgiving Sermon—returned home well is Still Living & preaching Constantly." See also Samuel A. Green, "Joseph Emerson's Journal of the Louisburg Expedition," *PMHS, 44* (1910–11), 65–84; and Nathan O. Hatch, "The Origins of Civil Millennialism in America: New England Clergymen, War with France, and the Revolution," *William and Mary Quarterly,* 3rd ser., *31* (1974), 407–30.

5. This victory and the subsequent successes of Warren for the crown made him a folk hero in the eyes of many Americans, as the newspapers of the period testify. Benjamin Colman was willing to designate him "a Father to these His Majtys Northern Colonies in America." See his letter to Warren, Aug. 17, 1747 (MS, Boston Public Library).

6. Below, p. 459. The letter in Appendix C contains a detailed account of the campaign. See also Louis Effingham de Forest, ed., *Louisbourg Journals 1745* (New York, 1932).

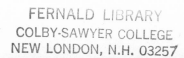

But providence seemed to have two faces. The joy over the success at Louisburg was soon mixed with other emotions. Word from the mother country told of a Jacobite rebellion led by the Stuart pretender to the throne. By late in the fall of 1745 the armies of Prince Charles Edward were invading England. Meanwhile the troops on Cape Breton had grown disgruntled after their victory when they were denied the right of plunder, and they had become nearly mutinous when the occupation dragged on, delaying their return home.[7] By 1746 rumors of a great French force assembled to revenge the loss of Louisburg were circulating throughout New England. The colonies began to lay plans for another larger assault upon Canada, a campaign which never materialized. The conflict with the French spread to other areas besides Canada; outlying parts of the English colonies increasingly came under attack. For example, in late 1745 the French with their Indian allies struck with surprise and success at Saratoga, carrying away many captives. In August 1746 Fort Massachusetts in the western part of the colony fell. Few areas seemed safe from encroachment.

Edwards weighed the remarkable deliverance at Cape Breton against the new threats and on balance declared the acts of providence sufficient to convince even an infidel of the existence of God and of his beneficence: "we live," he exclaimed, "in an age, wherein divine wonders are to be expected." On the other hand, he conceded that God might be using some of the events, especially the fresh activities of the antichristian coalition—the Roman Catholic pretender and the Catholic powers of France and Spain—to chastise "the nations of Great Britain" for their vice, wickedness, and apostasy. "It is a day of great commotion and tumult among the nations," he wrote, "and what the issue will be we know not: but it now becomes us, and the church of God everywhere, to cry to him, that he would overrule all for the advancement of the kingdom of Christ, and the bringing on the expected peace and prosperity of Zion" (below, pp. 459–60).

It was prayer that Edwards singled out as an appropriate activity for those tumultuous times. In prayer, the most universal act of worship, the church asked for divine favor and at the same time affirmed the reality of the divine being. Private prayer was fundamentally a matter of devotion, but public prayer was a social action with religious and ecclesiastical implications. Edwards was persuaded that praying Christians could exert a powerful influence upon the fortunes of the church and the world.

7. Leach, *Arms for Empire*, pp. 242–43.

This use of prayer was not new to Edwards; it had been an essential part of his religious exercises since childhood. Once he recalled that as young boys he and his schoolmates "joined together, and built a booth in a swamp, in a very secret and retired place, for a place of prayer." As a child he used to pray privately five times a day and often met with friends for social prayer. He described his life as continual communion with God. "And [I] was almost constantly in ejaculatory prayer, wherever I was. Prayer seem'd to be natural to me; as the breath, by which the inward burnings of my heart had vent." The topics occupying him in prayer were also those to which he directed his study. "I had great longings," he recollected, "for the advancement of Christ's kingdom in the world. My secret prayer used to be in great part taken up in praying for it."[8] When he faltered in his religious duties, he was not slow to chide himself. In his "Diary" for February 5, 1724, he wrote, "I have not, in times past, in my prayers, enough insisted on the glorifying of God in the world, on the advancement of the kingdom of Christ, the prosperity of the Church and the good of man."[9] Prayer became for Edwards an essential part of the business of religion, a means whereby rational creatures could glorify their Creator.

These judgments were not novel in New England. The standard textbook of Puritan theology defined prayer as "a devout presentation of our will before God so that he may be, as it were, affected by it."[1] Its author, William Ames (1576–1633), had stated that by its very nature prayer was a testimony to the glory and power of God. Practice followed theory in New England; public prayer was employed frequently for both religious and civil purposes. In the seventeenth century it became common practice to set aside special days for prayer appropriate to the needs or circumstances of the people, a pattern that persisted into the eighteenth century. The events of the 1740s evoked a similar response from New England.[2]

8. "Personal Narrative," in Levin, ed., *Jonathan Edwards*, pp. 24, 28, 31.

9. Dwight ed., *1*, 102.

1. John D. Eusden, ed., *The Marrow of Theology* (Boston, 1968), p. 258.

2. For example, see the published sermons of Thomas Prince, especially *Extraordinary Events the Doings of God, and marvellous in pious Eyes* (Boston, 1745); and *The Salvations of God in 1746* (Boston, 1746). It has been incorrectly suggested that JE was indifferent to such public occasions (Heimert, *Religion and the American Mind*, p. 126). In fact, a sequence of fast day sermons by him follows the progression of international events in this period. See the following sermons: Josh. 7:12, June 28, 1744, war with France; I Kgs. 8:44–45, Apr. 14, 1745, expedition against Cape Breton; II Chron. 20:20–29, Aug. 1745, return from Cape Breton; Is. 8:9–10, Sept. 19, 1745, war with the Indians; Matt. 16:18, Mar. 13, 1746, the rebellion; Neh. 4:14, June 1746, expedition to Canada; Rev. 17:11, July 10, 1746, expedition to Canada; Is. 33:

Edwards believed that the prayers of the saints were especially instrumental in the fortunes of the church because they constitute "one great and principal means of carrying on the designs of Christ's kingdom in the world."[3] Past experience of the church, he felt, confirmed that judgment. Therefore when the Great Awakening began to dissipate, he urged those who were interested in vital piety to pray for a new effusion of God's Spirit upon the land. Many wasted hours, he contended in 1743, might be spent profitably in such prayer:

> I have often thought it would be a thing very desirable, and very likely to be followed with a great blessing, if there could be some contrivance that there should be an agreement of all God's people in America, that are well affected to this work, to keep a day of fasting and prayer to God; . . . to address the Father of mercies, with prayers and supplications, and earnest cries, that he would guide and direct his own people, and that he would continue and still carry on this work, and more abundantly and extensively pour out his Spirit; . . . and erect his glorious kingdom through the earth.[4]

Perhaps a group of ministers might formulate a proposal for subscription by others and then make the whole affair public by printing an account of it.

On the basis of this suggestion in 1743, Edwards has been credited with originating the idea of the concert of prayer.[5] But the notion did not begin with him; a similar plan was already in operation in Scotland before his suggestion appeared in print. A number of prayer societies in Edinburgh had combined in a movement to select a special day to pray for an outpouring of God's Spirit. The leaders circulated a public announcement of their intentions which read as follows:

> *Edinbr. January* 21st, 1743.
> SOME Christian Societies in this Place who have of late observed, with no small spiritual Joy, the Outpourings of the Spirit from on High on several Corners of this wither'd Church, in Sincerity and

---

19–24, Oct. 16, 1746, arrival of French fleet; Is. 37:28–29, Nov. 27, 1746, confusion of French fleet; and Ex. 33:19, Aug. 1746, victory over the rebels (MSS, Yale coll.).

3. *Some Thoughts*; in *Works, 4,* 516. See JE's sermon on Rev. 8:2–3 preached in July 1742 (below, p. 441). The evangelicals had no monopoly on this belief. See Charles Chauncy, *The out-pouring of the Holy Ghost. A Sermon Preach'd in Boston, May 13, 1742. On a day of prayer observed by the first Church there, to ask of God the effusion of his Spirit* (Boston, 1742).

4. *Works, 4,* 520.

5. E.g., Heimert, *Religion and the American Mind,* p. 80.

Truth, and who long for the Coming of his Kingdom, to set a Day apart for praising and giving Thanks to his Name, for any remarkable Waterings he has given to some Spots of his Vineyard; and to pray that these may only be the Fore-runners of a plentiful Shower, to refresh the Whole.

That he would carry on this good and unexpected Work with such Power and Demonstration of the Spirit, that all Opposers, whether professed Enemies to his Kingdom, or mistaken Friends, may be at last obliged to own that it is *the Doing of the Lord, and wonderful in* their *Eyes.*

The Day proposed for this agreable Duty is the 18th of *February* next.

But if that Day does not suit with the Conveniency of any of the Societies, or private Christians, that desire to keep such a Day, they may chuse another more convenient for them.[6]

In Edinburgh a local concert preceded the larger effort of subsequent years.

Prayer societies had become prominent on both sides of the Atlantic during the revivals. These societies, nearly overlooked by historians, were an important institutional expression of the awakenings, although they were not unique to the eighteenth century.[7] Edwards recorded the increasing concern for prayer among the converted in Northampton and charted the ups and downs of the societies in his congregation.[8] The groups were usually homogeneous, composed of men or women, young or old, who met at designated times for corporate prayer. According to Edwards, the advancement of God's kingdom was a special concern of the societies. In later years these clusters of praying Christians provided a potential constituency for the proposed concert of prayer and a natural audience for the *Humble Attempt.*

Encouraged by the successes of the societies and by rising interest in a concerted effort of some kind, a group of Scottish ministers met in October 1744 and agreed to unite in prayer regularly at designated times and in quarterly meetings with the hope that God would revive his church throughout the world. Initially they did not publish their intentions,

6. Printed with John Willison's letter to Benjamin Colman, Feb. 28, 1743; in *The Christian History, 1,* 87.

7. *The Christian History* contains numerous references to the societies in both America and Scotland during the period of the awakening. E.g., *1,* 315–17, 349–51; *2,* 106–08, 326–27.

8. See his letter to Thomas Prince, Dec. 12, 1743; in *Works, 4,* 544. He reported that despite the decay of religion, "yet many societies for prayer and social religion were all along kept up."

but spread the concert by private conversation and correspondence
(HA; below, pp. 321–24). If successful, they planned to renew the
concert and to involve a wider segment of the Christian community.
John McLaurin (1693–1754), one of Edwards' earliest correspondents
in Scotland, was "the chief contriver and promoter" of the union;
others of his Scottish friends were also leaders of the movement.[9]

The proposal was immediately appealing and agreeable to Edwards,
who regarded the union as "exceeding beautiful, and becoming Christians" and especially appropriate to the present state of things. God of
late has shown "our weakness, infirmity, [and] insufficiency," he wrote
in November 1745, and therefore "it is apparent that we can't help
ourselves, and have nowhere else to go, but to God" (below, p. 445).
At the same time he asked his friends in Scotland for more details about
the concert.

Edwards became an organizer of the movement in America, promoting it among his acquaintances and associates. After hearing of the
proposal from abroad, he introduced it to his congregation, reading
parts of the letters in public and "using many arguments with them to
comply with the thing proposed." Many of the prayer societies in Northampton, he reported, followed the suggestion of special quarterly days
for prayer. Edwards circulated news of the affair among neighboring
ministers whom he thought likely to support the plan and urged them
to spread the word. He wrote to others farther away and asked them to
tell him of their activities on behalf of the concert. As of November
1745, however, he had mostly discouraging news to report concerning
the union. But, he added, "I shall not cease still to do what in me lies
to promote and propagate it, according as favorable junctures and
opportunities do present" (below, pp. 445–46). His report in May of
the next year was not much more encouraging. "With respect to the
Concert for Prayer, for the pouring out of the Spirit," he wrote, "the
People in this Town have of late more generally fallen in with it." The
last quarterly day "was pretty generally observed, in whole or part, as a
Day of Prayer, in private Societies, for the forementioned Blessing."[1]
The concert was far from an overwhelming success in Northampton.

9. John Gillies, ed., *Sermons and Essays by the late Rev. Mr. John M'Laurin, one of the Ministers
of Glasgow. To which is prefixed, some account of the Life and Character of the Author* (Philadelphia,
1811), p. viii. See Fawcett, *Cambuslang Revival*, pp. 224–27. John Wesley (1703–91), the founder of the Methodist movement, heard of the plan and immediately suggested that JE and
Gilbert Tennent in America be consulted. See his letter to Lord Grange, Mar. 16, 1745; in
John Telford, ed., *The Letters of the Rev. John Wesley* (8 vols., London, 1931), 2, 33–34.

1. Letter to unnamed minister at Glasgow, May 12, 1746; in *Christian Monthly History*,

Edwards worked for the union because he saw it as a solution to the religious problems plaguing New England. In place of ecclesiastical disruption and division, the plan offered a new basis for community and harmony. Christians engaged in prayer with one another would constitute "one family, one holy and happy society." Instead of religious drought in the land, the proposal held out the hope of a new era of the Spirit. If a union of praying Christians can be realized, he asked, "who knows what it may come to at last?" Perhaps the united prayers would even "open the doors and windows of heaven, that have so long been shut up, and been as brass over the heads of the inhabitants of the earth, as to spiritual showers" (below, pp. 446–47). Edwards wrote the *Humble Attempt* less than a year later as another effort to foster that union.[2]

The first part of the treatise contains his interpretation of the text for the discourse, Zechariah 8:20–22, and an account of the background of the concert of prayer. He explained the passage from Zechariah as a prophecy of the last prosperous times of the church on earth. Nothing in the experience of the Jews, not even the return from Babylon, and nothing in the early ages of the church has fulfilled the promises. Earlier periods of prosperity and deliverance were only types or anticipations of the last great age. According to Edwards, the future enlargement of the church will be inaugurated "by great multitudes in different towns and countries taking up a *joint resolution*, and coming into an express and visible *agreement*, that they will, by united and extraordinary *prayer*, seek to God that he would come and manifest himself, and grant the tokens and fruits of his gracious presence" (below, p. 314). The core of his argument for the concert was the idea that Christians must pray together for God's presence because he has withdrawn from the earth. From time to time, said Edwards, the prophets depict God as hiding from the church. At those moments the saints ought to wait for and seek God in a fervent and constant manner. Since union among Christians is pleasing to God, he argued, the churches of America cannot reject the proposal made by the ministers in Scotland.

Edwards began his account of the concert with the meeting held in October 1744 when the Scottish ministers set up the union for a trial period. Nearly two years later they met again and agreed to renew the concert and make it a public affair. Accordingly, they drew up a

---

No. 10 (Jan. 1746), p. 298. In the same issue, see JE's letter to William McCulloch of the same date, pp. 299–302, concerning the concert.

   2. See below, pp. 82–84, for a discussion of JE's composition of the HA.

Memorial which was printed and circulated among scattered evangelicals. Some five hundred copies were sent to America for distribution throughout the colonies, according to Edwards.[3] He included the text of the Memorial in the *Humble Attempt*.

The Memorial stated the rationale, objectives, and method of the concert. Its authors urged those agreeing with the proposal to publicize their cooperation. They especially encouraged ministers and teachers to publish "short and nervous scriptural persuasives and directions to the duty in view" and "to preach frequently on the importance and necessity of prayer for the coming of our Lord's kingdom" (HA; below, p. 326). The concert was not confined to "any particular denomination or party," but was inclusive in design, intended for all who had the interest of Christianity at heart.

In Part II of the treatise Edwards marshalled a variety of reasons for participating in the concert of prayer. The *Humble Attempt* was his answer to the call for "scriptural persuasives"; its basic line of argumentation was exegetical. Pointing to unfulfilled prophecies in the Bible, Edwards reasoned that the kingdom of God awaits a time of future prosperity greater than it has experienced in the past. The church of God has never been as extensive as it is depicted in the passages of the Old Testament which speak of its filling the entire world, surpassing all other monarchies in extent, and embracing the people of all nations. Nor have the New Testament prophecies about the universality of Christ's kingdom or its long duration been fulfilled. The church on earth has never included the fullness of the Jews and the Gentiles; nor has it witnessed a protracted period of prosperity. Christ's kingdom is to follow the destruction of Antichrist, an event which has not been completed, according to Edwards. Earlier ages have been mere anticipations of the glorious day.

The future kingdom of Christ, wrote Edwards, will be a paradise restored in which God will be "eminently glorified" and his people "unspeakably happy" (HA; below, p. 337). Knowledge and holiness will cover the earth when religion prevails again. The poor will become princes, and kings will bow as servants. Peace, love, and harmony will rule among the saints, false teaching and divisions will disappear from the churches, and superstition will give way to the

---

3. JE forwarded three copies to his close friend Joseph Bellamy (1719–90) and urged him "to dispose of two of 'em where they will be most serviceable. For my part," he wrote, "I heartily wish it was fallen in with by all Christians from the rising to the setting sun" (Letter of Jan. 15, 1747; Yale coll.).

pure worship of God. The family of man will be one and act as one, all members living as brothers. Prosperity, health, and long life will bring extraordinary joy to all beings on earth and in heaven. Surely, exhorted Edwards, such an ideal situation deserves the prayers of the church.

A further incentive to pray for the Spirit, according to Edwards, is the example of Christ who devoted his life and death to the goal of securing that blessing for his followers. He gave the Spirit to the church in small portions during earlier ages, but in the latter days he will bestow it in great abundance. Even if that age extends for only a thousand years, it will witness the greatest increase of the saints in history. It is possible, conjectured Edwards, that a hundred thousand times more converts will enter the church during the millennium than in all the ages since creation—a fitting end, in his view, to the activities of Christ's kingdom (HA; below, p. 343).

The "whole creation," wrote Edwards, is waiting for the day on which it will be delivered from the bondage brought by sin. Like a woman in labor, the universe struggles to be released from its unnatural bonds. The creatures of the universe were made for good ends by the Creator, and he will restore them to their proper functions in the future age of the church. The present commotions in the world serve a higher ultimate purpose, as the pains of travail precede the joys of birth. In the meantime all creatures wait and pray for that day.

In Edwards' view, the Bible is filled with "precepts, encouragements, and examples" stressing the necessity of prayer for the Spirit of God. In fact, he said, the people of God ought to be "importunate" in seeking that blessing. Repeatedly the Psalms and the Prophets depict deliverance as following the prayers of the faithful. The Scriptures suggest that when prayer fills the church, God is likely to answer the requests of his saints. Perhaps the present generation, Edwards speculated, is the one spoken of in the promises, for the prophecies describe the people as "destitute." Edwards judged the church at his time "in very low, sorrowful and needy circumstances" (HA; below, p. 352). At precisely such moments God commands his people to pray, and he stands ready to hear the cry for mercy. God is prepared to restore the church when he perceives that it earnestly seeks his Spirit.

Edwards viewed the contemporary situation as additional motivation to participate in the concert. The long list of evils threatening the world —the present "bloody war," the wickedness and vice filling the land and the nation, the infidelity and blasphemy of the age, the general contempt for religion, the decline of "vital piety," the struggles in the churches, the loss of respect for the ministry, the neglect of the ordinances, the lack of church discipline, and the religious excesses of all kinds—should compel the people of God to pray for a manifestation of the Spirit. Alongside these negative incentives for prayer there existed remarkable providences which were cause for Christians to believe that God will not let his church suffer forever—positive encouragements to pray. Most notable among these were the success at Cape Breton, the deliverances from subsequent French efforts on land and sea, the restoration of captives from Canada, and the recent revivals in the land. The evidences of mercy, Edwards believed, should evoke thanksgiving and prayer.

Edwards urged his readers to comply with the proposal for all of these reasons and for one more: the union of praying Christians will be beautiful, he said, because unity itself is "amiable" and consistent with God's plan for the creation. When the church throughout the world, diverse as it is, acts as one family, it is a mark of glory for its Head. By the act of united prayer the fractured church manifests the reality of the "body of Christ" (HA; below, p. 366). Spiritual union will lead to better relations among the separate parts of the church. Thus for Edwards the concert of prayer was both a means to an end and an end in itself.

The third and longest part of the *Humble Attempt* is a defense of the concert against a number of objections, practical and theoretical. The union in prayer had not been very successful in America during the two-year trial period. In the last section of the treatise Edwards dealt with some of the apparent reasons for that lack of success.

In answer to the charge that the designation of special days for regular observance was an imposition upon the consciences of men—a criticism Protestants traditionally leveled against the worship of the Roman Catholic Church—Edwards insisted the concert intended no such burden. The authors of the Memorial had no authority over the participants; they even recommended altering the pattern of observance wherever necessary or desirable. Surely no serious objection, Edwards said, can be made against establishing times and places for common prayer; otherwise all social worship is precluded. The principle of good order demands similar provisions. Furthermore, public fast days have never been subject to this criticism.

The concert is not "whimsical," contended Edwards. The proposal does not rest upon the assumption that God is more likely to hear prayers because they are offered at the same time. United prayer is beneficial for other reasons, principally because it promotes the unity of scattered Christians and nurtures confidence among them. Visible acts of worship, including corporate prayer, glorify God and encourage the saints by building mutual affection among the participants. "There is no wisdom," he philosophized, "in finding fault with human nature" (HA; below, p. 375).

Edwards rejected the epithet of "Pharisaism" as inappropriate for the concert. It makes no sense, he argued, to say that those who pray together publicly are making a show of their religious activities; the concert is not designed to restrict involvement to a small group, but rather to embrace as many people as possible. If the charge were valid, all special worship activities, whether fast days or days of thanksgiving, would be pharisaical. Nor is the idea of a concert new, he noted. The duty of prayer for the Spirit has been constant in the church, and Christians in many ages have appointed days for special worship.

Two other objections Edwards regarded as potentially more threatening to the cause of the concert, and he responded to both in greater detail, drawing directly upon his earlier reflections in the "Apocalypse." The first concerned the time for the beginning of Christ's future kingdom. Some interpreters of the Revelation on the basis of the hardships inflicted upon the witnesses in the vision of Revelation 11, concluded that the future kingdom would follow an age of calamity for the church.[4] Edwards, however, believed that their interpretation undermined the objectives of the concert and inevitably dampened their zeal for prayer, for if they prayed for the coming of the kingdom, they would be hastening upon themselves the age of persecution, according to their scheme. He tried to meet this difficulty at its root, namely, the interpretation of the account of the witnesses. He declared that the witnesses, representing the faithful, had been slain in the days before the Reformation. The church was then at its lowest point in the time of the crusades against the Waldenses and the Albigenses. The destruction of Antichrist began with the reformers, and now the church of Christ is gradually gaining ascendancy over her enemies as the vials are being poured out. God will not sacrifice these gains,

---

4. For example, see Samuel Sewall, *Phaenomena Quaedam Apocalyptica* (Boston, 1697). Thomas Goodwin, Peter Jurieu, and others were of the same mind. See Froom, *Prophetic Faith, 2,* 724–28. By contrast, Robert Fleming (1630–94) had argued that the slaying was already past. See *The Fulfilling of the Scripture* (Boston, 1743), a reprint of the work with an introduction by Thomas Foxcroft.

Edwards affirmed; nor will he return the saints to the earlier depths. The influence of the Antichrist has been permanently shaken, and the light of the gospel is dispelling the forces of the kingdom of darkness. The efforts of the Antichrist to defeat Protestantism have failed.

According to Edwards, these same interpreters misrepresent other parts of the Apocalypse. They confound the accounts of the battles between the forces of Antichrist and of Christ. In the Revelation there are two great battles, not one, which are depicted very differently in the visions. In the first the beast triumphs (Rev. 11), but the church of Christ is victorious in the second (Rev. 16 and 19). The second battle is the greater event in the book of Revelation, in Edwards' view. The commentators mistakenly confuse the meaning of the three woes (Rev. 9–11), all of which are inflicted upon Antichrist, contrary to their interpretations. Many exegetes have been too eager to pinpoint the exact time at which the 1260 days of the witnesses (Rev. 11:3) will end. Let it suffice to point out, Edwards suggested, that God in the past has sometimes shortened the days of the church's suffering and certainly can do so again. The rationale of the proposed concert, he maintained, was not inconsistent with a correct interpretation of the Revelation.

The other serious objection to which Edwards addressed himself was based upon the calculation of Moses Lowman that the fall of the Antichrist would not occur until after the year 2000. In defense of the concert Edwards parted company with Lowman, whose work he had earlier openly admired.[5] He attacked Lowman's interpretation because of its negative implications for prayer. Edwards charged that it is not reasonable to assume that God has revealed an exact date for Christ's coming in his kingdom (HA; below, p. 395). In fact, he has kept the matter hidden; nevertheless, he wants the church to pray that the kingdom come soon. There is an irony in this reprimand by Edwards in view of his own longstanding fascination with apocalyptic speculation. Even though he believed that the precise time of the fall of the Antichrist and the beginning of the kingdom had not been revealed, he was unwilling to place it far into the future. On the imminence of Christ's return he thought a majority of expositors agreed.

Edwards maintained that Lowman was mistaken in his identification of Constantine as one of the heads of the beast (Rev. 12:3), a part of the alliance of Satan against the church. He regarded Constantine as God's chosen vessel who had protected the saints from the heathen empire.

5. See pp. 22–25 and 55–59 for JE's earlier study and use of Lowman.

For him Constantine's appearance was a pivotal event in the history of the church. Edwards also contended that Lowman had miscalculated the beginning of the 1260 years of the reign of Antichrist and consequently had incorrectly identified the preceding world power. The beginning of the reign of Antichrist was more likely in 456 than in 756 since it was a time of spiritual domination, not temporal sovereignty. The latter he found inconsistent with the tone and intention of the book of Revelation. Therefore the rule of Antichrist was not fixed geographically to the city of Rome, as Lowman had suggested.

In order to discredit the basic assumptions on which Lowman rested his dating of the reign of Antichrist, Edwards took aim at the heart of his interpretation, the system of successive periods. Lowman's scheme, he wrote, "seems to me to be more ingenious than solid, and that many things might be said to demonstrate it not to be founded in the truth of things, and the real design of the divine author of this prophecy" (HA; below, p. 406). Lowman's association of the Saracens with both the fifth and sixth trumpets ignored the place and function of the Turks in western history—a clear distortion in Edwards' eyes. Lowman was inconsistent in allowing the period of the trumpets to close with conflicting events, the peace of the church and the rise of the Antichrist. These and other criticisms Edwards had noted earlier in his "Remarks on Lowman" (AP; below, pp. 251–52). By 1748 therefore he was challenging the leading features of Lowman's interpretation of the Revelation.

Edwards' own view of the fall of Antichrist underscored the gradualness of the historical process. With the fall of ancient Babylon as a prototype for God's activity, he hypothesized that a remnant of the Church of Rome may remain active in the world after the beginning of the destruction of Antichrist under the sixth vial. Perhaps the finishing stroke against the antichristian kingdom that leads directly to the millennium will come as late as Lowman suggests, namely, at the beginning of the "seventh thousand years," as many Jewish and Christian divines have argued (HA; below, p. 410). The destruction of the Antichrist is only one of the signs to be fulfilled before the millennium begins. Edwards complicated his apocalyptic timetable with this suggestion that the age of the Spirit might precede the millennium by a considerable distance in time. Even with the best of luck, he speculated, progress in the church will probably not be great enough for the millennium to begin until the year 2000. Here, some five years after he had published the bold prediction about the imminence of the millennium, Edwards withdrew that conjecture and returned to his earlier interpretation of the dating of the future glorious age.

But this apocalyptic reversal was no cause to neglect the concert. Edwards believed that an effusion of the Spirit is to accompany the destruction of the Antichrist under the sixth vial. God will destroy the new Babylon, the antichristian church, in the same manner as he did the ancient city—by drying up the river Euphrates. The "river" which serves mystical Babylon performs the same function as that which ran through literal Babylon of old. The river symbolizes the various revenues of the Roman Catholic Church and the wealth of the Catholic empires. When these supplies are dried up, the Antichrist will be weakened and ready for the final blow under the seventh vial. The sixth is a preparatory vial. Simultaneous with the weakening of the Antichrist will be the removal of other obstacles that have impeded the progress of Christ's kingdom, such as false doctrines and practices, divisions and contentions in the church. The saints have good reason to unite in the concert of prayer, for it seems evident, said Edwards, that "if the 6th vial han't already begun to be poured out, it may well be speedily expected" (HA; below, p. 421). Some fulfillment is apparent already from the changing relationship between the Pope and the Roman Catholic countries. The remarkable providences in North America, the reverses in South America, the losses of France in the East—these are portents of the impending destruction of the Antichrist. Even if the final destruction is distant, joint prayer may spark a revival which will further weaken the antichristian kingdom in the present age. Edwards concluded the *Humble Attempt* by reiterating his plea for compliance: surely no one, he exhorted, can reject this overture.

Within a month after he had submitted the text of the *Humble Attempt* to the printer, Edwards substantially changed the function of the "Apocalypse." In late 1747 he began to use the notebook as an apocalyptic ledger. In one list he collected contemporary evidence of the fulfillment of the sixth vial.[6] He searched newspapers and magazines and listened to reports from afar in the hope of documenting the reduction of the revenues and riches of the papacy. Through the next years he watched with delight the misfortunes of the Catholic powers—commercial, political, social, and military—confident that they betokened the approach of better times for the church. In a second list of

6. "An Account of Events Probably Fulfilling the Sixth Vial on the River Euphrates"; below, pp. 253–84.

contemporary events, Edwards tallied evangelical successes throughout the world, entering accounts culled from his reading, his correspondence, and his own experience.[7] He was convinced that the church would begin to prosper while her enemies suffered under the last three vials. Conversions of Indians, Jews, or Turks excited special attention because of traditional associations with those late stages in the apocalyptic timetable.[8] Edwards was not the only evangelical watching contemporary events, but it is a striking measure of the significance he attached to these affairs that he persisted with this apocalyptic bookkeeping throughout the years of great personal stress and turmoil, the period of the controversy in Northampton leading to his dismissal from his congregation. Perhaps his perception of the fulfillment of prophecy provided him some comfort in the midst of his own troubles.

The publication of the *Humble Attempt* was not Edwards' last effort to promote the concert of prayer. In subsequent years, as he kept his private record in the "Apocalypse," he continued to solicit public support for the union. For example, he sent Joseph Bellamy a copy of the *Humble Attempt* and requested, "Send me word whether the proposal for united prayer be complied with in your parts."[9] His letters to friends in Scotland between 1747 and 1749 contained numerous references to the concert and to the general state of religion.[1] Edwards functioned as an exchange point for information among evangelicals in America and abroad. He believed that the sharing of intelligence about scattered revivals was itself a means of grace. In mid-1749 he wrote:

> I was at the pains to extract from all the letters I received at that time, those things which appeared with a favourable aspect on the interest of religion in the world, and to draw various copies to send to different parts, to such as I supposed would be most likely to be entertained and improved by them, and to do good with them, and I believe they have been of great benefit, particularly to excite and encourage God's people, in the great duty of praying

7. "Events of an Hopeful Aspect on the State of Religion"; below, pp. 285–97.

8. See the two essays by Mukhtar Ali Isani, "The Pouring of the Sixth Vial: A Letter in A Taylor-Sewall Debate," *PMHS, 83* (1971), 123–29; and "The Growth of Sewall's *Phaenomena Quaedam Apocalyptica*," *Early American Literature, 7* (1972), 64–75. See also Increase Mather, *The Mystery of Israel's Salvation, Explained and Applyed: Or, A Discourse Concerning the General Conversion of the Israelitish Nation* (London, 1669); and Samuel Willard, *The Fountain Opened: Or, The Admirable Blessings plentifully to be Dispensed at the National Conversion of the Jews* (3rd ed., Boston, 1727).

9. Letter of Apr. 4, 1748 (MS, Yale coll.).

1. For example, see the letters in Dwight ed., *1,* 230–86.

for the coming of Christ's kingdom, and to promote extraordinary, united prayer in the method proposed in the Memorial from Scotland.[2]

In those years Edwards thought the concert was beginning to prosper in America, despite the fact that it was "in general a very dead time as to religion, and a time of the prevailing of all manner of iniquity."[3] Perhaps the concert did have some limited success in the colonies, but nothing comparable to the vision which had informed its authors and had filled the theological imagination of Edwards as he wrote in support of the Memorial.[4] The same might be said of the *Humble Attempt*. In mid-1749 Bellamy confided to Thomas Foxcroft that "to this day I beleive not half the Country have ever So much as heard of Mr. Edwards peice upon the *Scotland Concert*."[5] The concert and the treatise were far from successful in America. By the end of the 1740s Edwards' expectations for Christ's kingdom were also considerably more measured than his earlier prognostications.

5. *A Theology of the Apocalypse*

The "Apocalypse" was slated for one more use by Edwards, a project he sketched in a letter to the trustees of the College of New Jersey in October 1757 after he had been invited to assume the presidency of that fledgling institution. Writing from Stockbridge on the western frontier of Massachusetts where he had assumed a pastorate in 1751, Edwards enumerated several reasons for his hesitancy to accept the offer, including his plan for "a great work" of divinity in a "new method." For a long time, he confided, he had set his "mind and heart" on writing

2. Letter to William McCulloch, May 23, 1749; in Dwight ed., *1*, 276–77.

3. Letter to John Erskine, May 20, 1749; in Dwight ed., *1*, 275–76.

4. JE's assessment of the concert must be balanced against the relative lack of evidence of continuing widespread support for the affair. In Oct. 1748, an association of ministers in Massachusetts agreed "to be more especially fervent, in continual Prayer for the advancement of the kingdom of Christ" (Dwight ed., *1*, 282). In May 1749 JE mentioned to his Scottish correspondents several scattered ministers who were supporting the concert (ibid., 277–79), but by 1750–51 his references to the movement usually fall within the context of concern about slacking interest. In Scotland the concert was renewed in June 1754. See John Gillies, ed., *Historical Collections relating to Remarkable Periods of the Success of the Gospel and Eminent Instruments Employed in Promoting it* (2 vols., Glasgow, 1754), *2*, 402. Two years later John Brainerd wrote of plans in his synod to "come to Some Agreemt for extraordinary Prayer and Endeavours for a Reformation" (Letter to Eleazar Wheelock, Sept. 15, 1756; MS, Beinecke Library). On Feb. 11, 1757, JE wrote a letter to Thomas Foxcroft (MS, Yale coll.) expressing his hope for continued compliance with the Scottish plan, but by this time there were few others still aware of the movement.

5. Letter of May 6, 1749 (MS, Houghton Library).

a "*History of the Work of Redemption*" in which he would consider the whole of Christian theology in historical perspective. He proposed to examine "the grand design of God" as well as "all parts of the grand scheme" from eternity to the "consummation of all things; when it shall be said, *It is done. I am Alpha and Omega, the Beginning and the End.*" The materials in the "Apocalypse" were earmarked for this body of divinity because Edwards intended to deal with all successive dispensations in time, relying when necessary upon "history or prophecy."[6]

This proposed body of divinity was to be more than the series of sermons preached in 1739 and published posthumously under the name of the projected work. Edwards' plan called for a different method in which "doctrinal observations and dissertations" would be placed in "large MARGINAL NOTES at the bottom of the page."[7] Tentatively he had selected Deuteronomy 33:26 as a text for the treatise: "There is none like unto the God of Jeshurun, who rideth on the heavens in thy help, and in his excellency on the sky."[8] The universe, he explained, is like a "chariot in which God rides and makes progress towards the last end of all things." Deuteronomy 33:26, according to Edwards, signified "as much as that God governs the whole world for the good of his church . . . and every event in the universe is in subserviency to their help and benefit."[9] Edwards proposed to write theology in the form of universal history. Quite probably the "Extracts from Lowman" were compiled with this plan in mind, together with other notes he was taking; the excerpts would supply basic data for the historical framework of the discourse.[1]

6. Dwight ed., *1*, 569–70. As a young man in the months before he began the AP, JE had written, "There is a strange and unaccountable kind of enchantment, if I may so speak, in Scripture history; which, notwithstanding it is destitute of all rhetorical ornaments, makes it vastly more pleasant, agreeable, easy and natural, than any other history whatever" (Miscell. no. 6).

7. "Notebook on the History of Redemption, No. 1" (MS, Yale coll.), p. 103. The three notebooks related to the project are distinguished in the notes by their folder numbers. They reveal the close relationship between history and prophecy in JE's scheme.

8. "Notebook on Redemption, No. 1," p. 104.

9. "Miscellaneous Observations on the Holy Scriptures" (MS, Yale coll.), p. 169. Hereafter cited as the "Blank Bible." In this interleaved Bible JE wrote commentary on all parts of Scripture. He began to fill its more than 900 pages sometime after 1730; formerly the MS had belonged to his brother-in-law, Benjamin Pierpont. The contents of the "Blank Bible" form a tightly linked chain of commentary from which it is nearly impossible to extract a single entry without bringing to light several others that are closely related. This MS must be distinguished from the "Notes on Scripture" (MSS, Yale coll.), a numbered series of exegetical notes which JE began as a young man at the same approximate time as the AP and continued throughout his lifetime. Hereafter cited as the "Scripture."

1. See Appendix D, below, pp. 461–64, for a listing of some of the apocalyptic themes

The "History of Redemption" promised to be a final public expression of his lifetime of interest in the Apocalypse, the principal repository of prophecy, in his view, in the possession of the New Testament church. The sequence of the visions in the book of Revelation offered a natural organizational scheme for part of the proposed discourse. Edwards apparently planned such a use of the prophecy. In one of the project notebooks he wrote: "Another thing in these latter ages, which greatly makes way for the setting up of the glorious kingdom of Christ, is the remarkable diminishing of the ecclesiastical revenues of popish countries. Here shew this is the fulfilling of the SIXTH VIAL."[2] The contents of the "Apocalypse" were to be integrated into the body of divinity, a fitting conclusion for his reflections on the book of Revelation.

The sudden death of Edwards in 1758 left this project an unfulfilled promise. His death had another related but less obvious effect: the failure to complete the "History of Redemption" masked the significance of the apocalyptic factor in Edwards' theology by relegating much of the evidence of his commitment to biblical prophecy, including the "Apocalypse," to near oblivion.[3] This edition is one step toward correcting that situation.

By the 1750s Edwards possessed a coherent theology of the Apocalypse, the product of many years of reflection and writing.[4] Both the beginning and the end of history, according to him, fall within the theological perspective of the book of Revelation. All has proceeded from God by his pleasure, and ultimately all will return to him again. God's design for the universe was a product of his goodness, which he chose to communicate through the creation.[5] When rebellion blemished the creation, he determined to accomplish his ends through the work of Christ and the influence of his Spirit in the church. God directed the forces of nature and the events of history toward his objectives. Edwards

---

developed in the "Miscellanies" and the "Scripture." The appendix also contains a table indicating those passages in the book of Revelation on which JE commented in the "Blank Bible."

2. "Notebook on Redemption, No. 1," p. 8.

3. H. Richard Niebuhr was one of the earliest to perceive the importance of biblical eschatology for JE. See *The Kingdom of God in America* (New York, 1935), esp. pp. 141–50. His conclusions are different from those suggested here.

4. See James P. Martin, *The Last Judgment in Protestant Theology from Orthodoxy to Ritschl* (Grand Rapids, 1963), pp. 65–80, for an insightful assessment of the theological implications of JE's eschatological ideas.

5. During the same years JE was shaping his *Dissertation concerning the End for which God Created the World*, published posthumously in 1765 (Worcester rev. ed., 2, 191–257). It is a systematic statement of these themes.

was unbending in his commitment to the doctrine of providence, the natural extension of God's creative power throughout time. The doctrine of providence rested upon the twin assumptions of divine sovereignty and sufficiency. The special object of providential care was the church, guided at every moment, in good times and bad, by God's power, wisdom, justice, and mercy.[6]

Within this larger context the study of the Apocalypse became more than a matter of speculation about exegetical curiosities. Edwards' concern with the interpretation of the book of Revelation was itself a theological affirmation of sorts because it required of him confidence that the word of prophecy was a reliable guide for the affairs of the church. Apocalyptic speculation rested upon the presupposition that God had made known his intentions for the future in the book of Revelation and that in time he would unlock the secrets for his people on earth.[7] Therefore probing the mysteries of the book and correlating the prophecies with events in the life of the church constituted for Edwards a way of formulating statements about the sovereignty and sufficiency of God far more weighty than the details of the visions suggested. Conjectures and calculations about the Apocalypse were not idle amusements, but serious theological business. Concern with prophecy in Edwards' view was a mark of commitment and faith.[8]

In the same manner, Edwards' fixation upon the Antichrist and the activities of his kingdom was more than simply an expression of a culturally conditioned animosity or some kind of private preoccupation—although for Edwards it also may have involved a bit of both. In his theology of the Apocalypse the descriptions of the dangers facing the church from the antichristian forces played an additional theological role by compelling the saints to reflect upon the magnitude of the redemption effected by God on their behalf. Although the hatred and bigotry implicit in the negative judgments about the Roman Catholic Church were not mitigated one iota by this theological function, never-

6. See Seymour Van Dyken, *Samuel Willard, 1640–1707: Preacher of Orthodoxy in an Era of Change* (Grand Rapids, 1972), pp. 170–93, for an evaluation of the role of providence by an influential theologian of the generation preceding JE.

7. Concerning the "grand scheme" of all history, JE wrote: "In these days of the world, much more of it is discovered than had been in preceding ages; but till Christ came into the world, the grand mystery had been kept secret from ages and generations, from men and angels from the beginning of the world" ("Blank Bible," p. 478).

8. See Paul Ramsey, ed., *Freedom of the Will*, Vol. 1 of *The Works of Jonathan Edwards* (New Haven, 1957), pp. 245–47, for JE's connection of prophecy with the doctrine of God's foreknowledge of human events. Hereafter cited as *Works, 1*.

theless the constant concern with the beast was a subtle way of paying tribute to the God who triumphed over clever and unscrupulous enemies despite tremendous obstacles. Edwards' persistent attacks upon the Antichrist's claims and abuses were an affirmation of the truth of the divine attributes and accomplishments. For him the reality of the divine was mirrored even in the counterfeits of the beasts.

It is impossible to ignore the christological focus in Edwards' theology of the Apocalypse. Christ was the agent of the work of redemption through his life, death, and resurrection. His coming to earth brought an end to the earlier dispensations, and his ascension inaugurated the latter days of the church when all things ultimately will be restored. As the principal actor in the covenant of grace, he fulfilled the former promises of God and was himself the promise of things to come.[9] Theologically, the figure of the Lamb dominated the drama of the Apocalypse. The sacrifice of Christ, arranged in an eternal covenant of redemption between the Father and the Son, was effectual for all mankind. But the Son first suffered and then triumphed; so too his kingdom will experience hardship before the subsequent moments of glory. The Lamb that was slain in the visions, declared Edwards, is eventually victorious over the enemies of his church and will conduct his spouse to the glories of heaven.

In Edwards' view of the Apocalypse, Christ and the church were intimately related. As he was the primary agent of salvation, so the church—Christ mystical—upon his departure from the earth became the instrument through which the plan of God is carried forward. Those who experience grace in conversion unite with Christ and thereby share his suffering and glory. The union with Christ sustains and nurtures the church militant on earth, where suffering is common. But God has promised that the fortunes of believers will brighten in anticipation of the eternal glory of the church triumphant. As the bride of Christ, chaste and beautiful, the saints reject sin and seek holiness; they pray for his Spirit and attend upon the ordinances.[1] In this manner the church of Christ increases and spreads over the earth until the kingdom is universal. Then it can be said that the saints rule with Christ. After that, the Son delivers the kingdom to his Father, and the marriage of the Lamb is consummated in heaven.

In his theological reflections on the Apocalypse, Edwards tried to

9. Conrad Cherry has described JE's view of Christ as "God's covenant-event in history," in *The Theology of Jonathan Edwards: A Reappraisal* (Garden City, N.Y., 1966), p. 113.

1. See Thomas A. Schafer, "Jonathan Edwards' Conception of the Church," *Church History*, 24 (1955), 51–66.

hold in balance the dual eschatological themes of earthly prosperity and heavenly glory—sometimes a difficult task.[2] According to his understanding of the divine economy, the restoration of all things takes place gradually, from the time of the first promise of God through the various dispensations of salvation history. During the glorious age of the increase of the gospel, the earth will be restored to its primitive condition, or to at least a degree of it. Here Edwards was drawing heavily upon the Old Testament prophecies in the book of Isaiah. But the new creation will not be complete until God inaugurates the "new heaven and new earth," the eternal dwelling place of the saints. There the glory of God will be fully manifested, and the saints will live in bliss. Admittedly, at times it is difficult to distinguish the glories of one dispensation from those of another in Edwards' scheme because each anticipates the next, but he was never at a loss to identify his ultimate goal. Speaking of the "new heaven and new earth" described in Revelation 21:1, he wrote:

> It is the last that is said of the church, in this series of prophecies: 'tis set here as the end of all the foregoing revolutions, the highest reward of all their labors [and] sufferings, and the ultimate aim of all these wonderful successive dispensations of divine providence spoken of in the former part of the world. 'Tis after the general judgment, and manifestly different from the millennium (AP; below, pp. 141–42).

For him the eternal glory was the final goal of Christians. The accent upon the eternal rewards of grace did not remove the Christian from matters of earthly responsibility, in Edwards' opinion. In fact, the apocalyptic perspective heightened the pressures upon the Christian life, for God accomplishes his work of redemption through the human instrumentalities of the church by preaching, prayer, and the other ordinances.

Salvation is a progressive matter for Edwards. Christ's kingdom advances through time, but not in a straight line. The theme of restoration implies that progress in the work of redemption is circular in nature, bringing all things back to God, the initial point of departure. The final objective of the kingdom is not the exaltation of man, but the glorification of God, which was the original goal of creation too. It is God who rides in the chariot, not men. Edwards' related themes of

2. See Martin, *Last Judgment*, p. 76, for a different formulation of the same theological problem.

providence and universal restoration are controlling concepts in his theological perspective. God governs the totality of human experience. All must submit to his will and give him glory; "so there is nothing happens, except God first give the word" (AP; below, p. 120). Edwards chose the image of the wheel as a most apt representation of divine providence. All things in course, like a wheel, begin at one point and in time return to that point again. The events in the ages of the universe may be symbolized, he wrote, by a great wheel which goes through one revolution. "In the beginning of this revolution all things come from God, and are formed out of a chaos; and in the end, all things shall return into a chaos again, and shall return to God, so that he that is the *Alpha*, will be the *Omega*."[3] This vision of the beginning and the end controls Edwards' theology of the Apocalypse.

6. *Edwards' Sources*

Edwards spent a lifetime studying the book of Revelation, but the "Apocalypse" and the *Humble Attempt* reflect only a part of his investigations. The "Catalogue," that intriguing but uncharted map of his reading, provides additional clues to the full extent of his acquaintance with apocalyptic literature. It is the "Catalogue" that reveals his unending quest for books on a variety of subjects and establishes the fact that he obtained access to far more than he had in his own library. From his reading list it is apparent that Edwards knew and perhaps read the commentaries of William Whiston, Isaac Newton, Charles Daubuz, and John Lightfoot, that he was acquainted with the histories of Robert Millar and John Perrin, both anti-Catholic in perspective, and that he studied the volumes of Robert Fleming and Thomas Bray for themes related to the book of Revelation. None of these works was cited directly in the "Apocalypse" or in the *Humble Attempt*, but they constitute a part of Edwards' intellectual background. His other exegetical notebooks, especially the "Scripture" and the "Blank Bible," fill in the contours of his reading by showing that he had studied the works of Samuel Bochart, Francis Potter, Thomas Goodwin, Philip Doddridge, and many others on apocalyptic topics.[4]

The sources Edwards did cite in the "Apocalypse" and the *Humble*

3. "Scripture," no. 389; printed in Dwight ed., *9*, 402. No. 389 is an exposition of the vision of the wheels in Ezek. 1.

4. All of the authors cited here are dealt with elsewhere in this volume with one exception, John Lightfoot (1602–75), author of several volumes bearing on the relationship between Jewish and Christian writings. A full assessment of the impact of these and other authors upon JE awaits the publication of more of his private notebooks.

Attempt include a commentary on the book of Revelation, two popular annotations on the entire Bible, a number of historical volumes dealing with antiquity and Christian history, polemical works, some occasional tracts, religious magazines of the day, and newspapers—a representative cross section of his reading on apocalyptic issues. Only a few of the authors are widely known; most remain obscure figures, probably recognized by their contemporaries as much for their piety as for their scholarship, forgotten today outside the circle of those researching religious history. Collectively these sources shaped Edwards' interpretation of the Revelation.[5]

MOSES LOWMAN (1680–1752)

The volume Edwards cited most often in both the "Apocalypse" and the *Humble Attempt* was the *Paraphrase and Notes on the Revelation* by the Englishman Moses Lowman.[6] Lowman's life followed a pattern similar to that of many dissenting clergymen of his day. After studying theology at Leyden and Utrecht on the Continent, he served a congregation at Clapham in an unpretentious manner from 1710 until his death. His first love was "the study of *his Bible*," an activity he pursued with "unwearied application and diligence." By his scholarship he became "well known to the learned world."[7] In addition to the commentary on the Revelation, Edwards knew Lowman's *Dissertation on the Civil Government of the Hebrews* (1740), an exposition of the nature and function of the theocracy of ancient Israel. Lowman shared the strong anti-Catholic feelings of English Nonconformity, a sentiment he voiced in the sermon entitled *The Principles of Popery Schismatical* (1735).

Edwards first learned of the *Paraphrase and Notes* in 1737 through his uncle William Williams (1665–1741), who had heard from Benjamin Colman about a forthcoming exposition of the Revelation by a certain "Laman," a "work that was then adoing concerning which there was great expectation."[8] Edwards lost little time in securing a copy of the

5. In the following accounts, *The Dictionary of National Biography* has been used with the other studies cited in the notes.

6. The first and second editions (London, 1737 and 1745) were quartos with identical pagination, although the type was reset for the second. A third edition, an octavo, was printed in 1773.

7. Samuel Chandler, *The Character and Reward of a Christian Bishop. A Sermon Occasioned by the Death of the late Reverend Mr. Moses Lowman* (London, 1752), pp. 38, 40–41.

8. "Catalogue," p. 6. See ibid., pp. 8, 11, for two later references to the *Paraphrase and Notes*. On Colman, see Ebenezer Turell, *The Life and Character of the Reverend Benjamin Colman, D.D.* (Boston, 1749); and Clayton Harding Chapman, "Life and Influence of Rev. Benjamin Colman, D.D. 1673–1747," Diss. Boston Univ. School of Theology, 1946–47. Chapman wrote,

commentary, which he had in hand by mid-1738. In it he believed that he had found the best available interpretation of the Apocalypse, a volume that seemed tailor-made for his overlapping interests in history, chronology, and prophecy. Even the format pleased him: Lowman separated the text of the Revelation and an expository paraphrase of it, homiletical in character, from more technical scholarly comments in the footnotes. The notes included interpretations by earlier commentators, Lowman's own translations of difficult passages, and a range of supplementary information. Lowman added long excursuses on the historical periods represented by the visions of the Apocalypse, drawing upon both ecclesiastical and secular historians.

The first quotation from Lowman in the "Apocalypse," no. 74 in the series, was written in late 1738 or early 1739. After that, references to the *Paraphrase and Notes* become common in the numbered series as well as in Edwards' other biblical notebooks. For example, no. 78 in the "Apocalypse" refers to the "judicious" Lowman (below, p. 187). The first entry in the second manuscript of the "Scripture," no. 291, contains a direct reference to the commentary. In the series of sermons preached during 1739 Edwards cites approvingly the opinions of "a certain very late expositor" on the pouring out of the vials.[9] It was at the point of the fifth vial that Edwards' early apocalyptic calculations and Lowman's scheme of interpretation intersected. They agreed that the Reformation was the last predicted event in the visions which had already taken place, but they differed on the number of the vial that it represented. Edwards had associated the sixteenth-century Reformation with the second vial; Lowman linked it with the fifth. The two concurred, however, that another vial was soon to be poured.

Lowman's explanation of the visions appealed to his readers in part because it was straightforward. The first two chapters of the book of Revelation, according to him, told of the church at the time of the Seer himself. The balance of the Apocalypse described "the things that *shall be hereafter,* or to the State of the Church in the Ages to come, after the time of the Vision, with Cautions and Exhortations suitable to it."[1] Seven successive periods follow in the life of the church, according to Lowman's scheme. The first three of the seven correspond to the times

---

"From Colman's last will it is learned that the books he liked best and used the most were Pool's *Annotations*, Philip Henry's *Expositions* [read "Matthew" Henry], Burkit on the New Testament, the paraphrases of Guyse and Doddridge, and Lowman on the Revelation" (p. 273).

9. Worcester rev. ed., *1*, 462, 480.

1. *Paraphrase and Notes*, p. xxix.

of the seals, the trumpets, and the vials, those traditional conundrums confronting every interpreter of the book of Revelation. The period of the seals is the time of the church under the heathen Roman emperors, that of the trumpets extends from the reign of Constantine to the end of the Islamic invasions of the West with the victory of Charles Martel in the eighth century, and the era of the vials is the 1260 years the church suffers at the hands of the papacy. During the third period a faithful remnant of the saints persists, although they are sorely persecuted, and the destruction of the enemies of the church is gradually accomplished beginning with the commotions among the family of Charlemagne in 830 and culminating in the total ruin of mystical Babylon after the year 2000. Then comes the millennium, but after that follows a brief rebellion led by Satan. Christ crushes the revolt, and the final judgment ensues. Eternity begins for the saints and the reprobates, in heaven and hell respectively.[2]

One of Lowman's contemporaries said of his explanation of the prophecies that it was "formed upon a plan properly his own, . . . and if in some instances his observations may not be thought so clear and convincing, it is no more than what may be affirmed of all the learned men, who have wrote on that difficult subject, and what I apprehend will be the case of all who shall attempt to unfold those mysteries, even to the end of the world."[3] In 1739 Edwards found the scheme persuasive and quickly altered some of his own earlier views that conflicted with the interpretation. Some seven years later he filled nearly forty pages of the "Apocalypse" with extensive citations from Lowman's historical accounts, evidence of the continuing impact of the *Paraphrase and Notes* upon him.[4]

But Edwards did not agree with Lowman on every point in the explanation of the book of Revelation. In a brief section of the "Apocalypse" entitled "Remarks on Lowman," he offered a number of explicit criticisms of the scheme. He disagreed with the denial of synchronisms, observing that such repetitions are the "method of almost all the prophecies of Scripture" (AP; below, p. 251). Here Edwards was siding with Joseph Mede in the tradition. He disputed Lowman's correlation of the three woes under the last three trumpets with the various manifestations of the Saracen menace. The woes progressively destroy the enemies of the church, Edwards observed, not the church herself.

2. See the diagram of Lowman's interpretive scheme on p. 58.
3. Chandler, *Character and Reward*, p. 41.
4. "No. 94. Extracts from Mr. Lowman"; below, pp. 219–50.

SEVEN PERIODS OF THE APOCALYPSE
According to Moses Lowman

I	II	III	IV	V	VI	VII
Seals	Trumpets	Vials	Millennium	Satan Loosed	Judgment Day	New Heavens and New Earth

I Seals

1. 95–100 Christianity Prevails
2. 100–138 Destruction of Jews
3. 138–193 Famines

4. 193–270 Mortality and Pestilence
5. 270–304 Diocletian's Persecution

6. 304–323 Imperial Commotions

II Trumpets

1. 337–379 Intra-imperial Wars
2. 379–412 Invasion of Italy
3. 412–493 End of Roman Empire

4. 493–568 East-West Wars
5. 568–675 Rise of Mohammedanism

6. 675–750 Threat of Saracen Power

III Vials

1. 830–988 Commotion in Empire
2. 1040–1190 Crusades
3. 1200–1371 Guelph-Ghibelline Struggle

4. 1378–1530 Papal Schism
5. 1560–1650 Reformation, Turks, and Disease

6. 1670–1850 Invasion of Papal Dominions

7. 1850–2016 Utter Ruin of Roman Power

Finally, he questioned the exegesis of the seventh trumpet as introducing an interlude of peace and prosperity for the church, although the earlier woes had brought suffering on the saints. These criticisms Edwards developed more fully in his defense of the concert of prayer in the *Humble Attempt* (below, pp. 389–94).

The *Paraphrase and Notes* exerted a powerful influence upon Edwards' interpretation of the Revelation and had a direct impact upon the nature of the "Apocalypse." It was Lowman who persuaded Edwards to push forward his own interpretive scheme: the fifth vial had been poured and the sixth was impending—thereby preparing the logical and exegetical ground for him to begin assembling evidence related to the fulfillment of the sixth vial. Lowman confirmed Edwards in his conviction that the lowest days of the church were past and the times were becoming increasingly favorable for the saints.

MATTHEW POOLE (1624–79)

Matthew Poole was a seventeenth-century exegete and biblical annotator whose massive tomes were highly prized by many New England divines, including Edwards. He was educated at Emmanuel College, Cambridge, where his tutor was John Worthington (1618–71), the editor of the works of Joseph Mede. Following the restoration of the monarchy and passage of the Act of Uniformity in 1662, he resigned the only ecclesiastical living he ever held, a rectorship in London, and lived thereafter by means of a patrimony. Poole invested some of his energies in polemics: he attacked the unitarian cause, championed simplicity in public worship, and challenged the claims of the Roman Catholic Church. Two of his anti-Catholic publications, *The Nullity of the Romish Faith* (1666) and *A Dialogue between a Popish Priest and an English Protestant* (1667), produced a threat of assassination which forced him to flee to Amsterdam, where he later died.

Edwards was familiar with another side of Poole's endeavors, his biblical commentaries. In 1666 Poole began compiling the *Synopsis Criticorum aliorumque Sacrae Scripturae Interpretum*, a work eventually published in five folios, the product of more than ten years of labor.[5] Intended as a compilation of the best scholarship on the Bible, his massive commentary incorporated studies by English Protestants, continental scholars, Roman Catholic commentators, and Jewish

5. London, 1669–76. Four more editions appeared in less than forty years (Frankfort, 1678; Utrecht, 1684–86; Frankfort, 1694; Frankfort, 1709–12). All were folios except the fourth edition, which was in quarto.

rabbis. It was partially dependent upon an earlier but equally massive
Critici Sacri, a dependence that caused considerable difficulty in obtaining publication rights.[6] The *Synopsis,* written in Latin for the use of
scholars and divines, provided a wealth of critical and technical information. In the section on the book of Revelation, Poole surveyed more
than forty authorities and sources, summarizing viewpoints and
interpretations, but allowing differences to stand side by side. His
exposition of the Apocalypse occupies more than five hundred and
fifty columns.[7] The *Synopsis* received widespread acclaim during Poole's
lifetime and was regarded by many as without peer in scope and
sophistication.

After completing the *Synopsis* in 1676, Poole turned to another project he had contemplated for many years, a plan for providing unlearned
Christians with aids for scriptural study. He died before finishing the
popular commentary, but a group of interested ministers continued the
plan and within a few years published two folios entitled *Annotations
upon the Holy Bible.*[8] The exposition of the Apocalypse was written by
John Collinges (1623–90), like Poole a graduate of Emmanuel College
and a Presbyterian divine. This work was not simply an English translation of the *Synopsis;* it had a different rationale, namely, to give "the
plain sense of the Scripture, and to reconcile seeming contradictions
where they occurred, and . . . to *open Scripture* by *Scripture.*"[9] The
Annotations offered the reader a statement on the canonical authority of
each book, a discussion of the intention of the author, and an English
translation of the text with notes and commentary. The *Annotations*
joined a growing tradition of popular commentaries committed to the
Protestant ideal of placing the Bible into the hands of the common
people.[1]

Edwards became acquainted with both the *Synopsis* and the *Annota-*

6. *Critici Sacri: Sive Doctissimorum Virorum in SS. Biblia Annotationes, & Tractatus* (9 vols.,
London, 1660). These volumes, published by Cornelius Bee, were compiled by J. Pearson, A.
Scattergood, and F. Gouldman. As a result of the dispute, Poole wrote *A just Vindication of Mr.
Poole's Designe for printing of his Synopsis of critical and other commentators; against the pretences of Mr.
C. Bee, Bookseller* (1667).

7. *Synopsis,* 5 (1676), cols. 1659–2022. There is no conventional pagination; the two
columns of each page are numbered separately.

8. Two vols., London, 1683–85. The *Annotations* have been reprinted often, including
several nineteenth-century editions. The first edition has no pagination.

9. *Annotations, 1,* editors' preface.

1. In the preface the editors cited four previous works with the same intention: the *Paraphrase* by Desiderius Erasmus (c. 1446–1536), the Geneva Bible of 1560, the annotated translation of the Bible prepared by the Swiss Protestant Giovanni Diodata (1576–1649), and the
"Annotations" of 1657 compiled by the members of the Westminster Assembly.

tions as a young man. The former he noted on the letter sheet inserted in the "Catalogue": "Poole's *Synopsis* on the Apocalypse." There was a copy of the latter in Timothy Edwards' household, as the eulogy for Edwards' sister Jerusha attests.[2] Edwards apparently used the *Annotations* in the "Apocalypse" when he was writing the chapter by chapter exposition and the early entries in the numbered series (cf. below, p. 125). It is more difficult to establish a direct dependence upon the *Synopsis* in the "Apocalypse."[3] Both the *Annotations* and the *Synopsis* were concerned with the issues occupying his earliest reflections on the book of Revelation. Poole had underscored the insidious nature of the Antichrist and the antichristian forces, expounding at great length the dangers facing the church at the hands of her enemies and detailing the sufferings of the Christians who had been persecuted and martyred. His chronological discussions may have encouraged Edwards to become more specific in his own apocalyptic calculations.

Poole introduced Edwards to many of the leading commentators in the tradition by summarizing their views on major interpretive questions. In this way Edwards may have become familiar with the ideas of Joseph Mede, whom Poole often represented favorably.[4] Edwards sided with Mede on several disputed apocalyptic issues. But the use of such synoptic commentaries as Poole's complicates the identification of sources. On some occasions it is difficult, if not impossible, to determine whether Edwards derived an idea directly from a commentator or secondhand through another source. Mede's works, as a case in point, were available in the Yale College library, having arrived among the Dummer gift of books; but his principal ideas on the Apocalypse were equally accessible through the volumes of Poole.[5]

MATTHEW HENRY (1662–1714)

Another popular annotator of the Bible whose writings Edwards knew well was Matthew Henry, a prominent spokesman for English

2. Concerning Jerusha Edwards, who died on Dec. 22, 1729, it was written: "She seemed to be very conscientious in her ways, and delighted very much in reading books of divinity. According to my observation, she was very constant in the duty of secret prayer, and endeavored to be very secret therein, and would be often reading in the Bible, and made great use of Mr. Poole's *Annotations*" (MS, Andover coll.).

3. Sometime after the mid-1740s, JE worked through the first three volumes of the *Synopsis*, writing notes in the "Blank Bible" and the "Scripture." The *Synopsis* is also cited late in the "Miscellanies."

4. For example, see the *Annotations* at Rev. 8:9.

5. See Louise May Bryant and Mary Patterson, "The List of Books Sent by Jeremiah Dummer," in *Papers in Honor of Andrew Keogh*, ed. Mary Withington (New Haven, 1938), pp. 423–92.

Nonconformity.[6] Henry received his education from his father and from a private academy, after which he spent his lifetime as the minister of congregations at Chester and Hackney in London. He was highly successful as a pastor, preacher, and writer.

Matthew Henry's literary efforts went in two directions. On the one hand, he developed various devotional aids for the nurture of private and public piety, including a catechism, a hymnal, a prayer book, and a sacramental handbook. Edwards was well acquainted with this side of his work. For example, while a tutor at Yale College, he made an entry on the letter sheet in his "Catalogue" noting Henry's sacramental meditations, the *Communicant's Companion* (1704). Edwards was very familiar with the other major literary undertaking of Henry, the *Exposition of the Old and New Testaments*, a work he cited in the "Apocalypse" as "Henry's Annotations."[7] Like Poole in the *Annotations*, Henry designed the multivolume commentary on the entire Bible to promote both understanding and piety. It was said that he wrote the *Exposition* with Poole's *Synopsis* open in front of him, but the commentary seems more likely the product of his expository preaching because of the homiletical caste to its content and style. When Henry died before finishing the project, his friends were quick to suggest that it be continued by "those that have attended long upon the Ministry of good Mr. *Henry*" in order that "those precious Fragments" remaining from his reflections on the Bible might be communicated to the world.[8] William Tong (1662–1727), one of Henry's friends and associates, wrote the section in the *Exposition* on the Revelation. The work was completed in this manner and subsequently went through many editions.

Edwards cited the *Exposition* twice in the "Apocalypse." Both references are relatively late in the notebook, although he had become familiar with Henry's commentary many years earlier. The first cita-

6. Henry has attracted considerable biographical attention, including the publication by a contemporary, William Tong, *An Account of the Life and Death of the Late Reverend Mr. Matthew Henry* (1716). In the nineteenth century Samuel Palmer and J. B. Williams, successive editors of *The Miscellaneous Works of Matthew Henry* (1809), both wrote lives. Williams' account was abridged and issued by the American Tract Society as *Memoir of the Rev. Matthew Henry, the Commentator* (New York, n.d.).

7. The first volume was published in London in 1708. A uniform edition of the first five folios was issued in 1710. The sixth volume was ready for the press at Henry's death. One of the Yale College library volumes from the Dummer collection of books has "Henry's Annotations" cut into its leather binding, a likely indication of the common usage of this designation. JE referred to the work twice early in the "Catalogue" (p. 1 and letter sheet).

8. William Tong, *A Funeral Sermon Preach'd at Hackney, July 11, 1714* (London, 1714), p. 36. See also John Reynolds, *A Sermon upon the Mournful Occasion of the Funeral of the Reverend and Excellent Mr. Matthew Henry, Minister of the Gospel* (London, 1714), p. 37.

tion, written at the end of the "Remarks on Lowman," concerned the time of the millennium described in chapter 20 (AP; below, p. 123). The other reference in the "Apocalypse" was a late addition to no. 92 which Edwards used to support his optimistic reading of the apocalyptic timetable (below, p. 212). Edwards drew heavily upon Henry's *Exposition* in the "Scripture" and in the "Blank Bible," suggesting that this popular commentator was more influential upon his ideas and interpretations of the Bible than the infrequent use in the "Apocalypse" implies.

HUMPHREY PRIDEAUX (1648–1724)

By his own testimony, the "histories of past ages," especially those dealing with "the past advancement of Christ's kingdom" were "sweet" to Edwards, but considerable evidence suggests that for him "secular history was on the whole insignificant, or significant only as it illustrated, illuminated, impinged upon sacred history."[9] The historical volumes Edwards used as sources in the "Apocalypse" and in the *Humble Attempt*—for example, the works of Humphrey Prideaux—tend to confirm this judgment.

Prideaux was another scholar-divine, a man of accomplishment in both academic and ecclesiastical affairs.[1] He was educated at Christ College, Oxford, where he received the degree of Doctor of Divinity and was appointed as a Hebrew lecturer. When James II selected a Roman Catholic as dean of the college, Prideaux left to become a canon at Norwich and subsequently archdeacon of Suffolk. Following the Glorious Revolution, he swore allegiance to the crown and in 1702 was elevated to the deanery of Norwich. Prideaux's publications include a treatise defending the validity of Anglican orders against the attacks of the Roman Catholics and a biography, *The True Nature of Imposture Fully Display'd in the Life of Mahomet* (1697), which served as a vehicle for an attack upon the English deists.

In the "Apocalypse" and the *Humble Attempt,* Edwards cited Prideaux's *The Old and New Testament Connected in the History of the Jews and Neighbouring Nations,* a work of two parts, each in two volumes.[2] The *Connection* was reprinted frequently, and Edwards used more than one

9. "Personal Narrative," in Levin, ed., *Jonathan Edwards,* p. 35; and Gay, *Loss of Mastery,* pp. 96–97.

1. See *The Life of the Reverend Humphrey Prideaux, D.D. Dean of Norwich* (London, 1748), an anonymous biography attributed to Thomas Birch; and R. W. Ketton-Cremer, *Humphrey Prideaux* (privately printed, 1955).

2. London, 1716–18.

edition at different times. Eventually he owned a copy of the ninth edition which he cited in the notebook and the treatise.[3] In the *Connection* Prideaux set out to resolve some of the difficulties in scriptural history by exploring the historical period between the decline of ancient Israel and the birth of Christ. He conceived of his work as an "epilogue" to the Old Testament and a "prologue" to the New. Prideaux's narrative of the Jewish people in those years attempted to take into account the history of the entire ancient Near East. He was indebted in his scholarship to James Ussher's *Annales Veteris et Novi Testamenti* (1650–54), but he had little praise for other earlier chronologists.

Edwards was especially attracted to Prideaux's discussions of the prophecy of Daniel, including his sixty-page excursus on the complex vision of Daniel 9 contained in the fifth book of part one of the *Connection*. Prideaux believed that the vision told of a period of seventy weeks of years, or 490 years, in which the Jews were to be God's special people and Jerusalem his holy city, beginning with the time of Ezra. That Jewish dispensation ended with the crucifixion, and then Christ's kingdom began. Prideaux was reluctant, however, to probe far into the future on the basis of prophecy, being content to let the events themselves become the only "sure comments." In both the notebook and the treatise, Edwards drew upon Prideaux's dating of the seventy years of the Babylonian captivity of the Jews as an analogue to the 1260 days in Revelation 11:3 and the seventy weeks in Daniel 9:24 (below, pp. 109, 408). Prideaux reconciled the conflicting data on the captivity by concluding that whether the time was reckoned from the beginning of the bondage to the beginning of the restoration or from the end of the captivity until the completion of the restoration, in each case seventy years was involved. Edwards took note of Prideaux's descriptions of the multiple destructions of Babylon and Tyre (below, pp. 176, 409). He used Prideaux's chronological calculations to confirm his own judgment that the downfall of Antichrist's kingdom was not to be accomplished in one moment, but over an extended period of time.

ARTHUR BEDFORD (1668–1745)

Bedford was another historian quoted by Edwards in the "Apocalypse." He too was an Oxford graduate and a clergyman of the Church of England whose most prestigious ecclesiastical appointment came late in life with his selection as chaplain for Frederick, Prince of Wales.

3. London, 1725. JE's own signed copies of the ninth edition are at the Forbes Library.

Bedford was a logical choice for the post in the court of the heir apparent in view of his earlier published sermon entitled *King George the Security of the Church of England* (1717). His interests ranged widely: he joined the attack upon immorality on the English stage, worked for the reform of church music, and participated in the preparation of an Arabic psalter and a translation of the New Testament. Bedford planned to write on ancient chronology, but hearing that Isaac Newton was engaged in a similar task, he set aside the project. Later he resumed the plan and subsequently published *Animadversions upon Sir Isaac Newton's Book, intitled The Chronology of Ancient Kingdoms Amended* (1728) and a larger volume which Edwards quoted in the "Apocalypse," *The Scripture Chronology Demonstrated by Astronomical Calculations*.[4] The latter, a folio of more than eight hundred pages replete with charts, maps, illustrations, and numerous astronomical and chronological tables, spanned biblical history from the creation to the close of the New Testament canon. The *Scripture Chronology* belongs to the genre of chronological studies Edwards knew well; the "Catalogue" lists more than ten other works of the same kind.

In the *Scripture Chronology* Bedford hoped to vindicate the historical record of the Bible and to reestablish the case for its divine authorship by proving the reliability of the biblical chronology. As part of his argument he defended the Hebrew text of the Old Testament as more trustworthy than the Septuagint and the Samaritan version. He continued the polemic against Newton's work, which, he maintained, "tears up all former Learning by the Roots." The assaults against the Bible demanded in his view a strong counteroffensive. "If any Expression seem severe," he declared, "or written with too great a Warmth, the Reader will consider, that it is only where the Authority of the *Sacred Scriptures* is vindicated, and the Credibility of its History is asserted."[5]

Edwards quoted Bedford in nos. 70 and 71 of the "Apocalypse," copying out a detailed description of the physical arrangements of the camp of Israel in the wilderness and an ingenious resolution of the chronological puzzle posed by Revelation 9:15. In his other notebooks Edwards cited Bedford on a range of issues, a good indication of the broad impact of the work upon Edwards' interpretation of Scripture.

4. London, 1730. JE apparently learned of the volume in the early 1730s while reading the second volume of *The Present State of the Republick of Letters* (London, 1728), pp. 233–40. See "Catalogue," p. 4.

5. *Scripture Chronology*, p. vi.

LAURENCE ECHARD (1670?–1730)

Edwards knew more than one of the historical volumes by Laurence Echard, a clergyman of the Church of England who held minor benefices, but whose main interest was scholarship. Echard was a competent geographer, an able classicist, and a historian of diverse periods. For example, he wrote a history of the early church, a volume Edwards noted twice in the "Catalogue,"[6] and a popular three-volume history of England. He translated and edited other volumes, including a condensation of Walter Raleigh's *History of the World*.

In the "Apocalypse" Edwards cited still another work, *The Roman History*, of which the first two volumes were written by Echard[7] and the other three by an anonymous author. The volumes form a chronological continuum broken at five points: Augustus Caesar, Constantine the Great, the fall of Rome, Charlemagne, and the fall of Constantinople. Edwards used the materials from *The Roman History* late in the "Apocalypse" as supplementary data to support the interpretation of the fourth seal and the fifth trumpet summarized in the "Extracts from Lowman."[8] All five volumes of Echard's work were reissued rapidly in many editions, making nearly hopeless the task of determining precisely which edition Edwards used. Sets of the work are commonly composed of mixed editions, as in the case of the volumes in the early Yale library (second, second, fifth, fourth, and fourth respectively). Edwards used at least two different editions at times. His initial reference in the "Catalogue" is from his tutorship period (p. 2), but later in 1753 he mentioned the first volume of the work printed in 1734, that is, the eighth edition (pp. 31–32).

NATHANIEL LARDNER (1684–1768)

Lardner, like Lowman, studied theology at Leyden and Utrecht before becoming a minister of a dissenting congregation in England, a position he held until he resigned to have more time for his studies.[9]

6. *A General Ecclesiastical History from the Nativity of our Blessed Saviour to the First Establishment of Christianity by Humane Laws, under the Emperour Constantine the Great* (London, 1702). "Catalogue," pp. 1, 20.

7. London, 1695; and London, 1698.

8. Below, pp. 223 and 230. There are also several secondhand citations of Echard in the excerpts from Lowman.

9. See Joseph Jennings, *Memoirs of the Life and Writings of the late Reverend Nathaniel Lardner* (London, 1769); and Andrew Kippis, *The Life of Nathaniel Lardner, D.D.*, in *The Works of Nathaniel Lardner, D.D.* (11 vols., London, 1788). Lardner's works were reprinted three times in composite editions during the nineteenth century.

He gained considerable reputation as an apologist and scholar of antiquities by his attempts to meet the religious challenge of the Enlightenment. He wrote in defense of Christ's miracles and in support of a literal interpretation of the creation and the fall. His largest effort, *The Credibility of the Gospel History*, was a historical apology for the data of Christian revelation, a massive study in seventeen volumes published over a period of thirty years.[1] The *Gospel History* began as a series of lectures attempting to substantiate the external facts of the New Testament with passages from ancient authors. Lardner wrote his work to convince the common people of the validity of Christianity; in fact, the *Gospel History* was used primarily by scholars and clergymen. It earned Lardner a Doctor of Divinity degree from Marischal College, Aberdeen, in 1745.

In the "Apocalypse" Edwards referred to the "9th volume" of the *Gospel History*, the seventh volume in the second part of the work, a continuation of the catalogue of witnesses supporting Christian history (below, p. 215). Edwards used Lardner to support his own interpretation that the slaying of the witnesses had occurred before the Reformation. The references were part of a late addition to entry no. 92 written sometime after 1748. Edwards was favorably impressed with the *Gospel History*, as multiple references to it in the "Catalogue" suggest (pp. 11, 36). He wrote the following reminder to himself: "Read over Lardner a second time and sum up the evidence."[2]

JOHN FOXE (1516–87)

As indicated above (p. 4), Foxe exerted a formative influence upon the English apocalyptic tradition through the *Acts and Monuments*. At his death he was also writing a commentary on the book of Revelation, a little known work published posthumously as *Eicasmi seu Meditationes, in Sacram Apocalypsin* (1587). Foxe has attracted a great deal of biographical and critical attention.[3]

Edwards quoted the *Acts and Monuments* in the earliest section of the "Apocalypse." Undoubtedly he was familiar with the "Book of Martyrs" even as a youth, for among the Puritans of New England it was a standard piece of religious literature. Edwards turned naturally to

---

1. London, 1727–57.
2. "Subjects of Inquiry" (MS, Yale coll.), p. 17.
3. In addition to the works cited above (p. 4, n. 7), see an early life of Foxe in the 1641 edition of the *Acts and Monuments*; J. F. Mozley, *John Foxe and His Book* (London, 1940); and F. J. Levy, *Tudor Historical Thought* (Kingsport, Tenn., 1967).

its pages to illustrate his view on the deceits perpetrated by the Antichrist, using the citation to ridicule the doctrine of transubstantiation and to challenge the claims of the Roman Catholic priesthood (below, p. 112). The spirit of the "Book of Martyrs" informs the entire "Apocalypse."

It has been impossible to determine the precise edition quoted by Edwards because the *Acts and Monuments* was widely available in many forms during the eighteenth century. After the first edition of 1563, the work was expanded to more than twenty-three hundred folio pages and issued in three more editions during Foxe's lifetime and another five before the end of the seventeenth century. It was frequently abridged and abstracted. Edwards did not mention the *Acts and Monuments* in the "Catalogue," but in later years he did note two condensations of it (pp. 15, 17).

ARCHIBALD BOWER (1686–1766)

In late 1754 or 1755 Edwards made a passing reference in the "Apocalypse" to another polemical work he was reading, *The History of the Popes, from the Foundation of the See of Rome, to the Present Time*.[4] Portions of the bizarre career of its author, Archibald Bower, are shrouded in uncertainty and controversy. He was a Scot by birth, a Catholic by faith, and a Jesuit by profession, trained in both divinity and classics. Contact with the Inquisition in Italy apparently caused him to flee to England, where he converted to Protestantism. Later he changed his mind and returned to his mother church, only to become disaffected again. After the second renunciation he began to write the *History of Popery*, as Edwards called it. In time it was revealed as fraudulent, a translation of a work by the French historian Louis Tillemont (1637–98), and Bower was accused of being an agent of the Jesuits.

Edwards' first reference to the *History of Popery* was entered in the "Catalogue" in 1749 (p. 17). In subsequent years he seemed unaware of or uninterested in the controversy surrounding Bower. Edwards evidently thought highly of the volumes, for he took extensive notes from them on the growth of papal power in a separate manuscript entitled

---

4. Seven vols., London, 1748–66. A second edition printed in Dublin was begun in 1749 and a third in 1750. The work was issued in a new edition by Samuel Hanson Cox in the mid-nineteenth century (3 vols., Philadelphia, 1844–45). Bower's work must be distinguished from another publication referred to by the same name in the "Catalogue," pp. 12–13. The latter was a periodical edited by Henry Care, *The Weekly Pacquet of Advice from Rome: or The History of Popery* (1679–83).

"Episodes in [the] History of the Church."[5] The reference to the *History of Popery* in the "Apocalypse" is part of the only footnote in the notebook (below, p. 295, n. 8). The precise intention of Edwards' footnote remains unclear because it points to a set of supplementary sheets paginated consecutively with the second volume of Bower's work but not bound with it, having been sent separately to the subscribers. No extant copy of these pages has been located.[6]

JOHN WILLISON (1680–1750)

Another author whom Edwards cited was his Scottish friend and correspondent John Willison, a Presbyterian minister in Dundee.[7] A graduate of the University of Glasgow, Willison was a prominent clergyman in the Church of Scotland. Described as a "keen controversialist," he displayed that disposition in his public opposition to the Church of England and in his attacks upon the Church of Rome. He made his strong dislike for the Roman Catholic Church very evident in his published sermons, *Popery Another Gospel* (1745) and *A Prophecy of the French Revolution and Downfall of Antichrist* (1793), the latter a posthumous publication. Edwards, after reading the sermon against popery, sent it in 1747 to his father Timothy.[8]

Willison played a major role in the development of the revivals in Scotland during the 1740s. A senior member of the evangelical circle, he was one of the first outside the Church of England to invite George Whitefield into his pulpit.[9] He was deeply committed to the cause of the revivals and wrote in support of the movement. For example, he introduced the Scottish edition of Edwards' *The Distinguishing Marks of a Work of the Spirit of God*, which appeared in 1742,[1] and later wrote the preface for an edition of *Sinners in the Hands of an Angry God* (1745). During the same period he began to correspond with Edwards, sharing

---

5. "Notebook on Redemption, No. 3." See above, p. 50.

6. Another reference by JE to these same supplementary sheets in the "Blank Bible," p. 885, hints that somehow they may have alluded to the success of Protestantism in the towns of the Hanseatic League, the same region in which western Christianity expanded in the seventh century, the time being discussed by Bower in the parts of his volumes contiguous to the sheets.

7. See Hew Scott, *Fasti Ecclesiae Scoticanae: The Succession of Ministers in the Church of Scotland from the Reformation* (7 vols., Edinburgh, 1915–28), *5*, 320–22; and W. M. Hetherington, ed., *Practical Works, with an Essay on his Life* (Glasgow, 1844).

8. JE, "Account Book" (MS, Yale coll.), p. 34.

9. Fawcett, *Cambuslang Revival*, p. 110.

1. *Works, 4*, 213–88.

with him many interests. In 1749 he wrote, "I should be glad to do any thing in my power, for promoting the Concert for United Prayer, and Oh that it were spread both far and near; it would be a token of a general Revival of religion to be fast approaching."[2]

In the *Humble Attempt* Edwards quoted from *A Fair and Impartial Testimony, Essayed in Name of a Number of Ministers, Elders, and Christian People of the Church of Scotland, unto the laudable Principles, Wrestlings and Attainments of that Church; and against the Backslidings, Corruptions, Divisions, and prevailing Evils, both of former and present times,* an occasional tract in which Willison used a historical format to urge reformation upon the Church of Scotland.[3] From his perspective, true religion was in danger in the mid-1740s. His survey of the development of Christianity in Scotland from the third century until his own day was in effect a description of the religious decline of the national church, which, he warned, was "gradually drawing nearer to the Superstitions and Idolatry of *Rome*." He raised the specter of "an Inundation of *Popery*, that Antichristian, Tyrannical, Bloody, Blasphemous, Idolatrous and Damnable Religion" sweeping the land.[4] By God's mercy alone the nation had been spared a judgment. As a step toward reformation, Willison called for more national fasts and the setting of "Times of meeting for spiritual Conference, Fasting, Prayer and Wrestling for the Downpouring of the Spirit upon the whole Church and Land."[5] Edwards used an isolated account of the religious successes in Salzburg, Austria, from Willison's volume as further evidence of the mercies of God upon the contemporary church (below, p. 363).

JOHN ERSKINE (1720–1803)

In the "Apocalypse" Edwards quoted a sermon by another of his Scottish correspondents, John Erskine.[6] A son of Edinburgh by birth and education, Erskine after his university training served Presbyterian congregations at Kirkintilloch, Culross, and Edinburgh during a long and successful ministry. In the 1740s he had a full career ahead of him. His activities during that decade thrust him into the forefront of Scot-

2. Letter to JE, Mar. 17; in Dwight ed., *1*, 271. There is mention of another letter of May 10, 1748, in the AP (below, p. 271).

3. Edinburgh, 1744. This work was reprinted in the early nineteenth century (Pittsburgh, 1808).

4. *A Fair and Impartial Testimony*, p. 99.

5. Ibid., pp. 121–23.

6. See Henry Moncreiff Wellwood, *Account of the Life and Writings of John Erskine, D.D.* (Edinburgh, 1818).

tish evangelicalism. He became a prolific author and a regular correspondent of evangelicals on the European continent and in America, including Edwards after 1747.

In 1742 Erskine's publication of *The Signs of the Times Consider'd: or, the high Probability, that the Present Appearances in New-England, and the West of Scotland, are a Prelude of the Glorious Things promised to the Church in the latter Ages* announced his commitment to revivalism and his interest in apocalyptic speculation—concerns which Edwards shared. Erskine believed that the dispensations of his time were "a Prelude of greater Things yet to come." He hoped that the contemporary successes would encourage Christians to work and pray for further progress in the kingdom. The study of prophecies was also profitable and should be encouraged.[7] Some of Erskine's later publications signaled interests held in common with Edwards as, for example, *Considerations on the Spirit of Popery* (1778) and *Sketches and Hints on Church History, and Theological Controversy, chiefly translated and abridged from modern foreign writers* (1790, 1797).

Erskine and Edwards frequently exchanged publications and judgments about their readings.[8] It is likely that Erskine sent the copy of his sermon, *The Influence of Religion on National Happiness. A Sermon Preached before the Society for propagating Christian Knowledge, at their anniversary meeting, in the High Church of Edinburgh, on Monday, January 5, 1756,* which Edwards cited among the "Hopeful Events" in the "Apocalypse" (below, p. 297).[9] Erskine preached the sermon to point out the positive impact of religion upon the culture and to raise funds for the activities of the society. Edwards cited the activities of the Christians in London and Edinburgh as further evidence of the favorable state of religion in the late 1750s.

In the years after Edwards' death, Erskine continued his interest in the concerns of his late American friend. In conjunction with Jonathan Edwards, Jr., he was responsible for the posthumous publication of several volumes by Edwards, including the series of sermons preached in 1739 (above, p. 22). He continued to support the idea of a concert of prayer and in 1784 sent a copy of the *Humble Attempt* to Baptist ministers

7. *Signs of the Times,* pp. iii, 8.

8. JE had asked Thomas Prince to send a copy of the HA to Erskine, but Prince failed to do so. See JE's letter to Erskine, Aug. 31, 1748; in Dwight ed. *1,* 251. For an example of a packet of books sent by Erskine, see JE's letter to him, Apr. 15, 1755; in ibid., p. 545.

9. Edinburgh, 1756. This sermon was bound with an account of *The Present State of the Society in Scotland for Propagating Christian Knowledge.* The sermon was reprinted among his *Discourses Preached on Several Occasions* (2 vols., Edinburgh, 1798, 1804).

Photograph of manuscript page 7 in the "Notes on the Apocalypse"

Events of an hopeful aspect on the State of Religion

Boston Gazette march 18. 1748 London Jan 29. By a letter from Switzerland there is an account there one of the most considerable of the Romish cantons are going to embrace the Protestant Religion *—

The account in an extract of mr. Davidsons letter sent me by mr. Bromfield of Boston of the conversion of mr. West clerk of the privy Council & his writing in defence of Christian & also of mr. Little-tons writing (a noted member of the House of Commons) writing in defence of the same / the same in a letter to me from mr. McCulloch of Cambuslang dated Feb. 10. 1748.

The account mr. John Brainerd gives march 1748 of the Religious concern at Cape may & the account mr. Strong gives of the state of Religion among the Indians at Cranberry. —

The pious & charitable disposition of a number of Gentlemen in Boston & the zeal they shew for the promoting of the Gospel among the Indians

Evening Post march. 21. 1748. Petersburg Jan 8. The missionaries whom the Court maintains in the Go-vernment of Casan Risch — Nyogorad & Woronesch have sent hither a list of the persons as well mahometans as pagans who have been converted to the Christian faith within these last seven years amounting in all to 258357 souls. viz. 141844 males & 116513 of the other sex

*— Boston news-letter march. 29. London decem 12 we hear from Bern that some great Revolution in religious matters is expected on the Canton of Lucern the most power—

in the area of Northampton, England, an act which led to the revival of
the concert and the republication of the *Humble Attempt* (below, p. 87).[1]

OTHER AUTHORS

In the *Humble Attempt* Edwards made reference to several other
publications he had read, including the tract by James Burgh (1714–
75) entitled *Britain's Remembrancer: or, the Danger not over*, a contemporary
indictment of the immorality and irreligiosity of English society.[2]
Edwards used Burgh's work, a favorite among American evangelicals
throughout the eighteenth century, to support his assessment of the
times in which he was writing (below, p. 357).[3] In the treatise he also
recalled an earlier reading of *The Spectator*, the collaborative product of
Joseph Addison (1672–1719) and Richard Steele (1672–1729), two of
England's greatest writers and social critics in the Augustan age
(below, p. 376). Edwards' reading included the religious magazines of
the day, especially *The Christian History* and *The Christian Monthly
History*, which he cited several times in the *Humble Attempt*.[4] The "Apocalypse" also sets to rest an old stereotyped judgment about Edwards'
isolation from the contemporary world and his indifference to affairs
around him by revealing his consuming interest in the newspapers of
his day, which he searched for evidence to fit with his apocalyptic timetable.

7. *Note on the Manuscript and Texts*

The "Apocalypse" is a quarto of two hundred and eight pages,
measuring approximately $6\frac{1}{2}$ by 8 inches. Fifteen of the pages remain
blank, although Edwards was writing in the open sections in the year
before his death. The manuscript comprises six quires of unequal length
with the smallest, the second, containing only sixteen pages. Edwards
constructed the "Apocalypse" from folded half-sheets of foolscap, most
of which bear a London-GR watermark. The first quire is an exception,
being composed of Seven Provinces paper with one leaf of Crown-GR
sewn into the quire. In addition, eight unnumbered, unattached pages
displaying the Pro-Patria-GR watermark are at the end of the note-

1. Fawcett, *Cambuslang Revival*, p. 229. See also his letter to an unnamed correspondent,
Feb. 15, 1779 (MS, Boston Public Library), in which he shows his continuing fascination with
apocalyptic speculation.
2. London and Edinburgh, 1746.
3. Heimert, *Religion and the American Mind*, pp. 96–97.
4. See above, p. 31, n. 8, concerning these periodicals.

book.[5] The different batches of paper signal the composite nature of the manuscript and provide clues for dating the entries. The paper throughout is relatively coarse in texture and yellow in color, soiled by use and age.

Edwards' handwriting changed during the thirty-five years in which he wrote the "Apocalypse." His earliest entries are in a "round or circular" hand, the letters very small but well-formed.[6] By no. 34 in the series his hand shows an increasing angularity; he formed the letters less carefully, apparently writing with greater haste. By no. 42 he had also increased substantially the size of the characters and changed the spacing on a page. In the middle of the second quire, that is, at no. 70, Edwards was writing with his characteristic mature hand, a very "busy" but consistently legible script. The amount on each page decreased remarkably: in the earliest section of the notebook Edwards averaged more than 1150 words per page, but in the last four quires the average dropped to 430 words per page.[7]

The inks used by Edwards are an important tool for dating specific entries, but two nonchronological observations are in order. First and most obviously, in the manuscript he used several inks with marked differences in color, brilliance, and texture. Secondly, in the midst of this variety at least three sections of the "Apocalypse" are identifiable as units by their consistent appearance. Edwards wrote the first twelve and a half pages of the notebook with what now appears as a grayish brown ink, the fifty pages containing nos. 69–90 in the series with a rusty brown ink, and the forty pages of excerpts from Moses Lowman with an intensely black ink.[8] These uniform sections point to periods of concentrated study with the notebook.

Edwards took considerable pains in the construction of the "Apocalypse." He bound the manuscript with a sheet of coarse gray paper resembling wrapping paper and spanning both the front and the back of the assembled quires. After sewing the quires to the midpoint of the folded gray paper, he reinforced the spine with several narrow strips of similar paper stitched together as well as to the inside of the cover. Then he pasted an additional strip of tan paper approximately three

5. W. A. Churchill, *Watermarks in Paper in Holland, England, France, Etc., in the XVII and XVIII Centuries and their Interconnection* (Amsterdam, 1935), is a standard reference.

6. See Sereno Dwight's description of the handwriting in Dwight ed., *1*, 34.

7. See the photographs on pp. 72–73.

8. Inks take on a different appearance under the microscope. See William J. Barrow, "Black Writing Ink of the Colonial Period," *The American Archivist, 11* (1948), 291–307.

inches wide on the outside of the spine which overlapped both covers, thereby protecting the stitches and improving the appearance of the notebook. Edwards strengthened the covers by starching an additional sheet of heavy paper on the inside of each, his customary gluing process.[9] On the back cover is glued a section of a broadside printed by John Draper for the governor of Massachusetts. The front cover of the "Apocalypse" is missing, having broken away from the binding. The only marking on the back cover is "1." written in pencil, probably not Edwards' own notation.

The stitching in the "Apocalypse" also reveals the composite nature of the notebook. Edwards stitched each of the first three quires separately with a thin tan twine. Later he sewed the three together with a fine thread. Still later he attached the three quires to the spine of the notebook as it exists today. The last three quires have only a single stitching which holds the sheets of each together and attaches them to the larger notebook; they are not sewn to each other. The first three quires existed as a unit before Edwards added the last three and the cover. He paginated the entire volume at one time after he had finished its construction. The unattached and unnumbered pages at the end of the notebook (below, pp. 298–305) are not stitched to the manuscript, although Edwards did sew them together at the folds of the two half-sheets to form a signature.

The first quire of the "Apocalypse," the initial twenty-four pages of the manuscript, requires special comment. At present it comprises five folded half-sheets and two extra single leaves, the latter forming manuscript pages 1–2 and 17–18. Pages 1–2 were originally part of a sixth half-sheet in the quire; they are now broken away from the binding. There is no evidence to indicate the nature, use, or final appointment of the missing leaf.[1] Edwards sewed the second extra leaf, the piece of Crown-GR paper, into the quire in a reversed position so that page eighteen must be read before page seventeen. He transferred this leaf from the "Scripture" because of its similarity in content to the "Apocalypse"; it contains expository notes on Revelation 21:1 and Isaiah 42:4.

---

9. JE wrote on the cover of the second volume of the "Scripture," "If I live to make another book of this sort, to observe to cut the gashes for the stitching in deeper and not so near to the joinings of the stitch, that the book may open more freely and fully. And let the sheets be divided into twice so small divisions, and starch no paper on a paper cover, for that makes it crack. And if that don't do, try next stitching the backs of all the divisions of sheets to a slip of leather, and sew the cover over the leather."

1. Thomas Schafer has suggested that perhaps JE used the missing portion as a flyleaf after he began the notebook on the second recto of a separately folded half-sheet.

The manuscript is in good condition with only a few readings obstructed by soiled pages, torn margins, or wormholes. The ink on the first page, for example, is faded because page one has served as the cover for many years; the top margin of the second page is ragged and worn. Nevertheless, nearly the entire manuscript is intact and readable.

The most puzzling chronological problem concerning the "Apocalypse," the date of its beginning, has been solved thanks to the singular efforts of Thomas Schafer, who has established a chronology for the items written by Edwards before 1733. By the use of sophisticated techniques Schafer has constructed a closely reasoned literary history of Edwards' early years, including his work on the "Apocalypse."[2] The ink, the well-formed hand, the spacing of the lines, the Seven Provinces paper, and the contents themselves—all of these together place the beginning of the notebook in late spring or early summer of 1723.[3] Edwards wrote the earliest sections in a short time, possibly a month or less, as is evident by the striking consistency of the hand and ink throughout the opening exposition and the first sixteen notes in the series. The dependence of some of these entries upon Matthew Poole's *Annotations* makes it likely that Edwards composed them when he had ready access to his father's copy of Poole, that is, after May 1 when he returned from New York to Windsor. The remainder of the numbered series was written intermittently over many years. Schafer has placed nos. 17–26 of the series in September or October of 1723, the next seven entries between that October and June of 1724 when Edwards assumed responsibilities as a tutor at Yale, and nos. 34–39, 41, and the note on Isaiah 42:4 during the tutorial period.[4] From October 1726 until the

2. Schafer's studies revise the longstanding chronological assumptions formulated by Sereno Dwight (Dwight ed., *1*, esp. chs. 2–8) and reinforced by Egbert C. Smyth in a series of articles, including "Some Early Writings of Jonathan Edwards, A.D. 1714–1726," *Proceedings of the American Antiquarian Society*, new ser., *10* (1895), 212–47. Schafer's work undermines the argument for the extraordinary precocity of the young JE. See "The Role of Jonathan Edwards in American Religious History," *Encounter*, *30* (1969), 212–22, for some hint of the implications of Schafer's scholarship. His chronology of JE's early writings, which has influenced this editor greatly, will be forthcoming in the *Works*.

3. Schafer has dated the only two extant MS sermons written on Seven Provinces paper, Ps. 115:1 (MS, Yale coll.) and I Cor. 2:14 (MSS, Andover coll.), in the summer or fall of 1723. JE was evidently using the distinctive paper during the latter half of 1723, months which correspond with the period of JE's early entries in the AP.

4. JE's projects were interrupted when he became a tutor. He wrote in his "Diary": "*Saturday night, June* 6. This week has been a very remarkable week with me, with respect to despondencies, fears, perplexities, multitudes of cares, and distraction of mind: it being the week I came hither to New-Haven, in order to entrance upon the office of Tutor of the college" (Dwight ed., *1*, 103).

death of his grandfather Solomon Stoddard in February 1729, Edwards served as the associate minister at Northampton, during which time he wrote nos. 40 and 42–51.

After the death of Stoddard, Edwards introduced a change into his orthography as he searched for practical ways to save time in notetaking and sermonizing. In the "Apocalypse" abbreviations such as "Chh" for church and "G" for God first appear in no. 52.[5] Immediately following Stoddard's death, Edwards wrote little in the notebook, only three pages in as many years. Nos. 59–65 can be placed in late 1732 or early 1733 because of thematic parallels with the "Miscellanies" and with the sermon on Revelation 19:2–3 and because of their position at the beginning of the second quire of the notebook.[6] No. 68 reflects the rising expectations of the revival period of 1734–35. Edwards' citation of sources becomes chronologically significant in no. 70 of the series, in which he quoted Arthur Bedford's *Scripture Chronology*, a volume he was reading by 1736. In no. 74 he cited Lowman's *Paraphrase and Notes*, which he was studying by mid-1738. Several subsequent notes relating directly to Lowman's exposition of the Revelation mark a period of renewed activity in the notebook. Portions of nos. 78 and 87 are cited nearly verbatim in the series of sermons preached by Edwards in mid-1739.[7] The ink also ties nos. 69–90 into a contiguous time period. No. 90, which contains a specific allusion to the success of the Great Awakening, relates to the study question posed by the Hampshire Association of ministers in their meeting of October 13, 1741: "Q: Whither the Event Spoken of *Rev. 11. 7.* of the Slaying the Witnesses is come to pass—or is Yet to be Expected?"[8] In no. 93 Edwards expresses disenchantment with an "enthusiastical spirit" which deceived many people by counterfeiting the works of God, a note he sounded increasingly after 1741.

Several years may have elapsed between the writing of no. 93 and the "Extracts from Lowman" numbered as 94. The "Extracts" and the following "Remarks on Lowman" have a distinctive black ink, separate

5. Before this JE had employed an "X" for Christ and the ampersand, but now he began to use a variety of symbols. The abbreviations are to be distinguished from the shorthand he was using earlier. See William P. Upham, "On the Shorthand Notes of Jonathan Edwards," *PMHS*, 2nd ser., *15* (1902), 514–21.

6. The theme of no. 63 relates to a series of entries on hell or the eternity of torments in the "Miscellanies" between nos. 550–90. No. 565 had a cross-reference to no. 59 in the AP. See above, pp. 16–17, for JE's sermon on Rev. 19:2–3.

7. AP; below, p. 191, n. 2, and p. 199, n. 8.

8. "Record Book of the Hampshire Association of Ministers, 1731–1747" (MS, Forbes Library), p. 37.

pagination, and a different format from the preceding sections of the "Apocalypse," thereby signaling a change in Edwards' use of the notebook. At this time the "Apocalypse" became primarily a collection point for selected materials from his reading rather than a place for his own creative reflections on the Revelation. Edwards used the same ink of the "Extracts" and the "Remarks" in sermons written between August 1746 and October 1747 and in "Catalogue" entries from 1746 and 1747.[9] Although the principal function of the notebook had altered by 1748, in later years Edwards occasionally added comments to earlier notes. These additions appear in a separate section of the manuscript between the "Events Fulfilling the Sixth Vial" and the "Events of an Hopeful Aspect." The last addition was written by Edwards sometime before July 21, 1755, the date of a mistaken entry from the *Boston Evening-Post* which he subsequently canceled and entered properly among the "Events Fulfilling the Sixth Vial."

The two collections of contemporary events have sufficient internal evidence for dating. Edwards began the "Events Fulfilling the Sixth Vial" shortly after October 16, 1747, and continued it until his death; the last entry from the *Connecticut Gazette* is dated slightly more than three months before he died in Princeton. The "Events of an Hopeful Aspect" was begun about five months after the first list, and its last entry is a reference to a sermon by John Erskine published in 1756, a citation probably made by Edwards in late 1756 or early 1757.

The hand and ink of the unattached "Tractate on Revelation 16:12" place these pages in late 1746 or early 1747.[1] They parallel the fourth answer to the fifth objection in the *Humble Attempt* and may have served initially as a lecture on that subject. It is impossible to determine when Edwards placed these pages at the end of the notebook. It is also impossible to tell precisely when he assembled the entire notebook in its present form.

The history of the possession and use of the "Apocalypse" is a tale of some uncertainty. During Edwards' lifetime the notebook was normally

9. With the help of the microscope, sixteen sermons preached within fifteen months have been identified in the same ink, including five on Isaiah (6:3; 33:19–24; 55:2; 55:3; 64:5), one on Zech. 8:20–22 (see below, pp. 83–84), and David Brainerd's funeral sermon, delivered on Oct. 12, 1747 (MSS, Yale coll.). The same ink appears on p. 15 of the "Catalogue" in a selection from the *Boston Gazette* of Sept. 23, 1746, and in a reference to a letter from Thomas Prince dated Feb. 18, 1747, as well as on the back cover of JE's "Account Book" in an entry dated Apr. 2, 1747.

1. JE used a black ink similar to that of the "Extracts from Lowman." See above, n. 9.

in his own possession, although occasionally he lent some of his manuscripts to close associates, such as Samuel Hopkins.[2] Upon his death in
1758 all of his manuscripts, including fifteen quartos inventoried in his
estate, went by special bequest to his wife Sarah, who planned for
publication of selected items and authorized a biography based upon
the papers.[3] Sarah followed her husband to the grave within seven
months, but the family and friends of Edwards labored to complete her
plans.[4] Hopkins, who had been asked by her to write the biography,
kept the manuscripts in his possession for nearly a decade. Later he
recollected that he had "read them all," deriving "much pleasure and
profit."[5] Hopkins published the *Life* in 1765 and also edited for publication the treatises on *True Virtue* and the *End of Creation*.[6] In 1767 the
Edwards children entrusted the care of the manuscripts to Jonathan, Jr.
(1745–1801), the only son who had been trained theologically, with
whom the papers remained until his death. He was instrumental in the
publication of several additional volumes from the papers.[7]

The next person to use the collection of manuscripts was Sereno E.
Dwight (1786–1850), the son of Timothy Dwight, who was the president
of Yale College. Sereno Dwight prepared a new ten-volume edition of
the works of Edwards, including a major biography.[8] His edition made

2. For example, on two occasions JE lent a number of manuscripts to Hopkins ("Account
Book," pp. 71, 73). The relationship between the AP and Hopkins' later publication, *A
Treatise on the Millennium* (Boston, 1793), if any, remains uncertain.

3. See George Allen and George W. Hubbard, "Jonathan Edwards' Last Will, and the
Inventory of His Estate," *Bibliotheca Sacra, 33* (1876), 441. The quartos were not itemized.

4. In a letter to Thomas Foxcroft, Oct. 25, 1758 (MS, Houghton Library), Joseph Bellamy
wrote, "Mr. E. has left Many excellent Sermons & many volumes full of Curious Essays on
the Most important Points, which will be written out in fair hand for the press, if it be thought
that Subscriptions Can be obtained." Less than three months later, Foxcroft responded to
Bellamy with encouragement for the plan to publish JE's papers (Letter, Jan. 1, 1759; MS,
Beinecke Library).

5. Stephen West, ed., *Sketches of the Life of the Late, Rev. Samuel Hopkins, D.D.* (Hartford,
1805), p. 58.

6. See Levin, ed., *Jonathan Edwards*; and Worcester rev. ed., *2*, 191–304.

7. See a list of the publications issued during his custody, including the *History of Redemption*
(1774), in Ola E. Winslow, *Jonathan Edwards 1703–1758* (New York, 1940), p. 380. JE, Jr.,
was a tutor at Princeton in 1767–68, pastor of the White Haven congregation in New Haven
from 1769–96, minister at Colebrook, Connecticut, 1796–99, and president of Union College,
Schenectady, 1799–1801. See Tryon Edwards, ed., *The Works of Jonathan Edwards, D.D., Late
President of Union College. With a Memoir of His Life and Character* (2 vols., Andover, 1842). JE,
Jr., makes no mention of the manuscripts in his will (MS, Beinecke Library).

8. Dwight assembled another collection of papers for the biography which eventually
became the property of Andover Seminary (Andover coll.). Dwight, pastor of Park Street
Church in Boston from 1817–26, spent the years between 1826–33 in New Haven, where the
main body of manuscripts was located. See William T. Dwight, ed., *Select Discourses of Sereno*

no specific mention of the "Apocalypse" and even eliminated references to it. However, Dwight was familiar with the notebook, for on two occasions he observed that Edwards had examined the book of Revelation "at great length" and "with great care," a fact which he linked with the arguments in the *Humble Attempt*.[9] The publication of Dwight's edition reopened an old family argument concerning the ownership and publication rights of the manuscripts. The dispute remained unresolved until Tryon Edwards (1809–94) of New London, Edwards' great-grandson, was appointed "permanent trustee" of the papers.[1] Tryon Edwards' public statements about the unpublished materials attracted some attention to the collection.[2] For example, after a visit to New London, G. F. Magoun, an editor of *The Congregational Review*, singled out for special notice "a work on Revelations" and expressed the desire "that the work on the Apocalypse might be transcribed and given to the world, and that speedily."[3] That desire has remained unfulfilled for more than a century.

For the remainder of the nineteenth century, few specifics are available about the "Apocalypse." The notebook did escape the hands of Alexander B. Grosart (1827–99), who pirated several manuscripts to Scotland for a projected edition of Edwards' works,[4] only to fall prey to the casual custodianship of Edwards Amasa Park (1808–1900), a professor at Andover Seminary who contemplated a biography of Edwards. The "Apocalypse" remained closeted in Park's possession with other manuscripts for the last thirty years of the century.[5] When no biography was forthcoming, the family made arrangements to place the materials still in Park's possession and other items that had been returned from Scotland into the library of Yale University for safekeeping. Accordingly, in August 1900 the largest body of extant manuscripts again came to New Haven, including the "Apocalypse," which was inventoried as

---

Edwards Dwight, D.D., with a Memoir of His Life (Boston, 1851).

9. Dwight ed., *1*, 219, 246.

1. See Roger Sherman, a letter to Phoebe Farrar, Apr. 2, 1831 (MS of draft, Yale coll.).

2. Tryon Edwards, ed., *Charity and its Fruits* (London, 1851), pp. iii–iv.

3. "The Manuscripts of President Edwards," *The Independent*, no. 212 (1852), 208. Magoun also drew attention to the MSS in "President Edwards as a Reformer," *The Congregational Quarterly*, *11* (1869), 259–74; and "Unpublished Writings of President Edwards," *The Congregational Review*, *10* (1870), 19–27.

4. The only product of Grosart's effort was *Selections from the Unpublished Writings of Jonathan Edwards, of America* (Edinburgh, 1865). See also "The Handwriting of Famous Divines: Jonathan Edwards, M.A.," *The Sunday at Home*, *31* (1897), 459.

5. An inventory of materials for Park's projected biography (MS, Beinecke Library) compiled by William Edwards Park includes several indirect references to the contents of the AP.

follows: "Quarto. 'The Vials' (Fulfilling) Book I."[6] By this time the notebook was unknown to the general public, having been unavailable for more than three decades. In addition, few were any longer interested in it, for many shared the judgment of Alexander V. G. Allen, who said of Edwards' interest in biblical prophecy, "The fashion of it has passed away."[7]

The first sixty years of the twentieth century saw little concern with the "Apocalypse." Apparently only a few even knew of its existence. In 1934 W. J. B. Edgar of Princeton University listed "Notes on the Apocalypse" in his index to the Yale collection of manuscripts.[8] The bibliography of Ola E. Winslow's biography contains a reference to the "*Notes on Revelation*," but there is no mention of the manuscript or its contents in the body of her work.[9] Perry Miller's discussion of the millennial interests of Edwards passed over the "Apocalypse" in silence, as did C. C. Goen's influential essay on Edwards' eschatology.[1] Alan Heimert's study of eighteenth-century American religion refers to a "body of notes" on contemporary events, a reference derived secondhand from a brief mention of the "Apocalypse" by Ralph G. Turnbull.[2] Apart from the investigations of Thomas Schafer, no serious study had been directed toward the "Apocalypse" prior to the work of this editor.[3] This edition makes available for the first time a virtually unknown notebook.

There is no extant manuscript for the *Humble Attempt*. According to Sereno Dwight, the *Humble Attempt* originated with a series of sermons preached by Edwards to his congregation urging adoption of the proposed concert of prayer, then published by him "in the form of a Treatise," and "immediately republished in England and Scotland."[4] Unfortunately, no such series has been discovered among the papers of

6. L. F. Partridge, "Inventory of JE MSS" (MS, Yale coll.). Partridge was Park's amanuensis.

7. *Jonathan Edwards* (Boston, 1889), p. 240.

8. Typescript, Beinecke Library.

9. *Jonathan Edwards*, p. 374.

1. Miller, "End of the World"; and Goen, "Jonathan Edwards: A New Departure."

2. *Religion and the American Mind*, p. 67. See Ralph G. Turnbull, *Jonathan Edwards the Preacher* (Grand Rapids, 1958), p. 43. Harold P. Simonson, *Jonathan Edwards: Theologian of the Heart* (Grand Rapids, 1974), p. 169, also contains a secondhand reference to the AP.

3. See Stephen J. Stein, "A Notebook on the Apocalypse by Jonathan Edwards," *William and Mary Quarterly*, 3rd ser., *29* (1972), 623–34.

4. Dwight ed., *1*, 245. JE had preached other sermons on similar themes earlier. For example, see the sermon on Ezek. 36:36–37 (MS, Yale coll.), in Feb. 1746, with the following doctrine: " 'Tis the duty of God's people to be much in prayer for that great outpouring of the Spirit that God has promised shall be in the latter days."

Edwards, and the second edition of the *Humble Attempt* was not printed in England until 1789, thirty-one years after the original publication. The only editions ever published in Scotland were reprints of English and American collections of his works.[5] On Tuesday, February 3, 1747, Edwards did preach a single sermon on Zechariah 8:20–22, the biblical text for the treatise. The manuscript, a typical sermon booklet from the period comprising twenty pages approximately $3\frac{1}{2}$ by $4\frac{1}{2}$ inches, is part of the Yale collection of Edwards' papers in the Beinecke Library. Edwards constructed the booklet from assorted pieces of paper including two bidding prayers from his congregation and part of a letter from Timothy Woodbridge of Hatfield. The sermon manuscript constitutes only an outline, not a fully developed discourse.

The stated doctrine of the sermon, entitled by Edwards "Prayer for the Coming of Christ's Kingdom," is an anticipation of the theme of the *Humble Attempt*: " 'Tis a very suitable thing and well-pleasing to God, for many people in different parts of the world, by express agreement to unite in extraordinary, speedy, fervent and constant prayer for the promised advancement of God's church and kingdom in the world" (p. 5). The three sections of the sermon—the textual exposition, the doctrinal discussion, and the application—foreshadow the structure and substance of the treatise, although the *Humble Attempt* develops more fully certain ideas, omits others altogether, and adds a number with no counterparts in the earlier discourse. For example, Edwards singled out the idea of extraordinary, united prayer by the people of "different towns and cities" and "different countries" (p. 4) as a potential key to the unfulfilled promises of the future glorious time of the church. The six particular observations made in the textual section also have parallels in the *Humble Attempt*, sometimes in precisely the same language. The first sentence of the treatise is identical with the beginning of the sermon. By contrast, the sermon has few comments about the history of the concert, a subject treated in detail by the treatise. In the *Humble Attempt* Edwards vastly expanded the arguments for complying with the proposal, enlarged his defense of the ministers who had proposed the concert, and dealt with an even wider range of objections against the idea. Neither the interpretation of the slaying of the witnesses nor the exposition of the sixth vial—major arguments for cooperation in the *Humble Attempt*—figured at all in the sermon.

The sermon on Zechariah 8:20–22 was only one step toward the full

5. See Thomas H. Johnson, *The Printed Writings of Jonathan Edwards, 1703–1758: A Bibliography* (Princeton, 1940), esp. pp. 44–46.

text of the *Humble Attempt,* which was written during the following months. The task was completed .before September 23, when Edwards noted to a correspondent the "great deal of pains" he had taken to promote the concert in America: "I have written largely on the subject, insisting on persuasions, and answering objections; and what I have written is gone to the press. The undertaker for the publication encourages me that it shall speedily be printed."[6] In effect, the treatise was a reshaping of materials from this sermon and others, from the "Apocalypse" (most notably, the entries on the slaying of the witnesses and the interpretation of the sixth vial), and from his letters to correspondents in Scotland in which he had defended the concert and explained the "signal providences" of those times.[7] He organized these materials and wrote the *Humble Attempt* during a time with its own special anxieties. May 1747 brought the first visit of the ailing David Brainerd to the Edwards household. On July 25 the young missionary to the Indians returned to Northampton for a second sojourn, a stay that ended with his death in Edwards' home on October 9. These were unsettling times for the entire family, and yet there is evidence that during these very days Edwards was pushing forward on the *Humble Attempt.* He records that during Brainerd's last weeks the conversation frequently turned to the "future prosperity of Zion" on earth and to the lack of compliance with the proposed concert—evidence that Edwards' work was setting the agenda for the entire household.[8]

The printing of the *Humble Attempt* took longer than either Edwards or his printer expected. On August 20 *The Boston Weekly News-Letter* carried a full-column advertisement inviting subscriptions to the forthcoming publication "Prepared for the Press" and to be published "in a short Time." The proposed volume, the announcement promised, would be printed in octavo, making "about 12 Sheets," and if it did not exceed that, the book would be delivered to subscribers "at Six Shillings a Piece, old Tenor, stitch'd and cover'd with blue Paper."[9] The cost for binding was two additional shillings per volume. Persons subscribing for twelve copies would be given one additional without charge. Several

6. Letter to William McCulloch; in Dwight ed., *1,* 243.

7. For example, see letters to William McCulloch, Mar. 5, 1744, May 12, 1746, and Jan. 21, 1747, in Dwight ed., *1,* 211–19, 230–32, and *The Christian Monthly History,* No. 10 (Jan. 1746), 299–302; and to unnamed correspondents, Nov. 20, 1745, and May 12, 1746, in ibid., No. 8 (Nov. 1745), reprinted below, pp. 444-60, and in ibid., No. 10 (Jan. 1746), 296–99.

8. *Memoirs of the Rev. David Brainerd;* in Dwight ed., *10,* 399–400.

9. Page 2. The same advertisement appeared in the BNL of Sept. 3 and in a separate half-sheet flier. See a copy of the latter bound into the "Notebook on Redemption, No. 1" as pp. 73–74.

weeks later on September 24, a brief notice of the book appeared in the newspaper headed by the note: "Now in the Press and will speedily be publish'd." For the first time the forthcoming volume was identified by its *short* title, *A Humble Attempt to promote an explicit Agreement and visible Union of God's People thro' the World, in extraordinary Prayer, for the Revival of Religion, and the Advancement of Christ's Kingdom on Earth, pursuant to Scripture Promises and Prophecies concerning the last Time.*[1] But still more than three months passed before the book appeared in Boston. The five ministers signed the preface on January 12, 1748, and shortly thereafter the *News-Letter* announced that the *Humble Attempt* was "Just Published." The advertisement contained a postscript guaranteed to irritate parsimonious subscribers: "*N. B.*. The above Book rising higher in Pages than was calculated, the Price to Subscribers will be something more than was propos'd; and the Undertaker will deliver to them the Books at 7/6 a piece, stitch'd in blue Covers."[2] The delay in publication, not uncommon in that day, resulted in an actual date of publication in 1748, not 1747 as indicated on the title page.

Judging by its publication history, the *Humble Attempt* was not among the most popular works of Edwards, although it is fallacious to conclude that popularity is determined by a simple count of the editions and reprintings without data on the number of copies in each, information unavailable for Edwards' works. Apart from collected works, the text of the *Humble Attempt* went through seven editions in English, including the first of 1748 and two abridgements in 1814 and 1815. Only three were printed in America: the first, the third, which appeared in 1794 with Joseph Bellamy's sermon on *The Millennium* and David Austin's discourse on *The Downfall of Mystical Babylon*, and the 1815 abridgement, no. 60 in the publications of the New England Tract Society, which went through several printings. The others were published in England (1789, 1814, 1831, and 1902). The 1814 abridgement was translated into French in 1823. The *Humble Attempt* appeared in one form or another in all the collected editions of Edwards' works and their reprints throughout the nineteenth century and in the recent republication of the London edition of 1817.[3]

1. BNL, Sept. 24, 1747, p. 2; and the issues of Oct. 1 and 15.

2. BNL, Jan. 21, 1748, p. 2. After publication, JE arranged for Thomas Prince to send copies of the HA to his Scottish correspondents. Prince forgot, and JE made other arrangements (Dwight ed., *1*, 263). JE's "Account Book" has a tally sheet showing the disposition of some 45 copies of the HA through various agents (p. 38).

3. See Johnson, *Printed Writings*. The Burt Franklin Publishers of New York issued the reprint in 1968.

The liberties taken by nineteenth-century editors have been discussed in earlier volumes of this edition. The same freedoms plague the editions of the *Humble Attempt*. The editors frequently did not make the changes called for on the errata sheet, but consistently felt obliged to "improve" the text and syntax of the treatise. For example, the second edition rendered the corrected text of the first edition which reads "that when Antichrist's dominion began in *that place*, then the beast began; and when his reign ceases there, then the beast ceases" (below, p. 405) by the following: "that when Antichrist's dominion ceases in *that place*, then the beast ceases."[4] The first collected edition of Edwards' works and the Dwight edition which followed it restructured the third part of the *Humble Attempt*, relegating large parts of the text to the footnotes.[5] The first American edition and the later four-volume reprint of the Worcester edition—the latter something of a standard text—both omitted without comment the second answer to the sixth objection in part three.[6] This edition therefore is the first since the eighteenth century to print the entire text in its original arrangement.

The *Humble Attempt* received a mixed reception among its earliest readers. Edwards wrote the treatise for evangelical Christians already committed to the notion of the importance of the work of God upon the hearts of men. The five Boston clergymen who signed the preface to the first edition, all leaders of American evangelicalism, offered an equivocal or, at best, a restrained endorsement of the essay. They began the preface with a highly circuitous recommendation of the author's intention to promote "the increase, concurrency and constancy" of prayer for the advancement of Christ's kingdom, an objective no Christian of any party contested. But they were unable to recommend Edwards' "ingenious observations on the prophecies" in his interpretation of the slaying of the witnesses. Instead of ignoring the exegetical problem, they drew attention to the existence of a contrary viewpoint held by "many learned men" and told the readers to form their own judgment, quickly adding that the objective of "joint and earnest prayers for the glorious age" is worthy of support by all, regardless of exegetical opinions (HA; below, pp. 309–11).

When George Whitefield heard of Edwards' publication, he was

4. Northampton, Eng., 1789, p. 127. The third edition (Elizabethtown, 1794) followed the changed text (p. 262).

5. *The Works of President Edwards* (8 vols., Leeds, 1806–11), *2;* and Dwight ed., *3*.

6. *The Works of President Edwards* (8 vols., Worcester, 1808–09), *3*; and Worcester rev. ed., *3*.

quick to express skepticism to Thomas Prince. "What flourishing days are coming on," he wrote, "I know not—I have little or no insight into them, & therefore am no Judge of Dr. Mr. Edwards his opinion concerning the slaying of the Witnesses—However, I should be glad to see what He has wrote, & can heartily join with all those who pray for the coming of the latter day glory."[7] More than a year later, probably after he had read the *Humble Attempt* himself, Whitefield was even more reluctant to endorse its ideas. "I am afraid that some good men's calculations about the latter-day glory are premature, and that it is not so near at hand as some imagine. This is our comfort, a thousand years in the LORD's sight are but as one day."[8]

The *Humble Attempt* received its most enthusiastic response from the Scottish ministers who had sent the Memorial to America; they were delighted to enlist Edwards' pen in the cause. Thomas Gillespie (1708–74) of Carnock complimented the "great strength of reason" displayed in the treatise, which he read "with much satisfaction," including the discussions of the prophecies of the latter day.[9] John Willison sent word of his approval. "I wish it were universally spread," he wrote, "for I both love and admire the performance upon subjects so uncommon. I approve your remarks on Mr. Lowman. . . . I agree with you, that Antichrist's fall will be gradual, in the way you explain it."[1] A few years later John Gillies of Glasgow praised Edwards' "excellent performance" in the *Humble Attempt*, declaring it "a pious, learned and ingenious essay."[2] In America Jonathan Belcher (1682–1757), the royal governor of New Jersey in 1748 and a patron of evangelical piety, expressed similar approval: "I am much pleased with this proposal . . . and with your arguments to encourage and corroborate the design."[3]

The *Humble Attempt* split opinion among its first readers and among those who were to follow. John Sutcliff, a Baptist clergyman in England who edited the second edition, justified the reappearance of the work by observing the revival of interest in prayer meetings for the advancement of religion among the Baptists in England. But he added that he did not consider himself "answerable for every sentiment" in the treatise be-

---

7. Letter of Mar. 25, 1748 (MS, Boston Public Library).

8. Letter to unnamed correspondent, May 11, 1749; in *The Works of the Reverend George Whitefield* (6 vols., London, 1771–72), *2*, 252.

9. Letter to JE, Sept. 19, 1748; in Dwight ed., *1*, 260.

1. Letter to JE, Mar. 17, 1749; in Dwight ed., *1*, 272.

2. *Historical Collections, 2*, 401.

3. Letter to JE, May 31, 1748; in Dwight ed., *1*, 268.

cause the author and the editor must be distinguished. "Should any entertain different views respecting some of the *prophecies* in the inspired page, from those that are here advanced, yet, such may, and I hope will, approve of the general design." "Diversity of sentiments upon religious matters" is to be expected.[4] David Austin, the late eighteenth-century Calvinist and American millennialist who edited the third edition, published the "invaluable tract" with the hope that it would excite the use of the means for the advancement of Christ's kingdom. He found Edwards' arguments in 1794 "as applicable to the state of the Church, and of the world, now, as they were then" in 1748.[5] Much of the later support for the *Humble Attempt* came from those committed to revivalistic religion.[6] The editors of the Leeds edition added a caution: "How suitable the work itself is, in reference to the present state of things, we leave to the reader's own reflection."[7]

Sereno Dwight, editor and biographer, offered unqualified support for the treatise, describing the arguments of the *Humble Attempt* as "so clear and convincing, as wholly to supersede the necessity of any subsequent treatise on the subject." Edwards' opinions were "at the time wholly new to the christian world," according to Dwight, "and were at first regarded by many as doubtful, if not erroneous." But the critics have been silenced, he wrote in 1829; Edwards' view has created the "general conviction" that the period of the church's prosperity is at hand. As a result there is a "concentrated movement of the whole Church of God, to hasten forward the Reign of the Messiah." In his opinion, the *Humble Attempt* "has exerted an influence, singularly powerful."[8]

Most of Edwards' biographers have not been so complimentary to the work. Samuel Hopkins relegated all reference to the *Humble Attempt* to the list of Edwards' publications, a pattern followed by Ola Winslow.[9] Alexander V. G. Allen gave more space to the treatise, but he

4. 2nd ed., pp. iv–v.

5. 3rd ed., p. vii.

6. For example, see the later efforts to revive the concert in America: *A Concert for Prayer Propounded to the Citizens of the United States of America. By an Association of Christian Ministers* (Exeter, 1787); and *Circular Letters containing, An Invitation to the Ministers and Churches of every Christian Denomination in the United States, to unite in their endeavours to carry into Execution the "Humble Attempt" of President Edwards* (Concord, 1798). The 1902 edition of the HA, published by the Baptist Mission House in London, was prefaced with the hope that "God's Spirit may through it touch many a heart" (p. 4).

7. Vol. 2, p. 425.

8. Dwight ed., *1*, 246.

9. Levin, ed., *Jonathan Edwards*, p. 85. Hopkins added that in the treatise JE showed "his

judged it "a book of less interest and value" than the other writings of Edwards.[1] Perry Miller called it "a piece of propaganda," and Alfred O. Aldridge suggested that it was a "pamphlet, which now has value only as a curiosity."[2] By contrast, Alan Heimert made the *Humble Attempt* a crucial document in his controversial hypothesis concerning the role of evangelicalism in the formation of the American nation.[3] In recent years the only other praise for it has come from the twentieth-century representatives of conservative Protestantism.[4]

The texts in this volume conform to the editorial principles of the Yale Edition. The primary objective is to provide the reader with a modern critical edition retaining its eighteenth-century character. Authenticity and clarity have been equally important in the preparation of these texts which, unlike nineteenth-century editions, have not been changed when they offend literary, aesthetic, or theological sensitivities. The style sheet of the edition calls for silent and consistent modernization of spelling, especially of historical names and places, standardization of biblical citations and section headings, reduction in the use of italics, elimination of capital letters on substantives, and punctuation of the text in a manner that will facilitate understanding, not impede it.[5]

This first edition of the "Notes on the Apocalypse" has been prepared from the holograph manuscript located in the Beinecke Rare Book and Manuscript Library of Yale University. No previous edition or transcription of the notebook was known to exist prior to the editor's work.

The "Apocalypse" presents only a handful of special editorial problems. Conjectured and ambiguous readings are identified in the footnotes. Edwards' deletions on the manuscript appear in the apparatus only when they are potentially significant. Square brackets [ ] enclose interpolations by the editor in the text or in Edwards' notes; angle brackets < > in the footnotes signal Edwards' interlineations in the manuscript. This edition of the "Apocalypse" follows the order of the manuscript except at those points at which Edwards himself indicated

---

great acquaintance with Scripture, and his attention to, and good understanding of the prophetic part of it." See also Winslow, *Jonathan Edwards*, p. 379.

1. *Jonathan Edwards*, pp. 233–34.

2. Miller, *Jonathan Edwards* (New York, 1949), p. 198; Aldridge, *Jonathan Edwards* (New York, 1964), p. 34.

3. *Religion and the American Mind*, pp. 80–81.

4. For example, Fawcett, *Cambuslang Revival*, pp. 223–30; and Iain Murray, *The Puritan Hope: Revival and the Interpretation of Prophecy* (London, 1971), pp. 150–55.

5. See *Works*, *1*, 119–28; *2*, 75–82; *3*, 96–97; and *4*, 91-93; also Thomas A. Schafer, "Manuscript Problems in the Yale Edition of Jonathan Edwards," *Early American Literature*, 3 (1968–69), 159–71.

an intention to rearrange, as in entry no. 59. In several cases reordering would destroy the integrity of the numbered series, and therefore it has not been carried out, although such cases are footnoted. When rearrangements are chronologically significant, that too is indicated. At times Edwards left space in the manuscript with the apparent intent to write more later. Sometimes he did return for additional comments; at other times the spaces remained vacant. Later additions to the text that have substantive significance are annotated. One notable exception to this rule is the abundance of internal cross-references supplied by Edwards which need no comment. His corrections made at the time of the original composition are not regarded as later additions. The text of the "Apocalypse" is Edwards' own, mistakes and all. His grammatical errors are not marked by *sic*. What little punctuation he supplied is erratic, but it has been retained unless it creates confusion. The editor has supplied the balance of the punctuation. Occasionally a paragraph presents special problems in analysis or punctuation. Elliptical and defective sentences stand in the text as Edwards wrote them if they are clear. After all, the "Apocalypse" was a private notebook, not fair copy for the printer.

Edwards' use of written sources in the notebook seriously challenges the meaning of conventional forms of annotation. He paraphrased and edited as he quoted, without alerting the reader. The free style of quotation is especially evident in the "Extracts from Lowman," for which the editor has supplied cumulative footnotes at the beginning of the sections to identify the pages of the *Paraphrase and Notes* from which Edwards was drawing. The following parallel citations from Lowman and Edwards illustrate the liberties Edwards took with his sources.

Paraphrase and Notes, pp. 47–48.	"Apocalypse," p. 212.
In this Period of Time, the several sore Judgments of God were united, in the Punishment of a persecuting Empire, the Sword, Famine, and Pestilence. The Sword, and Famine, which were Judgments of the foregoing Seals, are continued in this, and the Pestilence is added to them. The Pestilence seems to be made the more distinguishing Judgment of this Seal. The Name of the Person sitting on the pale Horse was Death, which is the proper Expression in the Scripture-Language for the Plague,	In this period of time, the several sore judgments of God were united in punishing a persecuting empire: the sword, famine and pestilence. The pestilence seems to be made the distinguishing judgment of this seal.

as the Prophet *Jeremiah* uses the Word מות, Death, for the Plague; and the Seventy render דבר Pestilence, by Θανατον, Death. Accordingly, we find all these Judgments, in a very remarkable Manner, in this Part of History.

The State of the Empire was very much disturbed both by foreign Wars, and intestine Troubles; very few of the Emperors but met with a violent Death: so that besides thirty Persons who all pretended to the Empire at once, there were twenty acknowledged Emperors in the space of sixty Years, from *Caracalla*, A.D. 211. to *Aurelian*, 270. These intestine Divisions gave heart and strength to the Enemies of the *Roman* Empire, and great advantages to the *Persians*, and Northern Nations, against it; so that *Valerian*, in whose Reign the Persecution was very violent, was taken Prisoner by *Sapores*, (or *Sha Pur*) King of *Persia*, kept Captive by him, and treated with great Severity to his Death.

The state of the empire during this space was very much disturbed, both by foreign wars and intestine troubles; very few of the emperors but met with a violent death. So that besides thirty persons, who all pretended to the empire at once, there were twenty acknowledged emperors in the space of sixty years, from Caracalla, A.D. 211, to Aurelian, 270, which gave heart and strength and great advantages to the enemies of the Roman Empire against it, as the Persians and northern nations.

Valerian was taken captive by Sapores, king of Persia, and treated with great severity by him till his death.

The example is typical of Edwards in both private notebooks and published treatises.

This edition of the *Humble Attempt* reproduces the text of the first edition "Printed for D. HENCHMAN in Cornhil" in Boston. Edwards' own copy, signed "Jonathan Edwards's Book. 1751.," part of the collections of the Beinecke Library, has been used for the task. The text of the first edition has been followed as it is, with a few exceptions. The items noted on the errata sheet at the rear of Edwards' copy have been silently corrected, as have also a number of incorrect biblical citations, including the location of the text for the whole treatise on the first page, namely, Zechariah 8:20–22. The original punctuation stands unless it is confusing or unnecessary. Double punctuation at the end of a sentence has been eliminated. Italics have been substantially reduced so that proper names, titles of the deity, numbers, and geographical references no longer demand visual attention as in the eighteenth century. In this edition italics provide genuine substantive emphasis. Biblical citations have been identified by the editor in square brackets wherever possible; however, countless fragments of the discourse in the *Humble Attempt* as well as in the "Apocalypse" derive from the Bible but are not placed in quotation marks. Edwards' placement of biblical references remains as in the first edition if the referents are indisputable. Arbitrary movement of these references disrupts Edwards' sequence of thought and argument.

In earlier volumes of this edition in which the texts have been derived from first editions, the editors' footnotes stand at the bottom of the page in square brackets, and Edwards' own notes are without special designation. In this volume some adaptation of the footnoting procedure has been necessary because a manuscript and a first edition form the bases for the texts. Edwards wrote only one footnote in the "Apocalypse" and a mere handful in the *Humble Attempt*; therefore the editor's notes constitute the vast majority of all annotation in this volume. Here the editor's notes stand at the foot of the page without designation, and Edwards' notes are marked "—JE."

8. *Acknowledgments*

I am pleased to express my gratitude to many who have assisted in the preparation of this volume. John E. Smith of Yale University has provided guidance, support, and encouragement throughout the project. Sydney E. Ahlstrom, my mentor at the same university, has instructed, aided, and inspired in ways too many to mention. Thomas A. Schafer of McCormick Theological Seminary has generously shared his knowledge and time as well as his own research during the years and is acknowledged elsewhere, specifically in the footnotes. All of the above and those who follow have read portions of this volume at one stage or another and have offered helpful criticisms: C. C. Goen of Wesley Theological Seminary, David D. Hall of Boston University, Edmund S. Morgan and Norman Holmes Pearson of Yale University, and James Samuel Preus of Indiana University. With Wilson Kimnach of the University of Bridgeport I also have had many hours of valuable conversation about our parallel explorations in Edwards' manuscripts.

My work has been aided at every step by the indispensable assistance of librarians and their staffs at numerous institutions. Foremost among these for my research are the libraries of Yale University and Indiana University. At these two institutions respectively, the Beinecke Rare Book and Manuscript Library and the Lilly Library must be singled out for special thanks. In addition, I am pleased to acknowledge the cooperation of the following: the New York Public Library, the Boston Public Library, the John Carter Brown Library, the Forbes Library, the Massachusetts Historical Society, the Yale Divinity School Library, the Harvard Divinity School Library, the Houghton Library, the

Widener Library, and the Hills Library, Andover Newton Theological School.

Support of a different kind has come from the Department of Religious Studies at Indiana University, which granted research assistance at a crucial stage of manuscript preparation, and from the National Endowment for the Humanities, which awarded a nine-month fellowship to assist in my study of Edwards as a biblical exegete. Portions of the introduction were written during the leave made possible by that grant. The research assistance of Brenda Kennard cannot go unmentioned; nor can the kindness of Sally and Paul Sampley, who provided an appropriate retreat in the mountains of western Massachusetts for completion of the manuscript.

In small and large ways my wife Devonia has participated constantly in the work of this volume, offering both hands and heart to the task. Two others, Beth Ann and Stephen Michael, have given of their time to a cause about which they can only wonder.

Stephen J. Stein

Charlemont, Mass.
December 1974

"NOTES ON THE APOCALYPSE"

EXPOSITION ON THE APOCALYPSE[1]

VERSE 4.[2] The seven churches in Asia. But John dedicates this epistle to the churches in Asia, because they were the churches in which John was principally conversant, and in whose affairs he had for great part of his life been nextly concerned. 'Tis like these churches were the principal in all Asia, or at least of that part of Asia where John was acquainted. Christ bids him send these visions in an epistle to them, because he knew that they would be very useful to all Christians, as in the 3rd verse [and] ch. 22:7, and that these prophecies of the church were such as would more especially afford[3] many useful documents suited to their state and circumstances. And we have this epistle dedicatory at large inserted in this book because, on the other hand, the state of these churches was such, as would afford many documents especially useful to the church in future ages, in these different states and revolutions that are here prophesied of.

"Seven spirits" [v. 4]. When he speaks of seven spirits, he only speaks according to that symbolical vision that he had. There is no need that the vision should agree with the reality as to number or anything else any other way than symbolically.

The reason why the number "seven" is everywhere[4] put for perfection, is because in seven days all things were perfected and completed, both as to work and rest. So that the seventh number as well as the seventh day, is sanctified, that is, has a note of perfection put on it everywhere in Scripture.

1. In the MS there is no heading for this section. JE used this title in the "Scripture," Vol. 1, p. 9.
2. Here JE deleted "We are not to understand these seven churches which are in Asia of so many different states of the church in general."
3. MS: "to afford."
4. MS: "ever where."

These seven churches, seven being the number of perfection, seem to be a symbol of the universal church. Christ's walking in the midst of the seven golden candlesticks, and holding the seven stars in his right hand, signifies his presence in his church, and with his ministers [vv. 13–16]; so that this book is dedicated to the church of Christ in all ages.

"White like wool, as white as snow" [v. 14], signifying his eternity.

CHAPTER 2

Christ[5] foresaw that the same admonitions, instructions, encouragements, etc., that he was about to give to these seven churches would be very well adapted [to] the church under many of these changes: as that which is said to the church of Ephesus [vv. 1–7] is not only adapted to the state of that church, but is also suited to encourage the church, under those various temptations and persecutions that are prophesied of in this book, to assure Christians that Christ is not ignorant nor unobservant of their trials, but takes a merciful notice of their steadfastness and labor and patience at such times; particularly adapted [to] the state of Christians at the first Reformation, when once they began to discover popish lies, cheats and impostures, and found out the falseness of the pretenses of the Romish clergy to apostolical power and succession and infallibility and power of working miracles, etc.; and also [adapted] to the Dissenters in England in their casting off[6] prelacy, and [when they] rejected their pretended divine right and succession from the apostles, and their power of making laws to bind the conscience, for which they have suffered so much.

"Nevertheless, I have somewhat against thee, that thou hast left thy first love. Remember therefore, etc." [vv. 4–5]. This is suited to the degeneracy of the Reformed Church from the life and power of religion.[7] "But this thou hast, that thou hatest the deeds of the Nicolaitans" [v. 6], who taught the lawfulness of the common use of wives, and of things offered to idols. This likewise suits with the professors of the reformed religion, who hate the spiritual whoredom and adultery of the Romish Church.

What is said to the church of Smyrna suits also with the Reformed

5. MS: "~~John~~ ⟨X⟩." The first part of this sentence has been rearranged according to JE's directions.

6. MS: "of."

7. MS: "Re"; lacuna at margin. JE commonly used "religion" in this manner; see his sermon on Rev. 2:4–5 (MS, Yale coll.).

Church. They had to do with such as said they were Jews and were not, but were of the synagogue of Satan [v. 9]. So Protestants oppose those who hold themselves to be the only true church of God, who in the meantime are the church of the devil.

What is said to Pergamos seems very well to suit the case of the Church of England; "and where thou dwellest, even where Satan's seat is" [v. 13]. See no. 44.

CHAPTER 4[8]

By the rainbow which was round about the throne [v. 3], is signified the gospel or covenant of grace,[9] for the rainbow was the token of God's covenant to Noah. It was "like unto an emerald" [v. 3], which is so green that other things lose their greenness when compared with it. Green, being the most pleasing[1] color, and above all others easy and healthful to the eye, is a fit symbol of grace and mercy with which God is surrounded, and which he most especially doth exhibit unto us. By its being so exceedingly green, even like an emerald, is held forth the transcendent greatness and glory of the grace of God in the gospel. Green is a symbol of joy and prosperity. The trees and fields, when they prosper and flourish, are most green, and are said to rejoice and sing and clap their hands; hereby therefore is signified the joyful and glorious nature of the gospel. As greenness is caused on the face of the earth, by the kind influences of the sun, so[2] the joy and happiness of the gospel, is caused by the kind influences or grace and love of the Sun of[3] Righteousness. Therefore what color could have been so proper for this rainbow, as the wondrous greenness of the emerald?

The "four and twenty elders" [v. 4] represent the church of God, as appears by the 5th chapter, [the] 8th and 9th verses. The number is 24, because all the matters of the church of God run upon twelves, in all the visions of this book. As the Old Testament church was founded on twelve patriarchs, so the new upon twelve apostles of the Lamb, which is 24. For by these are represented the whole company of saints, both

8. JE did not comment on ch. 3 in the exposition.

9. MS: "Gr"; lacuna at margin. JE described the rainbow as a "covenant of grace" elsewhere. See Dwight ed., *9*, 181; and Stephen J. Stein, "Jonathan Edwards and the Rainbow: Biblical Exegesis and Poetic Imagination," *New England Quarterly, 47* (1974), 440–56.

1. Or: "pleasant." MS: "Ple"; lacuna at margin.

2. Conjecture for lacuna. The next phrase is written on the tattered top margin of p. 2 in the MS.

3. Or: "Saviour's"; conjecture for illegible words or word.

those that lived before, as well as since the coming of Christ. They are said to sit on four and twenty seats or thrones, and to be clothed with white raiment, and to wear crowns of gold,[4] because the saints are a royal priesthood. They are made kings and priests, and sit down in the kingdom, and reign forever with Christ [Rev. 5:10].

As there were seven lamps in the temple and tabernacle, so here [v. 5].

A sea, not as the ocean, or as pools, but as the sea in Solomon's temple: a "sea of glass" [v. 6], as Solomon's was a sea of brass. For everything that comes into the presence or before the throne of God, must be perfectly purified, and made free of all filthiness or stain. As[5] to the four beasts, see in the "Miscellaneous Reflections," no. ww.[6] See nos. 47, 49, 51, 70.

"And they rest not day nor night, etc." [v. 8]. God's glory is continually manifested anew every moment, by the new exhibitions of those attributes in God's providence, which manifestations stir up the saints to give glory to God. For "when those beasts give glory and honor and thanks, to him that sat on the throne, who liveth forever and ever, the four and twenty elders fall down before him, etc." [vv. 9–10].

CHAPTER 5[7]

There are things which do certainly prove the divinity of Christ. That he was "in the midst of the throne" [v. 6], the same throne mentioned in the beginning of the 4th chapter. And then he was in the midst of the four beasts, which must signify his possessing those four attributes of God.[8] And then he had seven horns, which doubtless signifies his perfection of power. And then the seven spirits of God were his spirit, not only as they are the saints', to help and assist and to dwell in them, nor as they were the prophets', to inspire them: but as a man's

4. MS: "God."

5. Conjecture for illegible word.

6. No. ww deals with the four beasts of Rev. 4:6–9, which JE equated with the living creatures of Ezekiel's vision (ch. 1) and with the ensigns of the camp of Israel (Num. 2). Ezekiel's creatures, responsible for the wheel of God's providence, according to JE, "are the emblems of something divine," namely, the wisdom, power, goodness, and justice of God. He linked the camp standards with the same attributes: Reuben's face of a man with wisdom, the lion of Judah with power, the ox of Ephraim with goodness, and the eagle of Dan with justice. See Mede, *Key* (1643), Pt. 1, pp. 30–38, for a fuller discussion of these associations.

7. Here JE deleted "A finite power may open a seal, but he that looses seven seals must certainly be omnipotent and omniscient."

8. See above, n. 6.

eyes are his own, he had seven eyes, which are the seven spirits of God. And then the four beasts worship him, and fall down before him [v. 8]; that is, that the manifestations of the infinite perfections of God do acknowledge him as their author.

"And we shall reign on earth" [v. 10], in that sense that is spoken of in the 20th chapter.[9]

Verse 3. "And no man in heaven, nor in earth, nor under the earth, was able to open the book, neither to look thereon"; that is, neither the angels, nor glorified saints in heaven, nor men on earth, nor the devils in hell, could foretell those futurities.

CHAPTER 6

By him that sat on the white horse cannot be meant Christ [v. 2]; the description is much too mean, and very unlike other descriptions of him.

Verse 8.[1] See concerning the pale horse, death and hell, no. 63; of the four first seals, see no. 70; concerning the third seal and black horse, etc., see nos. 74 and 94.

CHAPTER 7

"Till we have sealed the servants of our God in their foreheads" [v. 3]. Let not the church presently be the subject of these storms, lest it should be quite overthrown, and Christianity be quite extinct, and the very elect should be overpowered. But let Christianity be a little settled first, that when these storms do come, they may find the church so well stablished, as not to be entirely overthrown. Though it be exceedingly weakened and diminished, yet let it remain at least in that little number that is elected. See no. 43.

9. In Miscell. no. k JE stated his earliest understanding of the millennium. "By the saints' reigning on earth (as they sing in the 5th chapter of Revelation at the 10th verse), and so by their souls' living and reigning with Christ a thousand years (in the 20th chapter, wherein that is accomplished), can be understood nothing but their reigning in Christ, who then shall reign; for they are united to him, and being one with him, it may very properly be said that they reign. For it is just all one as if they reigned, as the saints on earth then shall; for the saints on earth shall reign no otherwise themselves. And besides, because of their communion with the saints on earth, whereby when those reign, these do in them: wherefore it is most properly said to be a revival of their souls; for the spirit of the saints and dead martyrs shall then be revived in the saints on earth, as if their souls descended from heaven and lived in them."

1. Here JE deleted "By the Hell that followed after, is not meant the hell of the damned, but Hades, the grave or state of the dead, the shades of death." He canceled the sentence when he wrote no. 63, which offers a different interpretation.

The "hundred and forty and four thousand" [v. 4] is the church which God had during the reign of Antichrist. And the "great multitude, which no man could number, of all nations and kindreds and peoples and tongues" [v. 9], that were clothed with white robes, and had palms in their hands, which were afterward, signifies that innumerable multitude of all nations that have been martyred, since the beginning of the Reformation.

"And have washed their robes, and made them white in the blood of the Lamb" [v. 14]. Not only purged from all filthiness of sin, but their garments, that were stained with their own blood, are now made white in the blood of the Lamb; and they are perfectly freed from all manner of trouble and affliction, as well as all sin. The "great tribulation" spoken of [v. 14], were the heathen persecutions.[2] See no. 68.

CHAPTER 8

The 6th seal ended with the end of the heathen persecutions, and the fixing the angels in their places to hold the four winds, and the voice that cried to them. The seventh seal begins with the silence that immediately ensued [v. 1]. See no. 6.[3]

That "voices and thunderings and lightnings and earthquake" [v. 5] were the changes by reason of the Arians, Julian the Apostate and the dividing the western from the eastern empire, etc.

And "the first angel sounded, and there followed hail and fire mingled with blood, and they were cast upon the earth. And the third part of the trees was burnt up, and all green grass was burnt up" [v. 7], that by which is meant those northern nations that infested the empire, such storms always coming from the north. In that respect, and for their multitude and the mischief they did, they were like hail; and for their making their way with fire and sword, they are resembled to a tempest of fire and blood. "And the third part of the trees were burnt up"; that is, great part of the prosperity [and] pleasant things in which they used to rejoice were destroyed. "And all green grass was burnt up"; that is, all the former glory and beauty of the empire was departed. See the beginning of the 4th chapter concerning the meaning of green grass.[4] See no. 12.

By the turning of the third part of the sea to blood [v. 8], is meant the

2. JE added this sentence when he wrote no. 68.
3. Here JE deleted "And 'to him was given much incense, etc.' [v. 3]; for the prayers of saints are perfumed with the abundant incense of Christ."
4. Above, p. 99.

empire's losing of whole states, kingdoms and governments to their enemies; for the Goths and Vandals set up kings and governments in many provinces of the empire. "And a third part of the creatures that were in the sea, and had life, died" [v. 9]; a third part of the subjects of the empire, were made subject to the rule of others. "And a third part of the ships were destroyed" [v. 9]. All those rich treasures and revenues, that used to [be] brought in from those parts of the empire, ceased. See nos. 13, 18.

The effect of the third trumpet was upon the rivers and fountains of waters [v. 10]; that is, their public nurseries and societies of rulers and chief men, were now filled with their enemies, so that those fountains by whose streams they were formerly made glad, were now bitter as wormwood [v. 11], because filled with their enemies. See nos. 14, 19.

The smiting of the fourth trumpet the third part of the sun, moon and stars [v. 12]. The fourth trumpet was the reduction of the Roman Empire down to its present states, to the dividing of it into ten kingdoms, and the lessening the imperial dignity, power and dominion to this low degree. See no. 15.

CHAPTER 9

By this "star" may be intended Mahomet, who fell from Christianity; "and to him was given the key" [v. 1]. Arabia, from whence these came, is the country of locusts. It was a wind that blew from Arabia, that brought the plague of locusts upon Egypt.

"And unto them was given power, as the scorpions of the earth have power" [v. 3], that is, of infusing deadly poison with their tails.

Verse 4. Here we have the good effects of the sealing the servants of God in their foreheads; those that had the seal of God in their foreheads, could not be hurt by them. They could not hurt them with the poison of their tails, that is, their[5] soul-killing religion; nor could they make them turn from the profession of the gospel. 'Twas only the insincere and hypocrites that they could cause to do this.

"And to them it was given that they should not kill them, but that they should be tormented five months" [v. 5]. And even them[6] they[7] could not make really to believe their religion (Those that really turned to their religion were killed.), but only compelled them outwardly to renounce Christianity and embrace Mahometanism, against the

5. Here JE deleted "false religion."
6. I.e., the servants of God.
7. I.e., the Mahometans.

convictions of their own hearts, and to the great torment of their consciences.

"And in those days shall men seek death, and shall not find it; and shall desire to die, and death shall flee from them" [v. 6]. That is, they shall wish for the truth of Mahometanism, and wish to be really convinced of it, that they might profess it without such internal torments of conscience.

Abaddon and Apollyon [v. 11], from *aubad* and $\dot{\alpha}\pi\acute{o}\lambda\lambda\nu\mu\iota$,[8] signifies "destroyer"; this is Mahomet. See nos. 4, 56; v. 15, see no. 71; vv. 10 and 19, see no. 42.

CHAPTER 10

"His right foot on the sea, and his left on the earth" [v. 2], to denote his sovereignty over both. And sware "that there should be time no longer" [v. 6]; or that the time should be no longer, that is, the time of all those long, numerous and tedious changes. When the seventh trumpet blows, [the] thing that is aimed at by them all shall be brought about: the overturning shall cease, and he shall rule and reign whose right it is. "The mystery of God shall be finished" [v. 7]. The meaning and end of all these mysterious providences of God, shall then be brought to light, and brought to pass. The time of all those things which have been prophesied of old, shall be finished; all these mysterious prophecies shall then be known by their events. The "time, times and half a time" [Rev. 12:14] shall see an end; the world shall then begin its sabbath of rest.

CHAPTER 11

"And I will give power to my two witnesses" [v. 3]. They are called "two" because that was the number that was constituted by the law of Moses, and the institution of the apostles in the New Testament, and by the law of all nations: for one witness, in the eyes of all laws, is no witness at all. See nos. 5, 33, 45.

"If any man will hurt them, fire proceedeth out of their mouth" [v. 5]. They shall be judged and condemned by their doctrine and preaching. If they will not receive their testimony, but instead of that persecute them for it, it shall be as fire to devour them, and bring down the wrath

8. The stem of the Hebrew אֲבַדּוֹן is אבד, for which the basic verbal idea in the Qal conjugation is "to perish." In the Piel and the Hiphil, it acquires the causative meaning "to destroy." Ἀπολλύων derives from the Greek ἀπόλλυμι, "to destroy." The Septuagint regularly translates אָבַד with some form of ἀπόλλυμι.

of God upon them. The threatenings, which are contained in that word which they preach, shall come upon them; for all that hear the Word of God shall be conquered by it. God's Word always comes as conqueror: those that are not conquered by conversion shall be conquered by destruction and the execution of its threatenings, of which this is a very apt visionary representation. See I Kgs. 19:17; Jer. 1:10, 5:14; and Hos. 6:5.[9]

"These have power to shut heaven, etc." [v. 6]. They have that privilege, that their cause shall never be unavenged. They shall receive no injury from their injuries, but what shall be fully punished; and their enemies shall be plagued, as often as ever they give occasion. For God will always be full on their side; wherefore 'tis best to let them alone. This could not be represented in a vision more appositely, than by their "smiting the earth with all plagues, as often as they will" [v. 6]. See no. 86.

Of their bodies lying unburied in the street [v. 8], see Miscell. no. uu.[1] See no. 1.

"And they ascended up to heaven in a cloud" [v. 12]. They are now got forever out of the reach of their enemies. Antichrist will never be able again to quell Christianity, and conquer the Reformation, do what he will.

"And the seventh angel sounded. And there were great voices in heaven, saying, The kingdoms of this world are become the kingdoms of our Lord, and of his Christ; and he shall reign forever and ever" [v. 15]. And now, according to the oath of the angel, that stood on the earth and the sea, the mystery of God is finished. I can see no reason for certainly concluding that the seven thunders are seven claps of this trumpet, nor why the seven vials should be all contained in it, any more than why all the succeeding parts of the book should.[2]

9. The biblical citations, later additions, emphasize the destructive potential of the prophetic word. For example, see JE's comment on Jer. 5:14 in the "Blank Bible," p. 529.

1. In no. uu entitled "APOCALYPSE" JE wrote, "By not suffering the dead bodies of the witnesses to be put in graves [Rev. 11:8–10], must be understood a mocking, reviling, and venting hatred and malice against them after dead; for they could not satisfy their rage and cruelty upon them by only killing them. And we know that thus the papists used always to do, very often venting their rage like fools upon their dead bodies, tearing and burning [them], sometimes digging them out of the earth on purpose to do these things to them, citing them to their bar after dead, and such like; also sometimes in not suffering any to bury them. Their anger and malice always used to be expressed so, that they used to curse and excommunicate them after dead, etc."

2. See Poole, *Annotations*, Vol. 2, at Rev. 11:15, for a summary of contrary viewpoints concerning the relationship between the seventh trumpet and the six vials.

"And the nations were angry" [v. 18]; for without doubt, the proud, the cruel, the haughty, the insulting and malicious Antichrist will be exceeding enraged, when he sees himself apace, irresistibly brought down. Rev. 16:10–11, "And they gnawed their tongues for pain, and blasphemed the God of heaven because of their pains and their sores." And Rev. 16:21, "And men blasphemed God, because of the plague of the hail." "And thy wrath is come" [v. 18], and now the turn is come for thy anger. The nations were angry with thy servants, and cruelly persecuted them, and then were angry with them; and now it is time for thine anger to be executed on them.

"And the time of the dead, that they should be judged" [v. 18]: not with a judgment of condemnation, but as God is said to judge the fatherless and the widow, that is, all the martyrs that have been persecuted and killed by Antichrist, and indeed, the martyrs by the heathen persecutions; for this is in answer to their prayer (ch. 6:10). [It] is time now that they should be righted, and have justice done them, and should be rewarded. See in what sense, in the exposition on the 20th chapter.[3]

"And the temple of God was opened in heaven, and there was seen in his temple the ark of his testament" [v. 19]. Hereby is denoted the wonderful discoveries that will be made when that time comes. Many things that puzzle our head now, shall be clearly discovered then. The glories of the gospel, which have a long time been hid, shall then abundantly more clearly shine forth than ever before; and men shall see plainly the very foundation and inward frame, of the wonderful doctrines of Christianity; and truth shall shine forth bright, pure and unmixed; and there [shall] be such discoveries, as to fill the world with joy and wonderment.[4] The ark was the most inward of all the things of the temple, and the most holy of all the holy things, as appears by its place, which was the holiest place in the whole temple.

"And there were lightnings, and voices, and thunderings, and an earthquake, and great hail" [v. 19]. It is evident that this chapter brings us down as far as the 20th chapter of this book. For the method of these visions is first, to give a more general representation of things, and then afterwards, a more distinct description of the particular changes and revolutions that are the subjects of them. Thus in this chapter, things are

3. Again JE had in mind Miscell. no. k, where he suggested that during the reign of the saints on earth the spirit of the martyrs will be revived and justice effected. It will be "as if they themselves should live and rule over their persecutors, for it is the same thing exactly."

4. In Miscell. no. 26, written shortly before JE began the AP, the millennium is described as a time of unprecedented learning in divinity and philosophy when "this lower world shall be all over covered with light."

more generally spoken to and run over, even the last overthrow of the enemies of the kingdom of Christ. But in the next chapter, things that were before but generally touched upon, are resumed, and we have a more particular description: the church's warfare with and conquest of heathenism, and Satan's ejection out of his kingdom. And then we have more generally, Satan's contrivance to regain his kingdom by the introduction of popery and antichristianism, and his persecution of the Protestants after the Reformation. And then in the next chapter,[5] the subject of popery is resumed; and there is a more distinct description of Antichrist. And then in the next chapter, things are brought down to the final destruction of Antichrist. But in the 15th and 16th chapters, this destruction of Antichrist is resumed and more particularly described, in the pouring out the vials, successively to the last stroke that is given, to her final overthrow.

And then in the seventeenth [chapter], there is yet a more particular description of Antichrist, not only a more particular vision, but an explication of the vision, which is such a key to the whole book, that it is impossible to be mistaken in the general meaning of it.[6] In the 18th chapter, we have the angel's proclamation of his overthrow; and in the beginning of the next, there is the universal joy that was caused by it, and the wedding of the Lamb. And from the 11th verse, we have another vision representing more particularly not only the destruction of Antichrist, but of all the church's enemies; and in the 20th chapter, a particular description of the glorious state of the church that followed, and of the general judgment; and then in the last two chapters, [a description] of the triumphant state of the church that followed. This, it is most evident, is the method of these visions.

CHAPTER 12

"A woman clothed with the sun" [v. 1], without doubt, with the gospel or the Lord Jesus Christ; for we are commanded to put on the Lord Jesus Christ. If the[7] gospel is the sun, the Old Testament institution was the moon; the light of that is as much inferior to the light of the New Testament, as the light of the moon is to the light of the sun. Before Christ came into the world, the church enjoyed but the moonlight, just enough to give them light, till the sun should rise. The Mosaic institutions shewn wholly by a reflected light. They were useful only as

5. I.e., ch. 13.
6. Below, p. 120.
7. Here JE deleted "New Testament."

they reflected the light of the gospel, and shadowed forth and typified[8] Christ. As the moon would be useless, except it reflected the light of the sun, the church now is got above these ordinances, and they are put under her feet.

"And upon her head a crown of twelve stars" [v. 1]. The doctrine of the twelve apostles, or the doctrine of the gospel, is the crown and glory of the church. Proverbs 1:9, "For they shall be an ornament of grace unto thy head, and chains about thy neck." The ministers of the gospel are represented as stars, in the first chapter; and without doubt, the twelve apostles may [be so represented], who are the chief of the ministers of the gospel. These twelve stars in this crown are instead of twelve shining gems.

"And she being with child cried, travailing in birth, and pained to be delivered" [v. 2]. "With child . . . in[9] birth," or Christ mystical. The ten persecutions,[1] especially the tenth, were the dreadful pains she endured in her travail with Christianity.

"And his tail," that is, his ecclesiastical men, and their tenets, and false doctrines (See Is. 9:15),[2] "drew the third part of the stars of heaven, and did cast them to the earth" [v. 4]. By "stars" is meant visible saints, or professors of the truth, as Daniel 8:10.[3] Christ is the sun, and saints are stars that shine by his light.

"And she brought forth a man child" [v. 5]. At last, after sore travail, this woman was delivered under Constantine. "And her child was caught up to God, and to his throne" [v. 5]. Though the serpent stood ready to devour it, yet he was disappointed; for God took him out of his reach. Paganism could never regain the empire more; it was in vain for the dragon to attempt that.

"And the woman fled into the wilderness" [v. 6], that is, presently after she was delivered; "and her child was caught up to God and his throne" [v. 5]. Soon after Christianity was well-established in the empire, the serpent still persecuting the woman, she flies into the wilderness, that she may be safe from him.

"And there was [war] in heaven, etc." [v. 7]. Here it is evident,

8. Here JE deleted "evangelical things."

9. MS: "with"; ellipsis added.

1. Tradition enumerated ten periods of persecution in the Christian church prior to the Edict of Milan in 313. See William H. C. Frend, *Martyrdom and Persecution in the Early Church, a Study of a Conflict from the Maccabees to Donatus* (Oxford, 1965).

2. MS: "his ~~followers his worshippers~~ ⟨Ecclesiastical men & their tenets and ~~Superstitions~~ fase doctrines vid Isai 9.15.⟩" These are later changes.

3. Years later JE wrote a related entry on Dan. 8:10 in the "Blank Bible," p. 620.

that the church's warfare with and victory over paganism is resumed, and more particularly described; for it is certain, that this war was before the woman's flying into the wilderness, mentioned in the foregoing verse. This appears by the 14th verse, where this flying into the wilderness is mentioned as being after this war.

"For the accuser of our brethren is cast down, who accused them before God day and night" [v. 10]. Great part of the work that Satan doth, is to render them as odious as possibly he can; and by this means he persecuted the church, by rendering of them odious by false accusations and false representations. And he endeavors to render them as odious as possibly he can, by tempting of them to sin, that he may have whereof to accuse them. See no. 52.

"And they overcame him by the blood of the Lamb, and by the word of their testimony" [v. 11]. By "the blood of the Lamb" may be partly intended their martyrdom; for in shedding their blood, they shed the blood of Christ (ch.11:8).

"That she might fly into the wilderness, into her place" [v. 14]. See Miscell. no. yy,[4] 1260 days. See Prideaux, Part I, p. 261, concerning the seventy years' captivity, and pp. 264, 265, 266, 267, 268. Concerning Babylon's destruction, see Prideaux, Part I, p. 271.[5]

"And the serpent cast out of his mouth water, as a flood after the woman, that he might cause her to be carried away of the flood" [v. 15]. That by this flood is intended popery is evident, because it is cast out during the woman's continuance three years and an half in the wilderness. This is a new contrivance for the destruction of the woman.

"And the earth helped the woman" [v. 16]; that is, the wonderful and signal providence of God appeared for her, to preserve her in the midst of so great a flood, and in the abolishing of popery as at the Reformation.

"And the dragon was wroth with the woman, and went to make war

4. No. yy, entitled "WOMAN IN THE WILDERNESS," reads as follows: "One meaning of the 'wilderness' [Rev. 12:6] may be the church of God in the valleys of Piedmont, where God always had an evangelical visible church; and the place prepared for her is that obscure, desolate, unknown, hidden place in the midst of those inaccessible mountains." After the cross-reference, JE deleted " 'Where she is nourished for a time, and times and half a time' [v. 14]. Here is one thing about the 1260 years of Antichrist's reign wherein expositors, in general, seem hitherto to have missed it: viz., they all have taken for granted, that the prophecy supposes some particular [year], wherein it may be said that Antichrist now begins, and another particular year, wherein it may be said he now ends."

5. *Connection*, Pt. I, Vol. 1 (1725), pp. 261–71. JE's reference to Prideaux, probably added in 1739, is jumbled on the MS.

with the remnant of her seed, which keep the commandments of God, and have the testimony of Jesus Christ" [v. 17]. That is, the dragon shall be exceedingly vexed and enraged, when he sees that this grand invention also fails, and all his contrivances are frustrated; the effects of which rage are these cruel and horrid persecutions, that have been since the Reformation. Or if by the "woman" we understand the Christians in the valleys of Piedmont, hereby is intended the persecutions of the Waldenses and Albigenses,[6] which perhaps were the most barbarous of any that ever were in the world. See no. 57.

CHAPTER 13

Concerning the number of the beast, see no. 61. "And the beast which I saw was like unto a leopard" [v. 2], which is spotted and gay, denoting as well the foolish gaiety of their worship, and the numerousness of their ceremonies, as their fierce cruel nature.[7] See no. 58.

"And her feet as the feet of a bear" [v. 2]. A bear's foot is like a man's and yet [it] tears to pieces. With their feet they will hug their enemies, and in the meantime kill them; for that is their way of killing— hugging to death. Hereby, therefore, is denoted the grand falsehood and hypocrisy of their proceedings.

"And his mouth as the mouth of a lion" [v. 2], that is, exceeding greedy and rapacious, whereby is denoted, whereby is signified: 1. their covetousness, 2. their devouring nature (How do they unjustly devour men's substance and estates; how many ways have they of devouring the riches of those miserable men that are deceived by them!), and 3. their great cruelty.

"And all the world wondered after the beast" [v. 3], as the vulgar will wonder at the external pomp and great shew of monarchs and

6. JE and other Protestants delighted in tales about these religious communities which arose in the Middle Ages, the former characterized by a drive against worldliness, the latter by a dualistic theology. Protestant historians romanticized both groups. For example, see Samuel Morland, *The History of the Evangelical Churches of the Valleys of Piemont* (London, 1658); Peter Allix, *Some Remarks upon the Ecclesiastical History of the Ancient Churches of Piedmont* (London, 1690), and *Remarks upon the Ecclesiastical History of the Antient Churches of the Albigenses* (London, 1692). JE knew Thomas Bray's work of the same stripe, *Papal Usurpation and Persecution, as it has been Exercis'd in Ancient and Modern Times* (2 vols., London, 1712), which contained John Perrin's work in translation, *The History of the Old Waldenses and Albigenses; Those Two Glorious Witnesses to the Truth of Christianity* (London, 1711). See the "Catalogue," letter sheet and p. 2.

7. In Miscell. nos. 12 and 13, JE linked ceremonies and persecution by contending that when the papists have power to establish rules about what is indifferent and to punish those who disobey, then they have power to persecute.

princes. They are foolishly deceived by this external glory, and think it is impossible there should be any in the world like him. And they say, "Who is like unto the beast? Who is able to make war with him?" [v. 4]. See nos. 2, 16.

"Lamb slain from the foundation of the world" [v. 8]. 1. He was the person typified, by the slaying of lambs from the beginning of the world. 2. He was slain in the decree, and according to the eternal agreement between the Father and him. 3. The efficacy of his death reached to the very first of mankind. 4. He was slain mystically in his members.

"He that leadeth into captivity shall go into captivity; he that killeth with the sword must be killed with the sword. Here is the patience and faith of the saints" [v. 10]. It is the consideration of this—that God will hereafter judge them and avenge them—and the faith of this, that makes them so patient under all these persecutions; not that the saints are desirous of revenge in the destruction of the persons that persecute them. For this vision don't speak of persons, but things. For the particular persons, both persecuting and persecuted, will be all gone out of the world before the accomplishment of this promise, which is at the destruction of Antichrist. But it is revenge on popery and antichristianism that they desire, the destruction and ruin of that, either in the destruction or conversion of papists; this is what ought to be desired, that the proud and cruel enemies of the church, should be either converted or destroyed. And those times will be glorious when it shall be so; those times are to be wished for, wherein the saints shall destroy the beast, as the beast has destroyed them.

"And I beheld another beast coming up out of the earth" [v. 11]. The former beast is the antichristian empire, and this the antichristian clergy, the same with the woman that rides the beast, the same with the false prophet that wrought miracles before him. See nos. 35, 37. The seven-headed beast is said to be "the first beast before him" [v. 12], because he is the same beast that was before him, only revived. This interpretation of this beast seems to be very evident. [Compare] the 14th verse of this chapter with the 20th verse of the 19th chapter.

Though the seven-headed beast be said to be "the first beast before him," yet 'tis evident that the two-horned beast is contemporary with him, because it is said he commanded them which dwell on earth, "to worship the first beast" [v. 12], which they could not do if he were ceased to be; and then because it is said, he wrought miracles "in [the] sight of the beast" [v. 14].

"And he doth great wonders, so that he maketh fire come down from heaven on the earth in the sight of men" [v. 13]. That is, they deceive men's sight, and make them think that they bring down fire from heaven on the earth. Fire from heaven is the wrath and judgment of God. They make men believe that they have the wrath of God at command, and can make men the subjects of it at pleasure, and can bring down eternal condemnation to everlasting fire, on the heads of whom they please by their bulls and anathemas. This is a great miracle indeed! How dreadfully does the world use to be frighted by the Pope's excommunications. He used to cause firebrands to be cast down from the top of steeples to represent fire from heaven.

Another miracle that they make men believe they work, is the changing of bread and wine into the body and blood of Christ, making ten thousand bodies of Christ, that shall yet be the same body, and the same with that in heaven. This is a miracle indeed! None of the prophets, nor apostles, nor Jesus Christ himself, ever did the like of this. This is a miracle that God himself cannot do! They make men believe that they make their Creator, as Bonner[8] said in his oration to the convocation:

> The dignity of priests, in some things, passeth the dignity of angels, because there is no power given to any of the angels to make the body of Christ; and therefore, the least priest can do what the highest angel cannot do. Wherefore the priests are to be honored above them, and all the kings of the earth; for a priest is higher than a king, happier than an angel, maker of his Creator.[9]

The creation of the universe in six days was a very wonderful work, but not worthy to be mentioned with this miracle.

Another miracle is infallibly to know the truth. Another miraculous power is the power of ordering the invisible world, delivering from purgatory, etc. Another is the pardon of sin; dispensations and indulgences; exorcism; and a power [to] infuse holiness into the dirt, stones, and walls, bells, water, etc. All these are greater works than ever were done by any of the prophets or apostles. And besides, there are other miracles which they frequently pretend to do. [See] no. 38.

"And deceiveth them that dwell on the earth by the means of those miracles, which he had power to do in the sight of the beast" [v. 14]. When once they have made the people believe that they can do such

---

8. Edmund Bonner (c. 1500–69), a prominent cleric in the anti-Protestant movement during the reign of Mary in England. He was an ardent champion of transubstantiation and other traditional doctrines of the Catholic Church.

9. Foxe, *Acts and Monuments* (1563), p. 928.

things, the gazing multitude are so much astonished, and so filled with admiration of their power, that they can lead them where they will, make them believe what they will. They pin their faith upon the priest's shews, and believe everything that the priest says to be true. "Had power to do in the sight of the beast" [v. 14]: not "had power to do," but had power to "in the sight of the beast," that is, had power to make them believe they could do.

"To the beast which had the wound by a sword, and did live" [v. 14]; that is, by that two-edged sword that proceeds out of the mouth of him that liveth, and was dead.[1]

Verse 17. "That no man should either buy or sell." And the Council of Lateran anathematized all that entertained the Waldenses, or traded with them; a synod of France, in express terms, forbid any commerce with Protestants in buying or selling. Pope Martin the Fifth[2] by his bull prohibited Roman Catholics "to suffer any heretics to have any dwellings in their countries, or to make any bargains, or use any trades, or to perform to them any civil offices."[3] Hereby is meant, in short, that they should deprive them of all their privileges, all benefit of human society, their natural rights and the comforts of their lives. Concerning the number of the beast, see Ezekiel 8:16.[4]

CHAPTER 14

"And I looked, and lo, a Lamb stood on the Mount Zion, and with him an hundred and [forty and] four thousand, having his father's name written in their foreheads" [v. 1]. These are that 144 thousand men-

1. Here JE deleted " 'And that no man might buy or sell, save he that had the mark' [v. 17]. They that were without the mark were excommunicated, and then all dealings with them were forbidden."

2. His reign (1417–31) marked a period of aggressive suppression of dissidents in the western church.

3. Poole, *Annotations*, Vol. 2, at Rev. 13:17.

4. This sentence is a later addition. JE wrote an entry on this passage in the "Blank Bible," p. 577, explaining that twenty-five is "the number of the false, idolatrous church, as 12 is of the true, being the root of 666, the number of the beast." He was citing Francis Potter's *An Interpretation of the Number 666* (Oxford, 1642). In a letter to William McCulloch on Oct. 7, 1748, JE commented, "Of all the conjectures concerning the number of the Beast, that I have lit on in my small reading, that of Mr. Potter's seems to me the most *ingenious*, who supposes the true meaning is to be found by extracting the root of the number. . . . Yet one reason why Mr. Potter's conjecture does not fully satisfy me, is, the difficulty about adjusting the fractions in the root, when extracted." See Dwight ed., *1*, 263–64; and Stephen J. Stein, "Cotton Mather and Jonathan Edwards on the Number of the Beast: Eighteenth-Century Speculation about the Antichrist," *Proceedings of the American Antiquarian Society, 84* (1975), 293–315.

tioned in the 7th chapter, that were then sealed, to preserve them from those storms that were coming. Now those storms are come. John beholds [the 144,000] standing with the Lamb on Mount Zion, and hears them singing. See no. 7.

"And I saw another angel fly in the midst of heaven, having the everlasting gospel to preach unto them that dwell on the earth, and to every nation and kindred and tongue and people, saying with a loud voice, Fear God, and give him glory, etc." [vv. 6–7]. This is doubtless at the Reformation. The 144 thousand are the church during the reign of Antichrist; but those of every nation, kindred, tongue and people to whom the angel preached the everlasting gospel, are contemporary with those of every nation, kindred, people and tongue that were seen after the 144,000. [See] chapter 7.[5]

It further appears that it is the Reformation, because there immediately after him follows "another angel, crying, Babylon is fallen, is fallen, etc." [v. 8].

"And the third angel followed, saying with a loud voice, If any man worship the beast and his image, and receive his mark in their forehead or in his hand, the same shall drink of the wine of the wrath of God" [vv. 9–10]. Before, Antichrist cursed all that would not receive this mark; [he] would not let them buy or sell without [it]. But now, all are cursed that have it, [cursed] to drink "the wine of the wrath of God, which is poured out without mixture, etc." [v. 10].

"Here is the patience of the saints. Here are they that keep the commandments of God, and the faith of Jesus" [vv. 12]. That is, they are supported and kept persevering by a belief of these things which are spoken of in the two foregoing [verses], and in the following verse, viz., the punishment of the wicked spoken of in the two foregoing, and the reward of the perseveringly godly that continue in the Lord all their life, and die in the Lord.[6]

"And another angel came out of the temple, crying with a loud voice to him that sat on the cloud, Thrust in thy sickle and reap" [v. 15]. This angel represents grace and faithfulness, which cry aloud for the salvation of the elect.[7]

"And another came out of the altar, which had power over fire, and cried with a loud cry to him that had the sharp sickle" [v. 18]. This

5. Above, p. 102.

6. Here JE deleted " 'And on the cloud one sat like unto the Son of Man, having on his head a golden crown, and in his hand a sharp sickle' [v. 14]. We may observe that Christ himself is immediately employed in gathering home the godly, but not in the destruction of the wicked, in gathering the [ungodly]."

7. Or: "church."

angel who cries aloud for the destruction of the wicked is justice; the angel that had the sharp sickle, that he cries to, was vengeance or vindictive wrath.

CHAPTER 15

"And I saw, as it were, a sea of glass mingled with fire" [v. 2]. A sea, in the same sense as the sea in the 4th chapter:[8] the end of it was to purify. "Mingled with fire," because fire is of a most purifying nature. Water purifies the outside, but fire purifies throughout the whole, inward and outward. Wherefore John the Baptist says, that he that comes after him shall baptize "with the Holy Ghost and with fire" [Matt. 3:11].

"And them that had gotten the victory over the beast, and over his image, and over his mark, and over the number of his name, stand on the sea of glass, having the harps of God" [v. 2]. They stood on the sea of glass, having been perfectly purged therein from all manner of filthiness. [They are] the same company of whom it is said, "These are they which came out of great tribulation, and have washed their robes, and made them white in the blood of the Lamb" (Rev. 7:14). These were literally baptized with fire, burning being the common method Antichrist used to martyr the saints; and if not literally with fire, yet with cruel persecutions, which in Scripture are frequently called fire. Persecutions and trials do purify the saints, as the furnace purifies gold. Job 23:10, "When he hath tried me, I shall come forth as gold." I Pet. 1:7, "That the trial of your faith, being much more precious than of gold which perisheth, though it be tried with fire." And they sing the song of Moses, the servant of God, as Moses and the children of Israel sang unto God, after they were baptized in the Red Sea [Ex. 15:1–21] (which was a type of the purifying of the saints, as appears by I Corinthians 1:1–2). So the saints, after they were baptized in this sea of glass mingled with fire, sing praise to God, as Moses sang to God, after the final deliverance of Israel from the persecuting Egyptians. So here, the spiritual Israel of God sing praises to him, upon their final deliverance from them that are spiritually called Egyptians. See no. 75.

"And one of the four beasts gave unto the seven angels, seven golden vials full of the wrath of God" [v. 7]. This beast was the eagle, or justice.

CHAPTER 16

Concerning the seven vials, see no. 86. Concerning the 3 first vials, see Miscell. no. xx.[9] [See] no. 23.

---

8. Above, p. 100.
9. According to no. xx, JE's earliest statement on the vials, two had been completed: the

"And the second angel poured out his vial upon the sea, and it became as the blood of a dead man, and every living soul died in the sea" [v. 3]. That is, all the men in this sea died as to popery, so that there was no more fish to be catched, nor merchandise to be brought in from this sea. See no. 17.

"And the fourth angel poured out his vial upon the sun" [v. 8], that is, the emperor and the civil power of Germany. "And power was given to him to scorch men with fire" [v. 8]. That is, they shall be exceedingly vexed and enraged, and yet shall not be able to revenge themselves; and this will scorch and torment them like fire.

"And men were scorched with great heat, and blasphemed the name of God" [v. 9]; that is, they shall vent their tormenting rage by cursing the Bible, which is that by which all this ruin is brought on Antichrist. This is what has sometimes been already done by papists. They shall curse the doctrines of the gospel which thus prevail, to the overthrow of popery; they shall curse the faith of Christians, and curse God's pure worship. And [they] shall inwardly fret at God, because he in his providence so orders things against them, and perhaps shall express their rage against him in words.

"And the 5th angel poured out his vial on the seat of the beast" [v. 10]. The seat of the beast is Rome, Italy and Spain. [See] no. 34.

"That the way of the kings of the East might be prepared" [v. 12]. That a door might be opened to the conversion of the Jews, and [the] ten tribes, and other eastern nations. And that nothing might hinder the Israelites' returning to their God and their land, which indeed would make way for the converting and enlightening of all the nations of Asia. See nos. 22, 24, 40, 54.

"Three unclean spirits like frogs" [v. 13], that delight in and live upon mud.

"Which go forth unto the kings of the earth and of the whole world, to

---

first in the days of Wycliffe, Huss, and Jerome of Prague, and the second at the time of Luther and the Reformation. The "rivers" on which the third was being poured "are those societies that are fountains of popery, fountains of popish doctrines and doctors, fountains of teachers of antichristianism; that continually send forth streams into every part to water the antichristian world, . . . those fountains at which the papists do continually drink. The water is the doctrine; the streams, or waterers, are the teachers." France has been "the grand fountain of popery; this has been the great river that has watered the antichristian world; this has been their market place, their great university, the seat and fountain of their learning and policy. Wherefore, the pouring out of the third vial may be the reformation of that kingdom and [its] casting off of popery." The third vial is not yet finished, JE wrote, for since the Reformation nothing has happened "any near great enough to answer the pouring out of one of the seven vials, especially the third; which is undoubtedly one of the greatest, or else there would not be such particular notice taken of it."

gather [them] to the battle of that great day of God Almighty" [v. 14]. For by this time Christianity shall begin to be spread into all the world, and there shall be an universal rising against it to oppose [it] in the various parts of Satan's kingdom. And the heathens and Mahometans shall join in the same design, with the remainder of the papists, and with joint forces shall endeavor to overthrow the truth.

"Armageddon" [v. 16], that is, *Har Megiddo*, or the mountain of Megiddo. See no. 8. See note on Judges 5:20, at the latter end of the note.[1]

Now is the time for their final overthrow; now they are gathered together against God. Wherefore now "the seventh angel pours out his vial into the air" [v. 17], that is, the universal kingdom of Satan, who is the prince of the power of the air.

"And the cities of the nations fell" [v. 19]. Besides the great city, the cities of the nations also fell; that is, besides the Church of Rome, or the antichristian kingdom of Satan, his other kingdoms or hierarchies among the nations also were overthrown.[2]

"And every island fled away, and the mountains were not found" [v. 20], signifying the whole[3] Jewish and antichristian world was overturned. By the islands being fled away and the mountains being not found, signifies the removal of all the great obstacles, stumbling blocks, prejudices, difficulties and objections that lay in the way of the truth, and obstructed the spreading of the gospel. All was made smooth and plain. The sea had no islands to obstruct the passage or prospect, or to interrupt the evenness of its surface; nor the land any mountains: they were all fled away, and were not found. Isaiah 40:4, "Every valley shall be exalted, and every mountain and hill shall be made low: and the crooked shall be made straight, and the rough places plain." [See] no. 30.

"And there fell upon men a great hail out of heaven, every stone about the weight of a talent"[4] [v. 21]. What temporal judgments may hereby be signified, we cannot tell. But[5] by this hail seems chiefly to be meant such strong reasons and forcible arguments and demonstrations,

1. This sentence, added in the 1730s, points to no. 211 of the "Scripture," a comparison of the battle ushering in the glorious times of the church with the victory of Barak and the Israelites over the army of Sisera. No. 211, derived from Bedford's *Scripture Chronology*, is printed in Dwight ed., *9*, 297–99.

2. Here JE deleted "The ecclesiastical polities of all nations and false religions fell to the ground; all these contrivances of the devil were entirely blown up."

3. Here JE deleted "heathen, Mahometan."

4. I.e., an indeterminate large weight.

5. Here JE deleted "as to spiritual matters."

that nothing will be able to withstand them; and [they] will irresistibly beat down and immediately batter to pieces the kingdom of Antichrist, and kill men as to popery, as at one blow, as if they were dashed to pieces by stones from heaven. For we know that Antichrist is to be destroyed by clear light, by the breath of Christ's mouth, [by the] brightness of his coming, that is, by plain reason and demonstration, deduced from the Word of God. We know likewise, that he is to be destroyed by the sword that comes out of the mouth of him that sits on the horse (ch. 19:15). And what is this but the Word of God, and the clear light of the gospel? What is meant by the overthrow of Antichrist, but the overthrow of falsehood, the abolishing their false doctrine and worship? And what can those hailstones be which dash falsehood to pieces, but clear proofs and plain manifestations of truth? [See] no. 26.

CHAPTER 17

"And upon her forehead was a name written, 'Mystery' " [v. 5]. Upon the Pope's mitre used formerly to be written, "Mystery." The word "mystery" was not used anciently, just as commonly as it is now, only for something that is intricate and difficult in its own nature; but [it was used] for anything that was kept secret and was not known, however easy it might be in its own nature. "Mystery" is, I think, everywhere in Scripture and in this book of the Revelation used in this sense. The Trinity would not be called a mystery for anything else, but because it was in a great measure concealed before Christ revealed it. Thus Christ, as God manifest in the flesh, is the great mystery of godliness, because Christ's coming was a thing very much spoken of in the world, expected by everybody. [Christ's coming] was the chief subject of the prophecies of the Old Testament; but the particulars of his incarnation, birth, life, death, resurrection, ascension and kingdom[6] were in great measure concealed, wondered at and not known. So Antichrist is the great mystery of iniquity, because his coming used to be very much spoken of. He was expected by all Christians, and is the chief subject of the prophecies of the New Testament. But who he was, and the manner of his coming, and what he should do, and the particulars of his reign and kingdom, were in a great measure concealed, till that wicked one was revealed. Yea, he was concealed for a long time after he had actually come, and reigned over the whole world, till at length this great mystery, Antichrist, was discovered, though he still acts under the pretense of being Christ's vicar and successor in his kingdom on

6. Here JE deleted "and the manner, design and effects of these things."

earth, is called "His Holiness" and pretends his church to be the only true church of Christ. Popery is the deepest contrivance that ever Satan was the author of to uphold his kingdom.[7] See nos. 3, 9, 28, 36.

"And the beast that was, and is not, even he is the eighth, and is of the seven" [v. 11]. In these two respects is he "the eighth, and yet of the seven." 1. Because although the Christian emperors might be called the 7th, because they differed very much from the 6th—in this respect, that they were of a religion so repugnant to the religion of the 6th, which necessarily caused great changes in their manner of government —yet they were the 6th form of government, to wit, emperors, and did not differ from them as to power or office; so that he was still but the 6th, and popes were the 7th. [2.] And because though he were a different head, yet he was a head of the beast; for the Christian empire was not the beast. Then was the time, when the beast was not, and wherein he was wounded to death. And perhaps it was partly to denote this, that at that time the seat of the empire was removed, so that Christianity never reigned in Rome.[8]

There are also two senses wherein it is said that "the beast was, is not, and yet is" [v. 8]. First, he was when the empire was heathen, is not when Christian and is again when antichristian. And 2ndly, the popish empire is not the beast, inasmuch as he is not pagan; but yet is the beast, inasmuch as he is pagano-Christian.

"And the ten horns which thou sawest are ten kings" [v. 12]. There was all along about ten independent, self-subsisting states, that were large enough to be taken notice of in this prophecy under the name of a kingdom. Though not the same kingdoms, but different and [at]

---

7. In Miscell. no. hh JE associated deceit with the Antichrist and the Church of Rome. "It is alleged against the Church of Rome being Antichrist—say they, how can he be Antichrist that professes Christ? To that it may be answered, that he is a great deal the more Antichrist for that, for he is a [great] deal the worse for it; and the worse he is, surely the more anti-Christ, against Christ. Now certainly, those wickednesses that are professed, established and commanded by that church, are much the worse for their profession of Christ, for their professing the fundamental articles of the Christian faith. They ever deny Christ, in being so contrary to him." The profession of Christ compounds the crime, according to JE; "thus the filthiness of a snake or toad is much more abominable for being joined with life, which is in itself excellent, than the same filthiness and shape would be in lifeless matter."

8. JE's attempt to solve this exegetical riddle relating to the traditional seven forms of government ruling over the city of Rome hinges on his distinction between the pagan emperors and the Christian emperors, both of whom were the sixth form of government over the city. The difference was that the Christian emperors ruled from Constantinople, not Rome. Therefore the popes were the seventh form of government in Rome, although when counted differently the sixth was the pagan empire, the seventh the Christian empire, and the eighth the papacy.

different times, yet there were but about ten. If there are several little states that depend upon or subsist very much by others, they are called all together one kingdom, of which I say there was all along about ten. If there were thirteen half the time, and seven the other half, if we give it one number[9] we must call it ten. And if there have been five or six different numbers, yet if taken together they make in the general ten; that is, if the excesses of those that exceed ten added do nearly answer the defect of those that are less than ten, the proportion of the length of their continuance being considered, then if we would give it in one number, we must call it ten. See nos. 10, 11.

"And the woman which thou sawest is that great city, which reigneth over the kings of the earth" [v. 18]. This verse is spoken the plainest of any one passage in the whole book, and is a key to the whole prophecy, whereby the general meaning of it may be unerringly discovered. 'Tis the only part of this prophecy that is spoken without allegory.

CHAPTER 18

"And the merchants of the earth" [v. 3] are the priests.

"Reward her even as she rewarded you, etc." [v. 6]. Not that we are to understand this as a command designedly to revenge upon the persons of men. The saints shall revenge themselves, no otherwise than by doing their utmost for the destruction of popery. They were the causes of her plagues, no otherwise than the two witnesses, who destroyed all that hurt them with fire out of their mouth, and by shutting heaven, etc.; of which, see the exposition of the 11th chapter.[1] Indeed, great plagues shall be brought on Antichrist, by means of the spreading of the gospel by their means; but 'tis God that will so order it. We are, therefore, to understand this only as a visionary representation, representing the word or command of his providence. For so there is nothing happens, except God first give the word: God shall give forth his command that it shall be that. Antichrist shall be exceedingly plagued by means of the saints, and the event of things shall obey.

"Therefore shall her plagues come in one day" [v. 8]. Though Antichrist's fall be very gradual, yet the great and finishing stroke to his overthrow shall be very sudden, as indeed shall every one of the seven strokes[2] that shall be given him, as have been the two past: the first by the Hussites and Wycliffites, etc., and the second at the Reformation, when great part of the world was at once become reformed.

9. I.e., as an average.
1. Above, pp. 104–07.
2. I.e., the seven vials.

"Death and mourning and famine" [v. 8]. Death which is the usual expression for the pestilence, as chapter 6:8.[3] Those that are converted and renounce popery, die as to Antichrist. And the truth shall prevail everywhere as a pestilence to Antichrist; and men shall die this death continually, as in a raging plague. Vast multitudes, yea, whole kingdoms, at once shall be swept away by this pestilence, as those that shall retain their antichristianism, shall be quite killed as to their power, influence, honor and hopes. They shall take a final leave of all those pleasant things they used to enjoy (mentioned in the following parts of this chapter), as a man does when he dies. It shall not be a sleep to revive again, but a death; for they shall fall and never rise more. They shall be in such a low, miserable, forlorn, despised state, as is fitly set forth by death. They shall have that internal pains and torments of mind, that are like the pangs of death, besides those many and dreadful external judgments that shall come upon them. Antichrist, as he is a body politic, shall forever die an eternal death. There may be many papists, vagabonds that shall be the scorn of the world; but there shall never more be a popish polity.

What a bitter grief, sorrow and mourning with these things loose in their minds! We have their lamentations in the ensuing parts of the chapter.

"And famine" [v. 8]. They shall be wholly deprived of all their fat benefices, rich revenues and great incomes on which they have lived so deliciously. They shall have all their delicious fare taken away, for Antichrist shall be stoned to death.

"And she shall be utterly burnt with fire" [v. 8]. As that which is burnt with fire vanishes away to nothing but ashes, so she—however stately or pompous she has been—shall be wasted, and quite consumed by her plagues and reduced to nothing but a despised, miserable, forlorn remnant, that shall be like ashes, which shall remain as trophies and objects of the triumph of the saints. And that they may have the full ruin and overthrow of Antichrist continually before their eyes, as the effects of it shall be beheld in the miserable state of this remnant, to raise in them admiration of the justice of God in the overthrow of her who in her lifetime was so proud, insulting and cruel, and [admiration of] God's mercy in the church's great deliverance. When they see how different her state is now to what it once was, when "she said in her heart, I sit a queen, and am no widow, and shall see no sorrow" [v. 7], they shall wonder when they consider that this is she, that made the nations to tremble.

3. Here JE deleted "This death here doubtless is the same sort of death."

Not but that there may also be a literal burning of Rome with fire; if that is to be yet, I think that can't be the principal thing that is aimed at here. There will doubtless be many of the judgments and calamities, spoken of in this book, externally inflicted on popish countries; but these are the least aim of the vision.

Verse 9. "And the kings of the earth." Hereby may partly be intended the priests, who reign as kings, and have hitherto kinged it over men's souls, that have rid the beast, and did what they would.

"When they shall see the smoke of her burning" [v. 9], the effects of her overthrow, the remaining marks and signs of her ruin.

"For no man buyeth her merchandise any more" [v. 11]. None will be such fools as to buy her pardons, indulgences, preferments, dispensations out of purgatory, and the like any more.

Verse 17. "And every shipmaster, etc." More especially the Jesuits and missionaries, who are about all over the whole world, under a pretense of zeal for men's souls, when they are only fishing for their estates.

Verse 21. "And a mighty angel took up a stone like a great millstone, and cast it into the sea, saying, Thus with violence shall that great city Babylon be thrown down, and shall be found no more at all." That is, first suddenly, second finally, third violently, with such force as they, with all their great power, with all their contrivance and cunning, shall not be able in the least to resist or retard, any more than a man can stop a millstone that falls down out of heaven.

[Verse] 23. "For by thy sorceries were all nations deceived." For their priests are but the instruments of the devil; they work by his power. The whole of their religion is his contrivance, and it is by the subtilty and craft of the devil that they have thus deceived all nations. 'Tis the devil that helps them in the propagation of his kingdom. Their whole constitution is a strange charm, and a politic device whereby all nations have been bewitched; it can't be better expressed than that the popish clergy have bewitched the nations.[4] [See] no. 39.

CHAPTER 19

Verse 3. "And her smoke rise up forever and ever"; that is, her memory should be most odious. She shall always be remembered as the object of the greatest scorn and detestation. Her memory shall [be] like a stinking scent rising up from her dead carcass, or like an offensive smoke rising from burning; her name shall stink to all generations. This

4. JE added this sentence when he wrote no. 39.

smoke is those visible marks of her ruin, that shall be continually before the eyes of all.

"And the four beasts fell down" [v. 4]; for the power, wisdom, justice and mercy will be all most gloriously manifested, in the destruction of Antichrist's and Satan's kingdom.

"For the Lord God omnipotent reigneth" [v. 6]. Now shall be brought to pass that which is so often spoken of in the Psalms and Prophets, of God reigning over all nations.[5]

"And I saw the beast, and the kings of the earth, and their armies gathered together" [v. 19]: not only the beast, but the powers of Satan's other hierarchies.

"And the remnant were slain with the sword of him that sat on the horse" [v. 21], that is, were slain as to antichristianism. Their life, as they were papists, was taken away by the sword, which is the Word of God.

CHAPTER 20[6]

"And I saw the souls of them that were beheaded, etc." [v. 4]. See Miscell. no. k;[7] see nos. 6, 21, 25, 27, 29, 48, 50, 55, 60, 66.

Concerning the time of the millennium.[8] "Mr. Broughton[9] observes the proportion of times in God's government since the coming out of Egypt: thence to their entering Canaan forty years; thence seven years to the dividing the land; thence seven jubilees to the first year of Samuel, in whom prophecy begun; thence to the first year of the captivity, seven seventies of years, i.e., 490; thence to the return one seventy; thence to the death of Christ seven seventies more; and from thence to the destruction of Jerusalem, 40 years." Henry, *Annotations* on Dan. 1: 1–7.[1]

Verse 14. "And death and hell (or Hades) were cast into the lake of fire"; that is, there shall be no more death, no grave, no separate state of souls. These shall be forever destroyed, and shall maintain their

5. E.g., Ps. 47:8; Is. 24:23.

6. JE wrote in the Table of the "Miscellanies" under "Millennium," "when it will begin, see exp. on Rev. Ch. 20," a probable reference to this location. He also wrote an entry in the "Blank Bible," p. 896, at Rev. 20:2 which reads, "Concerning the time when this thousand years is to begin, see Notes on Revelation, nos. 16, 21, 25, 27, 29, 35b, 50, 53, 60, 69."

7. In no. k JE suggested that the souls of the martyrs will be revived in the saints on earth during the millennium so that the martyrs will participate in the first resurrection, which is spiritual.

8. JE wrote this paragraph, rearranged according to his directions, in 1746 or 1747.

9. Hugh Broughton (1549–1612), a scholar of Jewish antiquity who wrote an exposition of the book of Daniel and *A Revelation of the Holy Apocalyps* (1610).

1. *Exposition*, Vol. 3 (1712), at Dan. 1:1–7.

terror nowhere else but in the lake of fire and brimstone, among the damned, where all that is evil in these shall yet be upheld. See no. 63.[2]

CHAPTER 21

This and the following chapter, doubtless gives a description of the church triumphant; this appears by the description of it, and because it is after the day of judgment. See no. 41;[3] see Miscell. no. 148 and "Scripture" no. 306.[4]

"And there was no more sea" [v. 1], which is dangerous, uncertain, unstable and never at rest, put into a ruffle by every wind; 'tis that from whence proceed all storms, clouds and tempests. Hereby is signified that all the changes, dangers, doubts, difficulties, storms and tempests, sorrows and afflictions of this world shall forever vanish and be abolished. And there shall be nothing but what is firm and stable as the earth. Water is the emblem of instability; Gen. 49:4, "unstable as water."[5] Of this, see further no. 72. See nos. 59, 62, 64, 65, 73a; see Miscell. no. 743.[6]

CHAPTER 22

"And in the midst of the street of it,[7] and on either side [of] the river, was there the tree of life" [v. 2]. The river ran along in the midst of the street; and all along on the banks thereof, on both sides thereon,[8] grew this pleasant tree of life.

---

2. JE added this paragraph when he wrote no. 63.

3. MS: "~~vid SS. p. 12~~ 41." This deletion confirms the provenance of the leaf sewn into the first quire. See above, p. 76.

4. These two references, later additions, point to discussions of the "new heaven and new earth." Miscell. no. 148 places that eternal abode outside the visible world "in the highest heaven." No. 306 in the "Scripture," a note on Rev. 21:22, describes the purity of that state. According to JE, the streets of gold like glass "most livelily represent the perfect purity of that city and its inhabitants," where the streets "are so pure, that their being like pure gold don't sufficiently represent the purity of them." No. 306 is printed in Dwight ed., *9*, 562.

5. JE added this sentence when he wrote no. 72.

6. In Miscell. no. 743 JE insisted that this earth cannot be "the place of the everlasting residence and reign of Christ and his church" because the Bible describes it as God's footstool or temporary dwelling. Also it cannot be the site of heaven because " 'tis a movable globe, and must continue moving always, if the laws of nature are upheld. . . . But it is not seemly, that God's eternal, glorious abode, and fixed and everlasting throne should be a movable part of the universe."

7. I.e., New Jerusalem.

8. Conjecture for illegible word.

APOCALYPSE SERIES[1]

1. CHAPTER 11:8. "Which[2] is spiritually called Sodom and Egypt." Sodom, for her spiritual filthiness and whoredom, so often spoken of in this book; and Egypt, for their keeping God's spiritual Israel in such cruel bondage and captivity. "Where also our Lord was crucified." He was literally crucified in the city, within its limits, in one of its provinces and by the civil power of it; and he was there crucified mystically in the persons of the multitude of martyrs. All the martyrs for the true religion that have perished out of her, either before or since Christ, are for number as nothing, not worth mentioning, if compared with those that have been martyred in her. The visible church in general, the whole mystical body of Christ, has been crucified in her by Antichrist.[3]

2. CHAPTER 13:5. "And there was given to him a mouth speaking great things and blasphemies"; that is, his proud and blasphemous boasts and pretenses, whereby he arrogates to himself the power and prerogatives of God, opposing and exalting himself above all that is called God, or that is worshiped, so that he as God sitteth in the temple of God, shewing himself that he is God. [He] pretends to the same power over the church[4] as Jesus Christ hath, pretending to have power to pardon sin, of managing the affairs of the invisible world, and to infallibility, which things are the prerogatives of God alone; so that he places himself in the church or the temple of God, in God's place, [and] presumes to mount Christ's throne. Yea, he places himself above God by pretending to a power of altering his laws at pleasure, dispensing with oaths taken by the name of God and vows made to him, dispensing with what God has positively forbidden, and making that

1. JE started this numbered series without beginning a new page of the MS. The title has been supplied.
2. I.e., "the great city," Rome for JE.
3. See Mede, *Key* (1643), Pt. 2, pp. 17–19, on the problems of comparing Jerusalem and Rome; echoed in Poole's *Annotations*, Vol. 2, at Rev. 11:8.
4. Here JE deleted "with which God the Father has invested his eternal Son."

unlawful which he has commanded; and by pretending to have the wrath of God at command, can make any man the subject of it at their will by excommunication; [and] by pretending to a power to create their Creator in transubstantiation, as in express terms they boast they can do. To suppose a power to do these things, supposes a superiority to God; thus Antichrist exalts himself above all that is called God or is worshiped. He also blasphemes God by cursing and anathematizing the sacred doctrines of the gospel, and by their idolatry, which is called blasphemy. Yea, their whole religion is blasphemy. Herein is probably contained their blasphemies against the church and saints, their malicious reviling and slandering them; for "blasphemy," in scripture phrase, is not only against God, but men.[5]

3. CHAPTER 17:3. "And I saw a woman sit on a scarlet-colored beast." The woman rides the beast, a very apt metaphor: all popish countries are priest-ridden. They lead the blinded people where they please, and do what they will with them, and a horse or ass is managed by his rider.

4. CHAPTER 9:13–14. "And I heard a voice from the four horns of the golden altar, which is before God, saying to the sixth angel which had the trumpet, Loose the four angels, etc." That is, God's mercy to the saints, and Christ's intercession for them, call for this punishment and vengeance on their enemies, which comes by the loosing [of] the four angels bound at Euphrates.

5. CHAPTER 11:1. "Rise, measure the temple"; intimating that they shall be kept to that measure, shall keep to the divine rule, shall neither add to nor diminish from the doctrines of the gospel.

6. CHAPTER 8:1. "And there was silence in heaven for about the space of half an hour." When we would judge how long a time this half hour signified, we must not compare it with prophetical days in other parts of this prophecy, but how long a time it was in comparison of the whole time, which the revelation of these visions to John took up: for this was half an hour of it. Wherefore, we are to understand it only of an indefinite short time.

7. CHAPTER 14:1. "144,000 having their Father's name written in their foreheads." Though the number of the professors of the true religion was but exceeding small in the time of Antichrist's height, yet it was large enough to be fitly represented by this number. The number of the Waldenses and Albigenses was so great, that as Perionius[6] says, a million of them were slain for their profession.

---

5. This sentence is a later addition.
6. MS: "Petrionius ~~one of them~~." Perhaps JE took the reference from the *Annotations,*

8. CHAPTER 16:16. Megiddo was the place where Sisera was discomfited by Deborah and Barak (Judg. 5:19), which victory was a very lively type of this victory of the saints over their enemies. Jabin and Sisera were a type of Antichrist: Jabin is the ten-horned beast, or the civil power; Sisera, the captain of his host, is the two-horned beast, or the Pope and his clergy, which are the captains of the host of Antichrist. Sisera had nine hundred chariots of iron, typifying the great power, tyranny and cruelty of Antichrist; he mightily oppressed Israel, as Antichrist mightily oppresseth and cruelly persecuteth the spiritual Israel of God. Sisera dwelt in Harosheth of the Gentiles; so Antichrist dwells in his new Gentile or heathenish church. He pretends to dwell in the holy catholic church, but he dwells in the synagogue of Satan. Deborah is a type of the church; she was a prophetess: so the church is the pillar and foundation of truth. She dwelt on a mountain, a type of Mount Zion, whereon stands the church of God, signifying the strength of the church's situation, having the Lord God for an impregnable mount of stone,[7] being built upon Christ, the Rock of Ages. She dwelt under the palm tree, another type to which Christ resembles his church: Canticles 7:7–8, "This thy stature is like unto a palm tree. I said I will go up to the palm tree. I will take hold of the boughs thereof." Barak is a type of Christ, who fights for his church and overcomes her enemies for her. Barak dwelt at Naphtali, the place where Christ chiefly resided. The song of Deborah, after the victory, signifies the church's great joy and singing and praising God, after this victory at Armageddon, spoken of in the 19th chapter.[8]

9. CHAPTER 17:10. "And there are seven kings." 1. Kings. 2. Consuls. 3. Tribunes. 4. Decemvirs. 5. Dictators. 6. Emperors. 7. Popes.

10. Thus, if we would tell how long the days are upon earth, if we give it in one number, we must say twelve hours, though they are of a hundred and eighty different lengths.

11. CHAPTER 17:12. The pretended division of the empire into ten kingdoms by Gensericus,[9] cannot be the division chiefly intended. Can we suppose that the whole empire, which continues for so long a time, would be called a ten-horned beast only because a conqueror once

---

Vol. 2, at Rev. 13:7, where Poole writes: "Perionius (one of their own) saith, That more than a Million were slain in these Wars of these poor People, meerly for not complying with the Church of *Rome* in their Apostacy." Joachim Perionius (d. 1559) was a French classicist and apologist for Roman Catholicism.

7. Conjecture for lacuna.

8. In the early 1730s JE continued his typological interpretation of Judg. 5 in the "Scripture." See Dwight ed., *9*, 297–99.

9. King of the Vandals (427–77) and conqueror of Rome.

divided it into ten different governments, which presently vanishes away again? How improper would it be, so often in prophecies both of Old Testament and New, to call that beast a ten-horned beast, and have him so represented in visions which, though his life is a thousand two hundred and sixty years, had not ten horns above forty or fifty of them, and that, when the beast was but a fetus, and only in embryo. Yea, I think it is pretty evident, that at the time of Gensericus, the beast was not in being, and that the forty and two months of his life and reign, had not yet commenced. And if so, it is impossible that these ten kings should be his horns; for all know that the Pope first obtained his supremacy and universal episcopacy in the year 606.[1] But if he was risen and at his height at the time of Gensericus' ten kings, yet they continued for so short a time that the beast could never be called ten-horned from them. 'Tis plain that the prophecy speaks of them as contemporary with the beast; that is, that they should rise [and] reign nearly together with the beast. And if they were contemporary, yet they could not be called horns of the beast or Antichrist; for they were not supporters of the Pope, cared nothing about him as we know of. They never agreed together to give their kingdom to the beast; nor are they those that will hate the whore, and "eat her flesh and burn her with fire" [ch. 17:16]. Neither are they properly horns of the empire; for they were none of themselves, but only foreign ravagers that overrun them, and conquered them, and kept them in bondage for a while.

But there has been for a long time, a division of the empire into various kingdoms; which division, for the main, has been permanent, and in the general has continued the same.

12. CHAPTER 8:7. The first trumpet was when the Goths and Vandals first came pouring into all parts of the empire, like a storm of hail, in the year 395 and several years after.

13. CHAPTER 8:8–9. The 2nd trumpet was when Rome was taken by Alaricus,[2] *anno* 410, after which the Goths obtained a seat and government in France, and the Burgundians and Vandals a seat near the river Rhone, and the Vandals a seat in Spain. By "seas" is signified kingdoms, states and governments. 'Twas the gathering together of the waters into one place, that God called seas [Gen. 1:9–10]. And the angel explains "waters" in these visions to be multitudes of people

1. See Nathaniel Stephens, *A Plain and Easie Calculation of the Name, Mark, and Number of the Name of the Beast* (London, 1656), for an example of the significance accorded the number 606 by Protestant commentators.

2. King of the Visigoths (370?–410).

(ch. 17:15). But it is not scattered waters or multitudes that God calls seas, but the gathering together of these waters or multitudes into one place, that is, into governments, states and commonwealths: these are called seas. See nos. 17, 18.

14. CHAPTER 8:10–11. The third trumpet was when Gensericus, *anno* 455, filled the public societies, courts and offices of the empire with Goths and Vandals; [he] filled the empire with a Vandalic magistracy. Public societies and offices are the rivers by which a land, nation or government is watered; but these rivers, being filled with their enemies, were made bitter. [See] no. 19.

15. CHAPTER 8:12. The 4th trumpet [was] when the empire was conquered by Odoacer,[3] *anno* 480, after which the empire immediately worked towards that division into various kingdoms, which for the main has continued ever since, and about 24 years after the reign of Antichrist commenced.[4] [See] no. 20.

16. CHAPTERS 13 and 20. The forty-two months began in the year 606, when the pope was first seated in his chair, and was made universal bishop. They will, therefore, end about 1866,[5] although I do not deny what by many is thought to be true, viz., that Satan's kingdom in the world will not be totally overthrown, his ruin will not receive its finishing stroke till the year two thousand; for this seems to be [to] me very probable, from ancient received traditions and some types in Scripture that seem to intimate it. Doubtless, the world is to enjoy a sabbath, after all this labor, these wearisome changes and overturnings; the world shall enjoy a rest in the peaceable reign of the saints. This the strain of all prophecy seems to hold forth to us.[6] The creature travails in pain, and groans for this manifestation of the sons of God, this rest that remaineth for the church [Rom. 8:19, 22]. The first 6000 years are 6 days of labor, and the seventh is a sabbath of rest. As the world was six days in making, so I believe that the kingdom of God, that it will be six days in making before 'tis finished. That is, things will be overturning six days in order to it; and the seventh day there shall be rest, putting a thousand years for a day, as the apostle Peter does,

3. The first barbarian ruler of Italy (476–93).

4. Here JE's chronology is potentially confusing. He dated the 4th trumpet about 24 years after the division of the empire at the time of Gensericus, the latter being an event he equated with the beginning of Antichrist's reign. See HA; below, p. 403.

5. Here JE deleted "when I suppose the fifth vial [poured] out upon his seat, and he shall be turned out of this chair again." This is JE's earliest reference to the 5th vial.

6. In Miscell. no. 45, entitled "Sabbath," JE argued that setting aside a seventh of time was agreeable to the scheme of the natural order.

when he is speaking of this rest of the world and glorious kingdom of Christ. II Peter 3:4, "And saying, Where is the promise of his coming; for since the fathers fell asleep, all things continue as they were from the beginning of the creation." And verse 8, "But, beloved, be not ignorant of this one thing: that one day is with the Lord as a thousand years, and a thousand years as one day." Our laboring 6 days and resting the seventh, I believe to be a type of the world's laboring 6 days and resting the seventh. Of this also the Jews' sabbatical year every seventh year, and especially their jubilee, at the end of seven times seven years, were lively figures. The jubilee, on many accounts, brightly represents this great jubilee. The Jews compassed the city of Jericho about 6 days, and the seventh the walls fell flat to the ground [Josh. 6]. I believe this matter was so ordered, upon this very account, to typify the downfall of the kingdom of Satan in the world, at the seventh thousand years, by means of the blowing the trumpet of the gospel and preaching the Word of God. God intended Jericho more especially for a type of Satan's kingdom, as appears, because there was such a curse laid upon him that should build it again.[7] And what further confirms that the sabbath of the world will begin near about the beginning of the seventh thousand years of the world, is because we are sure, it cannot be far from it. For we are come near it already; so that the beginning of this glorious time, cannot be very far on this side. And it is plainly inconsistent with the prophecies, that it should be so far off, as to be very far on the other side. See nos. 21, 25, 27, 35b, 50, 55, 60.

17. CHAPTER 16:3. There can be no difficulty why those states and kingdoms that fall off from popery should be called "sea"; that we have explained in the explanation of the trumpets. See no. 13. But the difficulty is why are they called "the" sea. How are those countries and kingdoms and states the sea of the empire, by way of distinction from other parts of the empire? I answer, those countries that are fallen off from popery, they are not properly pertaining to the empire. They are countries round about the empire and adjoining to it, as the sea is round about and adjoining to the land; but they are not properly parts of it. Perhaps they have generally, sometime or other, been conquered by the Romans, and so brought under their dominion; but they were never steadily pertaining to their empire, as the firm land. Thus [it was]

---

7. Here JE deleted "This was further shadowed forth by the legal cleansings and purifications, which were for seven days; he that was defiled, was to be unclean till the seventh day, and then was to be clean. They were to be unclean seven days, taking in the day they were defiled; but they were unclean but six whole days."

of England, Scotland, Holland, Sweden, Denmark, Prussia and the other Protestant principalities of Germany; they were not properly appertaining any otherwise, than as neighboring seas; that is, they were theirs to fish and to trade in. But now, every living soul has died in this sea of the empire, so that they can have no more fishing nor trading in these seas. The same is to be said of the sea, under the second trumpet; for then they lost many of the outskirts of the empire to their enemies.

18. CHAPTER 8:8. "And a great mountain burning with fire." By "mountains" is meant great and mighty men, exalted high above the plane of the common people. This "mountain burning with fire" is Alaricus. He is called a burning mountain, because of the destruction and ruin he made in the empire, burning and destroying where he came. Rome itself was burnt by him; 'twas he that was cast into this sea. Honorius,[8] to recover the empire, was glad to give him several countries belonging to the empire.[9] See no. 13.

19. CHAPTER 8:10. The star burning as a lamp is Gensericus. [See] no. 14.

20. CHAPTER 8:12. "The third part of the sun was smitten"; that is, after Odoacer, very much of the remaining greatness, glory and power of the empire was eclipsed and gone.[1]

21. CHAPTER 20. The marriage of Isaac and Rebecca is a very remarkable type of the marriage of Christ and the church [Gen. 24]. Isaac is a known type of Christ.[2] He was Abraham's only son, in whom his seed, that is, spiritual seed, was to be called; [he] was offered up a sacrifice to God, from whence Abraham received Christ in a figure. Abraham gave all he had to Isaac; so God the Father has made Christ heir over all things. Abraham's steward is the ministry, which Christ employs to bring home his spouse to himself. Rebecca was "very fair to look upon," and how beautiful is the church set forth in the Scripture to be in the eyes of Christ. And [she was] a pure virgin (Gen. 24:16); so the spouse of Christ is as a garden enclosed, a spring shut up, a fountain sealed. True believers are virgins that follow the Lamb, whithersoever he goeth. Abraham's steward presented her a chaste virgin to Isaac; so are ministers, the stewards of God's house, to labor, that they may

8. Roman emperor in the West, 395–423.

9. See Poole, *Annotations*, Vol. 2, at Rev. 8:9.

1. Above, p. 129.

2. JE wrote in no. 7 of the "Scripture," "Gen. 22:8. 'My son, God will provide a lamb for a burnt offering'; fulfilled in Christ."

present the church a chaste virgin to Christ. Abraham's servant adorned Rebecca with jewels of silver and gold and raiment (verses 22 and 53); so the bride, the Lamb's wife, shall be arrayed in fine linen, white and clean. The New Jerusalem shall be as a bride adorned for her husband. The king's daughter is all glorious within. She stands in gold of Ophir:[3] her clothing is of wrought gold, and she shall be brought unto the king in raiment of needlework. And God makes use of his ministers to adorn and beautify souls, that they may be fit to be the spouse of Christ; that is their work. Rebecca was willing to leave her father's house and her kindred and her country, never to return more, for the sake of Isaac, whom she had not seen. So believers forsake sin and their lusts, that are natural to 'em, that they are born with, and are naturally dear to them (See Ps. 45:10 note),[4] all for the sake of Christ; [they] remove their affections forever from the world, and hate father and mother and all, for the sake of him on whom they believe, having not seen. The spouse, in the 45th psalm, forgets her own people and father's house. There is something very significative in the blessing wherewith they blessed Rebecca. "Thou art our sister. Be thou the mother of thousands of millions, and let thy seed possess the gate of those that hate them" [Gen. 24:60]; which is gloriously fulfilled in the church, and no otherwise fulfilled to Rebecca, than in her spiritual seed. Isaac greatly loved Rebecca, as Christ loves the church, with a transcendent love.

It is taken notice of that "Isaac was forty years old when he took Rebecca to wife" (Gen. 25:20), which is six weeks of years. Now a day, or a year, or a week of years—they are all the same thing, with respect to the sabbath or rest amongst the Jews. There was a sabbath every seven days, every seven years and every seven weeks of years; and I take it, that the day or year or week of years alike, typify a thousand years of the world, the seventh of which is to be a sabbath. Then that marriage of the Lamb will come, spoken of chapter 19, typified by the marriage of Isaac and Rebecca.

So it [is] also taken notice of, that Isaac was sixty years old when Rebecca brought forth her two sons [Gen. 25:26]. So if we put a thousand for ten, and it is 6 thousand years when the time will come so often

3. An ancient region of uncertain location known for its production of fine gold.

4. This reference and the preceding complex objective clause are a later addition. At this location in the "Blank Bible," p. 421, JE explained the psalmist's directive as referring to "sin and the pleasures and profits thereof, the objects of our lusts, which may well be compared to our father's house and natural kindred, both because sin and corruption is what we have naturally, that which we are born with, and that we derive from our parents."

spoken of, wherein the church shall bring forth that with which she hath so long travailed.

The church was in bondage in Egypt 430 years, which is about 6 times seventy years, and then were delivered. There is very good reason why seventy years should represent[5] a thousand; for seventy years was the age of man in Moses' time, as well as now—as appears by the 90th psalm—as a thousand years was the primitive life of man.[6] Enoch, the seventh from Adam, was translated [Heb. 11:5; Jude 14]; the seventh generation in the line of the church is taken up into heaven.[7]

The time of the Israelites' journeying in the wilderness, before they were settled in the land of Canaan, it was forty years before Moses' death. And we may suppose, that it was about two years more before they had conquered Canaan, and were fully settled in the land, which makes 6 weeks of years. So it shall be 6 thousand years, before the church is settled in its peaceful and glorious state that is spoken of.

It is particularly taken notice of by Matthew, that the time of Christ's coming into the world, from Abraham (from whence the separation of that branch of mankind of whom came Christ, from the rest of the world began) was just 42 generations, that is, six weeks of generations [Matt. 1:17]. So we suppose that after 6 thousand years, Christ will gloriously come in his kingdom. See nos. 16, 25, 53, 69.

22. CHAPTER 16. As the land of Canaan is the most advantageously posited of any spot of ground on the face [of the earth], to be the place from whence the truth should shine forth, and true religion spread around into all parts of the world. There are three continents of the earth: the old continent, America and Terra Australis. This land is right in the center of the old and principal continent, between Europe, Asia and Africa, but most in Asia, because it is abundantly the largest. And [it is] lying at the end of the Mediterranean Sea, which opens the way from Canaan directly to America, and having the Red Sea and Persian Gulf touching its borders as much as the Mediterranean, according to Exodus 23:31 and other places, opening the way straight to Terra Australis, the third continent. A way into all parts of the globe of the earth, is easier from hence than from any other land whatever,

---

5. Here JE first wrote "typify" and later changed it to "represent."

6. See the note on Ps. 90:10, no. 203 in the "Scripture" (printed in Dwight ed., *9*, 356–57), for JE's related but later comment on the declining longevity of man.

7. This sentence is a later addition. JE wrote several eschatological notes on Jude 14. See nos. 188, 200, and 357 in the "Scripture" (Dwight ed., *9*, 557–58), and the "Blank Bible," p. 883.

yea, vastly easier from any other but the countries adjacent. [It is] more easy by land into either Europe, Asia or Africa, because it is in the middle between them: and also by water into Europe, on both sides, by the Mediterranean and Euxine Sea; into Africa, on both sides, by the Mediterranean Sea and Indian Ocean, the arms of which come quite up and touch the borders of the land; into Asia, on both sides, by the Euxine Sea and Indian Ocean, through the Persian Gulf or Red Sea; into America, direct through the Mediterranean Sea, or to the west side of America, through the Indian Ocean and the great South Sea; into Terra Australis, by the Indian Ocean. There is no need of fetching such a vast compass, round the Cape of Good Hope, or through the Straits of Magellan, and such immense round about ways as other nations must be obliged to. But here, let them go where they please, they are in the middle, and their passage is direct.

That God did take care of the situation of his people Israel, upon their account, for the advantage of spreading the truth and diffusing the influences of religion, I think is evident from Deuteronomy 32:8–9, and from Acts 17:26–27 and from Habakkuk 3:6.

Now the world has never enjoyed the advantages of this situation as yet. What advantage has it been to America, that the Mediterranean Sea opens from them to us; or what advantage has Hollandia Nova or Terra Australis Incognita,[8] from the Indian Ocean's reaching from them even to this land? Wherefore, we do believe that the most glorious part of the church will hereafter be there, at the center of the kingdom of Christ, communicating influences to all other parts.[9]

And it is the more evident, that the Jews will return to their own land again, because they never have yet possessed one quarter of that land, which was so often promised them, from the Red Sea to the river Euphrates (Ex. 23:31; Gen. 15:18; Deut. 11:24; Josh. 1:4). Indeed, it was partly fulfilled in Solomon's time, when he governed all within those bounds for a short time; but so short, that it is not to be thought that this is all the fulfillment of the promise that is to be. And besides, that was not a fulfillment of the promise, because they did not possess it, though they made the nations of it tributary.[1] [See] no. 24.

23. CHAPTER 16:4–7. This curse of the third vial is the same kind of

8. Both are early names for Australia.

9. See JE's later judgment in *Works*, *4*, 355; and above, pp. 18–19.

1. JE wrote concerning Deut. 11:24, "This is an instance of the gradual fulfillment of the promises that God makes to his church." The land will be fully given to the Jews only after the destruction of Antichrist, an example of his understanding of the progressive accomplishment of prophecy ("Blank Bible," p. 152).

curse, as that mentioned in the 3rd chapter of Isaiah, and the four first verses, and the same that is mentioned [in] Obadiah 1:8.

24. CHAPTER 16. We are not to suppose but that when the nation of the Jews are converted, other Christians will be as much God's Israel as they, and will have in every respect the same privileges. Neither can we suppose, that their church will have any manner of superiority over other parts of Christ's church, any otherwise than as that part of the church will be more glorious. Religion and learning will be there at the highest;[2] more excellent books will be there written, etc. Without doubt, they will return to their own land; because when their unbelief ceases, their dispersion, the dreadful and signal punishment of their unbelief, will cease too. As they have continued hitherto, with one consent, to dishonor Christ by rejecting the gospel, so shall they meet together to honor him, by openly professing of it with one mouth, and practice it with one heart and one soul, together lamenting their obstinacy, as it is said they shall (Zech. 12:11–12),[3] and together praising God for his grace in enlightening them. And as they have hitherto continued a distinct nation, that they might continue a visible monument of his displeasure, for their rejecting and crucifying their Messiah, so after their conversion will they still be a distinct nation, that they may be a visible monument of God's wonderful grace and power in their calling and conversion. But we cannot suppose they will remain a distinct nation, any more than the primitive Jewish Christians, if they continue dispersed among other nations.

But yet, we are not to imagine that the old walls of separation will be set up again. But all nations will be as free to come to Judea, or to dwell in Jerusalem, as into any other city or country, and may have the same privilege there as they themselves. For they shall look upon all the world to be their brethren, as much as the Christians in Boston and the Christians in other parts of New England look on each other as brethren.

25. CHAPTER 20. There are these remarkable periods of time: when Abraham was called, in the year of the world 2000; Solomon's glorious kingdom settled, and temple finished, in the year of the world 3000; Christ born in the year 4000; and the millennium to begin in the year 6000.

26. CHAPTER 16. 'Tis very agreeable to those expressions of Scripture, that speak of God's threshing the heathen in anger [Hab. 3:12], and dashing his enemies to pieces as a potter's vessel [Ps. 2:9].

2. Or: "height."
3. This reference and the preceding clause are a later addition.

27. CHAPTER 20. So it was forty years or six weeks of years, that David reigned over Israel, before the enemies of God's people were conquered by him; and then succeeded the peaceful and glorious state of the church under King Solomon. So the servant of Elijah, the seventh time he went to look towards the sea, saw the cloud from whence came the plentiful rain [I Kgs. 18:44]. So it was seven days that the children of Israel, that were as two flocks of kids, pitched against the great army of the Syrians that filled the country (I Kgs. 20:29).[4]

28. CHAPTER 17:5. As Babylon was the place where the apostasy of the world after Noah (which afterwards became so gross and universal) began, so the Church of Rome is the mother of the apostasy of the Christian church. In this sense, old Babylon was "the mother of harlots and abominations of the earth"; [she] was mother of heathenism and idolatry and all the devil churches. So is Rome in the Christian church. Thus Chaldea and Babylon is called "the land of graven images" (Jer. 50:38).

29. There were 6 remarkable periods of time in the church, before Christ came into the world: from Adam to the flood, from the flood to Abraham, from Abraham to David and Solomon and the temple, from David to the captivity into Babylon, from the captivity to Babylon to Christ.[5] The gospel times are the seventh. See chapter 20.

30. CHAPTER 16:19. "And the cities of the nations fell." There are many passages in Scripture which do seem to intend, that as well the civil as the ecclesiastical polities of the nations, shall be overthrown, and a sort of theocracy should ensue. Not that civil government shall in any measure be overthrown, or that the world shall be reduced to an anarchical state; but the absolute and despotic power of the kings of the earth shall be taken away, and liberty shall reign throughout the earth. And every nation shall be a free people, not only with a freedom from spiritual slavery, but from civil too, from the tyrannical and absolute power of men, as well as from the power of the devil. Kings shall rather be as the judges were before Saul (which government was that which was best pleasing to God), and as the kings of England now are in civil matters. There be no more kings after the manner that Samuel described (I Sam. 8:11 ff.). Not but that there may be different forms of

4. JE's sermon booklet on Rom. 12:18 (MS, Yale coll.) contains a rough draft for a portion of this note and for part of Miscell. no. 87, which Thomas Schafer has dated in the fall of 1723.

5. JE lists only five periods, having left out the time of Moses between Abraham and David. See the "Table of Contents" for the *History of Redemption*, Worcester rev. ed., *1*, iv.

government, very many; but none shall be tyrannical, or contrary to the true liberty (Dan. 2:44–45). Such kind of authority and power, is spoken of by Christ as a part of gentilism (Matt. 20:25). And undoubtedly, those frequent prophecies representing the glorious liberty of these times, wherein every man shall sit under his own vine and under his own fig tree, etc. [Mic. 4:4], are not understood only in a mystical and spiritual sense.[6]

31. CHAPTER 4:6–9. Of the 4 beasts. Relating to Miscell. no. ww,[7] where these beasts are compared to Ezekiel's living creatures which had calves' feet, inasmuch as the exercise and exertions of God's other attributes, were entirely and only upon the feet of goodness. Goodness is the only end why he has created the world, and the ultimate end of every dispensation of whatever nature, even the damnation of the wicked for the happiness of the blessed. God's power, wisdom and justice, are exerted wholly and ultimately upon the feet of goodness.[8]

32. [CHAPTER 9:19.] "And their power is in their mouth and in their tails, for their tails are like unto serpents." By their "mouth" is meant their army, by which they devoured and subdued men. And in these was their power; by these they wonderfully succeeded. Their "tails" is what comes afterwards, the effects and consequences of those conquests, their religion or the doctors of their religion. Their armies and warriors were the mouth, but the doctors of their religion were the tail, who infused poison more deadly than what was infused by the tails of scorpions. Is. 9:15, "The prophet that teacheth lies, he is the tail."

33. CHAPTER 11:3. "And I will give power to my two witnesses." By it may partly be intended those two nations, that were all along witnesses to Christianity, viz., the Waldenses and Albigenses.

34. CHAPTER 16:10. "And his kingdom was full of darkness, and they gnawed their tongues for pain." They shall be dreadfully confounded,

---

6. Above, p. 18.

7. In no. ww JE represented the second living creature, the calf or ox, as "the emblem of goodness amongst the Israelites and the nations round about. The Egyptians used to worship a bull or ox in remembrance of Joseph, for the plenty that he foretold and for his preserving corn in the midst of a famine. 'Tis very probable that for this reason those nations worshiped golden calves as emblems of goodness; the oxen, they plow the fields, from whence we receive the goodness of God. The ox is observed to be the most compassionate of all creatures. It is said that the feet of Ezekiel's living creatures were calves' feet (Ezek. 1:7), because all God's paths are mercy and truth. 'Twas alone the goodness of God that moved him to make the world, that moves him to preserve it; and all God's providential proceedings are upon the feet of goodness, even his damning sinners: though not in them, yet in others, as I could shew."

8. See Miscell. no. 87 for a discussion of God's motive in creating the world, and the sermon on Rev. 21:18 (above, pp. 15–16) for a homiletical treatment of the subject.

by those invincible arguments that shall be used against them. They shall be full of unsettledness, of self-contradiction and contradiction one of another, and shall be exceedingly divided in their schemes and the answers they shall give to the arguments, which shall be brought against them, as men stumble and run one against another in the dark. The prospect of this their confusion, will dreadfully vex and enrage them.

35a. CHAPTER 13:11. "And he had two horns like a lamb." By "horns," we know in Scripture, is commonly meant power. The Church of Rome pretends to all, by the power of Christ; all her laws, interpretations of Scripture, curses, tyrannies and persecutions are under a pretense of church power, and to be done by Christ's vicegerency. Antichrist, we know, claims the whole power of Christ, or the horns of the Lamb of God.

35b. CHAPTER 20. See no. 16, etc. So the Hebrew servant was to serve six years, and in the seventh was to be free for nothing (Ex. 21:2). Doubtless these servitudes and freedom years of release—jubilees—were types of spiritual servitude and freedom; and, I believe, the times did typify the times of the church's bondage, and her glorious liberty.

36. CHAPTER 17:1. "I will shew unto thee the judgment of the great whore that sitteth upon many waters." This whore includes in it not only false worship, but apostasy from God and falseness to him, the lawful husband. 'Tis adultery.[9]

One property of a whore is that she commits her wickedness in secret under a covert, and hides it with an external shew of modesty. Prov. 30:20, "Such is the way of an adulterous woman: she eateth and wipeth her mouth and saith, I have done no wickedness." Hereby is denoted the grand hypocrisy of the Church of Rome: she does all under the shew of sanctity and holiness, and being the spouse of Jesus Christ.

37. CHAPTER 13:11. "And I beheld another beast coming up out of the earth." This is he that is called Antichrist in Scripture, because of the perfect and universal contrariety of popery to Christianity, and its peculiar opposition to it, beyond all religions that ever were; and because this is the contrivance of the wit of hell in opposition to the gospel, the masterpiece of all his inventions against the interest of Christ, the most cunning and subtile, the most effectual, of longest duration, the

---

9. Here JE deleted "In the prophecies of the Old Testament, where the term is very frequently used, I think it is nowhere used in another sense." He also crossed out "Those nations, which time out of mind have worshiped false gods, are not called whores, at least except it be with respect to their having once at first been professors of the true God; but 'tis she, that having been married to God commits adultery, is called a whore."

fruit of the greatest and longest labors and study: so that however there have been a great many antichrists, this is the Antichrist.[1] Satan was dreadfully surprised by Christ's appearing in the world and the proclaiming [of] the gospel to all nations, and begun to look upon himself as totally overthrown. But he, at length, thought of one thing more as a means to defeat the design; and this was the last effort, and how wonderfully did he seem to succeed! Fitly, therefore, is this grand contrivance for opposing the gospel called antichristianism.

He is also called Antichrist, because he is Christ's rival. He disputes with Christ for the power and authority, for his throne and dominion; [he] sets up himself as being supreme head of the church, in opposition to him. He is Christ's rival for the same spouse, even the church; and Christ and he are fighting one with another, disputing who shall obtain her. Therefore, that part of the church that yielded to this rival of Christ, who had no right to her, is called the great whore; and they that were true to Christ, are called virgins, that follow the Lamb whithersoever he goeth. It is expressly prophesied, that Antichrist should be Christ's rival for his dominion and authority. II Thessalonians 2:4, "Who opposeth and exalteth himself above all that is called God or is worshiped." And that he should also be his rival for the church, his spouse, in the latter part of the same verse: "So that he as God, sitteth in the temple of God, shewing himself that he is God."

He is Antichrist inasmuch as he usurps Christ's offices in opposition to him. His prophetic office, pretending to infallibility, and to determine with absolute authority[2] what shall be believed by everyone; he is therefore called in the Revelation, the false prophet. He usurps his priestly office, pretending daily to offer up that expiatory sacrifice to God, which Christ alone can offer, even his own body and blood. Usurping his kingly office, assuming the keys of heaven and hell, and a power of disposing of the favor and anger of God, of pardoning sins, of delivering out of purgatory; usurping his throne as King of Kings, tyrannizing over princes themselves, and ruling the church as supreme head.[3]

38. CHAPTER 13:13. "And he doth great wonders, etc." Other pretended miracles are the frighting away of evil spirits by ringing of bells;

---

1. JE used this entry in 1739 when he wrote the series of sermons on the *History of Redemption*. See Worcester rev. ed., *1*, 457.

2. MS: "authoritive."

3. For additional comments upon the conflict between Christ and Satan, see Miscell. nos. 156 (*146*) and 158, entitled "Satan Defeated" and "Kingdom of Christ" respectively.

casting out devils from possessed persons; and the miraculous virtue that is pretended to be in their holy garments, holy ground, holy oil, in the consecrated elements, in relics, and innumerable such like charms. They have also very frequently pretended to work like miracles with Christ and his apostles, by healing the sick, opening the eyes of the blind, and the like; and [they] report many more of their former saints, that were pretended to be done by them. Yea, many of them have been really sorcerers, and have had help of invisible powers to do many false miracles.

39. CHAPTER 18:23. "For by thy sorceries were all nations deceived." Such charms as those mentioned in no. 38, are the sorceries and witchcrafts of this whore. All their worship and innumerable ridiculous ceremonies, and their muttering in an unknown tongue, is like juggling that they pretend has some great virtue and miraculous virtue. The wondering people are amazed at it, but the priests or sorcerers alone understand the mysteries.[4]

40. See CHAPTER 16:12.[5] "That the way of the kings of the East might be prepared." The 16th verse of the 20th [chapter] of Matthew seems to imply, that the Jews shall be some of the last that shall be converted to Christianity. It seems to me probable, that they shall be converted after the fall of Antichrist and the conversion of the civilized world and all Europe and perhaps most of Turkey, but before the conversion of the heathen nations, or at least before their general conversion.

41. CHAPTER 21:1.[6] "And I saw a new heaven and a new earth: for the first heaven and the first earth were passed away, and there was no more sea." To know what is meant by this "new heaven and new earth," is one of the most difficult points in the Bible. Undoubtedly the state and place of risen saints, is here called "a new heaven and a new earth." 'Tis not probable that this is materially the same earth that we now live upon, but only purged by fire and renewed; though perhaps it might well enough be so called, according to the language of Scripture in parallel cases. But yet we do not find that this earth is called another, different from what was before the flood or fall. This place, if it be the eternal abode of the blessed, as it seems, it will doubtless be vastly, immensely more glorious than it was before the fall. But, it seems to

---

4. JE compared the abuses of the Church of Rome with those of the apostatized Jewish church in no. 28 of the "Scripture" (printed in Dwight ed., *9*, 473–74).

5. No. 58 in the "Scripture" is a cross-reference to this entry. JE drew a single vertical line through this note. Here and elsewhere the precise meaning of his marking is uncertain.

6. See above, p. 76, concerning the provenance of this and the following note.

me, fire by purging could no more than bring it to its primitive state; and it would be as good as a new creation to make it so glorious. It likewise seems, by the 11th verse of the foregoing chapter, that this globe with all its appurtenances is clear gone, out of the way; and this is a new one, materially as well as in form.[7]

'Tis probable 'tis called by the name of a new earth, because 'tis the place of the habitation of bodies as well as souls, a place wherein their bodily senses shall be exercised. There shall be that whereon they shall tread with their feet, and an expanse over their heads. If we were in Jupiter or Saturn, that which would be under our feet would be called earth by us, and that which was over our heads, heaven. This is all that is meant by earth and heaven here, according to the vulgar meaning of the words. This, 'tis probable, will be some glorious place in the universe prepared for this end by God, removed at an immense distance from the solar system; though there is nothing said of such a remove in this prophecy, but it seems to suppose it in the same place. But the Scripture does not represent things, especially in prophecy and vision, according to philosophical verity, but as they appear to our eyes. So the earth is not represented as moving, but the sun. So if we should forsake this earth and go to an immense distance, we should look upon ourselves as keeping our station, after we had got at a little distance from the earth, and the earth as flying from us. Certainly we cannot gather [from] this manner of John's seeing those things in a vision, that this new heaven and new earth is in the same place. If we should be removed to any other earth or place, where there is footing underneath and heaven overhead, it would appear all one to us as to place; we should not appear higher nor lower. If I should tread upon the outermost surface of the universe, it cannot be supposed that I should seem higher to myself than here upon earth; nor would it be so philosophically. If I was in Saturn, the earth would be over my head, and very high in the heavens above me.

'Tis certain that this place shall be remote from the solar system, that is, that it will be distant from it, and therefore, not in the same place in any sense that is ever been wont to be used, in Scripture or in the world.

'Tis evident that this is here spoken of, as the eternal abode of the blessed. It is the last that is said of the church, in this series of prophecies: 'tis set here as the end of all the foregoing revolutions, the

7. In Miscell. no. 133 (*148*), JE wrote, "And besides, there are many places of Scripture that really do imply a final departure of the stars, as well as sun and moon; so that the heavens shall be new in all regards."

highest reward of all their labors [and] sufferings, and the ultimate aim of all these wonderful successive dispensations of divine providence spoken of in the former part of the world. 'Tis after the general judgment, and manifestly different from the millennium, spoken of in the foregoing chapter; this is spoken of as their eternal state. In the foregoing chapter, it was said they should reign with Christ "a thousand years," in the 6th verse; but in this state, it is said, "they shall reign forever and ever" (ch. 22:5). This is spoken of, as the greatest and highest reward of the saints (chs. 21:7, 22:14, 17); and that state which is opposed to it, is spoken of as the second death, and great punishment of the wicked (ch. 21:8, 22:11). But if it be their eternal state, I cannot imagine 'tis upon this individual globe of the earth, which is manifestly a fleeting thing in its nature, as is the whole solar system, and must necessarily come to an end. However durable the earth in particular may be made, yet it must run to ruin with the rest of the system. 'Tis manifest God did not make these fleeting systems for an eternal duration, as might be more fully shewn, if the place were proper for such a philosophical discourse.[8]

It may be here inquired, why the state of glorified spirits is not called another heaven and earth? The reason is good: because 'twould be very improper to represent the state of separate spirits by such things; we know that spirits don't walk upon an earth, nor live upon a ground.[9]

ISAIAH 42:4.[1] "And the isles shall wait for his law." This and such like prophecies of the gospelizing of islands, I believe to have a threefold accomplishment, to each of which the prophecies had an eye. By "isles" is meant any place beyond the sea, for they used to think the seashore the end of the world. And particularly, Europe is intended; and the conversion of that is principally aimed at in these prophecies.[2] And then they have a glorious accomplishment in the gospelizing the isles of Britain and Ireland, and making of them so glorious a part of the church. For as Greece was looked upon by the Jews, so were those islands by the Romans and other Europeans; they looked upon them as a little world

8. During his tutorship when he wrote this entry, JE was keeping a notebook on "Natural Philosophy" later printed as the "Notes on Natural Science" (Dwight ed., *1*, 702–61). See his comments on fixed stars, pp. 759–60.

9. For more on the condition of the glorified saints, see Miscell. no. 149 (*139*).

1. JE wrote in the "Blank Bible," p. 512, " 'Isles shall wait for his law' [Is. 42:4]. See in my book of notes on Revelation. By mistake there written, next page after number 40."

2. Before beginning the AP, JE had written in Miscell. no. g, "Where the Scripture speaks so much of the isles' conversion, is meant Europe, all which was looked upon and called islands."

by themselves, separated from all the rest of the world. But certainly these prophecies, many of them that speak of the glorious manifestation of God to the islands, do not only regard the first display of the gospel made soon after Christ's ascension; but by these glorious times they speak of, is intended also the times of the church's triumph at the millennium, and the times immediately foregoing, wherein these prophecies will be much the most notably accomplished. And what is peculiarly glorious in it, is the gospelizing the new and before unknown world, that which is so remote, so unknown, where the devil had reigned quietly from the beginning of the world, which is larger—taking in America, Terra Australis Incognita, Hollandia Nova, and all those yet undiscovered tracts of land—is far greater than the old world. I say, that this new world should all worship the God of Israel, whose worship was then confined to so narrow a land, is wonderful and glorious! And this I believe to be meant, in the third place, by the isles in these prophecies.

42. Chapter 9:19. "For their power is in their mouth and in their tails: for their tails were like unto serpents, and had heads, and with them they do hurt." We may be informed what these tails are by Isaiah 9:15. "The ancient and honorable, he is the head; and the prophet that teacheth lies, he is the tail." See no. 73.

43. Chapter 7:3. "Hurt not the earth, neither the sea, nor the trees, till we have sealed the servants of our God in their foreheads." By this hurting of the earth, the sea, and trees are meant those calamities that were to come upon the Roman Empire, and that part of the world where Christianity was settled, mentioned in the seventh and eighth and tenth verses of the following chapter, where we read how the earth and sea and trees were burnt, those calamities by which the Roman Empire was by degrees ruined. Care was first taken that God's elect, his true servants, might be safe in the midst of those calamities.

44. Chapter 2. The angels of the churches do no more represent real, particular persons, than the riders upon the horses in the 6th chapter signified particular, real persons, or [the] four angels that were bound in the river Euphrates in the 9th chapter, or the angel that preached the everlasting gospel to the whole world, represented any one real person.[3]

3. In Miscell. no. 162, entitled "Angels of the Apocalypse," JE wrote, "In these visions everything, almost, was represented as living, acting, speaking, mourning or rejoicing; those things that were without life, and other things to which personal acts cannot properly be attributed."

45. CHAPTER 11:3. "I'll give power to my two witnesses." Hereby it is with me undoubted, that respect is had to Moses and Elias. For these witnesses are two prophets, and the prophets that were Christ's two witnesses were Moses and Elias. Those were the prophets that came down from heaven to witness to Jesus Christ, as they did in talking with him at his transfiguration [Mark 9:2–10]; those are Christ's two witnesses, that John had seen there upon the mount. And then their deeds are the same with those of Moses and Elias: their destroying their enemies by commanding fire to devour them, and shutting heaven that it rain not, are the same that Elias did [I Kgs. 17; II Kgs. 1]; and turning the waters to blood, and smiting the earth with all plagues as often as they will, is as Moses did [Ex. 7–11]. But yet, I believe respect is also had to Zerubbabel and Joshua, because they are said to be the two olive trees and the two candlesticks, which in Zechariah seem to represent Zerubbabel and Joshua [Zech. 3–4], who were God's instruments for the rebuilding and re-establishing of the church after the Babylonish captivity, and probably instruments of upholding religion during the captivity, as these two witnesses are God's instruments for the preserving the church in its captivity to spiritual Babylon, and rebuilding and restoring of it after this captivity.

46. CHAPTER 20.[4] Concerning the thousand years, the sabbath of the world. Agreeable to other things that we mentioned, is that (Exodus 22:30) the firstlings of the cattle were to be with his dam seven days, and the 8th day was to be offered to God.

47. CHAPTER 4:6–9. Concerning the four beasts. It seems to me more probable that reference is here had to the standards of the four tribes,[5] because in the next chapter at the 5th verse, "the Lion of the tribe of Judah" is spoken of, where remembrance seems to be had of what was spoken of in this chapter, of the lion that was the standard of that tribe. He is called the lion of that tribe here, because he is the power of God, and because 'tis his power that there is occasion here to take notice of, his power to open the book.

48. CHAPTER 20:5. "This is the first resurrection." Verse 14, "This is the second death." We read here of the first and second death, and of the first and second resurrection. The first resurrection and the second death answer one to another. See [the] 6th verse. "Blessed and holy is he that hath part in the first resurrection; on such the second death hath no power." I think 'tis evident, the first resurrection is a

4. JE drew a slanted vertical line through this entry.
5. Above, p. 100, n. 6.

spiritual resurrection, and the second death is a spiritual and eternal death. The first death is a natural death, and the second resurrection a natural resurrection. He that is partaker of the first resurrection or regeneration, a resurrection to spiritual life—however he must die the first death, a natural death, yet he shall never die the second, or the spiritual and eternal death. As there is a spiritual resurrection, a first resurrection, of particular believers, so there is coming a spiritual resurrection of the world in general, spoken of in this chapter, a wonderful renovation of the world upon spiritual accounts. We may note, by the way, that the 6th verse is a certain proof of the perseverance of saints.

49. CHAPTER 4:6–9. The four beasts.[6] The four living creatures may possibly represent the angels, the ministers of the power and wisdom and justice and mercy of God,[7] because they are called cherubims in Ezekiel [10:15], and because they are said to fall down and worship, and in the 8th verse they sing "holy, holy, holy," the same song that the angels do in Isaiah 6:3. [See] chapter 8. There are these objections against it. That they are said to be "in the midst of the throne," as well as "round about the throne"[8] [Rev. 4:6]. And then we find a distinction made between these [beasts] and the angels in [the] 11th verse of chapter 5. I am ready to think they are only imaginary persons, not to represent any real beings. These four living creatures represent God's providence by persons; they are the four ministers of his providence: one the minister of his wisdom, another of his power, etc. So it is in Ezekiel; these are the living creatures that draw the wheel of providence [Ezek. 1]. And when they are represented as falling down and giving glory, the meaning of it is that God is glorified by the manifestations of those attributes in the creatures, and by all second causes, whereby he exercises those attributes which do, as it were, speak forth God's glory and worship him; as sun, moon, and stars and the inanimate world is sometimes represented as worshiping and praising God. There are a multitude of such imaginary persons in this book, that ben't designed to represent any one real person, nor many; and many imaginary things that represent not particular real ones.[9]

6. Here JE deleted "I am lately inclined to think that." He reworked this note several times.

7. Here JE deleted "rather than those attributes themselves." Earlier he had equated the beasts with the attributes of God; see above, p. 100, n. 6.

8. Here JE deleted "It may, therefore, have respect to both those attributes and the ministers of them."

9. Above, p. 143, n. 3.

50. CHAPTER 20. The seventh month amongst the Jews, was to begin with the feast of trumpets, wherein the silver trumpets were to be sounded. And trumpets were to be sounded throughout all their land; which signified the preaching of the gospel, and may possibly refer to the clear and glorious revelation of the gospel—that joyful sound—and of God's praise throughout the world, in the beginning of the seventh thousand years.

51. CHAPTER 4:6–9. Four Beasts. The ox is an emblem of goodness, because of his labors for the good of man. By the labor of the ox, we have the fruits of the earth, the effects of God's goodness. A calf [is an emblem] of mercy, because of its tenderness. If an ox is goodness, a calf is tender mercy and compassion, by a very fit analogy.

52. CHAPTER 12:10. "For the accuser of our brethren is cast down, etc." God tries the graces of his people by persecutions, that the truth and power of his grace in them may appear to his own glory, both before men, angels and devils. One end is that by such a discovery of the truth and strength of their faith and love, he may as it were triumph over Satan; and make him to see what a victory is obtained over him, by so rescuing those souls that were once his captives from his power; and convince him of the real success of his design of redeeming and sanctifying souls—notwithstanding all that he had done to [them], whereby he thought he had utterly ruined mankind, and put them past the possibility of cure. For this end God tried Job. God gloried in Job as a perfect and an upright man, that did good and eschewed evil [Job 1:8]. Satan don't own the truth of it, but charges[1] that Job was a hypocrite, and his service mercenary. But God tries Job with grievous affliction for Satan's conviction. So it is in the church in general, their trials being for Satan's conviction: it is represented by the like allegory, as though Satan accused them of hypocrisy and mercenariness, and God brought those great trials upon them, that he might glory in them over his and their adversary. The church in heaven now praise God, that Satan being sufficiently convinced, his mouth [was] stopped, and he was no longer allowed to accuse. The sins and shameful falls of God's people, gives Satan occasion to blaspheme God's name, as though God had no reason to glory in his pretended redemption of them from under his dominion, and from that corruption which he brought upon their natures. And this is one occasion of God's bringing such great afflictions and trials upon them, that by their enduring such a trial, God may glory over Satan. See II Sam. 12:14.

1. MS: "but ~~Charges Job~~ with ~~a hypocrisie and~~ [illegible word] that Job."

53. CHAPTER 20.[2] See no. 21. Elijah's servant went seven times to look towards the sea, at the end of the three years' famine; and the seventh time, he saw a cloud about as big as a man's hand (I Kings 18:43–44).

David was the seventh[3] (I Chron. 2:15).

I Kings 20:29, "And they pitched one over against the other, seven days. And so it was, that in the seventh day the battle was joined; and the children of Israel slew of the Syrians an hundred thousand footmen in one day."

Ex. 24:16, "And the cloud covered the mount six days, and the seventh day he called unto Moses out of the midst of the cloud."

54. CHAPTER 16:12. "And the 6th angel poured out his vial upon the great river Euphrates; and the water thereof was dried up, that the way of the kings of the East might be prepared." It is an allusion to the way wherein old Babylon came to be destroyed. They dried up the river Euphrates, whereby the way was prepared for the kings of Media and Persia, the kings of the East, with their armies to enter into the city, and to destroy it.

55. CHAPTER 20.[4] Ex. 24:16, "And the glory of the Lord abode upon Mount Sinai, and the cloud covered it six days, and the seventh day he called unto Moses out of the midst of the cloud."

56. CHAPTER 9:4. "The grass of the earth, nor any green thing, nor any tree." We may learn what is meant by these green things, by Ezekiel 20:47 compared with [Ezekiel] 21:3. See my notes upon it. There we learn that the righteous are intended by it.[5]

57. CHAPTER 12:12. "Rejoice, ye heavens, and ye that dwell in them; woe to the inhabiters of the earth, etc." Those that dwell in heaven, or the inhabiters of heaven, are commanded to rejoice. But woe is denounced to the inhabiters of the earth. By the "inhabiters of heaven" is meant all that belong to the church, the whole family in heaven and in earth. For this world is not the land of the church; 'tis not the church's proper country, as we have shewn elsewhere.[6] The

---

2. JE added to this entry over an extended period of time.

3. I.e., the seventh son of Jesse.

4. Although JE crossed out this entry, which duplicates part of no. 53, it has been retained because it is integral to the series.

5. Concerning Ezek. 20:47, JE wrote in the "Blank Bible," p. 588, " 'Every green tree and every dry tree,' i.e., both the righteous and the wicked. See Ezekiel 21:3 with Luke 23:31. The prophet (Ezek. 17:24) speaks of drying up the green tree, and causing the dry tree to flourish: meaning by the 'green tree,' the Jews who were visibly righteous and very self-righteous; and by the 'dry tree,' the Gentiles who were wicked."

6. In Miscell. no. 429, entitled "Ascension," JE had written that "the greatest part of the

"inhabiters of the earth" are, first, those that are not of the church, the men of this world that have their portion in this life; [and] second, those that are out of the appointed limits of the visible church. The appointed limits of the visible Christian church, were the limits of that principal part, the Roman Empire. The people of the Roman Empire were prophesied of as the future people of the Messiah (Dan. 9:26).[7] This is here in vision represented as heaven, upon two accounts. 1. Because 'twas the principal and highest part of this lower world, wherein the power and the wisdom of this lower world was principally seated, and that was the chief scene of action and of God's wonderful providence. It was *instar totius*; it was called *orbis terrarum*.[8] 2. Because it was the appointed place and possession of the Christian church till the last days, the dawning of the millennium. Christianity was soon propagated into all parts of the Roman Empire, till they got the possession of it in Constantine's time.

Satan was represented as being in heaven before, because the Roman Empire was yet in his possession; the Roman Empire was the seat of the dragon (ch. 13:2). And because his seat was amongst the saints, the Christian church and heathenism were mingled. And because of the power he had over the saints, by the authority and strength and wisdom of the empire, to persecute the church, he might well be represented as being in heaven, warring against the woman. But now he was cast to the earth: i.e., he was dispossessed of that power over the church, and his outward rule and influence was confined to his own visible kingdom. He was cast out from amongst the church, or to his heathenish kingdom; and then he was cast out of the empire.

"Woe to the inhabiters of the earth and of the sea! For the devil is come down unto you, having great wrath, because he knoweth that he hath but a short time" [v. 12]. "That he hath but a short time" to stay even upon earth, to which he is now cast down. He was cast out of heaven; but the time is coming when he shall be cast out of the earth too, when he shall be shut up in the bottomless pit, spoken of [in] chapter 20 at the beginning.

church is in heaven. There is the proper place of the church; there is their own country. There is the proper land of Israel; it is their home, their resting place. It is proper that when the Messiah, the promised King comes, that the place of his abode should be there, where is the proper abiding place of the church. Those that are here upon earth, are in a strange land: they are pilgrims and strangers, and are all going hence; and heaven is their country where they all tend."

7. See the "Blank Bible," p. 679, at Matt. 24:24–28, for a fuller discussion of this theme.

8. The two Latin phrases translate respectively, "an image of the whole" and "the circle of the world."

58. CHAPTER 13. This first beast [v. 1] don't represent any person or number or succession of persons; it don't so properly represent the antichristian civil power, nor yet the whole antichristian empire.[9] But 'tis an imaginary person representing, as it were, the genius of the antichristian world or of the[1] heathenish, devilish, antichristian Roman world, revived or continued under the profession of Christianity, an imaginary person, actuating and influencing, governing antichristianly in the Roman world. And it includes the antichristian religion and spirit, and all that belongs to it, as which is represented by the qualifications, the nature, kind, shape and properties of the beast; and includes all persons, men and devils, so far as they exercise antichristian power and influence in the world.

The second beast [v. 11] signifies the popish clergy, or the antichristian hierarchy.

Verse 12, "He exerciseth all the power of the first beast before." If by "before" be meant "before him" as to time, then the Holy Ghost has respect to this beast as being the old heathenish beast revived; and the meaning of it is that the Pope and his clergy exercise all the power that this beast was wont to do by the emperors and others, that had the power and influence of the empire in their hands, before it received its deadly wound. If by "before him" is meant only that John had in vision seen [it] first, then is meant that the Pope and his clergy engrossed the whole power and influence of the antichristian world and exercised it, so that all that the beast did, he did by them as by his hand. The genius of the antichristian world exercised his power in and through them, as they exercised all the power of the beast.

Verse 14, "That they should make an image to the beast, which had a wound by the sword and did live." Here, if the Holy Ghost has respect to this as being the old genius revived, then by making an image to him is [signified] the bringing in such a worship, such forms and ceremonies, etc., as was the form and shape of the beast before his deadly wound. See no. 67.

59. See CHAPTERS 21–22.[2] Begin this with what is said under number 65.[3] In those things that are said about the New Jerusalem, respect is

9. See above, p. 111, for JE's earlier opinion.

1. Here JE deleted "idolatrous."

2. In Miscell. no. 565, where JE depicted the happiness of the saints before the resurrection as an anticipation of their future rewards, there is a cross-reference to this entry.

3. No. 65 has not been transferred because it constitutes a separate entry in the series. No. 59, written by JE over an extended period of time, has been rearranged according to his directions.

had both to the happy state of the church here on earth, and also to its triumphant state after the resurrection. And therefore, there are some expressions that do agree only with the former; but there are many things too exalted for anything but the latter. See no. 84. The like is very common in prophecies in the Old Testament. Many prophecies have partly respect to the Jewish church returned from captivity in Babylon; but the things said are vastly too great to have respect to that only. So in prophecies that have respect partly to the Christian church that Christ first erected, [some] have expressions too great for that, and are fully accomplished in the blessed state of the church after the destruction of Antichrist. In some prophecies that do more immediately respect the state of the church begun in Constantine the Great's time, [some expressions] relate also [to] the glorious millennium, and even to the church after the resurrection. The prophecies about the destruction of Jerusalem and end of the world are mixed (in Matthew 24,[4] and so in the other evangelists). So we have many mixed prophecies. If these things here said, have only respect to the blessed state of the church on earth, they would be very hyperbolical. But this may be observed, that in all prophecies of future blessedness to the church or destruction of the wicked, there never is anything hyperbolical, taking in not only what they have more immediately, but more ultimately respect to.

'Tis common in scriptures, that have a double respect or an eye to several events, for there to be some expressions much more applicable to the one and not applicable to the other, unless it be in some more improper sense. And yet a respect to the other event, is not to be excluded; but an eye is had to both, even in those expressions, as particularly in the 8th psalm, where respect is had to two things which are represented and typified, the one by the other, viz., the creation of men and the incarnation of Christ. And those expressions there, that do abundantly in the most natural sense agree with the former, are by the Apostle in the second [chapter] of Hebrews applied to the latter.[5]

These two chapters describe the happy state of the church after the

4. By "mixed prophecies" JE intended "those parts of Scripture that have respect to various events," not simply one thing. See the "Blank Bible," p. 678–79.

5. JE wrote this paragraph after no. 73a on the MS. In a note on Ps. 8 in the "Blank Bible," p. 408, he described the twofold exaltation of man: at creation "God gave him dominion over this lower world and the other creatures in it"; in the incarnation, there was an "actual uniting the human nature to the divine, whereby the human nature was exalted not only to an honor and dominion that was an image of God's, but actually to God's honor and dominion, whereby he had indeed, in the most extensive sense, dominion over all the works of God's hands, and had all things put under his feet. . . . Hence we may understand why the Apostle applies this place as he does (Heb. 2:6)." See also Miscell. no. 702.

resurrection. But there are two resurrections: the first or the spiritual resurrection, and the literal resurrection; and a happy state of the church succeeds both. And respect is had to both these happy states in this description; this is a description of the state of the church in the new heaven and new earth, after the former heaven and earth are passed away. But there shall be a new heaven and new earth in two senses. First, the heaven and earth is to be renewed as to the spiritual state of things. The spiritual renovation of the world is in Scripture sometimes called creating a new heavens and new earth. And second, this heaven and earth will literally pass away; and the people of God will have a new habitation, a new world to them in the room of it. There will be a happy state of the church in both those new worlds, both which respect is had to in this description. This is a description of the happy state of the church after the judgment; but that destruction there shall be of the wicked, and rewarding and advancing of the righteous, which there shall be at the beginning of the glorious times of the church here on this earth, is a judgment of the world. Christ will make a very great distinction between his church and her enemies, in his dealings with them. 'Tis represented by gathering of the clusters of the vine of the earth, who are the wicked, and casting them into the wine press of God's wrath; and gathering the harvest of the earth, who are God's people, in the 14th chapter: after the same manner as Christ says, the tares shall be gathered in bundles to be burnt, and the wheat gathered into the barn at the day of judgment [Matt. 13:30]. This is called the coming of Christ (Rev. 16:15) and end of the world (Rev. 16:20). In predictions of the day of judgment, respect is had to this as well as to the day of the destruction of Jerusalem, and the day of the destruction of heathenism in the Roman Empire, which is represented as the day of judgment and end of the world (Rev. 6, latter end).[6]

And all parts of this description, are applicable to both those states of the church, though in different senses. That which is said in the 2nd verse of the 21st chapter, of the New Jerusalem's "coming down from God out of heaven," is applicable to the state of the church after the resurrection. For it signifies no more than this, that the saints' eternal house, which is not made with hands, is from God. They receive their glorious dwelling place, with all the glory and blessedness of it, as his

6. In the "Blank Bible," p. 889, JE noted that "we often find in the Old Testament, that the destruction of Jerusalem and the state of Israel, is represented as the dissolution of the world."

gift; 'tis what comes down from him. Seeing that the New Jerusalem is represented as being on earth, a new earth in its coming from God, 'tis fitly represented as coming down out of heaven. In what part of the universe soever this new earth shall be, God is above all; and he descends to dwell in the[7] third heaven.

Again, what is said in the 3rd verse, "Behold, the tabernacle of God is with men" [Rev. 21], is applicable to both states. It is very fitly and aptly spoken, to represent the glorified state of the church, when perfectly delivered from all sin and suffering. When the church comes to be glorified, then this will be much more fully accomplished than ever before. This is here indeed spoken as something new, in that state of the church which it is spoken of, as what had not been before; and it well may [be] of the glorified state of the church. The tabernacle of God will then be with men in a very new, and far more perfect and glorious manner, than ever it had been before. The tabernacle of God was with the church of Israel before Christ came. Lev. 26:11, "I will set my tabernacle among you, and my soul shall not abhor you." But God's tabernacle was with the church after Christ came, in a new and more perfect manner; and therefore, this is prophesied of as part of the glory of the gospel church. Ezek. 37:27, "My tabernacle also shall be with them: and I will be their God, and they shall be my people." Again the tabernacle of God shall be with men, yet in a new and more perfect manner, after the destruction of Antichrist and in the time of the millennium; and therefore, this is well foretold of in the description of that glorious time. Again the tabernacle of God shall be with men, yet in a new and far more perfect manner, in the triumphant state of the church after the general judgment. Then will be the first that the tabernacle of God shall be with men, in that so proper and perfect manner. The tabernacle of God is the human nature of Christ. But this never makes its settled and fixed abode with men, till after the general judgment; nor is it ever with men at all in its exalted, glorified state till then.

If it be said, how can this be spoken of as a thing new in the state of the church after the resurrection, for the tabernacle of God is with the souls of men before that: departed souls of saints go to be with Christ, with his human nature, which is the tabernacle of God, so that God's tabernacle's being with men is no new favor that is first then bestowed— to this I answer three things. 1. Though the tabernacle of God be with the souls of men, yet 'tis a new thing (excepting a few instances of particular persons before) that it should dwell with men in their com-

7. Here JE deleted "highest heavens."

plete nature, and that their inferior part, their bodies, should be advanced to this glory. 2. The tabernacle of God shall be with men after the resurrection, in a far more perfect and glorious manner, than ever before it was with the departed souls of saints. It may be spoken of as a thing new and distinguishing of that state; as well as new in the New Testament church, as distinguishing it from the church of the Jews; and as well as new in the millennium, as distinguishing it from what had ever been before. For there will undoubtedly be as great a difference in the perfection of the manner, wherein the tabernacle of God shall be with men after the resurrection from what ever was before in the heaven of the departed souls of saints; as in the manner of its being with men after Christ came, from what was before; as in the manner of its being with men in the time of the millennium, from what was in the gospel church before. 3. The glorified state of the separate souls of saints, is not here excluded in this description. The prophet in this vision has represented to him the state of God's people in glory, including the glory before and after the resurrection. Indeed, the glory here spoken of is represented in vision as being after the end of the world; and indeed, that is indeed the proper time of the church's glory, though God of his grace grants to his saints an anticipation of that glory in a degree,[8] before the end of the world, after their death. Thus the proper time of the redemption of mankind, was when Christ came into the world, and the gospel was preached, and the Christian church erected by him. But God granted an anticipation of it; many were redeemed before this, though but few in comparison of what were afterwards. Redemption is spoken of in the Old Testament as a thing future; so now we speak of the world of glory as a world to come, because the proper time of the church's glory is after the militant state of the church is finished, and after this world of probation is destroyed. Thus the proper time of day is after sunrising, but there is an anticipation. And therefore, if the whole state of the church's glory be represented in vision together, and in one with other visions representing the affairs of the church and God's various dispensations in their order, the proper place of it is here after the end of the world. This state of the church, which is here described, is represented as being the state of the church after the end of the world; but the world is at an end with particular saints when they die. Heaven and earth is passed away with them. 'Tis after the judgment, but judgment is passed upon them at death.

8. JE wrote the balance of this paragraph and the first sentence of the next after no. 63 on the MS.

Ch. 21:12, "And at the gates twelve angels."[9] This, it seems to me, may well be understood both of the[1] angels properly, the ministry of heaven, whom God empowers in the church here below, as it were, to stand at the gates to guard and defend his people as ministering spirits to them, and to bring in the elect into the church. And in heaven now before the resurrection, they, as it were, stand at the gates to bring in the souls of the saints as they die. And after the resurrection, they will still be ministering spirits to Christ and to his saints. And the place of a servant or minister is at the door; and they will there be employed in promoting and ministering to the happiness of the saints, leading and conducting them to the fountains of knowledge and blessedness: which may well be represented by their standing at the gates of the city, to introduce the righteous people of the new earth, of that heavenly land, into the city, and conduct them to the pleasures of it, as the porters of Jerusalem admitted Israel when they went up to the solemn feasts. And the angels sitting in the gates, may also represent their dignity and authority; the place of rulers and judges was wont to be in the gates, when they were in the execution of their office.

And it may also well be understood as representing the gospel ministry, which is represented by angels in the beginning of this book, and with a special reference to the twelve apostles, who were the twelve first ministers and heads and fathers of the gospel ministry, and those from whom all the rest are derived. Gospel ministers sit at the gates as judges and as servants or doorkeepers who have the keys of the gates which Christ has given to them, whose office it is to bring in and admit persons into the church, and to conduct souls to heaven. And in the triumphant state of the church after the resurrection, they may still be represented as being at the gates in the same manner, as they may still be said to be the foundations, which we have already explained.[2] They may be represented as being at the gates, as those that have been the means of bringing in all the inhabitants of the heavenly Jerusalem. And doubtless, those ministers that have been faithful and eminent instruments of doing this blessed work on earth, will have the highest place in glory. So the apostles are now, and ever will be in places of very high dignity in glory; and they shall, in a sense, sit in the gates, judging the twelve tribes of Israel to all eternity. And I believe that those who have [been] thus eminently instrumental of carrying the blessed work of the

9. JE wrote the rest of this paragraph and the next preceding no. 66 on the MS.

1. Here JE deleted "blessed."

2. See the next paragraph, which now comes after this reference because of JE's rearrangement.

gospel in this world, will be employed in still assisting and promoting the happiness of the saints in a glorified state, and so may as well as the angels be represented at the gates, introducing and conducting the inhabitants of the new earth to the pleasures of Jerusalem.[3] The higher any are exalted in glory, the more [they] will be like Christ, the head and highest of all, and will have his image in this respect, that they will be a means of the good and blessedness of the society.

Again[4] this city, New Jerusalem, is said to be built on the foundation of the apostles. This is, in a sense, true of the church in both states. The church in her ultimate glory may be said, in a sense, to be built on the foundation of the apostles; for it is through the word of the apostles, that they were brought to that glory. So elsewhere it is represented, as though when Christ should sit on the throne of his glory, the apostles should sit on twelve thrones, judging the twelve tribes of Israel.

Verse 24, "And the kings of the earth do bring their glory and honor into it." This is properly and literally true only concerning the church militant on earth,[5] and as it relates to that, signifies these things. 1. That the kings of the earth shall become members of the church, and so the church shall have this honor. Kings become her members with all their wealth and glory; it will be an ornament to the church, to have many of her members in such dignity and honor. 2. That these royal members shall, with their wealth and power, enrich and advance the church, that is, the other members. 3. That they shall use their wealth and dignity to promote the church's great ends and business, which is to glorify God.

The same thing in substance (though not circumstantially the same), may be predicated of the church in her ultimate glory, after the resurrection. The substance of the prosperity here predicted is this. 1. That the church shall have the ornament of having many of her members in great dignity and advancement: which never is so true as of the church in glory, where angels and archangels, thrones, dominions, principalities and powers are her members, and all the members shall reign as kings.

2. That they shall improve all that power, wealth and honor which

3. For more on the significance of the number 12 and the ministry, see JE's remarks on the twelve wells at Elim (Ex. 15:27) in no. 172 of the "Scripture" (printed in Dwight ed., *9,* 255–56).

4. JE wrote the remainder of this entry, with one noted exception, between nos. 63 and 64 on the MS.

5. JE marked the rest of this paragraph and the next three with a large "X." By the time he composed no. 838 of the "Miscellanies," he had apparently changed his mind. See below, n. 6.

God hath conferred upon them, for the promoting of the happiness of the community. This is also eminently true of the church triumphant. Those that shall be most highly advanced in glory, will improve their peculiar power and honor and benefits with which they are enriched, to the utmost for the good of the society. The angels, the princes of that land, princes of the new earth, will especially do so; they there, as well as here, will minister to the good of the saints.

3. They will all improve it, to promote the church's great end and business, namely, to glorify God. Thus we read, that in heaven they will cast down their crowns at the feet [of Jesus Christ], "and worship him that liveth forever and ever" (ch. 4:10).

But this well answers to something that shall be after the resurrection and general judgment, viz., that the kings of the new earth, or the world of the glorified church, the thrones, dominions, principalities and powers of the world to come, the greatest dignities, authorities and powers of all mere creatures in the universe, shall bring their glory and honor into the church of Jesus Christ. They shall be subject unto that Lamb of God, that is, the Head and Redeemer of the church of the saints. They shall with all their hearts devote themselves to him and to his service, and shall cast down their crowns at his feet; and he shall become their Head and King. See Miscell. no. 838.[6] And under him they shall be joined, and become one society with the saints, and in him shall serve them, and shall improve their mighty power and wealth and those glorious gifts with which their Creator has endowed [them], in ministering for the good of this society, and the glory and happiness of this city. See note on Psalms 89:27.[7] Angels are princes of the world (Dan. 10:13). It may [be] they are so often called thrones, dominions, authorities, etc., with respect partly at least to their dominion in the earth, their government and management of things here under God; and so they are kings of the earth.[8]

6. This reference, a later addition, points to JE's discussion of the angels as the ministers of God's providence in governing the world, "princes under God," having authority and dominion assigned to them. Theirs is an honored and exalted work, an image of the work of Christ who "has the vicegerency of the whole universe. . . . These seem in part to be signified by the kings of the earth that shall bring their honor and glory into the church; . . . they may be called ministers of the new earth."

7. This reference, a later addition, points to the "Blank Bible," p. 438, where JE wrote: "The kings and princes of the earth, are sometimes called the 'sons of God,' as Psalms 82:6; but God makes his Son the first-born of these sons. This is also true with respect to the thrones, dominions, principalities and powers in heavenly places, who are also called 'sons of God' (Job 38:7), and seem sometimes mystically to be bunched under this expression of 'kings of the earth.' See Exposition on Revelation, no. 59."

8. The last two sentences are later additions.

Ch. 21:25, "And the gates thereof shall not be shut at all." As it relates to the kingdom of glory, it denotes the free admittance of all that will to come and dwell in that city. We are all freely invited to the heavenly Jerusalem, to the eternal glory of God's people; the gates of heaven stand always open to us. We are freely invited to accept of and choose that glory, which the saints shall have after the resurrection, though it be future. This may well be represented in vision by the gates standing always open to receive all comers.

And then, hereby is signified the free access which the saints in glory shall at all times have to God and Christ, to have communion with them, and to see and enjoy them. For the matter is represented thus: not that all God's people shall be constantly in this city; but this New Jerusalem, where God dwells, shall be in the midst of them, as Jerusalem was in the midst of Israel of old. But the gates shall at all times be open to 'em; they shall have free access at all times, as having all a right in that holy city and the blessings of it. There is no need at all of understanding it only of the gates standing open to sinners; but it [may] very well be understood of their standing open to the saints, the inhabitants of that heavenly Canaan,[9] as the gates of Jerusalem stood open to the inhabitants of the earthly Canaan, when they went up to their solemn feasts. As 'tis said in Isaiah 26:1–2, "We have a strong city; salvation will God appoint for walls and for bulwarks: open ye the gates, that the righteous nation that keepeth the truth may enter in." There certainly Zion, or the church of God, is spoken of as having her gates open to the saints that are already saints; and it seems to me, that this place in the Old Testament is here alluded to by what immediately follows in the 27th verse. "And there shall in no wise enter into it anything that defileth, neither whatsoever worketh abomination, or maketh a lie."

It[1] also may signify the great safety in which they shall dwell; they never shall need to shut the gates for fear of any enemy.

Again it is said, that the leaves of the tree of life in this city, are "for the healing of the nations" (ch. 22:2). But this may be understood of the tree of life in the church in glory, as well as in the church on earth. Christ is the tree of life, and he heals men's souls here; but he more thoroughly heals them as they enter into glory. Then shall the church be thoroughly healed of all sin and suffering at the resurrection. It is not meant that they shall continue to have diseases, from time to time that shall need to be healed; but the leaves of this tree shall at once heal all

---

9. JE wrote the rest of this paragraph after no. 65 on the MS.
1. I.e., Rev. 21:25.

their diseases, as it follows in the next words, "and there shall be no more curse." And in the 4th verse of the 21st chapter, "There shall be no more death, neither sorrow nor crying; neither shall there be any more pain."

60. See Chapter 20. II Sam. 6:13, "And it was so, that when they that bare the ark of the Lord had gone six paces, he sacrificed oxen and fatlings."

61. See Chapter 13:18. " 'Tis the number of a man," i.e., supposing the wisdom of man to number and to find out; as "the rod of men and stripes of the children of men" [II Sam. 7:14], means such corrections as men can bear. Such a temptation "as is common to men" [I Cor. 10:13], intends a temptation that is not too great for men to overcome.[2]

62. Chapter 21:1. The "new heaven and new earth," as signifying the last and everlasting abode of the church, can't well be understood of this present globe and atmosphere renewed and purified; for the expression seems to denote that it is not anywhere in this visible world. For the expression "heaven and earth" signifies this visible world. The heavens that these new heavens are distinguished from, doubtless signifies those heavens that are to be seen here on the earth, and must include the heaven of sun, moon and stars. If the same sun, moon and stars remained, therefore it would not be said that there were new heavens; or if only the same fixed stars remained, that would shew it to be the same heavens, for they encompass and fill the whole sphere, and the heavenly bodies besides these are but few. If these remain, the heavens must be said to remain. However the sun and planets may be removed, they are only removed out of the heavens. The same heaven that before contained them remains, as is evident, because the sphere of the fixed stars which contains that heaven yet remains. The moving of sun, moon and planets out of the heavens, and bringing something else in their room, as long as the fixed stars remain, don't make a new heaven, any more than the changing of household goods makes a new house, when the same walls and roof, etc., remain. See nos. 64, 73a; and Miscell. nos. 634 and 743.[3]

63. See Chapter 6:8 and Chapter 20:14. The "death and hell"

---

2. For a fuller commentary on Rev. 13:18, see the "Blank Bible," p. 892.

3. In Miscell. no. 634 JE argued that the present globe cannot be the scene of the "new heaven and new earth." " 'Tis fit that in the consummation of all things, that all things should be gathered together to God, that the less should remove and be brought home to the greater, and not the greater change place to come to the less." Concerning no. 743, see p. 124, n. 6.

here spoken of are the same spoken of [in] Revelation 20:14, and are spoken of here as they are. They are as two persons, agents, two enemies of mankind. These two are here spoken of as acting in conjunction in destroying the fourth part of the earth at this time. These two are spoken of in the latter part of this verse, when it is said, "Power was given unto them, over the fourth part of the earth, to kill with sword, etc." These two are the same monsters that are at last punished, as two grand enemies of Christ and his people (ch. 20:14). These two are mentioned together. I Cor. 15:55, "O death, where is thy sting; O Hades, where is thy victory?" And they are the same two mentioned [in] Hosea 13:14. "I will ransom them from the power of the grave; I will redeem them from death. O death, I will be thy plagues; O grave, I will be thy destruction." This threatening the apostle John in Revelation 20:14 in vision sees accomplished.

64. CHAPTER 21:1. That this new heaven and new earth are entirely new, as to matter as well as to form, may be argued not only from the expression here used about the old heaven and earth, that they "were passed away," and in the foregoing chapter, [the] 11th verse, of their being "fled away, and there being found no more place for them"; both [of] which expressions plainly denote the whole thing's being removed and gone, and not of its remaining and being changed. This heaven and earth's passing away and fleeing away out of its place, are expressions that would not be used to denote only the ceasing of the form.

There is the like expression: II Pet. 3:10, "the heavens shall pass away." But it may also be argued from this, that we learn by the apostle Peter, that "the heavens and earth that [are] now, are reserved and kept in store as fuel" for the fire, in which ungodly men are to be destroyed [II Pet. 3:7]. And after that, the Apostle tells us we "look for new heavens and new earth, wherein dwelleth righteousness" [II Pet. 3:13]; he here supposes the other as being gone, being put to that forementioned use. See nos. 62 and 73a; and Miscell. nos. 634 and 743.[4]

65. Let number 59 begin with what is here said. CHAPTERS 21–22. We have here in these two chapters a description of the true Christian church in her future glory, including both her future glory in this world and that which is to come, both her glory after the first and also after the second resurrection. The glory of the church of Christ at the millennium is here brought in, because 'tis reckoned as a part of her future glory. 'Tis the earnest and image of her state of reward and

4. See above, n. 3.

complete blessedness; 'tis the dawning of that glorious eternal day. Neither, do I think, the glorified state of the spirits of just men is to be excluded.

66. See CHAPTER 20:4. Concerning the first resurrection. "The souls of them that were beheaded for the witness of Jesus, and for the Word of God, and which had not worshiped the beast, neither his image, neither had received his mark upon their foreheads or in their hands," or those that had been martyrs under Antichrist, might be said to rise and reign in the time of the millennium; as well as it [might] be said, that the antichristian church had shed the blood of the prophets and apostles (chs. 16:6, 18:20, 24).[5]

67. CHAPTER 13:14. See no. 58. "That they should make an image to the beast." The first beast is the genius of the antichristian empire, or the devil acting as the genius of that empire. The great red dragon is the genius, or the devil acting as the genius of the heathen empire; this dragon or genius of the heathen empire, gives to the beast his power, seat and great authority.

The second beast is the genius of the antichristian clergy. The image of the first beast that this last beast or the genius of the antichristian clergy made, that he gave life to, and power to speak and to cause that as many as would not worship it should be killed, is the Pope, who though he pretends to [be] Christ's vicar on earth, yet is indeed the vicar or image of the beast.

The first beast is here represented as the god of the antichristian world, who is Satan acting as the genius of the antichristian empire. The Pope is the vicar or image of this god.

The second beast is said to exercise all the power of the first beast before him. The Romish clergy pretend to exercise all the power of Christ; but indeed, they exercise the power of the devil.[6]

68. See CHAPTER 7. Here are in this chapter two visions of the church of Christ:[7] the first to the end of the 8th verse, the other from thence to the end of the chapter. In the first is represented the care that God took of his church before and in the storm; in the other is represented the happiness of the issue and the rewards God bestowed on his people after.

5. JE's figurative interpretation is confirmed by another comment on the same passage in the "Blank Bible," p. 885: "They lived in those that succeeded them in the same profession and the same spirit. This is according to the style of prophecy."

6. In Miscell. no. 475 JE wrote, "Blasphemy and persecution are joined together in Antichrist, that greatest of all persecutors."

7. JE marked the rest of this paragraph and the next with a vertical line.

The one seems to have respect to the state of the church in the time of those troubles that were coming, [and] God's care of it to protect and uphold it during those troubles. The other seems to have respect to the glorious state of the church after those troubles shall be at an end, when the church shall be brought out of great tribulation, and shall "wash their robes and make them white in the blood of the Lamb, and shall hunger no more, etc." [Rev. 7:14, 16]. God's people that suffered in the time of those troubles, shall be rewarded in their successors, in whom they are represented as still living, agreeable to a figure often used in this book. Here is represented the glorious increase of the church: that whereas during the times of tribulation in its suffering state, it was confined, as it were, only to the twelve tribes of the children of Israel, now in its state of liberty and triumph, it shall consist of all nations. Multitudes of nations that before never bare the name of Christians, and were not called of Israel, shall be brought in from all the ends of the earth. I don't think that the reward of martyrs in heaven is here to be excluded. But it seems to me, especially by the 9th verse,[8] the antithesis there seems to be, as their being so opposed in their number from those in the former vision: that whereas that was an 144,000, a distinct determinate number, this is a great multitude that no man can number; and also in that respect, that whereas those were only of the tribes of the children of Israel, these were of all nations, kindreds, people and tongues.

The two companies mentioned in these two visions, seem to coincide with those mentioned in the 14th chapter: the 144,000, the same with those spoken of from the 1st to the 5th verse; and the other "great multitude, which no man could number, of all nations and kindreds and people and tongues" [Rev. 7:9], the same with those that the angel preached the everlasting gospel to, spoken of in the 6th verse—this great multitude.

The former seems to have a special respect to those that adhered to Christ, through all degrees and steps of the apostasy and defection of the Christian world, and through the darkest times of popery, and that were preserved and protected of God, through all those judgments that were successively brought on the Roman Empire, whereby that empire was gradually brought to nought. This company that adhered to God during these times, was comparatively small and more confined, which is signified by their being only of the tribes of the children of Israel. The other seems to have respect to the vast increase of the

8. Here JE deleted "the glorious state of the church on earth is principally intended."

church, that there was by the preaching of the gospel, from the beginning of the time of the Reformation, and especially shews the glorious victory and rewards of those that suffered by the persecuting rage of Antichrist after that time. For the greatest persecutions of Antichrist have been since the beginning of the Reformation, since the gospel has ceased to be confined, and has been preached to all nations and kindreds and people and tongues.

In the time of great declension in Ahab's time, when idolatry prevailed in Israel and the church was almost hid, God reserved only seven thousand to himself that had kept themselves pure, who had not bowed the knee to Baal, and whose mouths had not kissed him [I Kgs. 19:18]. But in the time of degeneracy of the Christian Israel, God had reserved to himself above twice seven times ten thousand, who had not bowed the knee to Antichrist, and who were untouched virgins, whose mouths had not kissed that idol and rival of Christ, but followed the Lamb wheresoever he went; proportionable to the much greater extent of Israel under the New Testament than under the Old, or the greater number of those that bare the name of Christians, than of those that bare the name of Israelites in Ahab's time.

69. CHAPTER 20. See no. 21. On the 7th day after Christ had foretold of his coming in his kingdom, Christ was transfigured (Matt. 16:28, 17:1; Mark 9:1–2; Luke 9:27–28).[9]

70. Concerning the four beasts (See Miscell. no. ww),[1] and the four and twenty elders mentioned [in] Revelation 4, and the heads of the living creatures in Ezekiel [1], and the opening of the four first seals in Revelation 6. Bedford's *Scripture Chronology*, pp. 459–461.[2]

"The Levites were appointed to pitch on the three sides of the tabernacle, and Moses and Aaron before it (Num. 3:1–40). On the east side there were the tribes of Judah, Issachar and Zebulun. On the south side there were the tribes of Reuben, Simeon and Gad. On the west side were the tribes of Ephraim, Benjamin and Manasseh; and on the north side the camps of Dan, Asher and Naphtali. That there was an infinite wisdom concerned in the disposal of these camps, which knew all events to the end of the world, and was the same which appeared to Ezekiel and St. John, will appear by comparing them all together. In the wilder-

9. JE apparently reconciled for himself the conflicting testimony of the evangelists regarding the time of the Transfiguration. See his note on Luke 9:28 in the "Blank Bible," p. 719.

1. Above p. 100, n. 6.

2. Concerning Bedford, see above, p. 64. The recto of p. 460 in the *Scripture Chronology* is a full-page diagram of the camp of the Israelites.

ness there was a throne for the divine majesty, or the Holy of Holies, in the tabernacle. In Ezekiel and the Revelations there is a throne, expressly called so, and all these are supposed not to be vacant, but filled with the divine majesty, as it is particularly expressed by Ezekiel and St. John [Ezek. 1:26, 10:1; Rev. 4:2–10]. In the wilderness, and by St. John, this throne is placed in the midst of all. And all this to shew God's providence in and over his church, and that nothing happens to her but by his appointment and permission. Next to the tabernacle in the wilderness, was the camp of the Levites, including the priests as their principal part. Next to the throne in the Revelations are the four and twenty elders, like the heads of the four and twenty courses of the priests, appointed by David to attend upon the temple in their several turns (I Chron. 24:1–20). Beyond these in the wilderness are the twelve tribes of Israel, reduced into four armies or bodies, pitching at a convenient distance on the east, south, west and north sides, each having its particular standard under so many principal tribes, Judah, Reuben, Ephraim and Dan. Each of these principal tribes, as the head of each army, according to the ancient tradition of the Jews, had their own peculiar animals displayed on their banners: particularly Judah's ensign on the east was a lion, Ephraim's on the west was an ox, Reuben's on the south was a man, and Dan's on the north was a flying eagle. Thus when Ezekiel saw his vision with his face towards the north, the four faces of the cherub which he saw did exactly correspond thereto. For the face on the right hand or east was as a lion, that on the left hand or west was like an ox, that on the south, which he mentions first as being before him, was like a man, that on the north was like an eagle (Ezek. 1:4–10).

"The same order is also observed by St. John, as an introduction to his prophecies, or the opening of the seals, which immediately followed (Rev. 4:7, 6:7–8). And as the seat of St. John's visions was the Roman Empire, so this situation in the wilderness, and Ezekiel's vision, compared with his, do fix the history of the four first seals, and consequently serves as a key to all the rest. The first seal shews us 'a white horse; and he that sat on him had a bow, and a crown was given unto him; and he went forth conquering, and to conquer' [Rev. 6:2]. By this is meant Christ himself, who was perfectly clean and pure, and without spot or blemish. He is represented by St. John as a lion, the ensign of Judah on the east side, and is called 'the Lion of the tribe of Judah' (Rev. 5:5), to shew more expressly a correspondence of this seal with his authority and power. He first set up his kingdom at his resurrection and ascension, which begun in the East, and soon made a great progress, and after the destruction of his enemies the Jews, was still more and more advancing itself in the Roman Empire. The second seal shews a red horse, 'and power was given unto him that sat thereon to take peace from the earth, and that they should kill one another: and there was given unto him a great sword' [Rev. 6:4]. This is introduced by the second animal, an ox, whose station was on the west side of the camp of Israel, and the prophetic scenes. This fixes the history to the reign of Trajan, and his immediate successors of the Aelian family. He was born in Spain, the utmost parts of the West, and was the first Roman emperor that was not an Italian. And he and his successor Hadrian made the most dismal slaughters of the Jews, which ever were known, to the number, as some say, of twelve hundred thousand men." And the Jews also slew vast multitudes of the Roman subjects, as Lowman observes in his *Paraphrase and Notes on the Revelation*, pp. 42–43.[3]

See no. 74. "The third seal shews 'a black horse, and he that sat thereon had a pair of balances in his hand. And there was a voice in the midst of the four beasts, saying, A measure of wheat for a penny, and three measures of barley for a penny: and see that thou hurt not, or be not unjust in the oil and the wine' [Rev. 6:6]. This was introduced by the third animal, which had the face of a man, whose station was on the south side of the camp of Israel, and the prophetic scenes. This fixes the history to the beginning of the reign of Septimius Severus, who was born in the south part of the Roman Empire, even in Africa itself, and he and his successors under this seal were the only Roman emperors, who were of this extraction. And the care which he and his successors took to make good laws, and execute them impartially, particularly in relation to oil and wine, and to procure plenty of both, as retold by the historians of those times, doth perfectly agree with this prophecy. The fourth seal shews 'a pale horse, and his name that sat on him was Death, and Hell followed with him. And power was given unto them over the fourth part of the earth to kill with sword, and with hunger, and with death, and with the beasts of the earth' [Rev. 6:8]. This was introduced by the fourth animal, which was like a flying eagle, whose station was on the north side of the camp of Israel and the prophetic scenes, and fixeth the history to the beginning of the reign of Maximinus, who was born north as far as Thrace, and thus it was to continue during the reigns of his immediate successors. There were wars and murders,

---

3. This sentence is a later addition. On these pages Lowman discusses the mutual blood-letting by the Romans and Jews. See p. 219.

tyranny and cruelty, a pestilence for fifteen years together, and a famine consequent thereon, at which time it was no wonder, if the beasts of the earth increased upon them. So that it is evident, that the God that gave directions, how the Israelites should pitch their tents, was the God who appeared to Ezekiel and St. John, in visions agreeing therewith, and made them so exactly to agree with the history of future ages, and consequently knew in the beginning what should happen to the end of the world." Concerning the seals, see "Extracts from Lowman," no. 94, p. 219.

71. CHAPTER 9:15. "And the four angels were loosed, which were prepared for an hour, a day, a month, and a year, for to slay the third part of men." "An hour signifies 15 days, or the 24th part of a year; a day signifies one year; a month, 30 years; and a year, 365 years and a quarter, or 91 days—in all 396 years and 106 days, which was the exact space of time between the date of Ottoman's reign, May 19, 1301, to September 1, 1697, when Prince Eugene gained that famous victory over the Turks, which produced the treaty of peace at Carlowitz, in the following year."[4] Bedford, *Scripture Chronology*, p. 664, margin.[5]

72. CHAPTER 21:1. "And there was no more sea." As the creation of the world was a type of the new creation or work of redemption, so the dark chaos, which is called "the waters" [Gen. 1:2], is a type of that sin and misery which we are brought out of in the new creation, which is begun by causing the light to shine out of darkness. (See Miscell. no. 702, the 1st and 2nd pages in that number.)[6] These waters were in the creation (which is a type of the new creation in the souls of believers); [they] had their reigning power taken away, that they should not overwhelm and cover the whole world. They were limited to certain bounds, to represent how sin and misery in the saints, though limited and not suffered to reign, yet is not totally abolished in their present earthly state, or while they stay in this old creation. But now the church, in its

4. Prince Eugene (1663–1736) of the House of Savoy defeated the Turks at Zenta in 1697, thereby reducing the perennial menace to the Hapsburg dominions. The treaty was signed in 1699.

5. Bedford's note c, as cited.

6. In Miscell. no. 702 JE depicted the work of redemption as the great end of all God's providential dispensations, including creation. The details of creation "shadow forth" particulars concerning redemption. There are parallels, he said, between the primordial watery chaos and the darkness and confusion resulting from sin. Light first appeared at creation, and Christ the Light of the World inaugurated the redemption of the world. On the seventh day of creation, all things appeared good and God rested; analogously, the sabbath of the church will begin after the time of misery, after the first six thousand years of the world.

consummate and glorious state in another world, has all these things perfectly done away, so that the waters ben't only ruled and limited to certain bounds as before, but totally abolished. There is no more sea. See Miscell. no. 702, the 3rd page of that number.[7]

73a. CHAPTERS 21–22. See nos. 62 and 64. What is here called the new heaven and new earth, we are not to understand of a literal heaven and earth, but a spiritual and mystical heaven and earth, meaning no more than that new state of things in the spiritual world or in God's church, that was typified and represented by the old or literal heaven and earth. The new heaven and new earth signifies the church, with the spiritual things that appertain to it and concern it, in that state that it is brought into by the glorious work of redemption, the same with the New Jerusalem, spoken of in these chapters, with the spiritual possessions, privileges and blessings that belong to it, procured and wrought out in redemption, as is evident by Isaiah 65:17–19,[8] which is the place that John in these visions alludes to. "For, behold, I create a new heavens and a new earth; and the former shall not be remembered, nor come into mind. But be you glad, and rejoice forever in that which I create. For, behold, I create Jerusalem a rejoicing, and her people a joy; and I will rejoice in Jerusalem, and joy in my people. And the voice of weeping shall be no more heard in her, nor the voice of crying." Respect is evidently had to this place in Isaiah, by the 4th verse of the 21st chapter compared with it. "And God shall wipe away all tears from their eyes; and there shall be no more death, neither sorrow, nor crying. Neither shall there be any more pain; for the former things are passed away."

'Tis further evident, that 'tis a spiritual heaven and earth, by Isaiah 51:16. "And I have put my words in thy mouth, and have covered thee in the shadow of my hand. That I may plant the heavens, and lay the foundations of the earth, and say unto Zion, Thou art my people." The work of redemption is the new creation, of which the old creation was a type. The work of creating or making the old creation, was a type of this work of redeeming and spiritually creating; and also the work done, the old heavens and earth, was a type of the work done here in this new creation or new heavens and earth, which is spiritual. Of which, see

---

7. In no. 702 JE wrote, "Thus the remainders of waters in the creation, represent the remainders of sin and misery in the present state of the church. But in the future triumphant state of the church, there shall be no remains of these; and therefore, in the description of that, 'tis said there was no more sea."

8. In the "Blank Bible," p. 524, at Is. 65:17–18, JE wrote, "Christ speaks of himself as the restorer of the world after it has been destroyed."

Miscell. no. 702, the 1st, 2nd, 3rd and 4th pages of that number.⁹ And as the work or operation of the new creation or the new creating, is a spiritual operation, so it will necessarily follow that the work done, or the new heavens and earth, are also spiritual. For 'tis absurd to suppose, that 'tis a spiritual creating that brings into being a literal or corporeal heaven and earth. This great and glorious work wrought, that is the effect of this new and spiritual creating, now appears perfect and complete at the end of the world. Now it appears and stands forth finished. After the first heaven and first earth, the type and shadow, has vanished away, then the antitype succeeds.

As by the New Jerusalem in these chapters, is meant that spiritual society and state and possessions that was the antitype of the old literal, external Jerusalem, so by the new heavens and earth is meant that new spiritual world, that was the antitype of the old literal heavens and earth. 'Tis not necessary that we should suppose anything, in any respect externally like the old visible world, with a ground underfoot and an expanse or firmament overhead; as 'tis not necessary that by New Jerusalem we should understand anything externally like the old literal Jerusalem with walls, streets and buildings. We read in these three last chapters of Revelation, of two resurrections and two deaths and two Jerusalems and two heavens and earths; and in each of these, one is a literal and the other a spiritual. The first resurrection is a spiritual resurrection, the second a literal. The first death is a literal, the second a spiritual and eternal. The first Jerusalem is a literal Jerusalem; the New Jerusalem is a spiritual Jerusalem. The first heaven and earth is a literal heaven and earth; the new heaven and earth is a spiritual and eternal. See Miscell. nos. 634, 743, and 806.¹ See no. 85.

73b. CHAPTER 9:10, 19. See no. 42. The tails of the locusts, spoken of in the 10th [verse], that are said to be "like unto scorpions" and to have stings in them; and the tails of the horses, spoken of [in the] 19th verse, in which their power is said to be as well as in their mouths, and which [are] said to be like serpents, and to have heads with which they do hurt, is the religion of the Saracens and [the] Turks, their successors, which was taught them by their false prophet Mahomet. Is. 9:15, "The ancient

9. Above, n. 6 and 7. According to no. 702, in both the creation and the new creation, the Trinity consults together. In both creations there was a "vile original," life came by breath, and honor as well as responsibility were bestowed upon the creatures.

1. See p. 158, n. 3, concerning nos. 634 and 743. The latter contains a cross-reference to this entry. According to Miscell. no. 806, in Christ's redemption there is a remedy for every calamity caused by the fall. The dissolution of the universe is offset by the restoration of a new and more glorious heavens and earth.

and honorable, he is the head; and the prophet that teacheth lies, he is the tail." This false prophet was one of the lowest of the people, for he was a servant. And their religion may well be called the tail; for this was the consequence of their wars and victories, the establishment of their religion. This was the tail that their power and victory drew after it.

This tail was like a serpent, i.e., it was a devilish religion; it was the offspring of the old serpent, and that by which he maintained his power and exercised his cruelty on men's souls, and vented his poison. There was a sting in this tail, as very tormenting and as very mortal. This was the greatest mischief that attended their power and victories; it was a soul-killing religion. At last it bites like a serpent and stings like an adder. These tails had heads, that is, their mufti[2] and priests, that were the heads of their religion. Mahomet, himself of a tail, was turned into a head: of a vile, despicable slave, he became their great prophet and head of their religion.

74. CHAPTER 6:5–6.[3] See no. 70. "And when he had opened the third seal, I heard the third beast say, Come and see. And I beheld, and lo a black horse; and he that sat upon him had a pair of balances in his hand. And I heard a voice in the midst of the four beasts say, A measure of wheat for a penny, and three measures of barley for a penny; and see that thou hurt not the oil and the wine." "The horse on which this rider sat was of a black color, expressive of a time of mourning and affliction; and the person that sat upon him, had a pair of balances in his hands, but not as a common representation of exact justice, and righteous judgment, but to weigh corn and the necessaries of life, to signify great want and scarcity, and to threaten the world with famine, the next judgment of God to the sword."

"Black, in ancient prophecy, is an emblem of affliction; and, in particular, of affliction occasioned by famine: thus, in the expressions of Jeremiah, Lam. 5:10. 'Our skin was black like an oven, because of terrible famine.' And famine is expressed by the prophet Ezekiel, by eating bread by weight. 'Moreover, he said unto me, Son of man, behold I will break the staff of bread in Jerusalem, and they shall eat bread by weight, and with care; and they shall drink water by measure, and with astonishment; that they may want bread and water, and be astonished one with another, and consume away for their iniquity'" [Ezek. 4:16–17].

2. I.e., an interpreter of religious law.
3. This entry is an assortment of citations from Lowman's *Paraphrase and Notes*, pp. 43–47. JE rearranged the materials at will and later recopied some of the same items into the extracts below, p. 220.

'Tis said "the price of a measure of wheat should be a penny, and three measures of barley should cost the same price; i.e., the whole wages of a man's labor for a day, shall only purchase so much corn, as is an usual daily allowance; so that all he can get must be laid out on the necessaries of life, without any provision of other conveniences for himself or family. And a scarcity of oil and wine will make exactness in their measures very necessary also."

"The measure of wheat is a choenix,[4] and the price of a Roman denarius or penny; of which Grotius[5] observes, the Roman penny was the daily wages of a workman, and a choenix the allowance of corn for his daily provision. So that a penny for a measure of wheat, will in general appear a very excessive price; since corn, for a day's provision, would cost a whole day's wages. In another way of computation, if we reckon the measure of the choenix to be about a quart English, and the Roman penny or denarius to be about eight pence English, the nearest common computation of both, and there is no need of more exactness, corn at that price will be above twenty shillings (sterling)[6] an English bushel; which, when the common wages of a man's labor was but eight pence a day, shewed a very great scarcity of corn, next to a famine."

"According to the order of the prophecy we have observed in this book, the events in history to answer this prediction, are to be found in the next part of this period of the heathen Roman Empire, (to that intended under the foregoing seal, i.e.,)[7] after the reigns of Trajan and Hadrian. Now Antoninus Pius succeeded Hadrian, A.D. 138. Antoninus the Philosopher, partly with Verus, and partly alone, and after them Commodus, governed the Roman Empire, till within a few months of the reign of Severus, who began his empire, A.D. 193, a space of above 50 years."

"The state of the empire under the Antonine family, does properly and exactly answer this prophetic description. The testimony of Tertullian,[8] who lived in those times, is very plain, and allowed by Mr. Mede;[9] he mentions unseasonable weather and bad harvests, the judgments of God for persecuting the Christians. Aurelius Victor,[1] in the reign of Antoninus Pius, observes that the scarcity of provisions occasioned such

4. A dry measure for grain, approximately a quart.
5. Above, p. 7.
6. JE's interpolation.
7. JE's interpolation.
8. A third-century Christian theologian in North Africa.
9. Above, p. 5.
1. A Roman epitomator who wrote a history of the emperors in the second half of the fourth century.

a tumult in Rome, that the common people attempted to stone him, which he chose rather to suppress by fair means, than by severity. Julius Capitolinus[2] further observes, that Antoninus Pius was fain to supply the scarcity of wine and oil and corn out of his own treasury, and that famine was one of the evils with which the empire was afflicted in his reign. In the reign of his successor, Antoninus Philosophus, we have a like account of the scarcity of provisions, to a famine. Mr. Echard[3] has thus expressed it: 'The birth of this Prince Commodus was signalized by many deplorable disasters; particularly the river Tiber, by an inundation, overwhelmed great part of the city of Rome, bore along with it a multitude of people and cattle, ruined all the country, and caused an extreme famine. This inundation was seconded by earthquakes, burning of cities, and a general infection of the air, which immediately produced an infinite number of insects, which wasted all that the floods had spared.' This account seems to be taken from Capitolinus and Victor. In the next reign, of Commodus, Xiphilin[4] observes from Dio,[5] there was such scarcity of provisions, that the people of Rome rose, and actually killed Cleander, the emperor's favorite, in sedition."

"This scarcity of provisions, in every reign of the Antonines, continued to the empire of Severus, who heartily set himself to remedy so great an evil, and made it the great care of his life, which plainly shews it was a very pressing evil: and that through frequent wars, bad harvests, and a mismanagement of the public stores, scarcity of provisions was a distinguishing judgment of those times. So Aelius Spartian[6] observes, in the life of Severus. And thus also the reign of Severus appears a proper end to the judgment of this prediction." See no. 94, p. 220.

75. CHAPTER 15:2–3. "And I saw as it were a sea of glass mingled with fire; and them that had gotten the victory over the beast, and over his image, and over his mark, and over the number of his name, stand on the sea of glass, having the harps of God; and they sing the song of Moses, etc." The glass is the matter of the vessel that is the container. As the sea in Solomon's temple [I Kgs. 7:23], in which persons and things in and about the temple were washed and purified, so this sea of glass is that in which souls are purified. The laver in the tabernacle was made of

2. A biographer of the emperors active during the first half of the fourth century.
3. Above, p. 66. Here Lowman was citing Echard's *Roman History*, Vol. 2.
4. John Xiphilinos, a Byzantine monk and historian of the eleventh century who abstracted the Roman history by Dio.
5. Cassius Dio of Bithynia in the third century compiled a history of the Roman Empire.
6. Another biographer of the emperors working during the first half of the fourth century.

the molten looking glasses of the women [Ex. 38:8], glass not being in use; so the sea in the temple was made of polished brass. But this is made of glass or crystal (See ch. 4:6),[7] the better to represent the purity of it.

Those "that [had] gotten the victory over the beast" [Rev. 15:2], or those that had suffered martyrdom under his persecutions, are here represented as standing round about, upon the edge of this great vessel, as having been washed in it is said of the martyrs. Ch. 7:14, "These are they that came out of great tribulation, and have washed their robes, and made them white in the blood of the Lamb." The same are there represented as singing a triumphant song, as these here are. The washing in the brazen sea of old, typified the same thing as is represented in Christian baptism, viz., spiritual baptism. Those that stand on this sea, are those that have been purified in a spiritual baptism. And for a signification of the greater purity, this vessel is represented as not only made of clear glass or crystal, but crystal that was not only clear and transparent, but also flame, and sent forth rays of bright light like fire. [It is represented] by an appearance that there was nothing on this world pure enough, or excellent enough to resemble; as in the 21st chapter, the streets of the city are represented as pure shining gold, and yet as clear glass [Rev. 21:21].[8] What is purer than the light, or than fire? Agreeable to this, Christ says we must be baptized with the Holy Ghost and with fire [Matt. 3:11].

These martyrs had been baptized with fire, in two respects. They [had] been sanctified and cleansed by the influences of the Holy Ghost, that was powerful in its influences to destroy pollution as fire, and had enkindled a holy and purifying flame of divine love in their hearts. And also, as they had been baptized in the fire of persecution, which is called the "fiery trial," and which in Scripture is represented as that which purifies the souls of the saints, as a furnace does gold. And such sufferings are called "baptism." Thus Christ calls his own sufferings a baptism that he was to be baptized with; and he tells Peter that he shall be

7. For more discussion of the sea of glass, see JE's "Blank Bible," p. 888.

8. In no. 306 of the "Scripture," JE wrote as follows concerning these streets: "This does most livelily represent the perfect purity of that city and its inhabitants. In the most stately and magnificent cities in this world—however beautiful the buildings are, yet the streets are dirty and defiled, being made to be trodden underfoot. But the very streets of this heavenly city, are so pure that their being like pure gold don't sufficiently represent the purity of them; but they appear also like clear glass or crystal. If there be the least dirt or defilement, it discovers itself in that which is transparent; but these golden streets appeared perfectly clear without the least speck to lessen the transparency. . . . This is an evidence that what is treated of in these two last chapters of Revelation, is the heavenly state of the church" (printed in Dwight ed., *9*, 562).

baptized with his baptism, referring to the martyrdom that he was to suffer [John 21:18–19].

Here is also an allusion to the children of Israel's standing on the edge of the Red Sea, after they were come out of it, and there sung the triumphant song of Moses.[9] Their passing through the Red [Sea] typified the same with baptism, as is plain by the Apostle saying, the children of Israel were baptized in the sea [I Cor. 10:2]. And their coming up out of that sea, into which they were driven by the Egyptians, their enemies and persecutors, and having their persecutors dead in the sea, typifies the church's coming up out of great tribulation and affliction, which is often compared to floods of great waters, and particularly coming up out of persecution and triumphing over their persecutors, as these martyrs do.

76. CHAPTER 10:7. "But in the days of the voice of the seventh angel, when he shall begin to sound, the mystery of God should be finished." What this angel of the covenant so solemnly swears, shall at such a time be finished, is the suffering state of the Christian church; as what his people and all his holy ones, in both heaven and earth, are greatly concerned to be most fully assured of a certain fixed period to, as appears by Daniel 12:6–7. For this is only a repetition of the same oath of the same angel that is there mentioned, and also appears by Revelation 6:9–11, and which they needed an oath for their confirmation in, because this suffering state was to continue very long, even from Nero, the first persecuting Roman emperor, to the downfall of the Roman, idolatrous, persecuting power in the fall of the Roman antichristian church. See notes on Matthew 24:21–24 ("Scripture" no. 292).[1] This long continued suffering state of the church of God, is here called the "mystery of God," and in Daniel 12:6 that is here referred to, is called "these wonders," signifying that a state of such extreme suffer-

---

9. In the "Blank Bible," pp. 893, 898, JE commented on the typological significance of the song of Moses for the "victory over Antichrist, the spiritual Pharaoh, or king over that church that is spiritually called Egypt."

1. JE wrote no. 292 in the "Scripture" with Lowman's *Paraphrase and Notes* in hand. JE interpreted the prophecy of the "great tribulation" as a reference to the sufferings of both the literal and the spiritual Israel at the hands of Rome. The Christian church will live in tribulation until the spiritual Babylon, the Church of Rome, is overthrown. And the church's tribulation will not be short because the kingdom is built on the blood of its children. "This leads us," JE declared, "to interpret those things in the Old Testament that speak of the glory of the Christian church, of the state of the church in the millennium; for that is the time of her glory on earth. The time foregoing, excepting some intermissions by which God has graciously shortened those days, is the time not of her prosperity, but her great tribulation." See Dwight ed., *9*, 451–63.

ings of God's own people and of so long continuance, was a very mysterious and wonderful dispensation of providence. The afflictions of God's own people while the wicked prosper, is often spoken of in Scripture, as one of the most mysterious things of all God's providential dealings with mankind. The mystery of God shall be finished, when she is destroyed that has on her forehead written, "Mystery Babylon," etc. (Rev. 17:5).[2]

77. CHAPTER 16:13–21. "And I saw three unclean spirits like frogs come out of the mouth of the dragon, and out of the mouth of the beast, and out of the mouth of the false prophet. For they are the spirits of devils, working miracles, which go forth unto the kings of the earth and of the whole world, to gather them together to the battle of that great day of God Almighty, etc." Concerning the Pouring Out the Seventh Vial.[3] By the dragon here is meant the power or genius of heathenism and idolatry. The beast is the power of hypocrisy, or false Christianity. The false prophet is the power of false prophecy, or false ministry. This going forth of three unclean spirits out of the mouths of these three, to gather them together to battle against Christ and his church, probably[4] has a double aspect, and will have a twofold accomplishment.

1. In the gathering together of the subjects of the antichristian empire, and the union of all the antichristian powers in their last efforts against Christ and his church, before that event that will be the principal overthrow of the antichristian world. For the dragon, the beast and the false prophet are all united in the antichristian kingdom, as is represented all along in this book of Revelation. The spirit and power of heathenism, and of false Christianity, and of false ministry, do all meet in this church. See no. 93.

2. This will be accomplished in the last united efforts of Satan's kingdom through the whole world, or the last struggle of all false religions with their united strength against the true religion. All the false religion is supported by these three powers, viz., the power of heathenism, the power of hypocrisy, i.e., false Judaism and false Christianity, and the power of false prophecy. And the whole of Satan's visible empire upon earth, is mainly divided into these three great kingdoms, viz., his antichristian or false Christian kingdom, which is the kingdom of the beast, his Mahometan kingdom, or the kingdom of the false prophet (for

2. This sentence is a later addition.
3. JE intended this as a title. Subsequent pages of the entry on the MS have "The 7th Vial" at the top. No. 77 also has additional separate pagination.
4. MS: "probable."

the Mahometan world follow and worship Mahomet as the great prophet of God), and his heathen kingdom, or the kingdom of the dragon. 'Tis probable that all these will in some respect join together, and help one another at that time, as the enemies of the true religion are wont to do when Satan's kingdom seems to be in eminent danger; though they differ and at other times have great dissension among themselves (Is. 41:5–6, with the rest of the chapter). There will probably be a great deal of confederacy, caballing and leaguing together to help one another between the heathen, Mahometan and antichristian powers. Yet there is no necessity to suppose that they will meet in one army, and oppose the church in one body and in one place. They shall oppose it in different parts of the world, as if they had leagued together. The heathen probably will, at the same time, be in a vehement struggle against Christianity in America, and in the East Indies, and Africa, that the Mahometans and papists do in the other parts of the world, as if they had all agreed together to try their united strength against it. But the league shall not actually [exist] among them, but among those devils that lead them, the unclean spirits here spoken of, though there will be abundance of leaguing together on earth to help one another; and they shall be overcome and overthrown together.

The pouring out the seventh vial brings to pass the utter destruction of these united powers of the dragon, the beast and the false prophet. But this vial has respect to two things, viz., the overthrow of Satan's kingdom in the antichristian world, and also its overthrow through the world of mankind; as the fourth vial that poured out on the sun had a twofold accomplishment (See Lowman),[5] and the 6th vial on the river Euphrates probably respects a twofold event (See Notes),[6] and as the seven heads of the beast signified two things far more different one from the other than these [Rev. 17:9–10].[7]

'Tis said in the 14th verse, that these three spirits shall "go forth unto

---

5. *Paraphrase and Notes*, pp. 188–95. Lowman suggested that the fourth vial literally points to "intemperately hot and burning seasons, which should destroy the fruits of the earth," thereby producing famine and pestilence. Figuratively, the vial is a prediction of the widespread judgments of God upon his enemies. See p. 248.

6. Perhaps the reference is to Lowman's *Paraphrase and Notes*, p. 200, where the sixth vial is discussed, or to no. 292 in JE's "Scripture," sec. 12, where JE alludes to the twofold event (Dwight ed., *9*, 459–60).

7. JE wrote in the "Blank Bible," p. 894, "By this it is most manifest, that the Spirit of God may have an eye to several very different things in the same prophetic description. For this is a plain instance, against which there is no disputing. Seeing God himself tells us that it is so of one vision or prophetic description, why mayn't we suppose that it may be so with respect to others also?"

the kings of the earth and of the whole world." By this it seems that the event signified is to be of greater extent than of the Roman or antichristian empire. For though the Roman Empire was formerly called the whole world, when the earth was less inhabited, and men's commerce and intercourse in the world was far more confined, and the extent of the habitable world was less known than it is now; yet at the time when this is accomplished, the popish part of the world is far from being called or looked upon as the whole world. And 'tis reasonable to suppose, that there will be an accomplishment that answers the use of such an extensive and universal expression in the time of accomplishment. Here is a double expression, "the kings of the earth and of the whole world," which being taken together, seem to determine the meaning to the most extensive sense. Possibly by "the earth" is meant the countries under the dominion of the beast, as it often does in these prophecies; and the other expression that is added, "the whole world," intends that it shall not only be that, but all the rest of the world: as much as to say, not only the kings of the earth or the antichristian empire, but also the whole world.

But whether we understand these two expressions so, as one of larger extent than the other, or as synonymous, yet it is with me past doubt, that they will have a twofold accomplishment: one respecting the heathenism, and false Christianity, and false ministry or prophecy of the Roman earth or world; and the other with respect to the whole habitable earth in the overthrow of these three things—the heathenism, the Mahometanism, and the anti or false Christianism of the whole world of mankind.

And whether the accomplishment of these shall be both together, or whether the principal accomplishment [be] with respect to the former, viz., the antichristian world, I won't determine. Probably what in the 7th vial respects the downfall of Antichrist, may have its accomplishment a long time before the destruction of Satan's kingdom, in so vastly greater extent; and that one will make way for the other. And that then, at last, the remainders of the antichristian kingdom shall be utterly overthrown, at the same time that the rest of Satan's kingdom in the Mahometan and heathen world falls, even as the prophecies in the Old Testament of the destruction of old Babylon and of Tyre, two great types of Antichrist, though the prophecies[8] seem to be one, yet were accomplished in several overthrows. The chief destruction of Babylon was by Cyrus, and that is chiefly aimed at in the prophecies of

8. Conjecture for illegible word.

Babylon's downfall [e.g. Is. 13:19–22]; but there were many things in those prophecies that have respect to a more perfect destruction by Darius, many years after (See Prideaux).[9] And so of Tyrus. Many things in the prophecy of Tyre's destruction [Ezek. 26] were fulfilled in the destroying of the old city by Nebuchadnezzar, but yet other parts of the same prophecy were afterwards fulfilled by Alexander (See Prideaux).[1]

And that that event, which in the Revelation is principally pointed forth by the destruction of the mystical Babylon, is not the total and ultimate extirpation of the Romish Church (though it is its principal destruction, or the greatest revolution tending to its destruction), but that there will be another destruction after that by which her ruin shall be perfected, and the Romish religion shall be more entirely rooted out of the world, is confirmed by the things that are said upon occasion of [the] great event that is chiefly called the downfall of Babylon, in the 18th chapter of Revelation. For by what is there said, there shall not only yet remain many of the Church of Rome that shall bewail her overthrow. But that there shall be some kings amongst them. Vv. 9–10, "And the kings of the earth, who have committed fornication and lived deliciously with her, shall bewail her, and lament for her, when they shall see the smoke of her burning, standing afar off, etc." V. 11, "And the merchants of the earth shall weep and mourn." V. 15, "And the merchants[2] of these things, that were made rich by her, shall stand afar off." V. 17, "And every shipmaster, and all the company in ships, and sailors, and as many as trade by sea, stood afar off."

The Church of Rome will probably be so overthrown, that they will have no more courage to rise up to make any open war with the church of Christ by themselves. But when they see other parts of the kingdom of Satan, those of his Mahometan and heathen kingdoms, rising up in other parts of the world, their courage will be raised by it; and they will join in with them in another onset on the church. And then shall be their last overthrow; and with that overthrow, the millennium shall begin. 'Tis not to be supposed, that there will be any popish kings and kingdoms remaining in the world after the millennium is actually begun, and "the kingdoms of this world are become the kingdoms of

---

9. *Connection*, Pt. I, Vol. 1 (1725), pp. 267–69. See HA; below, p. 408.

1. Ibid., Vol. 2, pp. 690–94.

2. In the "Blank Bible," p. 894, JE equated the merchants of this prophecy with the clergy and teachers of spiritual Babylon.

our Lord, and of his Christ" [Rev. 11:15]. For if popish kings and kingdoms yet remained, a persecuting Romish power would yet remain; and so the church [is] not in the enjoyment of its rest or sabbatism.

'Tis an argument that the revolution spoken of under the seventh vial, shall reach further than the dominions of the Romish Church, because 'tis spoken of as the greatest revolution, remove or change in the state of the earth that ever was, since men were upon the earth. Rev. 16:18, "And there was a great earthquake, such as was not since men were upon the earth, so mighty an earthquake, and so great." The revolution that was in Constantine's time, is also represented by a great earthquake: ch. 6:12, "And I beheld, when he had opened the 6th seal, and lo, there was a great earthquake." But this earthquake is represented as far greater than that, or any other that ever was. But if the change that shall be at the pouring out of the seventh vial, reaches no further than the limits of the Romish Church, it can't be in any measure so great as that which was in Constantine's time: for that extended over the whole Roman Empire, east and west, but this only over a part of the western empire.

Doubtless that revolution that is to introduce the glorious state of the church and the world in the millennium, will be much greater and of greater extent than that which was in Constantine's time; for that was but an image and type of this. This in the millennium is the true glorious state of the church and world. This time is the proper and fit time for the church's glory and triumph, principally aimed at in all the prophecies of Scripture concerning the church's glory on earth; and all foregoing seasons of prosperity to the church, were but prelibations and shadows of this, that in Constantine's time was given, the time yet continuing that is meant by the time of the great tribulation of the church, spoken of by Christ and the prophets. The millennium is the proper time of this happy state of the church and world. In the beginning of the millennium, the church will be brought to this state, of which that in Constantine's time was a prelibation and type; for the millennium is the fit time of the remaining of this event in its actual accomplishment. And therefore then, even at the beginning of this time, the event will be accomplished in a degree so far beyond all preceding prosperous seasons, as that what shall then be, shall appear worthy to be the antitype of them all, and of which they were but forerunners and prelibations. Both these revolutions are represented as the conversion of the world, but yet the first so as to be only a type of the last. And therefore that which is called the world in the first, viz., the Roman Empire, is but a type of that which is called the world in the last, the latter being of vastly greater extent than the former: the former being the world, but only in some sense and typically; the latter being truly and literally the whole world, as 'tis fit the antitype should be.

The millennium is the sabbatism of the church, or the time of her rest. But surely the days of her sabbatism or rest don't begin, till she ceases to be any longer in travail. And the church don't cease to be in travail, till she has brought forth what she has for these many ages been in travail for; and that is doubtless something far greater than ever she brought forth heretofore, even while the days of her travail were yet continued. And therefore, when nothing is actually brought forth greater than anything past, the church can't be said to have brought forth; and so her rest is not begun. What the church has from Christ's time till now been travailing, has been the conversion of all nations, and the setting up the kingdom of him who is the rightful heir of the world through the world of mankind.[3] And as long as the church still remains struggling and laboring, to bring to pass this effect, her travail ceases not; as doubtless she will not cease continually to labor for it, till the kingdom of Christ is set up everywhere. As long as great part of the world yet remains under Satan's dominion in popery, Mahometanism, Judaism or heathenism, the church will still continue laboring to accomplish this effect, and won't rest, till all parts of Satan's kingdom are overthrown, and the kingdom of Christ everywhere established. And then will be her rest or sabbatism; and then will be her song of praise, which will last throughout the thousand years.

As the sabbatism or rest of the church can't begin, before the world of mankind is mainly settled in the profession of the true religion, because till then the church won't cease striving against false religion, so also because till then, false religion won't cease opposing and struggling against that, 'tis not probable that false religion and wickedness, the first-born of Satan, that spiteful, venomous serpent, will cease struggling and fighting against the true religion, as long as it is alive and continues to be upheld in any considerable part of the world. But as long as this is, the church won't be established in her sabbatism of rest.

The church from Christ's time to the millennium, is in a state of warfare, or her militant state; but during that sabbatism, [she] shall

3. See no. 613 in the "Miscellanies," where JE speaks of "a vastly more glorious propagation of the true religion before the end of the world."

be in a triumphant state. The proper time of the church's rest and triumph can't be said to be come, till all her enemies are subdued. As long as any considerable part of the world remains under the dominion of Satan, Michael and his angels will be at war with the devil and his angels; and the church will be going forth, fighting against her enemies with the sword of the Spirit, the sword of Christ's mouth, which is the Word of God. And then will begin the time of the church's rest and triumph.

Thus the rest of the children of Israel did not begin till the Egyptians had their last overthrow in the Red Sea, though there were many awful judgments on Egypt, and all her first-born were slain. And the children of Israel were brought forth, and in a sort delivered before this; but this was their final and perfect deliverance, that delivered them from all future attempts of the Egyptians against 'em, and all apprehensions or fears from them. And it was made known to them, that they should never see anything more of them forever. Then the children of Israel had their song of triumph, and then they had rest. Then they enjoyed a sabbath: that day that they came up out of the Red Sea, was the day of their sabbath; and their Sabbath forever after, was appointed to be kept in commemoration of that event. See Miscell. no. 691.[4] That sabbath of the Jews at the Red Sea, was a type of this sabbath of the world in the millennium; and that triumph of theirs at that time, a type of the church's triumph at this time, when especially they shall sing the song of Moses and of the Lamb.

So the time of the children of Israel's rest in Canaan, did not begin till Joshua had finished all his wars with the inhabitants, and had subdued the whole country. Though he had before that won that great victory at Gibeon, when the sun stood still, and afterwards that other great victory at the waters of Merom (Josh. 11), yet Joshua continued warring after that for some time, as in the following part of that chapter. And then, when the whole land was subdued, then we are told the land had rest. V. 16, "So Joshua took all that land, the hills, and all the south country, and all the land of Goshen, and the valley, and the plain, and the mountain of Israel, and the valley of the same." V. 23, "So Joshua took the whole land, according to all that the Lord said

---

4. No. 691 is a discussion of Deut. 5:15 and of the origin of the Sabbath. JE noted Arthur Bedford's suggestion that the Jewish Sabbath was instituted to remember the rescue from Egypt at the Red Sea. That deliverance is the principal type of Christ's work of redemption. The Christian Sabbath, in turn, is a commemoration of a vastly superior work, Christ's victory.

unto Moses; and Joshua gave it for an inheritance unto Israel, according to their divisions by their tribes. And the land rested from war." So Joshua 14:15, "And the land had rest from war." And ch. 21:43–44, "And the Lord gave unto Israel all the land, which he sware to give unto their fathers; and they possessed it, and dwelt therein. And the Lord gave them rest round about, according to all that he sware unto their fathers: and there stood not a man of all their enemies before them, and the Lord delivered all their enemies into their hand." So when the spiritual Joshua shall have subdued all the enemies of his spiritual Israel, throughout the whole land that he hath promised them, and hath given them the possession of all that land, then shall the church have rest from war, rest from all her enemies round about, and then shall begin her great sabbath of rest. The land that God has promised his church is the whole earth. Matt. 5:5, "Blessed are the meek, for they shall inherit the earth." [See] Ps. 37:11, 22.[5] The nation of Israel, whom God calls his son, his first-born, were heirs of the land of Canaan, that good land which was God's land, the land that God had set apart for himself. So the church of God, that consists of the children of God, that are "heirs of God and joint heirs with Christ" [Rom. 8:17], are heirs of the world as Christ is heir of the world. And therefore, God promises that he that approves himself one of these, shall inherit all things; and he will be his God, and he shall be his son.

Thus again, the rest of the children of Israel after David came to the crown, did not begin as long as David lived, though he had obtained many great victories over his enemies long before his death. It did not begin till David has conquered all his enemies on every side, from [the] river Euphrates to the land of Egypt, and all things were firmly settled in subjection to his crown. And then came on the reign of Solomon, whose name is peace, who was a prince of peace, and a man of rest, whose reign was a most eminent type of the millennium. And the things that are more immediately spoken of one, have an undoubted reference to the other, in the 72nd psalm where it is said (v. 8), "He shall have dominion from sea to sea, and from the river to the ends of the earth": which [words], as applied to the literal Solomon, are to be understood of all countries conquered by David on this side [of] the

5. The "meek," according to JE's comment in the "Blank Bible," p. 418, are those "that fret not themselves in any wise to do evil." When the glorious times of the church begin, "God's people shall be brought off from censoriousness, and bitter complaints of persecution, and other things inconsistent with meekness, that do now too much prevail amongst godly people and ministers." For more comments on the subject, see Miscell. no. 811.

river Euphrates to the Great Sea and Red Sea; but as they are to be applied to Christ, the true Solomon, are to be understood of all countries in the world, all continents contained between different parts of the ocean. As 'tis said (v. 11), "All kings shall fall down before him; all nations shall serve him." Ps. 2:8, "I will give thee the heathen for thine inheritance, and the uttermost parts of the earth for thy possession." The same words here used are used [in] Zechariah 9:9–10, where they are to be understood only of Christ. "Thy King cometh unto thee; he is just, and having salvation, etc., . . . and his dominion shall be from sea to sea, and from the river to the ends of the earth." As Solomon's reign of peace and rest, was not set up till all the nations of this his large dominion, in its utmost extent, had been subdued by David, and established firmly and quietly under his crown, so that there was no enlargement by war afterwards; so will not the millennium, typified by that reign, begin till all nations from one end of the earth to the other, are subdued by the spiritual David, and firmly and quietly established in subjection to his crown.

The sabbatism of God's people, or the day of her rest from labor, can't be supposed to begin, till they have finished their city and temple. These have been in building ever since Christ's time. The laboring and suffering time of the church, is to [be] continued till the city is completely finished, her gates set up. The foundation was laid in the blood of God's first-born, Jesus Christ, as Hiel the Bethelite laid the foundation of Jericho in his first-born [I Kgs. 16:34]. And from Christ's time to the millennium, the city is in building; and all the while the work is carried on by the blood of God's younger children, who are slain one after another, as it was in the building of Jericho.[6] And as Hiel set up its gates in his youngest son, so shall the suffering time of the church continue, till the last finishing stroke is done towards building the city of God, and the gates are set up. And then shall their death and sufferings cease, and rest shall follow. Though many great things may be done by the laborers towards building the temple long afore the topstone is brought forth, yet the time of their rest don't come, till this is done. The laboring time lasts till then.

And then besides, it is to be considered that the millennium that shall be after the beginning of the seventh thousand years, is not only the sabbatism or day of rest to the church, but to that which began to be, or

---

6. Concerning the place of bloodshed and suffering in the church, see JE's "Scripture," nos. 173 and 307 (printed in Dwight ed., *9*, 279–81, 287–88).

was created in the beginning of that week of millenniums, viz., this lower world. It shall be the day of rest and the holy day of the whole world; and therefore, it shall begin when holiness and spiritual rest begins to take place through the world in general. The Apostle tells us, that the creature is in bondage under the corruption and wickedness of mankind, and that the whole creation groans and travails in pain together, waiting for the manifestation of the sons of God (Rom. 8). And it will continue to groan and travail in pain, under the wickedness of its inhabitants, till its inhabitants are generally converted from their wickedness to Christianity. And then it shall enjoy its rest or sabbath; but this can't be while the greater part, or a very great part, of this lower creation continues to be inhabited and possessed by Satan and his followers, and a great part of God's good creatures here remain in their hands and under their dominion.

It can scarcely be reasonably supposed, that Satan's dominions all through the world will be thoroughly and perfectly subdued by one battle, and that he won't make any more attempts. But 'tis probable that the first great battle, in which place perhaps in some respects the most remarkable hand of God will give the greatest overthrow to the antichristian kingdom; and the next, to overthrow the kingdom of Satan through the world: and that both these, as two great parts of the same event, are prophesied of under one, as is common in scripture prophecy, especially the prophecies of the destruction of Babylon and Tyre,[7] which the destruction of Antichrist is especially compared to in Revelation. And the expressions used to describe it (Rev. 18), are taken from what is said by the prophets of the destruction of these two cities.

Thus the nations of Canaan were overthrown in two great battles: first, the Amorites, the principal of those nations, at Gibeon when the sun stood still, and God sent great hailstones upon them out of heaven, in which there was the most remarkable hand of God [Josh. 10]; and the other, at the waters of Merom, where a far greater number were overthrown than in the former battle [Josh. 11].

The event that the church has been laboring and in travail for, is that event that is accomplished by the sounding of the seventh trumpet. Rev. 11:15, "And the seventh angel sounded: and there were great voices in heaven, saying, "The kingdoms of this world are become the kingdoms of our Lord, and of his Christ; and he shall reign forever and ever." And therefore, the church's labor and travail is not over, nor her rest come, till this event be accomplished. But we must suppose,

7. MS: "AntiX." See p. 175.

that this will be accomplished in a greater extent at the sounding of the seventh trumpet than ever before, because 'tis spoken of as a new thing, that shall first be accomplished then. And by this world must be meant a much bigger world than the Roman world that became Christian in Constantine's time. And this event can't be looked upon to be accomplished, as long as such mighty empires as that of the Turks, and of the Chinese, and great Mogul, etc., remain in opposition to Christ's kingdom. Formerly the Roman Empire was called the whole world, when they had but little intercourse with other parts of the world, and were but little known to them. But 'tis far from being so now, since men's knowledge and commerce is vastly extended, and the globe of the earth is discovered quite round. It and almost all parts have intercourse one with another; which intercourse and acquaintance is daily increasing, and will doubtless be vastly augmented before the accomplishment of this event, and in all likelihood has thus increased, and will more increase, to make way for its accomplishment.

The universality of the event accomplished by the pouring out of the seventh vial, as reaching to Satan's kingdom through the world, seems to be denoted by its being poured out into the air, i.e., the atmosphere, which encompasses the globe of the earth, which is represented as what limits Satan's dominion as god of this world (Eph. 2:2).

And besides, if this ben't a prophecy of the destruction of Satan's kingdom through the world, we have no prophecy of it in this book, which is not credible, seeing the event is so exceeding great, and the design of the prophecy to give an account of the main events of providence, with relation to the church of Christ to the world's end, and especially to encourage the church with the hopes of that glorious event, that consists in the glory of Christ's kingdom in its last and most prosperous state.

We may further argue from the first sabbath, or seventh day of the creation, which was a type of this. God's great works in making the world were all wrought and finished before this, and on this day God saw all completely done. He beheld them very good, and rested and was refreshed. No part of the creation was done on the seventh day; there was nothing then to do but to rest, and rejoice in what was done and completely finished before. So in the millennium, which will begin in the seventh thousand years, God's spiritual work, his new heavens and new earth, so far as to be finished in this world, will be completely finished. The work of bringing the world into subjection to Christ, and establishing Christ's kingdom in the world will be done; and Christ and his church will then rest, beholding the work done, and all very good, rejoicing in it, as being now absolutely completed. See no. 83.[8]

78. CHAPTER 16:12.[9] See no. 54. "And the sixth angel poured out his vial upon the great river Euphrates; and the waters thereof were dried up, that the way of the kings of the East might be prepared." This is the last thing that makes way for the destruction of this spiritual Babylon, the last thing that shall be done against her, before the very stroke is given by which she shall be destroyed; and therefore, this is the last vial but one, that was poured out upon her. As of old, the last thing that was done to make way for the destruction of old Babylon, was the drying up the waters of the river Euphrates that run through the midst of the city, to prepare the way for the kings of the East to come into the city and destroy it. Babylon was destroyed by the kings of the East, by the kings of the Medes and other eastern nations. Jer. 27:7, "Many nations and great kings shall serve themselves of him." Jer. 51:11, "The Lord hath raised up the spirit of the kings of the Medes; for his device is against Babylon, to destroy it." And vv. 27–28, "Prepare the nations against her; call together against her the kingdoms of Ararat, Minni and Ashkenaz. Appoint a captain against her; cause the horses to come up as the rough caterpillars. Prepare against her the nations with [the] kings of the Medes, the captains thereof, and the rulers thereof, and all the land of his dominion." The Medes and Persians were both to the eastward of Babylon, and these princes that God raised up against her are spoken of as coming from the East. Is. 46:11, "Calling a ravenous bird from the East, the man that executeth my counsel from a far country." The prophets speak of drying up the river Euphrates to prepare the way for these. Is. 44:27–28, "That saith to the deep, Be dry, and I will dry up thy rivers; that saith of Cyrus, He is my servant, and shall perform all my pleasure." And in Jer. 51:31–32, "One post shall run to meet another, and one messenger to meet another, to shew the king of Babylon that his city is taken at one end, and that the passages are stopped: and the reeds they have burnt with fire, and the men of war are affrighted." And v. 36, "And I will dry up her sea, and make her springs dry."

Hence we may conclude that by the great river Euphrates, is meant something in the Church of Rome or spiritual Babylon, something wherein their outward good consists, or that has some way contributed to the convenience, comfort and outward prosperity and glory of that

8. MS: "83. Which add to this."
9. JE entitled the pages of this entry "The 6th Vial on the River Euphrates."

city, church or hierarchy, as the river Euphrates anciently was to the literal Babylon through the midst of which it [ran]. And something that comes constantly flowing, to be a continual supply to the city, as the waters of Euphrates were to that city, and [were] let into the midst of the city to that end. And also something that is a defense to it, to defend it against its enemies, as the waters of Euphrates, being instead of walls in certain places. So is this spoken of on which the 6th vial is poured: to the spiritual Babylon, 'tis something that has not only been a supply to it, but also a defense to it, because by the drying of it up, the way of her enemies is prepared to come in and destroy it. And 'tis probable that it is especially something that is for the supply of the king of the spiritual Babylon, viz., the Pope, and to add as it were to the glory of his palace: for the river Euphrates of old did not only run through the midst of the city Babylon, but through the midst of the palace of the king of Babylon, that part of his palace that was called the old palace standing on one side, and the other part called the new palace on the other, with communications from one part to the other across the river, both above the waters by a bridge, and under 'em by a vaulted or arched passage.

Hence, what can this river Euphrates be but the temporal supplies, wealth, revenues and incomes of the Romish Church? These are the waters by which that city is supplied and maintained. This is the river whence this spiritual Babylon is watered. These are the waters that they thirst after, and are continually drinking down to satisfy their thirst. These are continually flowing into that city from day to day, and from year to year, like the waters of a river. These may well be compared to the waters of a great river, if we consider how rich that church is and is represented to be in this book of Revelation, and how vast her continual incomes. Ecclesiastical persons possess a very great part of the wealth of the popish dominions. These are especially the waters that supply the palace of the king of this spiritual Babylon. The revenues of the Pope have been like the waters of a mighty river, coming into his palace from innumerable fountains, and by innumerable branches and lesser streams, coming from many various and different countries, as 'tis with the waters of a great river.[1]

Waters and rivers are in scripture language put for all temporal supplies (Prov. 9:17; Is. 33:16, 41:17, 43:20, 55:1, 58:11; Jer. 2:13, 18,

1. According to JE, the apostate Jewish church and the Church of Rome alike turned God's house into a "house of merchandise" and a den of thieves by their commerce in religion. See no. 330 in the "Scripture" (Dwight ed., *9*, 447).

17:8, 13).[2] Is. 5:13, "Therefore my people are gone into captivity; and their honorable men are famished, and their multitude dried up with thirst," i.e., were deprived of all supplies and supports of life. And so a time of famine is represented in Scripture by drying up the rivers of waters (Nahum 1:4), and by men or beasts[3] coming to the waters, or places where waters used to be, and finding none (Jer. 14:3).

And drying up the waters of a city or kingdom, is used in scripture prophecy for the robbing them of their wealth, as the Scripture explains itself in Isaiah 15:6–7. "For the waters of Nimrim shall be desolate: for the hay is withered away; the grass faileth; there is no green thing. Therefore the abundance they have gotten, and that which they have laid up, shall they carry away to the brook of the willows." And Hosea 13:15, "His spring shall become dry, and his fountain shall be dried up; he shall spoil the treasure of all pleasant vessels." And the drying up of waters, even the prophecies of Babylon's destruction, seems to be foretold, not only in a literal but also in a figurative sense, for the robbing of their treasures in Jeremiah 50:37–38, even as it seems there to be explained. "A sword is upon her treasures, and they shall be robbed; a drought is upon her waters, and they shall be dried up." Compared with Jer. 51:36, "I will dry up her sea, and make her springs dry." Babylon was situate on the river Euphrates, and so dwelt on many waters; but this is made use of to signify her being abundant in treasures, as well as large in dominions. Jer. 51:13, "O thou that dwellest upon many waters, abundant in treasures."

As the river that we read of in this book of Revelation, that runs through the holy city Jerusalem, the true church, signifies her spiritual supplies, those supplies that afford the inhabitants spiritual nourishment and satisfy their spiritual thirst, so the river that runs through the midst of that wicked city Babylon, the false church, represents her daily and carnal supplies which satisfy their carnal desires and thirstings. The true church is heavenly and spiritual. She is not of this world. She therefore seeks not the meat that perished [John 6:27], or the water which a man drink he shall thirst again [John 4:13]. But the false church is of this world, and seeks those things that are carnal: her nourishment and her wealth and glory, is that which is worldly. The wicked have their portion in this life. That the river (spoken [of in] Rev. 22), that waters the spiritual Jerusalem, signifies her spiritual supplies, by which she is nourished and satisfied, is abundantly evident from Scrip-

2. The biblical references are later additions.
3. Conjecture for illegible word.

ture. As particularly Ps. 46:4, "There is a river, the streams whereof make glad the city of God." And by what Christ says to the woman of Samaria [John 4:5–15]; and the promises of pouring waters on the thirsty and floods on the dry ground [Is. 44:3], and opening fountains in the wilderness, and causing streams in the desert [Is. 35:6]; and innumerable places that might be mentioned.

This heavenly Jerusalem is called in this book "the paradise of God" (Rev. 2:7), and therefore is represented as having the tree of life growing in it (Rev. 22:2). And in its being represented as though a river ran through the midst of it, there seems to be some allusion to the ancient paradise in Eden, of which we are told that there ran a river through the midst of it to water it (Gen. 2:10), i.e., to supply the plants of it with nourishment. And this river was this very same river Euphrates, that afterwards ran through Babylon, and in both is typical of the supplies of two opposite cities. In Eden, it typified the spiritual supplies and wealth of the true Christian church; in the other, the outward carnal supplies and incomes of the false antichristian church.

And the wealth of the Church of Rome, is very much its defense, as it is of any kingdom whatsoever. After the streams of her wealth and revenues are dried up, her walls will be as it were broken down. She will soon grow contemptible. And if at any time she shews her pride and resentment, and assumes as she used to do, it will not be endured at her hands by the kings and great men of the world; but they will fall upon her and destroy her.

By the "kings of the East" [Rev. 16:12], here it is not necessary that we should understand kings that dwell towards the eastern part of the world; for it may be a mere allusion to the way of destroying old Babylon that was done by neighboring kings of the East. But this is applied to the spiritual Babylon. There is no need to understand it any otherwise than that it shall be done by neighboring princes, by the princes of Europe, the princes that have formerly agreed to give their kingdom to the beast, who we are told are the same "that shall make her desolate and naked, and shall eat her flesh, and burn her with fire, and that God shall put into their hearts to fulfill his will" (Rev. 17:16–17).[4] As 'tis said of Cyrus, a king of the East that destroyed Babylon: Is. 44:28, speaking of the destruction of Babylon, "That saith of Cyrus, He is my shepherd, and shall perform all my pleasure."

And as the judicious Lowman supposes this vial is to be poured out

4. The Messiah, according to JE, has a dual role similar to that of Cyrus: to defeat the spiritual Babylon and to build up the spiritual Jerusalem ("Blank Bible," p. 894).

sometime after the year 1700,[5] so it seems already to have begun to be poured out, the kings of Spain and Portugal having lately dried up two great branches of the river Euphrates, by withholding great part of those incomes and revenues the Pope used to have from those countries. The principal fulfillment of this vial, probably is taking from the Roman Catholic powers the Spanish West Indies, which is also probably prophesied of in Isaiah 60:9.[6]

This that has been mentioned, seems to me to be the thing principally intended by the sixth vial. But yet it don't appear to me altogether improbable, that it may also have respect to another thing, somewhat nearer a literal accomplishment (As the seven heads of the beast signified two very diverse things, and as the vial on the sun had a twofold accomplishment. See Lowman.);[7] and that is the destruction of the Turkish Empire, and so letting in the true religion into those territories that lie on the eastern borders of the popish empire, whereby the Pope will, as it were, be compassed round with the true religion. His kingdom of darkness will be encompassed round with light, by which means that darkness will be less capable of being long maintained, or that kingdom of darkness of being long subsisting. Probably the princes that will possess the countries now under the Turks, after the destruction of their empire, will be of the true religion; and that they will have a great hand in the overthrow of this spiritual Babylon.

The Turkish Empire may be called the river Euphrates upon several accounts. 1. They are a people that come from the regions about the river Euphrates, as is represented in this prophecy (ch. 9:14–15). 2. They bound the antichristian Roman Empire on the eastern side, as of old. Euphrates used to be the boundary of the heathen Roman Empire. Rome, as to her antichristian power, is limited on the east by the Turkish Empire, as formerly her power under the heathen emperors was limited towards that part of the world by the river Euphrates. When the Turks were loosed from the river Euphrates, and so were no longer

5. "This period must, according to the series of the vials, fall in, I think, within some time between the years 1700 and 1900" (*Paraphrase and Notes*, p. 200).

6. In 1737 the Spanish government concluded a concordat with Rome during the pontificate of Clement XII (1730–40) giving the crown patronage rights within the church as well as the power to tax the clergy. Similar concessions were soon granted to Portugal. For the effect of these moves on papal finances, see Ludwig Pastor, *The History of the Popes from the Close of the Middle Ages* (40 vols., London, 1891–1953), *34*, trans. & ed. by Ernest Graf, pp. 479–93. The Roman Catholic powers were never driven completely from the Spanish West Indies during the eighteenth century. See J. O. Lindsay, ed., *The Old Regime 1713–63*, Vol. 7 in *The New Cambridge Modern History* (Cambridge, Eng., 1957), pp. 514–28.

7. Above, pp. 173–174, nos. 5 and 7.

confined to the borders of the empire, but have made such encroachments as they have done, the waters of the river Euphrates, the ancient boundary of the empire, did as it were break their ancient banks and overflowed, and extended themselves even to the Adriatic Sea and the borders of Germany, to the great straitening of the limits of the Roman Empire. Thus of old, the river Euphrates was the eastern boundary that God had set to the dominion of the children of Israel. And therefore, when their territories were overrun by the people that dwelt upon that river, 'tis represented by the waters of that river breaking their ancient banks, and coming and overflowing the land of Israel. Is. 8:7–8, "Now therefore, behold, the Lord bringeth up upon them the waters of the river, strong and many, even the king of Assyria, and all his glory. And he shall come up over all his channels, and go over all his banks. And he shall pass through Judah. He shall overflow and go over. He shall reach even to the neck; and the stretching out of his wings, shall fill the breadth of thy land, O Immanuel."[8]

The river Euphrates seems to be spoken of under this vial, as something that had remained hitherto as a barrier on the frontiers of the Romish dominion, to keep out the enemies that were on the eastern side of it; which barrier would be removed when its waters should be dried up, and so the way for these eastern enemies prepared. The river Euphrates was a defense to the city of Babylon, not only at those places where it run under the wall in running through the city; but its waters encompassed the city all round, by filling that vast moat or ditch that was made without its walls. The waters of rivers were commonly so used to defend cities. Is. 37:25, "I have digged, and drunk water; and with the sole of my feet have I dried up the rivers of the besieged places." And rivers on the frontiers of countries, are often a defense or barrier to those countries. So Jordan was a barrier to the inhabitants of Canaan on the eastern side; and therefore, when the time of their destruction came, God dried up her waters to prepare the way for the children of Israel, their enemies. So the river Nilus was a defense to the land of Egypt, and as a barrier to great part of that country on the eastern side, to defend 'em from the Assyrians and Chaldeans. And therefore, when God gave that land to be destroyed by those people, 'tis represented as though their rivers and brooks of defense were dried up. Is. 19:4–6, "And the Egyptians will I give over into the hand of a cruel Lord; and a fierce king shall rule over them, saith the Lord, the Lord of Hosts. And the waters shall fail from the sea, and the river shall be wasted and dried

8. See JE's explanation of Is. 8:7–8 in no. 293 of the "Scripture" (Dwight ed., *9*, 374).

up. And they shall turn the rivers far away, and the brooks of defense shall be emptied and dried up, etc." (This drying up the rivers of Egypt, also signifies the failing of the wealth of Egypt, as appears by the following verses, and so confirms the other sense of the effect of this vial.) See also Nahum 3:8. "Art thou better than populous No, that was situate among the rivers, that had the waters round about it, whose rampart was the sea, and her wall was from the sea?"[9]

So when the Turkish Empire is destroyed—if it be destroyed before Antichrist—they of the Church of Rome will probably find that their barrier on that side is removed. For although the Turkish Empire was set up in anger to the Church of Rome, so probably it will be taken away in wrath against the same. For whenever the Mahometan Empire is destroyed, it will doubtless be to make way for the kingdom of Christ's taking place in the room of it. And therefore, we may suppose that the true religion will then take place in those countries now possessed of Mahometanism. But the kingdom of Antichrist will be greatly exposed by such a letting in of light into such vast regions of the earth neighboring to it. Darkness is, and has all along been, its defense; and the more the antichristian empire is encompassed with darkness, the more secure it is.

This accomplishment of the pouring out the sixth vial, seems also to be already begun. The Turkish Empire has been weakening, ever since the Prince Eugene's famous victory over the Turks [in] 1697. They have been now for a long time greatly weakened by the Persians, and by the Muscovites under the late czar. But more especially in their present wars with the Turks, have they had extraordinary successes against them.[1] So their empire seems to [be] tottering and in greater danger of ruin than ever it has been. And probably the Russians, and the powers they may set up in Turkey when they have subdued it, are intended by the kings of the East spoken of. They are an eastern people. All their dominions are further east than the dominions of the bishop of Rome. They are as much an eastern people, with respect to the antichristian empire, as the Medes were with respect to the Babylonish. Their capital is much further east than Constantinople; and their dominions extend east, even to the borders of China. And they are not of the Romish

9. The last two sentences are a later addition.
1. See p. 165, n. 4, concerning Eugene's victory. Peter the Great (1672–1725) as czar worked to weaken the Turks. In the Russo-Turkish War of 1735–39, the Russians successfully invaded the Crimea, but most of their territorial gains were sacrificed in the Treaty of Constantinople which ended the conflict.

religion, and of late are much reformed. Their country is of late become much more a land of light than it was. They agree much more with the Protestants than the papists, and 'tis hopeful the reformation among them will yet be carried to a much greater height.[2] These, after their dominion is set up in the Turkish Empire, will probably join in with those princes of Europe that shall be the enemies of the whore, and greatly contribute to her destruction, when the days come that the kings that have formerly given their dominion to the beast shall hate the whore, and burn her with fire. And possibly the emperor of Muscovy, who lives to the northeast, is meant in Isaiah 41:25. See note in the place, "Scripture" no. 331.[3] See no. 89.[4] See also p. 253, this mark*.[5]

79. CHAPTER 14:8; CHAPTER 17:5; and CHAPTER 18:2. "Mystery, Babylon the great." "Babylon the great is fallen, etc."[6] The antichristian church is fitly called Babylon, as upon other accounts, so upon this, that Babylon was once Eden or the paradise of God. Eden was in the country of Babylonia, which was a type of the church of God. That city of God described in the two last chapters of Revelation, that is called the paradise of God, having the tree of life growing in and a river running through it, as the Garden of Eden had, which was the same river than ran through Babylon, that great city was Eden, or paradise turned into Babel. So this spiritual Babylon is the church of Christ apostatized, and turned into the antichristian church.

80. CHAPTER 8:10 and CHAPTER 16:4. That by "rivers and fountains of waters" is meant their chief cities and countries that are original seats of empire, fountains of power and dominion, according to Mr. Lowman is confirmed by II Samuel 12:27, where Rabbah, the chief city of the Ammonites, is called the "city of waters."[7]

2. The reforms in Muscovy under Peter the Great included the westernization of Russian culture and a program of attacks upon religious institutions. According to JE, "This emperor gave great encouragement to the exercise of the Protestant religion in his dominions." JE used these materials in the series of sermons on the *History of Redemption* in 1739. See Worcester rev. ed., *1*, 467–68.

3. JE explained Is. 41:25 in part as a reference to Cyrus, who destroyed Babylon. "But yet the Holy Ghost seems principally to have an eye here to some other prince, an antitype of Cyrus, that shall come from the northeast to destroy the spiritual Babylon, or antichristian church, which shall be raised up at the time when that glory shall be accomplished for the church." According to JE, the emperor of Muscovy fits the interpretation. See no. 331 of the "Scripture" (printed in Dwight ed., *9*, 388–89).

4. MS: "Here add Num. 89."

5. The last four short sentences are later additions.

6. In the "Blank Bible," p. 892, JE wrote, "Why the antichristian church is called 'Babylon,' see Rev. no. 79." See also no. 329 in the "Scripture" (Dwight ed., *9*, 534–35).

7. *Paraphrase and Notes*, p. 75.

81. CHAPTER 16:8–9. "And the fourth angel poured out his vial upon the sun: and power was given unto him to scorch men with fire, and men were scorched with great heat." There is all reason in the world to suppose with Mr. Lowman, that by the sun here must be meant the Pope, or the papacy, or the papal power.[8] For these vials are vials of wrath poured out on the papal kingdom, or antichristian world. By the luminaries of heaven, when spoken of in scripture prophecy with respect to the world of men in general, or with respect to a particular kingdom or empire, is meant the powers and authorities of the world or of that kingdom; as the luminaries of the literal heavens were wont among the heathen, to be worshiped as the authorities or gods of the world [that] governed all things here below. And among those, the chief is the sun; and therefore, anciently the sun used to be worshiped as the chief god. Now who is it therefore, that can be meant by the sun in the papal world, but the Pope? Who is he that has the chief authority in the papal kingdom, but the king or head of that kingdom? Who is he in the antichristian world, that is as the sun was in the heathen world, in which he is worshiped as the chief god, but only he that sitteth in the temple of God, shewing himself that he is God, and exalting himself above all that is called God or is worshiped?

And beside, we know that *Christ* has the place of the sun in the true church; he is called the Sun of Righteousness. And he often tells us that he is the light of the world [John 8:12], and "the true light that lighteth every man that cometh into the world" [John 1:9]. And therefore, who is he that is the sun of the false church, but *Antichrist*, he that pretends to be the vicar of Christ? In the description of the city of Jerusalem, in the two last chapters of this prophecy, we are told that the Lamb is instead of a sun. Ch. 21:23, They have "no need of the sun, for the Lamb is the light thereof." And therefore, who can be the sun in Babylon, the city that is opposite to Jerusalem, but Antichrist, the head of that church?

By this sun's scorching men with fire [ch. 16:8], is [meant], as Mr. Lowman observes, the popes' afflicting and tormenting their subjects by the use of their papal authority and the exercise of their pride, ambition, avarice and resentment.[9] And it seems to me probable, that the Holy Spirit among other ways, had an eye to this in particular, viz., their pursuing those that they were displeased with with the thunder and lightning of their excommunications and curses, which they rep-

8. Ibid., pp. 189–90.
9. Ibid.

resent as fire from heaven, i.e., as the wrath and curse of God, which is in Scripture so represented. For they suppose that they have the command of the fire of God's eternal wrath, to bring it down on any man's head they please. And these papal excommunications and curses, are called fire from heaven in this prophecy (ch. 13:13). Thus in the time of the Great Schism in the popish church,[1] when there was for a long time two and sometimes three popes at once, which was the time, according to Mr. Lowman, when this vial was poured out, these antipopes excommunicated and cursed one another, and all that adhered to them, and by this means kept all Europe in a flame, and brought innumerable distressing calamities on those that were of the antichristian church.

82. CHAPTER 16:10. The 5th Vial.[2] "And the fifth angel poured out his vial upon the *throne* of the beast (as it is in the original):[3] and his kingdom was full of darkness, and they gnawed their tongues for pain." The vial of God's wrath is poured out on the throne of the beast, i.e., on his authority and dominion, to weaken it and to diminish it, both in extent and degree. And their policy shall fail them, to maintain and support it. God will scatter darkness before them. They that have the management of the affair of the beast's kingdom, will stumble and be confounded in the enterprises, purposes and management of the affairs of the kingdom; as if the kingdom were full of darkness, and they could not see whither they went. Formerly their policy was successful; [it] was a light to guide 'em to attain their ends. But now they shall be like them that grope in the dark, signifying that all their wisdom and policy shall fail them in their endeavors to overthrow that by which their throne, their power and extent of their dominion shall be diminished. The Scripture takes notice of the great policy and subtilty of the powers that shall support this kingdom. Dan. 7:8, "And, behold, in this horn were eyes like the eyes of a man." So it is said of Antiochus Epiphanes, that great type of Antichrist. Dan. 8:23, "A king of fierce countenance, and understanding dark sentences, shall stand up." And v. 25, "And through his policy also, he shall cause craft to prosper in his hand." This understanding and policy is the light of this kingdom, as true wisdom is the light of the spiritual Jerusalem. And therefore, when this light fails them, then may the kingdom of this spiritual Egypt be said to be full of darkness; and they are hindered by it from per-

1. I.e., 1378–1417.
2. JE headed the pages of this entry with "The 5th Vial on the Throne of the Beast."
3. ἐπὶ τὸν θρόνον τοῦ θηρίου.

forming their enterprising, as the Egyptians were hindered from accomplishing anything or rising from their place, during that three days that the kingdom of Egypt was subject to the plague of darkness [Ex. 10:21–23].

The reformed church shall be defended from the fierce and violent designs of the men of that city, that is spiritually called Sodom (Rev. 11:8), as Lot's house, wherein were the angels, was defended from the Sodomites by their being smitten with blindness, so that they wearied themselves to find the door (Gen. 19:11). And as the city in which Elisha, the prophet and witness of the Lord, was defended from the Syrians, when they compassed it about with horses and chariots and a great host to apprehend him, by smiting them with blindness (II Kings 6:18). And as Elymas the sorcerer, who is said to be "full of all subtilty and mischief, a child of the devil, an enemy of all righteousness, that ceased not to pervert the right ways of the Lord," was smitten with blindness, so that "there fell on him a mist and darkness," that he could not see the sun; "and he went about seeking somebody to lead him by the hand," when he withstood the apostles Paul and Barnabas, seeking to turn away the deputy from the faith [Acts 13:6–12].

So God defended the children of Israel from Pharaoh the king, and from the army of Egypt, the country that is spoken of as a type of the antichristian church (ch. 11:8), when they pursued the children of Israel, after they had been partly delivered on the night of the Passover, before their complete deliverance when they came up out of the Red Sea. The pillar of cloud and fire, was a cloud and darkness to the Egyptians, so that they could not come near God's people to destroy them (Ex. 14:20[4] and Josh. 24:7). Ps. 35:4, 6, "Let them be confounded and put to shame that seek after my soul; let them be turned back and brought to confusion that devise my hurt; let their way be dark and slippery."

The Scripture teaches us, that God is wont in this way to defend his church and people from their crafty and powerful enemies. Job 5:11–15, "To set up on high those that be low, that those which mourn may be exalted to safety. He disappointeth the devices of the crafty, so that their hands cannot perform their enterprise. He taketh the wise in their own craftiness, and the counsel of the froward is carried headlong. They meet with darkness in the daytime, and grope in the noonday as in the night. But he saveth the poor from the sword, from their mouth, and from the hand of the mighty."

4. See JE's comments on Ex. 14:20 in the "Blank Bible," p. 59.

The church that was kept before under the power of the throne of the beast, shall now be out of his reach. The same that is spoken of here, as God's church's being secured by their enemies being smitten with blindness or covered with darkness, is signified (Rev. 11:12) by the witnesses being taken up to heaven in a cloud in the sight of their enemies, where they were out of their reach;[5] as the security of the godly from their enemies in the forementioned 5th chapter of Job, is in the 11th verse expressed by their being "set up on high," and by their enemies being confounded in darkness in the following verses.

Upon this account, "they gnaw their tongues for pain" [Rev. 16:10]. To have their dominion and authority so diminished by a revival of the church, and prevailing of the people of God, and to see them maintaining their ground, and remaining out of their reach while they are so confounded in all their politic and crafty devices and furious attempts against them, and to see 'em yet subsisting in an independency on them, in spite of all that they can do, will make 'em, as it were, bite their tongues for mere rage and vexation, agreeable to Psalms 112:9–10. "His righteousness endureth forever; his horn shall be exalted with honor. The wicked shall see it, and be grieved; he shall gnash with his teeth, and melt away. The desire of the wicked shall perish."

Thus their kingdom hath actually been filled with darkness; and they have been confounded in their devices and attempt to overthrow the Protestant church, from the first Reformation till their great frustration by King William and Queen Mary.[6] Remember when I have opportunity, and observe what particular events in history answer to the expression of "gnawing their tongues for pain," and particularly whether or no there are not instances of their executing their malice one on another under their disappointments, laying the blame to their own friends and true servants.[7] See no. 87.

83. [CHAPTER 16:13–21.] See no. 77.[8] That the calling of the Jews will not be till after the first and main destruction of Antichrist, appears

5. The safety of the saints, according to JE, is analogous to the security of Christ after his ascension: "The church shall come to such a state, that Antichrist by his persecutions shall not be able to suppress or destroy her" ("Blank Bible," p. 743).

6. William of Orange (1650–1702), a Protestant noted for his hostility to France, became co-sovereign of England with Mary his wife in 1689 at the invitation of Parliament. At the Battle of the Boyne he defeated the forces of the Stuart House and James II, a Roman Catholic.

7. In the "Blank Bible," p. 893, JE wrote, "They shall in their rage gnash their teeth; but those that they are enraged with, being out of their reach, they shall bite nothing but their tongues, and so instead of revenging their pain, they shall increase it."

8. MS: "Add this to Numb. 77."

pretty manifest to me by the following things. 1. Christ says that Jerusalem, after its destruction by the Romans, should "be trodden down of
the Gentiles, till the times of the Gentiles should be fulfilled" [Luke
21:24], meaning by "the times of the Gentiles" the same with the "time
and times and an half" [Rev. 12:14], and the same with the forty-two
months in the Revelation that Antichrist should tread down the spiritual
Jerusalem [Rev. 11:2]. See notes on Luke 21:24; and also Matt. 24:21
ff., "Scripture" no. 292.[9] So that the desolation of Judea by Rome or the
mystical Babylon, is in this respect to agree with its desolation by the
literal Babylon. The people were not restored till after Babylon, that
carried them captive, was destroyed by its first destruction, that destruction that was mainly respected in the prophecies, which seems to [be] a
type of the second restitution from the destruction by the mystical Babylon, or idolatrous Rome.

2. In the beginning of the 50th chapter of Jeremiah, both the restitu-
tions of Israel, that from literal Babylon and that from mystical Babylon,
seem to be spoken of under one; as is evident by the 4th verse, where
something is foretold concerning their restitution which was not accomplished, or at least accomplished but in a very low degree, in the
first restitution, viz., that both Judah and Israel should return together.
"In those days and in that time, saith the Lord, the children of Israel
shall come, they and the children of Judah together, going and weeping;
they shall go, and seek the Lord, etc."—speaking there of the destruction of Babylon. Therefore, inasmuch as this restitution that includes
both is spoken of as soon after the destruction of Babylon, therefore both
are to be after the destructions of these several Babylons that caused
their desolations.

And it seems by what the Apostle says, Romans 11:15. "For if the
casting away of them be the reconciling of the world, what shall the
receiving [of] them be, but life from the dead?" I say, by this it seems
that the world of the Gentiles shall be, as it were, revived from the dead
after this. By which it appears, that very great events for the advancement of religion and the kingdom of Christ shall be accomplished after
the calling of the Jews, which shall be extensive, that it may be called a
reviving of the world from the dead. And this last event must doubtless
be before the millennium begins. Probably it will be thus. First, Turkey

9. In the discussion of Luke 21:24 JE concludes, "Hence we may infer, that Antichrist will
fall and the Jews be called about the same time" ("Blank Bible," p. 732). In no. 292 he states
that the tribulation of the literal and the spiritual Jerusalem will continue until the fall of
Antichrist (Dwight ed., *9*, 458).

in Europe shall be overthrown, and the true religion established in those parts of Europe possessed by the Turks, which will be accomplished in pouring out the 6th vial. Concerning which, see no. 78. Nextly, Antichrist shall be overthrown, and the true religion embraced by the nations that formerly were the subjects of Antichrist. And perhaps religion shall begin to be gloriously propagated among heathen. Thirdly, the Jews shall be called.[1] And fourth, this will be succeeded by an universal propagation of religion through the vast regions of the earth, that had been many ages covered with ignorance and darkness, and had as it were lain dead in paganish and Mahometan barbarism and brutality (which are to revive from the dead, after this calling of the Jews), and [by] the last great battle, wherein the remains of Antichrist, Mahometanism and heathenism shall be united and shall be conquered. Which victory shall be the revival of the world from the dead, and is the first resurrection spoken of in Revelation 20. And then the millennium shall begin.

84. [CHAPTERS 21 and 22.] See no. 59.[2] That the things spoken of in the 21st and 22nd chapters of Revelation, concerning the new heavens and new earth, are fulfilled in different degrees, both in the glorious state of the church on earth before the last judgment, and also its state of consummate glory in heaven after the judgment, may be argued from this: that the new heavens and new earth, when spoken of elsewhere in Scripture, are in some places evidently meant of one, and in others of the other. When Isaiah speaks both of the new heavens and new earth, and also [of] the New Jerusalem (Is. 65:17–19 ff.), he evidently has respect to a glorious state of the church before the end of the world. It appears by verse 20. "The child shall die an hundred years old." And v. 21, "They shall build houses, and inhabit them: they shall plant vineyards, and eat the fruit of them." And so by many passages in this and the next chapter, which is a continuation of the same prophecy.[3] So when the prophet Ezekiel foretells of the New Jerusalem, he evidently

1. In the "Blank Bible," p. 806, JE wrote concerning the calling of the Jews, "So Christ's redemption and the glorious prophecies of the blessed fruits of it to Israel, respects mainly the spiritual Israel; yet through God's abundant grace, and that all things may be restored by Christ, in due time the external and literal Israel shall be restored by him. So likewise, as something equivalent to the restoration of the body, not only shall the spiritual state of the Jews be hereafter restored, but their external state in a nation, in their own land."

2. MS: "Add this to Num 59."

3. For example, JE wrote on Is. 66:1, "The glorious times shall come wherein the whole habitable world shall be blessed with honorable tokens of God's presence" ("Blank Bible," p. 525).

has respect to a glorious state of the church in this world [Ezek. 40–48]. But when the apostle Peter speaks of the new heavens and new earth, he has respect chiefly to the glorious state of the church after the end of the world, as is manifest by the context (II Pet. 3:13). So when the apostle Paul speaks of the Christian and spiritual Jerusalem, he calls heaven so (Gal. 4:26 and Heb. 12:22).[4]

85. CHAPTER 21. See no. 73a.[5] When the new heavens and new earth is spoken of [v. 1], thereby is meant the church with the spiritual things that appertain to it, or that concern its glorious state that it's brought into by the great restoration of Jesus Christ. But yet heaven, or the world which is the place in which the church shall dwell, and enjoy this glorious, renewed, restored state, is not to be excluded, but may also be supposed to be one thing meant by the new heavens and new earth. Like as when the New Jerusalem is spoken of [v. 2], thereby is meant Christ's spiritual Jerusalem or his redeemed church; but yet thereby is also meant heaven, the city which is the place where this church shall dwell, as is evident because heaven is often compared to a city, and is called the Mount Zion and heavenly Jerusalem in the 12th [chapter] of Hebrews.

86. CHAPTER 11:6. "These have power to shut heaven, that it rain not in the days of their prophecy: and have power over the waters, to turn them to blood; and to smite the earth with all plagues, as often as they will." These plagues that it is here intimated should be executed by the two witnesses on their enemies, during the days of their prophecy in sackcloth, in all likelihood are the same plagues that are mentioned in the 16th chapter, that were executed under the vials of the seven ages, which are called the seven plagues and the seven last plagues (ch. 15:1, 6, 8). Two of the plagues there mentioned, do consist in turning waters into blood, the same as one that is here mentioned. In the three first of these plagues, there is an allusion to the plagues of Egypt [Ex. 7–12]. So in what is here said of these two witnesses, there seems to be an allusion to Moses and Aaron smiting the land of Egypt with so many plagues during the bondage of God's people in Egypt, the type of the Church of Rome, and under Pharaoh, the type of Antichrist. This is an argument that some of those plagues were executed before the Reformation;[6] for the time of the prophecy of those two witnesses (so small a number) in sackcloth, was chiefly before the Reformation.

4. See JE's comments on Gal. 4:25–26 in the "Blank Bible," p. 837, and a full discussion of Heb. 12 on pp. 871–72.

5. MS: "add this to Num. 73a."

6. For JE's early view of this, see p. 115, n. 9.

And [it] was during that time chiefly that they executed that plague here spoken of, viz., of its not raining. For then, above all times after Christ's incarnation, were spiritual showers withheld from the earth.

87. CHAPTER 16:10–11. "And the 5th angel poured out his vial on the seat of the beast; and his kingdom was full of darkness; and they gnawed their tongues for pain, and blasphemed the God of heaven because of their pains and their sores, and repented not of their deeds." They blasphemed that holy religion of Christ, that gospel that had been the occasion of their sores and plagues. They were abundant in their solemn curses and anathemas pronounced against [it]. They cursed this holy religion of Jesus as from hell and as the religion of the devil, and damned all that professed it. Herein they did in effect blaspheme God, whose gospel this was. God looked on these curses as against him; 'tis against that Holy Spirit whose work [is] this religion. They thus cursed and blasphemed with great malice and spite, because it diminished their authority and glory, and contradicted their pride and avarice and other lusts, and was as a grievous sore and plague to them. And probably many of them did it against light, and so were guilty of the blasphemy against the Holy Ghost, as probably it was with Stephen Gardiner, a persecutor in England in Queen Mary's days.[7]

Thus the beast blasphemes, agreeable to what is said in Revelation 13:6. "And he opened his mouth in blasphemy against God, to blaspheme his name, and his tabernacle, and them that dwell in heaven." It appears by the words we are upon, that they were stirred up with rage to blaspheme that which tormented them. This was the reformed religion, and the gospel of Jesus Christ. Blasphemy in the New Testament, is commonly intended in this sense, a blaspheming God's people and the true religion; and this is called a blaspheming God.

"They repented not of their deeds" [Rev. 16:11]. Their impenitence and obstinacy, or their wicked deeds, especially appeared by what they did in the Council of Trent, presently after light was so clearly held forth to them by Luther and other servants of God, and they had been reproved and warned by them. Instead of reforming the church of its corruptions, this council only established and confirmed these corruptions, and added to them, and blasphemed God, [and] cursed the reformers and the reformed religion.[8]

7. Gardiner (c. 1490–1555), the Bishop of Winchester, was a leading opponent of the Protestant Reformation in England. He was imprisoned during Edward VI's reign but restored at the time of Mary and made Lord High Chancellor.

8. See Worcester rev. ed., *1*, 463, for JE's use of this paragraph in his sermons on the *History of Redemption.*

88. CHAPTER 14:8. "Babylon is fallen, is fallen." So chapters 16:19 and 18:2. The fall of Satan's visible kingdom on earth, even the whole of it, may fitly be called the fall of Babylon. For this visible kingdom began in the building of Babylon or Babel, and from thence it has spread abroad into all the earth. The whole world, as it were, belongs to those two cities that are opposite one to another, viz., Jerusalem and Babylon.

89. See no. 78.[9] CHAPTER 16:12. "And the sixth angel poured out his vial on the river Euphrates, etc." This seems also, in the third place, to have relation to that preparing of the way for Christ and his hosts, that is often spoken of in Scripture, as what shall be before the beginning of the glorious times of the church. Mountains shall be, as it were, leveled, and valleys exalted, and rivers dried up, to prepare the way for this glorious king of his church to come with his angels, the principalities and powers in heavenly places, and his ministers and saints, whom he has made kings and priests, to come and destroy Babylon, to prepare the way for that glorious king and those hosts that are with him, that we read of in the 19th chapter of Revelation, in that expedition of theirs against Antichrist that we there read of. These may be called "kings of the East" [Rev. 16:12] because Christ, the head of the whole army and King of Kings, was born and lived and died in the East. This vial has probably respect to the removal of the impediments that had before been in the way of the prevailing of the gospel. Those difficulties at which God's people used to stick, and particularly great and perplexing difficulties in the doctrines of religion—those being removed shall wonderfully prepare the way for Christ and his armies going forward to the destruction of their enemies, as the drying up of the river Jordan, that was an impediment in the way of Christ and his armies coming into Canaan to destroy their enemies there. But when this was dried up, the ark, and Joshua or Jesus, and the hosts of the Lord, came from the east and destroyed Jericho and the Amorites and the kings of Canaan with a mighty overthrow.[1]

This vial seems to have relation to the same thing with that spoken of in the 40th [chapter] of Isaiah. Vv. 3–5, "Prepare ye the way of the Lord; make straight in the desert an highway for our God. Every valley shall be exalted, and every mountain and hill shall be made low. And the crooked shall be made straight, and rough places plain. And the

9. MS: "This in addition to 78."

1. JE discussed the typological significance of the Jordan River with reference to the 6th vial in the "Blank Bible," pp. 174–75.

glory of the Lord shall be revealed, and all flesh shall see it together."
And Mal. 3:1, "Behold, I will send my messenger, and he shall prepare
the way before me." And Is. 42:15–16, "I will make waste mountains
and hills, and dry up all their herbs; and I will make the *rivers* islands;
and I will dry up the pools. And I will bring the blind by a way that
they knew not; I will lead them in paths that they have not known. I
will make darkness light before them, and crooked things straight.
These things will I do unto them, and not forsake them." And that Is.
11:15–16, "And the Lord shall utterly destroy the tongue of the Egyptian sea; and with his mighty wind shall he shake his hand over the
river, and shall smite it on the seven streams thereof, and make men go
over dryshod. And there shall be an highway for the remnant of his
people, which shall be left, from Assyria, like as it was to Israel in the
day that he came up out of the land of Egypt." And Is. 57:14, "Cast ye
up, cast ye up, prepare the way; take up the stumbling block out of the
way of my people." And Is. 62:10, "Go through, go through the gates;
prepare ye the way of the people. Cast up, cast up the highway; gather
out the stones; lift up a standard for the people." And Zech. 10:10–12,
"I will bring them again also out of the land of Egypt, and gather them
out of Assyria: and I will bring them into the land of Gilead and
Lebanon; and place shall not be found for them. And he shall pass
through the sea with affliction, and shall smite the waves of the sea; and
all the deeps of the river shall dry up. And the pride of Assyria shall be
brought down, and the scepter of Egypt shall depart away. And I will
strengthen them in the Lord; and they shall walk up and down in his
name, saith the Lord." See no. 91.[2]

90. CHAPTER 11:7–8 ff. The Slaying of the Witnesses.[3] I. The slaying
of the two witnesses is not a thing that yet remains to be accomplished,
at least in its principal accomplishment. 1. For if it yet remains to be
accomplished, it doubtless is to be in that great and last conflict, that
the church is to have with her enemies before the destruction of Antichrist. And so their ascending into heaven [Rev. 11:12], is to be accomplished in that glory of the church, that is to follow the destruction
of Antichrist. And the tenth part of the city falling [Rev. 11:13], signifies the downfall of Antichrist itself. And their ascending up to heaven in
a cloud, must signify the church's rising to that glorious state, that it

2. MS: "Add to this N. 91."
3. JE titled the pages of the entry with these words. His letter to William McCulloch, Mar.
5, 1744 (Dwight ed., *1*, 211–19), contains a parallel discussion. See also HA; below, pp. 378–
94.

shall be in when Antichrist shall fall. And we must suppose that it will be as it was in Constantine's time. As soon as that last and severest persecution by the heathen empire was ended, the heathen empire fell; and the church's glory and triumph followed.[4] And by that great earthquake spoken of (v. 13), wherein the tenth part of the city fell, must be the same earthquake with that spoken of (ch. 16:18), which was in the pouring out of the seventh vial, and attended or was the issue of that last battle of Christ's enemies with his church, by which "the great city was divided into three parts, and the cities of the nations fell, etc." [Rev. 16:19].

If the slaying of the witnesses and the things that shall attend it and be consequent upon it, remain yet to be accomplished, the accomplishment must needs be at that time and in those things. For the witnesses are slain in some great conflict that there shall be between the church and her enemies, and particularly in a great conflict with Antichrist or the beast, as appears by verse 7. "And when they shall have finished their testimony, the beast that ascendeth out of the bottomless pit, shall make war against them, and shall overcome them, and kill them." This making war, if it yet remains to be accomplished, doubtless signifies some great battle, some mighty battle, that shall be between Antichrist and the church. But if there were yet to be any such great conflict before the last that shall be, before the pouring of the seventh vial, 'tis not credible that no hint should be given of it in the 16th chapter of Revelation, where we have such an account in an orderly succession, of the great events by [which] Christ shall overthrow that kingdom of Antichrist and those great struggles by which they shall endeavor to uphold themselves. Mr. Lowman has made it plain, that all the vials are poured out but two.[5] And therefore, if there yet remains such a great conflict between Antichrist and the church, the issue of which shall be so very great, if the beast shall therein make war with the church or witnesses, and overcome them and kill them, and shall so greatly triumph over them, what *battle* can this be, but that mentioned in the 14th and 16th verses of the 16th chapter? "For they are the spirits of devils, working miracles, which go forth unto the kings of the earth and of the whole world, to gather them together to the *battle* of the great day of God Almighty. And he gathered them together unto [a] place called, in the Hebrew tongue, Armageddon." Where else is there any room for such a great conflict, or such a mighty event, under these

---

4. The last two sentences are a later addition.
5. For example, *Paraphrase and Notes*, pp. xxxii–xxxiii. See also above, p. 23.

two last vials? For the time of both these vials seems, at least great part of the time of both, to be taken up about that last great battle, the one in the preparation for it, and the other in the battle itself and the event of it.

And besides, if this battle wherein the witnesses shall be slain yet remains, it must [be] that last great battle; because after that is over, and the church has lain, as it were, dead three days and an half, it rises from the dead and ascends into heaven. And according to those that are in this scheme, the glorious times of the church do then begin. Therefore, by this scheme, this "making war" of the beast with the witnesses, must be the same "making war" with that which we read of in the 19th chapter of Revelation. V. 19, "And I saw the beast, and the kings of the earth, and their armies, gathered together to make war against him that sat on the horse, and against his army."

But this making war of the beast against the witnesses, cannot be the same with that great and last battle of Antichrist with the church. And therefore, it don't remain yet to be accomplished. They cannot be the same, for the things are said of one and the other; and their issue are in no wise compatible one with another. For in that last great battle, there is no appearance of such a sort of conflict of the church with her enemies in such sorrow. The armies of heaven don't conflict in blood, but in white raiment, betokening victory. Christ himself don't conflict in blood. His garments indeed are dipped in blood, but that is only in the blood of his enemies (Rev. 19:13).[6] But he is represented as coming forth to this battle in great pomp and magnificence, on a white horse, and on his head many crowns, and "on his vesture and on his thigh a name written, King of Kings and Lord of Lords" [Rev. 19:16]. And the saints that fight in this battle under him are represented, not as fighting in sorrow and blood, but in strength, glory and triumph. In their conflict with Antichrist before, they are represented as having their garments stained with their own blood; and therefore, when they get to heaven, they are represented as coming "out of great tribulation," having "washed their robes" and making them "white in the blood of the Lamb" (Rev. 7:14). But when they come forth to this last battle, they are represented as coming forth on "white horses, clothed in fine linen, white and clean" (Rev. 19:14).

6. In the "Blank Bible," p. 895, JE expressed a different opinion: "One thing that confirms me that the design here is not only to represent Christ's garment as dipped in the blood of his enemies, but also dipped in his own blood, was Joseph's garments being dipped in the blood of the kid that was slain in his room; in which affair Joseph was without doubt a type of Christ."

2. The event[7] of these two conflicts are quite the reverse, one of the other. In the conflict spoken of [in] chapter 11, the beast makes war with the witnesses, and overcomes them and kills them. The same is foretold in the 7th [chapter] of Daniel. V. 21, "I beheld, and the same horn made war with the saints, and prevailed against them." And Rev. 13:7, "And it was given unto him to make war with the saints, and to overcome them." But the issue of that last battle, that the church shall have with her enemies, is quite the reverse of this, in that the church shall overcome them. Rev. 17:14, "These shall make war with the Lamb, and the Lamb shall overcome them: for he is Lord of Lords, and King of Kings. And they that are with him are called, and chosen, and faithful." Compared with ch. 19:16 and following verses, and ch. 16:16–17. In the conflict that the beast shall have with the witnesses, [he] kills[8] them, and their dead bodies lie unburied, as if it were to be meat for the beasts of the earth and fowls of heaven [Rev. 11:7–9]. But in that last conflict, Christ and his church shall slay their enemies, and give their dead bodies to be meat for the fowls of heaven (ch. 19:17 ff.).[9]

There is no manner of appearance in the descriptions that are given of that last great battle, of any great advantages gained in it against the church, before they themselves are overcome, but all appearance of the contrary before. The descriptions in the 16th and 19th chapters of Revelation, will by no means allow of such an advantage as that, [namely,] the overcoming and slaying the church, and their lying dead for some time and unburied, that their dead bodies might be for their enemies to abuse and trample on and make sport with. In the 16th [chapter] of Revelation, we have an account of their being gathered together into the place called Armageddon; and then the first thing we hear of after that, is the pouring out of the seventh vial of God's wrath, and a voice saying, It is done [vv. 16–17]. And so in the 19th chapter, we have an account of the beast and the kings of the earth and their armies, being gathered together to make war against him that sat on the horse, and against his army. And then the next thing we hear of, is that the beast is taken, etc. (vv. 19–21). The event of the conflict of the beast with the witnesses, is the triumph of the church's

7. I.e., the results.
8. MS: "~~the~~ & kills."
9. JE wrote in the "Blank Bible," p. 895, "As David, when he fought with Goliath, said that he would give the carcasses of the hosts of the Philistines unto the fowls of the air, etc., so Christ, the true David, now calls on the fowls of the air to come to devour the carcasses of the enemies of his church."

enemies: when they of the peoples and kindreds and tongues and nations, "and they that dwell on the earth," shall see the dead bodies of the saints lying in the streets of the great city, and "shall rejoice over them, and make merry, and send gifts one to another" [Rev. 11:10]. But the event of that great and last battle, is quite the reverse, even the church triumphing over their enemies as being utterly destroyed. The church of God in this great invasion, in Ezekiel 38:8, 14, 39:29, are represented as dwelling safely; that the invasion there spoken [of], is the same as in Revelation 16 and 19, see "Scripture" no. 433, Book 3.[1]

3. These events that are consequent on the issue of the war with the witnesses, as described in the 11th chapter, do in no wise answer those that are represented as consequent on that last conflict of Antichrist with the church. 'Tis said that when the witnesses ascended into heaven, the same hour there was a great earthquake [Rev. 11:13]. But this don't seem to answer to what is described in chapter 16:18. "And there were voices and thunders and lightning; and there was a great earthquake, such as was not since men were upon the earth, so mighty an earthquake, and so great." 'Tis said that at the time of the first earthquake, that "the tenth part of the city fell" (Rev. 11:13). But how far does this fall short of what is described as attending the great earthquake. Ch. 16:19–20, "And the great city was divided into three parts, and the cities of the nations fell. And great Babylon came in remembrance before God, to give unto her the cup of the wine of the fierceness of his wrath. And every island fled away, and the mountains were not found." 'Tis said that of the earthquake, "and in the earthquake were slain of men seven thousand" (ch. 11:13). But how far is this from answering the slaughter, that is described (ch. 19:17 ff.). This seems a general slaughter of all God's enemies through the world, who are represented as gathered together against the church (chs. 16:14 and 19:19). But who can think that this, which is set forth in these places by such great expressions, should in the 11th chapter be called slaying seven thousand men?

4. If we read this very 11th chapter through, we shall see that the falling of the tenth part of the city, and the rising of the witnesses, and their standing on their feet and ascending into heaven [vv. 11–13], are

1. This sentence is a later addition. No. 433 suggests that the prophecy concerning Gog and Magog (Ezek. 38–39) refers to two battles in the Revelation: the conflict between the church and her enemies preceding the millennium and the struggle between the same foes immediately before the end of the world. The church emerges victorious from both, in contrast with her defeat at the time of the slaying of the witnesses. See Dwight ed., *9*, 409–12.

represented as entirely distinct from the accomplishment of the glorious state of the church, which shall be in the latter days. The judgments here spoken of as executed on God's enemies, are under another woe; and the benefits bestowed on the church, are under another trumpet. For immediately after the account of the rising and ascending of the witnesses, and the tenth part of the cities falling, and the slaying of seven thousand men, and the affrighting the rest, and their giving glory to the God of heaven, follow these words in the 14th and 15th verses: "The second woe is past; and behold, the third woe cometh quickly. And the seventh angel sounded; and there were great voices in heaven, saying, The kingdoms of this world are become the kingdoms of our Lord and of his Christ, and he shall reign forever and ever." And then in the following verses, we have an account of the praises sung to God on this occasion. And then in the last verse, we have a brief hint of that same earthquake, and that great hail, and those thunders, lightnings and voices that we have an account of in the latter part of the 16th chapter.

So that the earthquake mentioned in the last verse of the 11th chapter, is that great earthquake that attends the last great conflict of the church and her enemies, and not that mentioned in the 13th verse.

Neither can we reasonably suppose that those calamities and wars on God's enemies, signified by the falling of the tenth part of the city, and the slaying seven thousand men, are here spoken by way of anticipation among things that belong to the second woe, by reason of their relation to those other things, when indeed they belong to the third woe. For the words of the 14th verse will by no means allow such a supposition. For there, immediately after giving an account of those calamities, it is added, "The second woe is past; and behold, the third woe cometh quickly," making a most plain and express distinction between those calamities that had been already mentioned, and especially those that were just then mentioned in the very last words, and the calamities that belong to the third woe, that yet remain to be mentioned. For "being past," the prophet is to be understood [as intending] no other than "past" in the narration or representation; for it was not past any otherwise. And 'tis as much as to say, that an account has been given of the calamities of the second woe; now I proceed to give an account of the third woe, which shall soon follow it.

II. The time wherein the witnesses lay dead in the street of the great city [ch. 11:8–9], was doubtless the time wherein the true church of

Christ is lowest of all, and yields most to the power and prevalence of Antichrist, and has least of visibility, and is nighest of all extinct, and wherein there appears least hope of its ever flourishing anymore. Before this, they prophesied in sackcloth, but now they are dead. Before this, though they were kept low, yet there was life and power to bring plagues on their enemies; but now their enemies rejoice, as if they had never anymore to fear from 'em. But 'tis not likely that a time yet remains wherein the church of Christ will ever be reduced lower by a prevalence of popery, than it was before the Reformation; or so, but that there must remain more appearances, relics and monuments of the true religion, more of a remembrance of it, more of that light in the world, that will endanger popery and will tend to bring a return of Protestant principles. The death of the church was, in a great measure, its almost barbarous ignorance and blindness. As long as light and knowledge prevail in the world, true religion never can be buried so deep as it has been, or be so far out of hopes of a revival. Considering what the state of the world now is, and how near at furthest we must needs be to the downfall of Antichrist, 'tis next to impossible that things should come to such a state anymore before that time.

And then, it is scarcely agreeable to the analogy of God's dispensations, that it should be so. For the Reformation was the beginning of the fall of Antichrist. The vial[2] was poured out on his throne, whereby it was shaken and diminished, as a forerunner of its total overthrow.[3] It was the beginning of the church's revival, after it had for many ages been almost in a state of death. And 'tis not likely that Antichrist's great victory, and the greatest death of the church, yet remains. On the pouring out of the vial on the throne of the beast, his kingdom becomes full of darkness, so that the enemies of the church can no more perform their enterprises against the church. Their policy never shall serve 'em anymore, as it used to do. Thus it has proved hitherto time after time.

III. If the popish powers should prevail, and should by a wonderful turn of providence subdue all Protestant princes and countries, and by violent persecution extirpate Protestantism, and extinguish learning and knowledge and all monuments of the true religion, so that the state of the world should appear further from any hope of a revival of the true religion, than ever it has done yet, yet this would hardly answer the prophecy of slaying the two witnesses. For doubtless, one reason why

2. I.e., the fifth vial (Rev. 16:10–11).
3. Here JE deleted "It was, as it were, the dawning of the day before the glorious day of the."

they are called "two witnesses," is that the number of those that are of the true religion is so small. And therefore, though it was a sufficient number, yet it was a small number.[4] But since the Reformation, the number of those that are of the Protestant religion has been great, and sometimes thought to be equal to that of the papists. Therefore, the destroying those would not be a destroying a small number, as it were two witnesses, but a great multitude which no man can number.

IV. What was accomplished in the Reformation, exceeding well answers what is said in the prophecy of the rising and ascending of the witnesses, and their being set out of the reach of their enemies. See Lowman.[5]

V. If there has already been one accomplishment of this prophecy of the rising and ascending of the witnesses at the Reformation, there remains no other proper fulfillment of it yet behind (though there may be [a] dispensation that may bear a considerable analogy to it, and so, that the prophecy may have an indirect aspect upon); because henceforward, the witnesses are in heaven, so far out of the reach of their enemies, at least that they can't slay them anymore. They can no more see the church laying dead, for them to make merry over. See further no. 92.

91. [CHAPTER 16:12.] See no. 89.[6] Cyrus, the chief of the kings of the East that came into old Babylon and destroyed [it], when the river Euphrates was dried up to prepare their way, is spoken of in Isaiah as being in that matter a type of Christ. God calls him "his shepherd," to perform his pleasure, to say to Jerusalem, "Thou shalt be built, and to the temple, Thy foundation shall be laid" (Is. 44:28). God calls him "his anointed," or his messiah (Is. 45:1); and there God speaks of holding his hand, in the same manner as of the Messiah (ch. 42:6). And Is. 45:13, he is spoken of as one that God has raised up in righteousness, that he may build his city, and freely redeem his captives, or let them go without price or reward. Ch. 48:14, he is said to be one whom God hath loved, as the Messiah (ch. 42:1) is called God's elect, in whom his soul delighteth. And Is. 48:15, God says of him, "I have called him," as of the Messiah. [See also] Is. 42:6.

And God, in preparing Cyrus' way by drying up the river Euphrates, speaks in like terms as of his preparing the way of the Messiah, when he shall come to set up his kingdom in the world. As ch. 45:2, "I will go

4. Here JE deleted "that it was, as it were, but two in a great city."
5. *Paraphrase and Notes*, pp. 195–99.
6. MS: "add this to N. 89."

before thee, and make the crooked places straight." And v. 13, "I have raised him up in righteousness, and I will direct (or "make straight," as it is in the margin)[7] all his ways." This is like what is said of preparing the way of the Messiah, when he shall come to redeem his people out of captivity. Is. 40:3–4, "The voice of him that crieth in the wilderness, Prepare ye the way of the Lord; make straight in the desert an highway for our God. . . . The crooked things shall be made straight."

And since Cyrus is here a type of the Messiah spoken of in that 40th [chapter] of Isaiah, and the thing here spoken of Cyrus, viz., his coming to let go God's captives and restore Jerusalem, is also typical of that which is spoken of in that 40th chapter—that redemption of his captivated people, which the Messiah comes to perform; hence, 'tis but reasonable to suppose that the preparing the way of the one, and making straight his paths by making crooked things straight, when he comes to perform the typical redemption, is typical of that preparing the way of the other, that is spoken of in the same terms, when he comes to perform that redemption that is the antitype.

And therefore, 'tis but reasonable to suppose that this preparing the way of Christ, is one thing that is intended in Revelation 16, when a preparing the way for the destruction of the enemies of the church is spoken of, with reference to the preparing the way of Cyrus spoken of [in] Isaiah 45.

The other kings that are with their great King of Kings, are the people that follow on white horses, that we read of (Rev. 19:14). God's saints especially were eminent persons in the church, who at that day shall be made princes in all the earth, and shall then come to reign on earth. These are the kings and princes spoken of. Ps. 113:7–8, "He raiseth up the poor out of the dust, and lifteth the needy out of the dunghill, that he may set him with princes, even with the princes of his people." Job 36:7, "He withdraweth not his eyes from the righteous, but with kings are they on the throne." I Sam. 2:8, "He raiseth up the poor out of the dust, and lifteth up the beggar from the dunghill, to set them among princes, and to make them to inherit the throne of glory." I Pet. 2:9, "But ye are a chosen generation, a royal priesthood." Rev. 1:6, "And hath made us kings and priests, unto God and his Father."

And as Christ, when he shall come to the destruction of Antichrist, will come having on his head many crowns [Rev. 19:12], and "on his vesture and on his thigh a name written, King of Kings and Lord of Lords" [Rev. 19:16], because then he will come to take to himself his

7. See the margin at Is. 45:13 in the "Blank Bible," p. 514.

great power, and reign and appear in the glory of such a character, so his saints that shall follow him, have at that time especially given to them the title of kings; for then they will come to reign on earth, and to receive the fulfillment of those joyful expectations, which they express in their songs. In Rev. 5:10, "And hast made us unto our God kings and priests, and we shall reign on earth." And that Ps. 45:16, "Instead of thy fathers, shall be thy children, whom thou mayest make princes in all the earth." And that Dan. 7:27, "And the kingdom and dominion, and greatness of the kingdom under the whole heaven, shall be given to the people of the saints of the Most High, etc." Accordingly, they are represented as sitting on thrones, to reign and judge after Antichrist's destruction. Rev. 20:4, "And I saw thrones, and they sat upon them: and judgment was given unto them. And I saw the souls of them, etc.; . . . and they lived and reigned with Christ a thousand years." And because they come to judge the world, when they follow the King of Kings to Antichrist's destruction, they are represented as following on white horses [Rev. 19:14], as formerly judges were wont to ride on white asses, when going to sit on the judgment seat. Judg. 5:10, "Speak, ye that ride on white asses, ye that sit in judgment."[8]

92. [CHAPTER 11:7–8 ff.] See no. 90.[9] The grand objection against all this, is that it is said that the witnesses should prophesy 1260 days "clothed in sackcloth" [Rev. 11:3]; and when they have finished their testimony, the beast should make war against them, and kill them, etc. [Rev. 11:7]. And that it seems manifest, that after this they are no longer in sackcloth, for henceforward they are in an exalted state in heaven. And that therefore, seeing the time of their wearing sackcloth is 1260 days, which is the time of the continuance of Antichrist, hence their being slain and rising again, must be at the conclusion of this period, and at the end of Antichrist's reign.

In answer to which, I would say that we can justly infer no more from this prophecy than this, viz., that the 1260 days is the proper time of the church's trouble and bondage, or being clothed in sackcloth, because it is the appointed time of the reign of Antichrist. But this don't hinder but that God, out of his great compassion to his church, should in some respect shorten the days, and grant that his church should in some measure anticipate the appointed great deliverance that should be at the end of these days. As he has in fact done in the Reformation, whereby the church has had a great degree of restoration granted her, from the

8. The last two paragraphs have been rearranged according to JE's directions.
9. MS: "Join this to N. 90." See p. 201, n. 3.

darkness and power of Antichrist, before her proper time of restoration, which is at the end of the 1260 days. And so the church, through the compassions of her Father and Redeemer, anticipates her deliverance from her sorrows, and has in some respects an end put to her testifying in sackcloth, as many parts of the church are hereby brought from under the dominion of the antichristian powers into a state of liberty. Though in other respects, the church may be said still to continue in sackcloth and in the wilderness (as ch. 12:14), till the end of the days. And as to the witnesses standing on their feet and ascending into heaven [Rev. 11:11–12], I would propose that it may be considered whether anything more can be understood by it than the Protestant church, its being now able to stand on her own legs and in her own defense, and being raised to such a state that she henceforward is out of the reach of the Romish powers. That let them do what they will, they shall never anymore be able to get the church of Christ under their power, as they had before. As often times in the Scripture, God's people's dwelling in safety out of the reach of their enemies, is represented by their dwelling on high, or being set on high. As Ps. 59:1, 69:29, 91:14, 107:41; Prov. 29:25; and Is. 33:16. And as the children of Israel, when brought out of Egypt, were said to be carried on eagle's wings, that is lofty in its flight, [and] flies away toward heaven, where none of her enemies can reach her [Ex. 19:4].

I might here observe, that we have other instances of God's shortening the days of his church's captivity and bondage, either at the beginning or latter end, in some measure parallel with this. Thus the proper time of the bondage of the posterity of Abraham in Egypt, was 400 years (Gen. 15:13). But yet God in mercy, deferred the beginning of this bondage, whereby the time was much shortened at the beginning. So the time wherein it was foretold, that the whole land of Israel should be a desolation and an astonishment, and the land should enjoy her sabbaths, was seventy years (Jer. 25:11–12). And these seventy years are dated in II Chronicles 36:20–21 from Zedekiah's captivity. And yet from that captivity to Cyrus' decree, was but about 52 years, though it was indeed about 70 years before the temple was rebuilt and finished. So the proper time of the oppression and bondage of the Jewish church under Antiochus Epiphanes,[1] wherein both the sanctuary and host should be trodden underfoot by him, was two thousand and 300 days

---

1. Antiochus IV of the Seleucid dynasty in Syria (175–63 B.C.), a vigorous proponent of Hellenization, vented his hatred of the Jews when he sacked Jerusalem in 168 and erected an altar to Zeus in the temple. See JE's comments on these affairs in Dwight ed., *9,* 413–16.

(Dan. 8:13–14). And yet God gave Israel a degree of deliverance by the Maccabees. And they were "holpen with a little help"; and the host ceased to be trodden underfoot, before that time was expired (Dan. 11: 32, 34).[2]

We have another instance in the continuance of the children of Israel in their wanderings in the wilderness, under the awful tokens of God's anger. The proper time of this was 40 years, as it was threatened. Num. 14:33–34, "Your children shall wander in the wilderness forty years, and bear your whoredoms, until your carcasses be wasted in the wilderness. After the number of the days in which ye searched out the land, each day for a year, shall ye bear your iniquities, even forty years; and ye shall know my breach of promise." But yet these days of wrath were shortened. The first year of the forty, which was past before the threatening, "had been a year of triumph (as Mr. Henry observes) in their deliverance out of Egypt, and the last before the forty years was ended, was also a year of triumph, on the other side [of] Jordan. So that all the forty were not years of sorrow; and as the people came up out [of] Jordan into Canaan on the 10th day of the first month (Josh. 4:19), five days before the forty years was ended, to shew how little pleasure God takes in punishing, how swift he is to shew mercy, and that 'for the elect's sake the days of trouble are shortened' "[3] [Matt. 24:22].

Obj. 'Tis commonly so, that just before God appears for any remarkable salvation and comfort of his people, they are reduced to the greatest, their distress [is] the most; and so their necessity of divine help [exists] most clearly and remarkable. So just before the conversion, salvation and comfort of a particular soul. And God's dealings with his church are observably very parallel with his dealings with particular souls. So the last oppression of the children of Israel in Egypt, were the most severe; and the oppression of God's people by Antichrist, is evidently compared in Scripture to the oppression of Egypt. So the greatest oppressions of Israelites by the Midianites, were just before their deliverance. See Judges 6:1–11. The 10th persecution by Diocletian and his contemporaries in the government was the most severe of all. And the most severe and terrible sufferings of Christ himself, "the author and finisher of our faith" [Heb. 12:2], were his last sufferings and just before his exaltation. This seems to be God's declared method of dealing with his church (Deut. 32:36), which seems to be with a special eye to the

2. The rest of this entry has been rearranged according to JE's directions.
3. *Exposition*, Vol. 1 (1710), at Josh. 4:19.

great deliverance of the church in the latter days. To this objection, I would answer.

Ans. 1. In the first, as to the beginning of the deliverance, 'tis doubtless agreeable to God's common methods of dealing with his people, that their lowest state and the height of their calamity has immediately preceded their relief. But more generally, there is some space after this, sometimes a longer, sometimes a shorter space, before the complete salvation. So it commonly is with respect to the salvation and comfort of a particular soul that is converted. Commonly his greatest distress is just before the first dawn of light. But most commonly the first comforts, given at the very time of a sinner's conversion, are not so great as follow afterwards. And often great troubles and conflicts intervene. As we see, the greatest daylight succeeding a dark night, is not equal to what follows afterwards. It is but the dawning of the day, which though it be comparatively but a small light, yet is succeeded by no darkness equal to what was before, until the sun rises in the full blaze of day.

So it was with respect to the children of Israel's deliverance of Egypt. Their complete deliverance was not till Pharaoh and his host was overthrown in the Red Sea. Their beginning their journey on the night in which the first-born of Egypt were slain, was not the last or most glorious appearance of God for their salvation. Yea, we have reason to conclude that they obtained favor of the Egyptians, of the people in general excepting Pharaoh and perhaps a few about him, some time before, and so that they experience the happy effects of their favor in a mitigation of their bondage. See Ex. 10:7, 11:2–3, and 12:35–36.[4]

And then, it is further to be considered, that work of salvation that was then begun, did not wholly consist in the deliverance of the people from their Egyptian bondage, but in bringing [them] out of Egypt, carrying them through the wilderness, giving the victory over the enemies which should oppose them in their way, and carrying [them] on eagles' wings above the difficulties and dangers of that great and terrible wilderness, full of pits and drought and fiery flying serpents,

---

4. In a note on Ex. 11:2–3, JE observed that God took care that Israel should "be well paid by the Egyptians for their past services" with borrowed jewelry ("Blank Bible," p. 56). In no. 351 of the "Scripture," JE noted that according to Ex. 12:35–36 the church of Christ is adorned with the wealth of her enemies after she is redeemed from the tyranny of Rome, the spiritual Egypt. See Dwight ed., *9*, 252–53.

and giving them the victory over Sihon and Og [Num. 21:21–35], and the Moabites and Midianites on the other side of Jordan [Num. 31], and afterwards in dividing Jordan before them, and giving them such miraculous, glorious victories over the inhabitants of Canaan in their united strength, and finally giving them the possession of the land of Canaan, that land flowing with milk and honey, and giving them rest there. This is always spoken of as one work of salvation, in the preceding promises of God, and afterwards in the praises of the Jewish church in the Psalms, and in the mention that is frequently made of these things in other parts of the Scripture. And this work of salvation, in the whole of [it], is evidently a type of the great salvation of the church in the latter days. The victory that the church shall then obtain over her enemies, when it is said "the sun shall no more go down, nor the moon withdraw itself" (Is. 60:20), is evidently typified by Joshua's victory over the Amorites, when the sun and moon stood still (Josh. 10:12–14]. And indeed, it is expressly compared to it in Isaiah 28:21.

The children of Israel, after their departure out of Egypt, were very far from having that salvation and glory completed, that is a type of the latter-day glory. Their troubles were not over. They had many other and strong enemies to conflict with; they were soon met and opposed by the Amalekites [Ex. 17:8–16]. They had a sorrowful forty years to spend in a dreadful wilderness, and mighty conflicts with their enemies on both sides of Jordan to engage in, before they should be at rest. And their greatest affliction and distress, did not immediately precede this rest.

Again, if we consider the children of Israel's deliverance from the Babylonish captivity, their lowest state was not immediately before their complete deliverance and restoration, not to insist on the favor [and] relief they must be supposed to have by the advancement of Daniel, Shadrach, Meshach and Abednego. The restoration and deliverance of the church of Israel by Cyrus' decree, was but very partial; but a few returned at that time with Zerubbabel. It was the day of small things for a long time with them; and they still met with great troubles from their enemies, the Samaritans. And that which the Scripture itself calls the restoring and building Jerusalem (Dan. 9:25), was not till more than twenty years after, when Ezra went up with many of his people and Artaxerxes' ample commission.

So with respect to the troubles, deliverance and exaltation of David and his company [I Sam. 16–II Sam. 5] (which undoubtedly typified the church, first in its afflicted and persecuted [state], and then in its consequent glorious deliverance and prosperity). The greatest affliction which they suffered, at least by the persecutions of Saul, who in this case is a type of Antichrist, was not immediately preceding Saul's overthrow and David's advancement to the kingdom. David, before that for some considerable time, was out of Saul's reach; and his company greatly increased. Besides, when Saul was dead and David's promised advancement was begun, yet at first, even for seven years, it was very partial, reigning only over one tribe, and when all the other tribes still continued under the dominion of the house of his great persecutor.

'Tis true, it is commonly so, that just before the beginning of the deliverance of God's people from any great calamity, that their lowest state and greatest extremity is just before the dawning of the day. So it was just before the begun deliverance of the people in Egypt.[5]

So with respect to Christ himself, his greatest sufferings and lowest humiliation was just before his resurrection. But his resurrection did not complete his salvation; and the happy change God made in his state, that was not till 40 days after at his ascension, which was by far the most glorious part of it.

So it was with regard to the deliverance of the church of God from Antiochus' oppression and persecution, who is a great type of Antichrist, and designed evidently and remarkably as such, as much or more than any person spoken of in the Old Testament. The greatest extremity of God's people, was just before their begun deliverance by the Maccabees; but the death of Antiochus, and their complete deliverance and restoration, was not till some time after.

So when Christ came, the church of God in Israel was at its lowest state, just before what is called "the beginning of the gospel of Jesus Christ" [Mark 1:1], by the preaching of John the Baptist. But the completing of the glorious alteration in the state of things in Israel, intended to be in that age, and the actual introducing of the kingdom of heaven, was not till the pouring out of the Spirit on the day of Pentecost [Acts 2].

And with regard to the glorious revolution in Constantine's time, 'tis true that the 10th general persecution, which was the last preceding it, was far the most severe. But this began about the year 303, and lasted 10 years before "universally extinguished" (see Lardner's 9th volume, p. 339),[6] and so wholly ceased *anno* 313 (ibid., p. 382), but was abated before that time. And Constantine was not enthroned as emperor, both of the East and West, and the full restoration of Christians from

5. JE marked this paragraph with a vertical line.
6. *Gospel History*, Pt. II, Vol. 7 (1748).

banishment and bondage through the world [was not] till about 325, more than ten years [later] (Lardner, ibid., pp. 351 and 385 ff.).

Ans. 2. The church of God may suffer extreme oppression, and be brought very low just before the final destruction of Antichrist; but not directly by the power of Antichrist, but some other way, yet in general by things of the same tendency, and all by Satan, the grand adversary of God's church and head of all her enemies.

So it was after the deliverance out of Egypt, before the children of Israel were possessed of Canaan. They suffered extremely for 40 years in the wilderness. So it was with David after his begun deliverance from Saul. Just before his being made king over Israel, he was reduced to the last extremity by the Amalekites [I Sam. 30:1–31]; and then again, before the setting up his throne in Jerusalem over all Israel, he had much trouble from Ishbosheth and his adherents [II Sam. 2:8–4:12]. So after the partial restoration of the Jews by the decree of Cyrus, they suffered extremely from the Samaritans, and were well nigh overcome by their attempts and devices [Ezra 4], before the more complete restoration by Artaxerxes in Ezra's time [Ezra 7].

So since the Reformation, the church of God is now reduced very lower and to great extremity, through the prevalence of deism, atheism, heresy and profaneness.

Ans. 3. The same ends may be obtained. The church of God may be as much and in like manner prepared, for that great salvation she is to receive at the downfall of Antichrist, without her being brought to her lowest state, through the power and prevalence of her antichristian enemies. 'Tis manifest that immediately before that glorious event, the popish powers will collect all their strength. They will, in the height of the exercise of their malice and envy against God's will, rage in a most terrible manner, as Antiochus' rage was the greatest just before his death.[7] They shall join hand in hand; the combination will be exceeding strong. Their schemes shall be laid very deep; their preparations shall be immense. The devil will assist them to his utmost. All the powers of hell shall be awakened and engaged. Satan will engage other parts of his kingdom of darkness in the world, to engage in the help of the Romish power. Strong leagues and alliances shall be entered into. The ends of the earth, as it were, shall be stirred. Emissaries shall be most busily and successfully employed, in order to the most formidable and vast preparations. They shall be like Pharaoh with all the strength of Egypt, and his mighty host of chariots and horsemen, all ready for

7. Antiochus Epiphanes was reputed to have gone mad shortly before his death.

the battle, and in their own imagination sure of success, vaunting in themselves, in their greatly exceeding the people of God in external pomp and power, so that they shall seem as nothing to 'em. They, greatly irritated and enraged, shall come with whetted resolutions of the most merciless cruelties. The appearances will be such as strongly to impress the minds of God's people, with a sense of their enemies' power and their own comparative weakness, and the greatness of the sufferings intended them, and lively apprehensions of their danger, any otherwise than as their faith shall overcome all these threatening appearances, and fill 'em with holy fortitude. Probably some of God's people will suffer. The enemy shall begin to prevail and exercise their cruelties, raising the pride and vaunting of the enemy, and giving God's people a full idea of the extreme sufferings they are threatened with.

Now these things will be as good a preparation for the glorious deliverance and salvation, which God shall work for his people, and the triumph they shall have over them, as though their enemies should be suffered actually to prevail and conquer God's people, and reduce 'em to the most extreme distress, and to appearance hopeless and extreme,[8] immediately before their complete deliverance. Such a state of things with respect to God's people and their enemies, will be as good a preparation for the giving the world an affecting sense of God's glory as above that of his enemies', and [a sense] of the vanity of the pride and loftiness of men, and the folly of their envy, malice and self-confidence, and to give God's people a sense of God's great grace and mercy to them, and will as well prepare the way for the glory of their triumph, and for the increase of the ardor of their praises.

Such were the circumstance of the great salvation God wrought for Israel at the Red Sea, that perhaps the preparation for the manifestation of God's glory in that work, and the preparation of God's people for their deliverance, their victory over the enemies, and praises to their glorious deliverer, was as great as if Pharaoh had been suffered for a little season actually to prevail, and had taken Israel captive, and they had suddenly and in some wonderful way been rescued, and their enemies miraculously destroyed.[9]

93. CHAPTER 16:13–14. "And I saw three unclean spirits like frogs come out of the mouth of the dragon, and out of the mouth of the

8. Conjecture for illegible word.

9. Here JE deleted the following line which he rewrote below, p. 283: "*Boston Evening-Post*, July 21, 1755. Paris, May 9. All things are getting ready for the general meeting of."

beast, and out of the mouth of the false prophet. For they are the spirits of devils, working miracles, which go forth unto the kings of the earth and of the whole world, to gather them to the battle of that great day of God Almighty." One main thing here intended and represented, seems to me to be the great prevailing of the delusions of the devil in counterfeit illuminations, and false affections, and enthusiasm, by which the devil, imitating the great and wonderful works of God's Holy Spirit, shall deceive vast multitudes everywhere, and of all ranks and degrees, as they shall be led away by these things, and shall deceive others by hereby greatly prejudicing them against the power of godliness. Though this enthusiastical spirit shall operate different ways among different kinds of people, as it is not spoken as one spirit, but three unclean spirits out of the mouths of three different creatures.

NO. 94. EXTRACTS FROM MR. LOWMAN[1]

Concerning the four first seals, see no. 70, pp. 162 ff.

The FIRST SEAL.[2] Ch. 6:2. Representing a white horse, etc., "signifies the kingdom of Christ, or Christian religion prevailing against the opposition of Jews and heathens."

He that sat on the white horse had a bow, "an ensign of war; a crown, an ensign of command and victory; and he rode on a white horse, a symbol of joy and triumph. And, agreeable to this meaning, there was this motto: 'Go forth conquering, and to conquer.'"

The SECOND SEAL.[3] Ch. 6:3–4. "There went out another horse that was red. And power was given unto him that sat thereon, to take peace from the earth, and that they should kill one another; and there was given unto him a great sword." This prophecy refers "to the mutual slaughters of the Jews and heathen, the common enemies of the Christian faith, and persecutors of the Christian religion."

If this vision was before the destruction of Jerusalem by Titus,[4] as some have thought, "the dreadful slaughter of the Jewish nation in that war, may be described by it; in which, according to some, one million five hundred thousand, according to others, two millions of Jews were slain, besides the Romans slain by the Jews. But if this vision was in the time of Domitian's persecution," as is most likely, it probably refers to the mutual slaughters of Jews and heathens in the reigns of Trajan and Hadrian.[5] "In the latter end of the reign of Trajan, the

---

1. Above, p. 78. JE numbered the "Extracts" in succession with the preceding series, although they constitute a distinct part of the notebook. Footnotes have been kept to a minimum in this section because fuller bibliographical information is available in Lowman's commentary.

2. *Paraphrase and Notes*, pp. xxix, 39–40. This bibliographical reference and others in the following section indicate cumulative pages used by JE in the various subsections of the "Extracts." The supernumerals have been placed at the beginning of the respective subsection in order to facilitate the examination of JE's use of Lowman.

3. *Paraphrase and Notes*, pp. 41–43.

4. I.e., in 70 A.D.

5. Domitian reigned A.D. 81–96, Trajan 98–117, and Hadrian 117–38. Hereafter the names of emperors, kings, popes, etc., are not annotated unless there is occasion for confusion.

Jews rebelled in Egypt and Cyprus, and are reported to have put to death, with great marks of cruelty, four hundred and sixty thousand men; yet the Jews were everywhere subdued, and prodigious numbers slain by the Romans. In the reign of Hadrian, the Jews were led into a new sedition under a pretended messiah called Bar Chocab.[6] The whole Jewish nation rose against the Roman government, and for some time did great mischiefs to the Romans; but at last they were entirely cut off by the Romans, though with great loss to themselves. In these wars, besides what was lost on the Roman side, the Jews had a thousand cities and fortresses destroyed, with the slaughter of above five hundred and eighty thousand men. . . . This period of history was about forty years after the vision."

Ch. 6:5–6. "And when he had opened the THIRD SEAL."[7] See no. 74. "I beheld, and lo a black horse; and he that sat upon him had a pair of balances in his hands. And I heard a voice in the midst of the four beasts say, A measure of wheat for a penny, and three measures of barley for a penny; and see that thou hurt not the oil nor the wine." The color black is expressive of a time of mourning and affliction, and particularly affliction occasioned by famine. See Lam. 5:10. The pair of balances is "to weigh corn and the necessaries of life, to signify great scarcity, and to threaten the world with famine, the next judgment of God to the sword. Thus famine is expressed by the prophet Ezekiel (ch. 4:16)."

"The measure of wheat is a choenix, and the price of a Roman penny, which was wont to be the daily wages of a workman, and a choenix the allowance of corn for his daily provision. So that a penny for a measure of wheat was an excessive price; since corn, for one day's provision, would cost a whole day's wages. In another way of computation, if we reckon the measure of the choenix to be about a quart English, and the Roman penny to be about eight pence English, the nearest common computation of both, and there is no need here of more exactness, corn at that price will be above 20 shillings an English bushel, which, when the common wages of a man's labor was but eight-pence a day, shewed a very great scarcity of corn, next to a famine."

"Antoninus Pius succeeded Hadrian, A.D. 138. Antoninus Philoso-
138   phus, partly with Verus, and partly alone, and after
them Commodus, governed the empire, till within a few

---

6. Or Simon Bar Kochba, whose rebellion lasted from A.D. 132–135.

7. *Paraphrase and Notes*, pp. 43–47. See above, pp. 168–70, for footnotes identifying references in this subsection. JE had written the same discussion of the third seal as no. 74.

193   months of Severus, who began his reign, A.D. 193, a space
         of above 50 years."

"The state of the empire under the reigns of this Antonine family, does properly and exactly answer this prophetic description. Tertullian mentions unseasonable weather and bad harvests, the judgments of God for persecuting the Christians, . . . and speaks of a scarcity that was felt in every city. Aurelius Victor, in the reign of Antoninus Pius, observes that the scarcity of provisions occasioned such a tumult in Rome, that the common people attempted to stone him."

"Julius Capitolinus further takes notice, that Antoninus [Pius] was forced to supply the scarcity of wine, oil and corn out of his own treasury; and that famine was one of the evils with which the empire was afflicted in his reign. In the reign of his successor, Antoninus Philosophus, we have a like account of a scarcity of provision, to a famine." Echard,[8] from Julius Capitolinus, [relates] how that an inundation of the Tiber, and the infinite number of insects that followed, brought on an extreme famine. Aurelius Victor confirms this.

"In the next reign, [of] Commodus, Xiphilin observes from Dio, there was such scarcity of provisions, that the people of Rome rose, and actually killed Cleander, the emperor's favorite. This scarcity of provisions, in every reign of the Antonines, continued to the empire of Severus, who heartily set himself to remedy so great an evil: which plainly shews it was a very pressing evil; and that through frequent wars, bad harvests and a mismanagement of the public stores, scarcity of provisions was the distinguishing judgment of those times. So Aelius Spartian observes, in the life of Severus. 'And that he took such care as to this matter, that when he died, he left in the public stores provision enough for a public supply of the Roman people for seven years.'[9] And thus also the reign of Severus appears a proper end to the judgment of this prediction."

"He that sat on the black horse, having a pair of balances in his hand" [Rev. 6:5], probably signifies not only the great scarcity that was in the reign of the Antonine family, when they eat their bread by weight and measure, but also the great care that the two Antonines and Severus (though otherwise vicious) took for the exact administration of justice. As the seven heads of the beast [Rev. 13:1] signified two things, seven mountains and seven heads of government; and as the feet of the image, being part of iron and part of clay [Dan. 2:42], signifies

8. Above, p. 66. Here Lowman was citing from the second volume of Echard's *Roman History*.

9. This quotation is JE's translation of Spartian's Latin.

two things, viz., that the dominion should be partly strong and partly broken, and that the ten kingdoms should not mix one with another, so as to grow into one.[1]

Ch. 6:7–8. "And when he had opened the FOURTH SEAL,[2] . . . I looked, and behold a pale horse. And his name that sat on him was Death, and Hell followed with him. And power was given unto them over the fourth part of the earth, to kill with sword, and with hunger, and with death, and with the beasts of the earth." See Ezek. 14:21 and 33:27.

This has respect to the state of the empire next in order of time, under Severus, Maximin, Decius, Gallus, and Volusian, and Valerian, which begins about the year 211 and continued to the year 275.

211–275 "In this period of time, the several sore judgments of God were united in punishing a persecuting empire: the sword, famine and pestilence. The pestilence seems to be made the distinguishing judgment of this seal. The state of the empire during this space was very much disturbed, both by foreign wars and intestine troubles; very few of the emperors but met with a violent death. So that besides thirty persons, who all pretended to the empire at once, there were twenty acknowledged emperors in the space of sixty years,

211–270 from Caracalla, A.D. 211, to Aurelian, 270, which gave heart and strength and great advantages to the enemies of the Roman Empire against it, as the Persians and northern nations. Valerian was taken captive by Sapores, king of Persia, and treated with great severity by him till his death."

"Mr. Mede[3] observes from Dionysius of Alexandria,[4] that both war and famine were the judgments of these times. 'After these things,' says Dionysius, speaking of the persecution of Decius, 'war and famine came upon us.' Cyprian[5] takes notice of the more frequent wars and famines of those times. . . . Mr. Mede observes from Zonaras[6] and Lipsius,[7] that a pestilence arising from Ethiopia, went through all the provinces of Rome, and for fifteen years together incredibly wasted

---

1. This paragraph, a later addition, has been rearranged according to JE's directions.

2. *Paraphrase and Notes*, pp. 47–49.

3. Above, p. 5. In this section Lowman was citing Mede's *Clavis Apocalyptica*.

4. A pupil of Origen and bishop of Alexandria.

5. A third-century theologian and martyr, the bishop of Carthage during the Decian persecution.

6. A Byzantine canonist and historian of the twelfth century.

7. A humanist and philologist active in the late sixteenth century who wrote on Roman antiquity.

them. Neither did I ever read of a greater plague (saith an eminent man[8] in our age), for that space of time or land. This pestilence is mentioned by Zonaras, in the reign of Gallus and Volusian, about the year 251. The words of Zonaras are very agreeable to this prophecy: 'He (Gallus) was very severe to the Christians, many being put to death by a persecution, not less grievous than that of Decius; under him the Persians renewed their motions, and settled in Armenia. An almost innumerable company of Scythians fell upon Italy, and ravaged Macedonia, Thessaly and Greece. A part of them from Palus Maeotis,[9] brake through the Bosphorus into the Euxine Sea, and laid waste many provinces; and many other nations rose against the Romans. Moreover, a plague then infested the provinces, which beginning in Ethiopia, spread itself almost through the whole East and West, destroyed the inhabitants of many cities, and continued for fifteen years.' Zosimus,[1] an heathen historian, takes notice of the same calamity: 'While war raged in every part, a pestilence spread through all towns and villages, and destroyed the remainder of mankind; that so great a destruction of men, had not hitherto ever happened in former times.' I shall only add the short character of Eutropius,[2] of the times of these emperors, Gallus and Volusian; he observes, their reigns were only memorable for pestilence and grievous distempers."

Rev. 6:8.[3] "And Hell followed with him." One judgment that may very probably and naturally [be] signified by this, was men's being swallowed up and destroyed by earthquakes. Thus within these times, which Mr. Lowman fixes on as signified by the vision of this seal in the reign of Gordian, Echard says there were many terrible earthquakes, in which "many cities and towns of the empire were swallowed up and destroyed."[4] In these Hell did, as it were, open her mouth to swallow up the inhabitants of the earth.

Again Echard informs that, in the beginning of the reign of Gallienus, "Strange and dismal earthquakes overthrew the cities and stately edifices, destroying great numbers of people, and shaking the lands so terribly, that the hidden bowels of the earth, and stupendous caverns were laid open, from whence flowed vast streams of salt water. The sea

8. Lowman identified Lipsius in the margin.
9. The region surrounding the northern arm of the Euxine or Black Sea.
1. A fifth-century Greek historian of the Roman Empire.
2. A historian of Rome active in the fourth century.
3. The following two paragraphs, a later addition, have been rearranged according to JE's directions.
4. *Roman History*, Vol. 2 (2nd ed., London, 1699), p. 469.

251 (margin)

overswelled its banks, and broke into many continents, drowning coun-·
tries, cities and people."[5]

FIFTH SEAL.[6] From the year 275 to about 320. Ch. 6:11. "And white
robes were given to every one of them." "When persons were approved,
upon trial of their fitness for the priest's office, they were clothed with
white garments, the proper habits of priests. And rich garments, which
it was usual for princes to send as presents, according to the customs of
the eastern nations, were public marks of the prince's favor, and that
he designed to confer honor on the persons to whom he presented
them."

[SIXTH SEAL.][7] Ch. 7:1–3. "I saw four angels, . . . holding the four
winds. . . . And I saw another angel; . . . and he cried, saying, Hurt
not the earth, etc., . . . till we have sealed the servants of God in their
foreheads." "Constantine came to the whole power of the empire

323   about 323, and continued possessed of that power about 15
             years, to the year 337. During all this time, the empire had

337   a state of tranquillity unknown for many years. . . . The
profession of Christianity was greatly encouraged; the converts
to it from idolatry were innumerable, so that the face of religion
was, in a very short time, quite changed throughout the Roman Empire. Thus the providence of God, notwithstanding all opposition,
brought the Christian church to a state of great security and prosperity. But on the death of Constantine, the state of things soon altered
again."

[SEVENTH SEAL.][8] Ch. 8:1. "There was silence in heaven about the
space of half an hour." Like the silence in the temple, when the whole
congregation "prayed without, in silence, or privately to themselves,
while the priest offered incense in the holy place."

The FIRST TRUMPET.[9] Ch. 8:7. "There followed hail and fire mingled
with blood, and they were cast upon the earth. And the third part of
the trees was burnt up, and all green grass was burnt up." "A little
after the bloody intestine war," raised by Constantine's sons, one
against another, "all the Roman provinces were invaded at once, from
the eastern to the western limits, by the Franks, Almans, Saxons,
Quades, Sarmatians and Persians," wasting and destroying everywhere,

5. Ibid., pp. 492–93.
6. *Paraphrase and Notes*, p. 51.
7. Ibid., pp. 59–60, 69.
8. Ibid., p. 65.
9. Ibid., pp. 68, 70.

as though everything would be swallowed up. "This storm fell very heavy on the great men of the empire, and particularly on the family of Constantine, though so likely to continue, in so many of his own children and near relations; and yet, in 24 years after his death, these commotions put an end to his posterity, in the death of his three sons; and in three years more extinguished his family, in the death of Julian in a battle against the Persians. The following reigns of Jovian, Valentinian, Valens and Gratian, to the time that Gratian nominated Theodosius to the empire, are one continued series of trouble, by the invasion of the several provinces of the empire, and bloody battles in defense of them, for about the space of sixteen years, from the year 363 to the year 379."

363–379

The SECOND TRUMPET.[1] Ch. 8:8–9. "A great mountain burning with fire was cast into the sea. And the third part of the sea became blood; and the third part of the creatures, which were in the sea and had life, died; and the third part of the ships were destroyed." "A proper figurative representation of a further judgment, which should reach the capital city of the empire (See Jer. 51 : 25, 27 ff.), and many of the provinces; destroying their power and riches, dismembering them from the empire, and depriving it of all future support and assistance from them."

Theodosius "for some time preserved the empire from invasion, and left it to his sons, Arcadius and Honorius, A.D. 395." But then the empire, through their youth, weakness and mismanagement, "soon became a prey to the northern nations. Sigonius,[2] who has given us an accurate history of these times of the Roman Empire, observes that the empire itself began to shake on the death of Theodosius. Alaric, at the head of the Goths, invades Greece, lays waste the whole country, destroys the cities, puts to death all the males grown up to age, and gives all the women and children with the whole riches of the country in plunder to his army, according to Zosimus.

395

The year 400, or five years after the death of Theodosius, is marked out as one of the most memorable and calamitous that had ever befallen the empire. '*Annus hic fuit* (says Sigonius) *à Christo nato quadringentesimus, omnium, quos occidens vidit, maximè memorandus extitit. . . . Neque enim ullum sive bellicae calamitatis, sive barbaricae feritatis, sive vesanae cujusdam libidinis, excogitari exemplum potuit, quod non in ipsas provincias, civitates, agros, hominesque passim cum*

400

1. Ibid., pp. 71–73.
2. A sixteenth-century Italian humanist and editor of classical texts.

maximâ atrocitate sit editum.' Five years after, A.D. 405, Rhadagaise[3] entered Italy with an army of 200,000 men; and though he was defeated by Stilicho,[4] yet he had ravaged the country before his defeat with such success, that the heathen Romans publicly declared Rome was given up to destruction, because it had forsaken the worship of heathen gods."

"In the latter end of the year 406, the Alains, Vandals and other barbarous people, passed the Rhine, and made the most furious irruption into Gaul, that had yet been known, passed into Spain, and from thence over into Africa, so that the maritime provinces became a prey to them; the riches and naval power of the empire were much diminished, and almost quite ruined. But the heaviest calamity fell upon the capital and city of Rome itself. For Alaric enters Italy in the year 409, and after wasting all the country round about," plundering every town, and putting the inhabitants to the sword,[5] "at length laid siege to Rome, which was then afflicted both with famine and a pestilential distemper. The city was forced to save itself from this danger by all its riches, and purchased a peace of Alaric, on very hard conditions. He raises the siege for a while, but soon returns, is received into the city, and makes Attalus, the governor of Rome, emperor. Soon after he deposes Attalus, and makes peace with Honorius, on condition he should be acknowledged[6] his associate, and have Gaul given to him and to his army. However, not satisfied with Honorius, and his performance of the conditions agreed between them, he continues the siege of Rome, and at last takes it, and gives the plunder of it to his soldiers, which also occasioned its being set on fire and burnt."

"This calamity of the capital city of the empire, was followed by the spoil of the greatest part of Italy in like manner, in which the Christian bishops and their churches were principal sufferers."

The THIRD TRUMPET.[7] Ch. 8:10–11. "There fell a great star from heaven, burning as it were a lamp; and it fell upon the third part of the rivers, and upon the fountains of waters. And the name of the star is called Wormwood; and many men died of the waters, because they were made bitter." "Denoting a further judgment on the Roman Empire, on the capital and seat of the empire; signifying a thorough desola-

3. A Goth who formed a confederacy against Italy among the barbarian nations on the Danube.

4. A Vandalic Roman general.

5. These two phrases are JE's translation of Latin excerpts from Sigonio.

6. Here JE interlined "him."

7. *Paraphrase and Notes,* pp. 74–77.

tion and downfall, not only weakening it by dismembering its provinces, but putting an end to all power and authority of the government itself. We have here a prophecy which aptly expresses a judgment to come on the seat of the Roman Empire, which should destroy the power of it in its spring and fountain, and cut off all its necessary supports."

"The last period of history, correspondent to the foregoing prophecy, ended in the peace which Italy and Rome enjoyed, after the taking of Rome by Alaric, and dismembering many provinces of the empire, when Athaulphus[8] left Italy, and went to settle in Gaul. The

412

emperor Honorius returned joyfully to Rome, to the great satisfaction of the city, in the year 412. Yet though Rome and Italy recovered themselves into a pretty good state of peace and liberty, many of the provinces were quite dismembered from the empire denoted by the sea.[9] The Goths, Burgundians, Franks, Vandals, etc., possessed themselves of the better parts of France and Spain.

"Valentinian, son of Placidia, succeeded his uncle Honorius, about

425

the year 425. In his time began those new invasions of the empire, which put an end to the imperial dignity and

427

power of Rome, and founded a new kingdom in Italy itself. In the year 427, Genseric, with an army of eighty thousand, seized on Africa and founded a kingdom there. The Romans

449

had given up the defense of Britain, so that the Britons were forced to call in the Saxons to their aid, in the year 449.

451

Attila, though soundly beat at Chalons in the year 451, so that 170,000, according to some, 300,000, fell in battle, yet the next year, he marches with another numerous army into Italy, and destroys all before him."

"Rome and Italy were scarce freed from these troubles, when new evils succeeded. Genseric is invited from Africa to revenge the murder of Valentinian. He lands in Italy in the year 455, marches

455

directly to Rome, takes the city, and plunders it, carries away *all the public and private riches*,[1] makes an incredible number of citizens captives, and takes the empress Eudoxia (who had desired his assistance to revenge the death of Valentinian), together with her daughters along with her into Africa. The name of the Roman Empire continued for a few years longer, as in a dying condition, under

8. Brother-in-law and successor of Alaric.
9. The last four words are JE's addition.
1. JE's emphasis.

several successors, till the year 476. Odoacer, drawing together an army of the several nations in Germany, enters Italy, subdues the whole country, takes the city of Rome, and in it the emperor Romulus or Augustulus, whom he deposes, and takes to himself the title of king of Italy. Thus Italy, and Rome itself, became the possession of the conquerors; and the Roman name, power and empire were from that time extinct. Odoacer did not indeed continue his kingdom long; for Theodoric, at the head of the Goths in Illyricum, attacked Odoacer's new-founded kingdom in Italy, and according to Paulus Diaconus,[2] so fully with the consent of Zeno, then emperor of the East, that he made a grant of Italy to Theodoric. Theodoric engages Odoacer, overcomes him, and puts him to death; and so founded the Gothic

493
kingdom of Italy, A.D. 493, which continued many years under his successors, till it was subdued by Narses[3] for the emperor Justinian, A.D. 553. Thus Rome itself, and Italy, the seat of the empire, according to the prophetic description, became a prey to the barbarous nations, and followed the fate of the provinces. However, even under the Gothic kingdom, Rome, though it lost the supreme authority of empire, was permitted to retain some appearance of its ancient form of government and magistracy. Theodoric made Ravenna the seat of his kingdom; yet Rome retained its senate and consuls, and the image of its former government."

The FOURTH TRUMPET.[4] Ch. 8:12. "And the third part of the sun was smitten, and the third part of the moon, and the third part of the stars, etc."

"This figurative representation will very properly express the following period of history, and the true state of the city of Rome, once the imperial city, and mistress of the world. . . . In the reign of Justinian, emperor of the East, the new Gothic kingdom of Italy is overthrown, and new and great calamities befall that miserable country. In the

536
course of this war, Belisarius, the imperial general, takes Rome, A.D. 536. The next year, Vitiges, king of the Goths, besieges it with an army of 150,000 men. In this long siege, which continued above a year, the Romans were afflicted both with famine and pestilence, and suffered extremely, though at length the Goths were fain to raise the siege. Totilas, king of the Goths,

2. Paul the Deacon (d. c. 800), a chronicler known as the "Father of Italian History."
3. A general of the eastern empire.
4. *Paraphrase and Notes*, pp. 77–79.

afterwards takes Rome, A.D. 546; it is retaken by Belisarius
the next year, and again taken by Totilas about two years
after. During this war, which lasted for twenty years, Rome
was besieged and taken five times. The city and whole country suffered
all the evils of war in every place; and the event was to reduce Rome
to the lowest and meanest condition, in the loss of all authority and
power, being made entirely subject to the exarchate of Ravenna. For
Narses, having quite subdued the Gothic kingdom of Italy for the
emperor of the East, was constituted governor of the whole country,
with the title of duke of Italy, and all the governors of the several cities
were only inferior officers under him. A little after, the exarchate of
Ravenna was established by the emperor Justin II, Longinus is sent
into Italy. He appoints a new form of government. The seat of government was from that time fixed at Ravenna, and every city of Italy
entirely subjected to the exarch, both in things civil and military.[5]
Thus Rome lost all her dignity and authority. Her senate and consuls
were abolished; and it was put upon a level with all the lesser cities
and towns of Italy, and became only a small duchy of the exarchate."
Its affairs were no more subject to the administration of senate and
consuls, but to the duke, a Grecian, sent there by the exarch of Ravenna; and thus it was for a long time.[6]

FIFTH TRUMPET.[7] Ch. 9:5, 10. "Tormented five months." This seems
to be "an allusion to the time in which natural locusts are used to do
harm, and after which they die, as Bochart[8] observes."

"It is well-known, that the manner of the Arabians invading their
neighbors was by sudden incursions during the summer months, re-
tiring again, and dispersing themselves to their own homes during the
winter, and gathering together the next spring for a new summer's
invasion." See Lowman, p. 89.

Rev. 9:2.[9] "And he opened the bottomless pit; and there arose a
smoke out of the pit, as the smoke of a great furnace; and the sun and
the air were darkened by reason of the smoke of the pit." There was

546

5. This sentence is JE's translation.
6. This sentence is JE's translation.
7. *Paraphrase and Notes*, pp. 83, 89.
8. Samuel Bochart (1599–1667), a French orientalist and biblical scholar whose principal
works were the *Geographia Sacra* (1646, 1651) and the *Hierozoicon, sive Historia Animalium
Sacrae Scripturae* (1663). Here Lowman was citing the latter.
9. The following two paragraphs, a later addition, have been rearranged according to JE's
directions.

something remarkable in the time of the Saracen Empire, very remarkable, literally agreeing with this which is related in the *Roman History* begun by Echard, Vol. 4, p. 359. "The empire itself was weakened and almost destroyed by earthquakes, which were more frequent and destructive about this time than had been known in any age before. Syria and Palestine were most grievously shaken; innumerable multitudes of men perished, together with great quantities of buildings, both public and private. The same provinces were visited with so extraordinary a darkness, that for several days together in the month of August, there was little or no distinction between day and night. About the same time, a furious pestilence broke out in Calabria,[1] and passing through Sicily proceeded as far as Constantinople, where it raged with an insatiate thirst for three years together, insomuch that the living were hardly sufficient to bury the dead. It was observable that they who were seized with this contagion, and were doomed to die, had little crosses made as it were with oil imprinted on their clothes, and by no art whatever to be removed. Though it was acknowledged by all to be the immediate finger of God Almighty, yet it served rather to terrify than to reform mankind. The world, for the most part, was grown too obstinate to be reclaimed, though surrounded with judgments, which in various methods denounced the divine indignation."[2]

And another time, there is an account in the same history, and the same volume, p. 396, that it was so dark for seventeen days together, "insomuch that several ships lost their course for want of light, and fell foul on each other."[3]

SIXTH TRUMPET.[4] [Ch. 9:14.] "Loose the four angels, which are bound in the great river Euphrates." "According to Sir Isaac Newton, this has respect to the four kingdoms of the Turks seated upon Euphrates: that of Armenia Major, seated at Miyapharekin, Megarkin or Martyropolis; that of Mesopotamia, seated at Mosul; that of Syria, seated at Aleppo; and that of Cappadocia, seated at Iconium."

"Mr. Mede takes them to be the tetrarchy, or four governments of the Turks in Asia, Aleppo, Damascus and Antioch." These Lowman mentions, though not agreeable to his own scheme.[5]

1. The southernmost extension of the Italian peninsula.
2. *Roman History*, Vol. 4 (5th ed., London, 1720), pp. 359–60.
3. Ibid., p. 396.
4. *Paraphrase and Notes*, pp. 90–92.
5. Unlike Newton and Mede, Lowman took the number "four" as a symbol of universality. According to him, the four angels who represent the providence of God possess unlimited power.

(It seems to me, that by the river Euphrates, we need to understand no more than about the eastern boundaries of the empire, as formerly the river Euphrates was for a long time reckoned the eastern boundary of the Roman Empire, as it had been also of the kingdom of the Jews, as Lowman observes, pp. 91–92.)

Rev. 11:9. "And shall not suffer their dead bodies to be put in graves." With ch. 13:15–17, "And cause, that as many as would not worship the image of the beast, should be killed. And he causeth all, both small and great, rich and poor, free and bond, to receive a mark in their right hand or in their foreheads; and that no man might buy or sell, save he that had the mark, or the name of the beast, or the number of his name."

"To shew how exactly this persecuting power answers every particular of the prophetic description, I shall just mention the bull of Pope Martin V, which directs the persecution of the followers of Wycliffe, John Huss and Jerome of Prague. 'We will and command, that, by this our authority apostolical, yea exhort and admonish all the professors of the Catholic faith, as emperors, kings, dukes, princes, etc., that they expel out of their kingdoms, provinces, cities, towns, etc., all and all manner of heretics, according to the effect and tenor of the Council of Lateran.[6] . . . That they suffer none such within their shires or circuits, to preach or to keep either house or family, either yet to use any handicraft or occupation, or other trades of merchandise, or else to solace themselves any ways, or frequent the company of Christian men. And furthermore, if such public and known heretics shall chance to die (although not so denounced by the church), yet in this so great a crime, let him and them want burial. . . . The residue let the aforesaid temporal lords, etc., take amongst them, with condign punishments, without any delay to punish.'" Lowman, p. 148.

Ch. 15:5. "And after that I looked, and behold, the temple of the tabernacle of the testimony in heaven was opened." " 'The temple of the tabernacle of the testimony,' seems plainly to be meant of the most holy place [Num. 1:50]. The whole tabernacle [was called], 'the tabernacle of the congregation which is without the veil, which is before the testimony' (Ex. 27:21)." This "inmost part of the temple, the seat of God's glory and of the oracle, was opened, as when the high priest went into the Holy of Holies."

Ch. 15:6. "And the seven angels came out of the temple, having the seven plagues, clothed in pure and white linen, and having their

6. The Fourth Lateran Council of 1215, convoked by Innocent III.

breasts girded with golden girdles." These seven angels came "out of the most holy place, having received their instructions from the oracle of God himself. They appeared in habits, like those the high priest wore when he went into the most holy place, and consulted the oracle." [Lowman], pp. 169–170.

Ch. 15:8. "And the temple was filled with smoke from the glory of God, and from his power. And no man was able to enter into the temple, till the seven plagues of the seven angels were fulfilled." I.e., the cloud of glory filled the temple. This cloud of glory "expressed the presence of God, for protection and for judgment. The glory was a sign of protection, at erecting the tabernacle, and at the dedication of the temple. But in the judgment of Korah, the glory of the Lord appeared unto all the congregation, when he and his companions were swallowed up by the earth (Num. 16:19). In like manner, when the congregation murmured against Moses and Aaron, and 'were gathered together against them, they looked towards the tabernacle of the congregation, and behold the cloud covered it, and the glory of the Lord appeared' [v. 42]. This was the forerunner of a judgment, as well as to be a sign of favor." [Lowman], p. 171.

The FIRST VIAL.[7] Ch. 16:2. "And the first went, and poured out his vial upon the earth; and there fell a noisome and grievous sore upon the men which had the mark of the beast, and upon them which worshiped his image." King Pepin and Charlemagne his son were the chief instruments of raising the papal power to the greatest height. But this great power of the Pope, which they had established, was made use of to bring grievous calamities on that imperial family.

"We have already seen, that the Pope received the temporal power of Rome, together with the exarchate of Ravenna, as the
756   patrimony of St. Peter, about the year 756, by the assistance of Pepin, king of France.

"Charles the Great, son of Pepin, was proclaimed emperor by the Pope's means, A.D. 800. This prince carried the French
800   monarchy to a very large extent, having France, Germany and Italy within the bounds of his dominion. In quality of emperor, he confirmed the grant of the exarchate to the popes, and enlarged the donation of his father Pepin.

"Charles the Great, like another Constantine, seemed to have laid the foundation of a great and prosperous empire for his family, and a state of great outward prosperity for the church.

"But it appeared in a very few years, that notwithstanding all the

7. *Paraphrase and Notes*, pp. 172–77.

care of Charles the Great, and his son Lewis the Pious, that all sorts of corruptions gained ground, and continually prevailed both in church and state. The worship of saints and images, the doctrine of purgatory, and masses for the dead, the doctrine of the real presence, and adoration of the consecrated bread, the perfection and merit of a monastic life, the superstitious and idolatrous worship founded on these doctrines, became the sum of religion."

"The doctrine of the Pope's supremacy and power over the whole church, was carried to a great height; great indeed, as represented by the Roman writers. In particular, that the imperial dignity was conferred, and the translation made of the empire from the Greeks to the French, by the proper authority of the Roman bishops. . . . This authority is said to be seated in the Pope, and by divine right in him primarily. . . . Hence, the whole power of the emperors is said to be wholly from the grace of God, and of the apostolic see."

But this power was made use of against this family that so aggrandized it, to weaken and ruin it.

"It would be long to mention the intrigues by which the popes endeavored to weaken the imperial power, and render the emperors odious and contemptible, as a noted French historian (Mézeray)[8] observes. 'Pope Gregory [IV] had a great hand in the troubles of the emperor Lewis the Pious, son of Charles the Great; [he] gave secret encouragement to his sons in their unnatural rebellion, *833* and to Ebbo, archbishop of Rheims, and the bishops of France,[9] when they actually deposed him, A.D. 833.' "

"A little after this, Pope John VIII assumed the authority of giving the empire to Charles the Bald of France, in prejudice to the rights of Lewis of Germany, the elder branch. . . . 'He with the other prelates, judging they had more to get by Charles than Lewis, gave him the preference, and crowned him emperor on Christmas day, *875* A.D. 875.'[1] But Charles obtained this favor of the Pope, at the expense of the rights of the imperial crown and sovereign dignity; insomuch, that of a superior, which he was before, he became a sort of vassal. He also gave up many of the rights of the Gallican church, and promised by oath to protect the Pope against all persons.

8. François Mézeray (1610–83), a political pamphleteer and historian, who wrote the *Histoire de la France.*

9. MS: "French."

1. Lowman was citing Jean de Heiss, the seventeenth-century author of the *Histoire de l'empire.*

"These ambitious views and growing power of the bishops of Rome, greatly weakened the government and authority of that family, to which it owed its greatness and support. It proved a painful sore, and incurable ulcer, and was in great measure the cause of those many evils, which for so long a time afflicted the inhabitants of the earth, during the quarrels and contests between the successors of Charles the Great, which ended at last in their ruin, carried the crown of France to Hugh Capet, and transferred the kingdom to another family, and the imperial dignity to the Germans, another nation and people. And in these evils, Italy and Rome itself had their share, according to the righteous judgments of God.

"The sons of Lewis the Pious, among whom his empire was divided, could no more agree among themselves after their father's death, than they could with him while he was living; their differences were only to be decided by the sword. In the battle of Fontenay, A.D. 841, an

841   hundred thousand men were slain, a blow that so weakened the family of Charles the Great, that it could never after recover itself."

Charles the Gross united most of the dominions of Charles the Great. He

880   reigned over Germany, Italy and France. "He was crowned emperor by the Pope, A.D. 880, and received king of France,

884   A.D. 884, the French passing over Charles the Simple as too young for government. But he was soon forsaken by his

subjects, who chose in his room Arnold, his brother's natural son, about A.D. 887. And he was reduced to great misery and want,

887   insomuch that he had not a servant to attend upon him, nor a penny to buy him bread; only Luitprand bishop of Mentz

had any pity for him, and at last kept him from starving."

"At the death of Charles the Gross, the family of Charles the Great was reduced to two princes, Arnold natural son of Carloman, and Charles the Simple. But there were several persons of great power descended from some of the daughters of Charles the Great, as Eudes, earl of Paris and duke of France; Berenger, duke of Friuli; and Guy, duke of Spoleto in Italy. France chose Eudes for their king; this occasioned continued wars between him and Charles the Simple, till the death [of] Eudes, A.D. 898. But the differences between Berenger and

898   Guy in Italy were much longer, and afflicted all Italy with great calamities, in which Rome itself could not avoid a considerable share." . . . And it is observable that the

popes themselves, as they had "a very great hand in exciting these troubles, so they had a great share in them too. . . . The quarrel soon spread itself into the Roman Church. The parties of Pope Formosus and Sergius raged against each other with uncommon fury. Insomuch that Pope Stephen caused the dead body of Formosus to be dug out of its grave, and after condemnation to be thrown into the river Tiber; made all his acts null and void, and took care to make an emperor of his own party."

"It would be endless to mention all the calamities these civil contentions brought upon Italy for near fourscore years, till Pope *960* John XII, A.D. 960, implored the assistance of Otho the Great, emperor of Germany, who accordingly came and put an end to the troubles of Italy; in acknowledgment of which *962* service, he received the imperial crown from the Pope, A.D. 962.

"The forementioned calamities were great in themselves, and were also an occasion of many others; for these civil contentions had greatly weakened the western empire, so that the Normans were enabled to invade and ravage several parts of it; especially in France, where at last they forced a settlement, and erected a powerful dominion in Normandy. The mischiefs these Norman invasions caused in France, are not to be mentioned, says Mézeray, without horror. Their desire of plunder brought them into the richest provinces; the false zeal for their religion (They were then heathen.) made them cruel and bloody, especially to churchmen. . . . From sea to sea there was not a monastery that did not feel their rage, nor a town that was not ransomed, pillaged, or burnt twice, or three times; which, says our historian, made it sufficiently evident, it was one of God's terrible plagues.

"On the other hand, the Saracens ravaged Italy, fixed themselves at Tarento,[2] made excursions to the very gates of Rome, and carried off the riches of the churches without the gates of the city," or in the suburbs, and carried away even the silver doors of the Vatican itself.[3]

"About the same time the Hungarians, then a barbarous and brutal people, broke in upon the German dominions, and plundered Bavaria, Swabia, Franconia and Saxony. They afterwards marched into Italy, routed Berenger, cut his army to pieces and often renewed their incursions, to the great terror and ruin of the inhabitants of those countries which they invaded.

"This was the calamitous state of the western empire for above an

2. A seaport in southeastern Italy.
3. The last portion of this sentence is JE's translation of Sigonio.

962   hundred years, from the death of Lewis the Pious, A.D. 840, to the settlement of the German Empire in Otho the Great, A.D. 962."

The SECOND VIAL.[4] Ch. 16:3. "And the second angel poured out his vial on the sea; and it became as the blood of a dead man. And every living soul in the sea died."

"The difference between the expressions of earth and sea, under this and the former vial, may very probably mean, that the former judgments were chiefly inflicted on the inhabitants residing in the inland provinces of the western empire; but that the judgments of this vial are chiefly inflicted on such of the subjects of this empire, as went out by sea to foreign countries, and aboard fleets, especially on the Mediterranean Sea, which is used [to] be styled in Scripture 'the sea' and 'the great sea' " [e.g. Num. 34:6–7].

The history of the first vial "has brought us down to the latter end of the tenth century. Then the empire was fixed in Germany by Otho the Great, and the kingdom of France passed into the *987*   third race, the family of Capet, in which it still remains, about A.D. 987."

"From A.D. 1000 to 1100, the corruptions of true religion were greatly increased. A prodigious superstition spread every-
1000–1100 where during the 11th century, not only the lower sort and common people, but among persons of the first rank, even emperors and princes themselves. Pretended miracles, apparitions of departed souls, dreadful tales of the pains of purgatory, improved the people's superstition, and enriched the church. The whole of religion was placed in penances, masses, legacies to redeem souls from purgatory, pilgrimages, especially to the Holy Sepulcher at Jerusalem, which ended at last in the holy war.[5]

"This gave fair occasion to the popes to carry on their ambitious designs, and enlarge their authority in things temporal as well as spiritual. The antichristian power began now to exert itself above all that is called God, and to claim a power of choosing and deposing emperors, and to deprive princes of all rights by excommunication. Hildebrand was Pope, by the name of Gregory the VII. A.D. 1073, he *1073*   expressly claimed the authority of sovereign judge over all, of deposing emperors and absolving subjects from their allegiance. He actually used this power towards the emperor Henry IV,

4. *Paraphrase and Notes*, pp. 178–82.

5. I.e., the crusades.

1076

and other princes of Europe. In the year 1076, he held a council at Rome, of 110 bishops, who after mature debate, concluded the Pope to have reason to deprive the emperor of his crown, [and] absolve the princes and members of the empire from their oaths. This resolution the Pope put in execution; [he] excommunicated the emperor and all his adherents. Further,

1080

in the year 1080, he renewed his excommunication against the emperor, declares he had forfeited all the kingdoms of Germany and Italy, and all royal dignity, forbid all Christians to obey him, gives the kingdom of Germany to Rodolph,[6] exhorting all the princes to take arms against him. What troubles, what unnatural rebellions, what bloody wars this most extravagant claim of power occasioned, the historians of those times relate at large. They are such as in themselves might be esteemed justly a terrible judgment for this antichristian apostasy.

"This Pope[7] had other differences, with almost all the other Christian princes. He threatened to excommunicate Philip I, king of France, and usurped a full authority over the bishops and ecclesiastical affairs of France by his legates. And, in a word, he did all he could to become the only sovereign monarch of the universe."

"Besides all these flames which the ambition of the popes kindled in the western empire itself, it was the occasion of another most remarkable judgment, which fell grievously on the zealous abettors of superstition, and supporters of the papal authority. Pope Urban the II, next but one to this Hildebrand, continued the quarrel with the emperor, who supported Clement, formerly called Guibert, as Pope against him.

1096

"Pope Urban went into France, A.D. 1096, and held a council at Clermont. He proposed, with great earnestness, to raise an army, which should march into the Holy Land, to recover Jerusalem and the Holy Sepulcher out of the hands of Mahometans. It is incredible what effect so romantic a project had on the minds of a superstitious multitude. They received it as the will of God, and fell in with the Pope's proposal with wonderful zeal. The Pope, to encourage their constancy in such a resolution, promises free indulgence for their sins, to take them into the church's protection, both for their persons and fortunes."

The popes had great advantages from these *croisades* and voyages, to render themselves absolute. " 'Because they took the authority of com-

6. Rudolph of Rheinfelden (d. 1080), who was elected anti-king against Henry IV.
7. I.e., Gregory VII.

manding these expeditions of which they were the head, they had the persons and estates of those who took the cross in their protection. It made the use of indulgences and dispensations more common than before. Their legates had the management of the alms and legacies which were given for these wars; and it, moreover, gave the popes a pretense to raise the tenth on the clergy.'[8] In effect, no policy could have so well served the Pope's ambition, nor any means be better suited to render his authority supreme and absolute. We have an immediate instance of the truth of these observations. Clement, who disputed the papacy with Urban, had possessed himself of Rome; but Urban, by the help of those who had listed themselves for this holy war, assaulted Rome, and took it, and forced Clement to retire."

"An incredible number of persons soon prepared themselves for this holy war. Pope Urban traveled through Italy to raise money. The people listed themselves so fast in this spiritual militia, that the countries seemed to be deserted; and all the coasts and havens filled with people, setting out on this voyage to Asia. This first expedition is computed to consist of more than three hundred thousand men. They met with some success at first. Godfrey of Bouillon, their general, had the honor of receiving the title of king of Jerusalem, having taken it, *1099*   A.D. 1099. Yet their victories were so bloody, that in a very short time, there remained no more than five thousand horse and fifteen thousand foot of that numerous army."

"Another *croisade* was raised, A.D. 1100. This again consisted of above three hundred thousand more. In this expedition, not only *1100*   several great princes, but moreover many prelates, and even many great ladies, resolved to undertake the voyage."

"Thus, in about 4 years, six hundred thousand men were sent to perish, through the ambitious views of the popes.

"These expeditions continued for many years with an incredible effusion of blood. According to some authors, there perished above two millions of these enthusiasts. Others observe, there were hardly any men left in the West, and almost no persons seen, but either infants or widows.

"In fine, about the year 1190, the emperor Frederick, our King Richard, Philip Augustus of France and others, made an- *1190*   other fruitless and inglorious expedition; and after the loss of the greatest part of their armies, were forced to leave

8. Lowman was citing Mézeray. The "tenth" was a tithe.

what they had been so long contending for with so much bloodshed, in the hands of the Mahometans.

"This is a very remarkable part of history. It falls in exactly with the order and series of the prophecies, and is so memorable a judgment on the supporters of the papal apostasy, that I shall leave it to the reader's judgment, whether it does not give light to the time and contents of this second vial."

The THIRD VIAL.[9] Ch. 16:4–7. "And the third angel poured out his vial upon the rivers and fountains of waters; and they became blood. And I heard the angel of the waters say, Thou art righteous, O Lord, which art and wast and shall be, because thou hast judged thus. For they have shed the blood of saints and prophets, and thou hast given them blood to drink; for they are worthy. And I heard another angel out of the altar say, Even so, Lord God Almighty, true and righteous are thy judgments."

" 'Rivers and fountains of waters' may not unfitly signify the original countries or seats of empire, in distinction from the provinces, as fountains are the original of rivers, which run in one common collection of waters into the sea. *And as waters are necessary for life, when they are infected and become deadly, they are an emblem of such judgments as should cut off the very supports of life.*"[1]

"The judgments signified by the third vial, according to the order of the prophecies, will be the next remarkable judgment upon the followers of the beast, after the calamities of the holy war; which, according to the order of time, must be about A.D. 1200, for a proportional number of the 1260 years of this period.

1200

The contents of this vial, or the nature of the judgments signified by it, is shedding of blood, in recompense for the blood of the saints shed by authority of the beast. This judgment is chiefly to fall on those parts of the western empire, which were the original seat of the beast's residence and dominion."

"The persecuting power of popery was fully established, and raged with greatest fury, during this period of time. It was in this time they were most eminently distinguished for shedding the blood of saints and prophets.

"The Albigenses became numerous and powerful; they were spread through Languedoc, Provence, Dauphine and Aragon. They were

9. *Paraphrase and Notes*, pp. 182–88.
1. JE's emphasis. See above, p. 191.

protected by persons in power, in particular by Raymond, count of
Toulouse.[2] Pope Innocent III sent his legates to suppress
1198   them, about A.D. 1198. He gave them commission not
only to preach against the Albigenses, but to excite princes
and people to exterminate them by a *croisade*, in which he endeavored
to engage Philip Augustus, then king of France, and the great princes
and lords of his kingdom.

"Besides all former methods of proceeding against heretics, which
one would have thought were severe enough, this Pope Innocent the
Third found out, and established the new method of the Inquisition.
Father Dominic was made first inquisitor about A.D.
1216   1216. When he received his authority from the Pope,
he declared he was resolved to defend the doctrines of the
faith, meaning the corruption of the Romish Church, with the utmost
vigor; and that if the spiritual and ecclesiastical arms were not sufficient for this end, it was his fixed purpose to call in princes to take
arms against heretics, that the very memory of 'em might be destroyed.

"Thus, all the severe and bloody methods of persecution were set on
foot. A vast army of cross-bearers was raised: Mézeray says, they were
not less than five hundred thousand. They besieged Béziers,[3] took it,
and put above 60,000 to the sword, and proceeded with great cruelty,
till they had ruined the Count de Toulouse, and given his estate to
Montfort, general of the *croisade*, a reward for his services.

"The severest methods of persecution were established by the famous
Council of Lateran.[4] The poor Albigenses were everywhere a sacrifice
to the merciless rage of their enemies. The chief zeal of the church, in
those times, consisted in putting those they called heretics to death in
the most cruel manner they could invent. Thus they made themselves
worthy of the judgment, that God should 'give them blood to drink'
[Rev. 16:6].

"And we shall find this part of the prophecy as fully verified in the
events of providence as the former.

"There had been, for a long time, great contests between the emperors and popes about investitures. This contention had occasioned[5]
great confusion and disturbance. Parties were formed on each side,

2. Raymond (d. 1156), not to be confused with the crusader who founded a Latin state
around Tripolis in the Holy Land.
3. A city in southern France.
4. See p. 231, n. 6.
5. MS: "occasion."

distinguished by the names of Guelphs and Ghibellines: the Guelphs were the papal party, the Ghibellines the imperial.

"The emperor Frederick II was excommunicated, A.D. 1227, for not going in person to the holy war. This so angered the emperor, that he endeavored every way to mortify the Pope. He engaged several of the powerful noblemen of Rome against him, so that the Pope was forced to leave Rome, and retire to Perugia.[6] The Guelph and Ghibelline faction strove in every place to raise their own party, and to ruin the other; so that almost all the cities in Italy were in civil wars, and the blood of the citizens in almost every place, shed by their own hands.

1227

"However, the emperor embarked the next year for the Holy Land, but soon found the Pope had sent him into Syria, that he might make war against him the better in Italy. He therefore returned, recovered the places taken from him by the Pope, ravaged all the Pope's temporal dominions even to the gates of Rome. In the year 1237, he beat the army of the legate formed against him, after a furious and bloody battle, and put the general and other officers to death by the hands of the common hangman. The animosities of the Guelphs and Ghibellines were so outrageous, that not only the several cities of Italy were divided, but particular houses and families, so that they gave no quarter to each other.

1237

"The death of Frederick II, A.D. 1250, left the empire in great confusion; many pretended to the imperial dignity. These contests were sensibly felt in Italy; such cities as held of the empire, either formed themselves into commonwealths, or were governed by princes of their own. Pope Urban IV, jealous of the power of Manfred,[7] who had possessed himself of the kingdoms of Naples and Sicily, and to recover the power of the Guelph party, which was almost ruined, made an offer of the kingdoms of Naples and Sicily to Charles, earl of Anjou, brother to Lewis king of France, on condition he would bring sufficient forces into Italy, to support the almost ruined party of the Guelphs. Charles accepts the Pope's offer, [and] was crowned by Clement IV on condition to hold those kingdoms of the holy see, by homage, fealty and an annual rent. His army was joined by the Guelphs, defeated Manfred's army, and so got into possession of both the Sicilies. Upon this Conradin, duke of Swabia, son of the emperor Conrad, and last of the family, was en-

1250

6. An inland city in central Italy.
7. The son of Frederick II, a leader of the Ghibelline party.

couraged to enter into Italy by the Ghibellines, who were not able to
endure the power of the Guelphs, so greatly strengthened by the protection of Charles. Both sides came to a battle, in which Conradin was
beaten and taken prisoner, with Frederick of Austria who accompanied
him, and both had their heads cut off; so that the two great
1268   families of Swabia and Austria became extinct, A.D. 1268.
This dishonorable execution was by the Pope's advice."

"Rodolph of Hapsburg, afterwards emperor, who by transferring
these inheritances into his own family, raised the grandeur of the present
house of Austria, could not be persuaded to meddle with the affairs of
Italy; so that the government of most cities fell into several hands, just
as the contending parties could prevail over each other.

"The contest, upon the death of Rodolph, between his son Albert of
Austria and Adolph of Nassau, kept the affairs of Italy in pretty much
the same state. The feuds between the Guelphs and Ghibellines continued and increased."

"Pope Boniface VIII persecuted the Ghibellines and the cardinals
Colonna[8] with great severity. This more inflamed the parties against
each other; so that the Pope was taken prisoner by the Ghibellines, the
grief of which is supposed to have hastened his end. '*Dolore animi confectus
periit*,' says my author.[9]

"Pope Clement the V, a little time after, consulted his own safety,
and retired with the cardinals into France, where the court of Rome
continued for above seventy years, in a sort of banishment from their
own country and dominions;[1] in all which time, the Guelphs and
Ghibellines made war on each other, and Rome was in the greatest
confusion.

"The emperor Henry VII resolved to assert the rights of the empire
in Italy. Pope Gregory, on the other hand, by secret practices, raised a
powerful league against him. He engaged the king of Naples, the cities
of Florence, Siena, Lucca, Cremona, Padua and others to oppose him.
The city of Rome was in great distraction. The Colonnas, at the head
of the Ghibellines, seized on the Lateran, the amphitheater and other
principal places in the city. John, brother of the king of Naples, at the
head of the Guelphs, possessed themselves of the Capitol, [the] castle of
St. Angelo, the mole of Adrian and the Vatican. Platina has represented
the disorders of these bloody civil wars, as if the Italians were in every

8. A powerful noble family in Italy, usually siding with the Ghibelline faction.
9. Lowman was citing a history of the popes by Bartolomeo Platina, a fifteenth-century
Italian humanist and historian.
1. The "Babylonian Captivity" of the popes at Avignon, 1309–77.

place thirsting after each other's blood, without any bounds to their mutual rage and cruelty,"[2] continually killing one another in every city, yea, in every little castle. Old men were murdered, and little children dashed in pieces. Nor was there any sort of cruelty omitted.

"Benedict XII, in order to make as many friends as he could, and keep an interest in Italy against the emperor, published an edict, whereby he confirmed to all persons, who had seized on the governments of Lombardy, that they should have a just title by that grant to what they had usurped."

"The emperor, on the other hand, not to be outdone by the Pope in liberality, presented all who had seized on any part of the estate of the Pope or church, with a title to possess them as their own, by virtue of the imperial authority.

"Thus were the parties spirited up against each other. The contest continued for above an hundred years, [and] spread itself throughout all Italy; so that there was not a city, scarce a village or family, in which they did not shed each other's blood in this furious contention. It would be endless to mention particulars; I shall only take notice of one, the massacre in Sicily, usually called the Sicilian Vespers, *1282* A.D. 1282. Pope Nicholas had the chief hand in the plot, and managed the principal parts of it, though it did not break out till after his death, as Mézeray expressly declares. The French were murdered throughout the whole island. They massacred them at the very altars; they ripped up the women with child, and dashed out the children's brains against the stones. Eight thousand were murdered in two hours, and they spared the life but of one single person.

"When we see in history such bloody contentions, for so long a time, occasioned by the Pope's ambition, we have evident proof of this righteous judgment of God, that he gave them blood to drink, as they had shed the blood of his saints [Rev. 16:6]. We see their ambition proves as bloody and destructive to themselves, as to those whom they persecuted for their faithfulness in the cause of truth and righteousness. Here is a remarkable concurrence of persecution, on one hand, and of punishment by civil contentions and bloodshed, on the other; which are the distinguishing marks of this vial, as the time exactly answers to the series and order of the prophecies."

The FOURTH VIAL.[3] Ch. 16:8–9. "And the fourth angel poured out his vial upon the sun, and power was given unto him to scorch men

2. The remainder of the paragraph is JE's translation.
3. *Paraphrase and Notes,* pp. 188–94. See above, p. 192.

with fire. And men were scorched with great heat, and blasphemed the name of God, which had power over these plagues; and they repented not to give him glory."

"The sun, says Sir Isaac Newton,[4] is put in sacred prophecy, for the whole species and race of kings, in the kingdom or kingdoms of the world politic, shining with regal power and glory; and the scorching heat of the sun, for vexatious wars, persecutions and troubles inflicted by the king.

"Great troubles are often expressed in Scripture, by burning the inhabitants of the earth (Is. 24:6). Our Saviour uses the same figure in the parable of the sower, which he himself interprets of trouble and persecution" [Matt. 13:6–21].

"The time answering to the foregoing vial, brought us down to about
the year 1371, when the factions were so well quieted in
1371　　　　Italy, that the popes returned to Rome, from their banishment at Avignon in France." Agreeable to what Sir Isaac
Newton observes, of the signification of the sun in the style of prophecy, so the popes will most naturally be meant by the sun here. "So that, the power given to the sun 'to scorch men with fire' [Rev. 16:8], will most probably signify some great and grievous evils, brought upon the inhabitants of the earth by their hot and burning passions of ambition, envy and covetousness."

"Upon the death of Pope Gregory XI, which happened soon after his return to Rome, there followed a great schism, which was the most memorable event, and of greatest consequence in the history of those times," as Dupin[5] observes.

"The citizens of Rome, in order to fix the residence of the popes among themselves for the future, warmly pressed the choice of a Roman, or at least an Italian. They continually cried out, they would have a Roman Pope, and threatened the French cardinals to cut them in pieces, if they did not choose a Roman or Italian. At length the people broke into the conclave, and seized the cardinals, continually demanding a Roman Pope. Some of the cardinals' domestics having said to them, 'Have you not the cardinal of St. Peter?' Immediately, as if he had been duly elected, they clothed him[6] in the pontifical robes, placed him on the altar and proceeded to adoration, notwithstanding his own

---

4. See above, p. 6.

5. Louis Dupin (1657–1719), a French theologian and historian with Gallican and Jansenist leanings.

6. Bartolomeo Prignano (d. 1389), a native of Naples and archbishop of Bari.

declaration that he was no Pope. Yet the next day he caused himself to be proclaimed Pope, by the name of Urban VI. The cardinals then publicly owned him, yet privately writ to the king of France and other Christian princes, that it was a void and null election, which they did not intend should be acknowledged. Urban, trusting to his party at Rome, behaved with great insolence, and very much disobliged the cardinals. They retired from Rome to Fundi;[7] there they chose a new Pope, Robert, cardinal of Geneva, who took the name of Clement the VII.

"Thus a schism began, which continued many years, and divided the several kingdoms and states of Europe; some supporting the cause of Urban, others that of Clement, who left Italy, and placed his residence at Avignon."

Urban died A.D. 1389. "The Italian cardinals proceeded to a new election, and chose Boniface the IX, a Neopolitan. In the *1389* like manner, on the death of Clement, A.D. 1394, at Avignon, the cardinals of that party chose Peter Luna of Aragon who was named Benedict. Many attempts were made to heal this breach, but all to no purpose; a renunciation or cession of both the popes was proposed, but that suited the ambition of neither.

"The Romans, after the death of Boniface, chose Innocent VII, and after him Gregory XII, his successors. The mischiefs of these contentions were at last thought to require[8] general council. A *1409* general council was held at Pisa, A.D. 1409. The council deposed both popes, Gregory and Benedict, and chose a new Pope, Alexander V. The council consisted of 22 cardinals, 12 archbishops, 67 bishops, 85 deputies, a great number of abbots, proctors of orders and chapters, with 67 ambassadors of kings or sovereign princes. And yet both the popes found means to support themselves, and keep up a party, the one chiefly in Italy, the other principally in Spain. Alexander V, chosen by the council, was received by the greater part of the nations. Upon his death, John XXIII was chose in his place. There were now three successors to St. Peter, in three lines of succession, at the same time. John XXIII appointed a general council to *1414* be held at Constance, 1414. This council pressed him to resign, and declared he ought to do so, as well as Gregory and Benedict. John did all he could to avoid this ungrateful proposal; but finding he could not gain his point in the council, he retired from it.

7. A town in south central Italy.
8. Lowman reads "want."

The council notwithstanding continued, and cited John to appear. Upon his refusal, they declared him suspended from all government, spiritual and temporal; and at last, by a decisive sentence deposed him. Gregory renounced the papacy, and was confirmed a cardinal. But Benedict, continuing to oppose the council, was declared contumacious, a schismatic, and deposed.

"The next business was to choose a new Pope, to whom all would submit. The council unanimously chose Martin, A.D. 1417. This seemed to put an end to a long schism, and to restore the peace of the church. But it soon appeared, the ambition of the popes was restless, and a continued source of disorders and mischievous contentions.

1417

"Pope Eugene IV, who succeeded Martin V, was greatly displeased with the Council of Basel for maintaining the authority of councils to reform the church both in head and members. Therefore, A.D. 1432, he published an order to dissolve it. The council could not prevail upon the Pope to revoke the decree, yet continued to sit notwithstanding. They cited the Pope to appear before them. He was forced at last to revoke the dissolution, to allow and approve the continuation, with all that had been done by the council in that time; and the decree of the [Council of] Constance was renewed, for confirmation of the authority of general councils. Yet still new difficulties arose; the Pope translated the council from Basel to Ferrara, and opened a council there, January 10, 1438. Yet many bishops continue still at Basel, and proceeded so far as to depose Pope Eugene, and choose another Pope, who was called Felix V. Thus the schism was renewed by two popes, each at the head of a council: Pope Eugene presiding in the Council of Florence, to which place he had translated the council from Ferrara; and Pope Felix presiding in the Council of Basel. And at the same time Germany proposed to call a third general council, to examine the rights of the other two. This schism continued to the death of Eugene, A.D. 1447, Felix then resigning all his pretensions to Nicholas V, his successor.

1432

1438

1447

"From this time, though the schism was ended, the popes were more taken up with the wars of Italy, enterprises against the Turks, aggrandizing their temporal power, and establishing their own families, than in any care of religion; which proved the occasion of great disorders.

"Alexander VI was one of the worst of men; he dishonored his dignity, says Dupin, by ambition, avarice, cruelty and debauchery.

According to Mézeray, he was one of the most impious and vicious of men; and if there was anyone that exceeded him in his abominable crimes, it was his own bastard son Caesar Borgia.[9]

"The disorders and calamities occasioned by these contentions, which the ambition, tyranny and cruelty of the popes were the sole cause of, appear everywhere in the history of these times; neighbor princes and nations were divided by their quarrels, and they set the world about them in a flame, by the fire of their contentions. All the principal wars and quarrels of this age had their rise from the ambitious projects of the popes. This was the chief spring of these long and bloody wars about the kingdoms of Naples and Sicily: Pope Urban, to revenge himself of Jane, queen of Naples, offered the investiture of the kingdom to Charles of Durazzo, and persuaded him to attempt to dethrone her, though he was greatly obliged to her, and even designed by her for her successor. This ungrateful attempt, at the Pope's solicitation, made the queen change her mind, and adopt Lewis, duke of Anjou, for her heir. Charles of Durazzo was crowned in Rome, *anno* 1380, took Naples without

1380 resistance, and put Queen Jane to death, together with her husband, Otho of Brunswick. Upon this success of Charles, the duke of Anjou was somewhat in doubt, whether he should pursue his claim. But Pope Clement, who had no other way to depose Urban, used all endeavors to press him to it, that it seemed, says Mézeray, he valued not the ruin of the church, both in temporals and spirituals, if he could but establish himself."

"As these wars began, so they were kept alive by the intrigues of the popes for above 100 years, in which France, Spain and Germany had their share, as well as Italy.

"But these evils, great as they were, were not the only mischiefs the ambition and contentions of the popes caused in these times. The Council of Constance prosecuted[1] John Huss and Jerome of Prague with great severity, and a dishonorable breach of faith. They were both burnt by order of the council, notwithstanding the emperor's safe conduct. Such an unjust and perfidious declaration, 'that faith was not to be kept with heretics,' quite enraged the Bohemians. The emperor Sigismund, who succeeded his brother Wenceslaus in that kingdom, was fain to use the army he designed against the Turks to quiet the Bohemians. The Pope sent a legate to raise a *croisade* against them. There

9. The one-time archbishop of Valencia who pursued his political ambitions with notorious unscrupulousness after renouncing his vows.

1. Lowman reads "persecuted."

were many lesser skirmishes and battles with the Hussite general Ziska. At length an army of 40,000 horse, and as many foot, was sent against them, *anno* 1431, with the Pope's legate and many princes of Germany at the head of it. This great army was defeated by the Bohe-

1431   mians; and they were not at last subdued but with great difficulty, and by reason of differences among themselves, which were raised and managed by the Pope's agents, to weaken and destroy them.

"Nor were these all the fatal consequences of these ambitious contentions of the popes; they caused a schism between the Greek and Latin churches, and a war between the Christians of the eastern and western empires, which greatly weakened the Christian interest against their common enemies, the Turks. They kept up continual quarrels among the Christian princes, which [the] Turks, who were watching all opportunities, knew well how to improve. Mahomet[2]

1453   made great advances in Europe, and A.D. 1453, put an end to the eastern empire, by taking the city of Constantinople, which has continued to be the seat and capital of the Turkish Empire ever since. He soon passed over into Italy, took Otranto,[3] left a garrison in it; and nothing seems to have saved Italy from the greatest danger, but the death of Mahomet, and a dispute between his sons about the succession; for Mahomet was eagerly bent on taking old Rome, as he had already taken new Rome or Constantinople."

Some interpreters carry the meaning of the expressions in this prophecy, of the sun's scorching men with great heat, and men's being scorched with fire [Rev. 16:8–9], yet further, "and conceive they are to be understood in a literal sense also, for intemperately hot and burning seasons, which should destroy the fruits of the earth, [and] occasion famine and pestilential distempers. And it is certain, in the history of this period, that the prophecy is fully verified in this meaning too. Not to enter into a particular detail of the numerous instances the history of this period furnishes us with, there is one so remarkable above others, and which falls out at a time so proper to close this period, that I think it deserves particular notice.

"A new kind of disease invaded Germany this year, A.D. 1529, says a very judicious historian.[4] 'Men being taken with

1529   a pestilential sweating, either died in twenty-four hours; or if they sweated out the poison, they recovered by

2. Mohammed II (1432–81), the Ottoman sultan of Turkey known as "The Conqueror."

3. A seaport in southern Italy.

4. Johannes Sleidanus (1506–56), a chronicler of the German Reformation.

degrees their health again. But before any remedy could be found for it, many thousands perished. This distemper, in a very short time, spread itself from the ocean all over Germany; and with incredible celerity, like a fire raged far and near. It is commonly called "the sweating sickness" of England; for in the first year of the reign of Henry the VII of England, which was in the year of our Lord,

1486   1486, the same plague infested that country. And because there was no remedy known for such a new distemper, it swept away a vast number of people. At this time also there was a great scarcity of corn and wine; so that all the judgments wherewith God, in his anger, uses to punish an unthankful people, as the sword, pestilence and famine, fell upon Germany at one and the same time.'

"It appears this was a new distemper, and but lately known; yet it was not the first time this period or age was punished with it. 'There was a sweating sickness about 11 years before, *anno* 1517,

1517   being of that malignity, that it killed in the space of three hours. Many persons of quality died of it; it was so mortal among the vulgar sort, that in some towns it took away half the people, in others the third part.'[5]

"About 30 years before this, viz., the beginning of the reign of Henry VII, 'there reigned in the city, and other parts of the kingdom, a disease (says the Lord Bacon)[6] then new, which of the accidents and manner thereof, they called the sweating sickness. It was conceived to proceed from a malignity in the constitution of the air, and infinite persons died suddenly of it, before the manner of the cure and attendance was known.'

"Here we see a new pestilential distemper returning three times in about 40 years, and the last time not confined to a particular country, but spreading itself through most parts of Europe.

"I cannot leave this part of history, without the account a French historian gives us of it in his own country, as I think it greatly illustrates the propriety and elegance of the prophetic description.

" 'From the end of the year 1528 to the beginning of the year 1534,' says the historian,[7] 'heaven was so angry with France, that

1528–1534 there was a continual disorder of the seasons, or rather summer alone had taken all their places; so that for five years there was not two days of frost together. This intemperate heat enervated

5. Lowman was citing Herbert of Cherbury (1583–1648), poet, philosopher, and author of a life of Henry VIII.

6. Francis Bacon (1561–1626).

7. François Mézeray.

nature, if I may so express it, and made it impotent. It brought nothing to maturity; the trees blossomed immediately after the fruit. Corn did not increase in the ground for want of water. There was such a quantity of vermin, as eat up the young shoots; the harvest did not produce sufficient for the next year's seed. This scarcity caused an universal famine; after which there appeared a distemper called *troussegaland*,[8] and then a furious pestilence; by which three plagues, above a quarter part of mankind was carried away.'

"Thus literally, as well as in a figurative meaning, there was power given unto the sun [Rev. 16:8], to scorch men in this period."

Ch. 17:12. "And the TEN HORNS[9] which thou sawest are ten kings, etc."

"Ten in prophetic language, does not always mean a precise number, but it is used as a certain number for an uncertain, to express in general several or many. Ten times is the same as many times; ten women the same as many women; ten men mean several men; ten sons several sons."

"So that there seems to be no necessity of finding a precise number of ten different kingdoms, or just so many different governments, neither more nor less, erected on the ruins of the Roman Empire, in fact, in those times of disorder and confusion. They were shifting and variable; but that several new kingdoms were erected, when the northern nations divided the empire among themselves, is well-known in history, and evident in the several distinct governments of Europe at this day.

"Several interpreters have reckoned up the number of ten precisely with the time when, and the place where they were erected. . . . It may be sufficient here to mention the account given of them by Sir Isaac Newton.

1. The kingdom of the Vandals and Alans in Spain and Africa.
2. The kingdom of the Suevians in Spain.
3. The kingdom of the Visigoths.
4. The kingdom of the Alans in Gallia.
5. The kingdom of the Burgundians.
6. The kingdom of the Franks.
7. The kingdom of Britain.
8. The kingdom of the Huns.
9. The kingdom of the Lombards.
10. The kingdom of Ravenna."

8. I.e., a sporadic cholera.
9. *Paraphrase and Notes*, pp. 212–13.

REMARKS ON LOWMAN[1]

That there are no SYNCHRONISMS, or resumings of things before prophesied of more generally, to foretell them more particularly or in another manner, and declare something further concerning them, is contrary to the method of almost all the prophecies of Scripture, and plainly contrary to the manner of this prophecy of the Revelation.[2]

The several times of the prevailing of the SARACENS, are very improperly made distinct WOES, in those three great woes denounced [Rev. 8:13 ff.].[3]

It seems not reasonable to suppose [the] FIFTH TRUMPET no way affects the western empire [Rev. 9:1–12], which Mr. Lowman supposes the three foregoing trumpets do respect almost wholly. See Lowman, pp. 86–88.[4]

And besides, the WOE or the calamities brought on the Christian world by this trumpet, as Lowman limits it, were not greater, nor near so great, as the calamities under some of the former trumpets; whereas the prophecy represents these three last woes as vastly the greatest.

'Tis most evidently otherwise than Mr. Lowman supposes, that the THREE WOES are woes on the saints or church of God, and not on its enemies. These woes are denounced to the inhabitants of the earth. And this prophecy represents the inhabitants of the earth and the sea, as given over to God's judgments and plagues, when the servants of God were to be safe, being sealed in their foreheads, that woe might not befall them. Thus the first woe is described (ch. 9:1–11) as being only

1. See above, p. 57.

2. Lowman wrote, "So that there is no ground, I conceive, to consider the Prophecies which belong to these Periods as Synchronisms; on the contrary, each of these Prophecies seems fixed to that particular Period of Time to which they belong; which Periods are manifestly represented not as contemporary, but as an Order and Series of successive Times and Events" (*Paraphrase and Notes,* p. xi). Concerning synchronisms, see above, p. 5.

3. In the *Paraphrase and Notes,* p. 115, Lowman associated the first woe with the rise and progress of Mahometanism, the second with the Saracen threat to the western empire, and the third with a general state of affliction in the church.

4. On these pages Lowman discussed the religious and political successes of Islam in the East.

on those men that had not the seal of God in their foreheads. See v. 4. The second woe described (ch. 9:12–21), evidently is not on the church of God, but on idolaters. See vv. 20–21.

The SEVENTH TRUMPET is one of the WOE trumpets; and according to him, the woe that all the trumpets bring is on the church of God. And yet he himself supposes, that the seventh trumpet introduces a state of peace and prosperity to the church, which ends this period, as he supposes that the church's rest and happiness ends all the seven periods of this prophecy.[5] Those happy things spoken of chapter 11:15–19, are proclaimed on the sounding of this trumpet, which is evidently the great happiness of the church. And yet he supposes it to be a woe trumpet to the church.

Mr. Lowman confounds the order of the prophecies of this book more than former interpretations, especially in the 11th chapter.

Mr. Lowman himself makes many SYNCHRONISMS; as for instance, he supposes the latter part of chapter 6 and chapter 7:12 ff. to be contemporary. So he makes the 6th and 14th verses of chapter 12 to be contemporary. So he allows the prophecy of the two witnesses [ch. 11], and that of the woman in the wilderness [ch. 12], and that of the wild beast rising out of the sea and earth [ch. 13], and that of the woman on the scarlet-colored beast [ch. 17], and many others that might be mentioned, to be contemporary: i.e., that in these instances, different prophetical representations are given in the same book of prophecy of the same period and the same event, which is as much of a synchronism as I desire.

'Tis exceeding unlikely that the angel should swear so solemnly, that the time of the church's deliverance should not be yet, as Mr. Lowman interprets that chapter 10:6.[6]

Mr. Lowman supposes the period of the trumpets plainly follows the period of the seals, because it is expressly said that "when he had opened the seventh seal, there was silence in heaven for half an hour." And the next words are, "And I saw the seven angels, which stood before God; and to them was given seven trumpets" (ch. 8:1–2). But the words of the prophecy don't more plainly, nor so plainly, shew that the trumpets follow the seals, as they shew that the third woe follows the slaying and rising of the witnesses, which is contrary to what Mr. Lowman supposes.[7]

---

5. See Lowman's description of the happy ending of this period in the *Paraphrase and Notes*, pp. 167–71.

6. *Paraphrase and Notes*, pp. 101–02.

7. Ibid., pp. 64–66.

AN ACCOUNT OF EVENTS PROBABLY FULFILLING THE SIXTH VIAL ON THE RIVER EUPHRATES, THE NEWS OF WHICH WAS RECEIVED SINCE OCTOBER 16, 1747[1]

See above, p. 191,*. See before this date, *Gazette* of August 5, 1746.[2]

From the *Boston Gazette*, no. 1333, 1747. Amsterdam, July 12. "We have advice that the *S. Cajetan*, a Spanish register ship, going from Cádiz to La Veracruz, and esteemed worth 100,000 pounds, is taken in its passage by an English man-of-war."[3]

London, July 9. "They write from Vienna of June 28th, that the Jesuits' house having been fired by lightning on the 25th, the fire was communicated afterwards to the colleges, and from thence to the church. The flames were so fierce that almost the whole edifice was entirely reduced to ashes. The library, one of the best-chosen and most curious in Europe, was the greatest part of it consumed. While the body of the building was burning, the tower, of which the wooden roof had been already destroyed by the lightning, fell down with a terrible shock into the fine garden of the house, which were filled with the ruins. A great many people were killed or hurt by this accident."[4]

From the *Post-Boy* of October 19, 1747. Amsterdam, August 23. "The master of a ship arrived here reports that he met off Cape Finisterre an English man-of-war, and two privateers of the same nation, which had taken a Spanish ship laden with gold and silver; and off Goudstaart, ten other English men-of-war, having with them two French men-of-

---

1. See above, p. 46. The annotation in this section is confined to textual matters and authentication of JE's citations. A historical atlas or gazetteer may be a helpful aid on occasion.

2. This sentence is a later addition. The newspaper describes in detail British naval successes since the beginning of King George's War in 1744. For example, between March 1745 and April 1746, captured prizes were valued at more than nine million pounds. *The Boston Gazette, or Weekly Journal* (hereafter cited as BG), Aug. 5, 1746, p. 2.

3. BG, Oct. 6, 1747, p. 2.

4. Ibid.

war, two French India ships and a ship from Martineco."[5] The same is mentioned in the *Evening-Post*.[6]

Ibid. Bristol, August 29. "Thursday evening there was advice by the western post that the *Viper*, sloop of war of 14 guns, had taken in the Bay of Biscay, after a warm engagement of four hours, a large French ship called the *Hector*, burden 600 tons, 30 carriage guns, and 193 men; and brought her into Plymouth. She was homeward bound from the South Seas, had been five years on her voyage, and touched at the Canaries, where she landed the best part of her treasure, to the amount of two millions of piasters. However, we hear there has been discovered on board upwards of 40,000 pounds; and a great deal more, on closer search, is expected. The captain of the *Viper*, the boatswain and three other hands were killed in the engagement. And this morning came an account, that Commodore Acton with the *Kingston, Cumberland* and *Hardwick* privateers, had taken three Dutch ships, one of which was bound from the Canaries to Cádiz, having on board the treasure taken out of the *Hector*, and 400 hogsheads of wine, etc., which prize only is valued at 400,000 pounds."[7] The same is mentioned in the *Evening-Post* and *Gazette*.[8]

Evening-Post, October 19, 1747. Admiralty office, August 29. "On the 18th instant, at nine in the morning, His Majesty's ship the *Bellona*, commanded by the Honorable Captain Barrington, gave chase to a sail that was then standing to the eastward. About two o'clock he began to engage her closely, and continued so till past four, when she struck. She proved to be a French East India ship from Port Lorient, called the *Duke de Chartres*, mounted with 30 guns, and 195 men, burden about 700 tons; laden with beef, flour, brandy, wine and oil; and had also on board three mortars and a great number of shells. Captain Barrington has brought her into Mounts Bay."[9] The *Post-Boy* mentions the same, and gives an account of this ship's being part of a strong fleet going to the East Indies.[1] This capture is also mentioned in the *Gazette*.[2]

Evening-Post, October 12, 1747. London, August 6. "Yesterday in the afternoon, an express arrived at the admiralty office from Sir Peter Warren, who arrived with part of his fleet at Plymouth on Saturday

5. *The Boston Weekly Post-Boy* (hereafter cited as BPB), Oct. 19, 1747, p. 1.
6. *The Boston Evening-Post* (hereafter cited as BEP), Oct. 19, 1747, p. 1.
7. BPB, Oct. 19, 1747, p. 1.
8. BEP, Oct. 19, 1747, p. 1; BG, Oct. 20, 1747, p. 2.
9. BEP, Oct. 19, 1747, p. 1.
1. BPB, Oct. 19, 1747, p. 2.
2. BG, Oct. 20, 1747, p. 2.

last. . . . On July 27, he took the *St. Antonia*, laden with provisions and stores for the French East India settlements. . . . And she is brought into Plymouth."[3]

News-Letter, August 22, 1747. Spain. "This kingdom was never in a more distressed condition; our supplies from America come in very slowly. The last year considerably more was taken by the English than arrived on the king's account. As for our trade, we have scarce any left. The French would bring us goods, but we have no money to buy them. Our fruits, that used to be taken off by the English, now rot upon the trees, except a few that are smuggled through Portugal."[4]

In the *Evening-Post* of October 26. London, August 24. "Private advices from Madrid assure us, that Spain was never in a more distressed and uneasy situation than at present. Their supplies in America have come in very slowly; and, according to a computation made by the king's order, the English took considerably more last year than arrived safely in all the ports of Spain on the king's account."[5] And so further, as above, from the *News-Letter*.

News-Letter, November 5, 1747. London, August 28. "We learn by some private letters from Cádiz, that according to their last advices from the West Indies, the misfortune that has befallen the city of Lima has been very much increased by vast numbers, both of Spaniards and Indians, laying aside all regard to government; and with a contempt of the viceroy's order, seizing and plundering whatever came to hand of those rich effects, that had been with much difficulty saved out of the late general calamity. Which had obliged the viceroy to assemble a body of the militia out of the adjacent provinces, in order to cover the workmen that are employed in searching the rubbish of the old and laying out the streets of the new city, the houses of which are to [be] but one story high above the ground floor, and are not to be built of stone, brick or even timber, but of laths, reeds and plaster, to prevent future inconveniences."[6]

Post-Boy, November 9, 1747. From the Daily Gazetteer. London, August 14. "I believe every man that gives himself a moment's liberty to think and reflect, will agree with me that, previous to the setting out of the present war, the commerce of France was rising, and carrying on with an uncommon spirit; and that ours was proportionably decaying;

3. BEP, Oct. 12, 1747, p. 2.
4. BNL, Oct. 22, 1747, p. 1.
5. BEP, Oct. 26, 1747, p. 4.
6. BNL, Nov. 5, 1747, p. 1. See HA; below, p. 423, n. 1.

that we were subject to most of the disadvantages of war, while we had only the name of peace; that the difference is now essentially obvious; and that the French suffer all the inconveniences and expenses of a war, without the advantages that result to us therefrom. If our debts are increased by the war, so is our trade and acquisitions."[7]

Gazette, December 1. "By a vessel arrived at Marblehead in six weeks from Lisbon, we have advice that an English man-of-war, and a privateer of 50 guns of the same nation, had taken a Spanish man-of-war or galleon of 74 guns, bound from the West Indies, and was going in with her as his vessel was coming out."[8]

[The] *Evening-Post*, December 7, gives an account of a privateer belonging to New Providence, that brought in a Spanish ship with a valuable cargo, supposed to be worth 50,000 pound sterling.[9]

Ibid. Extract of a letter from Kingston, Jamaica. "The Spanish galley that was taken formerly by Captain Forest, and fitted out here as a privateer, came in yesterday from the southward, and has taken a large Dutch ship that sailed from hence about six weeks ago, as they said, for Curacao; but they found her going to La Veracruz, with 90 chests of arms on board. As she could not turn up here, they have sent her through the gulf, with a rich register ship which they also took, worth 80,000 pounds, as also a large Spanish schooner; and have sent them to South Carolina."[1]

[In the] *News-Letter* of December 17, 1747, is a very particular account of an extraordinary poll tax raised upon all sorts of persons in the king of France's dominions, and some other methods of raising money in France, causing a great surprise and consternation among the people.[2]

From the *Evening-Post* of January 4, 1748, and other public prints. Extract of a letter from Lisbon, dated October 31, 1747. "I shall conclude this letter with the agreeable advice that we have this day received by three expresses, which say, that as Admiral Hawke, with 18 ships of the line, was cruising about the Bay of Biscay, in hopes of meeting a large convoy from Brest to Martineco and St. Domingo, on the 7th instant he fell in with 6 French men-of-war, convoy to 20 transports bound for the East Indies. And after a short engagement,

7. BPB, Nov. 9, 1747, p. 1.
8. BG, Dec. 1, 1747, p. 3.
9. BEP, Dec. 7, 1747, p. 1.
1. Ibid., p. 2.
2. BNL, Dec. 17, 1747, pp. 1–2.

[he] took the 6 men-of-war and 15 of the transports, and sent a ship or two after the remaining 5. (See p. 260, *.) Two of the men-of-war he has sent to England with the transports, supported by two men-of-war of his squadron; the other 4 he has manned and keeps with him, and continues waiting for the above-mentioned convoy, which we think it will be a miracle if they should escape him."[3]

"We have likewise the pleasure to inform you, that the *Glorious*, a Spanish man-of-war of 74 brass guns, who has fortunately escaped three attacks of the English, in her voyage from the West Indies, immensely rich, arrived at the Groine, where she landed her money. But coming from thence for Cádiz, [she] was attacked by the royal family privateers, and soon after by the *Russel*, man-of-war of 80 guns, who took her and brought her safe into this river. We hear she has considerable effects concealed on board, besides cocoa, etc., so that she may turn out a valuable prize."[4] See p. 260, **.

Extract of another letter from Bellem, a league below Lisbon, November 6, 1747, N.S. "We could not omit communicating to you by this occasion a piece of intelligence which, we flatter ourselves, will prove as favorable as we could wish, for the general good of our nation: which is, that the French West India convoy, consisting of ten sail of men-of-war and about 200 merchantmen bound for America, fell in with 14 sail of our capital ships, upon which a long engagement ensued, the result whereof is not yet known. However, as we were of the stronger party, we may with God's assistance, reasonably flatter ourselves with success. This intelligence comes by three French vessels that appertained to the convoy, which making the best of their way at the commencement of the engagement, were afterwards picked up by a privateer, and are brought into this port. 'Tis said, the next morning several of the ships were disabled and dismasted, and that the *Neptune*, a large French ship of 74 guns, after several broadsides which our ships gave her, blew up. She, being the rearmost ship, ours all gave her broadsides as they passed her to attack the center and the van. We hope soon to be able to give you a more particular account of this action, as well as congratulate you upon our good success in it, which God grant, as it will almost debilitate the French from making any more naval armaments for time to come, and severely distress them in their American colonies."[5]

Extract of a letter from St. Christopher's, dated November 21, 1747.

3. BEP, Jan. 4, 1748, p. 4. JE drew a vertical line through this paragraph.
4. BEP, Jan. 4, 1748, p. 4.
5. Ibid.

"This day arrived an express from Admiral Hawke. He fell in with the French fleet off Brest; they were intended for these islands with their trade. He has taken two 74-, two 64-, one 70- and one 50-gun ships. The ship of 50 guns was the *Severn*, taken from us the last year. 'Tis a most excellent thing in that gentleman to send an express immediately, that our men-of-war may intercept the trade going to Martineco, and only under the convoy of two frigates. . . . This we have by an express from Hawke two days ago to Antigua, and all our ships are gone out to wait for them, as they go into Martineco.[6] . . . Captain Wall from St. Kitts brought the above-mentioned letters, and informs that Captain Hyndman, in a ship of 16 guns bound from London to St. Kitts, was arrived there, with one of the said French ships, about 300 tons, which he picked up on his passage."[7]

From the *Evening-Post* of January 11, 1748. "Friday last, Captain Slater arrived here in about eleven weeks from Bristol; by whom we have account from the prints, that . . . four East India ships were arrived safe at Lisbon, and that the company had received advice, that the French had laid siege to Fort St. David's three times in February last, and were twice beat off by the good dispositions of the governor. Notwithstanding which, they came the third time, with all the force they could collect together, intending to carry the place at all events. But at that very juncture, Commodore Griffins appeared before the place with 8 men-of-war; landed a 1000 men, and obliged the French to retire with great precipitation, leaving behind them their cannon, mortars, ammunition, baggage, etc. Since which, the commodore, being joined by two ships of war, and having got all the men that could be spared, was gone in his turn, to attack the French settlement at Pondichéry."[8]

From the *Boston Gazette,* January 19, 1748. New York, January 4. "On Wednesday last arrived here Captain Greenal, in a flag of truce, in about four weeks from Cape Francois; by whom we have an account, that some time before he left that place, part of a fleet of vessels was arrived there from old France, who informed that they sailed from Brest the 18th of October last N.S., in company with 180 sail of merchantmen, under convoy of 8 men-of-war and two frigates. And on the 22th, [they] fell in with an English squadron of 18 men-of-war. The

6. This sentence is from an extract of another letter from St. Christopher's, dated Nov. 22, 1747.

7. BEP, Jan. 4, 1748, p. 4.

8. Ibid., Jan. 11, 1748, p. 2.

French men-of-war then gave the signal for their convoy to make the best of their way off; and a very hot engagement immediately ensued, beginning about 11 o'clock in the morning. They could not tell what was the issue of the battle; but [they] fear that all the French men-of-war were either taken or sunk, as none of them were arrived at the cape the 5th of December, at which time about 100 sail of merchantmen were come in. They also inform that four days after that, a large part of the fleet fell in with twelve more English men-of-war, and those that escaped believed that the greatest number of them fell into the hands of the English."[9]

The same *Gazette* mentions one of that French fleet, being brought into New York, of 200 tons and 14 carriage guns. And she gave account "that Captain Obline took a snow[1] belonging to the same fleet, and drove four more ashore on Martineco; and [the *Gazette*] supposes all the men were lost, and were left by this prize in chase of another."[2]

Extract of a letter from Jamaica, dated December 10, 1747. "An express which arrived here (at New York),[3] on the 6th of December, brings the following list of the French men-of-war, taken by the English on the 24th of October, 1747, from the *Kingston Gazette*.

	Guns	[Men]
Le Grand Monarque	74	620
Le Terrible	74	620
Le Neptune	70	620
Le Trident	64	500
[Le] Tonond	80	750
Le Severn	50	480
[L'] Intrepid	74	620

As also the *Le Castre*, an old man-of-war laden with provisions, and 48 sail of merchantmen."[4] See p. 260, ††.

Boston Gazette, January 12, 1748. Admiralty office, October 1. "On the 17th past, Captain Shirley, commander of His Majesty's ship the *Dover*, brought into Plymouth the *Renomee*, a French man-of-war of 32 guns and about 300 men. . . . She had on board M. De Constans, who was going to his government of St. Domingo."[5]

9. BG, Jan. 19, 1748, p. 3.
1. I.e., a square-rigged ship.
2. BG, Jan. 19, 1748, p. 3.
3. JE's interpolation.
4. BG, Jan. 19, 1748, p. 3.
5. No copy located (here and elsewhere this notation means that the extant runs of colo-

From the *Boston Gazette* of January 26, 1748. New York, January 18. "Captain Maggee, who arrived here last Wednesday in twenty-four days from Barbados, informs us, that eighteen sail of the French fleet were sent into that island by our men-of-war, before he left it; . . . that several men-of-war were yet out in quest of more; and that they had accounts they had taken and drove ashore in all 32 sail."[6]

See p. 257, *. *Boston Gazette* of January 26, 1748. Extract of a letter from Madeira, dated December 5, 1747, N.S. "We have a report of Admiral Hawke's having met with and taken 6 French men-of-war, and as many Indiamen. But it is not confirmed. It's the more likely to be true, as the French knew of our fleet bound to India, and might endeavor to send a reinforcement before them."[7]

See p. 257, **. Afterwards came an account (as we were informed in the *Boston Gazette* of February 2, 1748) to New York, by a passenger that arrived thither from Madeira, "that they had found 111 chests of silver on board the *Glorious,* man-of-war that was lately taken and carried into Lisbon."[8]

See p. 259, ††. This account, as afterwards ratified by accounts from England, is this.

	Guns	Men
Le Monarque	74	686
Le Terrible	74	686
[*Le*] *Neptune*	74	686
Le Trident	64	650
Le Fougeux	64	650
Le Severn	50	550

And the admiral, on his return, also took two frigates and 9 merchantmen.[9]

Boston Weekly News-Letter, February 18, 1748. Venice, October 20. "By advices from Leghorn we learn, that Captain Hughes, of His Britannic Majesty's ship the *Essex,* has sent into that port two French ships laded with cloth, valued at 100,000 dollars, which he took near the Isle of Sardinia, being part of the Marseilles Turkey fleet."[1]

---

nial newspapers do not include the issue JE was citing). Notice of the same prize appeared in BEP, Jan. 11, 1748, p. 2.

6. BG, Jan. 26, 1748, p. 3.

7. Ibid. JE drew a vertical line through this entry.

8. BG, Feb. 2, 1748, p. 4.

9. BNL, Feb. 11, 1748, p. 2.

1. Ibid., Feb. 18, 1748, p. 1.

Ibid. London, October 27, 1747. "The *St. Joseph and the St. John,* a register ship from Maraca Goa, last from the Havana, having on board a great quantity of cocoa, and 60,000 dollars; and a tartan,[2] from the Canaries for Cádiz with cocoa, are both taken by the *Spence* sloop, and carried into Gibraltar."[3]

Observe the news in the *Gazette* of March 1, 1748, column 4, section 2; and see if it be confirmed.[4]

In the *Boston Evening-Post* of March 7, 1748, was an account that some of our men-of-war, cruising about the Isle of Corsica, had there taken several prizes, and two very rich, having a large quantity of silver on board.[5]

Boston Gazette, Tuesday, March 8, 1748. London, November 6. "We are assured, by passengers lately come over from St. Maloes, that notwithstanding the great success their privateers have had in taking English ships, yet the proprietors had in the whole lost very considerable sums of money by them, owing to the vigilant behavior of the British men-of-war in the channel service, who have lately taken all their privateers, except the *Grand Biche* and those lately sailed. The latter are quite new from the stocks, and fitted out at a prodigious expense, being their last effort in privateering. For as there is little doubt of their being soon taken by our many cruisers now out and going out, it will be impossible for them to fit out more for want of men."[6]

Boston Gazette, March 15, 1748. Admiralty office, London, February 1. "His Majesty's ships, the *Romney* and *Amazon,* cruising in the soundings, on the 23rd of last month, fell in with and took the *Count de Noailles,* privateer of 16 guns, belonging to Granville. And two days afterwards, the *Romney* and *Amazon,* being in company, met and took the *Geraldus,* a French East India ship of about 400 tons, laden with provisions, bound from Port Lorient to India. She came out with two other East India ships, but sailed so bad that she lost company with them, and was returning back to Port Lorient. The prize is come into Plymouth."[7]

Ibid. Milan, December 22. "According to advices from Admiral Byng, the English have lately taken off Genoa two French merchant

2. A sailing vessel with one mast, used especially in coastal areas.

3. BNL, Feb. 18, 1748, p. 1.

4. BG, Mar. 1, 1748, p. 2. This is an account of the British capturing a French fleet coming from the East Indies, heavily loaded with plunder.

5. BEP, Mar. 7, 1748, p. 2. JE erroneously cited the BNL of the same date, which does not exist.

6. BG, Mar. 8, 1748, p. 3.

7. Ibid., Mar. 15, 1748, p. 1.

ships, richly laden, together with several other vessels carrying provisions to that city."[8]

Ibid. Leghorn, December 22. "An English bomb vesssel has brought in here a bark,[9] which sailed from hence a few days before for Marseilles, with a very rich cargo. There are, among other things, eighty bales of silk."[1]

Ibid. London, November 12. "The two great blows given to the French navy by the admirals Anson and Warren and Hawke, have reduced their trading interest to the lowest ebb. The only dependence they had before was on their convoys, which, though few, were always very strong. But that advantage must now be entirely lost, by our taking so many of their men-of-war, and [by] all their West India ships [being] exposed to the English men-of-war and privateers. There are full two hundred sail of French ships expected home between this [date] and February, all richly laden. Fine encouragement for our marine officers to do their duty!"[2]

Ibid. London, January 11. "They write from Leghorn, that four French ships were taken, and carried into that port by some of our men-of-war. It is said they were bound from Turkey, and have valuable cargoes on board."[3]

Evening-Post, March 14, 1748. London, November 5. "There are accounts from several parts of France, that the vintage has failed this year, as well as their harvest; that the edicts, lately published in Holland, have prevented their receiving supplies of corn from the Baltic; and that our squadron in the Mediterranean, puts it out of their power to import any considerable quantities from Turkey. So that they have a very melancholy prospect before them, which in spite of their Te Deums for robbing their neighbors in Flanders, inclines the nation in general to express the most earnest desire possible, for the speedy conclusion of a general peace."[4]

Evening-Post, March 21, 1748. London, December 19. "It must afford

8. Ibid.

9. A sailing vessel with two square-rigged masts forward and a rear mast rigged fore-and-aft.

1. BG, Mar. 15, 1748, p. 1.

2. Ibid., p. 2.

3. Ibid. Here JE deleted "Ibid. London, January 29. By a letter from Switzerland, there is an account that one of the most considerable of the Romish cantons are going to embrace the Protestant religion." He rewrote it as the initial entry in the section of "Hopeful Events" (below, p. 285).

4. BEP, Mar. 14, 1748, p. 2.

every sincere lover of his country the highest pleasure, to contemplate the different situation of our own and the enemy's company, for carrying on the commerce of the Indies. . . . As to the affairs of our company, they are certainly in a very good posture, abroad and at home. . . . On the other hand, the concerns of the French company are equally distressed and irremediable in India and Europe; for since Le Bourdenay's being recalled, whose behavior incensed the subjects of the Mogul[5] against his whole nation, they have not above 5 ships of force, and these too, company's ships, in these seas. The *Lis*, which Le Bourdenay left behind him, being condemned in a Portuguese port as unfit for service; [and] the squadron under M. St. George, with seven of the company's ships laden with naval and military stores, demolished by Lord Anson, disappoints their hopes and must weaken them extremely, who from the nature and quantities of these supplies appear to be in want of everything. Besides, the blow lately given by Admiral Hawke, has hindered some attempt to lessen the fatal effect of the killing stroke before mentioned, so that nothing has been done towards replacing Bourdenay, or supplying the wants of their settlements, all this time increasing. It is out of their power to repair these losses immediately, or to equip and detach any squadron for this service; nor can they possibly furnish strength sufficient for the convoy of their homeward-bound ships in the company's service, so as to defend them against Commodore Boscawen's mighty force. In this dispute, therefore, notwithstanding all their skill, diligence and prodigious expense, the French are in a fair way to be ruined."[6]

Evening-Post, March 28, 1748. Leghorn, November 4. "Upon advice that a French man-of-war of 44 guns was sent into the Levant, to cruise against our privateers, the English detached two frigates from hence, which coming up with the Frenchman, engaged, took and carried her into Port Mahon."[7]

Boston Gazette, March 29, 1748. London, November 5. "Letters from several places in France complain much of the fall of the prices of wine and brandy, . . . and that they apprehend, should they have a war with the Dutch, many thousand families in that kingdom would be ruined, especially as they should have no market for the production of their vintage."[8]

5. I.e., the ruler of the Mongol state in India.
6. BEP, Mar. 21, 1748, pp. 1–2.
7. Ibid., Mar. 28, 1748, p. 4.
8. BG, Mar. 29, 1748, p. 2.

Gazette, April 5, 1748. London, December 1. "The *Hampshire*, man-of-war [commanded by] Captain Daniel, has taken and brought into Plymouth the *Castor*, a French man-of-war of 30 guns and 300 men. She was one that escaped Rear Admiral Hawke's squadron."[9]

Idem, ibid. "This morning arrived an express from Lewis in Sussex, to the owners of the royal family privateers, with the melancholy news that the *Nymphia*, prize from Lisbon, last from Portsmouth for London, is lost on the rocks near East Dean; and several of the people drowned. This ship was immensely rich; she was taken by the privateers in her passage from Cádiz to La Veracruz."[1]

Idem, ibid. December 5. "We hear that the money on board the *Nymphia* prize, was taken out at Portsmouth, so that the loss will not be so considerable, as was at first imagined."[2]

Concerning Admiral Knowles' taking Port Louis on Hispaniola, see the *Gazette*, no. 1457, of April 12, 1748, columns 4 and 5.[3]

Boston Gazette, April 19, 1748. London, February 4. "Yesterday a great number of sailors waited on His Majesty, to return him thanks for the order of council on Saturday last, for the speedy condemnation of prizes taken from the Genoese, which prizes amount to upward of 200,000 pounds."[4]

Ibid. Extract of a letter from Providence, dated March 25. "We have an account of two very rich French ships bound from Hispaniola to France, taken by Captain Braddock and Captain Miller, in a privateer ship and galley belonging to this place. Captain Braddock's prize is now in the harbor; her cargo consists of 100 large and 80 small casks of indigo, and about 400 hogsheads of sugar. The galley's prize was seen yesterday. She is a ship of about 700 tons; her cargo is of sugar, cotton, indigo and coffee."[5]

Ibid. Extract of a letter from Charlestown in South Carolina, dated March 1, 1748. "From Barbados there is advice, that His Majesty's ship *Mary Galley* had brought in there a polacre,[6] bound from Cádiz to La Veracruz, said to be worth 20,000 guineas."[7]

In the *Evening-Post* of April 18, 1748, was an account of some of

9. Ibid., Apr. 5, 1748, p. 2.
1. Ibid. JE necessarily complemented this entry with the following report.
2. BG, Apr. 5, 1748, p. 2.
3. No copy located. For a full description of the victory, see BEP, Apr. 11, 1748, pp. 1–2.
4. BG, Apr. 19, 1748, p. 2.
5. Ibid., pp. 2–3.
6. MS: "Polacco." A polacre is a ship with two or three masts.
7. BG, Apr. 19, 1748, p. 3.

Admiral Hawke's ships taking a French man-of-war of 74 guns called the *Magnanimous*, that was going with two other French men-of-war going from Brest to Cádiz, to strengthen a Spanish convoy to America.[8] This was afterwards confirmed by a ship from Lisbon to Boston, who said the ship was an eighty gun ship. This came in the *Gazette* of April 26.[9] See p. 266, *.

Boston Gazette of May 3. London, February 22. "Last Saturday came an account, that His Majesty's ships the *Roebuck* and *Loestaff*, part of Admiral Byng's squadron, had taken the *Brillant*, from Turkey bound to Marseilles, and carried her into Leghorn. She has on board about 90 bales of silk, and the whole cargo is valued at near 60,000 pounds sterling."[1]

Idem, ibid. February 24. "They write from Marseilles, that seventeen French ships, richly laden from the Levant, are taken by Admiral Byng's squadron."[2]

Idem, ibid. March 6. "On the 4th arrived at Portsmouth the *Union*, a French register ship of 30 guns [and] 115 men, from the Havana bound to Cádiz, taken the 27th last, about seven leagues from the latter port, by the *Bristol*, commanded by the Honorable Captain Montague. She had 360,000 dollars registered on board, cocoa, beside cochineal, Spanish snuff and hides."[3]

Idem, ibid. March 12. "By express from Bristol, we hear the *Tyger*, privateer [commanded by] Captain Siex, was arrived there with a Spanish register ship from the Havana, bound to Cádiz, which he took within eight leagues of that port. She is called the *Theresa*, and is a prize of considerable value, having on board 60,000 dollars, besides a rich cargo."[4]

"Letters from Constantinople and Malta assure, that Commodore Griffin had taken Pondichéry, and was preparing to undertake the recovery of Madras."[5] See further, p. 269, **.

"On the second instant, His Majesty's ship the *Monmouth*, commanded by Captain Henry Harrison, brought into Plymouth a French privateer of 20 carriage and 8 swivel guns and 136 men, called the

---

8. BEP, Apr. 18, 1748, p. 4.
9. BG, Apr. 26, 1748, p. 3.
1. Ibid., May 3, 1748, p. 1.
2. Ibid.
3. Ibid., p. 2.
4. Ibid.
5. Ibid.

Count de Maurepas, which she took on the 19th of last month, after a chase of three days."[6]

Ibid. Admiralty office, March 3. "Captain Edgecumbe of His Majesty's ship the *Salisbury*, has taken and carried into Plymouth, a French East India ship of 700 tons. She mounted 30 guns, and had 180 men on board, and was bound from Port Lorient to Pondichéry, laden chiefly with stores and ammunition and eight cases of silver."[7]

*Afterwards was a more particular and full account of this capture, from the admiralty office, March 4, in the *Gazette* of May 3, 1748; wherein was related that this ship had 686 men, "commanded by the Marquis d'Abert, *Chef d'escadre*; that she sailed from Brest the 13th of January O.S., in company with the *Alcide* of 64 guns, *L'Arc-en-Ciel* of 54 [guns], and a frigate, which were to be joined at Cádiz or the Cape de Verde Islands, by the *Conquerant* of 74, the *Content* of 64, and *L'Oriflamme* of 54 guns from Toulon, in order to proceed to the East Indies."[8]

In [the] *News-Letter* of April 29, 1748, is an account of a mutiny in Toulouse, on account of the great scarcity and want of bread in France.[9]

Evening-Post, May 2, 1748. "By a vessel[1] just arrived (at Boston)[2] from Antigua we are told, that Commodore Pocock had taken the island of St. Lucia from the French, demolished the fort, and drove the inhabitants off the island."[3]

News-Letter of May 5, 1748. London, March 6. On the 4th instant, "arrived the *Grand Biche*, a French privateer of 22 guns and 160 men, which was taken the 27th last, within sight of the Ushant, by Captain Campbell, in His Majesty's ship the *Bellona*, after a chase of 4 or 5 hours. When upon firing 14 guns, she struck."[4]

In both the *Evening-Post* of May 2, and also the *News-Letter* of May 5, was an account that the *Flora*, a French man-of-war of 36 guns, was taken by an English man-of-war and carried into Gibraltar.[5]

News-Letter of May 5. Boston. "Last Tuesday arrived here Captain Gardiner in twenty-four days from the West Indies, who confirms the

6. Ibid.
7. Ibid.
8. Ibid. See p. 265.
9. BNL, Apr. 29, 1748, p. 1.
1. JE substituted "vessel" for "gentleman."
2. JE's interpolation.
3. BEP, May 2, 1748, p. 2.
4. BNL, May 5, 1748, p. 1.
5. BEP, May 2, 1748, p. 2; BNL, May 5, 1748, p. 1.

accounts we have had, that the Dutch at Curacao had taken and seized in that harbor 4 or 5 French privateers, and a considerable number of their trading vessels. Among the former is the famous Captain Palanche, with his fine sloop and her consort. And the commanders with all the men were kept prisoners. [We hear] that they had received advice at Curacao from the governor of [St.] Eustatia, that Admiral Knowles with his squadron had taken Petit-Guivas, a French port of Hispaniola, not far from Léogane."[6] This was confirmed in the *Boston Gazette* of May 10.[7]

Gazette, May 10, 1748. Philadelphia, February 28. "From a gentleman in Barbados via Maryland, we have the following advices. . . . That Captain Broderick has taken off Martineco a French frigate of 18 guns, 9 and 12 pounders; that the famous Palanche of that place is said to be taken, and carried into Antigua by the *Centaur*, [commanded by] Captain Tyrrel; and that said ship had run down a large French privateer sloop off Martineco, only three of her hands saved; . . . that Captain Woolford of St. Kitts, has taken a register ship, reckoned very rich; and that a Spanish ship is sent into Barbados, taken by one of our men-of-war off of Martineco."[8]

Evening-Post, May 9, 1748. Lyons in France, February 20. "We learn by letters from Marseilles, that the apprehensions they were in of bankruptcies, upon the intercepting of the greatest part of the Levant fleet, appear not to be without foundation. For two of the greatest merchants of that city, who were in partnership, have broke for 1,300,000 livres which, 'tis thought, will occasion the failure of many other persons. There is also from Bordeaux, that seven considerable merchants became bankrupt there last week. We have similar accounts from most other trading towns."[9]

Boston Evening-Post, May 16, 1748. Extract of a private letter from Marseilles, February 18. "The English have taken several ships, richly laden, some bound to and others from the Levant, which has affected our trade to such a degree, that it has been resolved to put a stop to it for a time; and some ships that were actually freighted are now unloading. To add to our misfortune, and render a burden heavy enough in itself altogether insupportable, we are in the utmost distress (which is, indeed, the case of the whole country of Provence) for provisions.

6. BNL, May 5, 1748, p. 2.
7. BG, May 10, 1748, p. 3.
8. Ibid., p. 2.
9. BEP, May 9, 1748, p. 2.

268 "Notes on the Apocalypse"

We expect every day two very large ships with corn from Barbary. And if, by any disastrous accident, these should fall into the hands of the English, there are numbers of people here that must inevitably perish for want of bread."[1]

In the *Boston Gazette* of May 17, is a piece of news from The Hague, of Admiral Schryver with the English fleet taking a French fleet from the West Indies, which wants confirmation.[2] See below,*.

Evening-Post, May 23, 1748. Paris, March 11. "The king has caused an extraordinary assembly of the clergy to be convoked, to meet in the month of May next, in order to demand a free gift of twelve millions of livres. A tax has been just laid of 5 sols[3] per pound on wax candles, and one sol upon tallow candles; also one sol per pound on pasteboard, paper and hairpowder."[4] See p. 270, ††.

Ibid. Constantinople, January 30. "We have accounts of two good prizes made by His Britannic Majesty's ships, the one bound to Smyrna commanded by one Lefabre, the other by one Cournan for this port. The French here offer on several ships 35 percent insurance. None has appeared for some months at this scale. The French traders are in such a distressed condition, that they are obliged to raise money at 20 and 24 percent interest."[5]

Ibid. London, March 16. "They write from Leghorn, that His Majesty's ship the *Princessa*, had taken and brought into that port three French ships from Turkey, richly laden, bound to Marseilles, as also two ships from the coast of Barbary. Three French ships from Marseilles, bound to Martineco, are also taken by some of our men-of-war in the Mediterranean, and carried into Leghorn."[6]

Ibid. "There is advice from India, by way of Lisbon, that one of the French country ships, valued at near 200,000 pounds, has been taken by the English."[7]

See above,*. *Evening-Post*, June 6. Amsterdam, March 28. "A letter has been received here, which says, that the homeward-bound Martineco fleet, having been met with in its passage by the combined squadron of England and Holland, has been beaten and totally ruined; and

---

1. Ibid., May 16, 1748, p. 1.
2. BG, May 17, 1748, p. 2. JE marked this entry with a vertical line.
3. The sol was a French copper halfpenny.
4. BEP, May 23, 1748, p. 1.
5. Ibid.
6. Ibid., p. 2.
7. Ibid.

that a great number of ships have been taken. Those of the republic have got eight to their share."[8]

[In the] *Evening-Post*, June 6, is an account from the admiralty office, April 4. Captain Coats, with four ships of the line and one of 24 guns, met with a Spanish fleet of 9 Spanish men-of-war of the line, having under convoy about 27 merchant ships with which they sailed from Cádiz four days before; [and he] took out of the fleet five of the merchant ships, three being register ships bound to Veracruz.[9]

Ibid. London, April 14. "Letters from Paris by way of Holland, advise that one of their men-of-war of 80 guns and 600 men, from Cyprus in Turkey, is taken by one of His Majesty's ships of war."[1]

Evening-Post, June 27. "That Commodore Griffin had burnt two French men-of-war in the East Indies, viz., one of 74 guns, another of 50 guns, and taken one more; also retaken the *Princess Amelia*, Indiaman that fell into the enemies' hands after the taking of Madras; . . . that the five register ships taken by Commodore Coats were arrived at Lisbon."[2]

Gazette of June 28. Extract of a letter from a gentleman in New York, to his friend in Boston, dated June 23. "We had a privateer and 3 prizes come in this day with a joyful piece of news, that Mr. Osborne, the English admiral, has taken two French men-of-war of the line, and about 20 French merchantmen."[3]

Gazette, July 5. New York, June 27. "Thursday last arrived here the privateer ship *Antilope*. . . . She brings a report, that the English men-of-war who continue to cruise off and block up Martineco, have lately fell in with a French fleet of merchantmen from old France, under convoy of two men-of-war of the line and a frigate of 40 guns, and that they had taken the two men-of-war and most of the merchantmen, while some few with the frigate escaped."[4]

Ibid. Boston. "By letters from Antigua we have advice, that three French prizes taken by Admiral Osborne were arrived there, and thirteen at St. Kitts."[5]

See p. 265, **. *Gazette*, August 2, 1748. Paris, May 3, 1748. "The late

8. Ibid., June 6, 1748, p. 2. JE drew a vertical line through this entry.
9. BEP, June 6, 1748, p. 4.
1. Ibid.
2. Ibid., June 27, 1748, p. 2.
3. BG, June 28, 1748, p. 2.
4. Ibid., July 5, 1748, p. 2.
5. Ibid.

ill news from the Indies, which has been so industriously concealed, is at length brake out; and we are assured that the English have taken Pondichéry, several ships belonging to our India company and a vast quantity of rich effects."[6]

See p. 268, ††. *News-Letter*, August 4, 1748. London, May 21. "They write from Paris the 17th instant N.S., that a scheme has been presented to the Comptroller General of the finances, for erecting public granaries in the maritime provinces, which are to be maintained by a tax upon the religious houses and ecclesiastical revenues throughout the kingdom, with the addition of a royal bounty equal to the 4th part of the sums so raised."[7] See p. 273, *.

News-Letter, August 18. London, June 9. "By letters from Paris we have advice that, the royal commissaries have demanded in His Majesty's name, a free gift from the general assembly of the clergy, but to what amount is not yet known."[8] See p. 271, *.

Gazette, August 23, 1748. Extract of a letter from Barbados, to a gentleman in Williamsburg, dated June 22, 1748. "About a fortnight ago, the French homeward-bound fleet sailed from Martineco, consisting of 42 sail of ships; and as our squadron lay in readiness to intercept them, we have had the good fortune to take no less than 18, mostly rich and valuable prizes."[9]

News-Letter, August 25, 1748. Extract of a letter from Kingston in Jamaica, dated July 13, 1748. "We have received advice last night, that our men-of-war have met with the Spanish galleons, and had taken three of them, and the two men-of-war that convoyed them, and were in chase of the other nine galleons. And 'tis presumed they are taken also."[1]

Post-Boy, September 12. Extract of a letter from Paris, July 12. "An express from Count Dessaleaurs, our ambassador at Constantinople, is arrived by way of Poland, with dispatches which His Excellency has received from the East Indies by the way of Bagdat, concerning the expedition of the English against the town of Pondichéry. The contents are said to be, that the English have made themselves masters of the place, and entirely plundered and ruined it, in the same manner as M. de la Bourdenay dealt by Madras."[2]

6. BG, Aug. 2, 1748, p. 1.
7. BNL, Aug. 4, 1748, p. 2.
8. Ibid., Aug. 18, 1748, p. 1.
9. BG, Aug. 23, 1748, p. 1.
1. BNL, Aug. 25, 1748, p. 2.
2. No copy located. A briefer notice of the expedition is in BEP, Sept. 12, 1748, p. 2. JE drew a vertical line through this entry.

The taking of Pondichéry is confirmed by Mr. Willison of Dundee's letter of May 10, 1748 (p. 2, near the bottom).[3]

See p. 270, *. *News-Letter*, September 15, 1748. "They write from Paris, that the subscription for sixteen millions granted by the clergy to the king, by way of free gift, was filled up in less than 4 days."[4]

Gazette of September 20, 1748. Boston. "Last Lord's day arrived here from Newfoundland, Captain Freeman, with the rich Spanish prize he had taken, as heretofore mentioned, condemned at that place as a lawful prize. The said ship is said to be immensely rich, and Captain Freeman's conduct in taking her is much applauded."[5]

[In the] *Gazette* of August 30 is the following account, in a letter from Captain Freeman to his owners in Boston, from Newfoundland as follows. "The 10th of June we left Gibraltar; and on the 19th, in the latitude 36 north, off the isle of St. Mary's, we met with and took a rich Spanish merchantman, Don Antonia de Borges commander, from the Havana for Cádiz, with 110 men and 26 guns. By the best account we can get of her cargo, when she left the Havana, it was valued at three hundred thousand dollars. We have found on board her in specie 171,000 dollars; and her cargo is cochineal, snuff, hides, etc."[6]

Gazette, September 27. "Thursday last, in the evening, the money taken and brought in by Captain Freeman was landed on the long wharf, and carried in four carts, each with colors flying, under a guard of sailors, and was lodged, some in the house of one of the owners of the ship, and the rest in Captain Freeman's house."[7]

Gazette, October 4. Paris, August 2. "The king, having been informed of the famine at Bordeaux, which has caused more than 10,000 people to perish, has ordered his ministers to inquire into the cause of this calamity. M. d'Argenson, having in consequence hereof, wrote to the intendant of that city. This magistrate has accused four members of the parliament, among whom is the procureur and one of the advocates general. Upon which, the parliament received orders immediately to send these four magistrates to court, to give an account of their conduct. But being arrived at Compiègne, His Majesty, without vouchsafing to hear them, banished them into lower Normandy."[8]

3. No copy of the letter has been located. Concerning John Willison, see above, pp. 69–70. JE drew a vertical line through this entry.

4. BNL, Sept. 15, 1748, p. 2.

5. BG, Sept. 20, 1748, p. 1. JE marked this entry with a vertical line.

6. BG, Aug. 30, 1748, p. 2. After this entry, JE repeated a portion of the preceding paragraph from the BG of Sept. 20.

7. BG, Sept. 27, 1748, pp. 1–2.

8. Ibid., Oct. 4, 1748, p. 1.

News-Letter, October 13, 1748. London, August 13. "We hear, that four of our men-of-war have taken a Spanish ship, valued at 100,000 pounds."[9]

Gazette. October 25. Boston. "Last Saturday Captain Taylor arrived here from Jamaica, who informs that Admiral Knowles, being out on a cruise off the Havana, was engaged by 7 large Spanish ships of the line fitted out from the Havana in an extraordinary manner, and doubled-manned to engage him; that the engagement lasted from two in the afternoon till ten at night; and that one of the Spanish ships of 70 guns was taken. The rest, by favor of the night, got off."[1]

The above account in general was afterwards confirmed in the *News-Letter* of November 17, with a particular account of the names of each ship on both sides, with the number of guns. Only it was said that the ship which was taken, was but of 60 guns, and its name the *Conquestrador*. And it was added that the Spanish admiral's ship, the *Africa*, of 70 guns, being pursued, run into shoal water; and that the Spaniards, to prevent her being taken, burnt her; and that the rest of the fleet got into the Havana in a miserably shattered condition, having a 1000 of their men killed.[2]

Gazette, November 22, 1748. Paris, September 13. "Letters from Rochelle import that 5 ships are just arrived there from Martineco, the remainder of 12 which set out together from thence, the other seven having fallen into the hands of the English."[3]

News-Letter, February 9, 1748/9. There is occasional mention in a letter from Rome, of the Pope's proposals for the improvement of manufactures and trade in his dominions, to retrieve the state of that country and delivering it from frauds and oppression, etc., which, it is there said, are one great reason that the finest country in the world (meaning that part of Italy) is in a manner desolate.[4]

In one of the public prints in the summer, 1749, was an account of the revolt of the people of Chili from the king of Spain.[5]

Gazette, July 18, 1749. St. Johns in Antigua, June 16. "A gentleman from [St.] Eustatia informs us, that they have accounts from Curacao, that the Spaniards on the coast of Caracas, being joined by the Indians, have revolted, and disown their allegiance to the king of

9. BNL, Oct. 13, 1748, p. 2.
1. No copy located. A fuller account of the same engagement is in BEP, Oct. 24, 1748, p. 1.
2. BNL, Nov. 17, 1748, p. 1.
3. BG, Nov. 22, 1748, p. 1.
4. No copy located.
5. See the following paragraph.

Spain. The occasion of which was, the arbitrary and oppressive manner
the Biscayen Company has carried on their trade, to that part of the
continent, to whom it is farmed by the king of Spain. 'Tis said they
have destroyed all the vessels of the Biscayen Company that were
there; and for the encouragement of the natives, had chosen for their
head a descendant of the ancient Incas; and that there is now a free
trade, above 50 vessels having gone from Curacao for that purpose."[6]

Gazette, October 17, 1749. London, August 31. "From Paris, we are
informed . . . that the Comptroller General had demanded of the
French clergy a particular declaration of the amount of their several
revenues, in order, it is said, to subject that rich body to the payment of
the twentieth penny or one shilling in the pound, equally with the rest
of the nation."[7]

News-Letter, December 14, 1749. There is a circumstantial account of
the revolt of the country of the Caracas from the crown of Spain, in a
letter from Madrid dated September 2. The revolt was in April preceding.[8]

See p. 270, *. From the *Newcastle General Magazine*, sent me from
Scotland, pp. 442–443. Extracts of letters from Paris. "The Comptroller General has demanded of the clergy a particular declaration of the
amount of their revenues, in order, it is said, to subject that rich body
to the payment of the twentieth penny, or one shilling in the pound,
equally with the rest of the nation."[9] See p. 274, *.

August 22. "The king has sent circular letters to all the bishops in
the kingdom, importing that being desirous to maintain peace in the
church, he wills them to publish no mandates about religious controversies, without first obtaining His Majesty's approbation and permission. They are likewise required to be very cautious and moderate, in
refusing the sacraments to dying persons suspected or known to be
Jansenists. An edict is registered in parliament, and will be published in
a few days, for suppressing, in process of time, the convents of nuns. By
this new ordinance, all the monasteries of nuns are forbid to take in
novices before the age of 24 years and one day.

"The above edict will have very beneficial effects, both in church
and state. And as it is too common a practice with parents to put their
daughters into nunneries in their infancy, whereby they take a liking to

6. BG, July 18, 1749, p. 1.
7. Ibid., Oct. 17, 1749, p. 1.
8. No copy located. A similar account is in BEP, Feb. 12, 1750, p. 2.
9. *The Newcastle General Magazine*, 2 (1749), 442.

that way of life before they can know anything else, and so are wheedled to make their vows just before they become marriageable. The same edict enacts, that no child brought up in a nunnery shall be suffered to take the veil, till she has lived seven years in the world, after which she may return to the convent, if she likes it better."[1]

Weekly News-Letter, February 8, 1749/50. London, October 21. "Our correspondent at Paris acquaints us, that they talk there very much of great regulations, that will speedily be made in that kingdom with respect to religious houses; such as, that only two will for the future [be] permitted in each great town, and those of different orders. That men shall not be admitted to monastic vows before the age of 25 years, or women under 22, and that upwards of fifteen hundred convents, belonging to the mendicant orders will be absolutely suppressed. And some go so far as to say, that edicts for this purpose will be very speedily published."[2]

See p. 273, *. Paris, June 15. "We hear that, when the king's commissaries went a few days ago to the general assembly of the clergy, warm debates arose about the 20th penny, which the court intends to levy out of all church livings."[3]

Scots Magazine for January, 1751, p. 14. In an account there of the Pope's doing something disagreeable to the Republic of Venice, we have these words. "The republic's resentment against her ghostly father was immediately testified, by dismissing his minister, recalling hers from Rome, and suspending the payment of those pensions, which his subjects had from benefices within the Venetian territories."[4]

Ibid., concerning the affairs of Parma, p. 15. "That duke has obtained permission from the Pope, to lay a tax upon the clergy in his dominions, for enabling him to discharge the debts which were contracted during the last war."[5]

Ibid., p. 16. Concerning the affairs of Tuscany. "A mandate has been published with the Pope's permission, enjoining the clergy and all religious communities of both sexes in Tuscany, to give exact accounts of their revenues and pensions, to the end [that] they may be taxed for defraying the public charges of the state."[6]

1. Ibid., pp. 442–43.
2. No copy located.
3. No copy located.
4. *The Scots Magazine* (hereafter cited as SM), *13* (1751), p. 14. From "A summary or recapitulation of the Public Affairs of the year 1750."
5. Ibid., p. 15.
6. Ibid., p. 16.

Ibid., concerning the affairs of Rome, p. 16. The Pope, "instead of laboring to increase the power of his see and the temporal interests of the clergy in general, he has, with an appearance of frankness, consented to the diminution of both in several instances. In some former years, he had permitted a great number of holy days to be abolished through most of the states of Italy, which served only to fill the pockets of the monks, to render the people lazy, and discourage manufactures. This recapitulation already shews some cases, in which the privileges of the pontifical chair have been resigned, and allowance granted for raising taxes upon the clergy for supporting the governments under which they live. As indeed, it is surprising, that this body of men, who possess at least one third part of the lands in all popish countries, should have been so long exempted from bearing a share of so reasonable a burden. More instances of the same nature will occur in the histories of other states, which are yet to be mentioned. Besides these, the present Pope has suppressed several ridiculous objects of superstition called relics, which used to fatten the priests, and to make the laity stare."[7]

Ibid., p. 16. Concerning the affairs of the king of the Two Sicilies. "His Majesty, with the Pope's allowance, has also raised above a million of ducats from the clergy, for enabling him to fit out vessels against the corsairs of Barbary. In order to weaken the influence of the court of Rome in Naples and Sicily, where, in virtue of papal bulls, coadjutors were placed in the great livings, who succeeded of course upon the death of the incumbents, whether they were agreeable or not to the prince on the throne, the king has resolved to reserve such power in his own hands as may prevent that inconveniency, and not to suffer coadjutorships to be so frequent as they have been. It is some time since he sent a memorial to the Pope, demanding permission to suppress five convents of monks; but we have not heard what reception this has met with."[8]

Ibid., concerning the affairs of Spain, p. 17. "It is assured, that the king has established courts for deciding all ecclesiastical causes of a certain rank, without appeal to the Holy See; and that he has forbid any solicitations to be made to Rome, for benefices that become vacant in Spain."[9]

Boston Weekly News-Letter, May 23, 1751. A letter from Paris, dated December 22, N.S. "The Jansenists (who by the Jesuits, their original

7. Ibid.
8. Ibid.
9. Ibid., p. 17.

enemies) have been represented as the worst subjects His Majesty has, have now done an act sufficient to convince him and all the world of the contrary, having throughout the kingdom agreed to pay a ready obedience to His Majesty's ordonnance respecting ecclesiastical revenues, and not as of compliment, but of duty."[1]

"A rector of one of the Jesuit colleges lately advanced the following position. 'That 'tis heresy for anyone to assert, that the king has a right or power over the goods or revenues of ecclesiastics.' Whatever may be in the assertion, some think the position borders very close upon treason."[2]

Ibid. Paris, Alamain, January 11. "We hear from Lisbon, that the king of Portugal has formed a design to abolish the tribunal of the Inquisition in his dominions, in which undertaking every Frenchman, and we hope every true Christian in all nations, heartily wishes his success."[3]

Boston Evening-Post, June 10, 1751. London, March 25. "Our advices from Rome suggest that His Holiness is exceedingly alarmed at the steps taken in some, and about to be taken in other popish countries, in order to subject the ecclesiastics to an annual tax, proportionable to that levied on the laity, towards the expenses of the state, preventing the unequal distribution of the riches of the church, and putting a stop to the increase of idle and useless persons, by thrusting them for the ease of their respective families into convents."[4]

New York Evening Post. London, December 22. "Great pains are taking at Rome by the refractory clergy, backed by all the interest of the Jesuits, to engage His Holiness to espouse their oppositions (i.e., to the king of France's ordonnance respecting ecclesiastical revenues). But 'tis hoped by all who wish well to the peace of the church, and believed by such as sufficiently know His Holiness' great qualities, that he will not at all intermeddle in the affair, but suffer it to have its natural course."[5]

Boston Weekly News-Letter, Thursday, May 16, 1751. Nantes, a rich city in France, March 11. "We are in the utmost desolation and affliction, upon account of the damage done here and in our neighborhood by a violent hurricane. It began at the southwest on the 7th instant in the night, and at three o'clock next morning turned to the

1. No copy located.
2. No copy located.
3. No copy located. Notice of the king's design is in BEP, May 20, 1751, p. 1.
4. BEP, June 10, 1751, p. 4.
5. *New York Evening Post*, Apr. 29, 1751, p. 2.

northwest, accompanied with thunder, lightning and such terrible noises, both at sea and land, as seemed to proceed from an earthquake. We hear of a great deal of mischief from the country, such as the over-flowing of rivers, tearing up woods by the roots and overthrowing of houses. But the greatest damage that happened was in the road of Paimboeuf, where of 70 ships, there were only 4 which rode it out. Several were left upon the points of the rock; some were forced by the waves upon the quay, where they continue at this time upon dry land; some foundered at their anchors; and others were forced on the shore in different places and lost. It is said that 800 sailors were drowned at Paimboeuf. The land floods are daily increasing and bring down timber, trunks of trees, cattle, etc. The first chamber of insurance loses 1,200,000 livres, in consequence of this storm; and the whole loss to the town of Nantes is computed 10 millions of livres."[6]

Ibid. Paris, March 29. "It is assured that above 200 merchant ships have been cast away upon the coast of this kingdom by the late storms."[7]

Boston Gazette, June 25, 1751. "An expedient is talked of at Paris for composing the difference between the king of France and his clergy, the latter being willing, it is said, to give a declaration of their revenues, provided they be allowed to grant a supply to His Majesty, under the title of a free gift."[8]

The *Boston Weekly News-Letter* of July 25, 1751. "The king of Portugal talks of destroying the Inquisition, one of the most profitable milch cows, but the most curst of all the herd, that is now in possession of the venerable matron at Rome. At least it is agreed, that [if] he does not utterly demolish her, he will entirely deprive her of her horns, and all her power of doing mischief."[9]

"Summary of Public Affairs in 1751," in *Scots Magazine* for February, 1752.

In Tuscany. "About the middle of summer, an edict was published restraining the laity in that duchy from giving above a certain sum, by will or otherwise, to churches or convents. The Pope, judging this to be directly prejudicial to the interests of the clergy in general, has made strong representations to the emperor, for obtaining a revocation of the edict. But we do not hear of his having yet succeeded."[1]

6. BNL, May 16, 1751, p. 1.
7. Ibid.
8. BG, June 25, 1751, p. 1.
9. No copy located.
1. SM, *14* (1752), p. 63.

"The king of the Two Sicilies, . . . ever since his accession to the throne, has been gradually reducing the power and riches of the clergy within narrower bounds, and diminishing the papal influence in his dominions. Early in the year, he gave strict charge to the criminal court, to discourage all processes by which the clergy might become possessed of any more estates. And not long ago he issued orders, to prevent the Pope's disposing of such ecclesiastical benefices within the Sicilian territories as belonged to the bishops, in order to keep at home the large sums which went to Rome, when it was the only market for those benefices."[2]

"After the civil history of Italy, its natural history for the year under review seems to deserve particular notice. The earthquakes, which were frequent through so many places of Europe the preceding year, were almost confined to this country the last. Shocks began to be felt in the ecclesiastical state on the 11th of June N.S., which continued at short intervals, through different places of it, near five months, during which a great number of towns suffered much. Several of them were almost wholly laid in ruins; many of the inhabitants lost their lives; and the rest were obliged to flee, and live under tents in the open fields."[3]

In Portugal. "In order to reduce the number of the clergy, that hands may be found for trade and commerce, an ordinance has been published, which prohibits the ordaining [of] any priests and the receiving [of] any more into religious houses, without His Majesty's special license."[4]

In France. "It had been an ancient custom to receive occasional free gifts from the clergy, especially when the necessities of the states were urgent. But an assembly of that body having been convoked in 1750, the king signified his pleasure, that they should pay fifteen millions of livres per annum, for five years successively, and also that they should give up exact lists of their revenues, in order that a fixed annual sum might be laid upon them. The clergy remonstrated against this as an encroachment on their privileges, and insisted that His Majesty had not a right to tax the revenues of the church without their own consent. At the same time, they testified their fears, that the design of the court was to impose no lower a tax than that of the 20th penny, to which the rest of the kingdom was subject. His Majesty, in a letter directed to

2. Ibid., pp. 63–64.
3. Ibid., p. 64.
4. Ibid., p. 65.

them, disclaimed this intention, but not without informing them that he would have recourse to the means furnished by authority, if they persisted in not resolving to comply with his demand relating to lists of their revenues. Even this threatening not having produced obedience, at length, after sitting from the 15th of May to the 20th of September, the assembly was dissolved with marks of the king's displeasure. Since then, we have been told, that if the clergy did not comply, either their temporalities would be seized, or the intendants of the several provinces would receive orders to draw up the lists demanded. Sometimes the news would be, that the matter was adjusted. But this would soon appear, by succeeding accounts, to have been premature. Several of the bishops and deputies to the assembly, having been invited by circular letters from the court, met in Paris on the 1st of October last, when many proposals were laid before them. But such was the opposition of their sentiments, that they could agree upon nothing. According to very late advices, an *arret* of council was to be published, fixing the annual sum to be laid upon them at seven millions and $\frac{1}{2}$ of livres, and declaring the reason for demanding lists of their revenues to be, that this sum may be more equally proportioned than free gifts were."[5]

In *Scots Magazine* for February, 1752, p. 91. "His Sicilian Majesty has ordered, that, for the future, no layman shall be summoned to the court of Rome, for affairs relating to the spiritual jurisdiction."[6]

Boston Gazette of April 17, 1753. Extract of a private letter from Paris, dated December 27. "There are, so to speak, two camps in this city: one at the *palais,* the other at the archbishop's hotel; and in both they are busied in dressing their batteries. All the prelates, together with the devotees, compose the latter. It was said lately, in a company of the first distinction, that when the archbishop's temporalities were seized, they took away 100,000 pounds in ready money. A prelate of very high rank replied, that he had as many at his service. The eighteen archbishops and bishops, who went to Versailles with their pious and revengeful address, had dressed themselves in all their pontificals, to appear before the king. They were not, however, admitted to an audience. Only the Cardinal de Soubise was permitted to come into the king's closet, and with him His Majesty talked some time. Many of the peers, on receiving the summons to take their seats in parliament on the 18th, caused work all night to get their robes of ceremony ready, which cost upwards of 6000 livres. In short, the schism is made; and

5. Ibid., p. 67.
6. Ibid., p. 91.

we see no way to heal it. The court declares for the clergy, because they imagine they have less to fear from the parliament. But this conduct gives great offense to the bulk of the people, who makes the parliament's cause their own, and are most justly incensed against the archbishop and his clergy for so inhumanly refusing the spiritual assistances to which all the faithful, as such, have a just right."[7]

"Summary of Public Affairs in 1752," in *Scots Magazine* for January, 1753, p. 10. "They are repairing all the fortified places in Hungary, to which purpose is appropriated an annual sum of 120,000 florins, drawn from the abbeys and other religious communities, in virtue of an indulto[8] granted by the Pope."[9]

His Sardinian Majesty, "in order that the working hands may become more numerous, has afresh prohibited the leaving of estates to monasteries, and declared that all sums paid yearly by such monasteries to private persons, out of estates that have been left them for these uses, shall, after the death of such persons, be paid to the crown."[1]

"Since His Sicilian Majesty ascended the throne, he has been still gradually diminishing the papal influence in his dominions. To this end, he has ordered that for the future, no layman shall be summoned to the court of Rome, for affairs relating to the spiritual jurisdiction."[2]

In Portugal. "The power of the Inquisition is so much abridged, that it will not be able to do near so much mischief as formerly."[3]

Scots Magazine for June, 1753, p. 298. "An ordinance has been issued at Vienna, enjoining all superiors of communities, abbeys, monasteries and hospitals in lower Austria, who are exempted from any taxes, to shew within a month, by what title they enjoy such exemptions, what they paid for 'em, and for how long a time they were granted, the whole on pain of losing those privileges."[4]

Ibid., p. 299. "The sacred college at Rome, having dropped their opposition to the late agreement between the Pope and His Catholic Majesty, in relation to the collation of benefices, it has been ratified in form; meanwhile, the Holy See still reserves the nomination to 52 benefices."[5]

---

7. *The Boston Gazette, or Weekly Advertiser* (hereafter cited as BGA), Apr. 17, 1753, p. 2.
8. I.e., an ecclesiastical privilege.
9. SM, *15* (1753), p. 10.
1. Ibid., p. 12.
2. Ibid., p. 14.
3. Ibid., p. 15.
4. Ibid., p. 298.
5. Ibid., p. 299.

From the *New York Gazette* of December 24, 1753. "They write from Hamburg, that the disturbances [in Poland] are very far from being composed. . . . The nobility have no cause to be jealous of the power of the crown, and have seemed to turn their apprehensions towards the church, and are much displeased with the wealth and power of the clergy, notwithstanding that almost all the bishoprics and great preferments are enjoyed by the younger sons and brothers of noble houses; so that, in effect, it is [as] much their patrimony as if it was divided amongst them."⁶

From the *Boston Evening-Post*, March 11, 1754. Extract of a letter from Paris, dated November 4, 1753. "You know that it was the clergy, the bishops, who by their intrigues obtained the new commission court, which finds so much difficulty in getting its authority acknowledged. It seems, the Comptroller General would not be at the expense of this new tribunal; for all of it comes out of the clergy's fund. We are informed that even the archers who serve it go to M. de St. Julien, treasurer of the clergy, for their pay. . . . And as the hangman must be paid, the clergy have likewise taken this expense upon them. It is the clergy too who pay the members of the court: the president receives 6000 livres a month; each of the counselors of state who sit in it, 1000; the masters of requests, 2000 each; the attorney general, 4000. Then it costs the clergy about 74,000 livres each month for the salaries of the members, besides other expenses. . . . The clergy willingly pay this, because it prevents their being subjected to greater."⁷

From the *Boston Post-Boy* of March 11, 1754. Vienna, October 31. "The Franciscan fathers, who enjoyed considerable revenues and privileges, have been deprived of them, for permitting at one of their acts, a defense of the following thesis: 'That princes abuse their authority, in hindering their subjects from making donations or leaving legacies to religious houses or communities.' "⁸

Boston Evening-Post, April 29, 1754. Turin, January 7. "The nunciature (i.e., the office of the Pope's nuncio)⁹ continues shut up, and the king persists in his resolution that it shall not be opened again, unless the Pope acknowledges in His Majesty the same prerogative which other crowned heads have for a presentation to a cardinal's hat."¹

6. *The New York Gazette: or, The Weekly Post-Boy* (hereafter cited as NYG), Dec. 24, 1753, p. 2.
7. BEP, Mar. 11, 1754, p. 1.
8. BPB, Mar. 11, 1754, p. 1.
9. JE's explanation.
1. BEP, Apr. 29, 1754, p. 2.

New York Gazette, September 23, 1754. Rome, June 15. "The Pope has granted a bull, empowering the king of Spain to make use of 3 or 4 months' income of all benefices, both in his European and American dominions, to enable him to accomplish his great design of reducing the strength of the African infidels."[2]

Boston Post-Boy, October 14, 1754. London. "We have advice from Madrid, that His Catholic Majesty has issued an ordonnance, prohibiting all the religious houses from receiving any new nuns or monks, for the space of ten years."[3] See p. 283, **.

New York Gazette, January 6, 1755. Extract of a letter from The Hague,[4] dated September 26. "The clergy of France have spared no pains, to defeat the good understanding restored between the court and the parliament, so far they are from accommodating matters with this latter body. However, they now tremble in their turn at the projects, which the new Comptroller General of the finances is forming to affect their immense revenues, projects which the parliament will not fail of approving and confirming. The king himself, we are assured, is very much irritated with the manner of acting of these gentlemen, the prelates."[5]

From the *Boston Evening-Post* of March 24, 1755. Lisbon, October 1, 1754. "The king has caused an edict to be published, commanding the corregidor[6] in each division to take an exact account of all the lands held by religious communities, contrary to the law, or without His Majesty's permission, and to sequester the same forthwith. And 'tis said, a decree is soon to be published, for reducing the number of monks and nuns to the first institution of their respective orders and communities."[7] See what next follows *.

*From the *New York Mercury,* March 24, 1755. London. November 16. "All the letters from Lisbon concur in mentioning the edict, published by the king's order, to sequester the lands of the religious orders, which they hold contrary to the law, or not having the king's permission. This, with another order which is hourly expected, to reduce the number of religious, who within these few years have been greatly increased, to their original institution, will make a speedy diminution of those drones, who live only by the follies of other people. In this the

2. NYG, Sept. 23, 1754, p. 2.
3. BPB, Oct. 14, 1754, p. 1.
4. MS: "Paris."
5. NYG, Jan. 6, 1755, p. 2.
6. I.e., a civil magistrate.
7. BEP, Mar. 24, 1755, p. 1.

king of Portugal follows the new order in Spain, made since the ministry of Mr. Wall, whereby all the monasteries and nunneries are forbid to admit any persons into their orders for ten years."8 [See] p. 282, **.

Boston Evening-Post, July 21, 1755. "All things are getting ready for the general meeting of the clergy, who will be required to make the king a free gift suitable to the exigencies of the state. And M. Moreau de Seychelles, Comptroller General of the finances, has proposed in council that this article be brought on the tapis, previous to all other matters that are to be discussed by the clergy."9

Ibid. Rome, March 8. "The Cardinal of York has received advice, that the king of Spain has disposed of another benefice in his favor, worth six thousand crowns per annum."1

The *New York Gazette* of August 18, 1755. Paris, May 26. "The assembly of the clergy opens this day. The sum which His Majesty proposes to ask, is not certainly known; but it is said to be 15,000,000 [livres]. It is said, they are forbid to hold any debates relative to the certificates of confession, or the present circumstances of affairs; and the commissioners sent by the king, being provided with an exact list of the revenues of the clergy, are ordered to require them to give such an account themselves, in order to tax them the 20th penny, which demand occasioned the dissolution of the last assembly."2

Ibid. Paris, Alamain. "It is said, the free gift demanded of the clergy will be 37 millions, instead of 15."3

New York Gazette, March 1, 1756. There was an account in an extract of a letter from Madrid, dated October 13, of the king of Spain being offended with his father-confessor, Father Francis Ravago, a Jesuit; and of the said Jesuit's being removed from that place, which has been held by the society of Jesuits "for two centuries, and which has been the canal of all the riches that society possesses in the old and new world." And that there was no probability that any of that society would have that place anymore.4

In October, 1756, in my journey to Windsor and Northampton, [I] saw an account of a late great tax laid on the clergy in the kingdom of Naples.5

8. *The New York Mercury,* Mar. 24, 1755, p. 2.
9. BEP, July 21, 1755, p. 1.
1. Ibid.
2. NYG, Aug. 18, 1755, p. 1.
3. Ibid.
4. Ibid., Mar. 1, 1756, p. 1.
5. See BEP, Sept. 27, 1756, p. 1, for a notice of the proposed tax of three million ducats.

Connecticut Gazette of December 10, 1757. Rome, August 13. "The king of Spain, upon a survey which he had lately caused to be taken, of the estates of his subjects, finding the clergy much richer than the laity, desired leave of the Pope to lay a tax upon the former, the produce of which is to be applied against the Moors in time of war, and towards the relief of his subjects in time of peace. His Holiness has not only complied with so equitable a request, but lest any mistake should happen in drawing the brief, which might subject it to misinterpretation, has sent the rough draft to His Catholic Majesty, that he may make what alterations he shall think necessary."[6]

6. No copy located. The same report is in BEP, Nov. 28, 1757, p. 2.

EVENTS OF AN HOPEFUL ASPECT ON THE STATE OF RELIGION[1]

Boston Gazette, March 15, 1748. London, January 29. "By a letter from Switzerland, there is an account that one of the most considerable of the Romish cantons are going to embrace the Protestant religion."[2] See p. 286, *.

The account in an extract of Mr. Davidson's letter sent me by Mr. Bromfield of Boston, of the conversion of Mr. West, clerk of the privy council, and his writing in defense of Christianity; and also of Mr. Lyttelton's (a noted member of the House of Commons) writing in defense of the same. The same in a letter to me from Mr. McCulloch of Cambuslang, dated February 10, 1748.[3]

The accounts Mr. John Brainerd gives, March, 1748, of the religious concern at Cape May; and the account Mr. Strong gives of the state of religion among the Indians at Cranberry.[4]

1. See above, pp. 47–48.
2. BG, Mar. 15, 1748, p. 3.
3. This sentence is a later addition. No copies of the letters by Davidson or McCulloch have been located. This entry is clarified by a note in the "Catalogue," p. 16. "See an account of these two books [i.e., by West and Lyttleton] in an extract of a letter from Mr. Davidson, dissenting minister at Braintree in Essex, sent by Mr. McCulloch of Cambuslang, in a letter to Mr. Prince of Boston, and transmitted to me by Mr. Bromfield." Little is known about Thomas Davidson beyond what JE mentioned. Davidson was the author of a sermon entitled *The Real Christian Distinguished from Hypocrites, in a Discourse, from Revelations, Chap. iii. i* (2nd ed., Charleston, 1802). Edward Bromfield (1695–1756), a merchant in Boston, was a friend, correspondent, and agent of JE for years. See JE's letter to John Erskine, Aug. 31, 1748, for mention of him (Dwight ed., *1*, 252); and a funeral sermon preached by Thomas Prince, *The Case of Heman Considered* (Boston, 1756). JE referred to McCulloch's letter in another letter to him, May 23, 1749 (Dwight ed., *1*, 276–78). Gilbert West (1703–56) was converted from deism while "looking narrowly into the Bible in order to overthrow the doctrine of Christ's resurrection" ("Catalogue," p. 16). His *Observations on the History and Evidence of the Resurrection of Jesus Christ* (London, 1747) went through several editions. George Lyttleton (1709–73), a member of the powerful "Cobhamites" in the House of Commons, wrote a tract entitled *Observations on the Conversion and Apostleship of St. Paul. In a Letter to Gilbert West, Esq.* (London, 1747).
4. Brainerd (1720–81), a younger brother of David the missionary, was asked by the Society in Scotland for the Propagation of Christian Knowledge to continue his brother's work in New Jersey. John Brainerd had frequent contact with JE, including the communique

The pious and charitable disposition of a number of gentlemen in Boston, and the zeal they shew for the promoting of the gospel among the Indians.[5]

Evening-Post, March 21, 1748. Petersburg, January 8. "The missionaries whom the court maintains in the government of Casan, Risch-Nyogorod and Woronesch, have sent hither a list of the persons, as well Mahometans as pagans, who have been converted to the Christian faith within these last seven years, amounting in all to 258,357 souls, viz., 141,844 males and 116,513 of the other sex."[6]

See p. 285, *. *Boston News-Letter*, March 24. London, December 12. "We hear from Bern, that some great revolution in religious matters is expected in the canton of Lucerne, the most powerful of the Catholic members of the union, since within these 3 or 4 years past, there had been a demand from thence of no less than 30,000 Bibles; and that vast numbers were still continually sending [them] thither from Zurich and Basel."[7]

The accounts Mr. Buell gives in his letter to me of March 18, 1748, of the reviving of religion on Long Island and Shelter Island.[8]

---

mentioned here, a letter of Mar. 4, 1748. No copy of the letter has been located, but a portion is quoted by JE in his letter to William McCulloch, May 23, 1749 (Dwight ed., *1*, 276–78), including a reference to many in those parts "who are concerned for the prosperity of Zion." See also Thomas Brainerd, *The Life of John Brainerd, the Brother of David Brainerd, and his Successor as Missionary to the Indians of New Jersey* (New York, 1865). Job Strong (1716–98) of Northampton, a cousin of Brainerd, was one of the two candidates for the ministry recommended to the Commissioners in Boston to become missionaries to the Indians. He spent the winter of 1747–48 with John Brainerd in New Jersey and wrote a glowing report from Bethel concerning "the glorious work of Divine Grace among the Indians." See *Life of John Brainerd*, pp. 144–45. The BG, Mar. 29, 1748, p. 1, contains an extract from Strong's letter to his parents on Jan. 19, telling of the successes. Strong returned to Northampton in the spring and studied with JE, but delays forced him to give up his plans to become a missionary. On June 28, 1749, JE preached his ordination sermon at South Church in Portsmouth, *Christ the Great Example of Gospel Ministers* (Boston, 1750).

5. The New England Company was a leading sponsor of missionaries among the Indians. See William Kellaway, *The New England Company 1649–1776: Missionary Society to the American Indians* (London, 1961), esp. ch. 7. But a new effort developed after David Brainerd's visit to Boston in 1747 when "a considerable number in Boston, men of good substance and of the best character, and some of them principal men in the town, [resolved] to form themselves into a Charitable Society, that by their joint endeavours and contributions, they might promote the instruction and spiritual good of the Indians" (Dwight ed., *1*, 270).

6. BEP, Mar. 21, 1748, p. 1.

7. BNL, Mar. 24, 1748, p. 1.

8. No copy of the letter has been located. Samuel Buell, a graduate of Yale College, was a student and close acquaintance of JE. In 1742 he preached at Northampton with considerable success. See *Works*, *4*, 549–50. He spent some time itinerating in Virginia (below, p. 448) before he was ordained on Sept. 19, 1746, at East Hampton, Long Island, where JE

Boston Gazette, May 3. London, February 23. "Last Wednesday afternoon, a Jew, eminent for his great knowledge of the Hebrew and Chaldee languages, was after a proper confession of his faith publicly baptized, at the meetinghouse in Paul's Alley, Barbican."[9]

In [the] *Boston Weekly News-Letter*, May 5, 1748, was an account that Sir Richard Levinge, lately deceased, besides many other extraordinary legacies for pious uses, bequeathed "an estate of 93 pounds a year in the county of Westmeath, for maintaining and instructing poor children in the Protestant religion."[1]

The account Mr. McCulloch of Cambuslang gives me in his letter of February 10, 1748, that the Prince and Princess of Wales are both of them well-disposed persons, etc., (p. 4); and concerning the hopeful piety of the Princess Amelia (p. 5 ff.).[2] See p. 288, *.

News-Letter, October 20, 1748. London, August 9. Extract of a private letter from a member of the Charity[3] School Society in Ireland, to his friend in London. "The poor Irish continue to send such numbers of their children, that the four new schools opening next month will not hold them. We resolve not to check their spirit, but still continue to receive them to our reservoirs. Crowds of naked children are now in the workhouse, and several tailors employed to prepare that they mayn't go into these schools naked, as they came. There are piteous applications made for some, who are above the usual age to be admitted into them. In short, a great and promising harvest we have before us; and the same good providence of God, which hath hitherto blessed our endeavors, will still raise up more friends to carry on this design through the most distant parts of the kingdom."[4]

The account Mr. Buell gives in his letter of September 22, 1748, of the continuance of a religious concern at East Hampton, and of some religious concern at Bridgehampton; and the account there given from Mr. Prince, of the continuance of the work at Huntington.[5]

---

preached the sermon, *The Church's Marriage to her Sons, and to her God* (Boston, 1746). Buell's congregation experienced repeated revivals throughout the years.

9. BG, May 3, 1748, p. 1.

1. BNL, May 5, 1748, p. 1.

2. See above, n. 3; and Dwight ed., *1*, 262.

3. BNL reads "Charter." See M. G. Jones, *The Charity School Movement: A Study of Eighteenth Century Puritanism in Action* (Cambridge, Eng., 1938).

4. BNL, Oct. 20, 1748, p. 1.

5. No copy of Buell's letter has been located. In a letter to James Robe, May 23, 1749, JE wrote, "Mr. Buell, of East-Hampton, on Long Island, was here last week, and gave me an account of a very considerable work of awakening at this time in his congregation, especially among the young people; and also of a yet greater work at Bridgehampton, under the

The further account given of the good effect of Mr. West's conversion from deism, and his and Mr. Lyttelton's writings in defense of Christianity, on many of the great men of the nation, by Mr. Robe in his letter of April 7, 1748 (p. 7), and Mr. Erskine in his letter of April 6, 1748 (p. 2, about the middle).[6]

[See] p. 287, *. The good disposition of the Prince of Wales, is confirmed by Mr. Erskine in his letter of April 6, 1748 (last page, latter part). He also speaks of the religious disposition of the Princess Amelia (p. 2, past the middle), and gives a remarkable account of the conviction of the Princess Caroline (last page, latter part), which should be compared with the account Mr. McCulloch gives in his letter of February 10, 1748 (pp. 5–6).[7]

The account of the concern about religion in Mr. Randy's and Mr. Gray's parishes, in the shire of Angus in Scotland, in Mr. Erskine's letter forementioned (p. 2, past the middle).[8]

The account of a number of ministers in various parts of Scotland, uniting themselves in a kind of association, for the promoting [of] the interest of vital religion and the concert for prayer, in the aforesaid letter of Mr. Erskine (p. 2, latter part), and also Mr. McLaurin's letter of May 21, 1748 (latter end).[9]

The account of the piety of the Archbishop of Canterbury, in Mr. McLaurin's letter of April 4, 1748 (pp. 11–12), and also Mr. Erskine's letter of April 5, 1748 (p. 3, former part). Mr. McLaurin, in the place aforesaid, also speaks of the archbishop as "orthodox."[1]

The account given of the disposition of the king and Archbishop of Canterbury to comprehend the Dissenters, to allow the validity of Presbyterian ordination, and to set aside the laws obliging to the use of the Common Prayer and ceremonies, and entirely to abolish some of the ceremonies, in [a] letter from Mr. McLaurin of April 4, 1748 (pp. 8–10), and Mr. Robe's letter of April 7, 1748 (pp. 8–9), and Mr.

---

ministry of one Mr. Brown, a very pious and prudent young man, lately settled there. These congregations are both pretty large. He also gave account of religion's continuing in a very prosperous state, at a part of Huntington, another town on Long Island, where was a great and general awakening, last year" (Dwight ed., *1*, 280).

6. No copies of these letters have been located. Erskine's letter was summarized in JE's letter to him, Oct. 14, 1748, printed in Dwight ed., *1*, 265–70.

7. See above, n. 6, and p. 285, n. 3.

8. I. e., that of Apr. 6, 1748 (Dwight ed., *1*, 265).

9. No copy of John McLaurin's letter has been located.

1. No copies of the letters have been located. It seems unlikely that Erskine would have written to JE on successive days, but the references here and in the next entry are indisputable.

Erskine's letter of April 5, 1748 (p. 3, near the top). Mr. McLaurin speaks of several other bishops being with the king and archbishop in a design of this nature.[2]

The account given, that many of the clergy of the Church of England having lately appeared to preach the doctrines of grace, in Mr. Robe's letter of April 7, 1748.

The remarkable account of the piety of the Prince of Orange, Stadtholder of the United Provinces, and the wonderful interposition of divine providence in his advancement to the stadtholdership, etc., in answer to the extraordinary prayer of the churches in Holland united in a concert. The account given from a letter from Mr. Kennedy of Rotterdam, in Mr. Erskine's letter of April 6, 1748 (pp. 3–4).[3]

The account of an uncommon zeal, lately appearing among some of the magistrates in several parts of England, in putting the laws in execution against vice, in Mr. Robe's letter of April 7, 1748 (pp. 8–9). See p. 290, ††.

The account Mr. Emerson of Groton gives me, of several ministers falling in with the concert for prayer, in his letter of October 1, 1748.[4]

2. No copies of the letters have been located.

3. Hugh Kennedy (1698–1764) was pastor of the Scottish church in Rotterdam for twenty-seven years, during which time he actively promoted evangelicalism. He himself was a successful revivalist. In 1742 he wrote a preface for the Dutch translation of the accounts of the revivals in Cambuslang, reprinted in *The Christian History*, *1*, 287–92. Some of Kennedy's correspondence was published as *A Short Account of the Rise and Continuing Progress of a Remarkable Work of Grace in the United Netherlands* (2nd ed., London, 1752). See J. P. De Die and J. Loosjes, eds., *Biographisch Woorddenboek van Protestantsche Godgeleerden in Nederland* (Gravenhage, 1931), Vol. 4, pp. 725–28; William Steven, *The History of the Scottish Church, Rotterdam* (Edinburgh, 1832); and Fawcett, *Cambuslang Revival*, pp. 138–42. In Steven's *History*, p. 189, is the following entry from the minutes of the kirk session of June 1, 1747: "Ordered to note, that by commission from, and in the name of the members of the Consistory, Mr. Hugh Kennedy did, on the 17th May, congratulate his Most Serene Highness the Prince of Orange, (in his yacht here,) upon his accession to the Stadtholdership of the Seven United Provinces; and that his illustrious Highness returned a most gracious answer." See JE's later criticism of Kennedy in a letter to John Erskine, Nov. 23, 1752 (Dwight ed., *1*, 508–09).

4. Joseph Emerson (1724–75), a graduate of Harvard in 1743, served as a chaplain on the Louisburg expedition in 1745. A year later he organized the Second Church in Groton, Connecticut. See Clifford K. Shipton, *Sibley's Harvard Graduates*, *11* (Boston, 1960), 217–20. Following the commencement at Yale College in 1748, Emerson visited JE in Northampton and was attracted to his daughter Esther. Emerson's diary for these months has been edited by Samuel A. Green, *Diary Kept by the Rev. Joseph Emerson of Pepperell, Mass. August 1, 1748–April 9, 1749* (Cambridge, Mass., 1911). The following entries are found in it. "frid 30 I came home and attended the private Meeting at Ebenezer Gilsons. I read some out of Mr. Edwards Concert of Prayer. *October* Sat 1 I wrote two Letters in the forenoon one to Mr. Edwards, of Northampton the other to his Second Daughter a very desireable person, to whom I purpose by divine leave to make my addresses" (p. 9). Esther eventually married Aaron Burr, the second president of the College of New Jersey. No copy of Emerson's letter has been located.

†† *Weekly News-Letter*, October 6, 1748. London, August 8. "Yester-day ten barbers were convicted before Thomas Ellys, Esq., for exercising their trade on the Lord's day, and fined 5 shillings each."[5]

Boston Gazette, December 6, 1748. Philadelphia. "Yesterday about noon, arrived the Honorable James Hamilton, Esq., governor of this province. . . . We also hear that the Reverend Mr. Whitefield has preached to prodigious congregations in and about London, and was daily gaining the affections of people of all ranks; that he is made chaplain to the Right Honorable, the Countess of Huntingdon, at whose house he had several times preached, at her request, to many of the nobility, among whom were the earls of Chesterfield and Bath; and that after he had preached a farewell sermon to a very large and attentive auditory at St. Bartholomew's Church, London (in which he had a few Sundays before administered the sacrament to near a thousand com-municants), he set out for Scotland, and from thence intended for Ireland, and for this place next year."[6]

Boston Gazette, March 14, 1749. Bristol, November 5. "We hear that the Right Honorable, the Countess of Huntingdon has presented the Reverend Mr. Wesley with a living of 200 [pounds] per annum."[7]

Extract of a letter from a minister in the county of Norfolk in Eng-land, to Mr. Prince of Boston, in the year 1749. "The interest of religion at London, is in many places on the increase; and 'tis observed that for the most part, our successes there are by the means of younger ministers, of whom we have several there that do honor to the cause, and promise to do yet much more by and by. . . . Lyttelton has wrote in favor of Christianity with that fullness, clearness and strength of argument, that his piece, I hear, has already had a very good effect on Lord Cobham— lately one of the 'deistical club,' and who was extremely enraged at his brother Lyttelton for what he had done. But his lordship, being per-suaded to read his book himself, was obliged to yield, and has now also declared in favor of Christianity."[8]

5. BNL, Oct. 6, 1748, p. 1.

6. BG, Dec. 6, 1748, p. 1. The successes of Whitefield are detailed further in Aaron C. H. Seymour, *The Life and Times of Selina Countess of Huntingdon* (2 vols., London, 1840). On this particular incident, see Vol. 1, pp. 88–90.

7. BG, Mar. 14, 1749, p. 1. In 1749 at the urging of the Countess of Huntingdon, John Wesley and Whitefield mellowed on some of their theological differences and exchanged pulpits several times. During that period Wesley had extensive contact with the countess. See Nehemiah Curnock, ed., *The Journals of Rev. John Wesley* (8 vols., London, 1909–16), *3*, 452 n; and Luke Tyerman, *The Life and Times of the Rev. John Wesley* (3 vols., New York, 1872), esp. *2*.

8. No copy of the letter to Thomas Prince has been located. See above, p. 285, n. 3, on

Extract of a letter from Mr. Robert Cruttenden, to Mr. John Smith in Boston, dated London, March 15, 1748/9. "Not long after Mr. Whitefield's arrival, he was sent for by my Lady Huntingdon, who appointed him her chaplain and engaged his service, not only in staying in the family, but preaching to an auditory of the first distinction, who attended divine services at her ladyship's house. These have been daily increasing in their numbers, and are now no longer ashamed to avow and patronize that gospel, which I trust has been made the power of God to the awakening of some, and the conversion of others. As these are most of them equally distinguished by their superior understandings as well as stations, enthusiasm can have no place in this surprising change, which quite confounds our modern freethinkers, and is become the subject of conversation even in Caesar's household. When I mention the names of my Lord Chesterfield, the Earl of Bath, my Lord Bolingbroke, the Margraff of Lothian, and honorable women not a few, you will easily see that the cause in which he is embarked, is not like to be given up to a banter or a sneer, the strongest weapons which have hitherto been employed against it, and the only ones I believe it is likely to apprehend. Some of these ladies have even given their attendance at the Tabernacle. I own, sir, from these which I trust are but the beginnings of what God is about to do for us, I indulge myself in the prospect of much greater displays of the Redeemer's glory, when the scandal of the cross shall no longer blind the eyes of the great and honorable, the wise and prudent, from a professed subjection to the doctrines of the gospel. May I only be permitted to see these hopes confirmed! And I know nothing I desire to see more in this world. . . . Mr. Whitefield's constant attendance on that pious and truly honorable lady, three days a week and on Sabbath days, obliges him to employ the best assistance he can procure at those times for the Tabernacle."[9]

Concerning the extraordinary reception of Mr. Hervey's contemplation, especially by great men in England, though the book be so evan-

---

Lyttleton. Lord Cobham was Sir Richard Temple (1669–1749), leader of a parliamentary coalition.

9. No copy of the letter has been located. Cruttenden (d. 1763), a dissenting divine who left the ministry and went into business, lost his fortune when the South Sea bubble burst. Subsequently he published *The Experience of Mr. R. Cruttenden, as Delivered into a Congregation of Christ, in Lime-Street, under the Pastoral Care of the Reverend Mr. Richardson, prefaced and recommended by George Whitefield* (London, 1744). See Tyerman, *George Whitefield, 2,* 98. Smith (1704–68) was a Boston dry goods merchant, a close friend and correspondent of leading evangelicals including Whitefield, Watts, and JE. He made frequent business trips to England. See Shipton, *Harvard Graduates, 7,* 121–24.

gelical and Calvinistical, and very boldly and zealously testifies against Arminianism, see Mr. Willison's letter of March 17, 1749.[1]

Boston News-Letter, March 8, 1749/50. Extract of a letter from Petersborough, dated October 7. "We are assured by advices lately received from the office *de propaganda fide*, that within these six months last past, not only 16,179 men, but 7234 women, inhabitants of the cities of Casan and Orenburg, one part whereof were Mahometans, and the other perfect infidels, had abjured their respective impious sects, were all baptized and admitted members of the Christian church."[2] [See] p. 293, *.

Boston News-Letter, March 22. Extract of a letter from the Reverend Mr. Pearsall of Taunton in Somersetshire in England, October 31, 1749, to the Reverend Mr. Prince of Boston.

"I will lay open to you what I think is remarkable. And I will do it from the account which Dr. Doddridge sends me, who had the account from the person himself.

" 'There is a person who lays out himself for the conversion of the Jews, lately in London, and perhaps may be there still. He is one of the greatest and most surprising linguists in the world. He took an unaccountable fancy, without any reason that could be then assigned, of learning the languages used among the Jews, when he was but five years old: so that the pure Hebrew, the rabbinical, and the lingua Judaica, which is another different from both, and composed of the two former, and almost all the modern languages of the European nations are so familiar to him, that he can speak almost any of 'em as well as German, his native tongue. With this furniture and with great knowledge of God and love to Christ, and zeal for the salvation of souls, he hath spent 12 of the 36 years of his life in preaching Christ in the synagogues, in the most apostolical manner: warning the Jews of their enmity to God, of their misery as rejected by him, of the only hope that remains for them, but their returning to their own Messiah, and by seeking from him righteousness and life, and placing their souls under the sprinkling of the blood of that great sacrifice. [It is evident] that God hath in many places blessed his labors; so that there are in Germany, Poland, Hol-

---

1. Willison's letter (MS, Andover coll.) is printed in Dwight ed., *1*, 270–73. On Willison, see above, pp. 69–70. The work by James Hervey (1714–58) was two volumes: *Meditations Among the Tombs. In a Letter to a Lady*, and *Reflections on a Flower Garden. In a Letter to a Lady* (London, 1746). Both went through many editions. In the "Catalogue," p. 18, JE characterized the work "as the most polite of any that has been written in an evangelical strain" in England. See Hervey's *Life*, part of *The Works of the late Reverend James Hervey* (6 vols., Edinburgh, 1779).

2. BNL, Mar. 8, 1750, p. 2.

land, Lithuania, Hungary and other parts through which he hath traveled, about six hundred converts, many of whom are expressing their great concern to bring others of their brethren to the knowledge of that great and blessed Redeemer, and beseeching him to instruct their children, that they may preach Christ also.' Dr. Doddridge says further, that he heard one of his sermons as he repeated it in Latin; and that he could not hear it without many tears; and that he told him that sermon converted a rabbi, who was ruler of a synagogue.

"Thus far my good friend, Dr. Doddridge. I leave you to make your judicious remarks upon all this. But many of us are somewhat struck with the phenomenon, as it is something we have never heard the like of. We pray and hope that it may be the dawn of that blessed day, when God shall bring home the scattered of Israel, and the dispersed of Judah."3 See p. 295, **.

[See] p. 292, *. *Gazette* of July 17, 1750. From the *Universal Magazine* for April 30, 1750. "They write from Casan in Asia, that within six months 6672 men and women were converted to the Christian religion in those parts."4

Extract of a letter from Dr. Doddridge, in a postscript of a letter from Governor Belcher, dated August 20, 1750. "Nor did I ever know a finer class of young preachers for its number, than that which God has given me this year to send out into the churches. Yet are not all the supplies, here or elsewhere, adequate to their necessities; for many congregations in various parts of England remain vacant. But I hope God will prosper the schemes we are forming for their assistance.

"I bless God that in these middle parts of our island, peace and truth prevails in sweet harmony. And I think God is reviving our cause, or rather his own, sensibly, though in a gentle and almost unobserved manner."5

3. Ibid., Mar. 22, 1750, p. 1. Richard Pearsall (1698–1762) wrote several volumes, including one reprinted in New England: *The Power and Pleasure of the Divine Life* (Boston, 1755), which JE referred to late in the "Catalogue," p. 35. Philip Doddridge (1702–51) was a highly influential Nonconformist in England whose works JE knew well, including especially *The Family Expositor: or, a Paraphrase and Version of the New Testament: With Critical Notes; and a Practical Improvement of each Section* (6 vols., London, 1739–56). JE used the sixth volume of the *Family Expositor* extensively during the last year and a half of his life. On Doddridge, see Job Orton, *Memoirs of the Life, Character and Writings of the late Reverend Philip Doddridge* (2nd ed., London, 1766). The works of Doddridge have been collected in several editions. John D. Humphreys, ed., *The Correspondence and Diary of Philip Doddridge* (5 vols., London, 1829–31), contains several letters from Pearsall, but not the one in question. See JE's letter to John Erskine, July 5, 1750 (Dwight ed., *1*, 405–13), for another reference to the same materials.

4. BG, July 17, 1750, p. 2.

5. No copies of these letters have been located. Jonathan Belcher, a merchant, was the

When I was at Mr. Abiel Walley's in Boston, May 4, 1751, he read to me a passage of a letter to Mr. Prince, just then come over from his correspondent in Norwich in England, mentioning a late revival of religion in several parts of Holland.[6]

See also Mr. Davenport's letter to me dated April 26, 1751, and the printed accounts sent from Scotland in the paper entitled, "An Exhortation to the South Parish and the Hearers in the College Kirk," wherein are more full accounts.[7]

Scots Magazine for January, 1751, pp. 8–9. On the affairs of Russia. "The college established in the Asiatic provinces, for the propagation of Christianity, continues to meet with success in that work. During the first six months of the year, they baptized into the faith of the Greek Church 5344 persons, who were formerly pagans or Mahometans."[8]

From the *New York Gazette* of September 18, 1752, N.S. Letter from Amsterdam, June 19. "The disturbances between the clergy and the parliament of Paris, threaten very bad consequences to the Roman Catholic Church, which have extended so far as even to trouble the repose of the Pope. The Holy Father has heard with grief of the ravages which this dissension has made among his sheep, and sees with still more chagrin that these misfortunes proceed from the conduct even of those who are shepherds."[9]

From the *Scots Magazine* for February, 1752, p. 91. "We are told, that the prince of Transton, archbishop of Vienna, has lately published a pastoral mandate, directed to all the parish priests who have the care of souls in his diocese, in which he exhorts them to lay aside the ineffectual

colonial governor of Massachusetts from 1730–41 and of New Jersey from 1746–57. He was a strong supporter of evangelical causes and corresponded extensively with various religious leaders, including JE. JE quoted this entry verbatim in a letter to John Erskine, Nov. 15, 1750 (Dwight ed., *1*, 415–18). See ibid., pp. 266–68, for other letters from Belcher to JE.

6. No copy of the letter to Thomas Prince has been located. Walley (d. 1759) was a merchant in Boston and friend of JE. See also above, p. 33, n. 4.

7. No copy of the letter has been located. James Davenport (1716–57), earlier a minister at Southold, Long Island, gained notoriety during the Great Awakening with his inflammatory preaching and bizarre behavior. Arrest, dismissal, and sickness changed him, and by 1744 he printed *The Reverend Mr. James Davenport's Confession & Retractions* (Boston). He spent the rest of his life serving congregations in the New Jersey area. See Franklin Bowditch Dexter, *Biographical Sketches of the Graduates of Yale College with Annals of the College History* (6 vols., New York, 1885–1912) *I*, 447–50. JE quoted part of Davenport's letter in his letter to John Erskine, June 28, 1751 (Dwight ed., *1*, 458–62). The "Exhortation" (Glasgow, 1750–51) was a weekly religious newspaper edited by John Gillies, a minister in Glasgow, for his parishioners. Supportive of the cause of the awakenings, it furnished details of successful revivals in widely scattered areas. See Fawcett, *Cambuslang Revival*, pp. 172, 217.

8. SM, *13* (1751), pp. 8–9.

9. NYG, Sept. 18, 1752, p. 2.

doctrines of purgatory and adoration of saints, and to preach after the example of St. Paul, that sound faith which shews itself in a holy life."[1]

From the *Scots Magazine* for April, 1752, p. 205. "The missionaries employed by the Asiatic society in propagating the Greek religion, have sent advice that during the last six months of 1751, they converted and baptized 6417 persons of both sexes, who before had either been pagans or Mahometans."[2] There is the same account in the *Scots Magazine* for January, 1753, p. 6.[3]

See the account of the great spreading of the revival of religion in the Netherlands, in Mr. Erskine's letter of May 13, 1752.[4]

"The Summary of Public Affairs of the Year 1752," *Scots Magazine* for January, 1753. "The Protestants greatly increase in most of the hereditary dominions of the house of Austria."[5]

Boston Weekly Gazette of July 2, 1754. Paris, Alamain, April 1. "The number of Protestants in the Cévennes, has for some [time] past greatly increased."[6]

Boston Evening-Post, May 13, 1754. Vienna, March 6. "Last Sunday the Pope's bull and the queen's edict, for abolishing 24 holidays, that used to be observed yearly, were read in all our churches."[7]

See p. 293, **. *New York Gazette* of August 26, 1754. A paragraph of a letter of a baptized rabbi, Leopold Jacob de Dors, written at Osnaburg in Germany,[8] to a gentleman at Loen, by which a speedy conversion of the Jews is presaged. Translated out of the Dutch *Monthly State Secretary* for the month of March, 1754.

The above-named rabbi sets forth in the course of his letter: "In a council of the scattered Jewish church, assembled on matters of faith at Roda in Poland, the 4th of August, 1752, were assembled 548 rabbis; 53 whereof, with 15,000 of the principal Jews, separated themselves and sent a learned Jewish Christian from Poland, by way of Danzig and Amsterdam, to me with full power to offer unto me their undisguised confession of faith, contained in the five following articles.

1. SM, *14* (1752) p. 91.

2. Ibid., p. 205.

3. Ibid., *15* (1753), p. 6. This sentence is a later addition.

4. No copy of the letter has been located. JE referred at length to it in his letter to John Erskine, Nov. 23, 1752 (Dwight ed., *1*, 507–12). See his strictures there concerning the progress of the revivals in the Netherlands.

5. SM, *15* (1753), p. 10.

6. BGA, July 2, 1754, p. 1.

7. BEP, May 13, 1754, p. 2.

8. Osnaburg, as my gazetteer says, is one of the Hanse towns in Westphalia, most of which Hanse towns are Protestants. See *History of Popery*, Vol. 2, p. 568b. —JE. [See above, p. 69].

1. That the only true Godhead consists in three persons.
2. That the Messiah is the true Immanuel.
3. That this is certainly Jesus of Bethlehem.
4. That the Old Testment is a type of the New.
5. That the holy gospel is the true Word of God.

The various divisions and disputes in Christendom, put them at a stand what set of Christians to join, which made them apply to me to advise them which was the most essential way, and the Christian books [to be] brought into Hebrew when, as they promise, they would come into the true Christian dominions, with all their effects, in order to serve the Lord.

"Now, sir, as I have experienced the benefit in and by the holy religion you maintain, so I beg of you to favor me and those Jewish Christians with your protection, and to aid them in translating the Scripture into Hebrew in the city of Lingen, as also to let me have a speedy answer, etc."[9]

From the *Boston Evening-Post* of March 31, 1755. Ratisbon, January 14. "Several thousands of the inhabitants of the archbishopric of Salzburg, have declared themselves of the Protestant religion, and have demanded leave to exercise it publicly or to retire out of the country, by virtue of the right of transmigration, as was done in the year 1732. This affair occasions a great commotion, and the bishop and his chapter are extremely embarrassed to know how to act."[1]

From the *Boston Gazette* of March 25, 1755. An extract of a letter from a gentleman in London, to his correspondent in Boston, of the 13th of January, 1755, by Captain Gordon. "There is a great revival of religion in the west of England, under the ministry of a curate in the established church. Great part of the parish are under convictions; and the preaching of the gospel is attended constantly by upwards of a thousand souls, some of whom are daily applying personally to the minister under soul concern. The leaven is also spreading in six parishes round him; and eight of the clergy in that neighborhood are associated, and meet weekly to strengthen one another in the doctrines of the gospel and the things of God, and consult measures for promoting the good of souls. And what is most remarkable, God has seemed to work by himself; for they have no connection with any 'Methodists,' as they are here called, or dissenters of any denomination. And there is in some

9. NYG, Aug. 26, 1754, p. 2.
1. BEP, Mar. 31, 1755, p. 2. See HA; below, p. 363.

other places, a stirring among the dry bones in the establishment."[2]

See a further account of this, in a letter sent me by Mr. Davenport, containing an extract of a letter from Mr. Davies of Virginia to Captain Grant of Philadelphia, in which Mr. Davies transcribes a letter from a correspondent in England, giving an account of these things.[3]

This from a note in the margin of Mr. Erskine's sermon, on *The Influence of Religion on National Happiness*, p. 25. "Many worthy ministers and private Christians in London, of different denominations, deeply affected with the gross ignorance of multitudes in this land of gospel light, formed themselves into a society, August 1750, for promoting religious knowledge among the poor, distributing Bibles and other useful books. The printed accounts of their success occasioned the erecting a society in Edinburgh on a like plan, lst of January 1756."[4]

2. BGA, Mar. 25, 1755, p. 3.

3. No copies of the letters have been located. Samuel Davies (1723–61), trained at a "log college" founded by Samuel Blair, was ordained a Presbyterian evangelist in 1747 and sent to Virginia where he was responsible for founding the Presbytery of Hanover. A champion of religious toleration and civil liberty, he became president of the College of New Jersey following JE's death. See George William Pilcher, *Samuel Davies: Apostle of Dissent in Colonial Virginia* (Knoxville, 1971); and Wesley M. Gewehr, *The Great Awakening in Virginia, 1740–1790* (Durham, N.C., 1930). See JE's favorable assessment of Davies in Dwight ed., *1*, 518.

4. John Erskine, *Influence*, p. 25. See above, p. 70.

TRACTATE ON REVELATION 16:12[1]

"And the sixth angel poured out his vial upon the great river Euphrates, and the waters thereof, that the way of the kings of the East may be prepared."

Mr. Lowman, in his late, excellent exposition of the Revelation, has made it plain beyond all contradiction, that the five first vials are already poured out, and there remains only the sixth and seventh; so that this 6th vial upon the river Euphrates, is [the] next thing in the prophecies of the Revelation that remains to be accomplished. Mr. Lowman also shews with great evidence, that the fifth vial, the last before this, was poured out in the time of the Reformation; and he shews that there has ordinarily been about 200 years distance between one vial and another.[2] But it is now more than 200 years since the 5th vial begun to be poured out. He supposes the 6th vial will begin to be poured out sometime after the year 1700. It is therefore the more worth our while, to inquire what manner of events are signified by this 6th vial, seeing these events are what we have so much reason to expect a speedy accomplishment of.

And here is one thing, that is not so usually observed concerning this prophecy, that I think may be laid down for an evident truth, that may perhaps serve as a key to open the prophecy. And that is, that here is an allusion to the way wherein old Babylon was destroyed; which was by drying up the waters of the great river Euphrates which ran through the city, whereby the way of the kings of the East, the princes of Media and Persia, was prepared to come in under the walls of the city and destroy it.[3] That drying up the river Euphrates, was the last thing done by the besiegers of Babylon before its destruction, as this 6th vial is the last thing done against the spiritual Babylon, before her total destruction

1. See above, p. 79. These separate pages at the rear of the MS bear no heading. JE used the title "tractate" as a cross-reference in the "Blank Bible," p. 675. For discussions parallel to this essay, see no. 78, above, pp. 184–91; and HA, below, pp. 412–21.

2. *Paraphrase and Notes*, pp. 196–99. See above, "Extracts."

3. See above, no. 54, p. 147.

by the 7th vial. I need not strive[4] particularly to shew, that the anti-christian church is in this book of Revelation everywhere compared to Babylon, and called by the name of Babylon the Great, as the true church is called Jerusalem; because to mention all the places would be very tedious, and because none can be ignorant of it.[5] Seeing therefore these 7 vials are vials of wrath, which God pours out on Babylon (as 'tis called in this book), in order to her destruction, as all allow; and the destruction of this Babylon is what the Holy Spirit has here respect to; and this vial is the last before that which actually brings her destruction; and the destruction of old Babylon was by drying up the river Euphrates, to prepare the way for the kings of the East to come in to her destruction—I think it cannot be doubted but that here is an allusion to that event.

The prophecies of the Old Testament do represent old Babylon as being destroyed by the kings of the East. Is. 46:11, "Calling a ravenous bird from the East, the man that executeth my counsel from a far country," speaking of Cyrus. Jer. 27:7, "Many nations and great kings shall serve themselves of her," speaking of the destruction of Babylon. Jer. 51:11, "The Lord hath raised up the spirit of the kings of the Medes; for his device is against Babylon, to destroy it." And vv. 27–28, "Prepare the nations against her, with the kings of the Medes, and the captains thereof, and the rulers thereof, and all the land of his dominion." Media and Persia were both to the eastward of Babylon.

And the prophets also do take notice of God's drying up the river Euphrates, to make way for these enemies of Babylon to come in and destroy her. Is. 44:27–28, "That saith to the deep, Be dry, and I will dry up thy rivers; that saith of Cyrus, He is my servant, and shall perform all my pleasure." And Jer. 51:31–32, "One post shall run to meet another, and one messenger to meet another, to shew the king of Babylon that his city is taken at one end, and that the passages are stopped; and the reeds have they burnt with fire, and the men of war were affrighted." And v. 36, "I will dry up her sea, and make her springs dry."

Now therefore, since this is what this prophecy of the 6th vial has a plain reference to, I am humbly of opinion that the right way of going to work, in order to find the true meaning of this prophecy and to discover what that is appertaining to the Romish Church that is to be removed by this vial, answering to the removal of the river Euphrates in

---

4. Conjecture for illegible word.

5. MS: "⟨none can be ignorant of it⟩ ~~every one Knows it.~~"

the destruction of old Babylon, is to consider what the river Euphrates was to that city, or wherein it served Babylon and was a benefit to it, so that the drying of it up was a great judgment or calamity to it.

The river Euphrates served the city of Babylon two ways. 1. As a supply. 2. As a defense.

1. It served the city as a supply. The river Euphrates was let through the midst of the city by an artificial canal, and ran through the midst of the palace of the king of Babylon for that end: that the city and palace might have the convenience of its waters, and might be plentifully supplied by water from the river; and not for the convenience of navigation, for that was rendered impossible by the wall built over the river at each end of the city. And it was common thing for cities to be built by rivers and streams of water for the same end. Hence the temporal supplies of any people are very often in Scripture called "waters," as Isaiah 5:13. "Therefore my people are gone into captivity, and their honorable men are famished, and their multitude dried up with thirst," i.e., were deprived of the supplies and supports of life. So Isaiah 41:17, "When the poor and needy seek water, and there is none, and their tongue faileth for thirst, I the Lord will hear them; I, the God of Israel, will not forsake them." Waters are very often in scripture language used to signify both spiritual and temporal supplies, in places innumerable (Prov. 9:17; Is. 33:16, 43:20, 55:1, 58:11; Jer. 2:13, 18, 17:8, 13).

And therefore, one thing intended by the drying up the river Euphrates, when applied to the mystical Babylon or Church of Rome, must be meant a remarkably drying up or diminishing of her temporal supplies, and supports of power, learning and wealth, which may be accomplished by the taking away from the Church of Rome the supplies and help she has had from the principal powers that have hitherto supported her. Mr. Lowman, in his notes on Revelation 8:10 and 16:4, observes that by rivers and fountains of waters in prophecy, is sometimes meant chief cities and countries, that are original seats of empire, fountains of power and dominion.[6] As Joab, when he had taken Rabbah, the chief city of the Ammonites, sends messengers to David, saying, "I have fought against Rabbah, and have taken the city of waters" (II Sam. 12:27). The chief powers of Europe, that have for many ages been the main fountains of the supply and supports of the Church of Rome, are France, Spain and the emperor. This vial, therefore, may probably include the destroying or remarkably weakening and diminishing or taking away from the Church of Rome some or all of these. What has

6. *Paraphrase and Notes*, pp. 75 and 182–83. See above, no. 80, p. 191.

lately befallen the imperial power is well known.[7] And whether this mayn't probably be an effect of this vial beginning to be poured out on the rivers and fountains of the waters of the Church of Rome, I leave to be considered. And who knows what may yet further be in the issue of the present war,[8] with respect to the other two popish powers of France and Spain, as the vial goes on to be poured out. The one of which has, in a remarkable manner, been the fountain of power, policy and learning for the supply and support of the popish cause; the other, the fountain of her wealth.

And as by waters and rivers in scripture language, is meant supplies of any city or kingdom in general, so more especially are they used to signify their wealth and treasures. And the drying up the waters of a city or kingdom, is often used in scripture prophecy for the depriving them of their wealth, as the Scripture explains itself. So Jer. 50:37–38, "A sword is upon her treasures, and they shall be robbed. A drought is upon her waters, and they shall be dried up." So again, Is. 15:6–7, "For the waters of Nimrim shall be desolate; for the hay withereth away, the grass faileth; there is no green thing. Therefore the abundance they have gotten, and that which they have laid up, shall they carry away to the brook of the willows." And Hos. 13:15, "His spring shall become dry, and his fountain shall be dried up; and he shall spoil the treasure of all pleasant vessels."

The wealth, revenue and vast incomes of the Church of Rome, are the waters by which that Babylon has been nourished and supported. These are the waters that the members of the Romish hierarchy thirst after and are continually drinking down with an insatiable appetite. And they are waters that have been for many ages flowing into that spiritual city, like a mighty river, ecclesiastical persons possessing a very great part of the wealth of the popish dominions, as this Babylon is represented as vastly rich in this prophecy of Revelation, especially in the 17th and 18th chapters. These are especially the waters that supply the palace of the king of this spiritual Babylon, viz., the Pope, as the river Euphrates of old ran through the midst of the king of Babylon's palace, that part of his palace that was called the old palace being on one side, and the new palace on the other, with communications from one to the

7. Probably the loss of Silesia to Frederick the Great of Prussia (1712–86) in 1740 during the War of the Austrian Succession. For a time all of the dominions of Maria Theresa (1717–80) and the House of Hapsburg were threatened.

8. I.e., the War of the Austrian Succession, known in the American theater as King George's War.

other by a bridge over the water, and an arched passage under the water.[9] The revenues of the Pope have been like the waters of a mighty river, coming into his palace from innumerable fountains, and by innumerable branches and lesser streams, coming from many various and distant countries.

Therefore, we may suppose that the drying up of the river Euphrates by the 6th vial, will especially consist in drying up these waters. And agreeable to the significance of this vial, is the popish princes of late making bold with the treasures of the church, in taxing the clergy, as they have often done of late years, which formerly would have been looked on as an unpardonable sacrilege. And also the accounts we some years since had of the kings of Spain and Portugal, withholding great part of the incomes and revenues the Pope used to have from these countries, by strictly forbidding the people to go out of their own dominion for investitures, pardons, indulgences, dispensations and the like.[1]

But the main channel of this great river, seems to be the stream of their wealth from the Spanish West Indies. The silver and gold mines in this country are its main fountain, and indeed have been, for several hundred years, the chief fountain of the treasures of Europe. And if the Protestants that are at this day at war with those principal popish powers, France and Spain, should prevail, so far as to turn the stream of their wealth that flows from hence, away from that church into some other channel, as Cyrus, when he fought against Babylon, diverted the stream of Euphrates from the city [of] Babylon, this will be a great fulfillment of this prophecy.

2. As the river Euphrates served the city [of] Babylon as a supply, so another way it served them was a defense, or an obstacle in the way of its enemies, to hinder their access to it to destroy it. For at each end of the city, it served instead of walls; for the water ran under the walls. And when the waters were gone, the way for her enemies was prepared. There was nothing to hinder their coming in and destroying the city. And besides, there was a vast moat round the city, of prodigious width and depth, filled with the water of the river, to hinder the access of her besiegers; what moat was left empty when Cyrus had dried up the river, and so his way was prepared.

Therefore, there seems to be good ground for us to suppose, that by drying the river of Euphrates in this prophecy, to make way for her

9. Cf. HA; below, p. 413.
1. See no. 78, above, p. 188; and HA, below, p. 421.

enemies to destroy her, is meant the removal of those things that have been the main defense of the Church of Rome hitherto, and the chief obstacles on the way of the nations embracing the Protestant religion. The waters of rivers were commonly used to defend cities of old. Is. 37:25, "With the soles of my feet have I dried up the rivers of besieged places." Is. 19:4–5, "And the Egyptians will I give over into the hand of a cruel Lord. . . . And the water shall fail from the sea, and the river shall be wasted and dried up; and they shall turn the rivers far away, and the brooks of defense shall be emptied, and dried up."

Now if these things were accomplished that were before mentioned, the Church of Rome would be exceedingly weakened, and her main defense would be gone. If these main kingdoms that are the chief fountains of power, wealth, policy and learning were taken away from the Church of Rome, how exposed and defenseless would she be. If the main channels of her wealth were diverted from her into Protestant countries, how weak and despicable would she become, and how easy a prey to her enemies. And the way would be prepared remarkably for her enemies, called the kings of the East; by which, there is no necessity of understanding any civil powers coming from the eastern parts of the world, but only those powers that are enemies to the Church of Rome, as formerly the kings of the East were enemies to Babylon. For it seems to be a mere allusion to the way of destroying old Babylon.

Another thing that has hitherto been a great defense to the Church of Rome, and a great obstacle on the way of the prevailing of the Protestant religion, are those differences and controversies, sects and errors, among Protestants. These have been great stumbling blocks, and like mountains and rivers have, as it were, made the ground unpassable. And possibly these may be removed to prepare the way of God's people, by God's raising up some in his church, [who] shall in a wonderful manner set forth divine and Christian doctrines in a clear light, and unravel the difficulties that attend them, and defend them with great strength and clearness of reason; and so that voice be fulfilled: "Prepare the way of the Lord. Every valley shall be exalted; every mountain and hill shall be made low" [Is. 40:3–4].

And one thing more I would add, which may greatly prepare the way for the destruction of the Church of Rome; and that is the destruction of the Turkish Empire, and the establishing the true religion of those parts of the world. 'Tis darkness is the defense of the Church of Rome; and if God is pleased to let in light all around them, so that they shall be encompassed with it on every side, it may greatly prepare the way for her destruction. If those two great empires of Russia and Persia[2] (which are kingdoms of the East, with respect to Rome, and one of them the same country that formerly overthrew old Babylon), I say, if those should embrace the true religion (as one of them especially have of late gone far towards it), and should conquer the Turkish Empire, and let in the true religion there, how greatly would it be for the glory of the true church, and the strengthening of the true religion. And how much would it probably stir up the jealousy of the Church of Rome, who doubtless had much rather that the Mahometan religion should remain there as it is, than the Protestant religion let in instead of it. And if Russia and Persia professed the Protestant religion, [the Church of Rome] would esteem the Turks as their defense or barrier on the eastern side, against their encroachments.

Rivers are often a barrier to kingdoms. So the river Jordan was a barrier to Canaan; and therefore, when God brought in his people from the east to destroy the Canaanites under Joshua, Jordan was dried up to prepare their way [Josh. 3:14–17]. So the Rhine has been a defense to France on the eastern side. And the river Euphrates was the bounds of the kingdom of Israel in David's and Solomon's time, and was the boundary that God set to the dominion and possession of his people in the covenant with Abraham, and with the congregation in the wilderness. And therefore, when their territories were overrun by the Assyrians, a people that dwelt on that river, 'tis represented by the prophets, as the waters of the river Euphrates breaking their ancient banks, and coming and overflowing the land of Israel. Is. 8:7–8, "Now therefore, behold, the Lord bringeth up upon them the waters of the river, strong and many, even the king of Assyria and all his glory. And he shall come up over all his channels, and go over all his banks; and he shall pass through Judah. He shall overflow and go over. He shall reach even to the neck; and the stretching out of his wings shall fill the breadth of thy land, O Immanuel." So Euphrates was a long time the ancient eastern boundary of the Roman Empire. And therefore, when the Turks (a people that came from about that river) overran great part of that empire, even to the Adriatic Sea, this was, as it were, the waters of the river, breaking their ancient bounds and banks, and overflowing great part of the Roman Empire. And therefore, the destruction of that empire may fitly be compared to the drying up the river Euphrates.

And this perhaps, may be another thing implied in the pouring out of that vial, as Lowman makes it exceeding probable that the 4th vial has

2. Here JE deleted "should be enlightened with the light of the true religion."

respect to several diverse events, and as the seven heads of the beast by the angel himself is interpreted of two entirely diverse things (Rev. 17), viz., of seven mountains and seven different forms of government.[3] However, the whole meaning [of] this prophecy may be summed up in this: that it signifies the removal of those benefits to the new Babylon, which old Babylon anciently had by the river Euphrates, viz., its supply and its defense.

And as Mr. Lowman supposes, that the present time is the time when we may expect that this vial will be poured out, so I would leave it to be considered whether everything in divine providence have[4] the appearance of a beginning of the pouring out of this vial, and don't afford a prospect of its being speedily, more fully, poured out.

3. *Paraphrase and Notes*, pp. 188–95 and 210–12; and "Extracts," above, pp. 243–50.
4. Conjecture for lacuna.

AN HUMBLE ATTEMPT

Humble Attempt

To promote

Explicit Agreement

AND

Visible UNION

Of GOD's People in

Extraordinary Prayer

For the REVIVAL of *Religion* and the Advancement of *Christ's Kingdom* on Earth, pursuant to Scripture-Promises and Prophecies concerning the *last Time*.

By *Jonathan Edwards,* A. M.
Minister of the Gospel at *Northampton.*

With a PREFACE by several Ministers.

BOSTON, NEW-ENGLAND:
Printed for D. HENCHMAN in *Cornhil.* 1747.

THE PREFACE

T HE ruin of Satan's miserable kingdom, and the advancement of the universal and happy reign of Christ on the earth, were included and hinted in the sentence denounced on the serpent, that "the seed of the woman should bruise his head" [Gen. 3:15]. What was a terrible threatening to Satan, in the surprised ears of our first guilty parents, implied a joyful prophecy, to keep them from despair, and enliven their hopes for themselves and their descendants, of obtaining by this Seed of hers an eternal triumph over him who had so sadly foiled them. And 'tis likely, their hope and faith immediately arose, laid hold on the reviving prophecy, earnestly desired its happy accomplishment, and transmitted it to their posterity.

But though this prophecy was at first only delivered in the form of a threatening to Satan; it was afterwards directly given in the form of a promise to Abraham, though still in general terms, that "in his seed should all the nations of the earth be blessed" [Gen. 12:3]. Yet this general promise was more clearly by degrees explained in the following ages, to mean a divine king, no other than the Son of God assuming human nature of the seed of Abraham, Isaac, Jacob and David; that should be born of a virgin in Bethlehem of Judah; and at first despised, abused, rejected and put to death; but should rise to immortal life, ascend to heaven, and thence extend his blessed kingdom over all nations; not by outward force, but inward overcoming influence, by his Word and Spirit making them "his willing people in the day of his power" [Ps. 110:3]; and reigning in glorious light and holiness and love and peace forever: and the advancement of this universal and happy reign has been the earnest desire and prayer of the saints in all ages to the present day.

But how great the honor, and how lively the encouragement given in Scripture to those their prayers; by representing them as offered by Christ himself with the fragrant incense of his own merits and inter-

309

cession, on the golden altar before the throne, and ascending together in one grateful perfume to God [Rev. 8:3–4]! And how cheering to every saint is that promise of his, "From the rising of the sun, even to the going down of the same, my name shall be great among the Gentiles, and in every place incense shall be offered unto my name, and a pure offering" [Mal. 1:11]! How pleasing to God and the heavenly hosts to see, as the sun goes round the globe, this grateful incense rising from every part on high! And the more extensive and incessant are these prayers, ascending from the circle of the earth, the more does this blessed promise go into its desired fulfillment, and the holy God is more pleased and glorified.

To promote the increase, concurrency and constancy of these acceptable prayers, is the great intention both of the pious Memorial of our reverend and dear brethren in Scotland, and of the worthy author of this exciting essay. And this design we can't but recommend to all who desire the coming of that blissful kingdom in its promised extent and glory, in this wretched world.

As to the author's ingenious observations on the prophecies, we entirely leave them to the reader's judgment: with only observing, though it is the apprehension of many learned men,[1] that there is to be a very general slaughter of the witnesses of Christ about the time of their finishing their testimony to the pure worship and truths of the gospel, about 3 or 4 years before the seventh angel sounds his trumpet for the ruin of Antichrist [Rev. 11:3–15]; yet we cannot see that this is any just objection against our joint and earnest prayers for the glorious age succeeding, or for the hastening of it.

For if such a terrible time is coming in Europe, which we in depending America are like to share in; the more need we have of joining in earnest and constant prayers for extraordinary suffering graces for ourselves and others. And that such a time is coming on the members of Christ, is no more an objection against their prayers for the hastening of the following glory, than it was before the incarnation of him their Head, that his most bitter sufferings were to precede the spreading of his joyous kingdom among the nations. And the nearer the day approaches, the more need we have to be awakened to continual watchfulness and prayer.

May God pour out on all his people abundantly the "spirit of grace

1. E.g., above, p. 43, n. 4.

and supplications" [Zech. 12:10], and prepare them for the amazing changes hastening on the earth, both for previous trials and for following glories!

Boston, N. E.
January 12, 1747/8

Joseph Sewall
Thomas Prince
John Webb
Thomas Foxcroft
Joshua Gee[2]

---

2. Sewall (1688–1769) and Prince (1687–1758) were co-ministers at Old South Church in Boston. In the same city Webb (1687–1750) was the pastor of New North Church, Foxcroft (1697–1769) at First Church, and Gee (1698–1748) at Old North Church.

PART I

"THUS saith the Lord of Hosts, It shall yet come to pass, that there shall come people, and the inhabitants of many cities; and the inhabitants of one city shall go to another, saying, Let us go speedily to pray before the Lord, and to seek the Lord of Hosts: I will go also. Yea, many people and strong nations shall come to seek the Lord of Hosts in Jerusalem, and to pray before the Lord" (Zech. 8:20–22).

In this chapter we have a prophecy of a future glorious advancement of the church of God; wherein it is evident, something further is intended than ever was fulfilled to the nation of the Jews under the Old Testament. For here are plain prophecies of such things as never were fulfilled before the coming of the Messiah: particularly what is said in the two last verses in the chapter, of "many people and strong nations worshiping and seeking the true God," and of so great an accession of Gentile nations to the church of God, that by far the greater part of the visible worshipers of God should consist of this new accession, so that they should be to the other as ten to one, a certain number for an uncertain.[1] There never happened anything, from the time of the prophet Zechariah to the coming of Christ, to answer this prophecy: and it can have no fulfillment but either in the calling of the Gentiles, in and after the days of the apostles, or in the future glorious enlargement of the church of God in the latter ages of the world, so often foretold by the prophets of the Old Testament, and by

1. JE was echoing a common view that prophetic numbers were not always to be interpreted literally because they were frequently employed in the Bible in a figurative or symbolic manner. For a discussion of this principle applied to the book of Revelation, see Robert Fleming, *Apocalyptical Key. An Extraordinary Discourse on the Rise and Fall of Papacy; or, the Pouring out of the Vials, in the Revelation of St. John, Chap. XVI* (Philadelphia, 1843), pp. 7–8. Fleming's work was first printed in 1701.

the prophet Zechariah in particular, in the latter part of this prophecy. 'Tis most probable, that what the Spirit of God has chief respect to, is that *last* and greatest enlargement and most glorious advancement of the church of God on earth; in the benefits of which especially, the Jewish nation were to have a share, and a very eminent and distinguishing share. There is a great agreement between what is here said, and other prophecies, that most manifestly have respect to the church's latter-day glory: as that in Is. 60:2-4. "The Lord shall arise upon thee, and his glory shall be seen upon thee: and the Gentiles shall come to thy light, and kings to the brightness of thy rising. Lift up thine eyes round about, and see; all they gather themselves together, they come to thee." That whole chapter, beyond all dispute, has respect to the most glorious state of the church of God on earth. So ch. 66:8. "Shall the earth be made to bring forth in one day? Shall a nation be born at once?" V. 10, "Rejoice ye with Jerusalem, and be glad with her, all ye that love her." V. 12, "I will extend peace to her like a river, and the glory of the Gentiles like a flowing stream." Micah 4 at the beginning; "But in the last days it shall come to pass, that the mountain of the house of the Lord shall be established in the top of the mountains, and it shall be exalted above the hills, and people shall flow unto it; and many nations shall come and say, Come, and let us go up unto the mountain of the Lord, and to the house of the God of Jacob. And he shall judge among many people, and rebuke strong nations afar off; and they shall beat their swords into plowshares, and their spears into pruning hooks; nation shall not lift up sword against nation, neither shall they learn war anymore." See also Is. 2 at the beginning. There has been nothing yet brought to pass, in any measure to answer these prophecies. And as the prophecy in my text and the following verse does agree with them, so there is reason to think it has a respect to the same times. And indeed there is a remarkable agreement in the description given throughout the chapter, with the representations made of those times elsewhere in the Prophets; as may be seen by comparing v. 3 with Is. 60:14; v. 4 with Is. 65:20, 22, and 33:24; vv. 6–8 with Ezek. 37:2, 11–12, 21; v. 7 with Is. 43:5–6 and 49:12 and 59:19; vv. 12–13 with Hos. 2:21–22 and Ezek. 34:22–29; vv. 8, 12–13, with Ezek. 36:28–30; v. 13 with Zeph. 3:20 and Is. 19:24; v. 19 with Is. 61:3 and Jer. 31:12–14.

So that however the prophet, in some things that are said in this chapter, may have respect to future smiles of heaven on the nation of the Jews, lately returned from the Babylonish captivity, and resettled in the land of Canaan, in a great increase of their numbers and wealth, and the return of more captives from Chaldea and other countries, etc., yet the Spirit of God has doubtless respect to things far *greater* than these, and of which these were but faint resemblances. We find it common in the prophecies of the Old Testament, that when the prophets are speaking of the favors and blessings of God on the Jews, attending or following their return from the Babylonish captivity, the Spirit of God takes occasion from thence to speak of the incomparably greater blessings on the church, that shall attend and follow her deliverance from the spiritual or mystical Babylon, of which those were a type; and is, as it were, led away to speak almost wholly of these latter, and vastly greater things, so as to seem to forget the former.

And whereas the prophet, in this chapter, speaks of God's "bringing his people again from the east and west to Jerusalem" (vv. 7–8), "and multitudes of all nations taking hold of the skirts of the Jews" [v. 23]; so far as we may suppose that this means literally that nation of the posterity of Jacob, it can't have chief respect to any return of Jews from Babylon and other countries, in those ancient times before Christ; for no such things as are here spoken of, attended any such return: but it must have respect to the great calling and gathering of the Jews into the fold of Christ, and their being received to the blessings of his kingdom, after the fall of Antichrist, or the destruction of mystical Babylon.

In the text we have an account *how* this future glorious advancement of the church of God should be brought on, or introduced; viz., by great multitudes in different towns and countries taking up a *joint resolution,* and coming into an express and visible *agreement,* that they will, by united and extraordinary *prayer,* seek to God that he would come and manifest himself, and grant the tokens and fruits of his gracious presence.

Particularly we may observe,

1. The *duty,* with the attendance on which the glorious event foretold shall be brought on; viz., the duty of prayer. Prayer, some suppose, is here to be taken synecdochically,[2] for the whole of the worship of God; prayer being a principal part of the worship of the church of God, in the days of the gospel, when sacrifices are abolished: and so, that this is to be understood only as a prophecy of a great *revival* of religion, and of the true worship of God among his visible

---

2. I.e., as a figure of speech in which a part represents the totality.

people, the accession of others to the church, and turning of multitudes from idolatry to the worship of the true God. But it appears to me reasonable, to suppose, that something more special is intended, with regard to the duty of prayer; considering that prayer is here expressly and repeatedly mentioned; and also considering how parallel this place is with many other prophecies, that speak of an extraordinary spirit of prayer, as preceding and introducing that glorious day of revival of religion, and advancement of the church's peace and prosperity, so often foretold (which I shall have occasion to mention hereafter) and particularly the agreeableness of what is here said, with what is said afterwards by the same prophet, of the "pouring out of a spirit of grace and supplications," as that with which this great revival of religion shall begin (Zech. 12:10).

2. The *good*, that shall be sought by prayer; which is God himself. It is said once and again, "They shall go to pray before the Lord, and to seek the Lord of Hosts" [Zech. 8:21]. This is the good they ask for and seek by prayer, the Lord of Hosts himself. To "seek God," as the expression may perhaps be sometimes used in Scripture, may signify no more than seeking the favor or mercy of God. And if it be taken so here, "praying before the Lord," and "seeking the Lord of Hosts," must be looked upon as synonymous expressions. And it must be confessed to be a common thing in Scripture, to signify the same thing repeatedly, by various expressions of the same import, for the greater emphasis. But certainly that expression of "seeking the Lord," is very commonly used to signify something more than merely, in general, to seek some mercy of God: it implies, that God himself is the great good desired and sought after; that the blessings pursued are God's gracious presence, the blessed manifestations of him, union and intercourse with him; or, in short, God's manifestations and communications of himself by his Holy Spirit. Thus the Psalmist desired God, thirsted after him, and sought him. Ps. 63:1–2, 8, "O God, thou art my God; early will I seek thee. My flesh longeth for thee, in a dry and thirsty land, where no water is, to see thy power and thy glory, so as I have seen thee in the sanctuary. . . . My soul followeth hard after thee." Ps. 73: 25, "Whom have I in heaven but thee? And there is none upon earth that I desire besides thee." The Psalmist earnestly pursued after God, "his soul thirsted after him, he stretched forth his hands unto him," etc. (Ps. 143: 6). And therefore it is in Scripture the peculiar character of the saints, that they are those that seek God. Ps. 24: 6, "This is the generation of them that seek him." Ps. 69: 32, "Your heart shall live that seek

God." And in many other places. If the expression in the text be understood agreeable to this sense, then by "seeking the Lord of Hosts," we must understand a seeking, that God who had withdrawn, as it were hid himself, for a long time, would return to his church, and grant the tokens and fruits of his gracious presence, and those blessed communications of his Spirit to his people, and to mankind on the earth, which he had often promised, and which his church had long waited for.

And it seems reasonable, to understand the phrase, "seeking the Lord of Hosts," in this sense here; and not as merely signifying the same thing with praying to God: not only because the expression is repeatedly added to "praying before the Lord," in the text, as signifying something more; but also because the phrase, taken in this sense, is exactly agreeable to other parallel prophetic representations. Thus God's people's seeking, by earnest prayer, the promised restoration of the church of God, after the Babylonish captivity, and the great apostasy that occasioned it, is called their seeking God, and searching for him; and God's granting this promised revival and restoration is called his being found of them. Jer. 29:10–14, "For thus saith the Lord, That after seventy years be accomplished at Babylon, I will visit you, and perform my good word towards you, in causing you to return to this place. For I know the thoughts that I think towards you, saith the Lord, thoughts of peace, and not of evil, to give you an expected end. Then shall ye go and call upon me, and ye shall go and pray unto me, and I will hearken unto you; and ye shall seek me and find me, when ye shall search for me with all your heart; and I will be found of you, saith the Lord, and I will turn away your captivity." And the Prophets, from time to time, represent God, in a low and afflicted state of his church, as being withdrawn, and hiding himself. Is. 45:15, "Verily thou art a God that hidest thyself, O God of Israel, the Saviour." Ch. 57:17, "I hid me, and was wroth." And they represent God's people, while his church is in such a state, before God delivers and restores the same, as seeking him, looking for him, searching and waiting for him, and calling after him. Hos. 5:15, "I will go and return unto my place, till they acknowledge their offense, and seek my face: in their affliction they will seek me early." Is. 8:17, "I will wait upon the Lord, that hideth his face from the house of Jacob, and I will look for him." And when God in answer to their prayers and succeeding their endeavors, delivers, restores and advances his church, according to his promise, then he is said to answer, and come, and say, Here am I, and to shew himself; and they are said to find him, and see him plainly. Is. 58:9, "Then shalt thou call, and the Lord shall answer; and thou shalt cry, and he shall say, Here I am." Is. 45:17, "But Israel shall be saved in the Lord, with an everlasting salvation." And v. 19, "I said not unto the seed of Jacob, Seek ye me in vain." Ch. 25:8–9, "The Lord God will wipe away tears from off all faces, and the rebuke of his people shall he take away from off the earth. . . . And it shall be said in that day, Lo, this is our God, we have waited for him, and he will save us: this is the Lord, we have waited for him; we will be glad, and rejoice in his salvation." Together with the next ch., vv. 8–9, "Yea, in the way of thy judgments, O Lord, we have waited for thee: the desire of our soul is to thy name, and to the remembrance of thee. With my soul have I desired thee in the night; yea, with my spirit within me will I seek thee early. For when thy judgments are in the earth, the inhabitants of the world will learn righteousness." Is. 52:6–8, "Therefore my people shall know my name: therefore they shall know in that day, that I am he that doth speak: Behold, it is I. How beautiful upon the mountains are the feet of him that bringeth good tidings, that publisheth peace, that bringeth good tidings of good, that publisheth salvation, that saith unto Zion, Thy God reigneth! Thy watchmen shall lift up the voice; with the voice together shall they sing; for they shall see eye to eye, when the Lord shall bring again Zion."

3. We may observe *who* they are, that shall be united in thus seeking the Lord of Hosts: "the inhabitants of many cities," and of many countries, "yea, many people, and strong nations"; great multitudes in different parts of the world shall conspire in this business [Zech. 8:20–22]. From the representation made in the prophecy, it appears rational to suppose, that it will be fulfilled something after this manner; first, that there shall be given much of a spirit of prayer to God's people, in many places, disposing them to come into an express agreement, united-ly to pray to God in an extraordinary manner, that he would appear for the help of his church, and in mercy to mankind, and pour out his Spirit, revive his work, and advance his spiritual kingdom in the world, as he has promised; and that this disposition to such prayer, and union in it, will gradually spread more and more, and increase to greater degrees; with which at length will gradually be introduced a revival of religion, and a disposition to greater engagedness in the worship and service of God, amongst his professing people; that this being observed, will be the means of awakening others, making them sensible of the wants of their souls, and exciting in them a great concern for their

spiritual and everlasting good, and putting them upon earnestly crying to God for spiritual mercies, and disposing them to join with God's people in that extraordinary seeking and serving of God, which they shall see them engaged in; and that in this manner religion shall be propagated, till the awakening reaches those that are in the highest stations, and till whole nations be awakened, and there be at length an accession of many of the chief nations of the world to the church of God. Thus after the inhabitants of many cities of Israel, or of God's professing people, have taken up, and pursued a joint resolution, to go and pray before the Lord, and seek the Lord of Hosts, others shall be drawn to worship and serve him with them; till at length "many people" and "strong nations" shall join themselves to them; and there shall, in process of time, be a vast accession to the church, so that it shall be ten times as large as it was before; yea, at length, all nations shall be converted unto God. Thus "ten men shall take hold, out of all languages of the nations, of the skirt of him that is a Jew" (in the sense of the Apostle, Rom. 2:28–29), "saying, We will go with you; for we have heard, that God is with you" [Zech. 8:23]. And thus that shall be fulfilled, Ps. 65:2, "O thou that hearest prayer, unto thee shall all flesh come."

4. We may observe the *mode* of their union in this duty. 'Tis a visible union, an union by explicit agreement, a joint resolution declared by one to another, come into by being first proposed by some, and readily and expressly fallen in with by others. The inhabitants of one city shall apply themselves to the inhabitants of another, saying, Let us go, etc. Those to whom the motion is made, shall comply with it; the proposal shall take with many, it shall be a prevailing, spreading thing; one shall follow another's example, one and another shall say, I will go also [Zech. 8:21]. Some suppose, that those words, "I will go also," are to be taken as the words of him that makes the proposal; as much as to say, "I don't propose that to you, which I am not willingly to do myself, I desire you to go, and I am ready to go with you." But this is to suppose no more to be expressed in these latter words, than was expressed before in the proposal itself; for these words, "Let us go," signify as much, as that I am willing to go, and desire you to go with me. It seems to me much more natural, to understand these latter words as importing the consent of those to whom the proposal is made, or the reply of one and another that falls in it. This is much more agreeable to the plain design of the text, which is to represent the concurrence of great numbers in this affair; and more agreeable to the representation made in the next

verse, of one following another, many "taking hold of the skirt of him that is a Jew" [Zech. 8:23]. And though, if the words are thus understood, we must suppose an ellipsis in the text, something understood that is not expressed, as if it had been said, "Those of other cities shall say, I will go also"; yet this is not difficult to be supposed; such ellipses are very common in Scripture. We have one exactly parallel with it in Jer. 3:22. "Return, ye backsliding children, and I will heal your backslidings: behold, we come unto thee; for thou art the Lord our God," i.e., the backsliding children shall say, "Behold, we come unto thee," etc. And in Cant. 4:16, and 5:1. "Let my beloved come into his garden, and eat his pleasant fruits. I am come into my garden, my sister, my spouse," i.e., her beloved shall say, "I am come into my garden." We have the like throughout that song. So, Ps. 50:6–7, "The heavens shall declare his righteousness; for God is judge himself. Hear, O my people, and I will speak," i.e., the judge shall say, "Hear, O my people," etc. So Ps. 82:1–2. The Psalms and Prophets abound with such figures of speech.

5. We may observe the *manner of prayer* agreed on, or the manner in which they agree to engage in and perform the duty. "Let us go speedily to pray" [Zech. 8:21]; or as it is in the margin, "Let us go continually." The words literally translated are, "Let us go in going."[3] Such an ingemination[4] or doubling of words is very common in the Hebrew language, when it is intended that a thing shall be very strongly expressed; it generally implies the superlative degree of a thing; as the "Holy of Holies" signifies the most holy: but it commonly denotes, not only the utmost degree of a thing, but also the utmost certainty; as when God said to Abraham, "In multiplying, I will multiply thy seed" (Gen. 22:17), it implies both that God would certainly multiply his seed, and also multiply it exceedingly. So when God said to Adam, "In the day that thou eatest thereof, in dying thou shalt die" [Gen. 2:17] (as the words are in the original),[5] it implies, both that he should surely die, and also that he should die most terribly, should utterly perish, and be destroyed to the utmost degree. Yea, sometimes it seems to imply something else still: and in short, as this ingemination of words in the Hebrew, in general denotes the strength of expression, so it is used to signify almost all those things that are wont to be signified by the various forms

3. The Hebrew text combines the finite verb with the infinitive absolute, נֵלְכָה הָלוֹךְ. JE's reference to "the margin" probably refers to the printed text in the "Blank Bible," p. 650, where both "continually" and "going" are suggested substitutes for "speedily."

4. I.e., repetition.

5. מֹות תָּמוּת Again the Hebrew has an infinitive absolute with a finite verb for additional intensity of expression.

of strong speech in other languages: sometimes it signifies the utmost degree of a thing; sometimes certainty; sometimes the peremptoriness and terribleness of a threatening, or the greatness and positiveness of a promise, the strictness of a command, and the earnestness of a request. When God says to Adam, "Dying thou shalt die," it is equivalent to such strong expressions in English, as, "Thou shalt die indeed," or, "Thou shalt die with a witness." So when it is said in the text, "Let us go in going, and pray before the Lord," the strength of the expression represents the earnestness of those that make the proposal, their great engagedness in the affair; and with respect to the duty proposed, it may be understood to signify, that they should be speedy, fervent, and constant in it; or, in one word, that it should be thoroughly performed.

6. We may learn from the tenor of this prophecy, together with the context, that this union in such prayer is foretold as a *becoming* and *happy* thing, and that which would be acceptable to God, and attended with glorious success.

From the whole we may infer, that it is a very suitable thing, and well-pleasing to God, for many people, in different parts of the world, by express agreement, to come into a visible union, in extraordinary, speedy, fervent and constant prayer, for those great effusions of the Holy Spirit, which shall bring on that advancement of Christ's church and kingdom, that God has so often promised shall be in the latter ages of the world.

And so from hence I would infer the duty of God's people, with regard to the Memorial lately sent over into America, from Scotland, by a number of ministers there, proposing a method for such an union as has been spoken of, in extraordinary prayer for this great mercy.

And it being the special design of this discourse, to persuade such as are friends to the interests of Christ's kingdom, to a compliance with the proposal and request made in that Memorial, I shall first give a short historical account of the affair it relates to, from letters, papers and pamphlets, that have come over from Scotland; to which I shall annex the Memorial itself: and then I shall offer some arguments and motives, tending to induce the friends of religion to fall in with what is proposed: and lastly, make answer to some objections that may possibly be made against it.

As to the first of these things, viz., an historical account of the concert, which the Memorial relates to, the following observations may give a sufficient view of that affair.[6]

6. Above, pp. 36–40.

In October, A.D. 1744, a number of ministers in Scotland, taking into consideration the state of God's church, and of the world of mankind, judged that the providence of God, at such a day, did loudly call such as were concerned for the welfare of Zion, to united extraordinary applications to the God of all grace, suitably acknowledging him as the fountain of all the spiritual benefits and blessings of his church, and earnestly praying to him, that he would appear in his glory, and favor Zion, and manifest his compassion to the world of mankind, by an abundant effusion of his Holy Spirit on all the churches, and the whole habitable earth, to revive true religion in all parts of Christendom, and to deliver all nations from their great and manifold spiritual calamities and miseries, and bless them with the unspeakable benefits of the kingdom of our glorious Redeemer, and fill the whole earth with his glory. And consulting one another on the subject, they looked on themselves, for their own part, obliged to engage in this duty; and, as far as in them lay, to persuade others to the same: and to endeavor to find out and fix on some method, that should most effectually tend to promote and uphold such extraordinary application to heaven among God's people. And after seeking to God by prayer for direction, they determined on the following method, as what they would conform to in their own practice, and propose to be practiced by others, for the two years next following, viz., to set apart some time on Saturday evening and Sabbath morning, every week, for the purpose aforesaid, as other duties would allow to everyone respectively; and more solemnly, the first Tuesday of each quarter[7] (beginning with the first Tuesday of November then next ensuing), either the whole day, or part of the day, as persons find themselves disposed, or think their circumstances will allow: the time to be spent either in private praying societies, or in public meetings, or alone in secret, as shall be found most practicable, or judged most convenient, by such as are willing, in some way or other, to join in this affair: but not that any should make any promises, or be looked upon as under strict bonds in any respect, constantly and without fail to observe every one of these days, whatever their circumstances should be, or however other duties and necessary affairs might interfere; or that persons should look upon themselves bound with regard to these days in any wise as though the time were holy, or the setting them apart for religious purposes were established by sacred authority: but yet, as a proper guard against negligence and unsteadiness, and a prudent preservative from yielding to a disposition, that persons might be

7. I.e., a fourth of the year.

liable to, through the prevalence of indolence and listlessness, to excuse themselves on trivial occasions, it was proposed, that those that unite in this affair, should resolve with themselves, that if, by urgent business, or otherwise, they were hindered from joining with others, on the very day agreed on, yet they would not wholly neglect bearing their part in the duty proposed, but would take the first convenient day following, for that purpose.

The reason why Saturday evening and Lord's-day morning were judged most convenient for the weekly seasons, was, that these times being so near the time of dispensing gospel ordinances through the Christian world, which are the great means, in the use of which God is wont to grant his Spirit to mankind, and the principal means that the Spirit of God makes use of to carry on his work of grace, it may well be supposed that the minds of Christians in general will at these seasons be especially disengaged from secular affairs, and disposed to pious meditations and the duties of devotion, and more naturally led to seek the communications of the Holy Spirit, and success of the means of grace. And as to the quarterly times, it was thought helpful to memory, that they should be on one or other of the first days of each quarter: Tuesday was preferred to Monday, because in some places people might have public prayers and sermon on the stated day, which might not be so convenient on Monday, as on some day at a greater distance from the Sabbath.

It was reckoned a chief use of such an agreement and method as this, that it would be a good expedient for the maintaining and keeping up, amongst the people of God, that great Christian duty of prayerfulness for the coming of Christ's kingdom, in general, which Christ has directed his followers to be so much in, that it mayn't be out of mind, and in a great measure sink. Things, that we are too little inclined to, through sloth, carnality, or a fullness of our own worldly and private concerns, and that are to be attended at some seasons or other, and have no special seasons stated for them, are apt to be forgotten, or put off from time to time, and as it were adjourned without day; and so, if not wholly neglected, yet too little attended. But when we fix certain seasons, that we resolve, unless extraordinarily hindered, to devote to the duty, it tends to prevent forgetfulness, and a settled negligence of it. The certain returns of the season will naturally refresh the memory; will tend to put us in mind of the precept of Christ, and the obligations that lie on all his followers, to abound in such a duty, and renewedly engage us to the consideration of the importance and necessity and unspeakable value of the mercy sought; and so, by frequent renovation, to keep alive the consideration and sense of these things at all times. Thus the first promoters of this agreement judged, that it would be subservient to more abundant prayerfulness for effusions of the Holy Spirit, at all times through the year, both in secret and social worship; particularly as to this last, in congregations, families, and other praying societies. And then they also judged, that such an agreed union would tend to animate and encourage God's people in the duty proposed; and that particular persons and societies, knowing that great multitudes of their fellow Christians, in so many distant places, were at the *same time* (as a token of the union of their hearts with them in this affair) by agreement engaged in the *same holy exercise*, would naturally be enlivened in the duty by such a consideration.

It was not thought best, to propose at first a longer time for the continuance of *this* precise method, than two years: it being considered, that it is not possible, before any trial, so well to judge of the expedience of a particular method and certain circumstances of the managing and ordering such an affair, as after some time of experience. And it was not known, but that after longer consideration, and some trial, it might be thought best to alter some circumstances; or whether others, that had not yet been consulted, might not propose a better method. The time first agreed on, though but short, was thought sufficient to give opportunity for judgment and experience, and for such as were disposed to union in an affair of such a nature, in distant places, mutually to communicate their sentiments on the subject.

The way, in which those that first projected and came into this agreement, thought best for the giving notice of it and proposing it to others, was not by anything published from the press; but by personal conversation with such as they could conveniently have immediate access to, and by private correspondence with others at a distance. At first it was intended, that some formal paper, proposing the matter, should be sent about for proper amendments and improvements, and then concurrence: but on more mature deliberation, it was considered how this might give a handle to objections (which they thought it best, to the utmost, to avoid in the infancy of the affair) and how practicable it was, without any such formality, to spread the substance of the proposal by private letters, together with a request to their correspondents, mutually to communicate their thoughts. Therefore this was fixed on, as the method that was preferable at the beginning. Accordingly, they proposed and endeavored to promote the affair in this way;

and with such success, that great numbers in Scotland and England fell in with the proposal, and some in North America. As to Scotland, it was complied with by numbers in the four chief towns, Edinburgh, Glasgow, Aberdeen, and Dundee, and many country towns and congregations in various parts of the land: one of the ministers, that was primarily concerned in this affair, in a letter to one of his correspondents, speaks of an explicit declaration of the concurrence of the praying societies in Edinburgh, which they had made in a letter.[8] The number of the praying societies in that city is very considerable: Mr. Robe of Kilsyth (in a letter to Mr. Prince of Boston, dated Nov. 3, 1743) says, there were then "above thirty societies of young people there newly erected, some of whom consisted of upwards of thirty" members.[9] As to Glasgow, this union was unanimously agreed to by about forty-five praying societies there; as an eminent minister in that city informs, in a letter.[1]

The two years, first agreed on, ended last November. A little before this time expired, a number of ministers in Scotland agreed on a Memorial to be printed, and sent abroad to their brethren in various parts, proposing to 'em and requesting of 'em to join with them in the continuance of this method of united prayer, and in endeavors to promote it. Copies of which Memorial have lately been sent over into New England, to the number of near 500, directed to be distributed in almost every county in this province of the Massachusetts Bay, and also in several parts of Connecticut, New Hampshire, Rhode Island, New York, New Jersey, Pennsylvania, Maryland, Virginia, Carolina, and Georgia. The most (I suppose) of these were sent to one of the Congregational ministers in Boston, with a letter subscribed by twelve ministers in Scotland, about the affair: many of them to another of the said ministers of Boston; and some to a minister in Connecticut.[2] It being short, I shall here insert a copy of it at length. 'Tis as follows.

A Memorial from several ministers in Scotland, to their brethren in

---

8. John Willison of Dundee, in a letter to Benjamin Colman, Jan. 21, 1743, told of the plan in Edinburgh "to set a Day apart for praising and giving Thanks." The local societies hoped their religious successes were only "the Fore-runners of a plentiful Shower, to refresh the Whole." Here JE was using *The Christian History, 1,* 86–87. See above, p. 36, for the text of the letter.

9. See *The Christian History, 2,* 100–01, for an extract of the letter by James Robe, including this quotation.

1. Probably John McLaurin. See above, p. 38. No copy of the letter has been located.

2. The letter has not been located; nor have the ministers been identified. Thomas Prince is the most likely recipient among the Boston clergymen.

different places, for continuing a concert for prayer, first entered into in the year 1744.[3]

Whereas it was the chief scope of this concert, to promote more abundant application to a duty that is perpetually binding, *prayer that our Lord's kingdom may come,* joined with suitable praises: and it contained some

1. A short view of the concert, and the need of renewing it.

circumstantial expedients, apprehended to be very subservient to that design, relating to stated times for such exercises, so far as this would not interfere with other duties; particularly a part of Saturday evening, and Sabbath morning, every week; and more solemnly of some one of the first days of each of the four great divisions of the year, that is, of each quarter; as the first Tuesday, or first convenient day after:[4] and the concert, as to this circumstance, was extended only to two years; it being intended, that before these expired, persons engaged in the concert should reciprocally communicate their sentiments and inclinations, as to the prolonging of the time, with or without alteration, as to the circumstance mentioned: and it was intended by the first promoters, that others at a distance should propose such circumstantial amendments or improvements, as they should find proper: it is hereby earnestly entreated, that such would communicate their sentiments accordingly, now that the time first proposed is near expiring.

II. To induce those already engaged to adhere, and others to accede to this concert; it seems of importance to observe, that declarations of concurrence, the communicating and spreading of which are so evidently useful,

2. Declarations of concurrence, to be understood in a due latitude.

are to be understood in such a latitude, as to keep at the greatest distance from entangling men's minds: not as binding men to set apart any stated days from secular affairs, or even to fix on any part of such and such precise days, whether it be convenient or not; nor as absolute promises in any respect: but as friendly, harmonious resolutions, with

---

3. James Robe printed the text of the Memorial in *The Christian Monthly History,* No. 10 (Jan. 1746), 304–06. In 1754 John Gillies reprinted it in the *Historical Collections, 2,* 399–401. Both texts vary only slightly from that given by JE in the HA.

4. The meaning is, the first Tuesdays of February, May, August and November, or the first convenient days after these.—JE.

liberty to alter circumstances as shall be found expedient. On account of all which latitude, and that the circumstantial part extends only to a few years, it is apprehended, the concert cannot be liable to the objections against periodical religious times of human appointment.

III. It is also humbly offered to the consideration of ministers, and others furnished with gifts for the most public instructions, whether it might not be of great use, by the blessing of God, if short and nervous scriptural

3. The use of printed persuasives, etc., repeated from time to time.

persuasives[5] and directions to the duty in view, were composed and published (either by particular authors, or several joining together; which last way might sometimes have peculiar advantages) and that from time to time, without too great intervals; the better to keep alive on men's minds a just sense of the obligations to a duty so important in itself, and in which many may be in danger to faint and turn remiss, without such repeated incitements: and whether it would not also be of great use, if ministers would be pleased to preach frequently on the importance and necessity of prayer for the coming of our Lord's kingdom; particularly near the quarterly days, or on these days themselves, where there is public worship at that time.

IV. They who have found it incumbent on them to publish this Memorial at this time, having peculiar advantages for spreading it, do entreat that the desire of concurrence and assistance contained in it, may by no means

4. The extent of the desire of concurrence, etc.

be understood as restricted to any particular denomination or party, or to those who are of such or such opinions about any former instances of remarkable religious concern; but to be extended to *all,* who shall vouchsafe any attention to this paper, and have at heart the interest of vital Christianity, and the power of godliness; and who, however differing about other things, are convinced of the importance of fervent prayer, to promote that common interest, and of scripture persuasives to promote such prayer.

V. As the first printed account of this concert was not a proposal of it, as a thing then to begin, but a narration of it, as a design already set

5. I.e., brief but convincing arguments for support of the proposal. For example, James Robe cited a letter of Apr. 15, 1745, "from a valuable Correspondent, written in a most judicious and earnest Manner, with the most convincing Arguments to persuade good Christians zealously to comply with the Invitation." See *The Christian Monthly History,* No. 1 (Apr. 1745), 2. The text of the letter is printed in ibid., pp. 7–21.

5. Reasons for publishing this Memorial.

on foot, which had been brought about with much harmony, by means of private letters;[6] so the farther continuance, and, 'tis hoped, the farther spreading of it seems in a promising way of being promoted by the same means; as importunate desires of the renewing the concert have been transmitted already from a very distant corner abroad, where the regard to it has of late increased: but notwithstanding of what may be done by private letters, it is humbly expected, that a Memorial spread in this manner, may, by God's blessing, farther promote the good ends in view; as it may be usefully referred to in letters, and may reach where they will not.

VI. Whereas in a valuable letter,[7] from the corner just now mentioned as a place where regard to the concert has lately increased, it is proposed, that it should be continued for seven years, or at least for a much longer time than what was specified in the first agreement: those concerned in this Memorial, who would wish rather to receive and spread directions and proposals on this head, than to be the first authors of any, apprehend no inconvenience, for their part, in agreeing to the seven years, with the latitude above described, which reserves liberty to make such circumstantial alterations, as may be hereafter found expedient: on the contrary it seems of importance, that the labor of spreading a concert, which has already extended to so distant parts, and may, it is hoped, extend farther, may not need to be renewed sooner, at least much sooner; as it is uncertain but that may endanger the dropping of it; and it seems probable, there will be less zeal in spreading of it, if the time proposed for its continuance be too inconsiderable. Meantime, declarations of concurrence for a less number of years may greatly promote the good ends in view:

6. The number of years proposed.

6. The first printed account was *The Christian Monthly History*, No. 1 (Apr. 1745), in which James Robe announced that the movement had been underway since the previous October and spoke of possessing "several such excellent Letters" concerning its progress (p. 6). He devoted the entire issue to the topic.

7. JE's letter to an unnamed minister in Glasgow, probably John McLaurin, May 12, 1746; extracted in *The Christian Monthly History*, No. 10 (Jan. 1746), 296–99. In it JE wrote, "And in order to the promoting this Affair in *America*, I would humbly propose this, dear Sir, as a proper Expedient in order to it, *viz.* That the Concert which, with respect to the Term first agreed upon, expires the next *November*, be renewed and continued for seven Years, or, at least, for a much longer Time than what was specified in the former Agreement, &c." (p. 298).

though it seems very expedient, that it should exceed what was first agreed on; seeing it is found on trial, that that time, instead of being too long, was much too short.

VII. If persons who formerly agreed to this concert, should now discontinue it; would it not look too like that fainting in prayer, against which we are so expressly warned in Scripture? And would not this be the more
7. Some arguments against   unsuitable at this time, in any within the
discontinuing the concert.   British dominions, when they have the united calls of such public chastisements and deliverances, to more concern than ever about public reformation, and consequently about that which is the source of all thorough reformation, the regenerating and sanctifying influence of the almighty Spirit of God? August 26, 1746.

The minister in Boston forementioned (to whom most of the copies of this Memorial were sent) who, I suppose, has had later and more full intelligence than I have had, says, concerning the proposal, in a letter, "The motion seems to come from above, and to be wonderfully spreading in Scotland, England, Wales, Ireland, and North America."[8]

8. See above, p. 324, n. 2. No copy of the letter has been located.

PART II

MOTIVES TO A COMPLIANCE WITH WHAT IS PROPOSED IN THE
MEMORIAL

I NOW proceed to the second thing intended in this discourse, viz.,
to offer to consideration some things, which may tend to induce the
people of God to comply with the proposal and request, made to them
in the Memorial.[1]

And I desire that the following things may be considered.

1. It is evident from the Scripture, that there is *yet remaining* a great
advancement of the interest of religion and the kingdom of Christ in this
world, by an abundant outpouring of the Spirit of God, far greater and
more extensive than ever yet has been. 'Tis certain, that many things,
which are spoken concerning a glorious time of the church's enlargement and prosperity in the latter days, have never yet been fulfilled.
There has never yet been any propagation and prevailing of religion,
in any wise, of that *extant* and *universality*, which the prophecies represent. It is often foretold and signified, in a great variety of strong expressions, that there should a time come, when all nations, through the
whole habitable world, should embrace the true religion, and be
brought into the church of God. It was often promised to the patriarchs,
that "in their seed all the nations," or (as it is sometimes expressed)
"all the families of the earth, should be blessed." (See Gen. 12:3, 18:18,
22:18, 26:4, and 28:14.) Agreeable to this, 'tis said of the Messiah, Ps.
72:11, that "all nations shall serve him"; and in v. 17, "Men shall be
blessed in him, and all nations shall call him blessed." And in Is. 2:2
it is said, that "all nations shall flow unto the mountain of the house of
the Lord." And, Jer. 3:17, that "all nations shall be gathered unto the
name of the Lord to Jerusalem, and shall walk no more after the imagination of their evil heart." So it is said, that "all flesh shall come and

---

1. Above, pp. 40–42.

worship before the Lord" (Is. 66:23). And that "all flesh should see the glory of God together" (Is. 40:5). And that "all flesh should come to him that hears prayer" (Ps. 65:2). Christ compares the kingdom of heaven in this world "to leaven, which a woman took and hid in three measures of meal, till the whole was leavened" (Matt. 13:33). It is natural and reasonable to suppose, that the whole world should finally be given to Christ, as one whose right it is to reign, as the proper heir of him, who is originally the king of all nations, and the possessor of heaven and earth: and the Scripture teaches us, that God the Father hath constituted his Son, as God-man, and in his kingdom of grace, or mediatorial kingdom, to be "the heir of the world," that he might in this kingdom have "the heathen for his inheritance, and the utmost ends of the earth for his possession" (Heb. 1:2 and 2:8; Ps. 2:6–8). Thus Abraham is said to be "the heir of the world," not in himself, but in his seed, which is Christ (Rom. 4:13). And how was this to be fulfilled to Abraham, but by God's fulfilling that great promise, that "in his seed all the nations of the earth should be blessed" [Gen. 22:18]? For that promise is what the Apostle is speaking of: which shews, that God has appointed Christ to be the heir of the world in his kingdom of grace, and to possess and reign over all nations, through the propagation of his gospel, and the power of his Spirit communicating the blessings of it. God hath appointed him to this universal dominion by a most solemn oath (Is. 45:23). "I have sworn by myself, the word is gone out of my mouth in righteousness, and shall not return, that unto me every knee shall bow, every tongue shall swear." Compared with Phil. 2:10–11. Though this solemn oath of God the Father is to be understood in so comprehensive a sense, as to extend to what shall be accomplished at the day of judgment, yet it is evident by the foregoing and following verses, that the thing most directly intended, is what shall be fulfilled by the spreading of the gospel of his salvation, and power of the Spirit of grace, bringing "all the ends of the earth to look to him that they may be saved," and come to him for "righteousness and strength," that "in him they might be justified, and might glory" [Is. 45:22–25]. God has suffered many earthly princes to extend their conquests over a great part of the face of the earth, and to possess a dominion of vast extent, and one monarchy to conquer and succeed another, the latter being still the greater: 'tis reasonable to suppose that a much greater glory in this respect should be reserved for Christ, God's own Son and rightful heir, who has purchased the dominion by so great and hard a service: 'tis reasonable to suppose, that his dominion should be far the largest, and his conquests vastly the greatest and most extensive. And thus the Scriptures represent the matter, in Nebuchadnezzar's vision, and the prophet's interpretation (Dan. 2). There the four great monarchies of the earth, one succeeding another, are represented by "the great image of gold, silver, brass, iron and clay" [vv. 32–33]; but at last "a stone, cut out of the mountains without hands, smites the image upon his feet, which breaks the iron, clay, brass, silver and gold in pieces, that all becomes as the chaff of the summer threshing floors, and the wind carries them away, that no place is found for them; but the stone waxes great, becomes a great mountain, and *fills the whole earth*" [vv. 34–35]: signifying "the kingdom which the Lord God of heaven should set up in the world, last of all, which should break in pieces and consume all other kingdoms" [v. 44]. Surely this representation leads us to suppose, that this last kingdom shall be of vastly greater extent than any of the preceding. The like representation is made in the 7th chapter of Daniel; there the four monarchies are represented by four great beasts that arose successively, one conquering and subduing another; the fourth and last of these is said to be "dreadful," and "terrible," and "strong exceedingly," and "to have great iron teeth," and "to devour and break in pieces, and stamp the residue with his feet" [v. 7]; yea it is said (v. 23), that the kingdom represented by this beast shall "devour the whole earth"; but last of all "one like the Son of Man" appears, "coming to the ancient of days, and being brought near before him, and receiving of him a dominion, and glory, and a kingdom, *that all people, nations and languages* should serve him" [vv. 13–14]. This last circumstance, of the vast extent and universality of his dominion, is manifestly spoken of as one thing greatly distinguishing this holy kingdom from all the preceding monarchies: although of one of the former it was said, that it should "devour the whole earth," yet we are naturally led, both by the much greater emphasis and strength of the expressions, as well as by the whole connection and tenor of the prophecy, to understand the universality here expressed in a much more extensive and absolute sense: and the terms used in the interpretation of this vision are such, that scarcely any can be devised more strong, to signify an absolute universality of dominion over the inhabitants of the face of the earth (v. 27). "And the kingdom and dominion, and the *greatness of the kingdom under the whole heaven*, shall be given to the people of the most high God." Agreeable to this, the gospel is represented as "preached unto them that dwell on the earth, and to every nation, and tongue, and kindred, and people" (Rev. 14:6). The universality of the prevalence of true religion in the latter days, is sometimes expressed by its reaching to "the utmost ends of the earth" (Ps. 2:8), "to all the ends of the earth, and of the world" (Ps. 22:27, 67:7, 98:3; Is. 45:22), "all the ends of the earth, with those that are far off upon the sea" (Ps. 65:5), "from the rising of the sun to the going down of the same" (Ps. 113:3; Mal. 1:11), "the outgoings of the morning and of the evening" (Ps. 65:8). It seems that all the most strong expressions, that were in use among the Jews to signify the habitable world in its utmost extent, are made use of to signify the extent of the church of God in the latter days: and in many places, a variety of these expressions are used, and there is an accumulation of them, expressed with great force.

It would be unreasonable to say, these are only bold *figures*, used after the manner of the eastern nations, to express the great extent of the Christian church, at and after the days of Constantine: to say so, would be in effect to say, that it would have been impossible for God, if he had desired it, plainly to have foretold anything that should absolutely have extended to all nations of the earth. I question whether it be possible to find out a more strong expression, to signify an absolute universality of the knowledge of the true religion through the habitable world, than that in Is. 11:9. "The earth shall be full of the knowledge of the Lord, *as the waters cover the seas.*" Which is as much as to say, as there is no place in the vast ocean where there is not water, so there shall be no part of the world of mankind where there is not the knowledge of the Lord; as there is no part of the wide bed or cavity possessed by the sea, but what is covered with water, so there shall be no part of the habitable world, that shall not be covered by the light of the gospel, and possessed by the true religion. "Waters" are often in prophecy put for nations and multitudes of people: so the waters of the main ocean seem sometimes to be put for the inhabitants of the earth in general; as in Ezekiel's vision of waters of the sanctuary (Ezek. 47) which flowed from the sanctuary, and ran east, till they came to the ocean, and were at first a small stream, but continually increased till they became a great river; and when they came to the sea, the water even of the vast ocean was "healed" (v. 8), representing the conversion of the world to the true religion in the latter days. It seems evident, that the time will come, when there will not be one nation remaining in the world, which shall not embrace the true religion, in that God has expressly revealed, that no one such nation shall be left standing on the earth (Is. 60:12). "The nation and kingdom that will not serve thee shall perish; yea, those nations shall be utterly wasted." God has declared that heathen idolatry and all the worship of false gods shall be wholly abolished, in the most universal manner, so that it shall be continued in no place under the heavens, or upon the face of the earth (Jer. 10:11). "The gods that have not made the heavens and the earth, even they shall perish from the earth, and from under these heavens." V. 15, "They are vanity, and the work of errors, in the time of their visitation they shall perish." This must be understood as what shall be brought to pass while this earth and these heavens remain, i.e., before the end of the world. Agreeable to this is that, Is. 54:1–2. "Sing, O barren, and thou that didst not bear; . . . for more are the children of the desolate than the children of the married wife, saith the Lord: enlarge the place of thy tent, and let them stretch forth the curtains of thy habitation; spare not; lengthen thy cords, strengthen thy stakes." V. 5, "For thy Maker is thy husband; the Lord of Hosts is his name; and thy Redeemer the holy one of Israel; *the God of the whole earth shall he be called.*"

The prophecies of the New Testament do no less evidently shew, that a time will come when the gospel shall universally prevail, and the kingdom of Christ be extended over the whole habitable earth, in the most proper sense. Christ says (John 12:32), "I, if I be lifted up from the earth, will draw all men unto me." 'Tis fit, that when the Son of God becomes man, he should have dominion over all mankind: 'tis fit, that since he became an inhabitant of the earth, and shed his blood on the earth, he should possess the whole earth: 'tis fit, seeing here he became a servant, and was subject to men, and was arraigned before them, and judged, condemned and executed by them, and suffered ignominy and death in a most public manner, before Jews and Gentiles, being lifted up to view on the cross upon an hill, near that populous city Jerusalem, at a most public time, when there were many hundred thousand spectators, from all parts, that he should be rewarded with an universal dominion over mankind; and it is here declared he shall be. The Apostle, in the 11th [chapter] of Romans, teaches us to look on that great outpouring of the Spirit and ingathering of souls into Christ's kingdom, that was in those days, first of the Jews, and then of the Gentiles, to be but as the "first fruits" of the intended harvest, both with regard to Jews and Gentiles, and to look on the ingathering of those first fruits as a sign that all the remainder both of Jews and Gentiles should in due time be gathered in (v. 16). "For if the first fruit be holy, the lump is also holy; and if the root be holy, so are the branches." And in that context, the Apostle speaks of the fullness of both Jews and Gentiles, as what shall hereafter be brought in, as distinct from that ingathering from among both, that was in those primitive ages of Christianity: in v. 12 we read of the "fullness of the Jews," and in the 25th of the "fullness of the Gentiles": and there in vv. 30–32, the Apostle teaches us to look upon that infidelity and darkness, that first prevailed over all Gentile nations, before Christ came, and then over the Jews after Christ came, as what was wisely permitted of God, as a preparation for the manifestation of the glory of God's mercy, in due time, on the whole world, constituted of Jews and Gentiles. "God hath concluded them all in unbelief, that he might have mercy upon all" [Rom. 11:32]. These things plainly shew, that the time is coming when the whole world of mankind shall be brought into the church of Christ; and not only a part of the Jews, and a part of the Gentile world, as the first fruits, as it was in the first ages of the Christian church; but the fullness of both, the whole lump, all the nation of the Jews, and all the world of Gentiles.

In the last great conflict between the church of Christ and her enemies, before the commencement of the glorious time of the church's peace and rest, "the kings of the earth, and the whole world," are represented as "gathered together" (Rev. 16:14), and then the "seventh angel pours out his vial into the air," which limits that kingdom that Satan has, as god of this world, in its utmost extent; and that kingdom is represented as utterly overthrown (vv. 17 ff.). And in another description of that great battle, ch. 19, Christ is represented as riding forth, having on his head "many crowns" [v. 12], and on his vesture and on his thigh a name written, "King of Kings and Lord of Lords" [v. 16]. Which we may well suppose signifies, that he is now going to that conquest, whereby he shall set up a kingdom, in which he shall be King of Kings, in a far more extensive manner than either the Babylonish, Persian, Grecian, or Roman monarchs were. And in v. 17, and following, an angel appears "standing in the sun," that overlooks the whole world, calling on "all the fowls that fly in the midst of heaven," to come and "eat the flesh of kings," etc. And in consequence of the great victory Christ gains at that time, "an angel comes down from heaven, having the key of the bottomless pit, and a great chain in his hand, and lays hold on the devil, and binds him, and casts him into the bottomless pit, and shuts him up, and sets a seal upon him, that he should deceive the nations no more" [Rev. 20:1–3]. Satan being dispossessed of that highest monarchy on earth, the Roman Empire, and cast out, in the time of Constantine, is represented ch. 12, by his being "cast down from heaven to the earth" [v. 9]: but now there is something far beyond that; he is cast "out of the earth," and is shut up in hell, and confined to that alone, so that he has no place left him in this world of mankind, high nor low.

Now will any be so unreasonable as to say, that all these things don't signify more than that one third part of the world should be brought into the church of Christ; beyond which it can't be pretended that the Christian religion has ever yet reached, in its greatest extent? Those countries, which belonged to the Roman Empire, that was brought to the profession of Christianity, after the reign of Constantine, are but a small part of what the habitable world now is; as to extent of ground, they all together bear, I suppose, no greater proportion to it, than the land of Canaan did to the Roman Empire. And our Redeemer in his kingdom of grace has hitherto possessed but a little part of the world, in its most flourishing state, since arts are risen to their greatest height; and a very great part of the world is but lately[2] discovered, and much remains undiscovered to this day.

These things make it very evident, that the main fulfillment of those prophecies, that speak of the glorious advancement of Christ's kingdom on earth, is still to come.

And as there has been nothing as yet, with regard to the flourishing of religion, and the advancement of Christ's kingdom, of such extent as to answer the prophecies, so neither has there been anything of that duration, that is foretold. The prophecies speak of Jerusalem's being made "the joy of the whole earth," and also the "joy of many generations" (Ps. 48:2; Is. 60:15), that "God's people should long enjoy the work of their hands" (Is. 65:22), that they should "reign with Christ a thousand years" (Rev. 20) by which we must at least understand a very long time. But it would be endless to mention all the places, which signify that the time of the church's great peace and prosperity should be of long continuance: almost all the prophecies that speak of her latter-day glory, imply it; and it is implied in very many of them, that when once this day of the church's advancement and peace is begun, it shall never end, till the world ends; or, at least, that there shall be no more a return of her troubles and adversity for any considerable continuance; that then "the days of her mourning shall be ended" [Is. 60:20]; that her tribulations "should then be as the waters of Noah unto God, that as he has sworn that the waters of Noah should no more pass over the earth, so he will swear that he will no more be wroth with his people, or rebuke them" [Is. 54:9]; that "God's people should no

2. Here and elsewhere the meaning of "lately" or its adjectival equivalent "late" depends upon the larger context. In this passage JE depicted the voyages of exploration as relatively recent when viewed against nearly eighteen hundred years of Christian history.

more walk after the imagination of their evil heart" [Jer. 3:17]; that "God would hide himself no more from the house of Israel, because he has poured out his Spirit upon them" [Ezek. 39:29]; that "their sun should no more go down, nor the moon withdraw itself" [Is. 60:20]; that "the light should not be clear and dark" [Zech. 14:6] (i.e., there should be no more an interchange of light and darkness, as used to be) but that it should be all one continued day; "not day and night" (for so the words are in the original[3] in Zech. 14:7) alternately, "but it shall come to pass, that at evening time" (i.e., at the time that night and darkness used to be) "it shall be light"; and that "the nations should beat their swords into plowshares, and their spears into pruning hooks, and that nation shall not lift up sword against nation, nor learn war any more" [Is. 2:4; Mic. 4:3]; but that there "should be abundance of peace so long as the moon endureth" [Ps. 72:7]. And innumerable things of this nature are declared.

But the church of Christ has never yet enjoyed a state of peace and prosperity for any *long* time; on the contrary, the times of her rest, and of the flourishing state of religion, have ever been very *short*. Hitherto the church may say as in Is. 63:17–18, "Return, for thy servants' sake, the tribes of thine inheritance; the people of thy holiness have possessed it but a little while." The quietness that the church of God enjoyed after the beginning of Constantine's reign, was very short; the peace the empire enjoyed, in freedom from war, was not more than twenty years; no longer nor greater than it had enjoyed under some of the heathen emperors. After this the empire was rent in pieces by intestine wars, and wasted almost everywhere by the invasions and incursions of barbarous nations, and the Christian world was soon all in contention and confusion, by heresies and divisions in matters of religion.[4] And the church of Christ has never as yet been for any long time, free from persecution; especially when truth has prevailed, and true religion flourished. 'Tis manifest, that hitherto the people of God have been kept under, and Zion has been in a low afflicted state, and her enemies have had the chief sway.

And another thing, that makes it exceeding manifest that that day of the church's greatest advancement on earth, which is foretold in Scripture, has never yet come, is, that it is so plainly and expressly revealed

---

3. לֹא-יוֹם וְלֹא-לָיְלָה

4. I.e., the struggles among the sons of Constantine, the attacks upon the empire by the tribes of northern Europe, and the religious conflicts between the Nicene and Arian parties beginning in the fourth century.

that this day should succeed the last of the four monarchies, even the Roman, in its last state, wherein it is divided into ten kingdoms, and after the destruction of Antichrist, signified by the "little horn," whose reign is contemporary with the reign of the ten kings. These things are very plain in the 2nd and 7th chapters of Daniel, and also in the Revelation of St. John. And it is also plain by the 11th chapter of Romans, that it shall be after the national conversion of the Jews, which shall be as life from the dead to the Gentiles, and the fullness of both Jews and Gentiles should be come in, and all the nation of the Jews and all other nations shall obtain mercy, and there shall be that general ingathering of the harvest of the whole earth, of which all that had been converted before, either of Jews or Gentiles, were but the first fruits. And many other evidences of this point might be mentioned, which for brevity's sake I omit.

And thus it is meet, that the last kingdom which shall take place on earth, should be the kingdom of God's own Son and heir, whose right it is to rule and reign; and that whatever revolutions and confusions there may be in the world, for a long time, the cause of truth, the righteous cause, should finally prevail, and God's holy people should at last inherit the earth, and reign on earth; and that the world should continue in tumults and great revolutions, following one another, from age to age, the world being as it were in travail, till truth and holiness are brought forth; that all things should be shaken, till that comes which is true and right, and agreeable to the mind of God, which cannot be shaken; and that the wisdom of the ruler of the world should be manifested in the bringing all things ultimately to so good an issue. The world is made for the Son of God; his kingdom is the end of all changes, that come to pass in the state of the world of mankind; all are only to prepare the way for this; 'tis fit therefore that the last kingdom on earth should be his. 'Tis wisely and mercifully ordered of God that it should be so, on this account, as well as many others, viz., that the church of God, under all preceding changes, should have this consideration to encourage her, and maintain her hope, and animate her faith and prayers, from generation to generation, that God has promised, her cause should finally be maintained and prevail in this world.

Let it now be considered,

2. The future promised advancement of the kingdom of Christ is an event unspeakably happy and glorious. The Scriptures speak of that time, as a time wherein God and his Son Jesus Christ will be most eminently glorified on earth; a time, wherein God, who till then had

dwelt between the cherubims, and concealed himself in the Holy of Holies, in the secret of his tabernacle, behind the veil, in the thick darkness, should openly shine forth, and all flesh should see his glory, and God's people in general have as great a privilege as the high priest alone had once a year, or as Moses had in the mount; a time, wherein "the temple of God in heaven should be opened, and there should be seen the ark of his testament" (Rev. 11:19); a time, wherein both God will be greatly glorified, and his saints made unspeakably happy in the view of his glory; a time, wherein God's people should not only once see the light of God's glory, as Moses, or see it once a year with the high priest, but should dwell and walk continually in it, and it should be their constant daily light, instead of the light of the sun (Is. 2:5; Ps. 89:15; Is. 60:19), which light should be so much more glorious than the light of the sun or moon, that "the moon shall be confounded, and the sun ashamed, when the Lord of Hosts should reign in Mount Zion, and in Jerusalem before his ancients gloriously" (Is. 24:23).

It is represented as a time of vast increase of knowledge and understanding, especially in divine things; a time wherein God would "destroy the face of the covering cast over all people, and the veil spread over all nations" (Is. 25:7), wherein "the light of the moon shall be as the light of the sun, and the light of the sun sevenfold" (Is. 30:26), "and the eyes of them that see shall not be dim, and the heart of the rash shall understand knowledge" (Is. 32:3–4), "and they shall no more teach every man his neighbor, and every man his brother, saying, Know the Lord, because they shall all know him from the least to the greatest" (Jer. 31:34). And a time of general holiness, (Is. 60:21) "Thy people shall be all righteous"; and a time of a great prevailing of eminent holiness, when little children should, in spiritual attainments, be as though they were "a hundred years old" (Is. 65:20), and wherein "he that is feeble among God's people should be as David" (Zech. 12:8). A time wherein holiness should be as it were inscribed on everything, on all men's common business and employments, and the common utensils of life, all shall be dedicated to God, and improved to holy purposes; (Is. 23:18) "and her merchandise and hire shall be holiness to the Lord." Zech. 14:20–21, "In that day shall there be upon the bells of the horses, 'Holiness unto the Lord'; and the pots in the Lord's house shall be like the bowls before the altar; yea, every pot in Jerusalem and in Judah shall be holiness unto the Lord of Hosts." A time wherein religion and true Christianity shall in every respect be uppermost in the world; wherein God will cause his church to arise and shake herself from the dust, and put on her beautiful garments, and sit down on a throne [Is. 52:1–2]; and the poor shall be raised from the dust, and the beggar from the dunghill, and shall be set among princes, and made to inherit the throne of God's glory [Ps. 113:7–8]. A time wherein vital piety shall take possession of thrones and palaces, and those that are in most exalted stations shall be eminent in holiness. Is. 49:23, "And kings shall be thy nursing fathers, and their queens thy nursing mothers." Ch. 60:16, "Thou shalt suck the breasts of kings." Ps. 45:12, "The daughter of Tyre shall be there with a gift, the rich among the people shall entreat thy favor." A time of wonderful union, and the most universal peace, love and sweet harmony; wherein the nations shall "beat their swords into plowshares" [Is. 2:4], etc., and God will "cause wars to cease to the ends of the earth, and break the bow, and cut the spear in sunder, and burn the chariot in the fire" [Ps. 46:9]; "and the mountains shall bring forth peace to God's people, and the little hills by righteousness" [Ps. 72:3]; wherein "the wolf should dwell with the lamb" [Is. 11:6], etc., and wherein "God's people shall dwell in a peaceable habitation, and in sure dwellings, and quiet resting places" (Is. 32:17–18 and 33:20–21). A time wherein all heresies and false doctrines shall be exploded, and the church of God shall not be rent with a variety of jarring opinions; (Zech. 14:9) "the Lord shall be king over all the earth: in that day there shall be one Lord, and his name one." And all superstitious ways of worship shall be abolished, and all agree in worshiping God in his own appointed way, and agreeable to the purity of his institutions; (Jer. 32:39) "I will give them one heart and one way, that they may fear me forever, for the good of them and their children after them." A time wherein the whole earth shall be united as one holy city, one heavenly family, men of all nations shall as it were dwell together, and sweetly correspond one with another as brethren and children of the same father; as the prophecies often speak of all God's people at that time as the children of God, and brethren one to another, all appointing over 'em one head, gathered to one house of God, to worship the king, the Lord of Hosts [Zech. 14:16]. A time wherein this whole great society shall appear in glorious beauty, in genuine amiable Christianity, and excellent order, as "a city compact together" [Ps. 122:3], "the perfection of beauty" [Ps. 50:2], "an eternal excellency" [Is. 60:15], shining with a reflection of the glory of Jehovah risen upon it, which shall be attractive and ravishing to all kings and nations, and it shall appear "as a bride adorned for her husband" [Rev. 21:2]. A time of great temporal prosperity; of great health (Is. 33:24, "The inhabitant shall not say, I am sick."); of long life (Is. 65:22, "As the days of a tree, are the days of my people."). A time wherein the earth shall be abundantly fruitful; (Ps. 67:6; Is. 30:23–24; Amos 9:14 and many other places). A time wherein the world shall be delivered from that multitude of sore calamities that before had prevailed (Ezek. 47:12), and there shall be an universal blessing of God upon mankind, in soul and body, and in all their concerns, and all manner of tokens of God's presence and favor, and "God shall rejoice over them, as the bridegroom rejoiceth over his bride" [Is. 62:5], and "the mountains shall as it were drop down new wine, and the hills shall flow with milk" (Joel 3:18). A time of great and universal joy through the earth, when "from the utmost ends of the earth shall be heard songs, even glory to the righteous" [Is. 24:16], and God's people "shall with joy draw water out of the wells of salvation" [Is. 12:3], and God shall "prepare in his holy mountain, a feast of fat things, a feast of wines on the lees, of fat things full of marrow, of wines on the lees well refined" [Is. 25:6], which feast is represented (Rev. 19), as "the marriage supper of the Lamb." Yea, the Scriptures represent it not only as a time of universal joy on earth, but extraordinary joy in heaven, among the angels and saints, the holy apostles and prophets there (Rev. 18:20 and 19:1–9). Yea, the Scriptures represent it as a time of extraordinary rejoicing with Christ himself, the glorious head, in whom all things in heaven and earth shall then be gathered together in one. Zeph. 3:17, "The Lord thy God in the midst of thee is mighty; he will save; he will rejoice over thee with joy; he will rest in his love; he will joy over thee with singing." And the very fields, trees and mountains shall then as it were rejoice, and break forth into singing. Is. 55:12, "Ye shall go out with joy, and be led forth with peace; the mountains and the hills shall break forth before you into singing, and all the trees of the field shall clap their hands." Is. 44:23, "Sing, O heavens, for the Lord hath done it; shout, ye lower parts of the earth; break forth into singing, ye mountains; O forest, and every tree therein; for the Lord hath redeemed Jacob, and glorified himself in Israel."

Such being the state of things in this future promised glorious day of the church's prosperity, surely 'tis worth *praying* for. Nor is there any one thing whatsoever, if we viewed things aright, which a regard to the glory of God, a concern for the kingdom and honor of our Redeemer, a love to his people, pity to perishing sinners, love to our fellow creatures in general, compassion to mankind under its various and sore calamities and miseries, a desire of their temporal and spiritual prosperity, love to our country, our neighbors and friends, yea, and to our own souls, would dispose us to be so much in prayer for, as for the dawning of this happy day, and the accomplishment of that glorious event.

It may be worthy to be considered,

3. How much Christ prayed and labored and suffered, in order to the glory and happiness of that day.

The sum of the blessings Christ sought, by what he did and suffered in the work of redemption, was the Holy Spirit. So is the affair of our redemption constituted; the Father provides and gives the Redeemer, and the price of redemption is offered to him, and he grants the benefit purchased; the Son is the Redeemer that gives the price, and also is the price offered; and the Holy Spirit is the grand blessing, obtained by the price offered, and bestowed on the redeemed.[5] The Holy Spirit, in his indwelling, his influences and fruits, is the sum of all grace, holiness, comfort and joy, or in one word, of all the spiritual good Christ purchased for men in this world: and is also the sum of all perfection, glory and eternal joy, that he purchased for them in another world. The Holy Spirit is that great benefit, that is the subject matter of the promises, both of the eternal covenant of redemption, and also of the covenant of grace; the grand subject of the promises of the Old Testament, in the prophecies of the blessings of the Messiah's kingdom; and the chief subject of the promises of the New Testament; and particularly of the covenant of grace delivered by Jesus Christ to his disciples, as his last will and testament, in the 14th, 15th and 16th chapters of John; the grand legacy, that he bequeathed to them in that his last and dying discourse with them. Therefore the Holy Spirit is so often called "the Spirit of promise," and emphatically "the promise, the promise of the Father," etc. (Luke 24:49; Acts 1:4 and 2:33, 39; Gal. 3:14; Eph. 1:13 and 3:6). This being the great blessing Christ purchased by his labors and sufferings on earth, it was the blessing he received of the Father, when he ascended into heaven, and entered into the Holy of Holies with his own blood, to communicate to those that he had redeemed. John 16:7, "It is expedient for you, that I go away; for if I go not away, the Comforter will not come; but if I depart, I will send him unto you." Acts 2:33, "Being by the right hand of God exalted, and having received of the Father the promise of the Holy Ghost, he hath shed forth this which ye now see and hear." This is the sum of those gifts, which Christ received for men, even for the rebellious, at his ascension. This is

5. JE developed these themes in his first published sermon, *God Glorified in Man's Dependence* (Worcester rev. ed., *4*, 169–78).

the sum of the benefits Christ obtains for men by his intercession (John 14:16–17). "I will pray the Father, and he shall give you another Comforter, that he may abide with you forever; even the Spirit of truth." Herein consists Christ's communicative fullness, even in his being full of the Spirit, and so "full of grace and truth" [John 1:14], that we might of "this fullness receive, and grace for grace" [John 1:16]. He is "anointed with the Holy Ghost" [Acts 10:38]; and this is the ointment that goes down from the head to the members. "God gives the Spirit not by measure unto him" [John 3:34], that everyone that is his "might receive according to the measure of the gift of Christ" [Eph. 4:7]. This therefore was the great blessing he prayed for in that wonderful prayer, that he uttered for his disciples and all his future church, the evening before he died (John 17): the blessing he prayed for to the Father, in behalf of his disciples, was the same he had insisted on in his preceding discourse with them: and this doubtless was the blessing that he prayed for, when as our high priest, he "offered up strong crying and tears," with his blood (Heb. 5:6–7). The same that he shed his blood for, he also shed tears for, and poured out prayers for.

4. But the time that we have been speaking of, is the *chief* time of the bestowment of this blessing; the *main season* of the success of all that Christ did and suffered in the work of our redemption. Before this the Spirit of God is given but very sparingly, and but few are saved; but then it will be far otherwise; wickedness shall be rare then, as virtue and piety had been before: and undoubtedly, by far the greatest number of them that ever receive the benefits of Christ's redemption, from the beginning of the world to the end of it, will receive it in that time. The number of the inhabitants of the earth will doubtless then be vastly multiplied; and the number of redeemed ones much more. If we should suppose that glorious day to last no more than (literally) a thousand years, and that at the beginning of that thousand years the world of mankind should be but just as numerous as it is now, and that the number should be doubled, during that time of great health and peace and the universal blessing of heaven, once only in an hundred years, the number at the end of the thousand years would be more than a thousand times greater than it is now; and if it should be doubled once in fifty years (which probably the number of the inhabitants of New England has ordinarily been, in about half that time) then at the end of the thousand years, there would be more than a million inhabitants on the face of the earth, where there is one now. And there is reason to think that through the greater part of this period, at least, the number of

saints will, in their increase, bear a proportion to the increase of the number of inhabitants. And it must be considered, that if the number of mankind at the beginning of this period be no more than equal to the present number, yet we may doubtless conclude, that the number of true saints will be immensely greater; when instead of the *few* true and thorough Christians now in some few countries, every nation on the face of the whole earth shall be converted to Christianity, and every country shall be full of true Christians; so that the successive multiplication of true saints through the thousand years, will begin with that vast advantage, beyond the multiplication of mankind; where the latter is begun from units, the other doubtless will begin with hundreds, if not thousands. How much greater then will be the number of true converts, that will be brought to a participation of the benefits of Christ's redemption, during that period, than in all other times put together? I think, the foregoing things considered, we shall be very moderate in our conjectures, if we say, it is probable that there will be an hundred thousand times more, that will actually be redeemed to God by Christ's blood, during that period of the church's prosperity that we have been speaking of, than ever had been before, from the beginning of the world to that time.[6]

That time is represented in Scripture, as the proper appointed season of Christ's salvation; eminently the elect season, "the accepted time," and "day of salvation" (Is. 49:8, and so on to v. 23 and ch. 61:2 taken with the context, in that and the preceding and following chapters), "the year of Christ's redeemed" (Is. 63:4). This period is spoken of as the proper time of the dominion of the Redeemer, and reign of his redeeming love, in the 2nd and 7th chapters of Daniel, and many other places; the proper time of his harvest, or ingathering of his fruits from this fallen world; the appointed day of his triumph over Satan, the great destroyer; and the appointed day of his marriage with his elect spouse (Rev. 19:7). The time given to the Sun of Righteousness to rule, as the

---

6. JE's demographic speculations and projections illustrate an interest of Americans in the eighteenth century. Joseph Bellamy calculated that the population would double every fifty years in the millennium and projected accordingly that vast numbers would be converted. See *The Millennium* (Elizabethtown, 1794), pp. 38–42. Bellamy's sermon was first published in 1758. The 1794 printing accompanied the third edition of the HA. Samuel Hopkins also spoke of vast increases in the population during the millennium. See *Treatise on the Millennium*, pp. 73–74. See also the reflections of Ezra Stiles on New England's population, in Edmund S. Morgan, *The Gentle Puritan: A Life of Ezra Stiles, 1727–1795* (New Haven, 1962), pp. 139–42; and the views of the Jeffersonians on future increases, in Daniel J. Boorstin, *The Lost World of Thomas Jefferson* (Boston, 1960), p. 185.

day is the time God has appointed for the natural sun to bear rule. Therefore the bringing on of this time is called "Christ's coming in his kingdom"; wherein "he will rend the heavens and come down," and "the Sun of Righteousness shall arise" (Mal. 4:2 and Is. 64:1).

The comparatively little saving good there is in the world, as the fruit of Christ's redemption, before that time, is as it were granted by way of anticipation; as we anticipate something of the sun's light by reflection before the daytime, the proper time of the sun's rule; and as the first fruits are gathered before the harvest. Then more especially will be the fulfillment of those great promises, made by God the Father to the Son, for his pouring out his soul unto death (Is. 53:10–12); then "shall he see his seed, and the pleasure of the Lord shall prosper in his hand"; then "shall he see of the travail of his soul, and be satisfied, and shall justify many by his knowledge"; then "will God divide him a portion with the great, and he shall divide the spoil with the strong"; then shall Christ in an eminent manner obtain his chosen spouse, that "he loved and died for, that he might sanctify and cleanse her, with the washing of water, by the Word, and present her to himself, a glorious church" [Eph. 5:25–27]. He will obtain "the joy that was set before him, for which he endured the cross, and despised the shame" [Heb. 12:2], chiefly in the events and consequences of that day: that day, as was observed before, is often represented as eminently the time of the "rejoicing of the bridegroom." The foreknowledge and consideration of it was what supported him, and that which his soul exulted in, at a time when his soul had been troubled at the view of his approaching sufferings; as may be seen in John 12:23–24, 27, 31–32.

Now therefore, if it be so, that this is what Jesus Christ, our great Redeemer and the head of the church, did so much desire, and set his heart upon, from all eternity, and which he did and suffered so much for, offering up "strong crying and tears" [Heb. 5:7], and his precious blood to obtain it; surely his disciples and members should also earnestly seek it, and be much and earnest in prayer for it.

Let it be considered,

5. The "whole creation" is, as it were, earnestly waiting for that day, and constantly groaning and travailing in pain to bring forth the felicity and glory of it. For that day is above all other times, excepting the day of judgment, the day of "the manifestation of the sons of God," and of their "glorious liberty": and therefore that elegant representation the Apostle makes of the earnest expectation and travail of the creation, in Rom. 8:19–22, is applicable to the glorious events of this

day; "the earnest expectation of the creature waiteth for the manifestation of the sons of God. For the creature was made subject to vanity, not willingly, but by reason of him who hath subjected the same in hope. Because the creature itself also shall be delivered from the bondage of corruption into the glorious liberty of the children of God. For we know that the whole creation groaneth and travaileth in pain together until now." This visible world has now for many ages been subjected to sin, and made as it were a servant to it, through the abusive improvement that man, who has the dominion over the creatures, puts the creatures to. Thus the sun is a sort of servant to all manner of wickedness, as its light and other beneficial influences are abused by men, and made subservient to their lusts and sinful purposes. So of the rain, and fruits of the earth, and the brute animals, and all other parts of the visible creation; they all serve men's corruption, and obey their sinful will; and God doth in a sort subject them to it; for he continues his influence and power to make them to be obedient, according to the same law of nature whereby they yield to men's command when used to good purposes. 'Tis by the immediate influence of God upon things, acting upon them, according to those constant methods that we call the laws of nature, that they are ever obedient to man's will, or that we can use 'em at all. This influence God continues, to make them obedient to men's will, though wicked. Which is a sure sign that the present state of things is not lasting: it is confusion; and God would not suffer it to be, but that he designs in a little time to put an end to it, when it shall no more be so. Seeing it is to be but a little while, God chooses rather to subject the creature to man's wickedness, than to disturb and interrupt the course of nature according to its stated laws: but 'tis, as it were, a force upon the creature; for the creature is abused in it, perverted to far meaner purposes than those for which the author of its nature made it, and to which he adapted it. The creature therefore is as it were unwillingly subject; and would not be subject, but that it is but for a short time; and it, as it were, hopes for an alteration. 'Tis a bondage the creature is subject to, from which it was partly delivered when Christ came, and the gospel was promulgated in the world; and will be more fully delivered at the commencement of the glorious day we are speaking of; and perfectly at the day of judgment. This agrees with the context; for the Apostle was speaking of the present suffering state of the church [Rom. 8:18]. The reason why the church in this world is in a suffering state, is that the world is subjected to the sin and corruption of mankind. By "vanity" [Rom. 8:20], in Scripture, is very commonly meant sin and wickedness; and also by "corruption" [Rom. 8:21], as might be shewn in very many places, would my intended brevity allow.

Though the creature is thus subject to vanity, yet it don't rest in this subjection, but is constantly acting and exerting itself, in order to that glorious liberty that God has appointed at the time we are speaking of, and as it were reaching forth towards it. All the changes that are brought to pass in the world, from age to age, are ordered in infinite wisdom in one respect or other to prepare the way for that glorious issue of things, that shall be when truth and righteousness shall finally prevail, and he, whose right it is, shall take the kingdom. All the creatures, in all their operations and motions, continually tend to this. As in a clock, all the motions of the whole system of wheels and movements, tend to the striking of the hammer at the appointed time.[7] All the revolutions and restless motions of the sun and other heavenly bodies, from day to day, from year to year, and from age to age, are continually tending hither; as all the many turnings of the wheels of a chariot, in a journey, tend to the appointed journey's end. The mighty struggles and conflicts of nations, and shakings of kingdoms, and those vast successive changes that are brought to pass, in the kingdoms and empires of the world, from one age to another, are as it were travail pangs of the creation, in order to bring forth this glorious event. And the Scriptures represent the last struggles and changes that shall immediately precede this event, as being the greatest of all; as the last pangs of a woman in travail are the most violent [Rom. 8:22].

The creature thus earnestly expecting this glorious manifestation and liberty of the children of God, and travailing in pain in order to it, therefore the Scriptures, by a like figure, do very often represent, that when this shall be accomplished, the whole inanimate creation shall greatly rejoice: that "the heavens shall sing, the earth be glad, the mountains break forth into singing, the hills be joyful together, the trees clap their hands, the lower parts of the earth shout, the sea roar and the fullness thereof, and the floods clap their hands" (Is. 44:23, 49:13; Ps. 69:34–35, 96:11–12, and 98:7–8).

All the intelligent elect creation, all God's holy creatures in heaven and earth, are truly and properly waiting for, and earnestly expecting that event. 'Tis abundantly represented in Scripture as the spirit and character of all true saints, that they set their hearts upon, love, long, wait and pray for the promised glory of that day; they are spoken of as

7. See JE's comments on the vision of Ezekiel's wheels in the "Scripture," no. 389 (printed in Dwight ed., *9*, 400–07).

those that "prefer Jerusalem to their chief joy" (Ps. 137:6), "that take pleasure in the stones of Zion, and favor the dust thereof" (Ps. 102:13–14), "that wait for the consolation of Israel" (Luke 2:25 and v. 38). 'Tis the language of the church of God, and the breathing of the soul of every true saint, that we have in Ps. 14:7. "O that the salvation of Israel were come out of Zion! When the Lord bringeth back the captivity of his people, Jacob shall rejoice, and Israel shall be glad." And Cant. 2:17, "Until the day break, and the shadows flee away, turn my beloved, and be thou like a roe, or a young hart upon the mountains of Bether." And ch. 8:14, "Make haste, my beloved, and be thou like to a roe, or to a young hart upon the mountains of spices." Agreeable to this, was the spirit of old Jacob, which he expressed when he was dying, in faith in the great promise made to him and Isaac and Abraham, that "in their seed all the families of the earth should be blessed" [Gen. 12:3, 28:14]. Gen. 49:18, "I have waited for thy salvation, O Lord." The same is represented as the spirit of his true children, or the family of Jacob (Is. 8:17). "I will wait upon the Lord, that hideth himself from the house of Jacob, and I will look for him." "They that love Christ's appearing," is a name that the Apostle gives to true Christians (II Tim. 4:8).

The glorious inhabitants of the heavenly world, the saints and angels there, that rejoice when one sinner repents, are earnestly waiting, in an assured and joyful dependence on God's promises of that conversion of the world, and marriage of the Lamb, which shall be when that glorious day comes; and therefore they are represented as all with one accord rejoicing and praising God with such mighty exultation and triumph, when it is accomplished, in Rev. 19.

6. The Word of God is full of precepts, encouragements, and examples, tending to excite and induce the people of God to be much in prayer for this mercy.

The Spirit of God is the chief of the blessings, that are the subject matter of Christian prayer; for it is the sum of all spiritual blessings; which are those that we need infinitely more than all others, and are those wherein our true and eternal happiness consists. That which is the sum of the blessings that Christ purchased, is the sum of the blessings that Christians have to pray for; but that, as was observed before, is the Holy Spirit: and therefore when the disciples came to Christ, and desired him to teach them to pray (Luke 11), and he accordingly gave them particular directions for the performance of this duty. The conclusion of his whole discourse, in the 13th verse, plainly shews that the

Holy Spirit is the sum of the blessings that are the subject matter of that prayer about which he had instructed them. "If ye then being evil, know how to give good gifts unto your children, how much more shall your heavenly Father give the Holy Spirit to them that ask him?" From which words of Christ, we may also observe, that there is no blessing that we have so great encouragement to pray for, as the Spirit of God; the words imply that our heavenly Father is especially ready to bestow his Holy Spirit on them that ask him. Of the more excellent nature any benefit is that we stand in need of, the more ready God is to bestow it in answer to prayer: the infinite goodness of God's nature is the more gratified, and the grand design and aim of the contrivance and work of our redemption is the more answered, and Jesus Christ the Redeemer has the greater success in his undertaking and labors; and those desires that are expressed in prayer for the most excellent blessings are the most excellent desires, and consequently such as God most approves of, and is most ready to gratify.

The Scriptures don't only direct and encourage us in general to pray for the Holy Spirit above all things else, but it is the expressly revealed will of God, that his church should be very much in prayer for that glorious outpouring of the Spirit that is to be in the latter days, and the things that shall be accomplished by it. God speaking of that blessed event (Ezek. 36), under the figure of "cleansing the house of Israel from all their iniquities, planting and building their waste and ruined places, and making them to become like the Garden of Eden, and filling them with men like a flock, like the holy flock, the flock of Jerusalem in her solemn feasts" [vv. 33–38] (wherein he doubtless has respect to the same glorious restoration and advancement of his church that is spoken of in the next chapter, and in all the following chapters to the end of the book) he says, v. 37, "Thus saith the Lord, I will yet for this be inquired of by the house of Israel, to do it for them." Which doubtless implies, that it is the will of God that extraordinary prayerfulness in his people for this mercy should precede the bestowment of it.

I know of no place in the Bible, where so strong an expression is made use of to signify importunity in prayer, as is used in Is. 62:6–7 where the people of God are called upon to be importunate for this mercy: "Ye that make mention of the Lord, keep not silence, and give him no rest, till he establish, and till he make Jerusalem a praise in the earth." How strong is the phrase! And how loud is this call to the church of God, to be fervent and incessant in their cries to him for this great mercy! How wonderful are the words to be used, concerning the manner in which such worms of the dust should address the high and lofty one that inhabits eternity! And what encouragement is here, to approach the mercy seat with the greatest freedom, boldness, earnestness, constancy and full assurance of faith, to seek of God this greatest thing that can be sought in Christian prayer!

'Tis a just observation of a certain eminent minister of the Church of Scotland, in a discourse of his lately published on *social prayer*, in which, speaking of pleading for the success of the gospel, as required by the Lord's Prayer, he says, "That notwithstanding of its being so compendious, yet the one half of it, that is, three petitions in six, and these the first prescribed, do all relate to this great case: . . . so that to put up any one of these petitions apart, or all of them together, is upon the matter, to pray that the dispensation of the gospel may be blessed with divine power."[8] That glorious day we are speaking of is the proper and appointed time, above all others, for the bringing to pass the things requested in each of these petitions: as the prophecies everywhere represent that as the time, which God has especially appointed for the hallowing or glorifying his own great name in this world, causing "his glory to be revealed, that all flesh may see it together" [Is. 40:5], causing it "openly to be manifested in the sight of the heathen" [Ps. 98:2], filling the whole world with the light of his glory to such a degree that "the moon shall be confounded and sun ashamed" [Is. 24:23] before that brighter glory: the appointed time for the glorifying and magnifying the name of Jesus Christ, causing "every knee to bow, and every tongue to confess to him" [Rom. 14:11]. This is the proper time of "God's kingdom's coming," or of "Christ's coming in his kingdom": that is the very time foretold in the 2nd [chapter] of Daniel, when the "Lord God of heaven shall set up a kingdom" [v. 44], in the latter times of the last monarchy, when it is divided into ten kingdoms: and that is the very time foretold in the 7th [chapter] of Daniel, when there should be "given to one like to the Son of Man, dominion, glory and a

---

8. A quotation from a "Discourse on Social Prayer" by John Balfour, a minister at Nigg, Scotland, cited in a letter by an unnamed correspondent, Apr. 15, 1745, printed in *The Christian Monthly History*, No. 1 (Apr. 1745), 8–9. The Presbyterian church in Nigg experienced a revival under Balfour in 1739–41. See his account in ibid., No. 4 (Feb. 1744), 45–52; and No. 6 (Aug.–Dec. 1744), 39–45. Robe printed an essay by Balfour entitled, "Scripture-Persuasives and Directions to fervent and abundant Prayer for the publick Interest of Religion, contain'd in Remarks on the first three Petitions of the Lord's Prayer," in ibid., No. 10 (Jan. 1746), 307 ff. At his death Balfour left in manuscript "A Treatise on the Scriptural Authority for, and the advantage arising from, Christian Conference." See Scott, *Fasti Ecclesiae Scoticanae*, 7, 66.

kingdom, that all people, nations and languages should serve him; and the kingdom and dominion, and the greatness of the kingdom under the whole heaven shall be given to the people of the saints of the most high God" [vv. 13–14, 27], after the destruction of the little horn, that should continue "for a time, times, and the dividing of time" [v. 25]. And that is the time wherein "God's will shall be done on earth, as 'tis done in heaven" [Matt. 6:10]; when heaven shall as it were be bowed, and come down to the earth [Ps. 144:5], as "God's people shall be all righteous" [Is. 60:21], and " 'Holiness to the Lord' shall be written on the bells of the horses" [Zech. 14:20], etc. So that the three first petitions of the Lord's Prayer are in effect no other than requests for the bringing on this glorious day. And as the Lord's Prayer begins with asking for this, in the three first petitions, so it concludes with it, in these words, "For thine is the kingdom, and the power, and the glory for ever. Amen" [Matt. 6:13]. Which words imply a request that God would take to himself his great power, and reign, and manifest his power and glory in the world. Thus Christ teaches us that it becomes his disciples to seek this above all other things, and make it the first and the last in their prayers, and that every petition should be put up in a subordination to the advancement of God's kingdom and glory in the world.

Besides what has been observed of the Lord's Prayer, if we look through the whole Bible, and observe all the examples of prayer that we find there recorded, we shall find so many prayers for no other mercy, as for the deliverance, restoration and prosperity of the church, and the advancement of God's glory and kingdom of grace in the world. If we well consider the prayers that we find recorded in the book of Psalms, I believe we shall see reason to think, that a very great, if not the greater part of them, are prayers uttered, either in the name of Christ, or in the name of the church, for such a mercy: and undoubtedly the greatest part of that book of Psalms, is made up of prayers for this mercy, prophecies of it, and prophetical praises for it.

The prophets, in their prophecies of the restoration and advancement of the church, very often speak of it as what shall be done in answer to the prayers of God's people. (Is. 25:9, 26:9, 12–13, 16–21, 33:2; Ps. 102:13–22; Jer. 3:21; Is. 65:24, 41:17; Hos. 5:15 with 6:1–3 and 14:2–9; Zech. 10:6, 12:10 and 13:9; Is. 55:6 with vv. 12–13; Jer. 33:3.) The prophecies of future glorious times of the church are often introduced with a prayer of the church for her deliverance and advancement, prophetically uttered; as in Is. 51:9 ff., chs. 63:11–19, and 64 throughout.

In order to Christ's being mystically born into the world, in the advancement and flourishing of true religion, and great increase of the number of true converts, who are spoken of as having "Christ formed in them," the Scriptures represent it as requisite, that the church should first be "in travail, crying, and pained to be delivered" (Rev. 12: 1–2, 5). And one thing that we have good reason to understand by it, is her exercising strong desires, and wrestling and agonizing with God in prayer, for this event; because we find such figures of speech used in this sense elsewhere: so, Gal. 4:19, "My little children, of whom I travail in birth again, until Christ be formed in you." Is. 26:16–17, "Lord, in trouble have they visited thee; they poured out a prayer when thy chastening was upon them. Like a woman with child, that draweth near the time of her delivery, is in pain, and crieth out in her pangs, so have we been in thy sight, O Lord." And certainly it is fit, that the church of God should be in travail for that, which (as I before observed) the whole creation travails in pain for.

The Scriptures don't only abundantly manifest it to be the duty of God's people to be much in prayer for this great mercy, but it also abounds with manifold considerations to encourage 'em in it, and animate 'em with hopes of *success*. There is perhaps no one thing that so much of the Bible is taken up in the promises of, in order to encourage the faith, hope and prayers of the saints, as this: which at once affords to God's people the clearest evidences that it is their duty to be much in prayer for this mercy (for undoubtedly that which God does abundantly make the subject of his promises, God's people should abundantly make the subject of their prayers) and also affords them the strongest assurances that their prayers shall be successful. With what confidence may we go before God, and pray for that, of which we have so many exceeding precious and glorious promises to plead! The very first promise of God to fallen man, even that in Gen. 3:15—"It shall bruise thy head," is a promise that is to have its chief fulfillment at that day. And the whole Bible concludes with a promise of the glory of that day, and a prayer for its fulfillment. Rev. 22:20, "He that testifieth these things, saith, Surely I come quickly: Amen. Even so, come, Lord Jesus."

The Scriptures give us great reason to think, that when once there comes to appear much of a *spirit of prayer* in the church of God for this mercy, then it will soon be accomplished. 'Tis evidently with reference to this mercy, that God makes that promise (Is. 41:17–19). "When the poor and needy seek water, and there is none, and their tongue faileth for thirst, I the Lord will hear them; I, the God of Israel, will not forsake them; I will open rivers in high places, and fountains in the midst of the valleys; I will make the wilderness a pool of water, and the dry land springs of water; I will plant in the wilderness the cedar, the shittah tree, and the myrtle and the oil tree, I will set in the desert the fir tree, and the pine, and the box tree together." Spiritual "waters" and "rivers" are explained by the apostle John, to be the Holy Spirit (John 7:37–39). It is now a time of scarcity of these spiritual waters; there are as it were *none*: if God's people, in this time of great drought, were but made duly sensible of this calamity, and their own emptiness and necessity, and brought earnestly to thirst and cry for needed supplies, God would doubtless soon fulfill this blessed promise. We have another promise much like this, in Ps. 102:16–17. "When the Lord shall build up Zion, he shall appear in his glory; he will regard the prayer of the destitute, and not despise their prayer." And remarkable are the words that follow in the next verse, "This shall be written for the generation to come; and the people which shall be created, shall praise the Lord." Which seems to signify, that this promise should be left on record to encourage some future generation of God's people to pray and cry earnestly for this mercy, to whom he would fulfill the promise, and thereby give them, and great multitudes of others, that should be converted through their prayers, occasion to praise his name. Who knows but that the generation here spoken of may be this present generation? One thing mentioned in the character of that future generation, is certainly true concerning the present, viz., that it is destitute; the church of God is in very low, sorrowful and needy circumstances: and if the next thing there supposed, were also verified in us, viz., that we were made sensible of our great calamity, and brought to cry earnestly to God for help [Ps. 102:1–2], I am persuaded the third would be also verified, viz., that our prayers would be turned into joyful praises, for God's gracious answers of our prayers. It is spoken of as a sign and evidence, that the time to favor Zion is come, when God's servants are brought by their prayerfulness for her restoration, in an eminent manner, to shew that they favor her stones and dust; in the 13th and 14th verses of this psalm, "Thou shalt arise, and have mercy upon Zion; for the time to favor her, yea the set time is come; for thy servants take pleasure in her stones, and favor the dust thereof."

God has respect to the prayers of his saints in all his government of the world; as we may observe by the representation made, Rev. 8, at the beginning. There we read of seven angels standing before the throne of God, and receiving of him seven trumpets, at the sounding of which, great and mighty changes were to be brought to pass in the world, through many successive ages. But when these angels had received their trumpets, they must stand still, and all must be in silence, not one of 'em must be allowed to sound, till the "prayers of the saints" are attended to [v. 4]. The angel of the covenant, as a glorious high priest, comes and stands at the altar, with much incense, to offer with the "prayers of all saints" [v. 3] upon the golden altar, before the throne; and the smoke of the incense, with the "prayers of the saints," ascends up with acceptance before God, out of the angel's hand: and then the angels prepare themselves to sound. And God, in the events of every trumpet, remembers those prayers: as appears at last, by the great and glorious things he accomplishes for his church, in the issue of all, in answer to these prayers, in the event of the last trumpet, which brings on the glory of the latter days, when these prayers shall be turned into joyful praises. Rev. 11:15–17, "And the seventh angel sounded; and there were great voices in heaven, saying, The kingdoms of this world are become the kingdoms of our Lord and of his Christ; and he shall reign for ever and ever. And the four and twenty elders, which sat before God on their seats, fell upon their faces, and worshiped God, saying, We give thee thanks, O Lord God almighty, which art and wast and art to come, because thou hast taken to thee thy great power, and hast reigned." Since it is thus, that it is the pleasure of God so to honor his people, as to carry on all the designs of his kingdom in this way, viz., by the prayers of his saints, this gives us great reason to think, that whenever the time comes that God gives an extraordinary spirit of prayer for this promised advancement of his kingdom on earth (which is God's great aim in all preceding providences, and which is the main thing that the spirit of prayer in the saints aims at), then the fulfilling [of] this event is nigh.

God, in wonderful grace, is pleased to represent himself as it were at the command of his people, with regard to mercies of this nature, so as to be ready to bestow them whenever they shall earnestly pray for them (Is. 45:11). "Thus saith the Lord, the Holy One of Israel, and his Maker, Ask of me concerning things to come, concerning my sons, and concerning the work of my hands, command ye me." What God is speaking of in this context is the restoration of his church; not only a restoration from temporal calamity and an outward captivity, by Cyrus; but also a spiritual restoration and advancement, by God's commanding the heavens to "drop down from above, and the skies to pour down righteousness," and causing "the earth to open and bring forth salvation, and righteousness to spring up together" (v. 8). God would have his people ask of him, or inquire of him by earnest prayer, to do this for them; and manifests himself as being at the command of earnest prayers for such a mercy: and a reason why God is so ready to hear such prayers is couched in the words, viz., because it is prayer for his own church, his chosen and beloved people, "his sons and daughters, and the work of his hands" [v. 11]; and he can't deny anything that is asked for their comfort and prosperity.

God speaks of himself as standing ready to be gracious to his church, and to appear for its restoration, and only waiting for such an opportunity to bestow this mercy, when he shall hear the cries of his people for it, that he may bestow it in answer to their prayers. Is. 30:18–19, "Therefore will the Lord wait, that he may be gracious to thee; and therefore will he be exalted, that he may have mercy upon you; for the Lord is a God of judgment; blessed are all they that wait for him. For the people shall dwell in Zion at Jerusalem. Thou shalt weep no more; he will be very gracious unto thee, at the voice of thy cry: when he shall hear it, he will answer thee." The words imply as much as that when God once sees his people much engaged in praying for this mercy, it shall be no longer delayed. Christ desires to "hear the voice" of his spouse, "that is in the clefts of the rock, in the secret places of the stairs"; in a low and obscure state, driven into secret corners: he only waits for this, in order to put an end to her state of affliction, and cause "the day to break, and the shadows to flee away." If he once heard her voice in earnest prayer, he would come swiftly over the mountains of separation between him and her, "as a roe, or young hart" (Cant. 2:14–17). When his church is in a low state, and oppressed by her enemies, and cries to him, he'll swiftly fly to her relief, as birds fly at the cry of their young (Is. 31:5). Yea, when that glorious day comes, that I am speaking of, "before they call, he will answer them, and while they are yet speaking, he will hear"; and in answer to their prayers, he will make "the wolf and the lamb feed together," etc. (Is. 65:24, 25). When the spouse prays for the effusion of the Holy Spirit, and the coming of Christ, by granting the tokens of his spiritual presence in his church, saying (Cant. 4:16), "Awake, O north wind, and come, thou south, blow upon my garden, that the spices thereof may flow out; let my beloved come into his garden, and eat his pleasant fruits"; there seems to be an immediate answer to her prayer, in the next words, in abundant communications of the Spirit, and bestowment of spiritual blessings; "I am come into my garden, my sister, my spouse; I have gathered my myrrh with my spice; I have eaten my honeycomb with my honey; I have drunk my wine with my milk. Eat, O friends; drink, yea, drink abundantly, O beloved" [Cant. 5:1].

Scripture instances and examples of success in prayer give great encouragement to pray for this mercy. Most of the remarkable deliverances and restorations of the church of God, that we have account of in the Scripture, were in answer to prayer. So was the redemption of the church of God from the Egyptian bondage (Ex. 2:23 and 3:7). The great restoration of the church in the latter day, is often spoken of as resembled by this; as in Is. 64:1–4, 11:11, 15–16, 43:2–3, 16–19, 51:10–11, 15, 63:11–13; Zech. 10:10–11; Hos. 2:14–15. It was in answer to prayer, that the sun stood still over Gibeon, and the moon in the valley of Aijalon [Josh. 10:12], and God's people obtained that great victory over their enemies: in which wonderful miracle, God seemed to have some respect to a future more glorious event to be accomplished for the Christian church, in the day of her victory over her enemies, in the latter days; even that event foretold Is. 60:20. "Thy sun shall no more go down, neither shall thy moon withdraw itself." It was in answer to prayer, that God delivered his church from the mighty host of the Assyrians, in Hezekiah's time; which dispensation is abundantly made use of, as a type of the great things God will do for the Christian church in the latter days, in the prophecies of Isaiah. The restoration of the church of God from the Babylonish captivity, as abundantly appears both by scripture prophecies and histories, was in answer to extraordinary prayer; see Jer. 29:10–14, and 50: 4–5; Dan. 9 throughout; Ezra 8:21 ff.; Neh. 1: 4–11, 4: 4–5, and ch. 9 throughout. This restoration of the Jewish church, after the destruction of Babylon, is evidently a type of the glorious restoration of the Christian church, after the destruction of the kingdom of Antichrist; which (as all know) is abundantly spoken of in the Revelation of St. John, as the antitype of Babylon. Samson, out of weakness, received strength to pull down Dagon's temple, through prayer [Judg. 16:28–30]. So the people of God, in the latter days, will out of weakness be made strong, and will become the instruments of pulling down the kingdom of Satan, by prayer.

The Spirit of God was poured out upon Christ himself, in answer to prayer (Luke 3:21–22). "Now when all the people were baptized, it came to pass, that Jesus also being baptized, and praying, the heaven was opened, and the Holy Ghost descended in a bodily shape like a dove, upon him; and a voice came from heaven, which said, Thou art my beloved Son, in thee I am well pleased." The Spirit descends on the church of Christ, the same way, in this respect, that it descended on the head of the church. The greatest effusion of the Spirit that ever yet has been, even that which was in the primitive times of the Christian church, which began in Jerusalem on the day of Pentecost, was in answer to extraordinary prayer. When the disciples were gathered together to their Lord, a little before his ascension, "he commanded them that they should not depart from Jerusalem, but wait for the promise of the Father, which" (saith he) "ye have heard of me," i.e., the promise of the Holy Ghost (Acts 1:4). What they had their hearts upon was the restoration of the kingdom to Israel: "Lord," (say they) "wilt thou, at this time, restore again the kingdom to Israel" (v. 6)? And according to Christ's direction after his ascension, they returned to Jerusalem, and continued in united fervent prayer and supplication. It seems they spent their time in it from day to day, without ceasing; till the Spirit came down in a wonderful manner upon them, and that work was begun which never ceased, till the world was turned upside down, and all the chief nations of it were converted to Christianity. And that glorious deliverance and advancement of the Christian church, that was in the days of Constantine the Great, followed the extraordinary cries of the church to God, as the matter is represented in Rev. 6 at the opening of the fifth seal [vv. 9–11]. The church in her suffering state is represented crying with a loud voice, "How long, Lord, holy and true, dost thou not judge, and avenge our blood on them that dwell on the earth" [v. 10]? And the opening of the next seal brings on that mighty revolution, in the days of Constantine, compared to those great changes that shall be at the end of the world.

As there is so great and manifold reason from the Word of God, to think that if a spirit of earnest prayer for that great effusion of the Spirit of God which I am speaking of, prevailed in the Christian church, the mercy would be soon granted; so those that are engaged in such prayer might expect the first benefit. God will come to those that are seeking him and waiting for him (Is. 25:9 and 26:8). When Christ came in the flesh, he was first revealed to them who were "waiting for the consolation of Israel," and "looking for redemption in Jerusalem" (Luke 2:25, 38). And in that great outpouring of the Spirit that was in the days of the apostles, which was attended with such glorious effects among Jews and Gentiles, the Spirit came down first on those that were engaged in united earnest prayer for it [Acts 1:14]. A special blessing is promised to them that love and pray for the prosperity of the church of

God (Ps. 122:6). "Pray for the peace of Jerusalem. They shall prosper, that love thee."

7. We are presented with many motives in the dispensations of divine providence, at this day, to excite us to be much in prayer for this mercy.

There is much in providence to shew us our need of it, and put us on desiring it. The great outward calamities, in which the world is involved; and particularly the bloody war[9] that embroils and wastes the nations of Christendom, and in which our nation has so great a share, may well make all that believe God's Word, and love mankind, earnestly long and pray for that day, when "the wolf shall dwell with the lamb" [Is. 11:6], and "the nations shall beat their swords into plowshares" [Is. 2:4], etc. But especially do the spiritual calamities and miseries of the present time, shew our great need of that blessed effusion of God's Spirit: there having been, for so long a time, so great a withholding of the Spirit, from the greater part of the Christian world, and such dismal consequences of it, in the great decay of vital piety, and the exceeding prevalence of infidelity, heresy and all manner of vice and wickedness; and especially in our land and nation; of which a most affecting account has lately been published in a pamphlet printed in London, and reprinted in Scotland, entitled *Britain's Remembrancer*;[1] by which it seems that luxury, and wickedness of almost every kind, is well nigh come to the utmost extremity in the nation; and if vice should continue to prevail and increase for one generation more, as it has the generation past, it looks as though the nation could hardly continue in being, but must sink under the weight of its own corruption and wickedness. And the state of things in the other parts of the British dominions, besides England, are very deplorable. The Church of Scotland has very much lost her glory, greatly departing from her ancient purity, and excellent order; and has of late been bleeding with great and manifold wounds, occasioned by their divisions and hot contentions. And there are frequent complaints from thence, by those that lament the corruptions of that land, of sin and wickedness, of innumerable kinds, abounding and prevailing of late, among all ranks and sorts of men there.[2] And how lamentable is the moral and religious state of these American colonies? Of New England in particular? How much is that kind of religion, that was professed and much experienced and prac-

---

9. Above, pp. 31–33.
1. A work by James Burgh. See above, p. 61.
2. See John Willison, *A Fair and Impartial Testimony*. Above, p. 70.

ticed, in the first, and apparently the best times of New England, grown and growing out of credit? What fierce and violent contentions have been of late among ministers and people, about things of a religious nature? How much is the gospel ministry grown into contempt, and the work of the ministry, in many respects, laid under uncommon difficulties, and even in danger of sinking amongst us? How many of our congregations and churches rending in pieces? Church discipline weakened, and ordinances less and less regarded? What wild and extravagant notions, gross delusions of the devil, and strange practices have prevailed, and do still prevail, in many places, under a pretext of extraordinary purity, spirituality, liberty, and zeal against formality, usurpation, and conformity to the world? How strong and deeply rooted and general are the prejudices that prevail against vital religion and the power of godliness, and almost everything that appertains to it or tends to it? How apparently are the hearts of the people, everywhere, uncommonly shut up against all means and endeavors to awaken sinners and revive religion? Vice and immorality, of all kinds, withal increasing and unusually prevailing? May not an attentive view and consideration of such a state of things well influence the people that favors the dust of Zion, to earnestness in their cries to God for a general outpouring of his Spirit, which only can be an effectual remedy for these evils?[3]

Besides the things that have been mentioned, the fresh attempts made by the antichristian powers against the Protestant interest, in their late endeavors to restore a popish government in Great Britain, the chief bulwark of the Protestant cause;[4] as also the persecution lately revived against the Protestants in France,[5] may well give occasion to the people

3. For JE's analysis of the contemporary religious situation in New England, see above, pp. 29–31.

4. Prince Charles Edward of the deposed Stuart house, nominally a Roman Catholic, spearheaded the Jacobite rebellion of 1745–46, an attempt to repossess the throne of England for his father James (III) from the ruling Hanoverian dynasty. Undeterred by the earlier failures of his father and grandfather or by the lack of support from the French, the "Young Pretender" began an assault in July 1745. Five months later the Jacobite army controlled Scotland and invaded England. Then the fortunes of war shifted. By mid-December the army of Charles was retreating to Scotland. The *coup de grâce* for the Jacobite cause was delivered at the battle of Culloden on Apr. 16, 1746. See Charles Petrie, *The Jacobite Movement* (London, 1932), pp. 177–217.

5. During the reign of Louis XV (1715–74), the French Huguenots were subjected to intermittent religious oppression at the hands of the state and the Roman Catholic religious establishment. The persecutions from 1745–52 were particularly severe, including an incident at Vernoux where more than thirty Huguenots died. See Henry M. Baird, *The Huguenots and the Revocation of the Edict of Nantes* (2 vols., New York, 1895), *2*, 477–86. Colonial newspapers frequently reported atrocities attributed to the French; e.g., BNL, Feb. 5, 1747, p. 1.

of God, to renewed and extraordinary earnestness in their prayers to him, for the fulfillment of the promised downfall of Antichrist, and that liberty and glory of his church that shall follow.

As there is much in the present state of things to shew us our great need of this mercy, and to cause us to desire it; so there is very much to convince us, that God alone can bestow it, and shew us our entire and absolute dependence on him for it. The insufficiency of human abilities to bring to pass any such happy change in the world as is foretold, or to afford any remedy to mankind, from such miseries as have been mentioned, does now remarkably appear. Those observations of the Apostle (I Cor. 1), "The world by wisdom knows not God" [v. 21], and "God makes foolish the wisdom of this world" [v. 20], never were verified to such a degree as they are now. Great discoveries have been made in the arts and sciences, and never was human learning carried to such a height, as in the present age; and yet never did the cause of religion and virtue run so low, in nations professing the true religion. Never was an age wherein so many learned and elaborate treatises have been written, in proof of the truth and divinity of the Christian religion; yet never were there so many infidels, among those that were brought up under the light of the gospel. It is an age, as is supposed, of great light, freedom of thought, and discovery of truth in matters of religion, and detection of the weakness and bigotry of our ancestors, and of the folly and absurdity of the notions of those that were accounted eminent divines in former generations; which notions, it is imagined, did destroy the very foundations of virtue and religion, and enervate all precepts of morality, and in effect annul all difference between virtue and vice; and yet vice and wickedness did never so prevail, like an overflowing deluge. 'Tis an age wherein those mean and stingy principles (as they are called) of our forefathers, which (as is supposed) deformed religion, and led to unworthy thoughts of God, are very much discarded, and grown out of credit, and supposed more free, noble and generous thoughts of the nature of religion, and of the Christian scheme, are entertained; but yet never was an age, wherein religion in general was so much despised and trampled on, and Jesus Christ and God Almighty so blasphemed and treated with open daring contempt.

The exceeding *weakness* of mankind, and their *insufficiency* in themselves for the bringing to pass anything great and good in the world, with regard to its moral and spiritual state, remarkably appears in many things that have attended and followed the extraordinary religious commotion, that has lately been in many parts of Great Britain and America.[6] The infirmity of the human nature has been manifested, in a very affecting manner, in the various passions that men have been the subjects of, and innumerable ways that they have been moved, as a reed shaken with the wind, on occasion of the changes and incidents, both public and private, of such a state of things. How many errors and extremes are we liable to? How quickly overtopped, blinded, misled, and confounded! And how easily does Satan make fools of men, if confident in their own wisdom and strength, and left to themselves? Many, in the late wonderful season, were ready to admire and trust in men, as if all depended on such and such instruments, at least did ascribe too much to their skill and zeal, because God was pleased to improve 'em a little while to do extraordinary things; but what great things does the skill and zeal of instruments do now, when the Spirit of God is withdrawn?

As the present state of things may well excite earnest desires after the promised general revival and advancement of true religion, and serve to shew our dependence on God for it, so there are many things in providence, of late, that tend to encourage us in prayer for such a mercy. That infidelity, heresy and vice do so prevail, and that corruption and wickedness are risen to such an extreme height, is that which is exceeding deplorable; but yet, I think, considering God's promises to his church, and the ordinary method of his dispensations, hope may justly be gathered from it, that the present state of things will not last long, but that a happy change is nigh. We know, that God never will desert the cause of truth and holiness, nor suffer the gates of hell to prevail against his church; and that it has usually been so from the beginning of the world, that the state of the church has appeared most dark, just before some remarkable deliverance and advancement; "Many a time, may Israel say, Had not the Lord been on our side, then our enemies would have swallowed us up quick; . . . the waters had overwhelmed us" [Ps. 124: 1–4]. The church's extremity has often been God's opportunity for the magnifying his power, mercy and faithfulness towards her. The interest of vital piety has long been in general decaying, and error and wickedness prevailing: it looks as though the disease were now come to a crisis, and that things can't remain long in such a state, but that a change may be expected in one respect or other. And not only God's manner of dealing with his church in former ages, and many things in

6. E.g., the religious excesses accompanying the Great Awakening in America exemplified by the controversial activities of James Davenport. See *Works*, *4*, 60–65; and Gaustad, *Great Awakening*, pp. 37–41.

the promises and prophecies of his Word, but also several things appertaining to present and late aspects of divine providence, seem to give reason to hope that the change will be such, as to magnify God's free grace and sovereign mercy, and not his revenging justice and wrath. There are certain times, that are days of vengeance, appointed for the more special displays of God's justice and indignation; and God has also his days of mercy, accepted times, chosen seasons, wherein it is his pleasure to shew mercy, and nothing shall hinder it; they are times appointed for the magnifying of the Redeemer and his merits, and the triumphs of his grace, wherein his grace shall triumph over men's unworthiness in its greatest height. And if we consider God's late dealings with our nation and this land, it appears to me that there is much to make us think that this day is such a day: particularly God's preserving and delivering the nation, when in so great danger of ruin by the late rebellion;[7] and his preserving New England, and the other British colonies in America, in so remarkable a manner, from the great armament from France, prepared and sent against us the last year;[8] and the almost miraculous success given to us against our enemies at Cape Breton the year before,[9] disappointing their renewed preparations and fresh attempt against these colonies, this present year 1747, by delivering up the strength of their fleet into the hands of the English, as they were in their way hither.[1] And also in protecting us from time to time from armies by land that have come against us from Canada, since the beginning of the present war with France. Besides many strange instances of protection of particular forts and settlements, shewing a manifest interposition of the hand of heaven, to the observation of some of our enemies, and even of the savages. And added to these, the late unexpected restoring of the greater part of our many captives in Canada, by those that held them prisoners there.[2] It appears to me, that God

7. Above, p. 358, n. 4.

8. During the summer of 1746 a French fleet under the Duc D'Anville crossed the Atlantic with plans to avenge the earlier loss at Cape Breton. Storms and sickness battered the squadron. Ill fortune continued to plague the French off the coast of Nova Scotia when D'Anville died and the second in command committed suicide. More storms and losses caused the French to scuttle their plans. In mid-October the fleet divided, sailing for home and to the West Indies.

9. Concerning the campaign at Cape Breton, see above, pp. 32–34, and below, pp. 449–59.

1. I.e., the victory of the English admirals Anson and Warren off Cape Finisterre on May 3, 1747.

2. On Aug. 16, 1747, the French ship *Verd d'Grace* sailed into Boston harbor under a flag of truce, carrying 171 prisoners from Quebec. A few weeks earlier a vessel had departed for

has gone much out of his usual way, in his exercises of mercy, patience and long-suffering in these instances. God's patience was very wonderful of old, towards the ten tribes, and the people of Judah and Jerusalem, and afterwards to the Jews in Christ's and the apostles' times; but it seems to me, all things considered, not equal to his patience and mercy to us. God don't only forbear to destroy us, notwithstanding all our provocations and their aggravations, which it would be endless to recount; but he has, in the forementioned instances, wrought great things for us, wherein his hand has been most visible, and his arm made bare; especially those two instances in America, God's succeeding us against Cape Breton, and confounding the armada from France the last year; dispensations of providence, which, if considered in all their circumstances, were so wonderful, and apparently manifesting an extraordinary divine interposition, that they come perhaps the nearest to a parallel with God's wonderful works of old, in Moses', Joshua's, and Hezekiah's time, of any that have been in these latter ages of the world. And it is to my present purpose to observe, that God was pleased to do great things for us in both these instances, in answer to extraordinary prayer. Such remarkable appearances of a spirit of prayer, on any particular public occasion, have not been in the land, at any time within my observation and memory, as on occasion of the affair of Cape Breton.[3] And 'tis worthy to be noted and remembered, that God sent that great storm on the fleet of our enemies the last year, that finally dispersed, and utterly confounded them, and caused them wholly to give over their designs against us, the very night after our day of public fasting and prayer, for our protection and their confusion.[4]

Thus, although it be a day of great apostasy and provocation, yet it is apparently a day of the wonderful works of God; wonders of power and mercy; which may well lead us to think on those two places of Scripture, Ps. 119:126. "It is time for thee, Lord, to work, for they have made void thy law." And Ps. 75:1, "That thy name is near, thy wondrous

---

Canada with "60 or 70" French prisoners. Among the Englishmen exchanged was John Norton, captured the preceding year at Fort Massachusetts, who recorded his experience in *The Redeemed Captive. Being a Narrative of the taking and carrying into Captivity The Reverend John Norton* (Boston, 1748). See also BG, Aug. 18, 1747, p. 1; and BNL, Aug. 6, 1747, p. 4.

3. See below, p. 449.

4. Governor William Shirley of Massachusetts designated Thursday, Oct. 16, 1746, as a day of public fasting and prayer in view of impending danger from the French fleet off of Nova Scotia. Less than a month later, after storms and sickness had devastated the French, Shirley set aside Nov. 27 for public thanksgiving. See his *A Proclamation for a Publick Fast, October 6* (Boston, 1746), and *A Proclamation for a general Thanksgiving, November 7* (Boston, 1746).

works declare." God appears as it were loath to destroy us, or deal with us according to our iniquities, as great and aggravated as they are; and shews that mercy pleases him. As corrupt a time as it is, it is plain by experience, that it is a time wherein God may be found, and stands ready to shew mercy in answer to prayer. He that has done such great things, and has so wonderfully and speedily answered prayer for temporal mercies, will much more give the Holy Spirit if we ask him. He marvelously preserves us, and waits to be gracious to us, as though he chose to make us monuments of his grace, and not his vengeance, and waits only to have us open our mouths wide, that he may fill them.

The late remarkable religious awakenings, that have been in many parts of the Christian world, are another thing that may justly encourage us in prayer for the promised glorious and universal outpouring of the Spirit of God. "In or about the year 1732 or 1733, God was pleased to pour out his Spirit on the people of Salzburg in Germany, who were living under popish darkness, in a most uncommon manner; so that above twenty thousand of them, merely by reading the Bible, which they made a shift to get in their own language, were determined to throw off popery, and embrace the reformed religion; yea, and to become so very zealous for the truth and gospel of Jesus Christ, as to be willing to suffer the loss of all things in the world, and actually to forsake their houses, lands, goods and relations, that they might enjoy the pure preaching of the gospel; . . . with great earnestness, and tears in their eyes, beseeching Protestant ministers to preach to them, in places where they (when banished from their own country) came, in different places."[5] In the years 1734 and 1735, there appeared a very great and general awakening, in the county of Hampshire, in the province of the Massachusetts Bay in New England, and also in many parts of Connecticut.[6] Since this, there has been a far more extensive awakening of many thousands in England, Wales and Scotland, and almost all the British provinces in North America.[7] There has also been something remarkable of the same kind, in some places in the United Netherlands:[8] and about two years ago, a very great awakening and reformation of many of the Indians, in the Jerseys, and Pennsylvania, even among such

5. Willison, *A Fair and Impartial Testimony* (1744), pp. 99–100.

6. For JE's description and analysis of the awakening in the 1730s, see his *Faithful Narrative* in *Works*, 4, 97–211. C. C. Goen lists the communities which were affected by the revivals, according to JE, in ibid., pp. 19–25.

7. I.e., the awakenings of the early 1740s.

8. See AP; above, p. 289, n. 3.

as never embraced Christianity before:[9] and within these two years, a
great awakening in Virginia and Maryland.[1] Notwithstanding the great
diversity of opinions about the issue of some of these awakenings, yet I
know of none that have denied that there have been great awakenings
of late, in these times and places, and that multitudes have been brought
to more than common concern for their salvation, and for a time were
made more than ordinarily afraid of sin, and brought to reform their
former vicious courses, and take much pains for their salvation. If I
should be of the opinion of those that think these awakenings and
strivings of God's Spirit have been generally not well improved, and so,
as to most, have not issued well, but have ended in enthusiasm and
delusion, yet, that the Spirit of God has been of late so wonderfully
awakening and striving with such multitudes, in so many different
parts of the world, and even to this day, in one place or other, continues
to awaken men, is what I should take great encouragement from, that
God was about to do something more glorious, and would, before he
finishes, bring things to a greater ripeness, and not finally suffer this
work of his to be frustrated and rendered abortive by Satan's crafty
management; and that these unusual commotions are the forerunners
of something exceeding glorious approaching; as the wind, earthquake
and fire, at Mount Sinai, were forerunners of that voice, wherein God
was, in a more eminent manner; although they also were caused by a
divine power, as it is represented that these things were caused by the
"Lord passing by" (I Kgs. 19:11–12).

    8. How condecent,[2] how beautiful, and of good tendency would it be,
for multitudes of Christians, in various parts of the world, by explicit
agreement, to unite in such prayer as is proposed to us.

    Union is one of the most amiable things, that pertains to human

    9. Here JE had in mind the successes of David Brainerd. Ordained as a missionary to the
Indians in June 1744, Brainerd a year later established residences at Crossweeksung in New
Jersey and at the Forks of Delaware in Pennsylvania as centers for his activities. Before his
health failed, he published an account of his successes entitled *Mirabilia Dei inter Indicos, or the
Rise and Progress of a Remarkable Work of Grace Amongst a Number of the Indians in the Provinces
of New-Jersey and Pennsylvania* (Philadelphia, 1746). After Brainerd's death, JE edited his
journal. See *Memoirs of the Rev. David Brainerd*, in Dwight ed., *10*. The successes in New Jersey
and Pennsylvania are described on pp. 194–307.

    1. William Robinson, a prominent Presbyterian itinerant, sparked a revival in Maryland
in 1745 and was active at the same time in Hanover County, Virginia. His efforts in these
areas were continued by a stream of graduates from the "Log College" of William Tennent.
See William Henry Foote, *Sketches of Virginia, Historical and Biographical* (Richmond, Va.,
1966), pp. 119–32; and Gewehr, *Great Awakening*, pp. 50–52.

    2. I.e., suitable or appropriate.

society; yea, 'tis one of the most beautiful and happy things on earth, which indeed makes earth most like heaven. God has "made of one blood all nations of men, to dwell on all the face of the earth" [Acts 17:26]; hereby teaching us this moral lesson, that it becomes mankind all to be united as one family. And this is agreeable to the nature that God has given men, disposing them to society; and the circumstances God has placed them in, so many ways obliging and necessitating them to it. A civil union, or an harmonious agreement among men in the management of their secular concerns, is amiable; but much more a pious union, and sweet agreement in the great business for which man was created, and had powers given him beyond the brutes; even the business of religion; the life and soul of which is love. Union is spoken of in Scripture as the peculiar beauty of the church of Christ (Cant. 6:9). "My dove, my undefiled is but one, she is the only one of her mother, she is the choice one of her that bare her; the daughters saw her and blessed her, yea the queens and the concubines, and they praised her." Ps. 122:3, "Jerusalem is builded as a city that is compact together." Eph. 4:3–6, "Endeavoring to keep the unity of the Spirit in the bond of peace. There is one body, and one Spirit; even as ye are called in one hope of your calling; one Lord, one faith, one baptism, one God and Father of all, who is above all, and through all, and in you all." V. 16, "The whole body fitly framed together and compacted, by that which every joint supplieth, according to the effectual working in the measure of every part, maketh increase of the body, unto the edifying itself in love."

As 'tis the glory of the church of Christ, that she, in all her members, however dispersed, is thus *one*, one holy society, one city, one family, one body; so it is very desirable, that this union should be manifested, and become visible; and so, that her distant members should act as one, in those things that concern the common interest of the whole body, and in those duties and exercises wherein they have to do with their common Lord and Head, as seeking of him the common prosperity. It becomes all the members of a particular family, who are so strictly united, and have in so many respects one common interest, to unite in prayer to God for the things they need: it becomes a nation, in days of prayer, appointed by national authority, at certain seasons, visibly to unite in prayer for those public mercies that concern the interest of the whole nation: so it becomes the church of Christ, which is one holy nation, a peculiar people, one heavenly family, more strictly united, in many respects, and having infinitely greater interests that are common to the whole, than any other society; I say, it especially becomes this society, visibly to unite, and expressly to agree together in prayer to God for the common prosperity; and above all, that common prosperity and advancement that is so unspeakably great and glorious, which God hath so abundantly promised to fulfill in the latter days.

It is becoming of Christians, with whose character a narrow selfish spirit, above all others, disagrees, to be much in prayer for that public mercy, wherein consists the welfare and happiness of the whole body of Christ, of which they are members, and the greatest good of mankind. And union or agreement in prayer is especially becoming, when Christians pray for that mercy, which above all other things concerns them unitedly, and tends to the relief, prosperity and glory of the whole body, as well as of each individual member.

Such an union in prayer for the general outpouring of the Spirit of God, would not only be beautiful, but profitable too. It would tend very much to promote union and charity between distant members of the church of Christ, and a public spirit, and love to the church of God, and concern for the interest of Zion; as well as be an amiable exercise and manifestation of such a spirit. Union in religious duties, especially in the duty of prayer, in praying one with and for another, and jointly for their common welfare, above almost all other things, tends to promote mutual affection and endearment. And if ministers and people should, by particular agreement and joint resolution, set themselves, in a solemn and extraordinary manner, from time to time, to pray for the revival of religion in the world, it would naturally tend more to awaken in them a concern about things of this nature, and more of a desire after such a mercy; it would engage 'em to more attention to such an affair, make 'em more inquisitive about it, more ready to use endeavors to promote that which they, with so many others, spend so much time in praying for, and more ready to rejoice and praise God when they see or hear of anything of that nature or tendency: and in a particular manner, would it naturally tend to engage ministers (the business of whose lives it is, to seek the welfare of the church of Christ, and the advancement of his kingdom) to greater diligence and earnestness in their work: and it would have a tendency to the spiritual profit and advantage of each particular person. For persons to be thus engaged in extraordinarily praying for the reviving and flourishing of religion in the world, will naturally lead each one to reflect on himself, and consider how religion flourishes in his own heart, and how far his example contributes to the thing that he is praying for.

9. There is great and particular encouragement given in the Word

of God, to express union and agreement in prayer. Daniel, when he had a great thing to request of God, viz., that God by his Holy Spirit would miraculously reveal to him a great secret, which none of the wise men, astrologers, magicians or soothsayers of Babylon could find out, he goes to Hananiah, Mishael and Azariah, his companions, and they agree together, that they will unitedly desire mercies of the God of heaven, concerning this secret; and their joint request was soon granted [Dan. 2:16–19]; and God put great honor upon them, above all the wise men of Babylon, to the filling their mouths with praise, and to the admiration and astonishment of Nebuchadnezzar; insomuch that that great and haughty monarch, as we are told, fell upon his face and worshiped Daniel, and owned that "his God was of a truth a God of Gods," and greatly promoted Daniel and his praying companions in the province of Babylon [Dan. 2:46–49]. Esther, when she had a yet more important request to make, for the saving of the church of God, and whole nation of the Jews, dispersed through the empire of Persia, when on the brink of ruin, sends to all the Jews in the city Shushan to pray and fast with her and her maidens [Esth. 4:16]; and their united prayers prevail; so that the event was wonderful: instead of the intended destruction of the Jews, the Jews' enemies are destroyed everywhere, and they are defended, honored and promoted, and their sorrow and distress is turned into great gladness, feasting, triumph and mutual joyful congratulations.

The encouragment to explicit agreement in prayer is great from such instances as these; but it is yet greater from those wonderful words of our blessed Redeemer (Matt. 18:19), "I say unto you, that if any two of you shall agree on earth touching anything that they shall ask, it shall be done for them of my Father which is in heaven." Christ is pleased to give this great encouragement to the union of his followers in this excellent and holy exercise of seeking and serving God; an holy union and communion of his people being that which he greatly desires and delights in, that which he came into the world to bring to pass, that which he especially prayed for with his dying breath (John 17), that which he died for, and which was one chief end of the whole affair of our redemption by him (Eph. 1:7–10). "In whom we have redemption through his blood, the forgiveness of sins, according to the riches of his grace, wherein he hath abounded towards us in all wisdom and prudence; having made known to us the mystery of his will, according to his good pleasure, which he hath purposed in himself: that in the dispensation of the fullness of times, he might gather together in one all things in Christ, both which are in heaven, and which are on earth, even in him."

PART III

OBJECTIONS ANSWERED

I COME NOW, as was proposed, in the third place, to answer and obviate some objections, that some may be ready to make against the thing that has been proposed to us.[1]

Obj. I. Some may be ready to say, that for Christians, in such a manner to set apart certain seasons, every week, and every quarter, to be religiously observed and kept for the purposes proposed, from year to year, would be in effect to establish certain periodical times of *human* invention and appointment, to be kept holy to God; and so to do the very thing, that has ever been objected against, by a very great part of the most eminent Christians and divines among Protestants, as what men have no right to do; it being for them to *add* to God's institutions, and introduce their own inventions and establishments into the stated worship of God, and lay unwarrantable bonds on men's consciences, and do what naturally tends to superstition.

Ans. To this I would say, there can be no justice in such an objection against this proposal, as made to us in the forementioned Memorial. And indeed that caution and prudence appears in the projection itself, and in the manner in which it is proposed to us, that there is not so much as any color for the objection. The proposal is such, and so well guarded, that there seems to be no room for the weakest Christian that well observes it, so to mistake it, as to understand those things to be implied in it, that have indeed been objected against, by many eminent Christians and divines among Protestants, as entangling men's consciences, and adding to divine institutions, etc. Here is no pretense of establishing anything by authority; no appearance of any claim of power in the proposers, or right to any regard to be paid to their determinations or proposals, by virtue of any deference due to them, in any

1. Above, pp. 42–46.

respect, any more than to every individual person of those that they apply themselves to. So far from that, that they expressly mention that which they have thought of, as what they would propose to the thoughts of others, for their amendments and improvements, declaring that they choose rather to receive and spread the directions and proposals of others, than to be the first authors of any. No times, not sanctified by God's own institution, are proposed to be observed more than others, under any notion of such times being, in any respect, more holy, or more honorable, or worthy of any preference, or distinguishing regard; either as being sanctified, or made honorable, by authority, or by any great events of divine providence, or any relation to any holy persons or things; but only as circumstantially convenient, helpful to memory, especially free from worldly business, near to the times of the administration of public ordinances, etc. None attempts to lay any bonds on others, with respect to this matter; or to desire that they should lay any bonds on themselves; or look on themselves as under any obligations, either by power or promise; or so much as come into any absolute determination in their own minds, to set apart any stated days from secular affairs; or even to fix on any part of such days, without liberty to other circumstances, as shall be found expedient; and also liberty left to a future alteration of judgment, as to expediency, on further trial and consideration. All that is proposed is, that such as fall in with what is proposed in their judgments and inclinations, while they do so, should strengthen, assist and encourage their brethren that are of the same mind, by visibly consenting and joining with them in the affair. Is here anything like making laws in matters of conscience and religion, or adding men's institutions to God's; or any shew of imposition, or superstitious esteeming and preferring one day above another, or any possible ground of entanglement of anyone's conscience?

For men to go about by law to establish and limit circumstances of worship, not established or limited by any law of God, such as precise time, place and order, may be in many respects of dangerous tendency. But surely it cannot be unlawful or improper, for Christians to come into some agreement, with regard to these circumstances: for it is impossible to carry on any social worship without it. There is no institution of Scripture requiring any people to meet together to worship God in such a spot of ground, or at such an hour of the day; but yet these must be determined by agreement; or else there will be no social worship, in any place, or any hour. So we are not determined by institution, what the precise order of the different parts of worship shall be; what shall precede, and what shall follow; whether praying or singing shall be first, and what shall be next, and what shall conclude: but yet some order must be agreed on, by the congregation that unite in worship; otherwise they can't jointly carry on divine worship, in any way or method at all. If a congregation of Christians do agree to begin their public worship with prayer, and next to sing, and then to attend on the preaching of the Word, and to conclude with prayer; and do by consent carry on their worship in this order from year to year; though this order is not appointed in Scripture; none will call this superstition. And if a great number of congregations, through a whole land, or more lands than one, do by common consent, keep the same method of public worship; none will pretend to find fault with it. But yet for any to go about to bind all to such a method, would be usurpation and imposition. And if such a precise order should be regarded as sacred, as though no other could be acceptable to God, this would be superstition. If a particular number of Christians shall agree, that besides the stated public worship of the Sabbath, they will, when their circumstances allow, meet together, to carry on some religious exercises, on a Sabbath-day night, for their mutual edification; or if several societies agree to meet together in different places at that time; this is no superstition; though there be no institution for it. If people in different congregations, voluntarily agree to take turns to meet together in the house of God, to worship him and hear a public lecture, once a month, or once in six weeks; it is not unlawful; though there be no institution for it: but yet, to do this as a thing sacred, indispensable, and binding on men's consciences, would be superstition. If Christians of several neighboring congregations, instead of a lecture, agree on some special occasion to keep a circular fast, each congregation taking its turn in a certain time and order, fixed on by consent; or if instead of keeping fast by turns, on different days, one on one week, and one on another, they should all agree to keep a fast on the same day, and to do this either once or frequently, according as they shall judge their own circumstances, or the dispensations of divine providence, or the importance of the mercy they seek, do require; neither is there any more superstition in this than the other.

Obj. II. Some may be ready to say, there seems to be something *whimsical* in its being insisted on that God's people in different places should put up their prayers for this mercy *at the same time*; as though their prayers would be more *forcible* on that account; and as if God would not be so likely to hear prayers offered up by many, though they happened not to pray at the same time, as he would if he heard them all at the same moment.

Ans. To this I would say, if such an objection be made, it must be through misunderstanding. 'Tis not signified or implied in anything said in the proposal, or in any arguments made use of to enforce it that I have seen, that the prayers of a great number in different places, will be more forcible, merely because of that circumstance, of their being put up at the same time. It is indeed supposed, that it will be very expedient, that certain times for united prayer should be agreed on: which it may be, without supposing the thing supposed in the objection, on the following accounts.

1. This seems to be a proper expedient for the promoting and maintaining an *union* among Christians of distant places, in extraordinary prayer for such a mercy. It appears, from what was before observed, that there ought to be extraordinary prayers among Christians for this mercy; and that it is fit, that God's people should agree and unite in it. Though there be no reason to suppose that prayers will be more prevalent, merely from that circumstance, that different persons pray exactly at the same time; yet there will be more reason to hope, that prayers for such mercy will be prevalent, when God's people are very much in prayer for it, and when many of them are united in it. And therefore if agreeing on certain times for united and extraordinary prayer, be a likely means to promote an union of many in extraordinary prayer, then there is more reason to hope, that there will be prevalent prayer for such a mercy, for certain times for extraordinary prayer being agreed on. But that agreeing on certain times for united extraordinary prayer, is a likely and proper means to promote and maintain such prayer, I think will be easily evident to anyone that considers the matter. If there should be only a loose agreement or consent to it as a duty, or a thing fit and proper, that Christians should be much in prayer for the revival of religion, and much more in it than they used to be, without agreeing on particular times, how liable would such a lax agreement be to be soon forgotten, and that extraordinary prayerfulness, which is fixed to no certain times, to be totally neglected? To be sure, distant parts of the church of Christ could have no confidence in one another, that this would not be the case. If these ministers in Scotland, instead of the proposal they have made, or any other ministers or Christians in any part of the Christian world, had sent abroad only a general proposal, that God's people should, for time to come, be much more in

prayer for the advancement of Christ's kingdom, than had been common among Christians heretofore; and they should hear their proposal was generally allowed to be good; and that ministers and people, in one place and another, that had occasion to speak their minds upon it, owned that it was a very proper thing, that Christians should pray more for this mercy than they generally used to do; could they, from this only, have in any measure the like grounds of dependence, that God's people, in various parts of the Christian world, would indeed henceforward act unitedly, in maintaining extraordinary prayer for this mercy, as if they should not only hear that the duty in general was approved of, but also that particular times were actually fixed on for the purpose, and an agreement and joint resolution was come into, that they would, unless extraordinarily hindered, set apart such particular seasons to be spent in this duty, from time to time, maintaining this practice for a certain number of years?

2. For God's people in distant places to agree on certain times for extraordinary prayer, wherein they will unitedly put up their requests to God, is a means fit and proper to be used, in order to the *visibility* of their union in such prayer. Union among God's people in prayer is truly beautiful, as has been before observed and shewn; 'tis beautiful in the eyes of Christ, and 'tis justly beautiful and amiable in the eyes of Christians. And if so, then it must needs be desirable to Christians that such union should be visible. If it would be a lovely sight in the eyes of the church of Christ, and much to their comfort, to behold various and different parts of the church united in extraordinary prayer for the general outpouring of the Spirit, then it must be desirable to them that such an union should be visible, that they may behold it; for if it ben't visible, it can't be beheld. But agreement and union in a multitude in their worship becomes visible, by an agreement in some external visible circumstances. Worship itself becomes visible worship, by something external and visible belonging to the worship, and no other way: therefore union and agreement of many in worship becomes visible no other way, but by union and agreement in the external and visible acts and circumstances of the worship. Such union and agreement becomes visible, particularly by an agreement in those two visible circumstances, *time*, and *place*. When a number of Christians live near together, and their number and situation is convenient, and they have a desire visibly to unite in any acts of worship, they are wont to make their union and agreement visible by an union in both these circumstances. But when a much greater number of Christians, dwelling in distant places, so that

they can't unite by worshiping in the same place, and yet desire a visible union in some extraordinary worship; they are wont to make their union and agreement visible, by agreeing only in the former of those circumstances, viz., that of time: as is common in the appointment of public fasts and thanksgivings; the same day is appointed, for the performance of that extraordinary worship, by all those Christians, in different places, that it is intended should be united therein, as a visible note of their union. This the common light and sense of God's people leads Christians to, in all countries. And the wisdom of God seems to dictate the same thing, in appointing that his people, through the world, in all ages, in their stated and ordinary public worship, every week, should manifest this union and communion one with another, in their worship, as one holy society, and great congregation of worshipers, and servants of God; by offering up their worship on the same day; for the greater glory of their common Lord, and the greater edification and comfort of the whole body.

If any yet find fault with the proposal of certain times to be agreed on by God's people in different places, in the manner set forth in the Memorial, I would ask whether they object against any such thing, as a visible agreement of God's people, in different parts of the world, in extraordinary prayer, for the coming of Christ's kingdom? Whether such a thing, being visible, would not be much for the public honor of God's name? And whether it would not tend to Christians' assistance, quickening and encouragement in the duty united in, by mutual example, and also to their mutual comfort, by a manifestation of that union which is amiable to Christ and Christians, and to promote a Christian union among professing Christians in general? And whether we han't reason to think, from the Word of God, that before that great revival of religion foretold is accomplished, there will be a visible union of the people of God, in various parts of the world, in extraordinary prayer, for this mercy? If these things are allowed, I would then ask further, whether any method can be thought of or devised, whereby an express agreement, and visible union of God's people, in different parts of the world, can be come into, and maintained, but this, or some other equivalent to it? If there be any express agreement about any extraordinary prayer at all, it must first be proposed by some, and others must fall in, in the manner as is represented in my text. And if extraordinary prayer be agreed on and maintained by many in different places, visibly one to another, then it must be agreed in some respect, and with regard to some circumstances, what extraordinary prayer shall be kept up; and it must be seen and heard of, from one to another, what extraordinary prayer is kept up. But how shall this be, when no times are agreed upon, and it is never known nor heard, by those in different parts, nor is in any respect visible to them, when, or how often, those in one town or country, and another, do attend this extraordinary prayer? And the consequence must necessarily be, that it can never be known how far, or in what respect others join with them in extraordinary prayer, or whether they do it at all; and not so much as one circumstance of extraordinary prayer will be visible; and indeed nothing will be visible about it. So that I think that anybody that well considers the matter, will see that he that determines to oppose such a method as is proposed to us in the Memorial, and all others equivalent to it, is in effect determined to oppose there ever being any such thing at all, as an agreed and visibly united, extraordinary prayer, in the church of God, for a general outpouring of the Spirit.

3. Though it would not be reasonable, to suppose, that merely such a circumstance of prayer, as many people's praying at the same time will directly have any influence or prevalence with *God,* to cause him to be the more ready to hear prayer; yet such a circumstance may reasonably be supposed to have influence on the minds of *men;* as the consideration of it may tend to encourage and assist those in praying, that are united in prayer. Will any deny, that it has any reasonable tendency to encourage, animate, or in any respect to help the mind of a Christian in serving God in any duty of religion, to join with a Christian congregation, and to see an assembly of his dear brethren around him, at the same time engaged with him in the same duty? And supposing one in this assembly of saints is blind, and sees no one there; but has by other means ground of satisfaction that there is present at that time a multitude of God's people, that are united with him in the same service; will any deny, that his supposing this, and being satisfied of it, can have any reasonable influence upon his mind, to excite and encourage him, or in any respect to assist him, in his worship? The encouragement or help that one that joins with an assembly in worshiping God, has in his worship, by others being united with him, is not merely by anything that he immediately perceives by sight, or any other of the external senses (for union in worship is not a thing objected to the external senses), but by the notice or knowledge the mind has of that union, or the satisfaction the understanding has that others, at

that time, have their minds engaged with him in the same service: which may be, when those unitedly engaged are at a distance one from another, as well as when they are present. If one be present in a worshiping assembly, and is not blind, and sees others present, and sees their external behavior; their union and engagedness with him in worship, is what he does not see: and what he sees encourages and assists him in his worship, only as he takes it as an evidence of that union and concurrence in his worship, that is out of his sight. And persons may have evidence of this concerning persons that are absent, that may give him as much satisfaction of their union with him, as if they were present. And therefore the consideration of others being at the same time engaged with him in worship, that are absent, may as reasonably animate and encourage him in his worship, as if they were present.

There is no wisdom in finding fault with human nature, as God has made it. Things that exist now, at this present time, are in themselves no more weighty or important, than like things, and of equal reality, that existed in time past, or are to exist in time to come: yet 'tis evident that the consideration of things being present (at least in most cases) does especially affect human nature. As for instance, if a man could be certainly informed, that his dear child at a distance, was now under some extreme suffering; or that an absent most dear friend, was at this time thinking of him, and in the exercise of great affection towards him, or in the performance of some great deed of friendship; or if a pious parent should know that now his child was in the act of some enormous wickedness; or that, on the contrary, he was now in some eminent exercise of grace, and in the performance of an extraordinary deed of virtue and piety; would not those things be more affecting to the human nature, for being considered as things that are in existence, at the present time, than if considered as at some distance of time, either past or future? Hundreds of other instances might be mentioned wherein it is no less plain, that the consideration of the present existence of things, gives them advantage to affect the minds of men. Yea, 'tis undoubtedly so with things in general, that take any hold at all of our affections, and towards which we are not indifferent. And if the mind of a particular child of God is disposed to be affected by the consideration of the religion of other saints, and with their union and concurrence with him in any particular duty or act of religion, I can see no reason why the human mind should not be more moved by the object of its affection, when considered as present, as well in this case, as in any other case: yea I think we may on good grounds determine there is none.

Nor may we look upon it as an instance of the peculiar weakness of the human nature, that men are more affected with things that are considered as present, than those that are distant: but it seems to be a thing common to finite minds, and so to all created intelligent beings. Thus, the angels in heaven have peculiar joy, on occasion of the conversion of a sinner, when recent, beyond what they have in that which has been long past. If any therefore shall call it silly and whimsical in any, to value and regard such a circumstance, in things of religion, as their existing at the present time, so as to be the more affected with 'em for that; [he] must call the host of angels in heaven a parcel of silly and whimsical beings.

I remember, the *Spectator* (whom none will call a whimsical author) somewhere speaking of different ways of dear friends mutually expressing their affection, and maintaining a kind of intercourse, in absence one from another, mentions such an instance as this, with much approbation, viz., that two friends, that were greatly endeared one to another, when about to part, and to be for a considerable time necessarily absent, that they might have the comfort of the enjoyment of daily mutual expressions of friendship, in their absence; agreed that they would, every day, precisely at such an hour, retire from all company and business, to pray one for another. Which agreement they so valued, and so strictly observed, that when the hour came, scarce anything would hinder 'em. And rather than miss the opportunity, they would suddenly break off conversation, and abruptly leave company they were engaged with.[2] If this be a desirable way of intercourse of particular friends, is it not a desirable and amiable way of maintaining intercourse and fellowship between brethren in Christ Jesus, and the various members of the holy family of God, in different parts of the world, to come into an agreement, that they will set apart certain times, which they will spend with one accord, in extraordinary prayer to their heavenly Father, for the advancement of the kingdom and glory of their common dear Lord and Saviour, and for each other's prosperity and happiness, and the greatest good of all their fellow creatures through the world?

Obj. III. Some perhaps may object, that it looks too much like

---

2. Relying upon his memory, JE conflated two different accounts about the activities of separated lovers, in *The Spectator*, No. 241 (Dec. 6, 1711), p. 1.

Pharisaism,[3] when persons engage in any such extraordinary religious exercises, beyond what is appointed by express institution, for them thus designedly to make it manifest abroad in the world, and so openly to distinguish themselves from others.

Ans. 1. All open engaging in extraordinary exercises of religion, not expressly enjoined by institution, is not Pharisaism, nor has ever been so reputed in the Christian church. As when a particular church or congregation of Christians agree together to keep a day of fasting and prayer, on some special occasion; or when public days of fasting and thanksgiving are kept, throughout a Christian province or country: and though it be ordinarily the manner for the civil magistrate to lead in the setting apart such days; yet that alters not the case: if it be Pharisaism in the society openly to agree in such extraordinary exercises of religion, it is not less Pharisaism, for the heads of the society leading in the affair. And if that were now the case with the Christian church, that once was, for about three hundred years together,[4] that the civil magistrate was not of the society of Christians, nor concerned himself in their affairs; yet this would not render it the less suitable for Christians, on proper occasions, jointly, and visibly one to another, to engage in such extraordinary exercises of religion, and to keep days of fasting and thanksgiving by agreement.

Ans. 2. As to the latter part of the objection, there can be no room for it in this case. It can't be objected against what is proposed in the Memorial, that if persons should comply with it, it would look like affecting singularity, and open distinction from others of God's professing people, in extraordinary religion, such as was in the Pharisees of old: because 'tis evident, the very design of the Memorial, is not to promote singularity and distinction, but as much as possible to avoid and prevent it. The end of the Memorial is not to confine and limit the thing proposed, that it may be practiced only by a few, in distinction from the generality; but on the contrary to extend it, and make it as general among professing Christians as possible. Some had complied with the extraordinary duty proposed, and therein had been distinguished from others, for two years, before the Memorial was published; and they were more distinguished than they desired; and

---

3. I.e., sanctimonious and hypocritical religious behavior. This notion derives from the characterization of the Pharisees in the New Testament as a religious party devoted to the outward performance of the law while inwardly corrupt. See Matt. 23:23–33.

4. I.e., the first three centuries of Christian experience before the reign of Constantine, who granted imperial favor to Christianity and intervened directly in the affairs of the church.

therefore send abroad this Memorial, that the practice might be more spread, and become more general, that they might be less distinguished. What they evidently seek, is to bring to pass as general a compliance as possible of Christians of all denominations, "entreating that the desire of concurrence and assistance, contained in the Memorial, may by no means be understood, as restricted[5] to any particular denomination or party, or those who are of such or such opinions about any former instances of remarkable religious concern; but to be extended to *all*, who shall vouchsafe any attention to the proposal, and have at heart the interest of vital Christianity, and the power of godliness; and who, however differing about other things, are convinced of the importance of fervent prayer, to promote that common interest, and of scripture persuasives, to promote such prayer."[6]

Obj. IV. Another objection, that is very likely to arise in the minds of many against such extraordinary prayer as is proposed for the speedy coming of Christ's kingdom, is that we have no reason to expect it, till there first come a time of most extreme calamity to the church of God, and prevalence of her antichristian enemies against her; even that which is represented, Rev. 11 by the "slaying of the witnesses";[7] but have reason to determine the contrary.

Ans. It is an opinion that seems pretty much to have obtained, that before the fulfillment of the promises relating to the church's latter-day glory, there must come a most terrible time, a time of extreme suffering, and dreadful persecution of the church of Christ; wherein Satan and Antichrist are to obtain their greatest victory over her, and she is to be brought lower than ever by her enemies. Which opinion has chiefly risen from the manner of interpreting and applying the forementioned prophecy of the slaying of the witnesses. This opinion, with such persons as retain it, must needs be a great restraint and hindrance, with regard to such an affair as is proposed to us in the Memorial. If persons expect no other, than that the more the glorious times of Christ's kingdom are hastened, the sooner will come this dreadful time, wherein the generality of God's people must suffer so extremely, and the church of Christ be almost extinguished, and blotted out from under heaven; how can it be otherwise, than a great damp to their hope, courage and activity, in praying for, and reaching after the speedy introduction of those glorious promised times? As long as this opinion is retained, it will

5. The errata sheet did not locate this correction accurately.

6. The text of the Memorial; cited above, p. 326.

7. See above, pp. 43–44; and AP, pp. 201–08.

undoubtedly ever have this unhappy influence on the minds of those that wish well to Zion, and favor her stones and dust. It will tend to damp, deaden and keep down, life, hope and joyful expectation in prayer; and even in great measure, to prevent all earnest, animated and encouraged prayer, in God's people, for this mercy, at any time before it is actually fulfilled. For they that proceed on this hypothesis in their prayers, must, at the same time that they pray for this glorious day, naturally conclude within themselves, that they shall never live to see on the earth any dawning of it, but only to see the dismal time that shall precede it, in which the far greater part of God's people, that shall live till then, shall die under the extreme cruelties of their persecutors. And the more they expect that God will answer their prayers, by speedily bringing on the promised glorious day, the more must they withal expect, themselves, to have a share in those dreadful things, that nature shrinks at the thoughts of, and also expect to see things that a renewed nature shrinks at and dreads; even the prevailing of God's enemies, and the almost total extinguishing the true religion in the world. And on this hypothesis, these discouragements are like to attend the prayers of God's people, till that dismal time be actually come: and when that is come, those that had been prophesying and praying in sackcloth, shall generally be slain: and after that time is over, then the glorious day shall immediately commence. So that this notion tends to discourage and hinder all earnest prayer in the church of God for that glorious coming of Christ's kingdom, till it be actually come; and that is to hinder its ever being at all.

It being so, this opinion being of such hurtful tendency, certainly it is a thousand pities it should prevail and be retained, if truly there be no good ground for it.

Therefore in answer to this objection, I would with all humility and modesty, examine the foundation of that opinion, of such a dreadful time of victory of Antichrist over the church, yet to be expected: and particularly shall endeavor to shew that the "slaying of the witnesses," foretold Rev. 11:7–10 is not an event that remains yet to be fulfilled. To this end, I would propose the following things to consideration.

1. The time wherein the "witnesses lie dead in the streets of the great city" [Rev. 11:8], doubtless signifies the time wherein the true church of Christ is lowest of all, most of all prevailed against by Antichrist, and nearest to an utter extinction; the time wherein there is left the least visiblity of the church of Christ yet subsisting in the world, least remains of anything appertaining to true religion, whence a revival of it can be

expected, and wherein all means of it are most abolished, and the state of the church is in all respects furthest from anything whence any hopes of its ever flourishing again might arise. For before this, the witnesses "prophesy in sackcloth" [Rev. 11:3]; but now they are dead: before this, they were kept low indeed, yet there was life, and power to bring plagues on their enemies, and so much of true religion left, as to be a continual eyesore and torment to them; but now their enemies rejoice and feast, and have a general public triumph, as having obtained a full victory over them [Rev. 11:10], and having entirely extirpated them, and being completely delivered from them, and all that might give 'em any fear of being ever troubled with them any more. This time, wherever it be fixed, doubtless is the time, not only, wherein fewest professors of the true religion are left in the world; but a time wherein the truth shall be farthest out of sight, and out of reach, and most forgotten; wherein there are left fewest beams of light or traces of truth, fewest means of information, and opportunities of coming to the knowledge of the truth; and so a time of the most barbarous ignorance, most destitute of all history, relics, monuments and memory of things appertaining to true religion, or things, the knowledge of which hath any tendency to bring truth again to light; and most destitute of learning, study and inquiry.

Now, if we consider the present state of mankind, is it credible, that a time will yet come in the world, that in these respects exceeds all times that were before the Reformation, and that such a time will come before the fall of Antichrist, unless we set that at a much greater distance, than the farthest that any have yet supposed? 'Tis next to impossible, that such a change should be brought about in so short a time: it cannot be without a miracle. In order to it, not only must the popish nations so prevail, as utterly to extirpate the Protestant religion through the earth; but must do many other things, far more impossible for them to effect, in order to cover the world with so gross and confirmed a darkness, and to bury all light and truth in so deep an oblivion, and so far out of all means and hopes of a revival. And not only must a vast change be made in the Protestant world, but the popish nations must be strangely metamorphosed; and they themselves must be terribly persecuted by some other power, in order to bring them to such a change: nor would persecution without extirpation be sufficient for it. If there should be another universal deluge, it might be sufficient to bring things in the world to such a pass; provided a few ignorant barbarous persons only were preserved in an ark: and it would require some catastrophe, not much short of this, to effect it.

2. In the Reformation, that was in the days of Luther, Calvin and others their contemporaries, the threatened destruction of Antichrist, that dreadful enemy that had long oppressed and worn out the saints, was begun; nor was it a small beginning, but Antichrist hath fallen, at least, halfway to the ground, from that height of power and grandeur, that he was in before. Then began the vials of God's wrath to be "poured out on the throne of the beast" [Rev. 16:10], to the great shaking of its foundations, and diminution of its extent; so that the Pope lost near half of his former dominions: and as to degree of authority and influence over what is left, he is not now possessed of one half of what he had before. God now at length, in answer to the long continued cries of his people, awaked as one out of sleep, and began to deliver his church from her exceeding low state, that she had continued in for many ages, under the great oppression of this grand enemy, and to restore her from her exile and bondage in the spiritual Babylon and Egypt. And 'tis not agreeable to the analogy of God's dispensations, that after this, God should desert his people, and hide himself from them, even more than before, and leave 'em more than ever in the hands of their enemy, and all this advantage of the church against Antichrist should be entirely given up and lost, and the power and tyranny of Antichrist be more confirmed, and the church brought more under, and more entirely subdued than ever before, and further from all help and means to recover. This is not God's way of dealing with his people, or with their enemies: his work of salvation is perfect: when he has begun such a work he will carry it on: when he once causes the day of deliverance to dawn to his people, after such a long night of dismal darkness, he will not extinguish the light, and cause them to return again to midnight darkness: when he has begun to enkindle the blessed fire, he will not quench the smoking flax, till he hath brought forth judgment unto victory. When once the church, after her long labor and sore travail, has brought forth her man-child, and wrought some deliverance, her enemies shall never be able to destroy this child, though an infant; but it shall ascend up to heaven [Rev. 12:5], and be set on high out of their reach.

The destruction that God often foretold and threatened to ancient Babylon (which is often referred to in the Revelation, as a great type of the antichristian church) was gradually accomplished, and fulfilled by

various steps, at a great distance of time one from another: it was begun
in the conquest of Cyrus,[8] and was further accomplished by Darius,[9]
about eighteen years after, by a yet greater destruction, wherein it was
brought much nearer to utter desolation; but it was about two hundred
and twenty-three years after this, before the ruin of it was perfected,
and the prophecies against it fully accomplished, in its being made an
utter and perpetual desolation, without any human inhabitant, becoming the dwelling place for owls, dragons and other doleful creatures [Is.
34:13–15]. But yet when God had once begun to destroy her, he went
on till he finished, and never suffered her any more to recover and
establish her former empire. So the restitution of the Jewish church,
after the Babylonish captivity, was gradual, by various steps; there were
several times of return of the Jews from captivity, and several distinct
decrees of the Persian emperors, for the restoring and rebuilding Jerusalem, and reestablishing the Jewish church and state; and it was done
in turbulent times; there were great interruptions and checks, and
violent oppositions, and times wherein the enemy did much prevail:
but yet, when God had once begun the work, he also made an end; he
never suffered the enemies of the Jews to bring Jerusalem to such a
state of desolation as it had been in before, till the promised restoration
was complete. Again, the deliverance of God's church from the oppression of Antiochus Epiphanes[1] (another known type of Antichrist), was
gradual; they were first holpen with a little help, by the Maccabees;[2]
and afterwards the promised deliverance was completed, in the recovery of Jerusalem, the restoration of the temple, the miserable end of
Antiochus, and the consequent more full deliverance of the whole land.
But after God once began to appear for the help of his church in that
instance, after it seemed dead and past all hope, he never suffered
Antiochus to prevail against his people, to that degree, again; though
the utmost strength of this great monarch was used, from time to time,
in order to it, and his vast empire was engaged against an handful that
opposed them: God never forsook the work of his own hand; when he
had begun to deliver his people, he also made an end. And so Haman,

8. Cyrus the Great (d.c. 529 B.C.), king of Persia, conquered Babylon in 539.

9. Darius the Great (d. 486 B.C.), another Persian monarch, suppressed repeated revolts
against his authority in Babylon, including a rebellion in 521 during which he destroyed
the inner walls of the city.

1. See AP; above, p. 211, n. 1.

2. The family of Jewish patriots, also known as the Hasmoneans, who successfully led a
revolt against the Syrians (175–64 B.C.) and thereby checked the advance of Hellenism in
Palestine for more than a century.

that proud and inveterate enemy of the Jews, that thought to extirpate the whole nation, who also was probably another type of Antichrist, when he began to fall before Esther and Mordecai, never stayed, till his ruin, and the church's deliverance was complete. Haman's wife speaks of it, as an argument of his approaching inevitable full destruction, that he "had begun to fall" (Esth. 6:13).

3. If it should be so, that antichristian tyranny and darkness should hereafter so prevail against the Protestant church, and the true religion, and everything appertaining to it, as to bring things to the pass forementioned this would hardly so properly answer the prophecy of slaying the two witnesses [Rev. 11:3–12]; for doubtless, one reason why they are called "two witnesses," is that the number of the remaining witnesses for the truth, was, though sufficient, yet very small. Which was remarkably the case, in the dark times of popery: but since the Reformation, the number of those appearing on the side of true religion, has been far from being so small. The visible church of Christ has been vastly large, in comparison of what it was before: the number of Protestants has sometimes been thought near equal to that of the papists; and doubtless the number of true saints has been far greater than before.

4. It seems to be signified in prophecy, that after the Reformation Antichrist should *never* prevail against the church of Christ any more, as he had done before. I can't but think, that whoever reads and well considers what the learned Mr. Lowman has written on the five first vials, Rev. 16 in his late exposition on the Revelation,[3] must think it to be very manifest, that what is said v. 10 of the pouring out of the fifth vial "on the throne of the beast," (for so it is in the original)[4] is a prophecy of the Reformation. Then the vial of God's wrath was poured out "on the throne of the beast," i.e., according to the language of Scripture, on his authority and dominion, greatly to weaken and diminish it, both in extent and degree. But when this is represented in the prophecy, then it is added, "and his kingdom was full of darkness, and they gnawed their tongues for pain" [Rev. 16:10]. If we consider what is commonly intended by such like phrases in the Scripture, I think we shall be naturally, and as it were necessarily led to understand those words thus; their policy, by which heretofore they have prevailed, shall now fail them; their authority shall be weakened, and their dominion greatly diminished, and all their craft and subtilty shall not avail them to

3. See *Paraphrase and Notes*, pp. 172–99, for Lowman's interpretation of these five vials.
4. ἐπὶ τὸν θρόνον τοῦ θηρίου. See Lowman, *Paraphrase and Notes*, p. 196.

maintain and support the throne of the beast, or ever again to extend his authority so far as it had been before extended, and to recover what it lost; but all their crafty devices to this end shall be attended with vexatious tormenting disappointment; they that have the management of the affairs of the beast's kingdom, shall henceforward grope as in the dark, and stumble, and be confounded in their purposes, plots and enterprises; formerly their policy was greatly successful, was as a light to guide 'em to their ends, but now their kingdom shall be full of darkness, and their wisdom shall fail 'em in all their devices to subdue, and again to bring under the church of God. The Scripture takes notice of the great policy and subtilty of the powers that support this kingdom (Dan. 7:8), "and behold, in this horn were eyes like the eyes of a man." So it is said of Antiochus Epiphanes, that great type of Antichrist (Dan. 8:23), "a king of fierce countenance, and understanding dark sentences, shall stand up." V. 25, "And through his policy also, shall he cause craft to prosper in his hand." This understanding and policy is the light of this kingdom, as true wisdom is the light of the spiritual Jerusalem. And therefore when this light fails, then may the kingdom of this spiritual Egypt be said to be full of darkness. God henceforward will defend his people from these mystical Egyptians, as he defended Israel of old from Pharaoh and his host, when pursuing after them, by placing a cloud and darkness in their way, and so not suffering them to come nigh [Ex. 14: 24]. So he will protect his church from the men of "that city that is spiritually called Sodom" [Rev. 11:8], as Lot's house, wherein were the angels, was defended from the men of Sodom, by their being smitten with darkness or blindness, "so that they wearied themselves to find the door" [Gen. 19:11]; and as God defended the city in which was Elisha the prophet and witness of the Lord, from the Syrians, when they compassed it about with horses and chariots and a great host to apprehend him, by smiting them with blindness [II Kgs. 6:18]. The Scripture teaches us, that God is wont in this way to defend his church and people from their crafty and powerful enemies (Job 5: 11-15). "To set up on high those that be low, that those which mourn may be exalted to safety: he disappointeth the devices of the crafty, so that their hands cannot perform their enterprise: he taketh the wise in their own craftiness, and the counsel of the froward is carried headlong; they meet with darkness in the daytime, and grope in the noonday as in the night; but he saveth the poor from the sword, from their mouth, and from the hand of the mighty." Ps. 35:4, 6, "Let them be confounded and put to shame, that seek after my soul; let them be turned back, and brought to confusion, that devise my hurt. . . . Let their way be dark and slippery."

Upon the account of such defense of God's Protestant church, and disappointment and confusion of all the subtile devices, deep-laid schemes, and furious attempts of their antichristian enemies, to bring them under, and root them out, and their seeing them still maintaining their ground, and subsisting in an independency on them, in spite of all that they do, makes them as it were gnash their teeth, and bite their tongues for mere rage and vexation; agreeable to Ps. 112:9–10. "His righteousness endureth forever, his horn shall be exalted with honor: the wicked shall see it and be grieved, and gnash with his teeth and melt away: the desire of the wicked shall perish."

Hitherto this prophecy has been very signally fulfilled; since the Reformation, the kingdom of Antichrist has been remarkably filled with darkness in this respect. Innumerable have been the crafty devices, and great attempts of the Church of Rome, wherein they have exerted their utmost policy and power, to recover their lost dominions, and again to subjugate the Protestant nations, and subdue the northern heresy, as they call it. They have wearied themselves in these endeavors for more than two hundred years past. But [they] have hitherto been disappointed; and have often been strangely confounded. When their matters seemed to be brought to a ripeness, and they triumphed as though their point was gained, their joy and triumph has suddenly turned into vexation and torment. How many have been their politic and powerful attempts against the Protestant interest in our nation, in particular? And how wonderfully has God disappointed them from time to time! And as God has hitherto so remarkably fulfilled his Word in defending his Protestant church from Antichrist, so I think we have ground to trust in him, that he will defend it to the end.

5. The hypothesis of those that suppose the slaying of the witnesses is a thing that yet remains to be fulfilled, makes the prophecies of the Revelation to be *inconsistent* one with another. According to their hypothesis, that battle (Rev. 11:7) wherein the beast makes war with the witnesses, and overcomes them, and kills them, is the last and greatest conflict between Antichrist and the church of Christ, that is to precede the utter overthrow of the antichristian kingdom. And they must suppose so; for they suppose, that immediately after the sufferings the church shall endure in that war, she shall arise, and as it were ascend into heaven; i.e., as they interpret it, the church shall be directly ad-

vanced to her latter-day rest, prosperity and glory. And consequently, this conflict must be the same with that great battle between Antichrist and the church, that is described ch. 16:13, to the end, and more largely ch. 19:11, to the end. For that which is described in these places, is most evidently and indisputably the greatest and last battle or conflict that shall be between the church and her antichristian enemies; on which the utter downfall of Antichrist, and the church's advancement to her latter-day glory, shall be immediately consequent. And so the earthquake that attends the resurrection of the witnesses (ch. 11:13), must be the same with that great earthquake that is described (ch. 16:18). And the falling of the tenth part of the city [Rev. 11:13] must be the same with that terrible and utter destruction of Antichrist's kingdom (ch. 16:17–21).

But these things can't be. The battle (ch. 11:7) can't be the same with that last and great battle between the church and Antichrist, described chs. 16, and 19. For the things that are said of one and the other, and their issue, are in no wise consistent. In that battle (ch. 11), the church of God conflicts with her enemies in sorrow, sackcloth, and blood: but in the other the matter is represented exceedingly otherwise; the church goes forth to fight with Antichrist, not in sackcloth and blood, but clothed in white raiment, Christ himself before them, as their captain, going forth in great pomp and magnificence, upon a "white horse," and "on his head many crowns," and "on his vesture and on his thigh a name written, 'King of Kings and Lord of Lords' "; and the saints that follow so glorious a leader to this great battle, follow him on "white horses, clothed in fine linen, white and clean," in garments of strength, joy, glory and triumph [Rev. 19:11–18]; in the same kind of raiment, that the saints appear in, when they are represented as triumphing with Christ, with palms in their hands (ch. 7:9). And the issue of the latter of these conflicts, is quite the reverse of the former. In that battle (ch. 11:7), "the beast makes war with the witnesses, and overcomes them, and kills them": the same is foretold Dan. 7:21. "I beheld, and the same horn made war with the saints, and prevailed against them." And Rev. 13:7, "And it was given unto him to make war with the saints, and to overcome them." But in the issue of that last and great battle, which the church shall have with her antichristian enemies, the church shall "overcome them, and kill them." Rev. 17:14, "These shall make war with the Lamb, and the Lamb shall overcome them; for he is Lord of Lords, and King of Kings; and they that are with him, are called and chosen and faithful." Compared with ch. 19:16, and following verses, and ch. 16:16–17. In the conflict that the beast shall have with the witnesses, the beast kills them, and their dead bodies lie unburied [Rev. 11:7–8]; as though they were to be meat for the beasts of the earth and fowls of heaven: but in that last great battle, 'tis represented that Christ and his church "shall slay their enemies, and give their dead bodies to be meat for the fowls of heaven" (ch. 19:17–21). There is no manner of appearance, in the descriptions that are given of that last great battle, of any advantages gained in it, by the enemies of the church, before they themselves are overcome; but all appearance of the contrary. Be sure the descriptions in the 16th and 19th chapters of the Revelation will by no means allow of such an advantage, as the overcoming God's people, and slaying them, and their lying dead for some time, and unburied, that their dead bodies may be for their enemies to abuse, and trample on, and make sport with. In ch. 16 we read of their being gathered together against the church, a mighty host, into the place called Armageddon; and then the first thing we hear of, is the pouring out the seventh vial of God's wrath, and a voice saying, "It is done" [v. 17]. And so in the 19th ch. we have an account of "the beast, and the kings of the earth, and their armies, being gathered together to make war against him that sat on the horse, and against his army" [v. 19]. And then the next thing we hear of, is, that "the beast is taken, and with him the false prophet"; and that "these are both cast alive into the lake of fire"; and that "the remnant of their vast army are slain, and all the fowls filled with their flesh" [vv. 20–21]. The issue of the conflict of the beast with the witnesses, is the triumph of the church's enemies over God's people, looking on them as entirely vanquished, and their interest utterly ruined, past all possibility of recovery; "they that dwell on the earth shall see the dead bodies of the saints lying in the streets of the great city, and shall rejoice over them, and make merry, and send gifts one to another" [Rev. 11:10]. But the issue of that great and last battle is quite the reverse; it is the church's triumph over her enemies, as being utterly and forever destroyed.

Here if anyone shall say, that the ascension of the witnesses into heaven in the sight of their enemies, may, as has more generally been supposed, signify the church's last victory and triumph over her antichristian enemies, and final deliverance from them, and yet the battle between Antichrist and the witnesses, spoken of Rev. 11:7, wherein the witnesses are slain, may not be the same with that last and greatest battle between Antichrist and the church (chs. 16 and 19), that immediately precedes and issues in the church's final victory and deliverance; there may be two great battles, soon following one another, though both are not mentioned in the same place; one a conflict, wherein Antichrist prevails against the witnesses, and overcomes them, and kills them, and another that great battle described chs. 16 and 19 after the witnesses' resurrection, before their ascension into heaven, wherein they shall prevail and overcome their enemies, and kill them: I say, if anyone shall say thus, they will say that which the prophecies give no reason, nor allow any room to suppose. That last battle between the church and Antichrist, wherein Christ and his people obtain a complete victory, is evidently one of the greatest and most remarkable events foretold in all the Apocalypse: and there is no one thing, unless it be the consummation of all things, in the two last chapters, that is described in so solemn and august a manner. And the description shews that it is an event which with its circumstances must take up much time. There is vast preparation made for it by the church's enemies: the devils, in order to stir men up, and gather them together, to this "battle of that great day of God Almighty," "go forth unto the kings of the earth and of the whole world," to propagate various kinds of delusions, far and wide, all over the world; which undoubtedly must take up many years' time (ch. 16:13, 14). And then great preparation is made in the church of God, to make opposition (ch. 19:11–17). Now can any reasonably suppose, that in what is represented (ch. 11), of a great conflict between Antichrist and God's people, wherein the latter are overcome and slain, and lie dead three days (or three years) and an half, and their enemies triumphing over them, but God's people rising again from the dead in the midst of this triumph of their enemies, and ascending into heaven, while their enemies stand astonished and amazed spectators, that the manner of the description leaves fair room for us to suppose, that after this resurrection of God's people, they continue long before they ascend, to encounter with Antichrist in a new conflict, wherein their enemies, after long time to prepare, should engage with them with vastly greater preparation, strength, and violence than before, and should wage war with them with the mightiest army that ever was gathered against the church, and in the greatest battle that ever was fought?

And besides, the witnesses' ascending into heaven in the sight of their enemies, spoken of ch. 11, cannot be the same with the church's gaining a glorious ascendant over her enemies, in her final victory over Antichrist, spoken of chs. 16 and 19 because the descriptions of the events that attend the one and the other do by no means answer each other.

For, observe, 'tis said, that when the witnesses "arose, and stood on their feet, and ascended into heaven, the same hour there was a great earthquake" [Rev. 11:11–13]: but this don't seem to answer to what is described ch. 16:18. "And there were voices, and thunders, and lightnings, and there was a great earthquake, such as was not since men were upon the earth, so mighty an earthquake, and so great." 'Tis said that at the time of the first earthquake (ch. 11:13), "the tenth part of the city fell": but how far does this fall short of what is described, as attending the great earthquake? Ch. 16:19–20, "And the great city was divided into three parts, and the cities of the nations fell; and great Babylon came into remembrance before God, to give unto her the cup of the wine of the fierceness of his wrath; and every island fled away, and the mountains were not found." 'Tis said of the earthquake (ch. 11:13), "and in the earthquake were slain of men seven thousand": but how far is this from answering the slaughter described ch. 19:17 ff.? Which is represented as a general slaughter of the kings, captains, mighty men, horses and armies of the earth and of the whole world; so that all the fowls that fly in the midst of heaven, as far as the sun shines, are filled with the flesh of the dead carcasses, it being the "flesh of all men, both free and bond, both small and great" [Rev. 19:18]: (compare ch. 16:14). Who can think, that this great slaughter that is thus represented, should in ch. 11 be only called a "slaying seven thousand men"?

If we read this very eleventh chapter through, we shall see that the falling of the tenth part of the city, and the witnesses' rising and ascending into heaven, are entirely distinct from the final destruction of Antichrist, and that advancement of the church to her latter-day glory, that is consequent upon it. The judgments here spoken of, as executed on God's enemies, are under another *woe*; and the benefits bestowed on the church, are under another *trumpet*. For immediately after the account of the rising and ascending of the witnesses, and the tenth part of the city's falling, and the slaying of the seven thousand men, and the affrighting of the rest, and their giving glory to the God of heaven, follow these words in the 14th and 15th verses, "The second woe is past; and behold the third woe cometh quickly. And the seventh angel sounded; and there were great voices in heaven, saying, The kingdoms of this world are become the kingdoms of our Lord and of his Christ, and he shall reign forever and ever." And in the following verses, we have an account of the praises sung to God on this occasion. And then in the last verse, we have a brief hint of that same earthquake, and that great hail, and those thunders and lightnings and voices, that we have an account of in the latter part of ch. 16. So that the earthquake mentioned in the last verse of ch. 11 is that great earthquake that attends the last great conflict of the church and her enemies; and not that mentioned v. 13.

The three woes are the woes of God on Antichrist and his subjects; and the third and last of them evidently signifies the terrible judgments of God on Antichrist, by which God's wrath upon him shall be fulfilled in his utter destruction: but the calamities on Antichrist, spoken of as attending the rising and ascending of the witnesses, such as the falling of the tenth part of the city, and slaying seven thousand men, do not belong to this last woe, and therefore don't signify the final destruction of Antichrist: for the words of v. 14 will by no means allow of such a supposition; for there, immediately after giving an account of these calamities, it is added, "The second woe is past; and behold the third woe cometh quickly": making a most plain and express distinction between these calamities that had already been mentioned, and especially these that were just then mentioned in the very last words, and the calamities that belong to the third woe, that yet remain to be mentioned: for by being past, the prophet is to be understood no otherwise than past in the declaration and representation; it was not past in any other respect: 'tis as much as to say, thus an account has been given of the calamities upon Antichrist that belong to the second woe; now I proceed to give an account of those dispensations of providence that belong to the third and last woe, which shall prove Antichrist's final destruction, and end in the kingdoms of this world becoming the kingdoms of our Lord and of his Christ.

What was fulfilled in the Reformation, well answers the representation made concerning the witnesses (Rev. 11:11–12), of the Spirit of life from God entering into them, and their standing on their feet, and ascending up to heaven, in the sight of their enemies. A little before the Reformation, the state of the church of God, and of true religion was lowest of all, and nearest to utter extinction. Antichrist had, after great and long struggles, prevailed against the Waldenses, Albigenses and Bohemians.[5] The war with the Albigenses[6] seems especially to be in-

5. These religious groups all dissented from the official teachings of the western church during the late Middle Ages. On the Waldenses and Albigenses, see AP, p. 110, n. 6. The Bohemian Brethren, originally associated with the followers of John Huss, stressed the necessity of a disciplined and simple Christian life. Protestants viewed the three groups as faithful but oppressed precursors of the Reformation.

6. Pope Innocent III directed a crusade against the Albigenses during the first decades of the thirteenth century, lasting until 1218.

tended by the war of the beast with the witnesses spoken of v. 7. These were witnesses to the truth, that were the most numerous and considerable, and those that most tormented the Church of Rome. And the war that was maintained against them, was by far the greatest that ever Antichrist had against any of the professors of the truth, before the Reformation; and was properly the war of the beast; it was the Pope that proclaimed the war, and that raised the soldiers by his emissaries and priests, preaching the cross, gathering innumerable multitudes of pilgrims from all parts of Christendom, and raising one *croisade* after another, which were conducted and managed by the Pope's legates; and it was the Pope that paid the soldiers with pardons, indulgences, promises of paradise, and such like trumpery. When Antichrist had gradually prevailed against these witnesses, with much difficulty, and long continued violent struggling, and after innumerable vexatious disasters and disappointments; the church of God, in the time of Luther and other reformers, on a sudden, in a wonderful manner revives, when such an event was least expected (to the surprise and amazement of their antichristian enemies), and appears in such strength, that the reformed are able to stand on their own legs, and to withstand all the power and rage of the Church of Rome. Presently after this revival, the people of God are set on high, having the civil magistrate in many countries on their side, and henceforward have the power of many potent princes engaged for their protection: and this, in sight of their enemies, and greatly to their grief and vexation; who, though they from time to time exert their utmost, never are able to prevail against them, to bring them under any more, as they had done in former wars. Oftentimes in Scripture, God's church's dwelling in safety, out of the reach of their enemies, is represented by their "dwelling on high," or being "set on high"; as Ps. 59:1, 69:29, 91:14, 107:41; Prov. 29:25; Is. 33:16. The children of Israel, in their deliverance out of Egypt, from their cruel taskmasters, that would fain have brought 'em into bondage again, were said to "be carried on eagle's wings" [Ex. 19:4], that is lofty in its flight, flies away towards heaven; so that the Egyptians could not come at them: and they were protected by the cloud that went with them; as the witnesses are said to be caught up to heaven in a cloud [Rev. 11:12]. Compare this with Is. 4:5. "And the Lord will create upon every dwelling place of Mount Zion, and upon her assemblies, a cloud and smoke by day, and the shining of a flaming fire by night; for upon all the glory shall be a defense."

I shall not pretend to explain the mystery of the "three days and half" of the witnesses lying dead [Rev. 11:11], or to determine the precise duration signified by that mystical representation. Possibly no particular measure of time may be intended by it; and yet it not be without significancy.[7] As no particular number of persons is intended by the two witnesses; but in general, it intends a small number, and yet a sufficient number; and as small as might be, and yet be sufficient; as, less than two witnesses was not sufficient: so perhaps no particular duration of that low state that the church was in before the Reformation, may be intended by three days and half; but in general it may be hereby signified, that this time of the triumphing of the wicked, and extremity of God's church, should be but short. And possibly three days and half may be mentioned, because that is the utmost space of time that a dead body can be ordinarily supposed to lie without putrefaction; signifying that at this time the church should be brought to the very brink of utter ruin, and yet should be preserved and revive again. And half a day may be mentioned to signify the particular care of providence in exactly determining this time of his church's extremity. And probably there may be some reference to the three times (or three years) and an half of the witnesses' prophesying in sackcloth [Rev. 11:3]; the more apparently to shew the disproportion between the time of the church's welfare, and the time of her enemies' victory and triumph: the time of the church's affliction and conflict may be long; and in the issue she may be overcome; but the time of this victory shall be but short; in comparison with the other, but as a day to a year: she may as it were be killed, and lie dead, till she comes to the very brink of utter and hopeless ruin, but yet God will not suffer her to see corruption; but at that very time, when her enemies expected that she should putrefy, she shall rise; and be set on high, out of their reach, greatly to their astonishment.

The grand objection against all this, is, that it is said that "the witnesses should prophesy twelve hundred and sixty days clothed in sackcloth; and when they have finished their testimony, the beast should make war against them and kill them," etc. [Rev. 11:3, 7], and that it seems manifest, that after this, they are no longer in sackcloth, for henceforward they are in an exalted state in heaven: and that there-

---

7. Mr. Lowman, in the preface to his *Paraphrase on the Revelation*, page viii, observes as follows: "Prophetic numbers do not always express a determinate duration or space of time, any more than they always express a certain number. Prophecy, I acknowledge, uses numbers sometimes as other expressions, in a figurative meaning, as symbols and hieroglyphics. Thus the number 'seven,' sometimes does not denote the precise number seven: but figuratively denotes perfection, or a full and complete number: and the number 'ten,' sometimes does not mean precisely ten in number, but many in general, or a considerable number."—JE.

fore, seeing the time of their wearing sackcloth, is twelve hundred and sixty days, which is the time of the continuance of Antichrist; hence their being slain and rising again, must be at the conclusion of this period, and so at the end of Antichrist's reign.

In answer to which I would say, that we can justly infer no more from this prophecy than this, viz., that the twelve hundred and sixty days is the proper time of the church's trouble and bondage, or being clothed in sackcloth; because it is the appointed time of the reign of Antichrist. But this don't hinder but that God, out of his great compassion to his church, should, in some respect, shorten the days, and grant that she should, in some measure, anticipate the appointed great deliverance that should be at the end of those days. As he has in fact done in the Reformation; whereby the church has had a great degree of restoration granted, from the darkness and power of Antichrist, before her proper time of restoration, which is at the end of the twelve hundred and sixty days. Thus the church of Christ, through the tender mercies of her Father and Redeemer, in some respects, anticipates her deliverance from her sorrows and sackcloth: as many parts of the church are hereby brought from under the dominion of the antichristian powers, into a state of power and liberty; though in other respects, the church may be said to continue in sackcloth, and in the wilderness, till the 'end of days; many parts of it still remaining under grievous persecution.

What we render, "when they shall have finished their testimony" [Rev. 11:7], Mr. Lowman, from Mr. Daubuz, renders, "while they shall perform their testimony"; and observes, that the original may mean "the time of their testimony," as well as "the end of it."[8]

I might here observe that we have other instances of God's shortening the days of his church's captivity and bondage, either at the beginning or end, very parallel with what has been now supposed in the case of the witnesses. Thus the proper time of the bondage of the posterity of Abraham in Egypt, was four hundred years (Gen. 15:13). But yet God in mercy deferred the beginning of their bondage; whereby the time was much shortened at the beginning. So the time wherein it was foretold that the "whole land of Israel should be a desolation and an astonishment," and the land should enjoy her sabbaths, by the Babylonish captivity, was seventy years (Jer. 25:11–12); and these seventy years are dated in II Chron. 36:20–21, from Zedekiah's captivity; and yet, from that captivity to Cyrus' decree, was but fifty-two years; though it

---

8. Lowman, *Paraphrase and Notes*, p. 111. The Greek text reads ὅταν τελέσωσιν τὴν μαρτυρίαν αὐτῶν. Concerning Charles Daubuz, see above, p. 7.

was indeed seventy years before the more full restoration of the Jewish church and state by Darius' decree (Ezra 6). So the proper time of the oppression and bondage of the Jewish church under Antiochus Epiphanes, wherein "both the sanctuary and host should be trodden under foot by him," was two thousand three hundred days (Dan. 8:13, 14). The time from Antiochus' taking Jerusalem and polluting the sanctuary, to Antiochus' death, seems to have been about so long: but God shortened the days, by granting remarkable help to his people by means of the Maccabees, before that time: yea the temple and sanctuary were restored, and the altar rebuilt and dedicated before that time.

Upon the whole, I think there appears to be no reason from the prophecy concerning the two witnesses (Rev. 11), to expect any such general and terrible destruction of the church of Christ, before the utter downfall of Antichrist, as some have supposed; but good reason to determine the contrary. 'Tis true, there is abundant evidence in Scripture, that there is yet remaining a mighty conflict between the church and her enemies, the most violent struggle of Satan and his adherents, in opposition to true religion, and the most general commotion that ever was in the world, since the foundation of it to that time; and many particular Christians, and some parts of the church of Christ, may suffer hard things in this conflict: but in the general, Satan and Antichrist shall not get the victory, nor greatly prevail; but on the contrary be entirely conquered, and utterly overthrown, in this great battle. So that I hope this prophecy of the slaying of the witnesses, will not stand in the way of a compliance with the proposal made to us in the Memorial, as a prevalent objection and discouragement.

Obj. V. A late very learned and ingenious expositor of the Revelation, viz., Mr. Lowman, sets the fall of Antichrist, and consequently the coming of Christ's kingdom, at a great *distance*; supposing that the twelve hundred and sixty years of Antichrist's reign did not begin till the year seven hundred and fifty-six; and consequently that it will not end till after the year two thousand, more than two hundred and fifty years hence; and this opinion he confirms by a great variety of arguments.[9]

Ans. 1. If this objection be allowed to be valid, and that which ought to determine persons in an affair of this nature, and those things, concerning God's people praying for this glorious event, be also allowed to be true, which before were shewn to be the will of God abundantly re-

9. For example, see *Paraphrase and Notes*, pp. xxxi, 64, 103–07.

vealed in his Word, then the following things must be supposed; viz., that 'tis the will of God that his people be much in prayer for this event, and particularly that it is God's revealed will and purpose, that, a little before the accomplishment of it, his people be earnestly seeking and waiting, and importunately and incessantly crying to God for it; but yet that it was God's design, that before this time comes of extraordinary prayer and importunity of his church, for the bringing on this glorious event, his church should have it given 'em to understand precisely when the appointed time should be; and that accordingly he has now actually brought the fixed time to light, by means of Mr. Lowman. But is it reasonable to suppose, that this should be God's manner of dealing with his church, first to make known to them the precise time which he has unalterably fixed for the shewing this mercy to Zion, and then make it the duty of his church, in an extraordinary manner, to be by prayer inquiring of him concerning it, and saying, "How long, Lord!" and waiting for it, day and night crying to him with exceeding importunity that he would bring it on, that he would come quickly, that he would hide himself no longer, but would arise and have mercy upon Zion, and awake as one out of sleep, openly manifest himself, and make bare his holy arm for the salvation of his people [Is. 52:10]? That "they that make mention of the Lord should not keep silence, nor give him any rest, till he establish, and make Jerusalem a praise in the earth" [Is. 62:6–7]? And that the church should then say to Christ, "Make haste, my beloved, and be thou like a roe or a young hart on the mountains of spices" [Cant. 8:14]?

It may be many ways for the comfort and benefit of God's church in her afflicted state, to know that the reign of Antichrist is to be no more than 1260 years: and some things in general may be argued concerning the approach of it, when it is near: as the Jews could argue the approach of Christ's first coming, from Daniel's prophecy of the 70 weeks, though they knew not precisely when that 70 weeks would end [Dan. 9:24–27]. But 'tis not reasonable to expect that God should make known to us beforehand, the precise time of Christ's coming in his kingdom. The disciples desired to know this, and manifested their desire to their Lord; but he told 'em plainly that "it was not for them to know the times and seasons, which the Father hath put in his own power" (Acts 1:6–7); and there is no reason to think that it is any more for us than for them; or for Christ's disciples in these days any more than for his apostles in those days. God makes it the duty of his church to be importunately praying for it, and praying that it may come *speedily*; and not only to be praying for it, but to be seeking of it, in the use of proper means; endeavoring that religion may now revive everywhere, and Satan's kingdom be overthrown; and always to be waiting for it, being in a constant preparation for it, as servants that wait for the coming of their Lord, or virgins for the coming of the bridegroom, not knowing at what hour he will come. But God's making known beforehand the precise time of his coming, don't well consist with these things.

It is the revealed will of God, that he should be inquired of by his people, by extraordinary prayer, concerning this great mercy, to do it for them, before it be fulfilled. And if any suppose, that 'tis now found out precisely when the time is to be, and (the time being at a considerable distance) that now is not a proper season to begin this extraordinary prayer, I would, on this supposition, ask, when we shall begin? How long before the fixed and known time of the bestowment of this mercy comes, shall we begin to cry earnestly to God that this mercy may come, and that Christ would "make haste and be like a roe," etc. [Cant. 8:14]? For us to delay, supposing that we know the time to be far off, is not agreeable to the language of God's people in my text, "Come, let us go speedily, and pray before the Lord, and seek the Lord of Hosts" [Zech. 8:21].

Ans. 2. I acknowledge that Mr. Lowman's exposition of the Revelation is, on many accounts, excellently written, giving great light into some parts of that prophecy, and an instance of the fulfillment of that prediction, Dan. 12:4, "Many shall run to and fro, and knowledge shall be increased": and especially in his interpretation of the five first vials (which he supposeth already poured out) exceeding satisfying. But yet the opinion of Mr. Lowman, with regard to the particular time of the beginning and end of the time, times and an half of Antichrist's reign [Rev. 12:14], and of all others that pretend to fix the time, is the less to be regarded, because 'tis clearly revealed, and expressly declared by God, that that matter should be sealed up and hid, and not known till "the time of the end" [Dan. 12:9] of this time, times and an half. Daniel, in the last chapter of his prophecy [ch. 12], gives us an account, how the angel told him of a future time of great trouble and affliction to the church of God, and then said to him (v. 4), "But thou, O Daniel, shut up the words, and seal the book, even to the time of the end." And then the prophet proceeds to give an account of a vision that he had of one earnestly inquiring of the angel of the Lord how long it would be to the end of this remarkable and wonderful time of the church's trouble, saying, "How long shall it be to the end of these wonders" (vv. 5–6)?

The answer was, that "it should be for a time, times and an half," and that when so long a time was past, then this wonderful affliction and scattering of the holy people should be finished (v. 7). But then Daniel tells us, in the next verse, that he heard, but he understood not, and said, "O my Lord, what shall be the end of these things?" He did not understand that general and mystical answer, that those things should have an end at the end of a time, times and an half; he did not know by it, when this period would have an end: and therefore he inquires more particularly what the time of the end was. But the angel replies (v. 9), "Go thy way, Daniel, the words are closed and sealed up, till the time of the end." I don't know what could have been more express. The angel gently rebukes this overinquisitiveness of Daniel, very much as Christ did a like inquisitiveness of the disciples concerning the same matter, when he said to 'em, " 'Tis not for you to know the times and seasons, that the Father hath put in his own power" [Acts 1:7]. I think there can be no doubt but that this space, of a time, times and half of the church's great trouble, about the end of which Daniel inquires, is the same with that "time, times and half," that is spoken of ch. 7:25 and Rev. 12:14 as the time of Antichrist's reign, and the church's being in the wilderness; and not merely the time of the church's troubles by Antiochus Epiphanes. But we see, when Daniel has a mind to know particularly when this time would come to an end, he is bid to go away, and rest contented in ignorance of this matter: for says the man clothed in linen, "The words are closed up, and sealed, till the time of the end" [Dan. 12:9]. That is, very plainly, the matter that you inquire about, when the end of this time, and times and half shall come, shall not be known, but kept a great secret, till the time of the end actually comes, and all attempts to find it out before that shall be in vain. And therefore when a particular divine appears, that thinks he has found it out, and has unsealed this matter, and made it manifest with very manifold and abundant evidence, we may well think he is mistaken, and doubt whether those supposed evidences are truly solid ones, and such as are indeed sufficient to make that matter manifest, which God has declared should be kept hid, and not made manifest before 'tis accomplished. Mr. Lowman's own words in his preface, pp. xxiv–xxv, are here worthy to be repeated: "It will" (says he) "ever be a point of wisdom, not to be over-busy, or overconfident in anything, especially in fixing periods of time, or determining seasons; which it may be are not to be determined, it may be are not fit to be known. It is a maxim, of greater wisdom than is usually thought, 'Seek not to know what should not be revealed.'

Such are many future events. The precise time of our Saviour's coming to judgment, was not revealed, because not fit to be revealed. The uncertainty of his appearance was of greater service to preserve a care of religion, than the revelation of it would have been: for the uncertainty itself gives many useful exhortations; 'Watch, for ye know not what hour the Son of Man cometh' [Matt. 25:13]. Suppose then some of the events described in this prophecy should be of doubtful application, suppose the precise time of the downfall of the beast, the slaying and resurrection of the witnesses, and the beginning of the thousand years happy state of the church, should not be so determined, but it would admit of different calculations; may it not be wise, and therefore fit, it should be so? The certainty of those events in a proper time, though that time should not be precisely determined, will answer the greater ends of useful instruction. And if the revelation should go no further than this, it would yet be a revelation, of great benefit and advantage; as the certainty of the day of judgment in its proper time surely is, 'though of that day and hour knoweth no man'" [Matt. 24:36].[1]

Ans. 3. Though it is not for us to know the precise time of the fall of Antichrist, yet I humbly conceive that we have no reason to suppose the event principally intended in the prophecies of Antichrist's destruction to be at so great a *distance*, as Mr. Lowman places it; but have reason to think it to be much nearer. Not that I would set up myself as a person of equal judgment with Mr. Lowman in matters of this nature. As he differs from most others of the most approved expositors of the Apocalypse,[2] in this matter, so I hope it will not appear vanity and presumption in me, to differ from this particular expositor, and to agree with the greater number. And since his opinion stands so much in the way of that great and important affair, to promote which is the very end of this whole discourse, I hope it will not look as though I affected to appear considerable among the interpreters of prophecy, and as a person of skill in these mysterious matters, that I offer some reasons against Mr. Lowman's opinion. 'Tis surely great pity, that it should be received as a thing clear and abundantly confirmed, that the glorious day of Antichrist's fall is at so great a distance (so directly tending to damp and discourage all earnest prayers for, or endeavors after its speedy accomplishment) unless there be good and plain ground for it. I would therefore offer some things to consideration, which I think may justly

1. Ibid., pp. xxiv–xxv.
2. Here JE used the apocalyptic tradition in support of his interpretation.

make us look upon the opinion of this learned interpreter, of this happy event's being at so great a distance, not so certain and indubitable, as to hinder our praying and hoping for its being fulfilled much sooner.

The period of Antichrist's reign, as this author has fixed it, seems to be the main point insisted on in his exposition of the Revelation; which he supposes a great many things in the scheme of prophecies delivered in that book do concur to establish. And indeed it is so, with respect to the scheme of interpretation of these prophecies, which he goes into, and finds it requisite to maintain, in order to confirm this point. But there are several things in that scheme, that appear to me justly liable to exception.

Whereas 'tis represented (Rev. 17:10–11), that there are seven different successive heads of the beast; that five were past, and another was to come, and to continue a short space, that might on some accounts be reckoned a seventh; and that Antichrist was to follow next after this, as the eighth; but yet the foregoing not being properly one of the heads of the beast, he was properly the seventh; Mr. Lowman don't think with others, that by the seventh that was to continue a short space, which would not be properly one of the heads of the beast, is meant Constantine and the other Christian emperors; (for he thinks they are reckoned as properly belonging to the sixth head of the beast) but that hereby is intended the government that Rome was subject to under the Gothic princes,[3] and the exarchate of Ravenna,[4] after the imperial form of government in Rome ceased in Augustulus,[5] till the Pope was invested with his temporal dominion, called St. Peter's Patrimony, by Pepin king of France, in the year 756. And he supposes, that that wounding of one of the heads of the beast with a sword unto death, that we read of chs. 13:3 and 14, was not fulfilled in the destruction of the heathen empire, and the giving the imperial power unto Christians, but in the destruction of the imperial form of government, by the sword of the Goths, in the time of Augustulus.[6] But it seems to me to be very

---

3. I.e., the rulers of the Germanic peoples, the Visigoths and the Ostrogoths, who harassed the Roman Empire for several centuries before conquering it. Theodoric (d. 526), king of the Ostrogoths, was one of the most powerful to rule in Italy.

4. Following the Lombard invasions of the empire in the sixth century, the Byzantine emperor established a military governor over Italy called an "exarch," whose headquarters were in the city of Ravenna.

5. Romulus Augustulus, the "last" of the western Roman emperors (475–76), was ruling in 476 when the city of Rome fell to the forces of Odoacer.

6. For Lowman's discussion of the "heads of the beast," see *Paraphrase and Notes*, pp. xxi, 129, 211–12.

unlikely, that the Spirit of God should reckon Constantine and the Christian emperors as proper members, and belonging to one of the heads, of that monstrous wild and cruel beast, that is compared to a leopard and a bear, and a devouring lion, and that had a mouth speaking great things and blasphemies, and that rules by the power and authority of the dragon, or the devil [Rev. 13:2–5];[7] which beast is represented in this very 17th ch. as full of names of blasphemy, and of a bloody color [v. 3], denoting his exceeding cruelty in persecuting the Christian church. For Constantine, instead of this, was a member of the Christian church, and set by God in the most eminent station in his church; and was honored, above all other princes that ever had been in the world, as the great protector of his church, and her deliverer from the persecuting power of that cruel scarlet-colored beast. Mr. Lowman himself styles him "a Christian prince, and protector of the Christian religion."[8] God is very careful not to reckon his own people among the Gentiles, the visible subjects of Satan (Num. 23:9). "The people shall not be reckoned among the nations." God won't enroll them with them; if they happen to be among them, he will be careful to set a mark upon them, as a note of distinction (Rev. 7:3 ff.); when God is reckoning up his own people, he leaves out those that have been noted for idolatry. As among the tribes that were sealed (Rev. 7), those idolatrous tribes of Ephraim and Dan are left out, and in the genealogy of Christ (Matt. 1), those princes that were chiefly noted for idolatry, are left out. Much more would God be careful not to reckon his own people, especially such Christian princes as have been the most eminent instruments of overthrowing idolatry, amongst idolaters, and as members and heads of that kingdom that is noted in Scripture as the most notorious and infamous of all, for abominable idolatry, and opposition and cruelty to the true worshipers of God. And especially not to reckon them as properly belonging to one of those seven heads of this monarchy, of which very heads it is particularly noted that they had on them the names of "blasphemy" (Rev. 13:1); which Mr. Lowman himself supposes to signify idolatry.[9] It was therefore worthy of God, agreeable to his manner, and what might well be expected, that when he was reckoning up the several successive heads of this beast, and Constantine and his

7. The word *therion* [θηρίον in the Greek] signifies a wild savage beast, as Mr. Lowman himself observes, page 127.—JE.

8. *Paraphrase and Notes*, p. 69.

9. In ibid., p. 127, Lowman noted that because "Idolatry is a reproachful Contempt of the one true God, worshipping and serving the Creature more than the Creator, it is called Blasphemy in the Stile of Prophecy."

successors came in the way, and there was occasion to mention them, to set a mark, or note of distinction on them, signifying that they did not properly belong to the beast, nor were to be reckoned as belonging to his heads; and therefore are to be skipped over in the reckoning; and Antichrist, though the eighth head of the Roman Empire, is to be reckoned the seventh head of the beast. This appears to me abundantly the most just and natural interpretation of Rev. 17:10–11. 'Tis reasonable to suppose, that God would take care to make such a note in this prophetical description of this dreadful beast, and not by any means to reckon Constantine as belonging properly to him. If we reckon Constantine as a member of this beast having seven heads and ten horns, described ch. 17 and as properly one of his heads, then he was also properly a member of the great red dragon with seven heads and ten horns, that warred with the woman (ch. 12). For the seven heads and ten horns of that dragon, are plainly the same with the seven heads and ten horns of this beast. So that this makes Constantine a visible member of the devil: for we are told expressly of that dragon (v. 9), that he was "that old serpent, called the devil and Satan." And to suppose that Constantine is reckoned as belonging to one of the heads of that dragon, is to make these prophecies inconsistent with themselves. For here in this 12th ch. we have represented a war between the dragon and the woman clothed in the sun [v. 7]; which woman, as all agree, is the church: but Constantine, as all do also agree, belonged to the woman, was a member of the Christian church, and was on that side in the war against the dragon, yea, was the main instrument of that great victory that was obtained over the dragon there spoken of (vv. 9–12). What an inconsistency therefore is it, to suppose that he was at the same time a member and head of that very dragon, which fought with the woman, and yet which Constantine himself fought with, overcame, and gloriously triumphed over! 'Tis not therefore to be wondered at, that God was careful to distinguish Constantine from the proper heads of the beast; it would have been a wonder if he had not. God seems to have been careful to distinguish him, not only in his Word, but in his providence, by so ordering it that this Christian emperor should be removed from Rome, the city that God had given up to be the seat of the power of the beast and of its heads, and that he should have the seat of his empire elsewhere.

Constantine was made the instrument of giving a mortal wound to the heathen Roman Empire; and giving it a mortal wound in its head, viz., the heathen emperors that were then reigning, Maxentius and

Licinius.[1] But more eminently was this glorious change in the empire owing to the power of God's Word, the prevalence of the glorious gospel, by which Constantine himself was converted, and so became the instrument of the overthrow of heathen empire in the East and West. The change that was then brought to pass, is represented as the destruction of the heathen empire, or the old heathen world; and therefore seems to be compared to that dissolution of heaven and earth that shall be at the day of judgment (Rev. 6:12–17). And therefore well might the heathen empire under the head which was then reigning, be represented as "wounded to death" (ch. 13:3). 'Tis much more likely, that the wound the beast had by a sword, in his head, spoken of v. 14, was the wound that the heathen empire had in its head, by that sword that we read of chs. 1:16 and 19:15 that proceeds out of the mouth of Christ, than the wound that was given to the Christian empire and emperor by the sword of the heathen Goths.[2] 'Tis most likely that this deadly wound was by that sword with which Michael made war with him and overcame him and cast him to the earth (ch. 12:9), and that the deadly wound that was given him, was given him at that very time. 'Tis most likely, that the sword that gave him this deadly wound, after which he strangely revived, as though he rose from the dead, was the same sword with that which is spoken of, as what shall at last utterly destroy him, so that he shall never rise more (ch. 19:15, 19–21). This wounding of the head of the beast by the destruction of the heathen empire, and conversion of the emperor to the Christian truth, was a glorious event indeed of divine providence, worthy to be so much spoken of in prophecy. 'Tis natural to suppose, that the mortal wounding of the head of that savage cruel beast, that is represented as constantly at war with the woman, and persecuting the church of Christ, should be some relief to the Christian church: but on the contrary, that wounding to death that Mr. Lowman speaks of, was the victory of the enemies of the Christian church *over her*, and the wound she received *from them*.

'Tis said of that head of the empire that shall be next after the sixth head, and next before Antichrist, and that is not reckoned as properly one of the number of the heads of the beast, that "when it comes, it shall continue a short space" (ch. 17:10). By which we may well understand, at least, that it shall be one of the shortest in its continuance, of the successive heads. But the government seated at Ravenna, in the

1. Maxentius and Licinius were rival emperors defeated by Constantine in 312 and 324 respectively.
2. I.e., the Gothic invasions of the Roman Empire during the fourth and fifth centuries.

hands of the Goths, or of the deputies of the Greek emperors, (which Mr. Lowman supposes to be meant by this head) continued, as Mr. Lowman himself takes notice, very near 300 years.[3] And if so, its continuance was one of the longest of the heads mentioned.

And besides if the government that Rome was under, from the time that Augustulus abdicated, to the time when the Pope was confirmed in his temporal dominion, was meant by that seventh head that was to be between the imperial head and the papal, there would doubtless have been two different heads mentioned, instead of one, between the emperor and the Pope; viz., first, the Gothic princes, which reigned near an 100 years; secondly, the exarchs of Ravenna, which governed for about 185 years. The Gothic kingdom was much more properly a distinct government from the imperial, than the exarchate of Ravenna. For during the exarchate, Rome was under the government of the emperor, as much as it was in Constantine's time.

In Rev. 17:12 'tis said, the "ten horns are ten kings, which are to receive power as kings one hour with the beast," or (as Mr. Lowman says it ought to have been translated) "the same hour" or "point of time with the beast."[4] This will not allow the time when Antichrist first receives power as king, to be so late as Mr. Lowman supposes. This division of the empire into many kingdoms, denoted by the number ten, was about the year 456, after Gensericus had taken the city of Rome: but Mr. Lowman places the beginning of the reign of Antichrist in the year 756, which is 300 years later.[5] I know, such an expression as "in one hour," or "the same hour," may allow some latitude; but surely not such a latitude as this. This is a much longer time, than it was from the time of the vision to Constantine; much longer than the space of all the first six seals; longer than it was from Christ's ascension to Constantine; and near as long as the time of all the reigns of the heathen emperors put together, from Augustus Caesar to Constantine. An hour is everywhere, in the other places in this book of Revelation, used to signify a very short time; as may be seen in places cited in the margin.[6] And the expression, "the same hour," everywhere else in the Bible, intends near the same point of time.[7] The phrase "one hour" is

---

3. *Paraphrase and Notes*, p. xxi.

4. μίαν ὥραν μετὰ τοῦ θηρίου. In ibid., p. 213, Lowman wrote, "The Beast then, and the ten Kings or Kingdoms, are to be contemporary Powers, or to reign at the same time."

5. Ibid., pp. xxi, 106, 136–37.

6. Rev. 3:10, 8:1, 9:15, 11:13, 14:7, 18:10, 17, 19.—JE.

7. Dan. 3:6, 4:33, 5:5; Matt. 8:13, 10:19; Luke 7:21, 12:12, 20:19, 24:33; John 4:53; Acts 16:18, 33, 22:13; Rev. 11:13.—JE.

used several times in the next chapter [Rev. 18:10, 17, 19], speaking of the downfall of Antichrist:[8] and each time, evidently signifies a very short space of time. And there is no reason why we should not understand the same phrase in the same sense, when it is used here concerning the rise of Antichrist.

Mr. Lowman greatly insists upon it, that what is spoken as continuing 1260 days, is not so much any spiritual authority or ecclesiastical power of the Pope, over the nations of Christendom, as his temporal government and dominion in that individual city of Rome; and therefore to determine when these 1260 days or years began, and when they will end, we must consider when the Pope first received this his temporal power over this city of Rome, and the neighboring region, called St. Peter's Patrimony.[9] But I can see no good reason for this. Indeed it is strange, if it be so. God has been pleased in these revelations and prophecies, which he has given for the benefit of his church in *general*, to speak much concerning an antichristian power that should arise, that should persecute the saints, and "scatter the power of the holy people" [Dan. 12:7], and be an occasion of great affliction to the church of Christ; and in these revelations, in both Old Testament and New, has declared, and often repeated it, that his dominion shall continue so long, and no longer; and for the comfort of his church in general, Christ hath sworn with great solemnity, that the continuance of this persecuting power shall be thus limited (Dan. 12:7). Now it would be strange, if in all this the thing principally intended is not that dominion of this antichristian power that chiefly concerns the church of Christ in general, but merely his temporal dominion over one province in Italy, called St. Peter's Patrimony. Doubtless that dominion of Antichrist which the prophecies insist upon and describe, is the dominion whose duration and limits those prophecies declare. But the dominion of Antichrist which the prophecies insist upon and describe, is not any dominion over a particular province in Italy, but the dominion by which he succeeds the four great monarchies of the world (Dan. 7); the dominion by which he succeeds the dragon in "his power, throne and great authority" (Rev. 13:2); the dominion in which he has "power given him over all kindreds, tongues and nations" (v. 7); the dominion by which "the great whore sits on many waters" (ch. 17:1); which the angel explains to be "peoples and multitudes and nations and tongues" (v. 15); and the dominion in which he reigns over the ten kings, into

8. Rev. 18:10, 17, 19.—JE.
9. *Paraphrase and Notes*, pp. xxii, 106.

which the Roman Empire is divided (Rev. 13:1 and 17:3, 12–13). The beast that had ten horns, is not the city of Rome and the neighboring region, but the Roman Empire; they are the horns or the kings, not of the city, but of the empire. If we consider what is expressed in the passages themselves, which speak of the three years and half of Antichrist, they will lead us to understand something very diverse from the duration of his temporal dominion over St. Peter's Patrimony. In Dan. 7:25 "the time, times and an half," of the little horn, is expressly the continuance of time wherein "it shall be given to him to change times and laws, and wear out the saints of the Most High": and in ch. 12:7 'tis spoken of as the time of his scattering "the power of the holy people": in Rev. 11:2 the forty and two months is spoken of as the time of Antichrist's treading underfoot the court of the temple and the holy city; i.e., the external or visible Christian church abroad in the world, or the nations of Christendom. In v. 3 the 1260 days of Antichrist are spoken of as the time of the witnesses' prophesying in sackcloth; and in ch. 12:6 and 14, the time of the woman's being in the wilderness, which was through the great power that Antichrist had over the Christian world, and not his small temporal dominion in Italy.

'Tis true, some regard is had in the prophecies to the city of Rome, the city built on seven hills: which being the fountain of all rule and authority in the Roman monarchy, and the capital city of the empire, from whence the whole empire was denominated, and the place where the head of the empire usually resided, was properly made use of by the angel (Rev. 17:9, 18), to shew what empire Antichrist should rule over, and what city he should usually reside in. And this is all that can be meant by the words of the angel; and not that those streets and walls, and that very ground, were such main and essential things in what the prophecy intended by the beast; that when Antichrist's dominion began in *that place*, then the beast began; and when his reign ceases there, then the beast ceases. For if so, then it will follow, that the beast had his head wounded to death a second time, and ceased to be, when the popes resided at Avignon in France,[1] for the best part of a century; when not only the popes did not reside in Rome, nor in any part of St. Peter's Patrimony, nor any part of Italy; but some of them were neither Romans, nor Italians. Though the angel says of the great whore (Rev. 17:18), "The woman which thou sawest, is that great city which reigns over the kings of the earth": yet by the city, in this case, is not meant

---

1. A city in southern France which served as the seat of the papacy during the "Babylonian Captivity" of the popes, 1309–77.

so much what was contained within those Roman walls, as the Roman Empire; as is evident by ch. 11:8. "And their dead bodies shall lie in the street of the great city, which is spiritually called Sodom and Egypt." Here, by "the great city," neither Mr. Lowman himself, nor I suppose any other Protestant interpreter, understands the city of Rome, strictly speaking, but the Roman monarchy.[2]

And though it be true, as Mr. Lowman observes, the Pope's ecclesiastical monarchy, and power and influence through Christendom, was greatly established and advanced by Pepin's making him a temporal prince over the exarchate of Ravenna;[3] yet, I would ask, whether the Pope's power and influence in the world, and his ability to disturb the quiet of the nations of Christendom, and (as 'tis expressed in Daniel 7:25) "to change times and laws," and to carry his own designs, in the various countries and kingdoms of Europe, was not greater before Pepin, than it is now, and has been for a long time? And yet Mr. Lowman supposes that *now* is properly the time of Antichrist's reign, that the 1260 years of his reign continues, and will continue for about 270 years longer; though his power be now so small, and has been declining ever since the Reformation, and still declines continually.[4]

One thing that Mr. Lowman supposes confirms his opinion of so late a beginning of the 1260 years of the reign of the beast, is the order of the several *periods* of this prophecy, and the manner of their *succeeding* one another.[5]

As to his particular scheme of the seven periods, so divided and limited, and so obviously ranked in such order, and following one another in such direct and continued succession, and each ending in a state of peace, safety and happiness to the church of God, it seems to me to be more ingenious than solid, and that many things might be said to demonstrate it not to be founded in the truth of things, and the real design of the divine author of this prophecy. But now to enter into a particular and full examination of it, would be to lengthen out this discourse far beyond its proper limits. I would only observe (which directly concerns my present purpose) that to make out this scheme, Mr. Lowman supposes that the fifth and sixth trumpets, that bring on the two first woes, and the whole 9th ch. of the Revelation, altogether respects

2. See Lowman, *Paraphrase and Notes*, p. 111.

3. Ibid., pp. xx–xxii, 136–37.

4. Ibid., pp. 173–74, 204–05.

5. Concerning Lowman's views on the structure of the Revelation, see above, pp. 56–59, and ibid., the preface and esp. pp. xi and 106.

the Saracens.[6] But it appears to me not very credible, that the Saracens should have so much said of 'em in this prophecy, as to have a whole chapter taken up about them, and not a word in the whole prophecy be said about the Turks, who immediately succeeded them[7] in the same religion, and proceeding on the same principles, and were so much more considerable, and brought vastly greater calamities on the Christian world, and have set up and long maintained one of the greatest, strongest and most extraordinary empires that ever the world saw, and have been the most terrible scourge to Christendom, that ever divine providence made use of, and one of the greatest of all God's plagues on the world of mankind.

Mr. Lowman, in pursuance of his scheme, also supposes, (which is yet more incredible) this period of the trumpets ends in "a state of safety, peace and happiness to the church of God"; so that, on that occasion, "there are great voices in heaven, saying, The kingdoms of this world are become the kingdoms of our Lord and of his Christ" (ch. 11:15).[8] And yet he supposes, that it issues in setting up the kingdom of Antichrist;[9] and that about that very time, when these heavenly voices so joyfully proclaimed this, the beast was enthroned, and the time, times, and half, or 1260 days of his reign began, which is spoken of everywhere, as the time of the church's greatest darkness and trouble, the time wherein the little horn should "wear out the saints of the Most High" (Dan. 7:25), the time appointed for his scattering "the power of the holy people" (Dan. 12:7), the time of the woman's being in the wilderness (Rev. 12:6, 14), the time of treading underfoot the court of the temple (ch. 11:2), and the time of the witnesses' prophesying in sackcloth (ch. 11:3).

However, I do not deny that the time when Mr. Lowman supposes the reign of the beast began, even the time when Pepin confirmed to the Pope his temporal dominions in Italy, was a time of the great increase and advancement of the power of Antichrist in the world, and a notable epoch. And if I may be allowed humbly to offer what appears to me to

6. *Paraphrase and Notes*, pp. 80–97.

7. For though it be true, that the reign of Othman, or Ottoman, who began what they call the Ottoman Empire, was a long time after this; yet the Turks themselves, under other princes, in the government they set up in territories that had formerly been possessed by Christians, and in their overrunning and ravaging Christian countries, immediately succeeded the Saracens; and from thenceforward have been a terrible, and almost continual scourge to the church.—JE.

8. Preface of his *Paraphrase*, etc., pp. xiii, xiv, and xvi.—JE.

9. *Paraphrase and Notes*, pp. x–xxii.

be the truth with relation to the rise and fall of Antichrist; it is this. As the power of Antichrist, and the corruption of the apostate church, rose not at once, but by several notable steps and degrees; so it will in the like manner fall: and that divers steps and seasons of destruction to the spiritual Babylon, and revival and advancement of the true church, are prophesied of under one. Though it be true, that there is some particular event, that prevails above all others in the intention of the prophecy, some one remarkable season of the destruction of the Church of Rome and papal power and corruption, and advancement of true religion, that the prophecies have a principal respect to.

It was certainly thus with regard to the prophecies of the destruction of old Babylon, and the church's deliverance from captivity and oppression by that city and kingdom; which is abundantly alluded to in these prophecies of the Revelation, as a noted type of the oppression of the church of Christ by the Church of Rome, calling the latter so often by the name of Babylon, and the church of Christ Jerusalem. The captivity of the Jews by the Babylonians was not perfected at once, but was brought on by several notable steps. So neither was the restoration of the Jewish church, after the captivity, perfected at once. It was several times foretold, that the duration of the captivity should be 70 years; and also, that after 70 years were accomplished, God would destroy Babylon (Jer. 25:11–12 ff.). But this period had manifestly several different beginnings, and several endings. Thus from Jehoiakim's captivity [II Chron. 36:5–8] to Cyrus' decree, for the return of the Jews, and the rebuilding of Jerusalem [II Chron. 36:22–23], was 70 years. And from Zedekiah's captivity [II Kgs. 25:1–7] to Darius' decree (Ezra 6), 70 years. And from the last carrying away of all (Jer. 52:30), to the finishing and dedication of the temple [Ezra 6], was also 70 years. So also the prophecies of Babylon's destruction were fulfilled by several steps. These prophecies seem to have a principal respect to that destruction that was accomplished by Cyrus, at the end of the first 70 years forementioned: but there were other things in the very same prophecies, that were not fulfilled till the 4th year of Darius; when what remained of Babylon was subject to another dreadful destruction; which in a great measure completed its desolation; which was at the end of the second 70 years, and at the same time that the restoration of the Jews was perfected by the decree of Darius.[1] But yet, there were many other things contained in the same prophecies of Babylon's destruction, rendering it thence-

1. Prideaux's *Connection* (9th ed.), Part I, Vol. 1, pp. 183–184, 267–269, 271 and 272.—JE. [See above, p. 64 and AP, p. 109.]

forward perfectly and perpetually desolate, and the haunt of serpents and wild beasts, that were not fulfilled till more than 200 years after, in the time of Seleucus king of Syria.[2] So also it was with respect to the prophecies of the destruction of Tyre, in the 26th, 27th and 28th chapters of Ezekiel; from which many of the expressions used in the Revelation, concerning the destruction of the kingdom of Antichrist, are taken, and which is evidently made use of in Scripture as a type of the latter. These prophecies of the destruction of Tyre were fulfilled by various steps. Many things were fulfilled in the destruction of the old city of Nebuchadnezzar;[3] and yet other parts of the same prophecy were fulfilled by Alexander;[4] which was about 240 years afterwards.[5] And yet both these desolations are prophesied of under one.

And thus it seems to me very probable, that it will prove, with respect to the prophecies of the destruction of mystical Babylon. 'Tis I think pretty manifest by the prophecies, that this antichristian hierarchy and apostate church will at last be so destroyed, that there shall be no remainders of it left, and shall have as perfect a desolation, before God has done with her, as old Babylon had; there shall be no such thing as Pope or Church of Rome in the world.[6] It seems also pretty manifest that after that event that is chiefly intended in the prophecies of Antichrist's destruction, there will be some remains of the Romish Church. This appears by that most particular and large description of that destruction (Rev. 18). There it seems to be implied, not only that many shall yet remain of the Church of Rome, that shall bewail her overthrow, of her people and clergy (vv. 11, 15, 17–18); but that there should be some princes among them, "kings of the earth, that have committed fornication, and lived deliciously with her" (vv. 9–10); and it is exceeding improbable in itself, that every papist, in each quarter of the world, should be destroyed, or cease from the world, at one blow. And as long as so considerable a number remains, as may be gathered from the prophecy, they will doubtless have an hierarchy; and there will be one among them that will bear the name of a Pope. Although the Church of Rome shall be mainly destroyed, and the interest of popery shall be sunk very low in the world; so that there will yet remain such a

---

2. Prideaux, *Connection*, Part I, Vol. 2, pp. 808–812.—JE. [Seleucus I Nicator (d. 281), founder of the Seleucid empire in Asia, became governor of Babylon in 321 B.C.]

3. Ibid., Vol. 1, pp. 128–130.—JE.

4. Ibid., Vol. 2, p. 693.—JE.

5. Nebuchadnezzar, the king of Babylonia (605?–562), destroyed Tyre in 572 B.C. Alexander the Great, king of Macedonia (356–23 B.C.), sacked the city in 332.

6. See Rev. 18:21–23 and 19:20–21. Dan. 7:26–27.—JE.

thing as a papal church and hierarchy in the world, to be wholly extirpated at another period, sometime after that great overthrow principally insisted on in the prophecies. And this second destruction of Antichrist, or rather extirpation of his remains, together with the complete extirpation of all remains of Mahometanism, heathenism and heresy through the world, and the finishing stroke towards the overthrow of Satan's visible kingdom on earth, and so the beginning of the millennium, or spiritual rest of the world, may, for aught I know, be about the time Mr. Lowman speaks of;[7] agreeable to the opinion of the ancient Jews, and many Christian divines that have followed them, that the world would stand six thousand years; and then, the seventh thousand years should be the world's rest or sabbath.[8] The ruin of the popish interest is but a small part of what is requisite, in order to introduce and settle such a state of things, as the world is represented as being in, in that millennium that is described Rev. 20, wherein Satan's visible kingdom is everywhere totally extirpated, and a perfect end put to all heresies, delusions and false religions whatsoever, through the whole earth, and Satan thenceforward "deceives the nations no more" [v. 3], and has no place anywhere but in hell. This is the sabbatism of the world; when all shall be in a holy rest, when the wolf shall dwell with the lamb, and there shall be nothing to hurt or offend, and there shall be abundance of peace, and "the earth shall be full of the knowledge of the Lord as the waters cover the seas" [Is. 11:9], and God's people shall dwell in quiet resting places. There is not the least reason to think, that all this will be brought to pass as it were at one stroke, or that from the present lamentable state of things, there should be brought about and completed the destruction of the Church of Rome, the entire extirpation of all infidelity, heresies, superstitions and schisms, through all Christendom, and the conversion of all the Jews, and the full enlightening and conversion of all Mahometan and heathen nations, through the whole earth, on every side of the globe, and from the north to the south pole, and the full settlement of all in the pure Christian faith and order, all as it were in the issue of one battle, and by means of the victory of the church in one great conflict with her enemies. This would contradict many things in Scripture, which represent this great event to be brought to pass by a gradual progress of religion; as leaven that gradually spreads, till it has diffused itself through the whole lump; and a plant of

7. For Lowman's discussion of the time of the millennium, see *Paraphrase and Notes*, pp. xxxiii, 204–05.

8. JE's earliest reflections in the AP on the idea of the world's sabbath are on pp. 129–30.

mustard, which from a very small seed, gradually becomes a great tree (Matt. 13:31–33); "and like seed which a man casts into the ground, that springs and grows up, night and day; and first brings forth the blade, then the ear, then the full corn in the ear" [Mark 4:26–28]. And especially would this contradict the prophetical representation in Ezek. 47, where the progress of religion is represented by the gradual increase of the waters of the sanctuary; being first a small spring issuing out from under the threshold of the temple; and then, after they had run a thousand cubits, being up to the ankles; and at the end of another thousand cubits, up to the knees; and at the end of another thousand, up to the loins; and afterwards a great river, that could not be passed over; and being finally brought into the sea, and healing the waters even of the vast ocean. If the Spirit of God should be immediately poured out, and that great work of God's power and grace should now begin, which in its progress and issue should complete this glorious effect; there must be an amazing and unparalleled progress of the work and manifestation of divine power to bring so much to pass, by the year 2000. Would it not be a great thing, to be accomplished in one half century, that religion, in the power and purity of it, should so prevail, as to gain the conquest over all those many things that stand in opposition to it among Protestants, and gain the upper hand through the Protestant world? And if in another, it should go on so to prevail, as to get the victory over all the opposition and strength of the kingdom of Antichrist, so as to gain the ascendant in that which is now the popish world? And if in a third half century, it should prevail and subdue the greater part of the Mahometan world, and bring in the Jewish nation, in all their dispersions? And then in the next whole century, the whole heathen world should be enlightened and converted to the Christian faith, throughout all parts of Africa, Asia, America and Terra Australis, and be thoroughly settled in Christian faith and order, without any remainders of their old delusions and superstitions, and this attended with an utter extirpation of the remnant of the Church of Rome, and all the relics of Mahometanism, heresy, schism and enthusiasm, and a suppression of all remains of open vice and immorality, and every sort of visible enemy to true religion, through the whole earth, and bring to an end all the unhappy commotions, tumults, and calamities occasioned by such great changes, and all things so adjusted and settled through the world, that the world thenceforward should enjoy an holy rest or sabbatism?

I have thus distinquished what belongs to a bringing of the world from its present state, to the happy state of the millennium, the better to give a view of the greatness of the work; and not, that I pretend so much as to conjecture, that things will be accomplished just in this order. The whole work is not the less great and wonderful, to be accomplished in such a space of time, in whatever order the different parts of it succeed each other. They that think that what has been mentioned would not be swift progress, yea amazingly swift, don't consider how great the work is, and the vast and innumerable obstacles that are in the way. It was a wonderful thing, when the Christian religion, after Christ's ascension, so prevailed, as to get the ascendant in the Roman Empire in about 300 years; but that was nothing to this.

Ans. 4. There are, as I apprehend, good reasons to hope, that that work of God's Spirit will begin in a little time, which in the progress of it will overthrow the kingdom of Antichrist, and in its issue destroy Satan's visible kingdom on earth.

The prophecy of the 6th vial (Rev. 16:12–16),[9] if we take it in its connection with the other vials, and consider those providential events, by which the preceding vials have manifestly been fulfilled, I humbly conceive, affords just ground for such a hope.

'Tis very plain from this whole chapter, as also the preceding and following, that all these seven vials are vials of God's wrath on Antichrist; one is not poured out on the Jews, another on the Turks, another on pagans, another on the Church of Rome; but they all signify God's successive judgments or plagues on the beast and his kingdom, which is in this chapter and almost everywhere in this book, called "Great Babylon." And therefore undoubtedly, when it is said, "The sixth angel poured out his vial on the river Euphrates, and the water thereof was dried up, that the way of the kings of the East might be prepared" [Rev. 16:12]; by the river Euphrates is meant something some way appertaining to this mystical Babylon; as that river that ran through Chaldea, called Euphrates, was something appertaining to the literal Babylon. And 'tis very manifest, that here is in the prophecy of this vial an allusion to that by which the way was prepared for the destruction of Babylon by Cyrus; which was by turning the channel of the river Euphrates, which ran through the midst of the city, whereby the way of the kings of the East, the princes of Media and Persia, was prepared to come in under the walls of the city, at each end, where the waters used to run, and destroy it; as they did that night wherein Daniel interpreted the handwriting on the wall, against Belshazzar (Dan. 5:30). The

9. For JE's views on the 6th vial, see above, pp. 45–46, and AP, pp. 184–91 and 298–305.

prophecies of Babylon's destruction, do from time to time take notice of this way of destroying her, by drying up the waters of the river Euphrates, to prepare the way for her enemies (Is. 44:27–28). "That saith to the deep, Be dry, and I will dry up thy rivers; that saith of Cyrus, He is my servant, and shall perform all my pleasure." Jer. 51:31–32, "One post shall run to meet another, to shew the king of Babylon that his city is taken at one end, and that the passages are stopped, and the reeds they have burnt with fire, and the men of war are affrighted." And v. 36, "I will dry up her sea, and make her springs dry." The Medes and Persians, the people that destroyed Babylon, dwelt to the eastward of Babylon, and are spoken of as coming from the East to her destruction (Is. 46:11). "Calling a ravenous bird from the East, the man that executeth my counsel, from a far country." And the princes that joined with this ravenous bird from the East, in this affair of destroying Babylon, are called "kings" (Jer. 51:11). "The Lord hath raised up the spirit of the kings of the Medes; for his device is against Babylon to destroy it." V. 28, "Prepare against her the nations, with the kings of the Medes, the captains thereof, and the rulers thereof." The drying the channel of the river Euphrates, to prepare the way for these kings and captains of the East, to enter into that city, under its high walls, was the last thing done by the besiegers of Babylon, before her actual destruction: as this sixth vial is the last vial of God's wrath but one, on the mystical Babylon; and the effect of it, the drying up the channel of the river Euphrates, is the last thing done against it, before its actual destruction by the seventh vial, and opens the way for those that fight in a spiritual war against it, speedily to bring on its ruin.

Hence I think it may without dispute be determined, that by the river Euphrates in the prophecy of this vial, is meant something appertaining or relating to the mystical Babylon, or the antichristian church and kingdom, that serves that, or is a benefit to it, in a way answerable to that in which the river Euphrates served old Babylon, and the removal of which will in like manner prepare the way for her enemies to destroy her. And therefore what we have to do in the first place, in order to find out what is intended by the river Euphrates, in this prophecy, is to consider how the literal Euphrates served old Babylon. And it may be noted, that Euphrates was of remarkable benefit to that city in two respects: it served the city as a *supply*; it was let through the midst of the city by an artificial canal, and ran through the midst of the palace of the king of Babylon; that part of his palace called the old palace, standing on one side, and the other part called the new palace, on the other; with communications from one part to another, above the waters, by a bridge, and under the waters, by a vaulted or arched passage; that the city, and especially the palace, might have the convenience of its waters, and be plentifully supplied with water. And another way that the waters of Euphrates served Babylon, was as an *impediment* and *obstacle* in the way of its enemies, to hinder their access to it to destroy it. For there was a vast moat round the city, without the walls, of prodigious width and depth, filled with the water of the river, to hinder the access of her besiegers: and at each end of the city, the river served instead of walls. And therefore when Cyrus had dried up the river, the moat was emptied, and the channel of the river under the walls left dry; and so his way was prepared.

And therefore 'tis natural to suppose, that by drying up the waters of the river Euphrates, in the prophecies of the destruction of the new Babylon, to prepare the way of her enemies, is meant the drying up her *incomes* and *supplies*; and the removal of those things that hitherto have been the chief obstacles in the way of those that in this book are represented as at war with her and seeking her destruction (spoken of Rev. 19:11–21, and ch. 12:7), that have hindered their progress and success, or that have been the chief impediments in the way of the Protestant religion. The first thing is the drying the streams of the wealth of the new Babylon, the temporal supplies, revenues and vast incomes of the Romish Church, and riches of the popish dominions. "Waters" in scripture language very often signify provision and supplies, both temporal and spiritual; as in Prov. 9:17; Is. 33:16, 43:20, 55:1 and 58:11; Jer. 2:13 and 18, 17:8 and 13, and in other places innumerable. The temporal supplies of a people are very often in Scripture called "waters"; as Is. 5:13. "Therefore my people is gone into captivity, and their honorable men are famished, and their multitude dried up with thirst," i.e., deprived of the supports and supplies of life. And the drying up the waters of a city or kingdom, is often used in scripture prophecy, for the depriving them of their wealth, as the Scripture explains itself (Hos. 13:15), "His spring shall become dry, and his fountain shall be dried up; he shall spoil the treasure of all pleasant vessels." Is. 15:6–7, "The waters of Nimrim shall be desolate; for the hay is withered; the grass faileth; there is no green thing. Therefore the abundance they have gotten, and that which they have laid up, shall they carry away to the brook of the willows." By the "brook of the willows" there seems to be a reference to the waters of Assyria or Chaldea, whose streams abounded with willows (compare Ps. 137:2). So that the carrying away the treasures of Moab, and adding of them to the treasures of Assyria, is here represented by the figure of turning away the waters of Nimrim from the country of Moab, and adding them to the waters of Assyria, as the prophecy explains itself. Yea, even in the prophecies of the destruction of Babylon itself, the depriving her of her treasures, seems to be one thing intended by the drying up of her waters. This seems manifest by the words of the prophecy in Jer. 50:37, 38. "A sword is upon her treasures, and they shall be robbed; a drought is upon her waters, and they shall be dried up." Compared with ch. 51:13, "O thou that dwellest upon many waters, abundant in treasures": with v. 36, "I will dry up her sea, and make her springs dry." The wealth, revenues and vast incomes of the Church of Rome, are the waters by which that Babylon has been nourished and supported; these are the waters which the popish clergy and members of the Romish hierarchy thirst after, and are continually drinking down, with insatiable appetite; and they are waters that have been flowing into that spiritual city like a great river; ecclesiastical persons possessing a very great part of the wealth of the popish dominions: as this Babylon is represented as vastly rich, in this prophecy of the Apocalypse, especially in the 17th and 18th chapters. These are especially the waters that supply the palace of the king of this new Babylon, viz., the Pope; as the river Euphrates ran through the midst of the palace of the king of old Babylon. The revenues of the Pope have been like the waters of a great river, coming into his palace, from innumerable fountains, and by innumerable branches and lesser streams, coming from many various and distant countries.

This prophecy represents to us two cities very contrary the one to the other; viz., New Babylon and the New Jerusalem, and a river running through the midst of each. The New Jerusalem, which signifies the church of Christ, especially in her best estate, is described as having a river running through the midst of it (Rev. 22:1–2). This river, as might easily be made most evident, by comparing this with abundance of other scriptures, undoubtedly signifies the divine supplies, and rich and abundant spiritual incomes and provision of that holy city. Mr. Lowman, in his late exposition, says, "It represents a constant provision for the comfortable and happy life of all the inhabitants of this city of God."[1] And in his notes on the same place, observes as follows; "Water," (says he) "as necessary to the support of life, and as it contributes in great cities, especially in hot eastern countries, to the ornament of the place, and delight of the inhabitants, is a very proper represen-

1. *Paraphrase and Notes*, p. 179.

tation of the enjoyment of all things, both for the support and pleasure of life."[2] As the river that runs through the New Jerusalem, the church of Christ, that refreshes that holy spiritual society, signifies their spiritual supplies, to satisfy their spiritual thirst; so the river that runs through the new Babylon, the antichristian church, that wicked carnal society, signifies, according to the opposite character of the city, her worldly, carnal supplies, to satisfy their carnal desires and thirstings.

This New Jerusalem is called in this book the "paradise of God"; and therefore is represented as having the tree of life growing in it (chs. 2:7 and 22:2). And it being described, as though a river ran through the midst of it, there seems to be some allusion to the ancient paradise in Eden, of which we are told that there ran a river through the midst of it to water it (Gen. 2:10); i.e., to supply the plants of it with nourishment. And this river was this very same river Euphrates, that afterwards ran through Babylon. And in one and the other, it represented the divers supplies of two opposite cities: in Eden, it represented the spiritual supplies and wealth of the true Christian church, in her spiritual advancement and glory; and seems to be so made use of Rev. 22:1–2. In the other it represented the outward carnal supplies of the false antichristian church, in her worldly pomp and vain glory (ch. 16:12).

When the waters that supply this mystical Babylon, come to be dried up in this sense, it will prepare the way for the enemies of antichristian corruption, that seek her overthrow. The wealth of the Church of Rome, and of the powers that support it, is very much its defense. After the streams of her revenues and riches are dried up, or very greatly diminished, her walls will be as it were broken down, and she will become weak and defenseless, and exposed to easy ruin.

When Joab had taken that part of the city of Rabbah, that was called "the city of waters," whence the city had its supply of water, the fountains of the brook Jabbok being probably there; and which was also called the royal city, probably because there the king had his palace and gardens, on the account of its peculiar pleasantness; I say, when he had taken this, the conquest of the rest of the city was easy; his message to David implies that the city now might be taken at pleasure (II Sam. 12:27–28). 'Tis possible that by the pouring out of the sixth vial to dry up the river of the mystical Babylon, there may be something like the taking the city of waters in Rabbah: some one of the chief of the popish powers, that has been the main strength and support of the popish cause, or from whence that church has its chief supplies, may be de-

2. Ibid., p. 268.

stroyed, or converted, or greatly reduced. But this events must determine.

In the prophecies of Egypt's destruction, it is signified, that when their rivers and waters should be dried up, in that sense, that the streams of their temporal supplies should be averted from them, their defense would be gone (Is. 19:4–8). "The Egyptians will I give over into the hand of a cruel lord . . . and the waters shall fail from the sea, and the river shall be wasted and dried up, and the brooks of defense shall be emptied and dried up, and the reeds and flags shall wither; . . . everything sown by the brooks shall wither: . . . the fishers also shall mourn."

Those whose way was prepared to come in and destroy Babylon, by the drying up the river of Euphrates, were the army that was at war with Babylon, Cyrus the king, and his host, that sought her overthrow: so there seems to be all reason to suppose, that those whose way will be prepared to come in and destroy mystical Babylon, by drying up the mystical Euphrates, are that king and army that are in this book of Revelation represented as at war with Antichrist. And what king and army that is, we may see in chs. 12:7 and 19:11, to the end; Michael the king of angels, and his angels; he "whose name is called the Word of God," and "that has on his vesture and on his thigh a name written, 'King of Kings, and Lord of Lords' "; and the heavenly armies that follow him, "clothed in fine linen white and clean." Cyrus the chief of the kings of the East, that destroyed Babylon, and redeemed God's church from thence, and restored Jerusalem, seems in that particular affair very manifestly to be spoken of as a type of Christ: God calls him "his shepherd, to perform his pleasure, to say to Jerusalem, Thou shalt be built, and to the temple, Thy foundation shall be laid" (Is. 44:28). God calls him his messiah[3] (ch. 45:1); "Thus saith the Lord to his a-nointed" (in the original, "to his messiah"), "to Cyrus." He is spoken of as one that God had raised up in righteousness, that he might build his city, and freely redeem his captives, or let them go without price or reward (ch. 45:13). He is said to be one whom God has loved (ch. 48:14). In like manner as the Messiah is said to be God's elect, in whom his soul delighteth [Is. 42:1]. As by Babylon, in the Revelation, is meant that antichristian society that is typified by old Babylon; so by the kings of the East, that should destroy this antichristian church, must be meant those enemies of it that were typified by Cyrus and other chieftains of the East, that destroyed old Babylon; viz., Christ, who was born, lived,

3. לְמָשִׁיחוֹ

died and rose in the East, together with those spiritual princes that follow him, the principalities and powers in heavenly places, and those ministers and saints that are kings and priests, and shall reign on earth; especially those leaders and heads of God's people, those Christian ministers and magistrates, that shall be distinguished as public blessings to his church, and chief instruments of the overthrow of Antichrist.

As the river Euphrates served the city of Babylon as a supply, so it also was before observed, it served as an impediment or obstacle to hinder the access of its enemies: as there was a vast moat round the city, filled with the water of the river, which was left empty when Euphrates was dried up. And therefore we may suppose that another thing meant by the effect of the sixth vial, is the removal of those things which hitherto have been the chief obstacles in the way of the progress of the true religion, and the victory of the church of Christ over her enemies: which have been the corrupt doctrines and practices that have prevailed in Protestant countries, and the doubts and difficulties that attend many doctrines of the true religion, and the many divisions and contentions that subsist among Protestants. The removal of those would wonderfully prepare the way for Christ and his armies, to go forward and prevail against their enemies, in a glorious propagation of true religion. So that this vial, which is to prepare the way for Christ and his people, seems to have respect to that remarkable preparing the way for Christ, by leveling mountains, exalting valleys, drying up rivers, and removing stumbling blocks, which is often spoken of in the prophecies, as what shall next precede the church's latter-day glory; as Is. 42:13 ff. "The Lord shall go forth as a mighty man; he shall stir up jealousy as a man of war; . . . he shall prevail against his enemies. . . . I will make waste mountains and hills, and dry up all their herbs; and I will make the rivers islands, and I will dry up the pools; and I will bring the blind by a way that they know not, and I will lead them in paths that they have not known; I will make darkness light before them, and crooked things straight: these things will I do unto them, and not forsake them." Ch. 40:3–5, "Prepare ye the way of the Lord, make straight in the desert an highway for our God: every valley shall be exalted, and every mountain and hill shall be made low, and the crooked shall be made straight, and rough places plain; and the glory of the Lord shall be revealed, and all flesh shall see it together." Ch. 11:15–16, "And the Lord shall utterly destroy the tongue of the Egyptian sea, and with his mighty wind shall he shake his hand over the river, and shall smite it in the seven streams thereof, and make men go over dry-shod: and there shall be an highway for the remnant of his people which shall be left, from Assyria, like as it was to Israel, in the day that he came out of the land of Egypt." Ch. 57:14, "Cast ye up, cast ye up, prepare the way, take up the stumbling block out of the way of my people." And ch. 62: 10, "Go through, go through the gates; prepare ye the way of the people; cast up, cast up the highway; gather out the stones; lift up a standard for the people." Zech. 10:10–12, "I will bring them again also out of the land of Egypt, and gather them out of Assyria; and I will bring them into the land of Gilead and Lebanon; and place shall not be found for them. And he shall pass through the sea with affliction, and shall smite the waves of the sea; and all the deeps of the river shall dry up: and the pride of Assyria shall be brought down, and the scepter of Egypt shall depart away: and I will strengthen them in the Lord, and they shall walk up and down in his name, saith the Lord." And 'tis worthy to be remarked that as Cyrus' destroying Babylon, and letting go God's captives from thence, and restoring Jerusalem, is certainly typical of Christ's destroying mystical Babylon, and delivering his people from her tyranny, and gloriously building up the spiritual Jerusalem in the latter days; so God's preparing Cyrus' way, by drying up the river Euphrates, is spoken of in terms like those that are used in those prophecies that have been mentioned, to signify the preparing Christ's way, when he shall come to accomplish the latter event. Thus God says concerning Cyrus (Is. 45:2), "I will go before thee, and make crooked places straight." And v. 13, "I will direct," or "make straight" (as it is in the margin)[4] "all his ways." This is like ch. 40:3–4. "Prepare ye the way of the Lord; make straight in the desert an highway for our God. . . . The crooked things shall be made straight." Ch. 42:16, "I will make darkness light before them, and crooked things straight."

If any should object against understanding the river Euphrates in Rev. 16:12 as signifying what has been supposed, that when mention is made of the river Euphrates, in another place in this prophecy, 'tis manifestly not so to be understood, viz., in ch. 9:14. "Saying to the sixth angel which had the trumpet, Loose the four angels which are bound in the great river Euphrates": and that there is no reason to understand the river Euphrates in the vision of the sixth vial, as signifying something diverse from what is meant by the same river in the vision of the sixth trumpet:

I answer, that there appears to me to be good reason for a diverse

4. See the margin of the printed text in JE's "Blank Bible," p. 514, for this second translation.

understanding of the river Euphrates in these two different places: the diversity of the scene of the vision, and of the kind of representation, in those two divers parts of this prophecy, naturally leads to it, and requires it. It is in this book as it is in the Old Testament: when the river Euphates is spoken of in the Old Testament, both in the histories and prophecies, it is mentioned with regard to a twofold relation of that river: viz., 1st, with regard to its relation to Babylon. And as it was related to that, it was something belonging to that city, as its defense and supply, as has been represented. Thus the river Euphrates is spoken of in many places that have been already observed, and others that might be mentioned. 2ndly, this river is spoken of with regard to its relation to the land of Israel, God's visible people. And as it was related to that, it was its eastern boundary. It is so spoken of Gen. 15:18; Ex. 23:31; Deut. 1:7 and 11:24; Josh. 1:4; II Sam. 8:3; I Chron. 18:3; I Kgs. 4:21; Ezra 4:20. Agreeable to this diverse respect or relation of this river, under which it is mentioned in the Old Testament, so must we understand it differently in different parts of the prophecy of this book of Revelation, according as the nature and subject of the vision requires. In the 16th ch. where the prophecy is about Babylon, and the vision is of God's plagues on Babylon, preparing the way for her destruction, there, when the river Euphrates is mentioned, we are naturally and necessarily led to consider it as something belonging to Babylon, appertaining to the mystical Babylon, as Euphrates did to old Babylon. But we can't understand it so in the 9th ch., for there the prophecy is not about Babylon. To mention Euphrates there, as something belonging to Babylon, would have been improper; for the nature of the vision, and prophetical representation, did not lead to it, nor allow it. John had had no vision of Babylon; that kind of representation had not been made to him; there is not a word said about Babylon till we come to the second part of this prophecy, after John had the vision of the second book, and Christ had said to him, "Thou must prophesy again before peoples, and nations, and kings" (ch. 10:11). The scene of the vision, in the former part of the prophecy, had been more especially the land of Israel; and the vision is concerning two sorts of persons there, viz., those of the tribes of Israel that had the seal of God in their foreheads, and those wicked apostate Israelites that had not this mark. Compare ch. 7:3–8 and ch. 9:4. The vision in this 9th ch. is of God's judgments on those of the tribes of Israel, or in the land of Israel, which had not the seal of God in their foreheads. And therefore when mention is made (v. 14), of a judgment coming on them from the river Euphrates, this river is here spoken of in the former respect, viz., with regard to its relation to the land of Israel, as its eastern border; and thereby we must understand that God would bring some terrible calamity on Christendom from its eastern border, as he did when the Turks were let loose on Christendom.

If these things that have been spoken of, are intended in the prophecy of the sixth vial, it affords, as I conceive, great reason to hope that the beginning of that glorious work of God's Spirit, which in the progress and issue of it, will overthrow Antichrist, and introduce the glory of the latter days, is not very far off.

Mr. Lowman has, I think, put it beyond all reasonable doubt, that the 5th vial was poured out in the time of the Reformation.[5] It also appears satisfyingly, by his late exposition, that take one vial with another, it has not been 200 years from the beginning of one vial to the beginning of another, but about 180 years. But it is now about 220 years since the 5th vial began to be poured; and it is a long time since the main effects of it have been finished. And therefore if the 6th vial han't already begun to be poured out, it may well be speedily expected.

But with regard to the first thing that I have supposed to be signified by the effect of this vial, viz., the drying up the fountains and streams of the wealth and temporal incomes and supplies of the antichristian church and territories, I would propose it to consideration, whether or no many things that have come to pass within these twenty years past, may not be looked upon as probable beginnings of a fulfillment of this prophecy. Particularly what the kings of Spain and Portugal did some years since, when displeased with the Pope, forbidding any thenceforward going to Rome for investitures, etc., thereby cutting off two great streams of the Pope's wealth, from so great and rich a part of the popish world; and its becoming so frequent a thing of late for popish princes, in their wars, to make bold with the treasure of the church, and to tax the clergy within their dominions, as well as laity; or, which is equivalent, to oblige 'em to contribute great sums, under the name of "a free gift"; and also the late peeling and impoverishing the Pope's temporal dominions in Italy, by the armies of the Austrians, Neapolitans and Spaniards, passing and repassing through them, and living so much at discretion in them, of which the Pope has so loudly complained, and in vain; receiving nothing but menaces, when he has objected against giving liberty for the like passage, for the future.[6]

5. For Lowman's discussion of the 5th vial, see *Paraphrase and Notes*, pp. 195–99.
6. The deterioration of relations between Rome and several European monarchs during

These things make it hopeful that the time is coming when the princes of Europe, "the ten horns, shall hate the whore, and make her desolate and naked, and eat her flesh"; as Rev. 17:16, which will prepare the way for what next follows, "her being burnt with fire"; even as the sixth vial poured out, to consume the supplies of Antichrist, and strip him naked of his wealth, and as it were to pick his flesh off from his bones, will make way for what next follows, the seventh vial, that will consume Antichrist by the fierceness of God's wrath.

Besides these things that have been already mentioned, are also worthy to be considered the things that have lately happened to dry up the fountains and streams of the wealth of the antichristian dominions: as, the so far ruining the trade of France and Spain, that are the two chief popish kingdoms, the main support of the popish cause, and from whence the kingdom of Antichrist has had of late its main supplies. The almost miraculous taking of Cape Breton, in the year 1745, whereby was dried up one of the main sources of the wealth of the kingdom of France; and the no less, but yet more wonderful disappointment of the French, in their great attempt to repossess themselves of it, and the confounding of their great armada, under the Duke D'Anville, by a most visible hand of God against them, the last year;[7] and in now again baffling a second attempt of our obstinate enemies, this year, by delivering up their men-of-war, with their warlike forces and stores, in their way to America, into the hands of the English admirals Anson and Warren:[8] the strange and unaccountable consuming of the great magazines of the French East India Company, at Port Lorient, with their magnificent buildings, the last year; and its so wonderfully coming to pass, that scarce anything of the great stores there laid up, was saved out of the flames:[9] the awful destruction, by an earthquake, the last

---

the papacy of Clement XII (1730–40) had severe economic consequences for the papal states. Conflicts over the right to control and tax ecclesiastical incomes were constant. The papal states in Italy also suffered heavy losses during the early years of the papacy of Benedict XIV (1740–58) due to devastation by the armies in the War of the Austrian Succession. In 1745 Benedict wrote, "The Spaniards are the authors of our misfortune, but the Austrians expect to live entirely at our expense." See Pastor, *History of the Popes, 35,* 111.

7. Above, p. 361, n. 8.

8. On May 3, 1747, an English squadron under admirals Anson and Warren scattered a French fleet lying off Cape Finisterre, capturing a dozen or more of the vessels without great loss to the English. The French forfeited men and military supplies intended for a new assault upon the English in Canada. For their roles in the victory, both Anson and Warren were honored by the king. See BNL, Aug. 6, 1747, p. 2; Aug. 20, 1747, p. 1; and Sept. 10, 1747, pp. 1–2.

9. Boston newspapers reported the fire at Port Lorient on Mar. 24, 1746, which destroyed large stockpiles of war materiel. The port, located on the Bay of Biscay, served as the general magazine for several French naval squadrons. See BEP, June 23, 1746, p. 4.

year, of that great and rich city of Lima, the center of the South Sea trade, and the capital of Peru, the richest country in the world, from whence comes more of its silver and gold than any other country, from whence Spain is principally supplied with its wealth, and where the French had a great trade; the destruction of the city being attended with the destruction of all the ships in the harbor, which were dashed in pieces as it were in a moment, by the immediate hand of God; many of which were doubtless laden with vast treasures.[1] I might have mentioned the taking of Porto Bello, not long before this, by a very small force, though a place of very great strength, where the Spanish galleons used principally to go, to carry the wealth of Peru to Spain.[2] Besides the taking from the French and Spaniards so many of their ships, laden with vast riches, trading to the South Seas, the East and West Indies, and the Levant.

And here it is especially worthy of notice, that when the French seemed to have gotten so great an advantage of the English factory[3] at Madras, they were so frustrated of the benefit and gains they expected by it, by the hand of heaven against them, immediately pursuing the conquerors with tempest, wrecking their ships laden with our spoils; and after that, delivering up into the hands of the English their East India fleet, with their stores and immense treasures, intended for the confirming to themselves the advantage they seemed to have gained by the forementioned conquest;[4] at the same instant, also delivering into our hands their strong force intended for the regaining that great fountain of their wealth, which they had lost at Cape Breton. And since that, delivering into the hands of Sir Peter Warren so great a part of their vast and rich fleet from the West Indies.[5]

And one thing with relation to the taking of Cape Breton, though it may seem trivial, yet I don't think to be altogether inconsiderable in

1. An earthquake struck Lima on Oct. 28, 1746, causing violent waves which destroyed the vessels in the harbor. See BG, May 5, 1747, p. 3.

2. On Nov. 21, 1739, Admiral Edward Vernon captured Porto Bello, a Spanish port on the Isthmus of Panama. His attack provided an early indication of the determination of the English to pursue the imperial struggle in the Caribbean. See Leach, *Arms for Empire*, pp. 210–11.

3. I.e., trading station and settlement.

4. A French squadron captured the port of Madras in India on Sept. 10, 1746, and seized the goods of the East India Company. In October French vessels loaded with plunder were lost on the return voyage to Pondichéry when a gale struck the fleet off the Coromandel Coast. For a contemporary account, see BEP, June 22, 1747, p. 1.

5. During the summer of 1747 an English squadron under Admiral Warren preyed upon the French merchant fleet returning to France. Warren intercepted more than sixty vessels. See BNL, Aug. 20, 1747, p. 1; Aug. 27, 1747, p. 4; and Sept. 3, 1747, p. 3.

the present case; and that is, that hereby the antichristian dominions are deprived of a very great part of their fish, which makes no small part of the food and support of popish countries; their superstition forbidding them to eat any flesh for near a third part of the year. This they were supplied with much more from Cape Breton, than any place in the world in the possession of papists.[6] And the contention of France with the Dutch,[7] deprives 'em of most of their supply of this sort, which they had elsewhere. When the prophet Isaiah foretells the depriving Egypt of its wealth and temporal supplies, under the figure of drying up their rivers, this is particularly mentioned, that they should be deprived of their fish. Is. 19:4–8, "And the Egyptians will I give over into the hand of a cruel Lord. . . . And the waters shall fail from the sea, and the river shall be wasted and dried up; and they shall turn the rivers far away, and the brooks of defense shall be emptied and dried up. . . . The fishers also shall mourn, and all they that cast angle into the brooks shall lament, and they that spread nets upon the waters shall languish." This is expressed in the prophecies of drying up the waters, i.e., the supplies of Egypt; and this probably is implied in the prophecies of drying up the waters of that city that is spiritually called Egypt. And it may be noted, that this is not only a supply that the church of Antichrist has literally out of the waters, but is that part of their temporal supply which is eminently the supply and food of their antichristian superstition, or which their popish religion makes necessary for them.

These things duly considered, I imagine afford us ground to suppose, not only that the effect of this sixth vial is already begun, but that some progress is already made in it, and that this vial is now running apace. And when it shall be finished, there is all reason to suppose that the destruction of Antichrist will very speedily follow; and that the two last vials will succeed one another more closely than the other vials. When once the river Euphrates was dried up, and Cyrus' way was prepared, he delayed not, but immediately entered into the city to destroy it. Nor is it God's manner, when once his way is prepared, to delay to deliver his church and shew mercy to Zion. When once impediments are removed, Christ will no longer remain at a distance, but will be like a roe or a young hart, coming swiftly to the help of his people. When that cry is made (Is. 57:14), "Cast ye up, cast ye up,

6. See above, p. 32, n. 3.

7. The French invaded the United Netherlands in 1744 and again in 1746 and were successful in their military campaigns.

prepare the way," etc., "the high and lofty one that inhabits eternity," is represented as very near to revive the spirit of the contrite, and deliver his people with whom he had been wroth (vv. 15–21). When that cry is made (Is. 40), "Prepare ye the way of the Lord, make straight in the desert an highway for our God; every valley shall be exalted," etc., God tells his church, "that her warfare is accomplished," and the time to comfort her is come and that "the glory of the Lord now shall be revealed, and all flesh see it together" (vv. 1–5). And agreeably to these things, Christ on the pouring out the sixth vial, says, "Behold I come" (Rev. 16:15). The sixth vial is the forerunner of the seventh and last, to prepare its way. The angel that pours out this vial is the harbinger of Christ; and when the harbinger is come, the king is at hand. John the Baptist, that was Christ's harbinger, who came to level mountains and fill up valleys, proclaimed, "The kingdom of heaven is at hand" [Matt. 3:2]; and when he had prepared Christ's way, then "the Lord suddenly came into his temple, even the messenger of the covenant" (Mal. 3:1).

'Tis true, that we don't know how long this vial may continue running, and so Christ's way preparing, before 'tis fully prepared: but yet if there be reason to think the effect of this vial is begun, or is near, then there is reason also to think that the beginning of that great work of God's Spirit, in reviving of religion, which, before it is finished, will issue in Antichrist's ruin, is not far off. For 'tis pretty manifest, that the beginning of this work will accompany the sixth vial. For the gathering together of the armies on both sides, on the side of Christ and Antichrist, to that great battle that shall issue in the overthrow of the latter, will be under this vial; (compare Rev. 16:12–14 with ch. 19:11–21). And 'tis plain that Christ's manifesting himself, and wonderfully appearing after long hiding himself, to plead his own and his people's cause, and riding forth against his enemies in a glorious manner, and his people's following him in pure linen, or the practice of righteousness and pure religion, will be the thing that will give the alarm to Antichrist, and cause him to gather that vast host to make the utmost opposition. But this alarm and gathering together is represented as being under the sixth vial. So that it will be a great revival, and mighty progress of true religion under the sixth vial, eminently threatening the speedy and utter overthrow of Satan's kingdom on earth, that will so mightily rouse the old serpent, to exert himself with such exceeding violence, in that greatest conflict and struggle that ever he had with Christ and the church, since the world stood.

All the seven vials bring terrible judgments upon Antichrist; but there seems to be something distinguishing of the three last, the fifth, sixth and seventh, viz., that they more directly tend to the overthrow of his kingdom, and accordingly each of 'em is attended with a great reviving of religion. The fifth vial was attended with such a revival, and reformation, that greatly weakened and diminished the throne or kingdom of the beast, and went far towards its ruin. It seems as though the sixth vial should be much more so; for 'tis the distinguishing note of this vial, that it is the *preparatory* vial, which more than any other vial prepares the way for Christ's coming to destroy the kingdom of Antichrist, and set up his own kingdom in the world. A great outpouring of the Spirit accompanied that dispensation that was preparatory to Christ's coming in his public ministry, in the days of his flesh: so, much more, will a great outpouring of the Spirit accompany the dispensation that will be preparatory to Christ's coming in his kingdom.

And besides those things which belong to the preparation of Christ's way, which are so often represented by leveling mountains, drying up rivers, etc., viz., the unraveling intricacies, and removing difficulties attending Christian doctrines, the distinguishing between true religion and its false appearances, the detecting and exploding errors and corrupt principles, and the reforming the wicked lives of professors, which have been the chief stumbling blocks and obstacles that have hitherto hindered the progress of true religion; I say, these things, which seem to belong to this preparatory vial, are the proper work of the Spirit of God, promoting and advancing divine light and true piety, and can be the effect of nothing else.

And that the beginning of that glorious work of God's Spirit, which shall finally bring on the church's latter-day glory, will accompany that other effect of this vial, viz., the turning the streams of the wealth of the world, the bringing its treasures, and the gains of its trade and navigation, into the true Protestant church of Christ, seems very manifest, because this very effect is spoken of as that which shall be at the beginning of this glorious work. Is. 60:8–9, "Who are these that fly as a cloud, and as doves to their windows? Surely the isles shall wait for me, and the ships of Tarshish first, to bring thy sons from far, their silver and gold with them, unto the name of the Lord thy God, and to the Holy One of Israel, because he hath glorified thee." So that 'tis to be hoped that before this effect of this vial, which is now probably begun, is at an end, the Spirit of God will so influence the hearts of Protestants, that they will be disposed to devote to the service of God the silver and gold they take from their popish enemies, and the gains of their trade and navigation, both to the East and West Indies, so that "their merchandise and hire shall be holiness to the Lord" [Is. 23:18].

Agreeably to what has been supposed, that an extraordinary outpouring of the Spirit of God is to accompany this sixth vial; so the beginning of a work of extraordinary awakening[8] has already attended the probable beginning of this vial; and has been continued in one place or other, for many years past: although it has been, in some places, mingled with much enthusiasm, after the manner of things in their first beginnings, unripe, and mixed with much crudity. But it is to be hoped, a far more pure extensive and glorious revival of religion is not far off, which will more properly be the beginning of that work which in its issue shall overthrow the kingdom of Antichrist, and of Satan through the world. But God "will be inquired of for this, by the house of Israel, to do it for them" [Ezek. 36:37].

Ans. 5. If notwithstanding all that I have said, it be still judged that there is sufficient reason to determine that the ruin of Antichrist is at a very great distance, and if all that I have said, as arguing that there is reason to hope that the beginning of that glorious revival of religion, which in its continuance and progress will destroy the kingdom of Antichrist, is not very far off, be judged to be of no force; yet it will not follow that our complying with what is proposed to us in the late Memorial from Scotland, will be in vain, or not followed with such spiritual blessings, as will richly recompense the pains of such extraordinary prayer for the Holy Spirit, and the revival of religion. If God don't grant that greatest of all effusions of his Spirit, so soon as we desire, yet we shall have the satisfaction of a consciousness of our having employed ourselves in a manner that is certainly agreeable to Christ's will and frequent commands, in being much in prayer for this mercy, and much more in it than has heretofore been common with Christians: and there will be all reason to hope, that we shall receive some blessed token of his acceptance. If the fall of mystical Babylon, and the work of God's Spirit that shall bring it to pass, be at several hundred years distance, yet it follows not that there will be no happy revivals of religion before that time, that shall be richly worth the most diligent, earnest and constant praying for.

I would say something to one objection more, and then hasten to the conclusion of this discourse.

Obj. VI. Some may be ready to object, that what is proposed in this

8. I.e., the Great Awakening of the early 1740s.

Memorial is a *new thing,* such as never was put in practice in the church of God before.

Ans. 1. If there be something circumstantially new in it, this can't be a sufficient objection. The duty of prayer is no new duty: for many of God's people expressly to agree, as touching something they shall ask in prayer, is no new thing: for God's people to agree on circumstances of time and place for united prayer, according to their own discretion, is no new thing: for many, in different places, to agree to offer up extraordinary prayers to God, at the same time, as a token of their union, is no new thing; but has been commonly practiced in the appointment of days of fasting and prayer for special mercies. And if the people of God should engage in the duty of prayer, for the coming of Christ's kingdom, in a new manner, in that respect, that they resolve they will not be so negligent of this duty, as has been common with professors of religion heretofore, but will be more frequent and fervent in it; this would be such a new thing as ought to be, and would be only to reform a former negligence. And for the people of God in various parts of the world, visibly, and by express agreement, to unite for this extraordinary prayer, is no more than their duty, and no more than what it is foretold the people of God should actually do, before the time comes of the church's promised glory on earth. And if this be a duty, then it is a duty to come into some method to render this practicable: but it is not practicable (as was shewn before) but by this method, or some other equivalent.

Ans. 2. As to this particular method, proposed to promote union in extraordinary prayer, viz., God's people in various parts their setting apart fixed seasons, to return at certain periods, wherein they agree to offer up their prayers at the same time, it is not so new, as some may possibly imagine. This may appear by what follows; which is part of a paper, dispersed abroad in Great Britain and Ireland, from London, in the year 1712, being the latter end of Queen Anne's reign, and very extensively complied with, entitled, "A Serious Call from the City to the Country, to Join with them in Setting Apart some time, viz., from seven to eight, every Tuesday morning, for Solemn Seeking of God, Each One in his Closet, Now in this so Critical a Juncture."[9]

Jonah 1:6, "Call upon God, if so be that God will think upon us, that we perish not." What follows is an extract from it.

"You have formerly been called upon to the like duty, and have

9. JE was citing the excerpts of "A Serious Call" from *The Christian Monthly History,* No. 1 (Apr. 1745), 21–25.

complied with it; and that not without success. It is now thought highly seasonable to renew the call. It is hoped that you will not be more backward, when it is so apparent that there is even greater need. It is scarce imaginable how a professing people should stand in greater need of prayer, than we do at this day. You were formerly bespoke from that very pertinent text (Zech. 8:21), 'The inhabitants of one city shall go to another, saying, Let us go speedily to pray before the Lord,' or (as the marginal reading, more expressive of the original reading, is), 'continually, from day to day, to entreat the face of the Lord.' According to this excellent pattern, we of this city, the metropolis of our land, think ourselves obliged to call upon our brethren in Great Britain and Ireland, at a time when our hearts cannot but meditate terror, and our flesh tremble for fear of God, and are afraid of his righteous judgments: those past being for the most part forgotten; and the signs of the times foreboding evil to come, being by the generality little, if at all, regarded: we cannot therefore but renew our earnest request, that all who make conscience of praying for the peace of Jerusalem, who wish well to Zion, who would have us and our posterity a nation of British Protestants, and not of popish bigots and French slaves, would give us (as far as real and not pretended necessity will give leave) a meeting at the throne of grace, at the hour mentioned; there to wrestle with God, for the turning away his anger from us, for our deliverance from the hands of his and our enemies, for the turning the counsels of all Ahithophels,[1] at home and abroad, into foolishness; for mercy to the queen and kingdom; for a happy peace, or successful war, so long as the matter shall continue undetermined; for securing the Protestant succession in the illustrious House of Hanover (by good and evil wishes to which, the friends and enemies of our religion and civil rights, are so essentially distinguished), and especially for the influences of divine grace upon the rising generation, particularly the seed of the righteous, that the offspring of our Christian heroes may never be the plague of our church and country. And we desire that this solemn prayer be begun the first Tuesday after sight, and continued at least the summer of this present year 1712. And we think, every modest, reasonable and just request, such as this, should not on any account be denied us; since we are not laying a burden on

---

1. Ahithophel (אֲחִיתֹפֶל, literally "my brother is foolishness"), a royal counselor to King David, turned traitor and rebelled with the party of Absalom (II Sam. 15–17). Proverbial for his wisdom, he committed suicide when Absalom rejected his advice. Here JE capitalized upon the meaning of the name and upon the pattern of David's prayer (II Sam. 15:31).

others, to which we will not most willingly put our own shoulders; nay, indeed, count it much more a blessing than a burden. We hope this will not be esteemed by serious Protestants, of any denomination, a needless step; much less do we fear being censured by any such, as fanciful and melancholy, on account of such a proposal. We with them believe a providence, know and acknowledge that our God is a God hearing prayer. Scripture recordeth, and our age is not barren of instances of God's working marvelous deliverances for his people in answer to humble, believing and importunate prayer; especially when prayer and reformation go together; which is what we desire. . . . Let this counsel be acceptable to us, in this day of the church's calamity, and our common fears. Let us seek the Lord while he may be found, and call upon him while he is near [Is. 55:6]. Let us humble ourselves under the mighty hand of God [I Pet. 5:6]. Let us go and pray unto our God, and he will hearken unto us. We shall seek him and find him, when we search for him with all our hearts [Jer. 29:13]. 'Pray for the peace of Jerusalem: they shall prosper that love her' [Ps. 122:6]. And may Zion's friends and enemies both cry out with wonder, when they see the work of God; behold they pray! . . . 'What hath God wrought' [Num. 23:23]! Verily there is a God that judgeth in the earth" [Ps. 58:11].

"Postscript. It is desired and hoped, that if any are hindered from attending this work at the above-mentioned hour, they will nevertheless set apart an hour weekly for it."

God speedily and wonderfully heard and answered those who were united in that extraordinary prayer, proposed in the above-mentioned paper, in suddenly scattering those black clouds which threatened the nation and the Protestant interest with ruin, at that time; in bringing about, in so remarkable a manner, that happy change in the state of affairs in the nation, which was after the queen's death, by the bringing in King George the First, just at the time when the enemies of the religion and liberties of the nation had ripened their designs to be put in speedy execution.[2] And we see in the beginning of this extract, this which is proposed, is mentioned as being no new thing, but that God's people in Great Britain had formerly been called upon to the like duty,

---

2. The "black clouds" were the plans of the Jacobite party to place James (III) of the Stuart house on the throne when his sister Queen Anne (1702–14) died. His Roman Catholicism, which he would not surrender, was an obstacle to acceptance by many Englishmen. When the Jacobite cause failed because advisers surrounding the queen would not accept James, succession was secured for George of the house of Hanover.

and had complied, and that not without success. Such like concerts or agreements have several times been proposed in Scotland, before this which is now proposed to us; particularly there was a proposal published for this very practice, in the year 1732, and another in 1735.[3] So that it appears that this objection of novelty is built on a mistake.

3. JE derived this information about earlier concerts from *The Christian Monthly History*, No. 1 (Apr. 1745), 27.

THE CONCLUSION

AND now, upon the whole, I desire every serious Christian, that may read this discourse, calmly and deliberately to consider whether he can excuse himself from complying with what has been proposed to us and requested of us, by those ministers of Christ in Scotland, that are the authors of the late Memorial. God has stirred up a part of his church in a distant part of the world, to be in an extraordinary manner seeking and crying to him, that he would appear to favor Zion, as he has promised. And they are applying themselves to us, to join with them; and make that very proposal to us, that is spoken of in my text, and in like manner and circumstances. The members of one church, in one country, are coming to others, in other distant countries, saying, "Let us go speedily and constantly to pray before the Lord, and to seek the Lord of Hosts" [Zech. 8 :21]. Will it not become us readily to say, "I will go also?" What these servants of Christ ask of us, is not silver or gold, or any of our outward substance, or that we would put ourselves to any cost, or do anything that will be likely to expose us to any remarkable trouble, difficulty or suffering in our outward interest; but only that we would help together with them, by our prayers to God, for the greatest mercy in the world; and that a mercy which as much concerns us as them; for the glory of their Lord and ours, for the great advancement of our common interest and happiness, and the happiness of our fellow creatures through all nations; a mercy, which, at this day especially, there is great need of; a mercy, which we in this land do stand in particular need of; a mercy, which the Word of God requires us to make the subject matter of our prayers, above all other mercies, and gives us more encouragement to pray earnestly and unitedly to him for, than any other mercy; and a mercy, which the providence of God towards the world of mankind, at this day, does loudly call the people of God to pray for. I think, we cannot reasonably doubt but that these ministers have acted a part becoming disciples of the great Messiah, and ministers of his kingdom, and have done the will of God, and according to his Word, in setting forward such an affair at this day, and in proposing it to us. And therefore I desire it may be considered, whether we shall not really sin against God, in refusing to comply with their proposal and request, or in neglecting it, and turning it by, with but little notice and attention; therein disregarding that which is truly a call of God to us.

The ministers that make this proposal to us, are no separatists or schismatics, promoters of no public disorders, nor of any wildness or extravagance in matters of religion; but are quiet and peaceable members and ministers of the Church of Scotland, that have lamented the late divisions and breaches of that church.[1] If any shall say, that they are under no advantage to judge of their character, but must take it on trust from others, because they conceal their names; in answer to this, I would say, that I presume that no sober person will say that he has any reason to suspect 'em, to be any other than gentlemen of honest intention. Be sure there is no appearance of anything else, but an upright design in their proposal: and that they have not mentioned their names, is an argument of it. It may well be presumed, from the manner of their expressing themselves, in the Memorial itself, that they concealed their names from that, which perhaps may be called an excess of modesty; choosing to be at the greatest distance from appearing to set forth themselves to the view of the world, as the heads of a great affair, and the first projectors and movers of something extraordinary, that they desire should become general, and that God's people in various distant parts of the world should agree in. And therefore, they are moreover careful to tell us, that they don't propose the affair, as now setting it on foot, but as a thing already set on foot; and don't tell us who first projected and moved it. The proposal is made to us in a very proper and prudent manner, with all appearance of Christian modesty and sincerity, and with a very prudent guard against anything that looks like superstition, or whatsoever might entangle a tender conscience; and far from any appearance of a design to promote any particular party or denomination of Christians, in opposition to others; but with all appearance of the contrary, in their charitable request, that none would by any means conceive of any such thing to be in their view, and that all, of all denominations, and opinions concerning the late religious commotions, would join with them, in seeking the common interest of the kingdom of Christ. And therefore I think, none can be in the way of their duty, in neglecting a proposal in itself excellent, and

1. I.e., the secession in 1733 of some from the Church of Scotland who opposed patronage, and the subsequent ecclesiastical struggles.

that which they have reason to think is made with upright intentions, merely because the proposers modestly conceal their names. I don't see how any serious person, that has an ill opinion of late religious stirs, can have any color of reason to refuse a compliance with this proposal, on that account: the more disorders, extravagancies and delusions of the devil have lately prevailed, the more need have we to pray earnestly to God, for his Holy Spirit, to promote *true religion*, in opposition to the grand deceiver, and all his works; and the more such prayer as is proposed, is answered, the more effectually will all that is contrary to sober and pure religion, be extirpated and exploded.

One would think that everyone that favors the dust of Zion, when he hears that God is stirring up a considerable number of his ministers and people, to unite in extraordinary prayer, for the revival of religion and advancement of his kingdom, should greatly rejoice on this occasion. If we lay to heart the present calamities of the church of Christ, and long for that blessed alteration that God has promised, one would think it should be natural to rejoice at the appearance of something in so dark a day, that is so promising a token. Would not our friends that were lately in captivity at Canada,[2] that earnestly longed for deliverance, have rejoiced to have heard of anything that seemed to forebode the approach of their redemption? And particularly may we not suppose that such of 'em as were religious persons, would greatly have rejoiced to have understood that there was stirred up in God's people an extraordinary spirit of prayer for their redemption? And I don't know why it would not be as natural for us to rejoice at the like hopeful token of the redemption of Zion, if we made her interest our own, and preferred Jerusalem above our chief joy.

If we are indeed called of God to comply with the proposal now made to us, then let me beseech all that do sincerely love the interest of real Christianity, notwithstanding any diversity of opinion, and former disputes, now to unite in this affair, with one heart and voice: and "let us go speedily to pray before the Lord" [Zech. 8:21]. There is no need that one should wait for another. If we can get others, that are our neighbors, to join with us, and so can conveniently spend the quarterly seasons with praying societies, this is desirable; but if not, why should we wholly neglect the duty proposed? Why should not we perform it by ourselves, uniting in heart and practice, as far as we are able, with those who in distant places are engaged in that duty at that time?

If it be agreeable to the mind and will of God, that we should comply

2. Above, p. 361, n. 2.

with the Memorial, by praying for the coming of Christ's kingdom, in the manner therein proposed, then doubtless 'tis the duty of all to comply with the Memorial, in that respect also, viz., in endeavoring, as far as in us lies, to promote others' joining in such prayer, and to render this union and agreement as extensive as may be. Private Christians may have many advantages and opportunities for this; but especially ministers, inasmuch as they not only are by office overseers of whole congregations of God's people, and their guides in matters of religion, but ordinarily have a far more extensive acquaintance and influence abroad, than private Christians in common have.

And I hope that such as are convinced that it is their duty to comply with and encourage this design, will remember that we ought not only to go "speedily" to pray before the Lord, and to seek this mercy, but also to go "constantly." We should unite in our practice those two things, which our Saviour unites in his precept, praying and not fainting [Luke 18:1]. If we should continue some years, and nothing remarkable in providence should appear, as though God heard and answered, we should act very unbecoming believers, if we should therefore begin to be disheartened, and grow dull and slack, in our seeking of God so great a mercy. 'Tis very apparent from the Word of God, that God is wont often to try the faith and patience of his people, when crying to him for some great and important mercy, by withholding the mercy sought, for a season, and not only so, but at first to cause an increase of dark appearances; and yet, without fail, at last, to succeed those who continue instant in prayer with all perseverance, and will not let God go except he blesses. It is now proposed that this extraordinary united prayer should continue for seven years, from November 1746. Perhaps some that appear forward to engage, may begin to think the time long, before the seven years are out; and may account it a dull story, to go on, for so long a time, praying in this extraordinary method, while all yet continues dark and dead, without any dawnings of the wished-for light, or new promising appearance in providence of the near approach of the desired mercy. But let it be considered, whether it will not be a poor business, if our faith and patience is so short-winded, that we can't be willing to wait upon God one seven years, in a way of taking this little pains, in seeking a mercy so infinitely vast. For my part, I sincerely wish and hope, that there may not be an end of extraordinary united prayer, among God's people, for the effusions of the blessed Spirit, when the seven years are ended; but that it will be continued, either in this method, or some other, by a new agreement, that will be entered into, with greater engagedness, and more abundant alacrity, than this is; and that extraordinary united prayer for such a mercy will be further propagated and extended, than it can be expected to be in one seven years. But yet, at the same time, I hope, God's people, that unite in this agreement, will see some tokens for good, before these seven years are out, that shall give them to see, that God has not said to the seed of Jacob, "Seek ye me in vain" [Is. 45:19]; and shall serve greatly to animate and encourage 'em to go on in united prayers for the advancement of Christ's kingdom, with increasing fervency.[3] But whatever our hopes may be in this respect, we must be content to be ignorant of the times and seasons, which the Father hath put in his own power; and must be willing that God should answer prayer, and fulfill his own glorious promises, in his own time; remembering such instructions, counsels and promises of the Word of God as these. Ps. 27:14, "Wait on the Lord, be of good courage, and he shall strengthen thine heart; wait, I say, on the Lord." Hab. 2:3, "For the vision is yet for an appointed time; but in the end it shall speak, and not lie: though it tarry, wait for it; because it will surely come, it will not tarry." Mic. 7:7, "I will look unto the Lord, I will wait for the God of my salvation: my God will hear me." Is. 25:8–9, "God will wipe away tears from off all faces, and the rebuke of his people shall he take away from off all the earth; for the Lord hath spoken it. And it shall be said in that day, Lo, this is our God! We have waited for him, and he will save us: this is Jehovah! We have waited for him, we will be glad and rejoice in his salvation." Amen.

3. The HA has been associated with the growing interest of eighteenth-century evangelicalism in the missionary enterprise. See Earl R. MacCormac, "Jonathan Edwards and Missions," *Journal of the Presbyterian Historical Society, 39* (1961), 219–29. JE knew well the work of Robert Millar, *The History of the Propagation of Christianity, and Overthrow of Paganism* (2 vols., Edinburgh, 1723).

APPENDIXES

APPENDIX A

1. This outline underscores themes highlighted by JE.

439

APPENDIX B

1. Manuscripts exist in the Yale collection for all of the following except two sermons the sources of which are indicated. The dates for the sermons written before 1733 have been determined by Thomas Schafer.

Rev. 3:7—Mar., 1741. "How Christ is said to have the key of David. How when he opens, no man shutteth. How when he shuts, no man opens."

Rev. 3:12—July, 1740. "Those that are thorough Christians are properly deciphered by that, that they are they that overcome."

Rev. 3:15—1729–30. "A man had better be a heathen, than to differ from 'em only in common light and profession."

Rev. 3:20 [1]—Mar., 1734. "Nothing else is required of us in order to our having an interest in Christ, but that we should find it in our hearts to be willing that Christ should be ours, and we his."

Rev. 3:20 [2]—Sept., 1741. "Christ comes to the sinner's door."

Rev. 3:20 [3]—Feb.,1751. "The Lord Jesus Christ, by coming into the world and dying for sinners, has obtained salvation, for all such as will repent, and turn from their sins, and give their hearts to him."

Rev. 5:5–6—Aug., 1736. "There is an admirable conjunction of diverse excellencies in Jesus Christ, a Lion and a Lamb."

Rev. 5:12—1731–32. "Christ was worthy of his exaltation upon account of his being slain."

Rev. 6:13–17—July, 1754. "Though now many don't fear God's wrath, the time will come when they will be afraid."

Rev. 6:15–16—1731–32. "That wicked men will hereafter earnestly wish to be turned to nothing and forever cease to be, that they may escape the wrath of God."

Rev. 6:16 [1]—Dec., 1745. "When gospel graces come to [be] turned into wrath, that wrath is peculiarly dreadful."

Rev. 6:16 [2]—Jan., 1747. "The weight of rocks and mountains is light, in comparison of that wrath of God that shall hereafter come on ungodly men."

Rev. 7:1–3—Feb., 1741 (Fast for success in war). "In the time of great public commotions and calamities, God will take thorough and effectual care, that his servants shall be safe."

Rev. 7:17—Aug., 1740. "The Shepherd that leads and feeds the church of saints like a flock, is himself a Lamb."

Rev. 8:2–3—July, 1742. "The prayers of saints is a great and principal means of carrying on the great designs of Christ's kingdom in the world."

Rev. 12:1—July, 1741. "How the church of true saints by her union with Christ, is clothed in the sun; . . . that this is a great wonder."

Rev. 14:2—Nov., 1734 (Thanksgiving: Printed copy only, Dwight ed., *8*, 305–19). "The work of the saints in heaven doth very much consist in praising God."

Rev. 14:3 [1]—Nov., 1740 (Thanksgiving). "Those that [are] Christ's redeemed ones, in the holy praises they offer up to God, do sing a new song. No man can learn that song but they."

Rev. 14:3 [2]—Nov., 1741. "The nature of the redemption of God's elect. What is meant when they are said to be redeemed from the earth."

Rev. 14:4—Feb., 1756. "The saints are those that God has chosen out of all the world to be for him as his part and portion."

Rev. 14:13 [1]—1734–36. "How that those that die in the Lord are blessed, and those reasons given of their blessedness, viz., that they shall rest."

Rev. 14:13 [2]—Feb., 1736 (After the death of Mrs. Stoddard). "When the saints depart out of this into another world, their works do follow them."

Rev. 14:13 [3]—Feb., 1743. "The proper and appointed season of Christians' rest from the difficulties and labors of their course is after death."

Rev. 14:14 [1]—Oct., 1736. "Our Lord Jesus Christ is crowned with glory."

Rev. 14:14 [2]—Sept., 1741. "The great and apposite dispensations of God towards the elect and reprobates, at the time of the downfall of Antichrist."

Rev. 14:15—Jan., 1754. "The saints growing ripe for heaven."

Rev. 14:18–19—1724. "That God sometimes defers the punishment of sinners till they are fully ripe for destruction."

Rev. 15:7—Mar., 1746. "The wrath of God; . . . How God is here described as he that liveth forever and ever."

Rev. 17:11—July, 1746 (Fast for expedition to Canada). "The subject that I would now insist upon from these words is the fall of the Antichrist."

Rev. 17:14—1731–32. "Those that are Christ's and belong to him, 'tis of God that they are so. They that belong to Jesus Christ, they are faithful to Christ."

Rev. 18:20—Mar., 1733. "When the saints in glory shall see the wrath of God executed on ungodly men, it will be no occasion of grief to 'em, but of rejoicing."

Rev. 19:1—Nov., 1754 (Thanksgiving). "The work and business of saints and angels in heaven consists very much in praising God."

Rev. 19:2–3—1731–32. " 'Tis not inconsistent with the attributes of God to punish ungodly men with a misery that is eternal."

Rev. 19:5–6—Nov., 1748 (Thanksgiving). "Christ leads the heavenly assembly in their praises."

Rev. 19:11–12—June, 1734. "He that is to be the judge of men hath his eyes as a flame of fire."

Rev. 19:13—May, 1750. "Christ is, as it were, clothed with a vesture dipped in his own blood [and] in the blood of his enemies."

Rev. 19:15—Apr., 1734. "In hell is inflicted the fierceness of the wrath of a Being that is almighty."

Rev. 20:6—Aug., 1742. "The blessedness of the saints: that the second death hath no power over them . . . and that of their being priests and kings."

Rev. 20:11—Aug., 1741. "When God shall appear at the day, heaven and earth will flee away, as though they could not bear his dreadful and wrathful presence."

Rev. 21:2—Feb., 1742. "The glorious state. . . . What is here spoken of the church of Christ. Why called the holy city."

Rev. 21:6—Dec., 1744. "There is a time coming, when God's grand design in all his various works and dispensations, from age to age, will be completed, and his end fully obtained."

Rev. 21:8 [1]—Jan., 1745. "What is represented to us by the wicked being hereafter cast into a lake of fire and brimstone."

Rev. 21:8 [2]—Jan., 1745. "These shall have their part in this lake."

Rev. 21:8 [3]—Jan., 1745. "To warn my hearers to take heed to themselves."

Rev. 21:18—1723-24 (Two booklets). "That there is nothing upon earth that will suffice to represent to us the glories of heaven."

Rev. 22:3—1730-31. "The happiness of the saints in heaven consists partly in that they there serve God."

Rev. 22:3-5—Nov., 1753. "And there shall be no more curse in heaven."

Rev. 22:5—Aug., 1756. "The saints in heaven shall have light without any darkness."

Rev. 22:11-12—Nov., 1753. "The time will come that as men are at that time, whether good or bad, so they will be to all eternity; they will never change."

Rev. 22:12—Nov., 1753. "Christ will quickly come to judge men for what they do in the world."

Rev. 22:16-17—May, 1741. "Both the Bridegroom and the bride do, with united voice, freely and earnestly invite poor sinners to the entertainments of the wedding of the Lamb."

Rev. 22:17—1731-32. "Nothing is required in order to have all the blessings of the gospel but willingly receiving."

APPENDIX C

EDWARDS' LETTER TO A CORRESPONDENT IN SCOTLAND[1]

Northampton, Nov. 20, 1745

Rev. and most dear Sir,

I am greatly obliged to you for your large, friendly, profitable and entertaining letter of February last.[2] I esteem my correspondence with you, and my other correspondents in Scotland, a great honor and privilege; and hope that it may be improved for God's glory, and my profit. The church of God, in all parts of the world, is but one; the distant members are closely united in one glorious Head. This union is very much her beauty; and the mutual friendly correspondence of the various members, in distant parts of the world, is a thing well-becoming this union (at least when employed about things appertaining to the glory of their common Head, and their common spiritual interest and happiness), and therefore is a thing decent and beautiful, and very profitable.

When the day is so dark here in New England, it is exceeding refreshing and reviving to hear, by your and other letters, and Mr. Robe's history,[3] of religion's being to such a degree upheld in the power and practice of it, in those parts of Scotland, that have been favored with the late revival, and of such a number of the persevering subjects of it, and of the works now going on in the north of Scotland, under the labors and conduct of such pious, solid, judicious and prudent instruments, that Christ there makes use of; and one thing that has been very joyful to me, that I have been informed of in the letters I have received from you, and my other correspondents your dear neighbors and brethren, is that concert that is come into, by many of God's people in Scotland and England, for united prayer to God, for the pouring out of his Holy Spirit on his church and the world of mankind. Such an

1. Printed originally in Robe, ed., *The Christian Monthly History*, No. 8 (Nov. 1745), 234–54. John McLaurin of Glasgow was probably the unnamed correspondent. See below, p. 446, n. 5; and Dwight ed., *1*, 230–31.
2. No letter has been located.
3. I.e., *The Christian Monthly History*.

agreement and practice appears to me exceeding beautiful, and becoming Christians; and I doubt not but it is so in Christ's eyes. And it seems to me to be a thing peculiarly becoming us, in the state that things are in at the present day. God has lately done great things before our eyes, whereby he has shown us something of his wonderful power and mercy; but has withal so disposed things, that events have tended remarkably to shew us our weakness, infirmity, insufficiency, and great and universal need of God's help; we have been many ways rebuked for our self-confidence, and looking to instruments, and trusting in an arm of flesh; and God is now shewing us that we are nothing, and letting us see that we can do nothing. In many places where God of late wonderfully appeared, he has now in a great measure withdrawn; and the consequence is, that Zion and the interest of religion are involved in innumerable and inextricable difficulties. And it is apparent that we can't help ourselves, and have nowhere else to go, but to God. II Chron. 20:12, "We know not what to do; our eyes are upon thee." Now how fit is it that God's people, under such circumstances, should go to God by prayer, and give themselves more than ordinarily to that duty, and be uniting one with another in it, agreeing together touching what they shall ask, taking some proper course to act in it with a visible union, tending to promote their offering up their cries with one heart, and, as it were, with one voice. O that this duty might be attended with real meekness towards our opposers, lifting up holy hands without wrath; and that we may go to God, self-empty, brokenhearted, looking to God only through Christ, and without making any righteousness of our performances, or any exalting thoughts of ourselves for our secret or social religion, or our differing from others, in being either friends, or partakers of the late revival of religion.

I have taken a great deal of pains to promote a falling in with this concert in New England, at least so far as relates to the quarterly seasons agreed upon. I read those passages of your and your brethren's letters, that relate to this affair, publicly in my own congregation, using many arguments with them to comply with the thing proposed. And many praying societies here have complied. I gave an account of the affair to several of the neighboring ministers, that I thought most likely to fall in with it. Two of them seem to like it very well, and to determine to propose it to their people; but one of them, who seemed very much to approve of it, the next week was called away to serve as chaplain to the soldiers at Cape Breton, and is not yet returned, and so I suppose nothing is done there. When he was here, I talked with him about this affair, shewed him your letters, and urged, wherever he went, to give an account of this concert to the people of God, and to press their coming into it. He seemed forward to do as I desired; but I have not heard what he has done. I wrote to ———— about it, who was then in Connecticut, giving him an account of the proposal, desiring him to mention it to other ministers, that they might promote it among their people. He wrote me word back, that he had mentioned it to several ministers, and desired them to speak to others; but whether anything is done, I have not heard.[4]

I hope, dear Sir, that you will do what in you lies, still to uphold, promote and propagate this concert. I should be very sorry to hear of its sinking. I don't think it ought to be let fall, though you should meet with considerable difficulties and discouragements in the affair. Jacob [Gen. 32:24–28] and the woman of Canaan [Matt. 15:21–28], met with great discouragements, while they were wrestling for a blessing: but they persevered, and obtained their request. I should have more hope from the union, fervency and unfailing constancy of the prayers of God's people, with respect to the religious affairs of the present day, than anything else; more than from the preaching and writings of the ablest and best friends to the work of God's Spirit. For my part, I am not disheartened with respect to this concert, though I have met with great discouragements in my endeavors to promote it hitherto: I shall not cease still to do what in me lies to promote and propagate it, according as favorable junctures and opportunities do present. Please to remember me to the correspondent meeting in Glasgow,[5] that you speak of, as one whose heart is with them, particularly in the business of this concert. O that our hearts, and the hearts of all God's people everywhere might be united in such an affair, that we might be assisted to be in good earnest in it, and give God "no rest, till he shall establish, and make Jerusalem a praise in the earth" [Is. 62:7]! I desire you would mention it to this meeting, as my desire, that on the times agreed on for this united prayer, they would pray for America and New England, and (if it be not too much to ask) that they would sometimes think of me in their addresses to heaven. I am sensible it would be too much for me to expect, that they should commonly mention me in particular in their prayers; it would be impracticable for such societies, in all their prayers, to pray particularly for every minister, that is sensible of the worth of the prayers of God's people, and would highly prize them. But I should esteem it a great privilege, to be sometimes thought of by the Christian people there, in their prayers to God. I hope the time is hastening, when God's people in all the different parts of the world, and the whole earth shall become more sensibly, as it were, one family, one holy and happy society, and all brethren, not only all united in one Head, but in greater affection, and in more mutual correspondence, and more visible and sensible union and fellowship in religious exercises, and the holy duties of the service of God; and so that in this respect, the church on earth will become more like the blessed society in heaven, and vast assembly of saints and angels there.

I am persuaded that such an agreement of the people of God in different

4. The associates and correspondents mentioned by JE in this paragraph remain unidentified.

5. John McLaurin met with his acquaintances in Glasgow once a week "to receive and communicate religious intelligence." See Fawcett, *Cambuslang Revival*, p. 224.

parts, to unite together, to pray for the Holy Spirit, is lovely in the eyes of Jesus Christ the glorious Head of the church. And if endeavors are used to uphold, and promote, and enlarge such a concert, who knows what it may come to at last? Who knows but that by degrees, it may spread all over the British dominions, both in Europe and America, and also into Holland, Zealand, and other Protestant countries, and all over the visible church of Christ, yea, far beyond the present limits of the visible church? And how glorious a thing will this be, to have the people of God everywhere, thus agreeing together, touching such a thing that they would ask! And what blessed fruits and consequences might reasonably be hoped for, from such united prayers! Might it not be hoped, that they would open the doors and windows of heaven, that have so long been shut up, and been as brass over the heads of the inhabitants of the earth, as to spiritual showers; and that God, in answer to such prayers, would speak the word, and say, "Drop down ye heavens from above, and let the skies pour down righteousness" [Is. 45:8]?

As there is great need of God's people's uniting their cries to God for spiritual blessings at this day,[6] so I can't but think that there is much in the present aspects of divine providence to encourage them in it. For although there are many dark clouds, and God's Spirit is greatly withdrawn from some places where it has lately been remarkably poured out, and Satan seems at present greatly to rage and prevail; yet God is still carrying on his work, if not in one place, yet in another. Though it seems in some measure to cease in the west of Scotland, yet it is carried on in the north, and breaks out in some parts of the United Netherlands.[7] And since the work has ceased very much in New England, it has broke out wonderfully in Virginia, and has prevailed there, for, I suppose, more than a year and half. The work that is lately broke out among them, was begun by the labors of one Mr. Robinson, a young minister that went down among them from Pennsylvania, the last year, and spent much time in preaching there, with great success, multitudes being greatly awakened as he preached from place to place, a great thirst appearing in the people after the means of grace, and eagerness to hear the Word preached, and fondness towards the instrument of their awakening. This Mr. Robinson, by all that I can learn of him, from those whose intelligence and judgment I rely upon, is a man of sprightly abilities, fervent piety, and very solid, judicious and prudent.[8]

The governor[9] encouraged Messrs. Tennent and Finley[1] to preach in

6. See above, pp. 29–31, for JE's analysis of the contemporary religious situation.
7. See AP; above, p. 289, n. 3.
8. Concerning William Robinson, see HA; above, p. 364, n. 1.
9. William Gooch, governor of Virginia.
1. Gilbert Tennent (1703–64), Presbyterian minister at Philadelphia, and Samuel Finley (1715–66), pastor at Nottingham, Pennsylvania, and later president of the College of New Jersey (1761–66), were both successful itinerant revivalists.

Virginia, and invited them to make his house their home, when it was in their way. Accordingly they continued preaching for some time in the country with great success; and, by the last accounts that I heard, the work continued to go on wonderfully there. Mr. Buell,[2] I hear, is gone down into those parts, designing to continue there this winter. He is one that you have probably heard of, has been a zealous and successful preacher in New England.

Besides the work in Virginia, Mr. William Tennent[3] in the Jerseys, has lately had great success among his people; a greater work having lately been carried on among them than at any time these seven years past. And the above-mentioned Mr. Robinson, besides his success in Virginia, has lately had great success in the parts below Philadelphia, in Pennsylvania. The provinces of New Jersey, Pennsylvania, Maryland and Virginia, are become exceeding populous; and there are great numbers in those provinces that shew a forwardness to hear the Word preached; but there are few ministers. "The harvest is plenteous, but the laborers few" [Matt. 9:37].

The ministers of the three forementioned presbyteries, that are friends to the late work, who have lately formed themselves into a new synod, who had their first meeting September last, at Elizabethtown, in New Jersey,[4] I say, these ministers taking into consideration the very calamitous circumstances of those provinces, by reason of the scarcity of ministers, have formed a design of erecting a college there, for the educating young men for the ministry, hoping, through the influence of some particular gentlemen, to obtain a charter for the establishment of such a society from the king.[5] I think the design to be very glorious, and very worthy to be encouraged, and promoted by all the friends of Zion. In the meantime, these ministers have determined that private academies should be kept in certain ministers' houses, for the instructing and educating young candidates for the ministry, till this design of a more public school can be ripened. Accordingly they have determined that such academy should be kept by Mr. Dickinson, Mr. Burr, Mr. Blair and Mr. Finley;[6] all of them excellent men, well capable of, and fitted for such business.

2. See AP; above, p. 286, n. 8.

3. William Tennent (1673–1745), Presbyterian minister at Neshaminy, Pennsylvania, founder of the "Log College," and leader of the New Light cause in the Middle Colonies. See further, Charles Hartshorn Maxson, *The Great Awakening in the Middle Colonies* (Chicago, 1920), esp. ch. 3; and Martin Ellsworth Lodge, "The Great Awakening in the Middle Colonies," Diss. Univ. of California, Berkeley, 1964, esp. chs. 10, 14.

4. On Sept. 19, 1745, ministers from the presbyteries of New York, New Brunswick, and New Castle formed the synod of New York. See Maxson, *Great Awakening*, pp. 88 ff.

5. This movement led to the chartering of the College of New Jersey (later Princeton College) in 1746.

6. Jonathan Dickinson (1688–1747), a Presbyterian minister at Elizabethtown, New Jersey, the moderator of the Synod of New York, became the first president of the College of New Jersey. Aaron Burr (1715–57), a pastor at Newark, New Jersey, succeeded Dickinson

Besides those things that have a favorable aspect on the interest of religion in these parts, among the English, and other inhabitants of European extract, Mr. Brainerd,[7] a missionary employed by The Society in Scotland for Propagating Christian Knowledge, to preach to the Indians, has lately had more success than ever. This Mr. Brainerd is a young gentleman of very distinguishing qualifications, remarkable for his piety, and eminent zeal for the good of souls, and his knowledge in divinity, and solidity of his judgment, and prudence of conduct. And I hope he will be improved to be a great blessing. 'Tis pity but that he should have all the encouragement from those that employ him, that shall put him under the best advantage in his work.

While I am speaking of the late wonderful works of God in America, I cannot pass over one, which, though it be of a different kind from those already mentioned; yet is that wherein the Most High has made his hand manifest, in a most apparent and marvelous manner, and may be reckoned among the evidences of its being a day of great things, and of the wonderful works of God in this part of the world. What I have reference to, is the success of the late expedition, from New England, against Cape Breton; a place of vast importance, and a place from whence New England, and all the English colonies on the American continent, have been chiefly, and almost only infested by our French enemies since the beginning of the war. I have had much opportunity to be well-informed of the circumstances of this affair, about twenty of my parishioners being present at the siege and surrender of the place; and among others, a major of one of the regiments, and the general's chaplain, both worthy pious men.[8] There was very discernibly an extraordinary spirit of prayer given the people of God in New England, with respect to this undertaking, more than in any public affair within my remembrance; and many praying pious persons were immediately concerned in it; and among others, several of the chaplains and principal officers. Some of the chief officers that I am well acquainted with, and conversed with a little before they embarked, seemed to have special and extraordinary assistance, to commit themselves to God in the undertaking, to resign their lives to his disposal, and trust in him; and I was informed of the same in many others. Providence made provision for the expedition, by giving us an extraordinary plenty the summer before; and they were remarkable providences that led us into the design. The state of the place was strangely concealed from us, which if it had been known, would have effectually prevented the design. We seemed to be under great advantages

in the presidency. Samuel Blair (1712–51), a product of the "Log College" himself, served a congregation at Fagg's Manor, Pennsylvania. Concerning Finley, see above, p. 447, n. 1.

7. See HA; above, p. 364, n. 9.

8. Seth Pomeroy (1706–77) and Joseph Hawley (1723–88) respectively. See Louis Effingham de Forest, ed., *The Journals and Papers of Seth Pomeroy* (New Haven, 1926).

to be informed; for we had many that very lately had been prisoners there, and others that had traded, and been very conversant there, and some that had dwelt there a considerable time, and our governor[9] and general assembly were very diligent in making inquiry, and all seemed to be well-satisfied that we had full information; and yet the representations that were relied upon as true, were exceeding wrong. It was unaccountable, that so many that had been conversant there, should be kept in such ignorance. If one half of the strength of the place had been known, the expedition had never been thought of; or if they had imagined the number of soldiers and inhabitants there, or if the expensiveness of the undertaking had been conceived of, it never would have been meddled with; for it soon abundantly exceeded the expectations of our general assembly. After all, when the affair was first proposed to the assembly, it was not fallen in with; it was thought too great an undertaking. But afterwards, the affair was unexpectedly reconsidered, and then it was carried by a majority of one single vote among fourscore representatives; and such a majority would not have been obtained, had not several of the members of the house, that were against it, been at that time providentially absent; nor yet would it have been, had it not been so ordered, that one of the voters present, that had been against it on a committee, changed his mind, and voted for it in the house. After the affair was determined, it was surprising to see how the people were spirited to offer themselves. When the determination of the General Court was first noised abroad, it was not known but that men would be impressed into the service; and many, through fear of being impressed, hid themselves, particularly there were many in a neighboring town, viz., Westfield, that were so afraid of being obliged to go in the expedition, that they ran away, and hid themselves in the woods; and yet afterwards, when orders came for enlisting volunteers, eleven of those same persons that had hid themselves, came and voluntarily offered their service. There were also several such instances in other towns.

We were marvelously smiled upon in our preparations for the expedition; so that within two months, from the resolution of the government (which was January 29), the whole military force was under sail. It was wonderful, that during this whole time of preparation, which was in those usually stormy months of February and March, we had a constant series of moderate and fair weather, such as was scarce ever known at that time of year: so that there was hardly any impediment from the weather to our officers, in going about and enlisting, or our soldiers in marching, or our coasters in bringing provisions, or the Committee of War in their various preparations, till all were ready to sail; not so much as the loss of one day, either by snow, rain or cold. Some who have preserved an account of the weather, for more than twenty years, have been surprised to behold the difference between the

9. I.e., William Shirley of Massachusetts. See John A. Schutz, *William Shirley: King's Governor of Massachusetts* (Chapel Hill, N.C., 1961), esp. pp. 80–103.

months of February and March this year, and the foregoing ones; this a continued course of good weather, those as continually intermixed with storms of snow, or rain, or severity of cold. And we seemed in other respects to be strangely succeeded in our preparations. Some have been heard to express themselves with wonder, how things would happen; just as they wanted some kind of materials or provision, an unexpected vessel would come in, and bring them.

It was strange, that while this affair was managing in New England, and the whole country full of the noise of it, it should be concealed from our French enemies, in Cape Breton and Canada. It was very early known in Albany, a place where the Indians that live in Canada, are abundantly conversant; so that it was very much concluded by some of the most discerning and judicious of our rulers, that they had notice of our design in Canada, long before our forces embarked; which, if it had been, would in all probability have frustrated the whole design. But it proved afterwards, that it was wonderfully concealed from them, not only till our forces sailed, but a long time after, till it was too late for them to send any succors to their friends. And the design was also kept wholly concealed from the French in Cape Breton; which was in some respects more wonderful, especially considering, how many friends they had, French and Indians in Nova Scotia, on the borders of New England; and not only so, but the Indians in the eastern parts of this province, that have always been friends with the French, and have since openly sided with them, and must needs know of our design. 'Tis unaccountable, that none of these should inform our enemies.

Our soldiers were wonderfully preserved from the smallpox, which is a distemper very fatal to the people of New England, and was in Boston, as our troops were gathering there, both by land and water, and continued all the while they were quartering and anchoring there; very few of the officers or soldiers having had it. And 'tis thought the time was never known, when so many persons, in so many different parts of the town, were ill with this distemper, and it was notwithstanding stopped in its progress. If it had prevailed, and got among the soldiers, it would unavoidably have put an end to the expedition.

When the expedition was first determined by our authority, they were not sure they should have the assistance of one man-of-war; without which our forces would (as it proved by what appeared afterwards) [have] been easily swallowed up by their enemies. Indeed the governor, soon after the expedition was fully determined, dispatched a packet for England, to the Lords of the Admiralty, desiring their assistance. And it was so ordered in providence (which was perhaps much in favor to the design), that there had been a change made a little before in the Board of Admiralty, and such commissioners introduced, that were thought to be much spirited for the interest of the nation, and sincerely to seek the success of the war against the French.

However, if we had had no assistance of men-of-war, till those arrived that the Lords of the Admiralty sent, it would have been too late (as events proved), to have saved our forces from their enemies. Our governor at the same time that he sent a packet to England, sent another to the West Indies to Commodore Warren, in hopes of persuading him to send some assistance of men-of-war; but the commodore sent back the packet boat with a denial, thinking himself not warranted to come without orders from England. But so wonderfully was it ordered, that within a few days after the messenger was sent back with his discouraging answer, the commodore received express orders from the Lords of the Admiralty, forthwith to come to Boston, to act in concert with our governor, for the defense of these northern English set-tlements; not that they knew anything of the intended expedition against Cape Breton, but only expected, that the French would that spring make an attempt on Annapolis,[1] and would endeavor extraordinarily to annoy our seacoasts. Thus the designs that our enemies were forming against us, were made an occasion of their ruin, and our great advantage. They were taken in the pit that they had digged; for had it not been for their extraordinary designs against us, Commodore Warren would not have had orders at that time to come hither, which if it had not been, our forces must have fallen a prey to the French, and Cape Breton not have been taken. The commodore having received these orders, with all speed sent the news of it to Governor Shirley; which, when it arrived, was like life from the dead to him and others, that were ready to sink in distress and discouragement.

Commodore Warren, after receiving the forementioned orders, soon set sail, with three ships from the West Indies, for Boston. But still if he had not been prevented from coming to Boston, as he intended, before he went to Cape Breton, he would have been too late there, to have prevented the *Vigilant* (a strong ship from France of 64 guns, with all manner of warlike stores) from getting into the harbor, which, if it had done, would (as is judged on all hands) prevented the taking of the place. But so wonderfully was it ordered, that Commodore Warren in his voyage hither, near Cape Sable[2] on April 12th, met with a fisherman, who informed him of our army's being gone to Canso[3] the week before; that on board the fisherman, there was one of the best of pilots, who had got out of the way of our Committee of War, to avoid being pressed for the service. On which information, and being now furnished with a good pilot, so wonderfully thrown in his way, the commodore dropt his design of coming to Boston, tacked about, and went directly to our forces to Canso, to their great joy; and then without stopping there, went on to his station before Louisburg, to block up that harbor. The commodore also, by the said fisherman, sent his order for the

1. A port on the western coast of Nova Scotia located on the Bay of Fundi.
2. The southernmost point on Nova Scotia.
3. The small port at the eastern tip of Nova Scotia.

king's ships that should be found in these ports, forthwith to follow them. The order came to the *Eltham*, a forty gun ship at Piscataqua, after she was actually got to sea, having set sail for England, as convoy to the mast fleet. The order reached her by a boat, sent after her from the shore, before she was got quite out of call, on which she bore after the commodore, and quickly joined him; so that now our army had four men-of-war, under God, to protect them.

It was remarkable, that when so many vessels sailed from this province, New Hampshire and Connecticut, being in all about 80 sail, in a time of year that used to be the most turbulent and tempestuous of any, all arrived safe (through a course of five or six hundred miles on the ocean) at Canso, the place of concourse, a place about sixty miles on this side Cape Breton, without the loss of more than one soldier, and three seamen, and fifteen sick. And 'tis to be observed, that the Connecticut forces very narrowly escaped being taken by a French ship of force, that came in sight of them in their voyage; but were kept in play by some vessels of ours, of inferior force, till the fleet of transports got out of reach. And 'tis remarkable, that of all the vessels that have been employed in this affair (who had their voyages at a very difficult time of year), transports and vessels of force from New England, packet boats to and from England and the West Indies, men-of-war from the West Indies and England to Cape Breton, not one of them failed in any of those voyages, either by being cast away or taken.

It seemed to be ordered wholly in favor to the design, that our forces that went from this government, were detained by contrary winds for near three weeks at Canso; for if they had sailed before, as appeared, they would have found the harbors and bays full of ice, and could not have landed, so that they would only have discovered themselves to the enemy, and given them timely notice to prepare for their defense, without being able to come near them, which (as after-events confirm) would wholly have defeated the design: and besides, the weather, while they lay in Canso harbor, was exceeding bad, being very cold, with storms of snow, so that if the wind had been fair, and they could have landed at Cape Breton, they could not have lived ashore, so ill provided as they were with tents. By this means the enemy would have had a vast advantage against them; but God held them at Canso, till the Connecticut forces and Commodore Warren were come up, and till the bays were clear of ice, and till the time was come that he intended the weather should be good, so that our men could live ashore, and then the wind sprung up fair to carry them to Cape Breton.

While our forces lay at Canso, their cruisers were succeeded to intercept and take many French vessels that were coming to Cape Breton, and in them to take some things that the army greatly needed; and particularly it is judged by some of the officers that were there, that are persons of good judgment, that the army could not have subsisted (so exposed as they were to cold at that time of year in that cold climate), without the rum they took from the enemy.

It was very strange, that when our army lay so long at Canso, within sight of the island of Cape Breton, they should be wholly concealed from the French on that island; so that the people of Louisburg had no notice of the expedition against them, till they were surprised with the sight of the fleet coming upon them, and entering the bay where they landed.

Our forces, when they went from Boston, had orders to land in the night, and go upon a certain plan of operations, established on the false representations we had had of the state of the place. Accordingly they set sail from Canso, with a design to land in the night, and prosecute their plan, which, if they had done, it is judged it would have proved fatal to the design; therefore divine providence prevented it, by causing the wind suddenly to die away, in the midst of their way from Canso to Chappe-rouge Bay, where they intended to land, so that they could not land in the night, but were obliged to land in the daytime, which proved greatly for their advantage.

When they came into the bay, about five miles from Louisburg, in the daytime, in the sight of their enemies, the French were seized with such surprise, that they seemed hardly to know what they did, and were left to act very foolishly. They sent out eighty-eight persons to resist their landing, when, if they had consulted their interest, they should have sent seven or eight hundred, which might have rendered the landing of our men extremely difficult. These eighty-eight men were left to discover themselves, and appear openly; whereas if they had concealed themselves, and lain in ambush, as there were places enough convenient for their so doing, they might have cut off many of our men. Our men were, on this occasion, wonderfully animated with courage, and between twenty and thirty that first landed, boldly encountered those eighty-eight of the French, and killed eight of them, without the loss of a man on their side, and drove the rest back to the town in a great fright, setting all the city and garrison into a terrible consternation; so that in their fright they immediately deserted the Grand Battery, a fort about a mile and half from the city, on the other side the harbor, a fortress of great strength, and the principal fortification that defended the harbor, furnished with thirty-two great cannon, thirty of them forty-two pounders, a fortress which might have maintained itself alone against all our army. Our men soon perceiving the fortress to be deserted, took possession of it the next morning; and without this, none imagines that ever the city would have been taken. It was principally by the weapons the French left there, that our army annoyed their enemies; and all say they could have done nothing without them. And if the French had kept this fort, they would have had the advantage vastly to have annoyed our army in their siege, and kept them at a distance from the city. 'Tis not imagined, that the French would ever so foolishly have left this fortress, had it not been for their surprise, through the unexpected arrival of our forces, and those that came out to resist our landing, being driven back in so great a fright: so that here appeared the advantage of the above-mentioned concealment of the expedition; and also hereby it appears, how it was in favor to us, that the French came out to oppose our forces at their landing as they did.

The enemy spiked up their cannon before they left the fort, but did not do it effectually. Our men soon got them all clear again. They carried away most of their powder, or threw it into the sea; but left what was much more needed by our men, viz., their balls, suited to the bores of their huge pieces (for our army had none such), and shells, that happened to be suited to the bores of our mortars; and did not knock off the trunnions of their cannon, nor destroy the carriages.

It was a remarkable favor of providence, that our men discovered that the Grand Battery was deserted, and took possession of it, just as they did; for if this discovery had been delayed but an hour or two longer, the enemy would have repossessed themselves of it, and so our whole design probably have been defeated. For just after our soldiers had taken possession of this fort, the enemy, being on consideration aware of their fatal error in leaving of it, were coming out in great numbers in many boats to recover it, but were repulsed by a handful of our men.

Soon after the siege began, the officers of the army, in a council of war, had determined a general assault to be made by scaling the walls; which, though it appeared to be a very adventurous and dangerous attempt, yet was thought necessary to hasten the taking of the city, because, from what they had heard, they were in daily expectation of a strong French fleet, greater than our naval force before the harbor could resist.[4] But just as they were going to put this in execution, the officers, unexpectedly, changed their minds, and presently after several men-of-war arrived from England, to add to our naval strength,[5] and put the army out of fear of the French fleet; and so this desperate attempt was prevented, which if it had gone on, would have proved fatal to our army, as all are sensible since the strength of the city is fully known.

When the army began to fall short of ammunition, and were like to be run out, God sent the *Vigilant*, the strong French ship from France before mentioned, with all manner of warlike stores, and plenty of ammunition, which fell into the hands of our fleet, and so our army was supplied with what they wanted, to enable them to carry on the siege, which otherwise they could

4. The commodore also was in expectation of orders from England, sending him elsewhere. —JE.

5. With orders to the commodore to continue in his present station, at assisting in the siege of Louisburg.—JE.

not have done.[6] This ship, and her warlike stores, was intended to be improved against the English settlements. Thus again our enemies fell into the pit which they digged.

Another remarkable incident, by which that which our enemies had done, was an occasion of a great advantage to our army against them, was this: the French, for some reason or other, had sunk a number of cannon in the sea by the Lighthouse Point, over against the Island-Battery (a strong battery that defended the mouth of the harbor). These cannon were providentially discovered by our men, which gave them the hint of erecting a battery on the Lighthouse Point. Accordingly they got up these cannon out of the water; and though while they were at work at it, they were right before the mouths of the cannon of the Island-Battery, within about half a mile, yet they went through with the business, without the loss of a man. The enemy in the city also seeing what they were about, came out a great number of them in boats to resist them; but after they were landed, our men ran between them and their boats to hinder their return. Upon which the French immediately fled to the woods, and so the town was weakened; and then our men erected a battery on the Lighthouse Point, which being higher ground than the Island-Battery, they had great advantage to annoy them from thence, and did greatly annoy and distress them, which was one of the chief means of their being brought to capitulate.

Our soldiers seemed to be inspired with resolution, eagerness and activity, in a kind of miraculous manner, greatly to the surprise of their enemies, and were marvelously supported, during the long siege of seven weeks, under their extraordinary and herculean labors and fatigues—in carrying stores, drawing cannon by their own strength over hills and valleys, among rocks, and even drawing great 42 pounders, for two miles, through morasses, up to the middle in mire, and in digging trenches, and erecting batteries, and watching continually against the enemy, not only in the town, but the French and Indians from the country, in the woods, that were lurking about them seeking advantages against them—our men being unexperienced in war, having never seen a siege before in their lives, and very few of them ever before engaged in any warlike enterprise of any kind, and a great many of them never heard the report of a cannon before.

But the miracle of their preservation, in the midst of so many continued great dangers, was yet greater. Our nearest batteries were erected within thirty rods of the town wall; and the enemy were constantly, day and night, discharging their cannon and small arms from the town wall, and their mortars from the many strong fortifications in and about the town; and the air was, as it were, continually full of bombs, and other instruments of death, and our soldiers were abundantly exposed at their batteries, and moving

6. And the ship itself was added to our fleet, and was the strongest and best ship in the whole fleet.—JE.

from place to place. But yet the whole number that were killed by the enemies' fire, from the town and forts, during the whole siege (excepting what were killed at an unsuccessful attempt, made in the night, on the Island-Battery), did not amount to twenty. Our men at length were so used to their bombs and cannonballs, and found them harmless for so long a time, that they learned at length but little to regard them; so wonderfully did God cover their heads.

Things were wonderfully ordered from time to time, so as tended to keep up the courage of the army, during this long siege, and to revive their spirits, and give new life to them, when their spirits and courage began to fail; when they were very much beat out, and things looked dark, something new that was prosperous or promising would happen to encourage them, either some additional force would arrive, some men-of-war would be added to the fleet, or some new prizes would be taken, or some remarkable advantage gained against the enemy. And as was observed, that such things happened from time to time, at critical seasons, when most needed to encourage the army. Once in digging a trench, our men came upon a rock, which they fatigued themselves in vain, in endeavoring to remove, and labored till they were quite discouraged; and just as they had left it, there came a bomb from the enemy, and fell under that very rock, in the most suitable spot, so as at once to do their work for them, and cast the rock quite out of the way; so that then their work lay fair before them, and they went on with digging their trench.

There once happened something very discouraging to the army, and that was, that they split their large mortar, that they chiefly depended on, and had none but small mean ones left. But it so wonderfully happened, that a mortar of just the same size, was that very day put on board at Boston, to be sent to them, without the people at Boston knowing anything of this special need; which mortar they soon joyfully received; and it was with that mortar, that they afterward chiefly distressed the enemy, from the battery they had erected at the Lighthouse Point, and drove them from the Island-Battery, that defended the mouth of the harbor.

God's providence in disposing the circumstances of the surrender of the place, was wonderful. There was an army that had gathered, and laid siege to Annapolis, in Nova Scotia, the last spring, in expectation of a strong naval force from France to assist them, as had been before determined by the French. This army was made up partly of French and Indians from Canada, and partly of the Indians of Nova Scotia, that are at war with us. This army was disappointed of the expected ships from France; some of them were taken by our squadron, under Commodore Warren (the *Vigilant* forementioned was one of them), others were driven away. And the French at Cape Breton sent for this army to come to their relief; so that siege was raised, and Annapolis and Nova Scotia saved, and the army were on their way to Cape

Breton, and if they had arrived before the surrender of the city, they had, in all probability, disappointed our enterprise. But our fleet and army before Louisburg, being wearied with the length of the siege, the sea and land officers met in council, and determined, without further delay, to make a general assault upon the city, and attempt to take it by storm. But this desperate attempt was wonderfully and happily prevented; for just as the council of war was broke up, before Commodore Warren was gone off the ground, came out a flag of truce from the city, desiring a cessation of acts of hostility, till they might meet together, to consider what proposals to make to the English, as terms of the surrender of the city; and the consequence was, that they soon agreed to give up the city, and all its fortifications, and king's stores, and the whole country depending, on condition of their being transported, with their movable effects, to France. Thus God gave into our hands the place of greatest importance of any that the French have in North America, the principal fountain of the king of France's wealth, from these parts of the world, and the key to all his northern colonies, and the chief annoyance of the British colonies. When our men entered the city, they were amazed at the strength of it, and to see how they should have been exposed, if providence had not prevented their design that was resolved upon, of scaling the walls. The walls, which were of a most prodigious thickness, they found to be about 25 foot high, very much higher than they imagined, by reason of a trench, of about 12 foot deep, and a vast wraith under the walls, that they were not aware of; so that their ladders would have proved vastly too short; and it would have been a wonder if so much as one of the land army had got into the city. And, besides the strength of the place, it was found, that there were many more soldiers, and others, capable of bearing arms, in the city and country about, than in our whole army.

Another wonderful circumstance of the taking of this place, was this, that during this long siege, our army had almost a constant series of fair good weather, there being scarce any rain, so as to incommode our army during the whole time, which was to the amazement of the French; for it was a time of year, wherein, in all former years, used to be almost perpetual rains and fogs. And the French inhabitants agreed, that there never had been any instance of such weather at that time of the year, since the place was settled. And it was apparent to the French, by this and other things, and much taken notice of by them, that God fought for the English, and some of them said, "that their God was turned an Englishman." Though it was constantly such good weather, during the seven weeks of the siege, yet (as the major general of the army told me) as soon as ever they had entered the city, before the general had reached his quarters, it began to rain, and continued raining almost constantly for eight days together, which, if it had been before the surrender of the city, would have filled our trenches with water, have stopt all business, and extremely incommoded and distressed the army (who were very ill-provided with tents, and very many of them at that time sick), and must have confounded the whole affair. Some of the French took notice of this, and said one to another, "If we had held out a little longer, we should have done well enough"; but others replied, "No; for if the English had continued in the siege, it would still have been fair weather." Thus the clouds and winds, and sun, moon and stars in their courses, from the beginning, fought for us. While we were preparing in New England, for two months, was a constant series of good weather, in February and March, such as was never known at that time of year. And the winds and weather favored us in all our voyages, that were made about this affair; while God detained the army for three weeks at Canso, till the harbors at Cape Breton were cleared of ice; when good weather was not needed, then was a constant series of bad weather, but after they landed at Cape Breton, till the city was surrendered, was again constant good weather; but as soon as they entered the city, and did not stand in need of good weather any longer, then they had no more of it.

This place, since it has fallen into our hands, has proved a snare to our enemies abroad; for they not knowing that it was taken, nor imagining that it could be taken, have resorted thither, as they used to do, with their wealth, from the East and West Indies; two East-India ships and one South-Sea man, immensely rich, besides several other vessels, have come there, into our mouths. And now we are freed from the noise of the archers, or gunners, on board their ships of war, that infested us, and made havoc on our coasts the last year.

Thus, Sir, I have given you a particular account of this affair, it being perhaps a dispensation of providence, the most remarkable in its kind, that has been in many ages, and a great evidence of God's being one that hears prayer; and that it is not a vain thing to trust in him; and an evidence of the being and providence of God, enough to convince any infidel; and a great argument with me, among other things, that we live in an age, wherein divine wonders are to be expected; and a dispensation wherein God has so apparently manifested himself, that it appears to me it ought not to be concealed, but to be declared in the world amongst his people, to his praise.

We have lately heard of the Pretender's eldest son his entering Scotland, and being joined there by a number of Highlanders.[7] How far God may punish the nations of Great Britain by him, we cannot tell. We have not yet heard of the rebellion's being suppressed, but are ready to hope, by the aspect of affairs, from what we hear, that it is done before this time. It is a day of great commotion and tumult among the nations, and what the issue will be we know not: but it now becomes us, and the church of God everywhere, to cry to him, that he would overrule all for the advancement of the kingdom

7. See HA; above, p. 358, n. 4.

of Christ, and the bringing on the expected peace and prosperity of Zion.

I desire, honored Sir, that you would favor me with some further accounts of the progress of religion in the north of Scotland, and in the Netherlands, and in general of the state of things on your side the world, relating to late revivals of religion. And please send me a particular account of things relating to the concert for joint prayer, whether it be like to be upheld, how far it is spread, etc. And remember in your prayers, dear Sir,

> Your respectful, affectionate and obliged
> Brother and servant,
> Jonathan Edwards

APPENDIX D

APOCALYPTIC THEMES IN OTHER NOTEBOOKS

1. The "Miscellanies"

See especially entries with the following headings.[1]
Angels of the Apocalypse
Antichrist
Calling of the Gentiles
Calling of the Jews
Coming of Christ
Conflagration
Consummation of All Things
Delivering up the Kingdom
Dispensation
End of the Creation
End of the World
Eternal Torments
Future State
Glorious Times of the Church
Hades
Happiness of Heaven
Heaven
Hell
Hell Torments
Immortality
Interpretation of Scripture
Israel
Judgment Day
Kingdom of Christ
Lord's Day
Millennium
Misery of Damned

1. The specific entries under each heading may be located by using the "Table" prepared by JE for the "Miscellanies."

New Heavens and New Earth
Progress of the Work of Redemption
Prophecies of the Messiah
Resurrection
Saints in Heaven
Satan Defeated
Scripture
Types

2. The "Scripture"

See, for example, the following entries.[2]

3 (Luke 14:22–23), calling of Gentiles
4 (Matt. 21:40–41), destruction of Jerusalem
10 (Matt. 9:10), calling of Gentiles
12 (Matt. 8:25), distress before deliverance
16 (Ps. 48:7), redemption from the East
19 (Jer. 13:11), union of Christ and church
25 (Mark 4:26–28), growth of kingdom
28 (Luke 11:44), apostasy of church
33 (Mark 12:24), future state
37 (Jer. 16:16), victory over Satan
39 (Matt. 15:21–22), exorcism of antichristianism
40 (Luke 15:21–22), calling of Gentiles
41 (Luke 17:20), growth of kingdom
42 (Luke 17:30 ff.), destruction of Jerusalem
50 (Eph. 4:13), union of Christ and church
52 (Jas. 2:19), exorcism of antichristianism
58 (Matt. 20:16), victory over Satan
70 (Acts 1:15), significance of "twelve"
73 (Num. 23:23), victory over Satan
77 (Gen. 2:17), second death
80 (Judg. 16:25), victory over Satan
85 (Cant. 6:13), church militant–church triumphant
91 (Eccles. 2:16), future state
93 (I Sam. 17:25), victory over Satan
104 (Jude 9), union of Christ and church
125 (Ruth 1), calling of Jews and Gentiles
129 (Gen. 15:17), deliverance
158 (I Cor. 15:28), Christ as King
172 (Ex. 15:27), significance of "twelve"
173 (Josh. 6:26 & I Kgs. 16:34), blood of martyrs

2. Most of these notes are printed in Dwight ed., *9*, and can be located by means of the canonical reference.

197 (Matt. 16:28), Christ's coming
207 (Josh. 10:12–14), struggle with enemies
210 (Ps. 68:8–9), victory over enemies
211 (Judg. 5:20), struggle with enemies
214 (Is. 33:17), eternal punishment
227 (Heb. 6:4–6), apostasy from church
236 (Jer. 30:21), gospel times
255 (Is. 51:9), types of antichristianism
256 (Ex. 36:5), types of antichristianism
265 (II Pet. 1:11 ff.), Christ's coming
266 (Ex. 33:18 ff.), heaven
269 (Zech. 1:8), victory over enemies
271 (Rev. 12:1), stages of church
273 (I Kgs. 7:15 ff.), heaven
274 (Jonah 2:6), eternal punishment
276 (Gen. 19:24–28), conflagration
279 (Dan. 7:13), Christ's coming
281 (I Kgs. 3:1), calling of Gentiles
289 (Heb. 13:12–14), calling of Gentiles
292 (Matt. 24:21–24 ff.), times of persecution
294 (Jer. 5:22), victory over enemies
295 (Luke 10:38 ff.), external vs. spiritual worship
298 (Ps. 17:4), victory over enemies
302 (Gen. 14:15–16), victory over enemies
306 (Rev. 21–22), heaven
307 (Num. 19), stages of church
312 (Heb. 9:28), Christ's coming
317 (Is. 40:1–2), supplies of church
319 (Ps. 68), judgment day
321 (Mal. 4:1–2), Christ's coming
328 (Ps. 19:4–6), gospel times
329 (II Thess. 2:7), Christianity and antichristianity
330 (Matt. 21:12–16), apostasy from church
331 (Is. 41:25), sixth vial
348 (Gen. 9:12 ff.), heaven
351 (Ex. 12:35–36), tyranny of Rome
354 (Gen. 7:8–9, 14–16), judgment day
355 (Gen. 18), victory over enemies
357 (Jude 15), judgment day
359 (Gen. 19:23–24), eternal punishment
368 (John 2), supplies of church
384 (Ex. 2:5 ff.), times of persecution
388 (Ex. 10:21–23), eternal punishment

389 (Ezek. 1), providence in history
395 (Cant. 2:7), times of persecution
396 (Zech. 14:16–19), judgment day
413 (Dan. 9:27), abomination of desolation
414 (Matt. 16:28), end of world
433 (Ezek. 38–39), Gog and Magog
462 (Prov. 30:27), providence
464 (Matt. 16:28), Christ's kingdom
470 (Rev. 22:11), sealing the unjust
471 (Ex. 12:2), day of the sabbath
475 (Ex. 25:23–40), light of the church
483 (Hab. 3:2), deliverance
484 (I John 2:18), Antichrist
504 (Eph. 2:7), ages to come

3. Annotations on the Apocalypse in the "Blank Bible."[3]

Ch. 1:4, 8, 10*, 13, 15, 18.
Ch. 2:1, 7*, 10, 14–15, 17(4), 17*, 24(2), 26*, 27*.
Ch. 3:4 (3), 5, 5*, 10(2), 12(3).
Ch. 4:3, 3*, 4, 6(3), 6*, 7, 8, 11.
Ch. 5:8, 11*, 12.
Ch. 6:9, 12, 14.
Ch. 7:8, 11*, 16, 16–17, 17.
Ch. 8:13.
Ch. 9.
Ch. 10:1, 1–2, 3, 3–4, 6(2).
Ch. 11:1, 3(2), 7(3), 12*, 13, 19.
Ch. 12:1, 1*, 5*, 7, 8–9, 10, 14.
Ch. 13:5*, 6, 10(2), 14, 18(3).
Ch. 14:1, 5, 10, 13(2).
Ch. 15:2(2), 3(2).
Ch. 16:6, 6*, 10, 15, 17, 18*, 21.
Ch. 17:5, 9–10, 12, 17.
Ch. 18:3, 20.
Ch. 19:5, 12*, 13, 14, 17.
Ch. 20:4(2), 5(2), 6(2), 9*, 12, 14.
Ch. 21:1, 1*, 2(2), 11(2), 14, 16, 18*, 21*, 23(2), 23–24, 24*.
Ch. 22:1, 2, 3–4(2), 5*, 11, 14(3), 16, 17, 19*.

3. This is a list of the entries on the verses of the book of Revelation written by JE in the "Blank Bible." The parentheses indicate multiple notes on a given text. The asterisks point to cross-references on the margins of the small printed Bible. No attempt has been made to indicate the date of the entries or the variations in length and content. Some notes comprise several paragraphs; others are only a single line. In addition, JE wrote five general comments dealing with such questions as canonicity and authority. The more than ninety cross-references to the AP appearing in the "Blank Bible" are not listed here.

GENERAL INDEX

The General Index contains only selective entries in three specific areas: references to the Deity, geographical names, and biblical characters or events. See the entries for "God," "Christ," and "Holy Spirit" for discussions of particular aspects of the Deity. See the Index of Biblical Passages *for the locations of other biblical items.*

Aaron, 198
Abaddon, 104
Abelove, Henry, 25 n.
Aberdeen, Scotland, 324
Abraham, 135, 136, 309
Absalom, 429 n.
"Account Book" (JE), 69 n., 79 n., 80 n., 85 n.
Account of the Life and Death of the Late Reverend Mr. Matthew Henry (Tong), 62 n.
Account of the Life and Writings of John Erskine (Wellwood), 70 n.
Act of Uniformity, 59
Acton, Commodore, 254
Acts and Monuments (Foxe), 4, 67, 68, 112 n.
Adam, 136
Addison, Joseph, 74
Adolph of Nassau, 242
Adoration of the saints, 294–95
Adriatic Sea, 189
Aelius Spartian, 170, 221
Affection, ways of expressing, 376
Affliction. *See* Persecution
Africa, 133–34, 174, 411
Africa, 272
Ahithophel, 429
Ahlstrom, Sydney E., 92
Alains (Alans), 226, 250
Alaricus (king of the Visigoths), 128, 131, 225, 226, 227
Albany, New York, 451
Albert of Austria, 242
Albigenses, 43, 110, 126, 137, 239–40, 390–91
Alcasar, Luis de, 4
Alcide, 266
Aldridge, Alfred O., 89
Alexander V (pope), 245
Alexander VI (pope), 246
Alexander the Great, 176, 409

Allegory, 12, 146
Allen, Alexander V. G., 82, 88–89
Allen, George, 80 n.
Allix, Peter, 110 n.
Almans, 224
Alpha and Omega, 49, 54
Althaus, Paul, 3 n.
Amazon, 261
Amelia, Princess, 287, 288
America: millennium in, 26, 28; location of work of God, 26, 328, 361, 362, 449; relation to Canaan, 133–34; reign of the devil in, 143; struggle against Christianity, 174; relation to Europe, 310; concert of prayer in, 324, 327 n., 447; low moral and religious state, 357; Great Awakening in, 359–60, 363; conversion of, 411; prayer for, 446
American Opinion of Roman Catholicism in the Eighteenth Century (Ray), 8 n.
Ames, William, 35
Analogy of God's dispensations, 381
Andover Seminary, 80 n., 81
Angels, 154, 156 n., 347, 376
Angels of the Apocalypse, 143 n.
Anglicanism. *See* Church of England
Animadversions upon Sir Isaac Newton's Book (Bedford), 65
Annales Veteris et Novi Testamenti (Ussher), 64
Annapolis, Nova Scotia, 452, 457
Anne (queen of England), 428, 430 n.
"Annotations" (Henry). See *Exposition* (Henry)
"Annotations" of 1657, 60 n.
Annotations upon the Holy Bible (Poole), 56 n., 60–61, 77, 105 n., 113 n., 125 n., 126–27 n., 131 n.
Anson, Admiral, 262, 263, 361 n., 422
Anti-Catholicism in New England, 8–9
Antichrist: associated with the papacy, 3,

Colors, interpretation of: white, 98, 224; green, 99, 147; black, 168, 220. *See also* Black horse; Rainbow; Red horse; White horse

Commentatio ad loca Novi Testamenti (Grotius), 7 n.

Commerce in religion, 185 n.

Committee of War, 450, 452

Commodus (emperor of Rome), 170, 220, 221

Common Prayer, 288

Communicant's Companion (Henry), 62

Concert for Prayer Propounded, 88 n.

Concert of prayer: origins associated with JE, 36; promotion and support in Scotland, 36–37, 39–40, 48 n., 70, 71, 288, 321–24; limited success in America, 38, 48; as solution to religious problem, 39, 41–42, 43, 434–36; promoted and defended by JE, 39–46, 47–48, 59, 82, 84; support in Massachusetts, 48 n.; similar effort in Holland, 289; historical account of, 320–24; promoted privately at first, 323–24; trial period of two years, 323–24; described in Memorial, 324–28; not limited to any denomination or party, 326, 433; objections against answered by JE, 368–431; early efforts on behalf of, 377–78; Lowman's views seen as obstacle to, 398–99; earlier efforts at union in prayer, 428–31; to continue seven years, 435; beautiful and becoming, 444–45; supported by ministers, 445–46; JE requests information concerning, 460; mentioned, 289 n. *See also* Memorial; Prayer

Confession of faith by Jewish Christians, 295–96

Congregational Review, 81

Connecticut, 324, 363, 445, 453

Connecticut Gazette, 284

Connection (Prideaux). See *Old and New Testament Connected* (Prideaux)

Conquerant, 266

Conquestrador, 272

Conrad (Holy Roman emperor), 241

Conradin (duke of Swabia), 241, 242

Considerations on the Spirit of Popery (Erskine), 71

Constance, council at, 245, 246, 247

Constans, M. De, 259

Constantine: ends persecution, 2; Lowman's view criticized, 44–45, 401; protects and delivers the church, 108, 356, 377 n., 400; time of, 150, 177–78, 183, 202, 215, 403; struggles in family, 224,

225, 336; extent of church during reign, 332; relation to heads of beast, 399–402; gave wound to heathen Roman Empire, 401–02; conversion of, 402; mentioned, 66, 232, 335

Constantinople, 66, 190

Constantinople, treaty of, 190 n.

Content, 266

Conversion(s): of Jews, 19, 287, 292–93, 295–96; of the isles, 28; pattern of, 212–13; as a type of church's salvation, 214; notable examples in England, 288, 291; in Asia, 293, 294; of the world, 347. *See also* Revivals of religion

Cooper, William, 21 n.

Cornhill in Boston, 91

Coromandel Coast, 423

Correspondence and Diary of Philip Doddridge (Humphreys), 293 n.

Cotton, John, 5, 8

"Cotton Mather and Jonathan Edwards on the Number of the Beast" (Stein), 113 n.

Count de Maurepas, 266

Count de Noailles, 261

Counterfeit illuminations denounced by JE, 218

Cournan, Captain, 268

Covenant of grace, 52, 99, 341

Covenant of redemption, 52, 341

Covenant with Noah, 99

Cox, Samuel Hanson, 68 n.

Cranberry, New Jersey, 285

Creation: end or goal of, 16, 41, 50, 53, 137; compared to false miracles, 112; a type of work of redemption, 165, 166–67, 183–84; waits for the glorious day, 344–47

Credibility of the Gospel History (Lardner), 67, 215 n.

Critici Sacri, 60

Cromwell, Oliver, 6

Crossweeksung, New Jersey, 364 n.

Crown-GR paper, 74, 76

Crusades, 237–38, 240–41, 247–48, 391

Cruttenden, Robert, 291

Culloden, battle of, 358 n.

Culross, Scotland, 70

Cumberland, 254

Curnock, Nehemiah, 290 n.

Cutler, Timothy, 9

Cyprian (church father), 222

Cyrus: destroyed Babylon, 175, 187, 302, 382, 412–14; as type of Christ, 208–09, 417–19; restored church from temporal calamity, 353; decree of, 393, 408; preparation of his way, 424; men-

Prayer (*continued*)
53, 83, 351; urged by JE, 24, 30; for military campaign, 33; defined by Ames, 35; at stated times, 35, 322–23, 325–26, 365, 369, 372–74; for God's presence, 39, 315–17, 354–55; a duty in the church, 43, 314–15, 319–20, 322–23, 428; associated with incense of Christ, 102 n.; encouraged in the Bible, 309–10, 356–57; pleasing to God, 310, 320; joint resolution by many, 317–19; importunity in, 348–49; examples in the Bible, 350, 355, 366–67; motivated by acts of providence in the present, 357–63; as remedy for present evils, 358; for downfall of Satan and Antichrist, 358–59, 396; answered on occasion of expedition against Cape Breton, 362, 449, 459; beauty of union in, 364–67, 372; awakens religious concerns, 366; promotes mutual charity and affection, 366, 371–72, 374–76; defended by JE, 373–74, 376, 396, 427, 434; discouraged by misinterpretation of prophecy, 378–79; union is no new thing, 428. *See also* Concert of prayer

Prayer, concert of. *See* Concert of prayer

Prayer societies: in Scotland, 36, 321, 324; membership and activities, 37; in Northampton, 37, 445; relation to concert, 323, 434; among youth, 324

Preaching, 53, 146, 293. *See also* Ministers of the gospel

Premillennialism, 7 n.

Presbyterian ordination in England, 288

Present State of the Republick of Letters, 65 n.

Present State of the Society for Propagating Christian Knowledge, 71 n.

"President Edwards as a Reformer" (Magoun), 81 n.

"Pressing into the Kingdom" (JE), 19–20

Preus, James Samuel, 92

Prideaux, Humphrey, 63, 109, 176, 408 n., 409 n.

Prignano, Bartolomeo, 244 n.

Prince, Thomas: signs preface to HA, 21 n., 311; letter to, 26 n., 37 n., 87, 290, 292, 294, 324; supports revivalism, 31 n.; sermons by, 35 n., 285 n.; involved with distribution of HA, 71 n., 85 n.; letter from, 79 n.; account of revival at Huntington, 287

Prince, Thomas, Jr., 31 n.

Princessa, 268

Princess Amelia, 269

Princeton, New Jersey, 79

Princeton College, 82, 448 n. *See also* College of New Jersey

Principles of apocalyptic interpretation illustrated: spiritual sense, 2, 137; literal sense, 16; metaphorical sense, 16; symbolical sense, 97; visionary representation, 105, 120, 143; mystical sense, 137, 384, 391–92, 397, 412

Principles of Popery Schismatical (Lowman), 55

Printed Writings of Jonathan Edwards (Johnson, T.), 83 n., 85 n.

Private academies, 448

Proclamation for a general Thanksgiving (Shirley), 362 n.

Proclamation for a Publick Fast (Shirley), 362 n.

Pro-Patria-GR paper, 74

Prophecy: JE's interest in, 1, 15, 51; for guidance and benefit of the church, 23, 30, 404; fulfillment of, 47; and theology, 49; multiple meanings of, 150, 398; the method of, 251; of church's advancement, 312–14, 329–37, 350; of Babylon's destruction, 408–09. *See also* Prophetic numbers

Prophecy of the French Revolution and Downfall of Antichrist (Willison), 69

Prophetic Faith of Our Fathers (Froom), 2 n., 43 n.

Prophetic numbers: interpretation of, 97–98, 312 n., 392 n.; number seven, 18, 97, 98, 100–01, 105, 123, 136, 147; number twenty-four, 99; number twelve, 99, 108; number *666,* 113 n.; number forty, 136; number four, 230 n.

Providence: cannot be thwarted, 11, acts or dispensations of, 20, 22, 142, 165 n., 207, 357–63, 369, 370, 390; favorable toward New England, 33; double aspect of, 34; remarkable, 42, 46, 361, 449; JE's commitment to, 51; the ultimate aim of, 53, 104, 353; represented as a wheel, 54, 100 n., 145; manifests attributes of God, 100; associated with four beasts, 100 n., 145; preserves the church, 109, 163, 224, 392; ordered by God, 116; the word of, 120; includes afflictions, 173, 407; blesses missionary endeavors, 287; and Prince of Orange, 289; signs in the present, 305; encourages prayer, 360, 430, 432; dispensations at Cape Breton, 362, 455, 457–59; and Constantine, 401, 402; hoped for, 435. *See also* God

INDEX OF BIBLICAL PASSAGES

DATE DUE